STEWARDS
OF
SPLENDOUR

Natural resource regions, Province of British Columbia, 2022

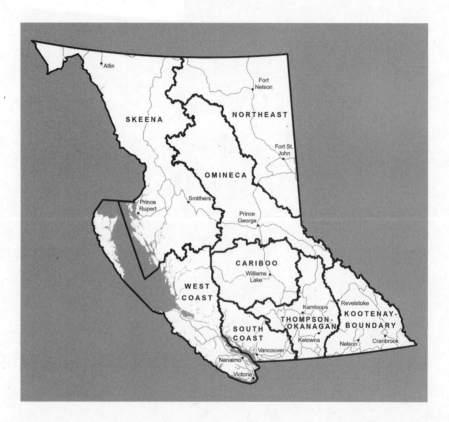

Data source: Forests Tenures Branch, Ministry of Forests. Map by GeoBC, 2022.

STEWARDS
OF
SPLENDOUR

A HISTORY OF
WILDLIFE AND PEOPLE
IN BRITISH COLUMBIA

JENNIFER BONNELL

ROYAL **BC** MUSEUM

VICTORIA, CANADA

Stewards of Splendour
A History of Wildlife and People in British Columbia

Published by the Royal BC Museum, 675 Belleville Street, Victoria, British Columbia, v8w 9w2, Canada.

The Royal BC Museum is located on the traditional territories of the Lekwungen (Songhees and Xwsepsum Nations). We extend our appreciation for the opportunity to live and learn on this territory.

Cover and interior design and typesetting by Lara Minja/Lime Design Inc.
Substantive editing by Eva van Emden
Copy editing by Alison Jacques
Index by Stephen Ullstrom

Library and Archives Canada Cataloguing in Publication

Title: Stewards of splendour : a history of wildlife and people in British
    Columbia / Jennifer Bonnell.
Names: Bonnell, Jennifer, 1971– author. | Royal British Columbia Museum,
    publisher.
Description: Includes bibliographical references and index.
Identifiers: Canadiana (print) 20230229611 | Canadiana (ebook) 20230229697 |
    ISBN 9781039900004 (softcover) | ISBN 9781039900011 (EPUB) |
    ISBN 9781039900028 (EPUB)
Subjects: LCSH: Wildlife conservation—British Columbia—History. |
    LCSH: Animals—British Columbia—History. | LCSH: Indigenous peoples—
    British Columbia—History. | LCSH: Environmental management—
    British Columbia—History. | LCSH: British Columbia—Population—
    Environmental aspects.
Classification: LCC QL84.26.B7 B66 2023 | DDC 333.95/41609711—dc23

10 9 8 7 6 5 4 3 2 1

Printed and bound in Canada by Friesens.

MIX
Paper from
responsible sources
FSC
www.fsc.org   FSC® C016245

To all the British Columbians who work for wildlife

in their jobs, on the side,
on their lands and traditional territories,
with their hands and with their minds.

CONTENTS

PART FIVE

Rising Stakes, Changing Roles, 1992–2022

Illustrations

Maps, Graphs and Plates

PLATES (following page 278)

Foreword

Stewards of Splendour is an outstanding 250-year history of people and wildlife in British Columbia. "Saddle up," readers, because Jennifer Bonnell holds nothing back. She lets us know that we are at a critical point in our relationship with nature.

Climate change and biodiversity loss are impacting human existence at global scales. Bonnell has captured stories of loss, conflicting values, cooperation and hope. From the deep roots of Indigenous cultures to the emerging identity of what it means to live in the province now known as British Columbia, it is time to change the narrative from one of decline and loss to one of recovery and health. Bonnell's history reveals the many diverse perspectives at play in the recent past of wildlife management practice, and she shows us ways to come together and make change through more collaborative and holistic stewardship. The spotlight on "change makers" in the book's conclusion demonstrates that history does not have to repeat itself. It is our responsibility now to start writing a new future, based on our shared passion for fish and wildlife, that will ensure healthy ecosystems and support healthy communities and healthy economies.

Bonnell's expertise in environmental and social history, her ability to connect with the hearts of the storytellers and her dedicated archival and academic research have resulted in a rich narrative about the relationship of people and wildlife in this province.

This impressive social history could not come at a better time, as the people of British Columbia focus their efforts toward meaningful reconciliation among First Nation, provincial and federal governments; improved ecosystem health and the safeguarding of biodiversity; and re-envisioning the natural resource sector for more sustainable outcomes.

In our respective roles as co-chairs of the Together for Wildlife strategy's Minister's Wildlife Advisory Committee and executive director in the Ministry of Land, Water and Resource Stewardship, we are witnessing recent positive changes: the passing of the Declaration Act, the province's acceptance of the recommendations of the Old Growth Strategic Review, the international Global Biodiversity Framework (GBF) and the establishment of a provincial target to protect 30 per cent of land and freshwater by 2030, as well as the ongoing implementation of the Together for Wildlife strategy.

Together, these initiatives will move us closer to a sustainable relationship with nature.

In our individual roles and the work that we do together, we have witnessed what happens when peoples' values come together around a deep connection with and love for wildlife. This book solidifies our long-standing connection to place and wildlife, from the deep spiritual and cultural connections of Indigenous Peoples to the settlers and immigrants drawn and inspired by "super, natural British Columbia." The stories here capture this shared passion.

Sadly, there is another common theme throughout the narrative: diminishing wildlife populations and habitats, and conflicts driven by different attitudes and beliefs—including those that see wildlife as "generous relatives," those that value wildlife principally in terms of human benefit and those that award little value to wildlife at all. The generations living on this planet today are most familiar with these stories of loss, frustration and conflict. It is the exceptions that we must look to and emulate.

The reader will see how different social systems, unbalanced authority and a lack of clarity in objectives divide people, but also how a shared appreciation of wildlife can bring people together for tangible change. The power of Indigenous leadership, the role of rod and gun clubs and conventions, the work of the Royal BC Museum and universities, the creation of naturalist organizations and conservation organizations—all have helped us to move beyond the post–World War II era of "development at all costs," when river basins were viewed as "power trenches." We see a shared conservation ethic evolving.

Success stories across the decades have common elements: collaboration, influence of decision makers, commitment to outcomes. The opportunity to reverse the trajectory of diminishing wildlife comes when people align around a shared trust in information. We have come to recognize that such information must be grounded in multiple ways of knowing: individual experiences of being on the land through time, whether hunting and fishing or hiking; generational knowledge shared through oral history; or studies designed with Western science and Indigenous knowledge systems together. Given the unprecedented loss of wildlife, habitat and biodiversity, it is imperative to learn from these lessons of success, to get past differences and find ways to work together. As the author points out, we've known for a long time what needs to be done.

Our message to you: read the book! Take the time to understand our past and begin to change the future. As "stewards of splendour," with a provincial motto of "splendour without diminishment," how effective have we been? The reviews are in and the response is "mixed." We are the province with Canada's greatest biodiversity. It is time to become better stewards of its gifts.

With increasing global and local action to halt and reverse biodiversity loss, to mitigate climate change through wetland restoration and other nature-based solutions, and to reconcile with Indigenous Peoples, there are signs of hope. And, as stated by one of the book's interviewees, "We will build our hope as we go."

We recognize there is greater complexity with the knowledge of cumulative effects and their impacts on people and wildlife. We need to align across multiple authorities, knowledge systems and values to advance change where there is common ground: fish, wildlife and habitat.

The book ends with very encouraging stories about change makers, people dedicated to the protection and conservation of wildlife. How to begin to make change? Bonnell suggests revitalizing local-level initiatives to bring people together, build better relationships, initiate long-term planning and invest in our future.

Stewards of Splendour is Bonnell's distillation of 250 years of wildlife management. It is her call to action to come together for wildlife. What will your action be?

Chief Harry Nyce (Simoogit Hleek)

Nisga'a hereditary chief; director of fisheries and wildlife, Nisga'a Lisims Government; co-chair, Minister's Wildlife Advisory Committee

Jennifer Psyllakis

Executive director, Wildlife, Habitat and Species Recovery, Ministry of Land, Water and Resource Stewardship

Nancy Wilkin

Director, Office of Sustainability, Royal Roads University; co-chair, Minister's Wildlife Advisory Committee

Acknowledgements

Stewards of Splendour was published with financial support from the Wildlife, Habitat and Species Recovery Branch of the BC Ministry of Land, Water and Resource Stewardship and from the Office of the Vice-President, Research and Innovation, and the Faculty of Liberal Arts and Professional Studies at York University.

The work of researching and writing this book has been a great pleasure from start to finish. The project provided an opportunity to reconnect with my home province, to meet a great number of dedicated wildlife advocates and professionals, and to better understand changing relationships with wildlife in a place that means so much to me.

The project emerged out of reconnections with old friends and past experiences. During a visit home to Vancouver Island in December 2017, my friend Paul Chytyk suggested we meet up with Tom Ethier, a mutual friend I hadn't seen in over two decades. Paul and I had worked with Tom in the early 1990s when he was leading a research study of northern goshawk laingi subspecies for the BC Ministry of Environment in the old-growth forests of northern Vancouver Island and Haida Gwaii. I worked with Tom for two field seasons before taking up other work that would ultimately lead to my current position as an environmental historian at York University in Toronto.

In the time that had passed since those goshawk years, Tom had taken on various leadership roles within the Ministry of Forests, moving into the position of assistant deputy minister in 2012. Given my own work on the history of environmental concerns, he asked if I would consider writing a report for the ministry on the history of wildlife work in the province. He had in mind not a government history but a more expansive accounting of the wide range of historical actors that had worked to understand and conserve wildlife in British Columbia, including Indigenous communities, fish and game associations, naturalists, conservation organizations, industry representatives, scientists and policymakers within and beyond government. This book—much longer than any report—is the result of Tom's original vision for the project and his patience in allowing both timelines and word limits to stretch as the project developed. I have both Tom and Paul to thank for the serendipity of that 2017 meeting and the ideas it generated.

Jennifer Psyllakis (currently executive director of wildlife, habitat, and species recovery for the BC Ministry of Land, Water and Resource Stewardship) picked up where Tom left off in her former role as director of wildlife and habitat for the BC Ministry of Forests. Jen oversaw the research stage of the project and reviewed early drafts of the book, shaping its tone, content and direction in important ways. Her commitment to the project, on top of a very demanding job, and her openness to its evolution from report to book were an enormous source of support to me. It was a pleasure and a privilege to work with and learn from her as the book developed.

Rod Silver, retired former manager of the Habitat Conservation Trust Fund (now Foundation), was this project's guardian angel, and to him I owe my greatest thanks. One of a number of influential wildlife biologists I had been advised to interview for the project, Rod stepped up as an early champion of the work, offering his assistance and his extensive network of "wildlife people" throughout the province. He went on to provide guidance and advice at every stage of the project. In the months of research through 2019 and 2020, he sourced relevant archival documents and scientific and government reports, reached out to government and university librarians on my behalf, and paved the way for me to meet and speak with some of the most respected hunter-conservationists, scientists and wildlife advocates in the province. He read and commented on the first drafts of every chapter and then found the time and energy to bring the same considered attention to the revised versions. In a very significant way, Rod shaped the content of this book, drawing my attention to key individuals, issues, victories and turning points in the history of wildlife conservation in the province. I have digital folders full of articles he sent me throughout the research and writing phase of the project, many of which are referenced in the pages that follow. One memory crystallizes his unflagging support, good humour and generosity: the emails I received from him from a hospital gurney in Victoria as my first submission deadline neared. Forced, like many, to endure lengthy pandemic wait times for an otherwise routine procedure, he occupied himself by connecting me with some of the professional photographers who donated their work to the project. In Rod I found an indefatigable champion of both BC wildlife and the memory of those who sought to understand and protect it. I couldn't have asked for a better source of support for this project.

Dennis Demarchi—like Rod, a historian in his own right—made generous loans from his personal BC wildlife history collection, facilitated connections with wildlife biologists in his network, secured image permissions and provided thoughtful and timely answers to my many questions about the history of wildlife work in the province.

Almost eighty people from all regions of the province contributed their time and knowledge as interviewees. They included retired and active government biologists, managers and conservation officers; Indigenous leaders, knowledge keepers, and land and wildlife managers; hunters and anglers; and representatives from industry and conservation organizations. Some passed away before the book was completed. Their generosity in sharing their time with me, through in-person and telephone interviews and email correspondence, helped to ground this book in the personal experiences of British Columbians who have dedicated their lives to wildlife conservation. I am especially grateful to the Indigenous leaders and land managers who found the time to explain their historical relationships with wildlife and their efforts over many decades to reclaim management authority over the land and wildlife within their traditional territories.

Thanks to the directors and staff of the community museums, archives, and historical societies across the province who shared material from their collections for the benefit of this book. I am grateful, as well, to all the First Nations representatives who considered my requests to reproduce historical images of community members and, in every case, offered their permission. This book is richer for the inclusion of those images. Thanks to Susan Westmacott and Sarah MacGregor of GeoBC, the province's excellent geospatial data office, for their skilled and responsive work in constructing many of the beautiful maps that illustrate the text. Taylor Starr and Cristina Wood, PhD candidates in history at York University, provided valuable research assistance.

It was a great pleasure to work closely with the team at the Royal BC Museum. Eve Rickert and later Jeff Werner capably shepherded the book through the publication process. Art and images curator India Young hunted through the Royal BC Museum and Archives collections to locate many of the historical images that accompany the text. Thank you, India, for your knowledgeable suggestions and willingness to track down "just one more image." Kelly-Ann Turkington provided careful guidance on image permissions. Eva van Emden's sharp editorial eye made this a better book. Her serendipitous knowledge of BC wildlife helped me to puzzle out some remaining questions. It was Eva, for example, who pointed to the vestigial ivory in the canine teeth of elk that made them such valuable (and unsustainable) trade items in the nineteenth century. Copy editor Alison Jacques and proofreader Andrea Zanin completed the final polish. Designer Lara Minja made it beautiful. Stephen Ullstrom built an index I love. Thanks to all of you for the work you do collectively to bring books into the world.

Family and friends make the process of writing a book (especially during a global pandemic) less isolating. Love and thanks to my family in BC who shared my excitement about this project and celebrated my progress through the many stages of research, writing and editing. My family in Toronto tolerated my absences through the research phase of the project in 2019, endured one-sided conversations about wildlife browse and hydro dams, and put up with the project's hold on me through the pandemic years. For their welcome distraction and unwavering love and support, I am grateful.

SPLENDOR SINE OCCASU

Designed in 1895, the British Columbia Coat of Arms gives pride of place to wildlife. Supporting the provincial shield, the Roosevelt elk of Vancouver Island and the bighorn sheep of mainland British Columbia represent the two colonies that formed the province. BC Ministry of the Provincial Secretary and Travel Industry, ca.1940. Royal BC Museum, I-29220.

— INTRODUCTION —

When clergyman Arthur Beanlands of Victoria designed British Columbia's coat
of arms in 1895, he made explicit reference to wildlife as supporters of the
province's development. Buttressing the province's central shield, the wapiti
(Roosevelt elk) stag of Vancouver Island and the bighorn ram of mainland
British Columbia represent the union of the two colonies in 1866. Together
with the wavy blue bars of the sea below the Union Jack, the representation
of the elk and the bighorn sheep signals the permanence of the natural world
within the provincial identity. The setting sun amplifies this message of
permanence and abundance—referencing simultaneously the continuity of
the province's resources and the popular slogan that "the sun never sets on
the British Empire." Maintaining its stability and glory even while setting,
the sun reinforces the provincial motto, *Splendor sine occasu*, a Latin phrase
meaning "splendour without diminishment."[1]

Stewards of Splendour picks up on the symbolism of the province's motto.
"Splendour" is the word that early settler British Columbians reached for in
describing the beauty of this place, not only in its mountaintop vistas and
sparkling coastlines but also in the richness and bounty of its biological life.
"Splendour without diminishment" reflects the ideals of early collectors
and conservationists who sought to understand and protect the province's
wildlife. It also signals the responsibility of stewarding or caring for a place
of such enormous biological diversity. However, it is difficult to interpret
the province's motto today as more than an ironic reminder of all that has
been lost.

As this history shows, British Columbians have not always lived up to
their responsibility as stewards of splendour. Thousands of years of adaptation and experimentation, guided by cultural systems steeped in values
of relationship and reciprocity with the natural world, allowed Indigenous
groups to become adept cultivators of wildlife abundance within their traditional territories. Indigenous governance systems for regulating access to
fish and wildlife in some parts of the province would later form the basis

for provincial systems of trapline and guide-outfitting territories. By the early nineteenth century, however, competitive commercial hunting and fishing among fur trade companies, followed by unregulated wildlife exploitation in the early years of European settlement, prompted urgent calls for conservation. Habitat loss and technological change in the latter half of the twentieth century generated similar demands to consider the needs of wildlife in the expansion of industry, agriculture, residential and recreational development.

As biodiversity loss has reached alarming heights in the early twenty-first century, British Columbians have become more aware of their collective responsibility to care for the non-human occupants of the province and the habitats they depend on. Since the 1990s, the extraordinary advancement of Indigenous rights in Canada and associated implications for landownership and management authority have contributed to this shift. Across the province, the revitalization of Indigenous land and wildlife stewardship systems has ushered in a new regime of collaborative and Indigenous-led wildlife conservation. These changes bring some circularity to this narrative and, in the context of international commitments to biodiversity protection and climate change mitigation, lay the groundwork for British Columbians to renew their commitment as stewards of the country's most biologically rich province.

Scope and Sources

This book explores British Columbians' changing relationships with wild animals and their habitats from the period of pre-contact Indigenous history, prior to 1774, to the present. From the early provincial game legislation of 1904 to the 2020 ban on grizzly bear hunting, wildlife has been a subject of polarizing debate in British Columbia. Regardless of where people fall in these debates, many carry a passion for wildlife. More than any other place in Canada, a recent study found, British Columbia's diverse and highly secular society demonstrates a "pervasive, distinctive, and reverential approach to the natural world."[2] From recreational and subsistence hunters and anglers to birdwatchers and wildlife program enthusiasts, British Columbians care deeply about the prospects of what have become known as "charismatic" wildlife species—the large mammals, birds and valued fish species that drive tourism revenue, support Indigenous cultures and inspire a sense of awe and wonder among those who experience them.

As British Columbians confront a changing climate and growing biodiversity loss, an understanding of the history of efforts to conserve the province's wildlife, with its successes and missteps, will provide important context for the difficult decisions that lie ahead. This book draws on this history with the aim of softening, however slightly, the divides between hunters and naturalists, rural and urban dwellers, and Indigenous and non-Indigenous wildlife advocates. Finding ways to work together to privilege the needs of wildlife will be more essential than ever as British Columbia's growing human population and changing climate alter the livability of remaining animal habitats.

"Wildlife" in this history refers generally to the vertebrate wild animals that occupy the province, including native and some non-native mammals, birds, freshwater fish, reptiles and amphibians. The emphasis throughout is on terrestrial wildlife species, although marine mammals, seabirds and **anadromous** fish such as salmon play an important role in this story. Invertebrates (including insects and shellfish) and plants, although proposed for addition to the BC Wildlife Act in 2004, are beyond the scope of this history.

The "people" side of this story is equally encompassing. The book reaches beyond the scope of government wildlife programs to provide an expansive history of human relationships with wildlife over two and a half centuries. It considers three principal groups: the First Peoples of the province; the European and American explorers and traders who arrived in the late eighteenth and early nineteenth centuries; and the settlers from Europe, the Americas and Asia whose populations expanded through the late nineteenth and twentieth centuries. Following the creation of the province of British Columbia in 1871, the book turns its focus to the experiences of individuals, communities and organizations with interests in and connections to wildlife, including hunters, anglers, trappers and guide outfitters; Indigenous communities; naturalists and wildlife biologists; government wildlife staff; natural resource industries; and wildlife conservation organizations. Throughout, it follows the ways these groups sought to shape and deliver, or respond to the consequences of, wildlife management policies and practices in the province.

"Government" in this book includes the early colonial administrations of Vancouver Island and British Columbia and the provincial, federal and First Nations regimes that followed. Given the provincial government's primary role in the management and conservation of wildlife and in the regulation of industrial activities on the land base, its changing policies and practices feature prominently in this account. Overlapping provincial and federal jurisdiction for some wildlife species, such as migratory birds, marine mammals and anadromous fish, bring federal fisheries and wildlife officials and policies into the narrative. Overall, this book takes an agnostic approach to changing political administrations. Since the dissolution of the Social Credit Party in 1991, BC has oscillated between Liberal and New Democratic Party governments that have both struggled to enact successful environmental reforms. While the NDP has more consistently prioritized environmental concerns, both parties have forwarded environmental mandates and principles. Their approaches, however, have differed, with the Liberals generally preferring fast executive solutions over the NDP's longer, collaborative processes. In the end, neither party has succeeded in balancing a growing human population and a natural-resource-dependent economy with the effects of those developments on the land and the wildlife it supports. As this history shows, dedicated efforts by individuals and organizations within and outside of government have educated British Columbians about the needs of wildlife and have protected some of its most significant wildlife habitats and species. This book is indebted to their work.

A wide range of sources inform my analysis, including relevant historical, legal and scientific literature, memoirs and biographies, government and stakeholder data and published reports. To gain a sense of changing concerns, methods and experiences with respect to wildlife in the province, I interviewed over eighty wildlife advocates and professionals, including retired and active wildlife managers, biologists and conservation officers, Indigenous leaders and wildlife specialists, representatives from industry and conservation organizations, and individual hunters, anglers and naturalists.

With respect to the names of Indigenous groups, I use the names that people have given themselves as much as possible. In the first usage (and where it seemed appropriate to do so), I also present the most well-known alternative (e.g., Nlaka'pamux [Thompson]). For broader ethnic groups, where both the names and sometimes the territorial boundaries have changed over time, I use the names and boundaries identified in Robert Muckle's 2014 *The First Nations of British Columbia* for consistency. The names of specific First Nations are drawn from Crown-Indigenous Relations and Northern Affairs Canada's regularly updated database of First Nations, which reflects the preferences submitted by individual First Nations. Guidelines from the British Columbia government's *Writing Guide for Indigenous Content*, produced in consultation with a team of Indigenous public servants, also inform my approach.[3]

The Setting: British Columbia's Extraordinary Biological Diversity

Any assessment of historical relationships with wildlife must begin by pointing to British Columbia's exceptional status as the most biologically diverse of Canada's provinces and territories. As University of British Columbia forest ecologist Fred Bunnell commented in a 1980 conference presentation, "if diversity or variety is indeed the spice of life, then life in British Columbia is markedly more spicy than elsewhere in Canada."[4] Occupying 10 per cent of Canada's land area, BC hosts as much as 71 per cent of its bird and mammal species—the highest levels of avian and mammalian diversity in the country. Many of these species are **endemic**, or locally unique, to the province. Twenty-four of BC's 142 mammals are found nowhere else in Canada, and some species, like the endangered Vancouver Island marmot, are found nowhere else in the world.[5] Among the province's bird species, 162 breed only in British Columbia.[6]

This astonishing variety originates in the province's highly varied topography and intricate energy flows—in the ability of the land, in other words, to sustain life. A complex glacial history contributed to the province's characteristic long, rugged, indented coastline, numerous coastal islands and mountain ranges, which, "oriented perpendicular to prevailing winds . . . generate a range of vegetation types from rain forest . . . to desert."[7] Of Canada's eight forest types, five occur in BC. Among these, the province's remaining old-growth coastal rainforests are exceptionally rich in biological diversity and represent roughly one-quarter of all remaining coastal temperate rainforests in the world. Other biologically rich environments include the grasslands in the southern and northeastern Interior, and the estuaries and wetlands of the province's coastal areas and major river systems.[8]

British Columbia's extraordinary biodiversity elevates the stewardship responsibility that it shoulders, not only nationally but globally. Steep and inaccessible terrain in parts of the province provide a last refuge for some species, like California bighorn sheep, that were once widespread elsewhere. The province is one of the last places in the world with a complex of large predator-prey systems. It has some of the last freshwater ecosystems naturally without fish, which provide important refuge for amphibian and invertebrate species. Finally, ten vertebrate animal species in BC are considered to be globally "imperilled," meaning that the province carries a share of the global responsibility for conserving them.[9]

Changing Human Populations, Changing Relationships with Wildlife

Large and diverse human populations also characterize the history of what is now known as British Columbia. In the years immediately before contact with Europeans in the 1770s, this was the most heavily occupied region in what would become Canada, with an estimated 200,000 to 400,000 people concentrated along the coast and major river systems. Approximately two hundred distinct nations spoke over thirty Indigenous languages. From the coastal regions through the interior and into the boreal regions of the north, these nations employed a diversity of stewardship practices to maintain and enhance wildlife populations within their territories. Despite over two centuries of colonization, dispossession and government-enforced assimilation, the descendants of many of these peoples still live in communities within their original territories. Many remain active stewards of the lands, fish and wildlife within their traditional territories.

Beginning in the mid-1770s, contact and exchange with European explorers and traders initiated nearly a century of intensive commercial hunting and trade of a range of wildlife species including sea otter, beaver and other fur-bearing mammals; elk and mule deer; waterfowl; and salmon. The formation of the Crown colony of British Columbia in 1858 set the conditions for European colonization and the corresponding dispossession and marginalization of Indigenous Peoples. Agricultural settlement by European, American and central Canadian migrants proceeded very slowly at first; by the 1890s, the pace had quickened, resulting in expanding settler populations on southern Vancouver Island, the Lower Mainland and the southern Interior. The province's settler population has expanded steadily

| Indigenous Peoples' settlement and occupation, to 1774 | European-Indigenous trade, 1774–1858 | Early non-Indigenous settlement, 1858–1904 | Expanding non-Indigenous settlement and population growth, 1904–present |

This timeline provides a general overview of the time periods of Indigenous and non-Indigenous settlement in what is now British Columbia. Image courtesy of the author.

ever since. In keeping with historical geographer Cole Harris's terminology, I describe this early period of in-migration as one of "resettlement" in recognition of the long prior history of Indigenous settlement, including permanent village sites on the coast and established seasonal sites in other parts of the province.

Where these growing human populations congregated continues to shape human-wildlife relationships in important ways. Among Canadian provinces, only Ontario matches British Columbia for the predominance of its urban population. Following historical European settlement patterns of congregation in the southwestern portion of the province, by 2001 over 70 per cent of British Columbians occupied the urban centres of southern Vancouver Island and the Lower Mainland.[10] This concentration of urban development in the province's southwest has had negative consequences for the more sensitive wildlife species in the region. It has also created on-going political dynamics around wildlife and resource management that differ markedly from those in neighbouring, more rural jurisdictions such as Alaska and Montana. BC's politics surrounding resource extraction and conservation have tended to pit a politically powerful urban south-west against the views, and often the interests, of hinterland residents. The province's economic dependence on forestry, hydroelectric development, mining and more recently oil and gas industries has further reinforced this urban-rural divide, concentrating power and decision-making in the south-west while placing a disproportionate burden on rural residents to shoulder the effects of these extractive industries. While these developments have generated local jobs and economic investment, the benefits for hinterland communities have proved difficult to sustain. In recent years, catastrophic wildfires and insect infestations, as well as industrial disasters such as the 2014 Mount Polley tailing dam breach, have had profound consequences for rural livelihoods and communities.[11] The disproportionate effects of these

Indigenous and settler populations in British Columbia, 1871–1981

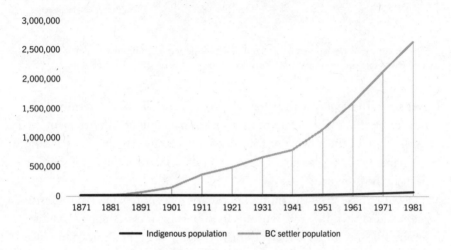

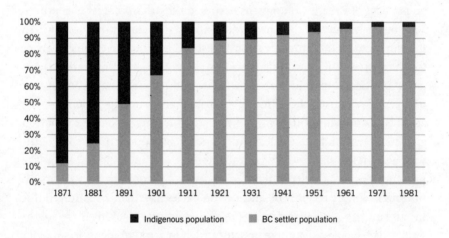

Data source: Graph data adapted from Jean Barman, *The West beyond the West: A History of British Columbia* (Toronto: University of Toronto Press, 1991), 363, table 5 (British Columbia Population by Ethnic Origin, 1871–1981). Image courtesy of the author.

BC land tenure ratios

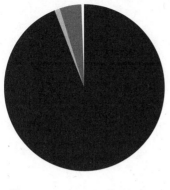

British Columbia's high proportion of Crown land in relation to other provinces is in part a product of its geography. A small proportion of arable land, in particular, reduced the amount of Crown-to-private land conversions. Data source: GeoBC and BC Land Title Register, 2016–22. Image courtesy of the author.

■ Provincial Crown land, 89,200,000 ha

▨ Federal Crown land, 1,070,000 ha

▨ Private land, 4,300,000 ha

☐ First Nations Treaty Settlement lands, 300,000 ha

developments have featured significantly in the history of wildlife management and conservation over the past century. They are worthy of our attention as we contemplate the decades ahead.

Another artifact of BC's colonial history that has had an outsized and ongoing effect on wildlife and wildlife management is the province's unusually high ratio of Crown-to-private land. The vast majority of BC's land mass—94 per cent—is provincial Crown land; federal Crown land constitutes an additional 1 per cent.[12] Just 5 per cent of the province has been converted to private (fee simple) ownership, mostly in the coastal areas and valley bottoms of the southern half of the province. Neighbouring Alberta, by comparison, is 70 per cent Crown land; New Brunswick, just 48 per cent. BC's high Crown land quotient is in part a product of its geography: three-quarters of its land base is above 1,000 metres in elevation and more than 17 per cent of the province is rock, ice or tundra.[13] The resulting scarcity of agricultural land (less than 3 per cent of the province's land area is considered suitable for crop production) placed hard limits on land conversions for agricultural settlement in the late nineteenth and early twentieth centuries. Furthermore, a Crown land base dominated by forests set the conditions for a provincial economy largely dependent, by the early twentieth century, on resource rents and forestry jobs and investment.

Land cover types in BC as percentage of total area of province

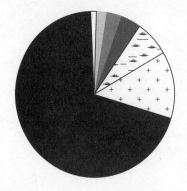

Wildlife and people compete for access to the small percentage of ecologically productive lands in the province, including river valleys, grasslands and estuaries. Data source: M.A. Austin and A. Eriksson, *Biodiversity Atlas of British Columbia* (Victoria: Biodiversity BC, 2009).

☐ Grasslands (1%)

▨ Human-dominated land* (2%)

▨ Fresh water (3%)

▨ Glaciers (4%)

⊟ Wetlands (7%)

⊞ Alpine (13%)

■ Forest and other** (70%)

*   Areas mapped as urban, agriculture, recreation (e.g., golf courses) or mining

** All areas not mapped into the other six categories; the vast majority is forest.

Like other colonial administrations in Canada and the United States, British Columbia considered wildlife to be a "public trust resource," meaning that it was owned by no one and "held by government in trust for the benefit of present and future generations." In keeping with English common law traditions, wildlife was considered "to be part of the land" (with the exception of marine fisheries). Crown ownership and authority over land, in other words, extended to the wildlife that it supports. Only once an animal is legally captured or killed can it be "owned" by an individual. This North American **"public trust doctrine,"** still the foundation of wildlife legislation in the province, differs from many other countries, where wildlife, alive or dead, is considered the property of the individual landowner.[14]

Because the Canadian Constitution grants authority to the provinces for lands and resources within their boundaries, provincial governments generally held, and continue to hold, the primary responsibility for wildlife management in Canada, including licensing hunters and fishers, developing hunting regulations and conducting enforcement and research. Wildlife habitat also fell, for the most part, under provincial control, given the province's ownership of the lion's share of Crown lands. Federal government jurisdiction over wildlife applied to the small percentage of federally owned Crown land in the province: national parks, airports, Indian reserves, federal harbours and military lands. Species that ranged across provincial or national boundaries also fell under federal jurisdiction. This latter specification allowed for large areas of federal management authority, including the province's coastal fisheries, whales and migratory birds and, by the early 2000s, a growing number of species at risk.

That the vast majority of the province's land base, and the wildlife that it supports, falls under public ownership has powerful implications for management. One of the central responsibilities of the provincial government is to manage the public land base in the interests of all British Columbians. The biophysical composition of the province, however, and the relative value of its natural resources have contributed to the weighting of some interests over others.

Since the early twentieth century, the dominance of the forest industry in the province has meant that other less intensive and less lucrative uses of the land—including hunting, fishing, tourism, recreation and Indigenous cultural and subsistence activities—have received at best only secondary consideration. Intensive agriculture and urbanization have exacted their own tolls on wildlife (and wildlife users) by **alienating** or converting for human uses the limited low-elevation habitats on which wildlife depend. The growth of coal and metal mining in the province since the late 1960s, while directly affecting less than 1 per cent of the provincial land mass, has incurred wider societal and environmental costs through incidents of surface and groundwater contamination.

A latecomer in comparison with other provincial industries, the expansion of oil and gas extraction in the northeast since the early 1970s introduced seismic lines and roads that have facilitated predator access for caribou and other **ungulates** (hooved mammals), altered wetland hydrology and fragmented grassland habitat for songbirds and other species. As the pressures on provincial landscapes have increased, government ability to effectively manage the cumulative effects of these industries and to maintain wildlife populations "for the benefit of present and future generations" has been compromised by fluctuating budget allocations and political will.

Super, Natural British Columbia?

As the province's motto and coat of arms suggest, BC has long recognized its origins in the fur trade and the historical dependence of its settler and Indigenous populations on its biological diversity and abundance. Since the late 1970s, tourism marketing for the province has referenced these historical celebrations of abundance through the use of the trademarked "Super, Natural British Columbia" in bumper stickers, travel brochures and websites.[15] And yet, as this history shows, wildlife abundance in the province has never been guaranteed, nor permanent. Mule deer declines and sea otter population crashes within the context of colonial market hunting, and more recent declines of mountain caribou and salmon populations, demonstrate the dangers of placing faith in what historians and other scholars have described as a "**myth of superabundance**"—the idea that the natural wealth of the North American continent was "so vast as to be inexhaustible."[16] Many species currently at risk in the province were never abundant to begin with—making them especially susceptible to changing habitat conditions, invasive species and, especially in the case of reptiles, human collectors.

The concept of **shifting baselines** is relevant here in describing changing expectations of what constitutes ecosystem health. Developed in the mid-1990s by UBC global fisheries scientist Daniel Pauly, "shifting baseline syndrome" describes a long-term pattern of amnesia wherein each generation of people sees the natural world they grew up within as the "normal state of nature" and measures declining natural abundance or integrity against that baseline. With each new generation, the baseline shifts, permitting what Pauly describes as "a gradual accommodation of the creeping disappearance." Each generation, in effect, redefines what is "natural," or normal, and in doing so, fails to recognize longer-term declines in ecosystems or species. As J.B. MacKinnon notes in his 2013 book, *The Once and Future World*, we "[forget] what the world used to look like." A "knowledge extinction," in MacKinnon's words, accompanies and facilitates the physical losses of biodiversity and ecosystem integrity.[17]

Since the 1990s, scientists have worked to counter this tendency to overlook longer-term population changes by factoring historical hunting and fishing statistics and other evidence into modern population assessments—in effect, shifting the baselines back as far as historical data permits. Inconsistencies and omissions in historical record keeping, and

Bumper stickers and road maps like this one featured the memorable "Super, Natural British Columbia" tourism slogan. Royal BC Museum, CM/B1599.

the absence of records of pre-contact Indigenous harvests, limit both the extent and the accuracy of historical population estimates. The problem of forgetting past abundance, however, remains highly relevant in public perceptions of nature. Failures to notice long-term changes in the natural world have prompted global conservation organizations to promote understanding of shifting baselines syndrome as a "cure for planetary amnesia."[18]

British Columbians, however, have not always forgotten, and some have remembered more than others. Across the province (and Canada more generally), wildlife conservation has enjoyed several distinct periods of heightened public awareness and political action: 1) in the 1910s, with the activities of the federal Commission of Conservation (1909–21), the completion of two major international treaties to protect fur seals and migratory birds, and the expansion of enforcement and licensing requirements for resident and non-resident hunters; 2) in the late 1960s and 1970s, when concerns about land conversions and logging damage to fish-bearing streams prompted a range of legislative and policy responses; and 3) in the late 1980s and 1990s, when the accelerating loss of BC's old-growth forests led to massive public protests and the reform of provincial forestry practices. As this history shows, however, these spikes in public and political support for conservation measures are only part of the story.

While conservation has attracted varying levels of government investment over time, it has never been the purview of government alone. Indigenous communities have long-established practices and beliefs that have supported the conservation and enhancement of fish and wildlife populations. Those who make their living from the land, including farmers, ranchers, trappers and guide outfitters, have employed conservation practices to varying degrees to ensure the sustainability of the natural systems they depend on. Ranchers in the BC Interior, for example, have embraced sophisticated mechanisms to protect riparian areas and guard against overgrazing and ecological damage by their cattle. Even through decades of enormous industrial and infrastructure expansion, such as the late 1950s and 1960s, naturalists, fish and game associations and conservation organizations persisted in the implementation of water controls, prescribed burns, fish ladders and other measures to nurture and regenerate wildlife habitat.

Defining Terms

Throughout the text, bolded terms indicate key concepts, initiatives or legislation of significance to the history of human-wildlife relationships in the province. Definitions of these terms are collated in the glossary at the end of the volume. Four concepts in particular are worth highlighting here, as they represent different ways of thinking about and approaching wildlife that emerged in particular historical moments and often existed simultaneously.

The first is **stewardship**. Defined as "an ethic and practice to carefully and responsibly manage natural resources and ecosystems for the benefit of current and future generations," stewardship is perhaps the best word in the English language to describe the complex and varied relationships that Indigenous British Columbians held, and continue to hold, with the lands and waterways that constitute their traditional territories.[19] Beginning in the 1990s, the term came to describe initiatives by conservation organizations and private landowners, notably ranchers and farmers, to voluntarily care for their properties with the long-term health of wildlife and ecosystems in mind. Since 2000, it has been associated with efforts by First Nations in BC to reclaim traditional roles of monitoring, protecting and caring for territorial lands and the fish and wildlife that depend on them.

The second term is **conservation**. Originating in the context of unregulated exploitation of natural resources across North America in the late nineteenth century, conservation historically described "the planned and efficient use of natural resources, so as to ensure their permanence." At the core of early conservationist thought was a recognition of limits. Early twentieth-century proponents such as US Forest Service chief Gifford Pinchot, forester and wildlife conservationist Aldo Leopold and, in British Columbia, writer and sport fisher Roderick Haig-Brown countered the prevailing myth of superabundance. Generally interchangeable with the idea of "wise use," conservation in practice aimed to stamp out wasteful practices and to sustainably allocate trees, wildlife, water and other resources. "By taking no more from nature in a given time period than nature itself could replace in that period," conservationists argued, wildlife and other resources could be sustained over the long term.[20]

But conservation was not defined by pragmatic economic thinking alone. Within wildlife conservation especially, many proponents believed that the protection of sentient, living creatures was an "admirable goal in itself," regardless of an animal's usefulness to humans.[21] This moral component to conservationist thought also found expression in concern for future human generations. Haig-Brown, for example, likened conservation to a "religious concept" for its acceptance of "moral and practical restraints that limit immediate self-interest." Because conservation was predicated on "a sense of responsibility . . . for the needs of future people," he argued, it "must always be as much an act of faith as an intellectual exercise."[22] Today, conservation practice draws on science and changing societal values to respond to the effects of human activities on ecosystems, effects that have intensified with the growth of human populations and advances in technology.[23]

Related to conservation is the third concept, that of **preservation** or protection. Many early Canadian conservationists spoke of conservation and
preservation interchangeably. Nineteenth-century game ordinances, for example, like the colony of Vancouver Island's 1859 Act for the Preservation
of Game, established what can be considered conservation measures in
their restrictions on deer and game bird hunting during breeding seasons.
Conservation and preservation, or protection, began to acquire distinct tra-
jectories with the proliferation of "game protective societies" in the southern
half of the province after 1890. Formed in response to the perception that
commercial, Indigenous and settler hunters used wildlife wastefully, these
societies aimed to protect wildlife not for everyone's use but rather for the
use of what were considered to be a more disciplined class of sport hunters.
Privately owned game reserves of the same period—or "preserves," as they
were often called—employed private game wardens to protect members' investments in exotic game transplants and fish and game propagation. These
more exclusive connotations of game preservation and protection were carried through in early twentieth-century provincial game legislation, which
placed progressive restrictions on commercial and subsistence hunting
while promoting hunting for sport. While conservation and protection/
preservation initiatives are generally aligned in their desire to restrict commercial hunting, conservation as a term does not carry the same freighted
emphasis on sport hunting to the exclusion of other uses.

The trajectory of the two concepts widened further during the wilderness campaigns of the 1970s and 1990s, when "preservation" and "protection" became more concretely associated with efforts to protect nature from
extractive uses for the benefit of a growing class of urban recreationalists.
In sum, the terms "protection" and "preservation" have historically implied
benefits "for some," while conservation has implied benefits "for all." A pres-
ervationist logic that aims to simply protect and "set aside" valued habitats
has been generally dismissed as inequitable by today's scientists, Indigenous
leaders and wildlife advocates. Preservationists' emphasis on a "hands off"
approach to ecosystem management, critics argued, was not only inequitable but inadequate. Protection is an important tool in meeting broader
wildlife conservation objectives, but efforts cannot stop there. Border-
crossing animal populations and landscape-level threats such as wildfire,
invasive species and climate change make a more active managerial stance
essential to the success of wildlife conservation initiatives. For Indigenous

managers, maintaining an active human presence within protected areas is essential to the revitalization of cultural uses of land and wildlife.

The fourth term is **wildlife management**, which describes efforts to balance the needs of wildlife with the needs of people according to the best available science. Like conservation, the concept of wildlife management arose in particular historical circumstances. The publication of Aldo Leopold's influential *Game Management* in 1933 launched the discipline of scientific wildlife management, which Leopold defined as "the art of making land produce sustained annual crops of wild game for recreational use." Rather than relying on reactionary methods such as game refuges and hunting regulations to protect specific game species, Leopold argued, wildlife managers could employ a range of techniques to enhance wildlife habitat on public and private lands. Leopold believed that game could be restored "by the creative use of the same tools which have heretofore destroyed it—axe, plow, cow, fire, and gun."[24] Creative use of the axe could reduce ingrowth of trees into grasslands, while the plow, used judiciously, could create food sources for deer and game birds. Attention to proper cattle stocking rates and enforcement of rotational grazing would benefit wild ungulates and other species. Managers could employ prescribed burns to stimulate the early **seral-stage** vegetation that attracted grouse, moose and deer. Finally, prudent hunting regulation could be used to limit the populations of prolific game species or to reduce the effects of predators in specific areas. By applying these methods in combination, land managers could restore game species and improve wildlife diversity while increasing the productivity of their land.

In British Columbia, Leopold's five tools were taken up by UBC zoologist Ian McTaggart Cowan and the first generation of government wildlife biologists beginning in the 1940s. In effect, scientific wildlife management became the accepted body of methods to achieve the objectives of wildlife conservation. By the 1970s most, but not all, wildlife managers held credentials as professional biologists, and a separate Conservation Officer Service handled the enforcement and public education components of the work. Today, wildlife management incorporates a range of positions, including conservation officers, researchers, biologists, managers and a new generation of Indigenous guardians. Leopold's five tools still form the foundation for wildlife management training, policy and practice across North America, although Indigenous knowledge has gained significant ground in recent decades as a deeply local and millenniums-old corrective to the "one size fits all" nature of mainstream management principles.

The practice and the theory of wildlife management was challenged in the 1960s and 1970s by a generation of environmentalists, naturalists and writers such as John Livingston and Farley Mowat who believed that humans had intervened too much already in natural systems and that predator-prey systems and other ecosystem dynamics would naturally rebalance themselves if left to recover.[25] This non-interventionist stance, often associated with urban advocates of conservation, remains a potent force in public discourse about wildlife. As the cumulative impacts of resource extraction, agriculture and urban expansion, climate change and invasive species alter or destroy the conditions for wildlife survival, however, scientists stress that the need for intervention has never been greater. Like the province's first game manager, Arthur Bryan Williams, who worked to rein in unsustainable hunting practices in the early twentieth century, today's wildlife work concentrates primarily on mitigating both the foreseeable and unintended consequences of human activities.

Contents

This history of over 250 years of wildlife management in British Columbia is presented in five parts. Part One, "Indigenous Wildlife Stewardship," explores Indigenous Peoples' interactions with wildlife prior to contact with Spanish explorers in 1774 in the area that became British Columbia. It explores how the diverse groups of Indigenous Peoples in the province were not only deeply knowledgeable and versatile users but also active managers of wildlife.

Part Two, "Euro-American Trade and Settlement: Competition and Perceptions of Abundance, 1774–1904," follows the expansion of commercial trading relationships in the eighteenth and nineteenth centuries and the dramatic changes experienced by resident peoples and wildlife with the growth of European settlement. Chapter 2 highlights the role of Indigenous hunters, trappers and suppliers of the maritime fur trade. The consequences of the trade for animal populations and Indigenous Peoples foreshadowed changes to come when wildlife became a common property resource "open to all" within the new colony of British Columbia. Chapter 3 explores the context for the colony's first game laws, including efforts by fish and game protection associations to curb the worst abuses of market hunting and arrest the decline of overharvested birds and mammals.

Part Three, "Early Wildlife Conservation and the Rise of Scientific Management, 1905–1965," follows the efforts of the province's first game and forest warden to develop and enforce hunting regulations, implement experimental conservation measures and establish licensing systems to fund the warden's activities. Chapter 4 examines the implications of efforts to circumscribe market and subsistence hunting for Indigenous and rural residents. Chapter 5 documents the role of science in the professionalization and modernization of wildlife management in the postwar period. The careers of zoologist Ian McTaggart Cowan and his colleagues at UBC epitomized these changes, nurturing the development of institutions like the Royal BC Museum and their reference-species collections and training a new generation of wildlife and fisheries biologists. As chapters 6 and 7 show, their work articulated a growing ecological perspective as a countercurrent to the period's prevailing enthusiasm for rapid infrastructure expansion and resource extraction.

Part Four, "Making Space for Wildlife, 1966–1991," charts an emergent environmental awareness among the general public and growing demands from wildlife organizations to give fishing, hunting and wildlife-viewing interests a seat at the table in resource allocation decisions. With accelerating urbanization, changes in public attitudes toward wild animals influenced the rise of the animal rights movement and forwarded powerful critiques of fur-bearer trapping and predator control. Knowledge about wildlife and their habitat needs took great leaps forward in this period, but mechanisms for protecting wildlife habitat across the landscape remained very limited. Chapter 8 explores government and non-government responses to the twin problems of land alienation and expanding access to wildlife populations. Chapter 9 turns to efforts by fish and game associations, naturalists and government wildlife programs to challenge forestry practices destructive to fish habitat. In the same period, Fraser River First Nations fought federal allocation rationales that saw in-river Indigenous fisheries receive the brunt of conservation regulations for dwindling salmon runs.

Part Five, "Rising Stakes, Changing Roles, 1992–2022," documents rising threats to biodiversity in the province and the efforts of a new generation of wildlife professionals and Indigenous leaders to protect threatened and culturally significant wildlife species and ecosystems. Chapter 10 explores the ways that environmental and animal rights organizations, whose policies reflected growing public opposition toward hunting and trapping, came into conflict with established conservation groups. Chapter 11 examines the rise and fall of BC's Forest Practices Code (FPC), recalled by many as a high-water mark for ecosystem-based management in the province. The career of wildlife ecologist Fred Bunnell reflects the expansion of knowledge around wildlife-forestry interactions. His collaboration with fellow scientists, First Nations and industry leaders propelled significant changes in forestry practices by the early 2000s. In chapter 12, women and Indigenous professionals ask different questions and shape new approaches. The final chapter charts the astonishing changes over the past three decades with respect to Indigenous rights and title in the province and their implications for shared and Indigenous-led management of wildlife and wildlife habitat. Throughout the book, inset features profile key individuals, species and initiatives that illustrate the successes and challenges of wildlife management in different periods. The individual experiences and perspectives highlighted here bring nuance to the often polarizing perspectives around wildlife and wildlife management in the province.

— PART ONE —

INDIGENOUS WILDLIFE STEWARDSHIP

1

Wildlife Stewardship among Indigenous Peoples before 1774

To describe the Indigenous Peoples of the area now known as British Columbia as "hunter-gatherers" is to greatly oversimplify the complex relationships they held and continue to hold with the province's diverse ecosystems. As Indigenous elders, knowledge keepers and allied academics have laboured to show for decades, British Columbia's most productive landscapes—its low-elevation meadows, marshes, river valleys and estuaries—resembled a garden more than a wilderness. Indigenous Peoples cultivated plants in environments across the province—seeding, digging, pruning and harvesting selected crops—but they also cultivated *animals*, actively tending and enhancing the populations of certain species, like shellfish, and creating conditions for abundance among salmon, ungulates and waterfowl. The Indigenous Peoples in what is now British Columbia, in other words, were active stewards of the lands they occupied. Drawing on detailed observation and experience of changes in natural systems over many generations, they used proven techniques and complex customary arrangements to ensure the long-term sustainability of the species they harvested.

This chapter draws on published works by Indigenous elders and hereditary leaders, as well as by Indigenous and non-Indigenous scholars (primarily anthropologists, archaeologists, ethnobotanists and ethnobiologists), to explore the principles and practices that governed human relationships with wild animals before contact with European traders and explorers in the 1770s. These relationships evolved over thousands of years of living within changing ecosystems in what would become British Columbia. The chapter sets the frame for the extent and rapidity of the changes that followed, for Indigenous communities and the animals they depended on, over the course of the next two and a half centuries.

Knowledge about pre-contact Indigenous practices and ways of life is partly facilitated by the relative recency and incompleteness of Euro-American colonization in the province. First Nations in BC experienced the effects of colonization and epidemic disease more than two centuries later than their counterparts in the eastern parts of the continent. For coastal societies especially, historians generally agree that the fur trade of the late eighteenth and nineteenth centuries "produced no major revolution" but instead "brought . . . an increase in wealth in [societies] already organized around wealth."[1] As Richard Atleo (Umeek) writes of his Nuu-chah-nulth ancestors in this period, "they continued to eat their own foods, live in their own homes, speak in their own ancient languages, and perform their ancient rituals and ceremonies, which were now enhanced by the influx of new material goods, such as blankets and iron tools."[2]

In the north especially, the slow and limited encroachment of settlers and resource extraction activities meant that many Indigenous communities experienced their traditional territories as relatively intact into the 1950s. As Robin and Jillian Ridington note, the Dane-zaa (Beaver) people of the Peace River valley "rarely encountered white people" until the completion of the Alaska Highway in 1942.[3] The late Gitxsan leader Neil J. Sterritt, Gitxaala anthropologist Charles Menzies and Nuu-chah-nulth elder Richard Atleo (Umeek) make similar observations about the belated impact of colonization within their communities in the northwest.[4] (Areas farther south, such as southern Vancouver Island and the Lower Mainland, the Okanagan and the Kootenays, experienced the loss of homelands, life-sustaining salmon runs and other plant and animal resources decades earlier.) Elders like Atleo's grandfather Chief Keesta, who was born in Ahousaht in the 1860s and lived into the early 1950s, remained, in Atleo's words, "firmly in the grasp of their ancestral ways." Too old to attend Western schooling by the time the first mission school was built in Ahousaht in 1896, he and his peers maintained their language and their familiarity with the teachings of their ancestors.[5] Subsequent generations would not be so fortunate.

Some of these elders and hereditary leaders, including Pacheedaht Chief Queesto of southwest Vancouver Island, Okanagan elder Harry Robinson and Ahousaht Chief Earl Maquinna George, worked independently or with interpreters and ethnographers to prepare their memoirs.[6] Others, such as the hereditary leaders of the Dane-zaa, Secwépemc (Shuswap), and Gitxsan and Wet'suwet'en, worked with elders and allied anthropologists to produce collective histories. Some managed to pass their knowledge on to their children.[7] Elders like the late Xenaksiala/Haisla hereditary leader Cecil Paul, for example, used knowledge passed down from family members to recover from the trauma of residential school and to nurture what W̱SÁNEĆ (Saanich) scholar Nick Claxton has described as an "Indigenous resurgence" among their peoples.[8] It is these sources, combined with a growing body of scholarship on the nature of Indigenous wildlife stewardship systems, that form the basis for the conclusions in this chapter.

Not all of the province's nearly two hundred First Nations are represented in the discussion that follows. While the chapter aims for regional and cultural representation, its examples are mostly limited to published sources (some unpublished materials, such as statements of cultural principles and dissertations accessible on First Nations and university websites, have also been consulted). The conclusions presented here proceed from the assumption that the general principles of respect, reciprocity and responsibility that guided stewardship practices across the wide range of First Nations represented in this chapter extended to their neighbours as well.

Indigenous Peoples of British Columbia

Prior to contact with Europeans in 1774, the area of northwestern North America now known as British Columbia was home to some of the largest and most diverse populations of Indigenous Peoples on the continent. No other region of Canada was so heavily occupied; about 40 per cent of all Indigenous people in Canada lived in what is now British Columbia. While pre-colonial population levels fluctuated and remain a source of debate, most anthropologists agree that the Indigenous population of the province likely ranged from 200,000 to 400,000 people, with the highest proportion along the coast and the major river systems.[9] Some areas of the coast, such as Haida Gwaii and the outer coast of Vancouver Island, were much more heavily populated than they are today.[10]

British Columbia was, and remains, a place of many Indigenous nations. The great variety of languages, ways of life, and artistic and ceremonial activities practiced in different parts of the province are indicative of the extraordinary diversity of its First Peoples. The diversity of languages

First Peoples in British Columbia

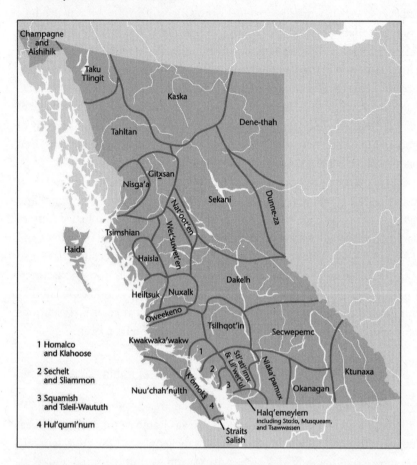

This map identifies major ethnic groups based on shared territory, language and culture. Some are represented today by a single nation; others comprise many smaller nations. Reprinted with permission from the Publisher of *The First Nations of British Columbia: An Anthropological Survey* by Robert J. Muckle © University of British Columbia Press 2014. All rights reserved by the Publisher.

here was greater than anywhere else in Canada, with over thirty native languages spoken across the province.[11] Many of these peoples still live in communities within their original territories. Detailed exploration of this diversity is beyond the scope of this chapter, but some generalizations can be drawn by dividing the province into three main cultural areas: the coast, the southern Interior and the northern Interior.[12]

The mild climate and abundant resources of the coast supported the largest populations of Indigenous Peoples and the greatest variety of languages and customs. Peoples of the coast centred their economies on the rich seasonal offerings of the sea and the forest, including salmon, shellfish, waterfowl, seals and whales. While plant and animal resources were generally more bountiful here than in other parts of the province, availability was limited to specific seasons and a limited number of conveniently located, resource-rich sites. As population densities on the coast increased over time and people established large permanent village sites, complex systems of ownership developed to control access to land and sea resources.

Indigenous Peoples of the coast: Gitxsan, Haida, Haisla, Halq'emeylem, Heiltsuk (Bella Bella), Homalco, Hul'qumi'num, Klahoose, K'ómoks (Comox), Kwakwaka'wakw (Kwakiutl), Nisga'a, Nuu-chah-nulth, Nuxalk (Bella Coola), Oweekeno, Sechelt, Tla'amin (Sliammon), Squamish, Straits Salish, Tsimshian and Tsleil-Waututh. The Taku Tlingit are sometimes considered to be within the northwest coast culture area and sometimes within the Subarctic.[13]

SPECIES PROFILE: Eulachon (*Thaleichthys pacificus*)

Eulachon, or oolichan, is a small fish in the smelt family that continues to be highly valued by Indigenous Peoples in BC. Like salmon, eulachon are anadromous: they live in salt water but spawn in fresh water, migrating in early spring to the major river systems along the BC coast. Known as "salvation fish" by some coastal nations, eulachon were the first fish to return to the river after winter. Their annual return brought an important source of fresh protein to Indigenous communities and a source of prey for birds, otters, wolves and other wildlife.

Described by historians as "one of the most concentrated sources of wealth in Indigenous North America," eulachon was, and remains, a valued trade item. Dried or rendered into oil (the fish are so oily during their reproductive phase that they will burn if lit, giving them another common name: "candlefish"), eulachon were the namesake for the "grease trails" used by Indigenous traders to bring eulachon grease to the Interior and goods and supplies back to the coast. The vitamin-rich grease provided a flavourful condiment to accompany dried salmon and acted as a preservative for berries, smoked cockles and other perishable foods over the winter months.

Nuxalk woman with eulachon catch near Bella Coola, ca.1920. Royal BC Museum, H-06863. Reprinted with permission from the Nuxalk Nation.

Thirteen major rivers in the province's northwest, including the Nass, Kitimat, Kitlope and Klinaklini, hosted large Indigenous eulachon fisheries. Less desirable as a target of settler commercial fisheries than salmon and herring, eulachon runs remained largely intact into the mid-twentieth century. This comparatively low commercial interest was among the factors that enabled the Nisga'a to obtain an exclusive right to the Nass River eulachon fishery in 1886. Familiar with eulachon life cycles and their sensitivity to changing ecological conditions, Nisga'a hereditary leaders argued that "any systematized endeavour to place the oolichan on the market would result in its extinction."[14]

Other northwestern nations would face more substantive obstacles in protecting their ancestral eulachon fisheries. In Haisla and Xenaksiala territory, the damming of the Kemano River in 1954 to power an aluminum smelter altered river flows, washing away the small, weak-swimming fish as they entered the river to spawn. By the early 1970s, municipal sewage and pulp and paper mill effluents had contaminated the fishery on the adjacent Kitimat River. While efforts to regulate water flows on the Kemano saw modest improvements in eulachon returns, runs on the Kitimat

River never recovered. "They took away . . . something so precious to our culture," Xenaksiala elder Cecil Paul commented in 2019.[15]

Since the early 1990s, nearly all of BC's historically abundant eulachon runs have declined precipitously. Only the Nass River run on the north coast remains relatively healthy. For the Nuxalk people of Bella Coola, the eulachon failed to return to the Bella Coola River in the spring of 1999 and have returned in numbers too low to harvest ever since. The expansion of commercial shrimp trawl fisheries in the mid-1990s have been implicated in the collapse. Before the regulation of these fisheries for eulachon conservation in the early 2000s, trawlers netted tons of eulachon as unwanted bycatch, wiping out juveniles and adults alike. In 2011, the Committee on the Status of Endangered Wildlife in Canada (COSEWIC) declared both the Fraser River and central Pacific Coast eulachon populations as endangered, attributing their decline to a combination of factors, including commercial fisheries bycatch, logging and shoreline development, pollution and climate change.

Today only ten eulachon runs remain on BC rivers.[16] Because of the importance of the fish to Indigenous societies and the accumulation of ecological knowledge that accompanied their harvest, more information is available about the spawning and life cycle of eulachon—including exact migration routes, spawning times and run sizes—than about any other fish species in the province. Nations like the Nuxalk have led the effort to conserve and restore eulachon to their territories, collecting cultural knowledge about the fish alongside data on river flows, water temperatures and fish movements. Since 2012, the eulachon returns to the Bella Coola River have slowly begun to increase. The reasons for their decline, however, are complex and overlapping, with the role of such factors as climate change still poorly understood. The known sensitivity of the fish to high flow rates and changing water temperatures makes the work of restoring them to the waters of a climate-altered coast all the more complicated.[17]

In the southern Interior cultural area, Indigenous populations were smaller than on the coast, concentrated primarily along the Fraser and Columbia River systems. Annual salmon runs on the Fraser and Columbia rivers and their tributaries were central to southern Interior economies, together with deer, bear, elk and waterfowl. For much of the year southern Interior peoples travelled within and beyond their territories in family groups to hunt, fish, gather plant and animal resources, and trade with neighbouring nations, returning to live in small villages of partially underground pit houses over the winter months.

Indigenous Peoples of the southern Interior: Ktunaxa (Kutenai or Kootenay), Nlaka'pamux (Thompson), Syilx (Okanagan), Secwépemc (Shuswap), St'atl'imx (Lillooet), Tsilhqot'in (Chilcotin) and, in some interpretations, the southern Dakelh (Carrier).[18]

The northern Interior of the province was the least populous of the three cultural areas. Here, Indigenous Peoples spoke Athapaskan languages and centred their economies around mobile or nomadic hunting, fishing and gathering. Salmon were important along major rivers that emptied into the Pacific Ocean, and nations with easy access to the sea shared cultural commonalities with the coastal peoples. Most groups, however, depended more heavily on other resources, such as moose and caribou.

Indigenous Peoples of the northern Interior/Subarctic: Dene-thah (Slavey), Dane-zaa (Beaver), Kaska, Nat'oot'en (Babine), Sekani, Tahltan, Wet'suwet'en and, in some interpretations, the northern Dakelh (Carrier).[19]

Indigenous Stewardship Practices

The Indigenous Peoples in what is now called British Columbia have relied on and helped to sustain the biodiversity of their homelands for at least ten thousand years and probably much longer. From permanent winter village sites along the coast, or along rivers and lakeshores, First Nations peoples would (and still do) travel to specific sites throughout their territories to access various seasonal resources as they became available. These seasonal rounds involved the harvesting of specific resources at particular times of year from a range of different habitats, from tidal estuaries to valley bottoms to mountaintops.[20] In the northern Interior, for example, family groups moved throughout the year from traplines to fish camps to hunting ranges, hunting for caribou in the fall as the animals migrated southward from the tundra to the boreal forest, trapping fur-bearers over the winter, and fishing and gathering edible and medicinal plants from when the ice broke up in April through the summer months.

These seasonal movements were dictated by a deep ecological knowledge of place. Hunters, for example, drew on a vast store of experiential knowledge gained from observing animal habits and behaviour in different seasons and climatic conditions.[21] Many animal species acted as ecological indicators in peoples' seasonal rounds. As ethnobiologists Trevor Lantz and Nancy Turner have shown, "the songs of certain birds, or the appearance of certain types of butterflies or other insects, are signs of seasonal change or of the time for some important harvest event."[22] The Secwépemc, for example, recognized the call of the western meadowlark (*Sturnella neglecta*) in late April as the best time to harvest desert parsley.[23] Knowledge of seasonal change was also reflected in Indigenous languages. The Nuu-chah-nulth of Vancouver Island's northwest coast, for example, used the word "Naa'sQaʔitkquisHicit" to refer to these cycles of seasonal change through the year and the reliance of humans and animals on these changes.[24]

Indigenous Peoples were, and remain, not only deeply knowledgeable and versatile users but also active *managers* of the province's biodiverse ecosystems. Considerable evidence exists that First Nations actively stewarded plant and animal populations to enhance their productivity. Indeed, recent scholarship by, and in collaboration with, Indigenous knowledge keepers in several areas of the province has expanded overly simplified representations of Indigenous Peoples as "hunter-gatherers" to build an understanding of these peoples as active resource managers and cultivators of their homeland territories.[25] Indigenous strategies to produce a greater variety and abundance of foods and material in easily accessible and predictable locations had the effect, this scholarship has shown, of not only maintaining and enhancing wildlife populations but also increasing the diversity of wildlife habitats.[26]

Two concepts are central to the discussion that follows. The first, **Indigenous management**, refers to the economic allocation of natural resources and the regulation of human access that flows from hereditary leaders' ownership and authority over a particular territory. The second, **Indigenous stewardship**, refers to the responsibility that comes with those hereditary rights. Anthropologist Richard Daly, who worked with the Gitxsan and Wet'suwet'en nations in preparation for *Delgamuukw v. British Columbia* (1997), described Indigenous stewardship as "the managers' responsibility . . . to answer for their actions to their own social group and to the ecological and spiritual authority of the territories they manage."[27] Management and stewardship responsibilities often corresponded with

watershed boundaries. Among the Haisla, for example, watershed stewardship areas, or wa'wais, followed "the tops of mountains around the different
drainable basins of the rivers." Hereditary wa'wais owners are bound by
traditional laws, or nuyem: "a code of stewardship that has detailed prescriptions for how the land, waters and wildlife are to be harvested, shared
and respected."[28] Marianne and Ronald Ignace describe a similar system
of watershed-based stewardship among the Interior Secwépemc peoples.[29]

Stewarding Coastal Wildlife

On the coast, Indigenous societies came to divide their time between large
permanent winter villages and specific, resource-rich sites accessed seasonally for whale and seal hunting, eulachon or halibut fishing, and clam,
berry and root gathering. These sites were limited in number and highly
valued. Streams with large populations of salmon or eulachon, for example,
could be kilometres apart, while elk or deer were relatively scarce beyond
the forest clearings where they grazed.[30] Dependence on a finite number
of productive sites led to complex systems of ownership over land and sea
resources, wherein extended family groups or "houses" controlled specific
resource sites within larger, clan-owned territories. These systems of land
tenure provided the basis for the sustainable management of valued wildlife
populations.[31] House members hunted, fished and gathered not only to meet
the daily dietary needs of their house groups but also to produce a surplus
for trade with other groups and as a means of acquiring wealth and status.

The potlatch was one such mechanism wherein hereditary chiefs demonstrated their wealth and prestige by hosting lavish feasts where food and
goods were given away and rights and uses of specific territories and resources reaffirmed. Among the Stó:lō, for example, wealth produced by families at
the mouth of the Fraser River, such as dried clams and woven bullrush mats,
was exchanged for the right to access family-owned salmon fishing sites in
the Fraser Canyon. Families who did not fulfil their social obligations risked
losing access rights to distant resources.[32] Farther north, Gitxsan chiefs used
the formal institution of the potlatch to introduce the foods present and the
"specific mountain or creek that it came from," verifying in the process their
authority and jurisdiction over a specific territory.[33] In both cases, hereditary
chiefs thus had strong incentives to maintain and enhance the productivity
of plant and animal populations within their territories.[34]

Stó:lō men dip netting for salmon on the Fraser River, ca.1880. Prime fishing locations like this were owned and stewarded by family lineages. Photo by Charles Macmunn. Royal BC Museum, A-06077. Reprinted with permission from the Stó:lō Nation.

Within many BC First Nations, hereditary chiefs continue to carry ancestral responsibilities into the present. As the late Gitxsan hereditary chief Bill Blackwater Jr. (Chief Mauus) explained, "one of the main mandates of the Gitxsan Chiefs [is] to make sure that . . . every beautiful living thing, whether it be wildlife or plants, is available for future people. My chief name, Mauus, never goes away. When I pass on, someone else will take that name on. He or she will also have the same responsibility that I have . . . to make sure that [those] resources are protected . . . for future generations to come."[35]

Efforts to increase output of plant and animal resources at specific sites had the corollary effect of improving habitat conditions for valued species. The Kwakwaka'wakw (Kwakiutl) peoples of northeastern Vancouver Island, for example, created "clam gardens" by rolling large rocks to the low tide line to catch sand and gravel in terrace-like structures (some of which are still visible at low tide today). Designated stewards tended these terraced clam beds by regularly aerating the soil with digging sticks, clearing away obstructions such as shells and sticks and selectively harvesting larger clams to give juvenile ones more space to grow. These efforts extended and enhanced sandy areas for clam production, creating an abundant, predictable and easily accessible shellfish resource for nearby villages.[36]

Cultivated spaces like clam gardens, and the "root gardens" of edible water plants that the Kwakwaka'wakw, Nuu-chah-nulth and other northwest coast groups tended in coastal estuaries, had the associated benefit of attracting geese and waterfowl. "Garden hunting" at both kinds of sites not only protected plant and shellfish output but also provided additional sources of dietary protein.[37] These examples—together with the network of stone fish traps, tended berry patches, crabapple "orchards" and eelgrass meadows along the coast—provide evidence of Indigenous resource management systems across a complex network of cultivated landscapes. As UBC anthropologist Charles Menzies, a member of the Gitxaala Nation of the northwest coast, writes, millenniums of "interaction and purposeful intervention" shaped the environments of coastal societies.[38]

Maintaining Salmon Abundance

One of the indicators of successful wildlife management is the sustainability of the harvest over time. The Indigenous salmon fishery along BC's coast and major rivers is a good example of successful management. Analyses of pre-contact Indigenous population levels in the province and dietary intake of fish protein point to very high annual salmon harvests—harvest levels that were comparable to or higher than late twentieth-century commercial harvests for all five species of salmon in the province.[39] High Indigenous population levels on the coast, combined with the technological capability to seriously impact fish populations (salmon weirs, for example, sometimes extended across rivers bank to bank, blocking all incoming fish), created the possibility of overexploitation. And yet, as anthropologist Michael Kew has argued, Indigenous fishing practices had the effect of stimulating rather than depressing salmon productivity, allowing for high annual salmon harvests over many centuries.[40]

Chief Old Fort Michel (right) of Lake Babine Nation drying spring salmon from the Babine River, June 1926. Photo by Frank Cyril Swannell. Royal BC Museum, sw-02975. Reprinted with permission from the Lake Babine Nation.

Complex systems of fisheries management contributed to maintaining and possibly enhancing the populations of harvested species over time. As Ahousat Chief Earl Maquinna George wrote in 2003, "there is a name for 'conservation' in the Nuu-Chah-Nulth language: *7u<u>h</u>-mowa-shitl* ('keep some and not take all'). . . . People knew how much [fish] they could use, and they didn't ever use it all."[41] Cultural rituals and Indigenous leadership played important roles in fisheries management. In many Indigenous groups, leaders were responsible for the opening of the salmon fishery through first salmon ceremonies, where the first fish of the season was prepared in a special manner and shared among community members. These ceremonies were typically performed several days (and up to two weeks) after the beginning of the salmon run, allowing salmon to run freely until the fishery was officially opened and thereby protecting their ability to reproduce.[42]

Ownership of fishing sites and equipment by extended family groups also reduced pressure on salmon populations. Among the Gitxsan and Nisga'a of the northwest coast, for example, hereditary chiefs controlled access to fishing sites and smokehouses on their traditional territories. Among the Cowichan, non-intensive forms of fishing such as gaffing were open to all, but more intensive harvesting technologies like fishing traps belonged to specific family groups.[43] Cultural expectations of redistribution ensured that fish harvests were shared throughout the community. At potlatches, or community feasts, hereditary leaders acquired status through generous gifts of dried salmon and other valued resources. Ensuring the ongoing productivity of salmon harvests at fishing sites under their jurisdiction was an important part of maintaining that status.[44] In other cases these practices are reflected in language and in traditional roles. The Heiltsuk people of Bella Bella, for example, use the word "miaisila" to refer to someone designated as the guardian of a fish-bearing river.[45]

Careful observation and experience with animal populations over many centuries also led to practical methods to ensure their continuity. Hereditary leaders or fisheries guardians who monitored in-river salmon weirs, for example, worked with a knowledge of when the run started and ended, opening the weir after a certain time to allow passage of fish to spawning grounds. In Secwépemc territory, the pole-and-lattice weirs that spanned the South Thompson River incorporated trap doors that were left open during the day to allow salmon to proceed to upriver spawning grounds.[46] For the Tsleil-Waututh Nation of Burrard Inlet in North Vancouver, trapping salmon at in-river weirs presented an opportunity to target male fish for harvest, allowing greater numbers of egg-bearing females to pass through the weir to upriver spawning grounds.[47] Reef nets used in ocean fisheries by the Coast Salish peoples of southern Vancouver Island allowed for conservation needs in similar ways, permitting a portion

Fish weir on the Spallumcheen/Shuswap River operated by the Secwépemc people of Splatsín, ca.1900. Photo by C.W. Holliday. Enderby and District Museum & Archives, edms photo #3994. Reprinted with permission from Spatsin te Secwépemc.

of the catch to pass through a built-in "escape" hole at the bottom of the net.[48] As W̱SÁNEĆ scholar Nick Claxton explains, "it was a spiritual belief that the schools of salmon were families and that if some of the salmon could escape then those particular lineages would perpetuate themselves."[49]

Unlike most modern commercial fishing operations, where mortality rates are high for non-targeted juveniles and "bycatch" species, Indigenous fisheries typically employed a selective harvest that permitted the release of non-target ages and species. Live trap ocean fisheries like the W̱SÁNEĆ reef nets allowed non-targeted fish to be released unharmed, with minimal handling.[50] In-river fisheries permitted even greater selectivity by targeting specific runs of fish on their return to their streams of origin. As Gitxaala scholar Charles Menzies explains, "when harvesting occurs at the mouth of a creek, the harvester knows exactly which spawning population is being targeted. Harvesting at close range ensures that the fisher can target a particular species . . . or size of fish."[51]

Menzies describes his people's ancestral use of stone traps located in the intertidal zone near the mouths of salmon-bearing streams and rivers. Consisting of stacks of stones arranged in a semicircular design, the traps caught fish behind the wall of stones when the tide receded.[52] During the incoming and high tide, the structures became submerged, allowing fish to "advance freely up the estuary and into the stream without obstruction."[53] Hereditary leaders used such technology to regulate the harvest based on observations of spawner abundance. Fishers selected by species and age, leaving non-target and juvenile fish to escape the trap as the tide rose. The use of weirs, stone traps and reef nets persisted in some areas until the 1880s and even the early 1900s, when colonial regulations and the effects of epidemic disease brought an end to many live trap Indigenous fisheries technologies.[54]

Management of the salmon fishery also required conservation responses in times of scarcity. As Nuu-chah-nulth Chief Earl Maquinna George recalls, "there were years when no fish came up the rivers. The word for this is wikĬns7ii ('cycle never arrived')."[55] In these times, people turned to other foods, especially shellfish. The labour-intensive nature of the Indigenous fishery meant that a low return on effort in times of scarcity prompted a shift to other resources, allowing stocks to recover.[56] But reducing pressure on salmon resources was not the only conservation strategy. Groups also drew on acquired ecological knowledge to stimulate salmon productivity. The Tla'amin Nation of the northern Sunshine Coast refrained from eating female fish or their eggs during the first half of the fishing season, returning them live to the river instead.[57] Secwépemc chiefs at Adams Lake insisted on extreme caution during spawning season, requiring community members to switch from poles to paddles to propel canoes over spawning shoals.[58] Habitat and stock enhancement were other strategies used to augment salmon populations. The Nuu-chah-nulth, for example, transported salmon eggs and smolts in moss-lined boxes to depleted waterways. They and other northwest coast nations improved spawning habitat by removing woody debris from stream beds and actively shaping creeks to increase spawning areas.[59]

These conservation practices, combined with relatively limited cultural impacts on riparian ecosystems, allowed Indigenous groups to maintain a highly productive fishery over thousands of years while avoiding long-term negative effects on populations of salmon and other valued fish species.[60]

Stewarding Animals on the Land

Similar stewardship practices existed for valued terrestrial animal species. Among the Nuxalk and Kwakwaka'wakw, for example, access to mountain peaks and valleys for mountain goat hunting was controlled by hereditary chiefs whose status depended on the sustainability of the hunt.[61] Other sources suggest that in times of scarcity, hunters responded by reducing pressure on game populations. Heiltsuk hunters, for example, rotated harvest areas to allow heavily hunted deer populations to recover.[62] Other nations, like the Kaska Dena of northern British Columbia, guarded large game animals against overharvest by adhering to more formalized protected areas strategies.

In the ancient Kaska Dena practice of dechin, elders or prophets within the community designated areas for protection with dechin, or "sticks," arranged in a cross formation. The markers indicated that the area was a sacred place to be protected. Wilderness guide and conservationist Wayne Sawchuk described the experience of encountering the remains of a dechin in his 2004 book on the Muskwa-Kechika watersheds within Kaska Dena traditional territory: "as [we rode] into the flats near the confluence we noticed a curiously carved pole and crossbar leaning against a spruce tree. It was very old, nearly rotted into the ground." William Davis, an Indigenous guide accompanying the expedition, identified it as a dechin. "That cross," Davis explained, "means that this is a sacred place, a place you protect. It's a place where you don't hunt, unless you need to, and then the animals will always be there to feed the people if times get hard." Similar principles of caring for the land and future generations continue to guide present-day Kaska Dena land stewards in their work to protect their ancestral territories.[63]

The seasonality of the hunt also mattered. Gitxsan Chief Tenimget referenced historical practices in an interview in the 1980s, noting that "we have always limited our hunting to the fall and winter, when the young are no longer dependent on their mothers."[64] Indigenous Peoples drew on generations of acquired ecological knowledge to monitor the health of animal populations. Northern caribou hunters, for example, examined animal fat as an indication of population well-being and the quality of surrounding range conditions.[65]

While peoples of the northwest coast used hereditary systems of land-ownership to regulate access to wildlife within house territories, Interior

Tahltan hunters on the way to the hunt, ca.1900. Andrew Jackson Stone Fonds. Royal BC Museum, D-08958. Reprinted with permission from the Tahltan Central Government.

nations generally viewed land and hunting territories as communal property open to all members of a nation.[66] Within those nations, chiefs of local communities carried the responsibility to monitor wildlife populations and manage allocations accordingly. Some nations supplemented the political role of the chiefs with knowledgeable community members who acted as stewards of game populations. The Secwépemc, for example, designated experienced adults as yecwmínmen, or caretakers, of valued wildlife and plant species within a particular watershed. Trappers acted as yecwmínmen of the watersheds through which they ran their traps. As elder Joe Stanley Michel recalled, families who trapped in a given valley "had to look after that valley, as well." Yecwmínmen also assumed broader roles, monitoring fish and game populations at specific locations and communicating their assessments to hereditary leaders to inform decisions about when and where a hunt or a fishery might begin.[67]

These practices of monitoring animal populations and regulating access are representative of historic and ongoing Indigenous philosophies of stewardship across the province. Such philosophies were predicated on a regular and active wildlife harvest. As Chief Tenimget asserted, "we look after our land by using it." For Tenimget and many other Indigenous leaders, regular hunting stimulated productivity within animal populations and provided a point of contact in maintaining long-term relationships with valued species. Indigenous communities fished, trapped and hunted for many different species, but "within limits that allow for regeneration."[68]

Certainly, evidence of overhunting exists. Hunting methods such as fire drives, where fire was used to channel animals into areas where they could be slaughtered, sometimes resulted in the destruction of large numbers of deer and other animals.[69] Archaeological records suggest that the combined effects of overhunting and climate change resulted in the extinction of more than 70 per cent of large mammal species across North America after the Ice Age.[70] Analysis of early European records also points to the scarcity of large ungulate species in places like the Columbia River basin at the time of contact.[71] Later, the disappearance of elk from the southern Interior in the 1860s has been attributed to a combination of overhunting by Interior Indigenous groups with newly acquired firearms and the susceptibility of elk to bovine diseases that arrived with the first cattle ranches in the region.[72]

On the whole, however, the story of Indigenous relationships with wildlife in pre-contact British Columbia seems to be one of adaptation. In the Interior

and in the north, especially, Indigenous people responded to resource depletion at least in part by moving on; traditions of regional movement in seasonal rounds allowed for the renewal of valued wildlife populations.[73]

Beyond seasonal movement, however, ancestral stories and oral histories from across the province point to the process of learning from times
of scarcity. In many of these stories, taking too much or otherwise disre-
specting animals results in their disappearance, with severe consequences
for the human societies that depend on them. A good example is Neil J.
Sterritt's telling of an ancient Gitxsan story, wherein children's mistreat-
ment of steelhead trout leads to a poor salmon season and starvation for
the people. The story concludes with the halayt, or shaman, advising village
leaders to remind their children of the "need to respect the laws and values
of our ancestors."[74] In this story and the many others like it, the moral of
the story serves as a reminder of cultural values of reciprocity and respect
for non-human species. These values, in turn, set a foundation for systems
of land tenure and resource allocation, and practices of conservation and
habitat enhancement, that together ensured the sustainability of valued
animal populations.

Burning to Enhance Wildlife Habitat

Hereditary chiefs and designated stewards also played active roles in the
management of wildlife habitats, most commonly through the application
of fire. Evidence from a range of sources—including Indigenous oral
histories, early explorer and settler accounts, archaeological records,
and fire scar and tree ring analysis—shows that BC First Nations made
deliberate use of fire across the province, but especially in the southern
Interior. Here, human-set fires augmented natural wildfires common
in many plant communities in the region, including grasslands, boreal
forest and Douglas fir–ponderosa pine forests. Interior peoples used fire
to stimulate the growth and quality of valued food plants, such as berries
and edible bulbs; to control forest insects; and to check the encroachment
of forests and sagebrush within meadows and wetlands. Among the Syilx
people of the Okanagan, designated Firekeepers or Kou-Skelowh carried
the responsibility to "purify the land" by setting fire to berry bushes and
hillsides, renewing growth, clearing brush and creating natural fireguards.
Before setting the fires, descendants of the last Syilx Firekeeper recall, lines

of Kou-Skelowh would walk through the area beating drums to warn birds, mammals and other animals.[75]

Periodic burning also "promoted and renewed the habitat that made valued game possible."[76] The Nlaka'pamux (Thompson) peoples, for example, set fires in valley bottoms in spring and fall to control ponderosa pine ingrowth and create openings for the bunchgrass ecosystems that elk and other ungulates depended on.[77] In the spaces that fire opened up, deer and elk sought out sunlight-dependent sedges, grasses and shrubs; grizzly and black bears found berries and roots; and mountain goats and sheep accessed high-elevation swards.[78] Many non-game species also benefited. As scientists have since shown, fires of intermediate frequency and size support high levels of plant and animal biodiversity. While some species tolerate fire better than others, the patchwork of habitats that regular, low-intensity fires produce supports a wider range of species than areas with less disturbance.[79]

The Ktunaxa people of southeastern British Columbia used this knowledge of the role of fire in enhancing habitat productivity to lure game into Rocky Mountain passes. Hunters set fires along river valleys in the spring to produce succulent grassy corridors, enticing bison and other game into the meadows and trench valleys of the Rockies, where steep valley walls and snowdrifts made animals easier to hunt. These methods produced a predictable and accessible source of game close to winter encampments.[80] Fire-scarred trees in the Canadian Rockies, researchers have found, suggest that fires occurred with double the frequency along valley corridors than in more remote areas. As environmental historian Stephen Pyne concludes, the great grassy valleys of the Rockies "were maintained, if not created, by fire-wielding humans."[81]

Further north, First Nations peoples of the Peace River area made frequent use of fire, producing extensive grasslands that, as archaeologists have shown, supported bison and other wildlife populations for thousands of years.[82] As Alexander Mackenzie reported in 1793, the prairie near Fort St. John was "so crowded with animals as to have the appearance . . . of a stall-yard, from the state of the ground, and the quantity of dung which is scattered over it."[83] The Dane-zaa and other Peace River peoples continued ancestral practices of spring burning into the 1940s, clearing travel routes and maintaining habitat for moose, hare and lynx.[84]

Indigenous use of fire was much less frequent within the rainforests of the coast. Smaller burns, however, continued to be applied to specific sites.

The Haida, for example, used fire to maintain salal and huckleberry patches in specific places. Inland along the major river valleys of the northwest coast, Gitxsan and Wet'suwet'en trappers burned underbrush to create "roads" for animal movement, setting snares along the fire-opened passageways. Valley bottoms within the Skeena-Bulkley corridor still bear evidence of long-term fire use to create meadows for deer and bear, maintain berry patches and control insect outbreaks within the forests.[85] Human use of fire on the coast was most prevalent in the arid southeastern tip of Vancouver Island and the Gulf Islands. Here, the W̱SÁNEĆ and Lekwungen (Songhees and Xwsepsum Nations) peoples regularly set controlled fires to enhance the growth of food plants, to improve deer habitat and to maintain open habitats that facilitated hunting. Like the grassy trench valleys of the Rockies, the Garry oak savannahs of Victoria and southeastern Vancouver Island, rich in acorns and edible bulbs such as blue camas (*Camassia quamash*), were maintained and expanded by burning (see plate 1).[86]

Fires in each of these places were not set casually; instead, people selected specific sites, times and conditions for burning. Evidence from oral histories shows that some northwest coast groups burned berry harvest areas in the fall, choosing a time just before a rainfall to allow for greater control. In the southern Interior cultural area, the Secwépemc typically burned in cycles of ten to twenty years, selecting the moderately dry and gentle wind conditions of mid-spring.[87] Others burned in the early spring when the ground was wet and ridge-top snow lines created a natural barrier.

Because European colonial settlement and associated fire-suppression policies extinguished Indigenous landscape burning practices from the early 1900s on, little evidence survives of controlled burning techniques among First Nations in BC. Evidence from neighbouring peoples in Montana and Alberta shows that a detailed knowledge of winds, the burn frequency of a given site and the relative humidity of fuel types governed decisions of when and where to burn. These techniques, together with the use of firebreaks and wetted conifer boughs to control or extinguish flames, were likely also employed by Indigenous Peoples in BC. Like other methods they employed to enhance wildlife populations and improve habitats, Indigenous Peoples drew on detailed knowledge of natural systems and generations of observation and experimentation to modify landscapes to their benefit.[88]

Stewardship as a Cultural Responsibility:
Animals as "Generous Relatives"

Indigenous Peoples tended and maintained animal populations not only to ensure their own survival but also because they felt it was their responsibility to do so. Stewardship practices, in other words, were rooted in a larger philosophy of respect for living things and the environments that sustained them. Though cultures and belief systems differed across the province, Indigenous Peoples shared common principles of reciprocity and responsibility toward the plant and animal species on which they depended. Ethnobotanist Nancy Turner explains: "animals, fish, trees and other plants . . . were regarded in traditional worldviews as generous relatives, willing to give themselves to people within a reciprocal system that demanded proper care and respect in return." This understanding of animals as "generous relatives" meant that they had the power "to influence human lives in positive or negative ways, depending on whether the humans were worthy and behaved properly towards them."[89] Indigenous fishers and hunters were therefore motivated to ensure that such animal relatives "were able to thrive and have their needs met." By regularly fulfilling these expectations, they understood that animals would, in turn, "support the interests and needs of humans by presenting themselves more abundantly for harvest."[90]

Stories of transformation from humans to animals, and animals to humans, underscored this sense of kinship and mutual obligation. In many Indigenous stories from the distant past, animals have human form and live in human-like societies, only gradually assuming their present animal forms. In other stories, humans are transformed into animals and live among them, returning to the human world to teach people how to treat animals of that particular species respectfully based on their personal experiences.[91] As Kwakwaka'wakw clan chief Adam Dick explained, "we had the same voice at the beginning of time—all the animals, the people."[92] Critically, animals were not "like" people; they *were* people. Richard Atleo (Umeek) elaborates: Nuu-chah-nulth peoples "know and experience [other life forms, including animals and plants] as *quuʔas*, as people like themselves."[93] An understanding that all of the animals and plants had their own societies, each with particular social rules and conventions for relationships with humans, guided the actions of Indigenous hunters and fishers.[94] Because animals were once (and could still be) humans in a different form, hunters perceived them as "intelligent, social, and spiritually powerful" animal people to whom they had particular obligations.[95]

Secwépemc scholars Marianne and Ronald Ignace describe this relationship between Indigenous Peoples and other life forms as "reciprocal accountability." The idea of an animal "giving itself up" to responsible hunters or fishers is expressed as "kecmentsút" in the Secwépemc language.[96] For an animal to give itself to the hunter, the hunter must approach it with a "clean mind and body."[97] As Robin and Jillian Ridington note, for northern Dane-zaa hunters there is "no such thing as luck in the hunt. A hunter is successful because the animal recognizes him as a good [and generous] person."[98] Accepting an animal's gift graciously involved killing it quickly, thanking it (and the Creator) for its gift, treating animal remains properly by disposing of them in appropriate ways and avoiding any waste of animal meat. Sharing the gift with other community members extended this principle of respect into social relations. Hunting and fishing became in this context "ritual and spiritual acts" through which communities maintained relationships with the sentient environment around them.[99]

Recognition of this reciprocity formed the basis for laws to govern those relationships. As Gisday Wa and Delgam Uukw, hereditary chiefs of the Gitxsan and Wet'suwet'en nations, explained in their opening statement to the Supreme Court of British Columbia in May 1987, "the land, the plants, the animals and the people all have spirit—they all must be shown respect. This is the basis for our law."[100] Such laws, according to Nuu-chah-nulth elder Richard Atleo (Umeek), aimed to "maximize the wellbeing of all life forms, human and nonhuman."[101] As Xenaksiala elder Cecil Paul confirms in his stories about the consequences of mistreating frogs, this sense of reverence for life—what the Nuu-chah-nulth describe as "iisʔak," or sacred respect—extended to all life forms, not just game species.[102]

Ritual practices of respect and reciprocity often had the effect of conserving animal populations and protecting habitats. Among these, giving thanks and avoiding waste or needless suffering were ways to honour the animal's gift and to avoid offending powerful animal relatives. Avoiding the needless killing of any life form supported the belief that all plants and animals had their own families and societies "parallel to and as important as those of people."[103] In the instance of the salmon reef net described above, for example, the hole in the bottom of the net reflected a respect for salmon families and lineages: allowing a portion of the catch to escape allowed some members of salmon families to carry on their family lineages.[104] Such practices had the effect of preventing overharvesting and waste.

Failure to meet these reciprocal obligations might lead animal relatives to refuse to give themselves in future, or to impose sanctions, including misfortune, illness or death, on the hunter or his family. As Tahltan elders told ethnographer James Teit in the 1910s, AtsEntma, the meat mother, held the power to "make game scarce" as a warning or punishment when "someone had not treated the animals respectfully or had failed to make full use of them as food."[105] Success in hunting, and in life, meant actively maintaining harmony among human and animal relatives.[106]

Conclusion: "Our Box Was Full"

Indigenous societies prior to contact with Europeans did not live a romantic existence of consistent ecological harmony.[107] Salmon failed to return some years, and game populations fluctuated for a range of reasons, including localized overhunting. Resulting periods of scarcity led to reliance on a wide range of plant and animal resources. Harvest technologies such as fishing weirs and fire drives, furthermore, had the potential to overexploit animal resources. Overwhelmingly, however, evidence suggests that Indigenous societies were able to maintain wildlife abundance and diversity over many centuries. This is true even in coastal areas, where relatively high Indigenous populations produced correspondingly high levels of exploitation of salmon and other animal species.

Cultural systems of ownership of land and sea resources reduced pressure on animal populations. Detailed observation of and experience with the fluctuations in natural systems over many generations allowed people to make adjustments in times of scarcity. This ecological understanding, combined with an underlying ethic of respect for other species, produced beliefs and practices that fostered wildlife conservation.[108] As Nancy Turner and Fikret Berkes remark, "it is difficult, if not impossible, to identify intention to conserve as separate from a belief system that values and recognizes as kin all lifeforms, from frogs to wolves to cedar trees. Nevertheless, this system, within its cultural contexts, seems to have worked well for people in maintaining their resources over a long period of time."[109]

For Charles Menzies and many other Indigenous leaders and knowledge keepers, the active management and stewardship of their territories over millenniums produced an environment that supported wildlife abundance and human well-being. As the Gitx̱san and Wet'suwet'en maintain, "our box was full."[110] In the two and a half centuries that followed, European traders, profit-seekers and, later, settlers would approach the Indigenous territories of what would become British Columbia with a different kind of land ethic, one that privileged extraction and control over respectful use and reciprocity. The following chapters explore the effects of these conflicting perspectives on the diverse ecosystems and wildlife species of the province.

— PART TWO —

EURO-AMERICAN TRADE AND SETTLEMENT

Competition and Perceptions of Abundance, 1774–1904

2

The Wildlife Trade

Indigenous Hunters and Euro-American Traders, 1774–1858

Wildlife was the "first wealth" that drew Europeans to what would become British Columbia.[1] Commercial harvesting practices driven by external markets and blending Indigenous and European economies had dramatic impacts on commercially valuable species in the region. For the most part, the effects of the commercial hunt on wildlife populations were relatively short-term; animal populations could recover from heavy exploitation if hunting pressure was redirected. Competition between fur trade companies in the early years of the trade, however, led to highly unsustainable hunting practices that sought to "get the fur out" before competitors could do the same. The result was the **extirpation** (removal from its historical range) of the sea otter from the coast and localized extirpations of beaver. Other species, such as mule deer and elk, were also hit hard by the trade to provision fur trade posts and, later, mushrooming gold rush towns. These losses had repercussions for BC ecosystems. The sea otter, for example, is instrumental in maintaining kelp forest ecosystems through sea urchin predation. The habitat engineering of beaver, similarly, has been shown to have positive effects on waterfowl abundance and diversity, and on trout and salmon populations.

This chapter examines the precarious monopoly on trade held by the **Hudson's Bay Company (HBC)** after 1821. While the monopoly allowed for the implementation of limited conservation measures in the north-central parts of the province, competition from American trappers continued to fuel unsustainable practices in the south. Both Indigenous and European hunters and traders were complicit to varying degrees in the overexploitation of animal resources in this period. For Indigenous hunters and traders, participation in the trade expanded opportunities for wealth generation through the extension and intensification of established pre-contact trade networks.[2] For European and Euro-American traders, individual incentives to overhunt and corporate incentives to outcompete outweighed concerns for sustainability. Not until the signing of the **Oregon Treaty** in 1846, which removed American competitors, did a complete HBC trade monopoly enable more effective conservation. As the period of HBC control waned in the 1850s, however, unregulated hunting and habitat destruction by gold miners and independent traders intensified threats to wildlife populations.

"Soft Gold": The Commercial Hunt for Sea Otters, 1785–1825

The arrival of Russian, Spanish and British explorers to the Pacific Coast in the eighteenth century signalled the beginning of change in Indigenous Peoples' economies and relationships with wildlife in what would become British Columbia. In 1740, Danish sea captain Vitus Bering led a Russian expedition to what is now identified as the Alaskan coast. Bering's recognition of the economic potential of the sea otter, whose thick silky coat would fetch high prices in China and Europe, initiated a 150-year period of exploitation. Spanish and British expeditions followed in the 1770s, the Spanish aiming to extend their sovereignty north from California, and the British in search of a northwest passage between Europe and Asia. British expeditions to the northwest coast between 1778 and 1780 returned not only with sea otter pelts but also with detailed charts of the coast and how to get there, setting off a rush for sea otter furs over the next four decades.[3]

The first British fur trade vessel arrived at Nootka Sound in 1785. American boats followed, most originating in Boston, and came to dominate the sea otter trade by 1801. The Nuu-chah-nulth of northwestern Vancouver Island became central suppliers and brokers of this trade, driving fur prices higher as the trade progressed and controlling large regional trading networks. Chief Wickaninish of Clayoquot Sound and Chief Muquinna of Nootka Sound, for example, gained wealth and status by controlling trading networks that extended to the east coast of Vancouver Island and beyond.[4] In the peak years of the trade, between 1792 and 1812, roughly 10,000 to 15,000 sea otters were killed annually on the BC and Alaska coasts, and coastal Indigenous societies and British and American fur trade companies alike benefited from the wealth of pelts that had come to be known as "soft gold."[5]

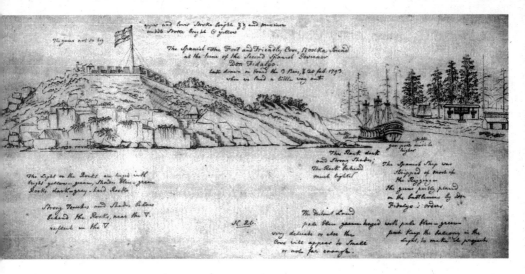

Spanish fort San Miguel at Nootka in 1793, by Sigismund Bacstrum. Royal BC Museum, PDP01329.

Although contact between Indigenous societies and early explorers and traders was generally peaceful—oriented as these exchanges were toward trade rather than settlement—the presence of newcomers produced misunderstandings and occasional conflict. Conflict sometimes occurred over access to traditional fishing and gathering sites. The Spanish fort at Yuquot (Friendly Cove) on Nootka Island, for example, occupied an important Nuu-chah-nulth fishing site. Spanish captain Francisco de Eliza reported in 1791 that Mowachaht Chief Muquinna and his people "do not cease in coming to question me daily about when we will leave," arguing that they were unable to find adequate food elsewhere on their lands.[6] Given coastal peoples' reliance on a finite number of productive sites and the complex systems of extended family ownership that governed access to those sites, going elsewhere to fish was not always an option, and displacement from sites like this could result in significant material hardship.[7] When the Spanish finally abandoned the fort in 1795, Chief Muquinna and his people destroyed the buildings and reconstructed their own structures on the site.[8]

The steady decline of sea otter populations after 1810 saw American traders turn their attention to northern fur seals and markets for "land furs" such as beaver and river otter.[9] Competition from the HBC, which arrived on the coast in 1821, eventually forced out American traders and reoriented the trade to land-based furs. Although sea otters were hunted only periodically through the nineteenth century, the high profit gained from even a single pelt meant their numbers continued to fall. By 1929, sea otters had been completely extirpated from the BC coast.

SPECIES PROFILE: Sea Otter (*Enhydra lutris*)

The sea otter (*Enhydra lutris*) once occupied coastal areas of the North Pacific from northern Japan across eastern Russia and Alaska and down the northwest coast of North America into Mexico. Among the largest members of the weasel family (Mustelidae), sea otters differ from other marine mammals in relying not on blubber to keep warm but instead on their exceptionally thick fur. Occupying coastal areas, they forage in the nearshore on marine invertebrates such as sea urchins, molluscs and crustaceans, using rocks as tools to smash open hard-shelled prey.[10]

Indigenous Peoples hunted sea otter throughout their range but likely without significant reductions in their overall population.[11] For the Nuu-chah-nulth, Haida and other coastal First Nations, sea otter pelts were valued gifts at potlatches to mark coming-of-age ceremonies, weddings and funerals. The warm, luxurious pelts were also used in chiefs' regalia.

The commercial hunt for sea otter pelts that began in the Aleutian Islands in the 1740s reduced sea otter populations from an estimated 150,000 to 300,000 worldwide to a remnant 1,000 to 2,000 individuals living within a fraction of their historic range.

In 1911, Russia, Japan, Great Britain (for Canada) and the United States signed an international treaty that placed a moratorium on the hunt. However, the hunting ban was both too late for sea otter populations in British Columbia and largely in-effective, in that it failed to protect sea otters close to shore, where they primarily occur.[12] Although a small population survived off the west coast of Vancouver Island, the last member of this colony was killed near Kyuquot in 1929.

Restoration efforts began in the late 1960s, when 89 sea otters were relocated from Alaska to the northwest coast of Vancouver Island. By 2013, this population had increased to over 5,600 individuals, and it reoccupied former habitats as far north as Cape Scott and the Hope Islands. A second colony, discovered on the central BC coast in 1989, brought the provincial total to almost 7,000 at last count in 2013. Sea otters now occupy two-thirds of their former range in the northern Pacific with a total population of approximately 128,000 as of 2018.[13]

The reintroduction of sea otters to British Columbia has been linked to significant improvements in the health of coastal ecosystems. Sea otters are a classic example of a keystone species, in that their presence produces important effects throughout the ecosystem. Sea otters eat mussels and sea urchins. By keeping those popula-tions in check, they open up space for other species and maintain the viability of kelp forest ecosystems. Sea urchins destroy kelp forests by grazing on the lower stems of kelp and causing it to drift away and die. An absence of otters leads to

Current and historical range of sea otter (*Enhydra lutris*) in British Columbia

Data source: Fisheries and Oceans Canada, "Trends in the Growth of the Sea Otter (Enhydra lutris) Population in British Columbia, 1977 to 2017," Canadian Science Advisory Secretariat, Science Advisory Report 2020/036 (June 2020). Map adapted by GeoBC in consultation with Linda Nichol, 2022.

the formation of "urchin barrens," areas with abundant sea urchins and little kelp. Kelp forests are extremely productive ecosystems, providing habitat and nutrients for other species and absorbing carbon dioxide from the atmosphere through photosynthesis. In addition to their influence on ecosystem health and diversity, sea otters may help mitigate the effects of climate change.

While sea otter populations in BC are growing and appear viable, the fact that only two main colonies exist (along the west coast of Vancouver Island and a small section of the central British Columbia coast) makes them vulnerable to threats such as disease, parasites and, most significantly, the possibility of a major oil spill. Even a small amount of oil reduces the insulation provided by their fur and can cause hypothermia. The 1989 *Exxon Valdez* oil spill in Alaska, for example, wiped out almost half of the sea otter population in Prince William Sound. Entanglement in fishing nets is another significant cause of mortality for sea otters. In recognition of these vulnerabilities, Canada identified the sea otter as a species of "special concern" under the Species at Risk Act (SARA) in 2009.[14]

Sea otter rehabilitation efforts have also generated management concerns among some coastal First Nations, who have linked their return with declining size and abundance of shellfish on coastal beaches. On the west coast of Vancouver Island, for example, where sea otter populations have increased significantly in recent years, the Nuu-chah-nulth Tribal Council has sought a return of their traditional stewardship authority in order to strike a better balance between otter populations and the availability of the crab, urchins and abalone that they depend on.[15]

Fur, Game and Salmon: Indigenous Hunters and the Hudson's Bay Company, 1821–1858

Just as the highly competitive sea otter trade was beginning to peak on the coast in the early 1800s, interior fur traders extended their explorations into the upper Peace River area and then west of the Rockies to the coast along the province's major river corridors. While Indigenous trade networks had allowed for the indirect exchange of furs and other provisions for European trade goods before this time, the establishment of trading posts created new opportunities for direct trade and greater integration between traders and Indigenous communities. The "fur trade" that resulted is perhaps best described as the "wildlife trade": Indigenous hunters and fishers traded not only pelts but also enormous quantities of salmon, venison and other meats and skins both for export and to provision a burgeoning number of trading posts across the province.

Effects of the Trade on Wildlife Populations

Competition between fur trade companies in the early nineteenth century had decimated fur-bearer and ungulate populations east of the Rockies. Similar patterns emerged as fur trade companies moved into the upper

Peace River watershed surrounding Fort St. John, home of the Sekani and Dane-zaa people and reputed as the "best beaver country" in the province. Competition for furs quickly intensified as HBC traders encroached on established North West Company (NWC) traders in the 1810s. As historian Georgiana Ball has shown, HBC incursions into the region brought not only traders but also outside trappers. Recognizing that Plains Indigenous groups like the Dane-zaa were "not primarily interested in trapping as long as bison were available," trading companies brought experienced Haudenosaunee (Iroquois) and Anishinaabe (Ojibwe) hunters from the east to trap beaver with an effective combination of castoreum (a powerful attractant from the glands of the beaver) and steel traps.[16] Trader Daniel Harmon recalled in 1820 that outside trappers wreaked "great havock [*sic*] among the game, destroying alike the animals which are young and old."[17] The encroachment of outside trappers on traditional family-owned hunting territories may have contributed to the erosion of Indigenous resource tenures in some areas.[18] At the very least, these incursions were met with considerable resistance by resident groups. In Dakelh (Carrier) territory west of the Rockies, for example, encroachments by Iroquois trappers on family-owned beaver streams led to the killing of an Iroquois trapper and his family by Dakelh trappers in 1818.[19]

Competition for furs not only threatened local animal populations and the Indigenous communities that depended on them; it also placed significant financial strain on competing companies as they expanded rapidly westward, trading at a loss if necessary to capture commercial relationships with Indigenous trappers before their competitors. The situation ultimately led the two dominant companies, the HBC and NWC, to amalgamate under the HBC name in 1821.

Diversification of wildlife products was key to the long-term survival of the Hudson's Bay Company in the Pacific Northwest. Chief factors sent a steady stream of animal parts and skins for trial in the English market in the 1820s. If the iconic product of the nineteenth-century trade was the beaver fur hat, it headed a list that included a large number of other wildlife products: bearskins for fur coats, deer antlers for knife handles, "sea horse teeth" (walrus tusks) for dentures, isinglass (a gelatin extracted from the float bladder of the sturgeon) used to clarify wine and beer, and trumpeter swan down for powder puffs.[20]

Granted the exclusive right to trade with Indigenous groups west of the Rockies for twenty-one years, the newly amalgamated HBC extended its control over all major rivers of the province. The company eyed its new **"Columbia Department,"** encompassing the northern Interior posts of New Caledonia south to Oregon, as a source of beaver and other furs to allow for the recovery of severely depleted populations east of the Rockies.[21] In the northern Interior especially, a relatively sustainable beaver trade followed the removal of outside trappers and the return to Indigenous territorial management of beaver harvests.[22]

Exclusive trading rights enabled the HBC both to regulate the supply of furs in order to keep prices high and to create new markets for other wildlife products. By the 1830s, Columbia Department traders gathered skins from over sixty animal and bird species, including bear, fox, "panther" (cougar), grebe, loon and elk, as well as feathers from goose, swan and eagle.[23] In this way, fluctuations in the market, and fluctuations in animal populations, could be accommodated by shifting hunting pressure to other species.[24]

Reduced competition also presented the opportunity to restore beaver populations in depleted districts, such as the upper Peace. Here the HBC applied some of the conservation measures implemented in districts farther east, like offering higher prices for smaller furs like marten and muskrat to relieve pressure on beaver populations.[25] Some of these measures were applied in localized areas west of the Rockies as well. In 1822, for example, HBC Governor George Simpson imposed a general ban on the purchase of lower quality "summer-killed" beaver pelts in all HBC territories, including the New Caledonia district of north-central BC. A ban on steel leghold traps in the same year, aimed at reducing indiscriminate killing of beaver, also applied to the north-central regions of the province. To be sure, conservation measures were a business tactic meant to increase the value of animals taken and the sustainability of HBC profits, rather than an altruistic response to fur-bearer population losses. Nevertheless, historians have pointed to these measures as the first effort by Europeans to enact a systematic wildlife management policy in North America.[26]

Conservation policies, however, did not always translate into conservation practice. One of the reasons for this was a reluctance among individual traders to slow fur production. As Lorne Hammond has shown, "the number of furs brought in influenced not only an individual trader's prestige but also the calculation of his pension."[27] It was not in the trader's interest,

Posts and routes of the Columbia Department, 1825–1850

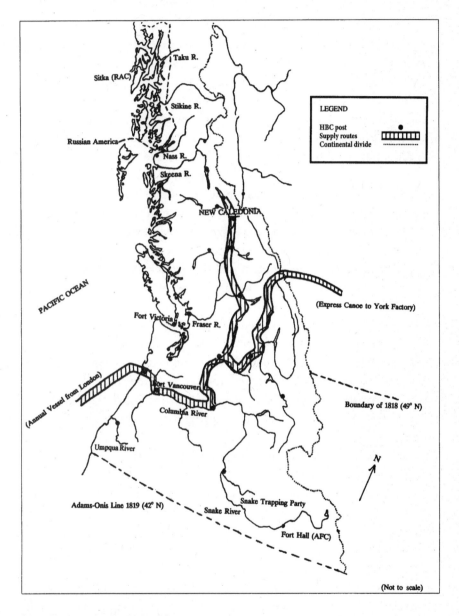

Map courtesy of Lorne Hammond.

in other words, to reduce production (and profits) in one year to ensure a sustainable harvest for their successors.

The reality of ongoing competition among trading companies also hindered conservation initiatives. As Georgiana Ball argues, conservation measures could only be implemented effectively under the conditions of monopoly control.[28] Encroachments by American traders in the south and along the coast, and by Russian traders in the north, made the HBC monopoly precarious at best. Even in the New Caledonia district of north-central BC, Indigenous traders had the option to use long-established trading networks to bypass HBC posts and trade with American ships stationed on the coast. Competition with American traders not only undid the effects of conservation measures but also led the HBC to pursue deliberate policies of fur-bearer extermination in the southern Interior. Better to trap out these areas, the logic went, than to leave animals for the enrichment of competitors. By 1827, beaver were on the verge of extirpation from the areas surrounding the Kamloops and Okanagan posts.[29] Farther south, in the Lower Columbia, an area that would later be annexed by the United States, the HBC hired Iroquois and Métis trappers to create a "fur desert" as a buffer against the encroachment of American trappers. Not until the 1840s, when an agreement with Russian traders and the signing of the Oregon Treaty removed both Russian and American competitors, did the HBC achieve a complete monopoly on trade in the province.[30]

As precarious as the HBC monopoly was on the coast, so was the position of its resident employees. Traders occupying posts in the northern Interior were often desperately short of food. In addition to hunting pressure, local animal populations were subject to migration and rapid population fluc-tuation because of a range of factors, including predation and disease; severe winters often significantly reduced the availability of large mammals.[31] Bison and other large game populations had been severely depleted in the upper Peace region by the early 1800s, contributing to the closure of several forts in the 1820s.[32] The employees of McLeod's Lake Post (140 kilometres north of today's Prince George), meanwhile, "lived almost exclusively on fish, rotten or fresh, and made up shortfalls with pemmican [a calorie-rich mixture of animal fat, dried meat and dried berries] from the plains," while Fort St. James was "notoriously difficult to provision."[33] Mutual aid between traders and area Indigenous groups became essential for the survival of both

Gitxsan Chief Daniel Wiik'aax [Wecahk] of Kisgegas with furs, ca.1914. Royal BC Museum, A-06042. Reprinted with permission from the Gitxsan Huwilp Government.

groups in these circumstances, and traders found themselves dependent on local First Nations for supplies of meat as well as furs.

As Marianne and Ronald Ignace have shown, this dependence on Indigenous provisioning reflected not only a shortage of labour power at the forts but also an acknowledgement of Indigenous control over access to wildlife and other resources on their territories. Traders were generally not entitled to hunt or fish for their own provisions, unless they had married local Indigenous women. Instead, they purchased or traded for fish and game harvested within largely intact Indigenous management regimes.[34] Beginning in the 1820s and 1830s, the introduction of livestock and vegetable gardens at some trading posts allowed for greater self-reliance. Trade with Indigenous partners for furs and other wildlife continued, but HBC employees could move away from the "feast-or-famine economy" of subsisting on ungulates and other wildlife.[35]

For First Nations of the southern coast and major inland rivers, the "fur trade" is better described as the "salmon trade." The HBC experience at Fort Langley is a case in point. When the HBC established the fort in Stó:lō territory in 1827, the company's expectations that the Stó:lō would begin trapping beaver were met with indifference. The Stó:lō economy was based primarily on fishing and not trapping, and the trade goods the HBC offered were interesting but not essential. Fur-bearers in coastal areas, furthermore, with the exception of the increasingly scarce sea otter, were generally fewer and lesser in quality than their interior counterparts. These circumstances, combined with Stó:lō reluctance, ultimately led the HBC to shift from furs to salmon at Fort Langley. Similar developments occurred at the Kamloops and Thompson River posts in the southern Interior, where Secwépemc and surrounding nations became major suppliers of salmon.[36] By the 1830s the HBC had become a major broker of salmon, and later lumber and other provisions, both for export (to Pacific markets in Hawaii, Alaska and San Francisco) and for provisioning its network of inland forts east of the Rockies. For its Indigenous trading partners, the trade did not transform traditional economies as much as it expanded and supported existing activities and trade networks.[37]

Effects of the Trade on Indigenous Societies

For its Indigenous participants, the wildlife trade both enriched and disrupted aspects of their cultural and economic life. For coastal societies in particular, the sea otter trade and the salmon and provisions trade that followed reinforced existing hierarchies and cultural practices, allowing leaders of extended families to accumulate and distribute more wealth and to gain status by holding larger and more frequent potlatches. Greater wealth also allowed for expansions in artistic production and ceremonial life among the Haida and other northwest coast groups.[38]

BC First Nations incorporated the European trade into their existing trade economies and the social obligations that accompanied them. This was especially true with the land-based trade, where the establishment of permanent trading posts with resident traders in the early 1800s led Indigenous families to cement trading relationships through intermarriage. Within the first year of HBC's operation at Fort Langley, for example, "nearly all of the fort's men married into Stó:lō families." As historian Keith Carlson explains, just as pre-contact intermarriage between villages granted in-law families access to prime fishing or hunting sites, so intermarriage with HBC employees became a way to gain access to useful and prestigious European trade items, including wool blankets, steel axe blades and fish hooks.[39] Cultural adaptation went both ways. NWC and later HBC traders

Sekani women with Hudson's Bay Company manager, Fort Grahame, ca.1910. Note the
similarities in the way they are dressed, an indication of cultural adaptations on both sides
brought about by the fur trade. As Sekani elder Ray Izony points out, the HBC manager wears
what appears to be an Athabascan firebag around his neck. Six decades later, the area where
they stood would be completely inundated by the construction of dams on the Peace River.
Royal BC Museum, F-04337. Reprinted with permission from the Tsay Keh Dene First Nation.

were quick to adopt Indigenous forms of commerce, diplomacy and social
relations in order to secure important trading relationships. Indigenous
communities, who greatly outnumbered traders in this period, did not rad-
ically alter their cultures or economies to meet the demands of the trade.

While the fur trade allowed for considerable continuity with pre-
contact life, the presence of European traders also brought significant social
change. Time spent hunting and trapping to provision HBC posts, and the
growing expansion of Indigenous labour at the posts in agricultural work,
coal mining, canoe repair and other tasks, meant fewer hands to assist in
seasonal food-gathering activities and the stewardship of clam gardens
and other resource sites.[40] Depopulation and destabilization of Indigenous
communities in the wake of repeated outbreaks of epidemic disease through
the nineteenth century greatly exacerbated these effects. With European
traders, too, came access to guns and alcohol, which led to profound
changes and weighted the outcomes of long-standing territorial conflicts

in some areas. On the coast, for example, access to muskets allowed the Kwakwaka'wakw to displace the K'ómoks (Comox) peoples of Cape Mudge and Campbell River. In the Interior, the gun- and horse-owning Blackfoot pushed the formerly plains-dwelling Ktunaxa west through the mountains to the Kootenay River. Farther north, incursions from Cree and Assiniboine middlemen destabilized trapping and trading patterns in the Peace River area, with the result that Sekani hunters moved into the foothills of the northern Rockies in search of fur.[41]

Changes in traditional hunting practices also accompanied the trade. Why, given established relationships of respect with "animal peoples," did Indigenous hunters participate in the overexploitation of fur-bearers and game species to the point of near or total extirpation? Prior to European contact, the beaver had been an important source of food and blankets for many groups. Its sedentary habits made it easy to locate and trap; for these same reasons, it could easily be overhunted. Indigenous nations with high dependence on beaver, therefore, regulated their harvest carefully. The Dakelh of the northern Interior, for example, strictly controlled harvests through family ownership of beaver streams. As trader Daniel Harmon reported in 1820, encroachment on these streams by neighbouring groups was "frequently punished by death."[42] Why, then, would the opportunities of the fur trade lead so many to overhunt the animals that sustained them? For outside trappers working in the upper Peace in the early 1800s, the answer is perhaps more discernible: Haudenosaunee and Anishinaabe trappers depleted beaver in these areas "because they had no vested interest in the country."[43] For resident hunters and trappers, however, the reasons were more complex.

Most significantly, circumstances had changed. The competitive atmosphere of the trade, especially in the period before the HBC merger, led to encroachments from other groups that destabilized family-owned hunting territories in some areas. The Cree, for example, encroached on the Dane-zaa and Sekani.[44] In the rapidly changing environment of the early fur trade, animals that had once been hunted for food and clothing were now hunted to exchange for useful and prestigious trade goods. Pelts from highly valued species such as sea otter and beaver brought high returns in trade goods, which met growing demands for potlatch gifts among coastal nations.[45] The widely shared belief that animals "gave themselves up" to hunters when the circumstances were right may have facilitated overhunting, particularly as access to new technologies like steel traps improved success and the growing need for provisions at HBC forts increased hunting pressure.[46] On the coast, as we have seen, competition led to the decimation and ultimate extirpation of sea otter populations. The story is different in the northern Interior, where adaptations by the HBC and Indigenous trappers led to localized recoveries of beaver and other game populations by the 1850s. As Hammond observed, of the more than sixty forms of wildlife recorded in HBC trade accounts, none are extinct, and population declines in recent years are better linked to habitat loss than any long-term effects of the trade.[47]

A range of factors would bring about decline in the fur trade in the province through the 1840s and '50s. The waves of epidemic disease that ravaged Indigenous communities in the 1830s and '40s caused massive population loss and corresponding disruptions to seasonal hunting, fishing and harvesting activities, which meant fewer pelts for HBC traders. At the same time, consumer demand in Europe had shifted. By the 1840s, the popularity and relative affordability of silk hats had displaced beaver hats on the London market.[48] While the HBC would continue to operate in the province as a procurer of furs and other wildlife products well into the twentieth century, the loss of its trade monopoly in 1858 and the influx of independent traders and settlers that followed would have serious consequences for the sustainability of the animal trade and animal populations alike.

Quick Riches, Big Changes: The Fraser River Gold Rush

In 1858, news of the presence of gold on the bars of the Fraser River launched rapid changes for the HBC, Indigenous Peoples and relationships with wildlife in the province. That spring, some 10,000 miners, mostly from California, travelled by boat up the Fraser River past Fort Langley to the lower reaches of the Fraser Canyon in Nlaka'pamux territory. An additional 15,000 arrived by fall. Not surprisingly, Indigenous Peoples of the Fraser and Thompson rivers did not look favourably on intruders arriving to seize resources that they "not only owned but knew the value of."[49] The Nlaka'pamux, for example, had mined and traded placer gold from the Thompson River for two years before being overrun by newcomers.

HO! FOR FRAZER RIVER.

"Ho! For Frazer [sic] River." News of gold discoveries on the Fraser River triggered a mass migration of prospectors from California and neighbouring states. Illustration by J. Ross Browne, from "A Peep at Washoe," *Harper's Monthly Magazine* 22 (December 1860), 4. Image courtesy of Wikimedia Commons.

Miners intruded on village sites and cultivated areas with brazen disregard for Indigenous inhabitants. Their activities disrupted the Nlaka'pamux salmon fishery, occupying fishing sites and destroying spawning grounds by diverting creeks and rivers to wash gravel through mining sluices. Efforts to stop miners from proceeding upriver and attempts to impose taxes on those working Nlaka'pamux-owned ground were rebuffed with threats of violence. Several incidents of sexual assault on Nlaka'pamux women, combined with the massacre of a group of unarmed Syilx (Okanagan) people at Okanagan Lake, confirmed the gravity of these threats.[50]

Tensions ultimately erupted in August 1858 in what has become known as the **Fraser Canyon War**. When the Nlaka'pamux were suspected in the death of two French miners in July, hundreds of miners organized themselves into military companies and marched upriver to exact revenge. They killed at least thirty-six people over eight days of fighting, including women, children and five chiefs, and wounded many more. As they retreated downriver, the miners burned five Nlaka'pamux villages to the ground. A truce was finally called when, upon threat of further violence, the Nlaka'pamux agreed to grant miners access to their territories and resources.[51]

By the mid-1860s, the Fraser River gold rush had run its course, and miners shifted their attention to gold strikes in the Cariboo, the Kootenays and later the Skeena and Omineca rivers.[52] But the events on the Fraser in 1858 would have much longer-term consequences for the HBC, Indigenous Peoples of the region and, ultimately, the wildlife species they sought.

For Sir James Douglas, governor of the fledgling British colony of Vancouver Island and chief factor of the HBC territory that encompassed the Fraser River, the brewing violence in the Fraser Canyon prompted fears that the American miners might win the war and encourage American annexation of the region. In early August 1958, he received authorization to extend British sovereignty from Vancouver Island to the mainland, converting the HBC territory of New Caledonia into the new Crown colony of British Columbia. The British colonial office also sought to profit from the gold rush: Douglas promptly claimed the land and minerals for the Crown and required all incoming miners to purchase licences from Victoria. With little military capability to assert British sovereignty on the mainland, however, Douglas could do little to prevent the violence. By the time he arrived in Nlaka'pamux territory to assess the situation, the conflict was over.[53]

Conclusion: Monopoly Rescinded

The gold rush, and the resulting creation of the colony of British Columbia in August 1858, had immediate and lasting consequences for the HBC. Douglas became governor of the new colony on the condition that he sever his connections with the fur trade company. Seemingly in the same breath, Britain cancelled the HBC's exclusive rights to trade in the region. As Britain eyed settlement and free enterprise for its Pacific Northwest colonies, the HBC's monopoly trade over the region's resources seemed like an artifact of the past.

The HBC's trade privileges, of course, existed in relationship with the Indigenous hunters, fishers and trappers who supplied the trade. With the HBC's loss of those privileges, Indigenous people lost their privileged position as procurers of wildlife and other products. And wildlife itself, newly subject to British common law, became a resource "open to everyone." This designation would have profound implications for wild animal populations and the Indigenous Peoples who depended on them, coinciding as it did with the arrival of hungry miners and independent traders eager to exploit the province's resources. As Georgiana Ball explains, centuries of Indigenous family ownership of hunting territories and almost four decades of HBC monopoly trading control gave way to "ineffectual control by [an] uncertain public authority."[54]

For the Nlaka'pamux and their Secwépemc and Syilx allies, the encroachment of American miners on their territories and the violence that resulted marked the beginning of successive waves of British and Canadian settlers who made similar claims to territory and resources. While not all Indigenous groups in the province encountered gold miners or settlers directly in this period, their presence brought devastation of a more insidious kind in the massive smallpox epidemic of 1862. On Vancouver Island, news of the rush attracted large numbers of Indigenous people from the northwest coast to camp on the outskirts of Victoria in hopes of profiting from trade with the ballooning numbers of newcomers in the city.[55] When a prospector from San Francisco arrived in the city with smallpox in the spring of 1862, the disease reached the camps. Authorities in Victoria drove sick Indigenous people from the city, sending the disease with them to their home communities and infecting others at stopping points along the way.[56] By 1863, large areas of southeastern BC were almost completely depopulated. The epidemic reached all parts of the province within two years, killing at least 30,000 people, or 60 per cent of the Indigenous population of the era.

As the miners moved on to gold strikes farther north, settlers followed in their wake. In subsequent years, the dispossession of Indigenous Peoples of their lands and established stewardship regimes, and the opening of a free market in wildlife, would produce urgent demands for conservation measures in the developing British colony.

3

The Wildlife Commons

Overexploitation in the Early Settlement Period, 1859–1904

T his chapter begins with an overview of European resettlement activities
after 1858 and the corresponding dispossession and marginalization of
Indigenous Peoples. These developments provide crucial context for the
shift in wildlife consumption that followed. In the absence of HBC monopoly
rights to the trade in wildlife, the game and fur-bearer species in the colony
became a common property resource, open to everyone.[1] Heavy reliance on
selected wildlife species for food in the early settlement period, combined
with ongoing commercial exploitation of fur-bearers and big-game species
for furs, horns, hides and trophy heads, led to significant declines of freshwater fish, resident and migratory game birds, beaver and ungulate species.

This **"wildlife commons"** was temporary and geographically dependent:
it describes a period in the province's history where newcomers largely un-
familiar with the extent and limitations of local wildlife populations, and
motivated by requirements for subsistence and income, took advantage of
a vacuum in the regulation of access to wildlife. As Indigenous Peoples lost
access to and management authority over their traditional territories—in
the southern half of the province, especially—the absence of effective rules
governing access to wildlife created "free for all" conditions that significantly reduced populations of hunted species. A series of ad hoc and mini-
mally enforced game protection ordinances enacted through the latter half
of the nineteenth century did little to arrest the decline of wildlife populations. Not until the early twentieth century would more robust regulation
and enforcement of hunting and fishing begin to close the wildlife commons, with disproportionate effects on rural and Indigenous communities.

Dispossession and Resettlement after 1858

Following the formation of the Crown colony of British Columbia in 1858, settlers from Great Britain, the western United States and Upper Canada began to arrive to take up land in the new colony. By 1866, when the colonies of Vancouver Island and British Columbia united, pockets of European and Euro-Canadian resettlement had been established on Vancouver Island, in the Fraser Valley and in the Kootenay, Okanagan and Thompson River valleys.[2] Five years later in 1871, on the promise of a rail link to central Canada, BC joined Confederation. Under the terms of the British North America Act of 1867, the new province of British Columbia had the right to the ownership and management of its lands and wildlife, while the federal government held jurisdiction over inland and coastal fisheries.

In many of these locations, settlers took advantage of sites that had been previously cleared by Indigenous burning. The dramatic population loss that resulted from the 1862 smallpox epidemic and preceding disease outbreaks, combined with sporadic warfare among Indigenous nations, resulted in the abandonment of a number of Indigenous settlements in the southern and eastern portions of the province. This absence facilitated the tendency of incoming settlers to view these spaces not as landscapes cultivated by Indigenous Peoples but rather as sites cleared by divine providence for the purposes of European settlement. James Douglas admired the "park-like" appearance of the Garry oak savannahs of Victoria in the 1840s, the "extensive spaces" of which, as Captain George Vancouver had described fifty years earlier, "wore the appearance of having been cleared by art."[3]

Unlike the prairie lands east of the Rockies, British Columbia's mountainous topography limited the opportunities for agricultural settlement. Consistent with its fur trade roots, the province's economy in the period of early settlement depended on resource exports of fur, gold, fish, coal and timber. Not only was suitable agricultural land limited in quantity, but it was also made less available through patronage policies that granted land and resource tenures to political favourites. In a practice that rankled incoming settlers, public figures linked to the colonial government in Victoria were rewarded for their loyalty with long-term leases to timber, grazing and mineral resources and large parcels of prime agricultural land, some of which they resold to incoming settlers at higher prices.[4] Railway companies may have profited the most from these incentives to settlement and

Pamphlets like this one attracted potential settlers from the United States, Britain and northern Europe to a land of agricultural bounty open for the taking. *Canada West: The Last Best West*, produced by the Department of the Interior, 1909. Image courtesy of Library and Archives Canada, e011181929.

resource development, when later in the century millions of acres of Crown land, including valuable valley lands, were set aside for proposed railway lines—only a handful of which were ever constructed.[5]

Despite these hard limits on the amount and availability of land suitable for agriculture, colonial visions of agricultural settlement as the pathway to a successful society remained steadfast in the early years of settlement. These ideals would have lasting effects on the distribution of land in the province. To prevent land speculation and encourage agricultural development, the provincial government required owners to "improve" the land by clearing and building on it. The limited quantity of suitable land for agriculture, however, meant that only a small fraction of the land was transferred to private landowners for farms or townsites. (The province continues to hold 94 per cent of BC land as Crown land.)[6] With farming and settlement

identified as the highest and most desirable use of land, the colonial government followed established models in central Canada of relegating other
land uses, such as mining, grazing and forestry, to a system of resource
tenures where ownership of the resource, and the land it was drawn from,
would rest with the Crown.[7]

The limits of BC's attractions as a destination for agricultural settlement,
combined with opportunities elsewhere, meant that settlement was initially
slow and sporadic. The slow influx of colonists, miners and trappers in the
1860s and '70s nevertheless created new tensions in the relationship with
Indigenous Peoples. In place of the economic cooperation of the wildlife
trade period came economic rivalry with a growing population of newcomers.[8] Land grants to political favourites meant that in places like the
Okanagan and the grasslands of the middle Fraser basin—environments
that had long sustained Indigenous cultivation—hunting, fishing and, later,
livestock raising were taken over by large settler-owned ranches.[9] On southern Vancouver Island, localized overgrazing by pigs and sheep destroyed
cultivated camas beds and competed with wildlife for browse.[10]

Treaties and Reserves

Resettlement of the colony produced little of the bloodshed so prevalent
south of the border. "Had it not been for the ravages of several decades of
introduced diseases," BC historian Wilson Duff concluded about this period,
Indigenous Peoples of the province "would have been a greater force when
the settlers began to arrive."[11] However, like the conflicts occasioned by incoming gold seekers in 1858, repeated encroachments by settlers claiming
lands and resources produced bitterness, alarm and in some cases retalia-
tion by Indigenous nations. A rare example of the latter was the Tsilhqot'in
(Chilcotin) War of 1864, in which members of the Tsilhqot'in Nation killed
fourteen road construction workers and five settlers who encroached on their
territory without permission. The arrest and subsequent execution of six
Tsilhqot'in chiefs at what they understood to be peace talks led to an apology
and exoneration of the chiefs by the BC government in 2014, 150 years later.[12]

HBC Chief Factor and Vancouver Island Governor Sir James Douglas
had tried to avoid such conflict by signing treaties with Indigenous groups
that recognized the ownership they held in their lands. Between 1850 and
1854, Douglas signed fourteen treaties with First Nations around Victoria,

Nanaimo and Fort Rupert (near Port Hardy) on Vancouver Island. These land surrender treaties established Crown sovereignty over all lands, enclosing Indigenous village sites and agricultural fields onto reserves while extinguishing Aboriginal title over the remainder of their traditional territories.[13] First Nation signatories to what became known as the "**Douglas treaties**" retained the right to "hunt over unoccupied lands and to carry on fisheries as formerly."[14] As settlement spread into the Cowichan Valley and Salt Spring Island by 1860, Douglas's efforts to sign further treaties were denied by the imperial government, which refused to send funds for land purchases. When Douglas retired in 1864, his successors chose to ignore the problem of settler-Indigenous conflict, in part by denying the existence of Aboriginal title.[15] Small reserves continued to be allocated, often with little consultation, but no further treaties were signed in the province.

The exception was **Treaty 8**, a land surrender agreement signed in 1899 by the federal government and the Dane-zaa and Dene-thah (Slavey) peoples of the northeast with surprisingly little participation from the province.[16] Initiated following a Dane-zaa blockade of northbound gold prospectors at Fort St. John, the treaty guaranteed signatory Indigenous nations hunting, fishing and trapping rights throughout their traditional lands, "saving and excepting such tracts as may be required or taken up from time to time for settlement, mining, lumbering, trading or other purposes."[17] As Robin and Jillian Ridington argue in their history of the Dane-zaa, it is very unlikely that the eight Dane-zaa chiefs who signed the agreement—none of whom spoke English—were aware of these terms or of the treaty's work in extinguishing title to their territories. From a Dane-zaa perspective, the agreement, like one they had signed recently with the encroaching Saulteau people, was about "peace, friendship, and the sharing of land."[18]

Waves of smallpox, measles, influenza and tuberculosis continued to bring about steep population declines among Indigenous communities through the late nineteenth century, with a low point of about 20,000 Indigenous men, women and children in 1911. This decline was made more apparent by the enormous growth of the settler population in the same period. When BC entered Confederation in 1871, Indigenous people constituted 71 per cent of the population. The completion of the railway in 1885 brought a rapid increase in settler arrivals. By the beginning of World War I in 1914, British, European and Asian settlers made up 95 per cent of the BC population.[19]

BC politicians acted on the perception, and the reality, of a declining Indigenous population by taking steps to reduce the size and value of existing reserves and to deny the creation of new ones. Reserves in BC were already considerably smaller than their counterparts in other parts of the country, averaging twenty acres per family compared with the minimum of 160 acres reserved for families on the Prairies (in part a factor of the relative agricultural potential of the land). Reserve size varied in different parts of the province, too: some interior groups received larger tracts for ranching and trapping; the fishing cultures of the coast and major salmon-bearing rivers received much smaller allotments.[20] As UBC legal historian Doug Harris has shown, the majority of the province's reserves were intended as "fishing stations" to provide access to saltwater and anadromous fish, clam beds, and marine mammals such as seal. Their small size was predicated on the assumption that the fishery would provide a sufficient livelihood for reserve inhabitants.[21] As early as the 1860s, BC Governor Joseph Trutch removed what he considered to be "excess land" from many reserves using the argument that the land could be put to more "productive use" by neighbouring white settlers. Further reductions occurred through the nineteenth and early twentieth centuries.

Fences and Fines

The constraints of small reserve spaces were further amplified by access restrictions off-reserve. Especially in the southern reaches of the province where settler populations were higher, Indigenous communities found their seasonal movements—and the livelihoods supported by those movements—increasingly curtailed. In places like southeastern Vancouver Island, the lower Fraser Valley and the productive valleys of the southern Interior, growing numbers of settlers pre-empted land surrounding reserves.[22] As fences were erected to contain livestock and demarcate property, Indigenous people increasingly faced accusations of trespass and the threat of jail time for accessing hunting, fishing and food-gathering sites within their traditional territories.[23] St'at'imc (Lillooet) Chief Peters expressed a common sentiment among southern Interior Indigenous leaders in 1914: "we have a hard time to make our living—the whites tied up the salmon and the whites tied up the game, and the whites . . . have tied up everything outside the Reserves marked on this map."[24]

Circumstances differed along much of the coast and in the central and northern Interior, where the delayed arrival of settlers enabled the persistence of traditional Indigenous economies. On the coast, continued access to ancestral fishing sites allowed many First Nations to "catch and cure the bulk of their winter food" and sell portions of their catch (however illegally) to white communities.[25] Participation in the commercial fur-seal hunt brought income to coastal First Nations like the Nuu-chah-nulth in the 1880s and 1890s, while hunting land mammals for food and fur continued largely unimpeded into the early twentieth century. People of the central and northern Interior, meanwhile, continued to participate in the fur trade and maintained seasonal rounds of hunting, trapping and fishing into the 1950s. Even in these more remote areas, however, expanding government regulation and competition from white trappers and fishers in the early twentieth century would gradually undercut the ability of Indigenous communities to maintain their traditional livelihoods.[26]

As settlers took up more land in desirable southern districts, Douglas-era understandings that permitting hunting on unoccupied Crown land, even for non-treaty nations, gave way to a new regime wherein hunting off-reserve was subject to provincial game regulations.[27] A 1910 document titled "Declaration of the Indian Chiefs in the Southern Interior of British Columbia" illustrates the resulting hardships for Indigenous communities. "In many places," the chiefs wrote, "we are debarred from camping, traveling, gathering roots and obtaining wood and water as heretofore. Our people are fined and imprisoned for breaking the game and fish laws and using the same game and fish which we were told would always be ours for food. Gradually, we are becoming regarded as trespassers over a large portion of this our country."[28] Increasingly, reserve lands became the only spaces where First Nations members could fish and hunt year-round, free of allegations of trespass and infringement from game laws. Resulting overharvest of wildlife in and around reserves not only compounded hardships for Indigenous communities but also reinforced settler beliefs that Indigenous people lacked the ability to manage wildlife populations.[29]

Vocal protests and repeated petitions by Indigenous leaders led the federal and BC governments in 1912 to create the Royal Commission on Indian Affairs, commonly known as the **McKenna-McBride Commission**, to review reserve allotments across the province. While Indigenous leaders wanted the federal government to address their land claims and eliminate reserves altogether, the BC government sought to free up existing reserve lands for agriculture and industrial development.[30] The Commission responded by further reducing the size of many reserves based on their criteria of proper land use—namely farming and resource extraction. As Jean Barman writes, the Commission "removed 47,000 acres of mostly good land from reserves in return for 87,000 generally poor acres. The value of land taken away was three times that added to reserves." By the time the Commission completed its work in 1916, Indigenous people were left with 843,000 acres of reserve land, comprising less than 0.4 per cent of the province.[31]

"From the late 1860s, Native leaders [in British Columbia] had protested their small reserves in every way they could, claiming, fundamentally, that their people would not have enough food and that their progeny had no prospects. In retrospect, they were right. The spaces assigned to Native people did not support them, although the mixed economies they cobbled together, the revised diets they ate, and the accommodations and settlements they lived in had allowed some of them to survive."

—R. Cole Harris, *Making Native Space: Colonialism, Resistance, and Reserves in British Columbia* (Vancouver: UBC Press, 2002), 291.

The dispossession and marginalization of Indigenous Peoples in this period, and through the twentieth century, was justified by dominant political beliefs in the superiority of European people, cultures and institutions. A right to ownership in land, for example, had to be demonstrated through European definitions of productive land use, such as cultivation, mining or logging. The colonial government used this logic to dock reserve lands used for less intensive purposes, like hunting and berry-picking. The belief that Indigenous people were doomed to disappear reflected not only very real and discernible population declines in the nineteenth century but also foundational beliefs in European superiority. "Uncivilized" Indigenous cultures were doomed, according to this logic, to give way to what was understood as the natural progress of civilization.[32]

Catastrophic population loss and the loss of traditional territories had a destabilizing effect on Indigenous Peoples' traditional resource management regimes and habitat enhancement activities. As Douglas Deur has shown, population losses, and later the loss of children to residential school, greatly reduced the labour and knowledge needed for maintaining clam gardens and other managed resources. Between the 1870s and 1900, Indigenous nations in the southern Interior were forced to abandon the seasonal burning activities long used to maintain berry patches and hunting grounds. Settlers' destruction of fishing weirs and barring of access to ancestral fishing, waterfowl hunting and gathering sites created hardship for many and prompted numerous petitions by Indigenous leaders.[33]

Privileging the Commercial Catch

Over the same period, competition from cannery-owned fishing fleets operating near the mouths of the Fraser, Skeena and Nass rivers threatened upriver Indigenous fisheries.[34] Pressure from salmon canneries for priority access to sockeye in particular contributed to a series of dominion fisheries regulations that restricted Indigenous access. As Doug Harris has shown, this was a major change; fisheries regulations had generally exempted Indigenous fisheries before the canning industry became a dominant force in the provincial economy.[35] In 1888, fisheries officials introduced the concept of an **Indigenous food fishery** that permitted fishing for consumption but not "for sale, barter or traffic." Indigenous fishers who had formerly

Label from McLellan's Cannery on the Nass River, ca.1900. Royal BC Museum, I-61302.

A Secwepemc woman preparing a deer hide, Kamloops, 1898. Photo by Harlan Ingersoll Smith. American Museum of Natural History—Research Library, item 411796. Reprinted with permission from Tk'emlúps te Secwepemc First Nation.

supplemented their income by selling to the canneries now had to turn to the canneries for commercial licences. In subsequent decades Indigenous fishers would find it increasingly difficult to obtain commercial licences that were, in theory at least, open to all.

Furthermore, the failure to protect Indigenous fisheries meant that commercial drift net and seine fishers encroached on important Indigenous fishing grounds and intercepted large numbers of returning fish before they entered the rivers.[36] Despite the existence of a reserve system predicated largely on access to fisheries, the Department of Fisheries refused to grant Indigenous communities exclusive access to tidal and in-river fisheries on their reserves.[37] By 1894, Indigenous fishers required a permit to fish for food on reserves, and regulations prohibited the use of spears, traps or pens. Even the use of dip nets at ancestral fishing sites required special permission from fisheries officials. As anthropologist Kimberly Linkous Brown points out, the effect was to replace selective, live-capture Indigenous fisheries technologies with "mixed stock" tidal gill net fisheries that killed fish of different species and age classes "indiscriminately."[38]

In the early twentieth century, as Indigenous populations began to re-cover from the effects of successive waves of epidemic disease, access to wildlife within a greatly reduced land base would nevertheless provide a vital source of resilience and opportunities for passing on knowledge.[39] The persistence of seasonal rounds incorporating harvests of salmon, shellfish and game for subsistence and for trade, combined with wage labour in commercial fishing, logging and other industries, supported Indigenous families and communities through a period of wrenching change.

Resettlement activities in the late nineteenth century did not in them-selves have dramatic effects on wildlife populations. The removal of forest cover, the draining of wetlands and the alienation of valued valley-bottom lands for crop production and livestock grazing had localized effects on wildlife abundance, but the extent of settlement was not yet great enough to cause significant reductions in wildlife populations in most parts of the province.[40] Far more consequential than habitat loss in this period was the unregulated hunting of wildlife for food and profit.

Hunting for the Table and the Market

Early European settlers and Indigenous residents relied on wildlife for subsistence and as a source of revenue. Given the limited agricultural potential of much of the province, the development of local sources of agricultural produce and meat took time. Cash was in short supply for most settlers and, especially in more remote areas, the cost of imported food was prohibitive. Settlers turned instead to local populations of wildlife that they could harvest themselves or purchase or barter for from game provisioners. As Blanche Norcross recalled in her history of the Cowichan Valley on Vancouver Island, "what appeared on the table was very largely limited to what the country provided. There was plenty of game and, for those who lived near the sea, clams in abundance. . . . Cash was scarce, but no one went hungry."[41]

The ease of access to free food literally "from the doorstep" in some cases was reinforced by a general sense of animal abundance. Port Alberni resident Hazel Hill described the Alberni Valley in the 1870s as "simply swarming with game," while Winnifred Ariel Weir of Invermere noted that homesteaders in the 1880s seeking meat for the table "had only to step to the door of their home in the early morning or evening and wait. Deer and elk were never far off, and a single shot could provide dinner for many days."[42] Others spoke of the "myriads" of ducks, geese and other wild fowl. Father Adrien-Gabriel Morice, missionary at Fort St. James, noted that grebes on Stuart Lake "abound to such an extent that, for a fortnight or so, they are daily taken by the hundred in a single locality."[43]

Wildlife also provided a source of income. "Hunting was a combination of business and pleasure," Norcross recalled of the Cowichan Valley. "A man could not only supply his own table while getting some sport, but he could make a little cash in Victoria by the sale of fresh venison or grouse."[44] For new arrivals especially, market hunting provided a vital source of income and met steady demands for wild protein in urban centres. Immigrant and Indigenous hunters alike supplied game markets in Victoria and other towns with venison, bear meat, grouse and other game birds from surrounding areas. Hunters also sold their catch directly at railway platforms and even door-to-door, as writer Edgar Fawcett recalled of Victoria in the 1860s. Cheap wild foods, he wrote in 1912, "were a godsend to early residents." The Songhees people "would sell at your door grouse and wild ducks at 35 to

A hunting party near Kamloops, ca.1880. Royal BC Museum, B-08285.

50 cents a pair, venison by the quarter at 5 to 8 cents a pound, a salmon at 10 cents and oysters and clams for 25 cents a bucket."[45]

Unlike the decades before 1858, when the HBC held monopoly rights to the trade in wildlife, wildlife had become "a common property resource, open to everyone."[46] Resulting pressures on wildlife populations in more populated areas led to the passage of the province's first game protection laws. In the spring of 1859, the colony of Vancouver Island passed the **Act for the Preservation of Game,** which prohibited hunting of deer and elk from January to July and outlawed the sale or purchase of a number of waterfowl and upland game birds and their eggs during the breeding season. The colony of British Columbia passed similar legislation in 1865, and a single ordinance for the united colonies replaced its predecessors in 1867. Significantly, the preamble to the act pointed to the importance of "birds and beasts of game" as a "source of food . . . and occupation" for many residents of the colony.[47]

As historian George Colpitts has observed, these early game laws and those that followed in the 1870s and '80s recognized the importance of wild meat as a food source for the settler population. Unlike their European predecessors, which had reserved game for a privileged minority, early game laws in BC and other parts of North America were written with the assumption that wildlife belonged to everyone: anyone who needed meat had the right to hunt and use wild animals. Reflecting the seeming abundance of New World wildlife, the coveted personal freedoms of a pioneer population and a general lack of capacity for enforcement, nineteenth-century ordinances sought to curb the worst abuses and halt the decline of overharvested game species around settler population centres. (Indigenous hunters and settlers in more remote districts were generally exempted from game laws in this period). Even the commercial hunt remained largely unregulated over these decades. Although restricted to open seasons for the most valued of game species, market hunters and butchers could continue to sell or barter wild animal meat to a hungry and growing settler population.[48]

INDIVIDUAL PROFILE:
John Fannin and the Origins of the Royal BC Museum

Like many others who arrived in the province in the mid-nineteenth century, John Fannin followed a dream of gold and adventure across the continent to the Cariboo region of British Columbia in the early 1860s. He used his wilderness experience to take up contract work as a surveyor for the BC government in the 1870s before accepting a position as the province's official taxidermist and museum curator in 1886.

The Provincial Museum of Natural History and Anthropology, initially a single room in one of the former BC legislature buildings, was the largest expression of a wave of natural history societies and museums that formed across the province in the last decades of the nineteenth century. Founded in response to concerns that European and American collectors were appropriating BC wildlife specimens and Indigenous artifacts for export to foreign museums, the museum aimed to promote investment and settlement in the province through displays of the "natural wealth" of its resources and the superabundance of its wildlife populations. Fannin, who had explored regions as remote as the upper Stikine in the province's northwest, donated his own large collection of mounted birds and animals as the basis for the museum's collection.

Early specimen collectors like Fannin lay the foundation for the development of wildlife knowledge in the province. Like other collectors of the period, including

Curator John Fannin in his taxidermy workshop at the Provincial Museum, ca.1890. Photo by Albert H. Maynard. Royal BC Museum, G-03172.

artist-naturalist Allan Brooks of the Okanagan, Fannin was both an ardent hunter and a talented naturalist with an insatiable curiosity for the natural world. His knowledge of natural history and skill as a taxidermist, writer and public speaker led him to publish many papers on natural history, earning him the respect of naturalists and scientists across the continent. In 1891, Fannin published the first catalogue of birds in the province, stimulating interest in provincial wildlife and specimen collection expeditions by major museums in the United States.

The museum continued to expand under Fannin's leadership. His work to establish the **Natural History Society of British Columbia** in 1890 generated new sources of bird and mammal specimens from across the province. These specimens provided important source data for scientific studies of species' physical charac- teristics and distribution; they continue to be used for reference and research to- day. Inspired by visits to natural history museums in Europe and the United States, Fannin continued to produce captivating exhibits and dioramas until his death in 1904. In 1968, the museum that took its origins from his collections moved to its current purpose-built facility. In recognition of the museum's centennial and its growing international significance, Prince Philip, the Duke of Edinburgh, conferred its designation as the Royal British Columbia Museum in 1987.[49]

As settlement of the southern parts of the province increased rapidly between the 1890s and the 1910s, pressures on valued game species became more acute.[50] Access to improved and more affordable firearms, such as the breech-loading rifles available after the American Civil War, allowed for more hunters and shorter reloading times; as a result, there was a great- er toll on animal and bird populations. The completion of the Canadian Pacific Railway (CPR) line from the Kicking Horse Pass to Vancouver in 1885, its Crowsnest line to Kootenay Landing in 1898 and smaller regional lines across the province created access corridors into previously distant hinterlands for miners, big-game hunters and market hunters.[51] On south- ern Vancouver Island, for example, the extension of the E&N Railway from Nanaimo to Victoria in 1888 led to the localized eradication of blue grouse along the railway allowance. "At least 1500 to 2000 guns left Victoria by the E&N railway" over the first three days of the hunting season, a local game guardian estimated in 1909, and hunters "cleaned up everything that they were allowed to shoot from Victoria to Cowichan . . . for a half mile at least on each side" of the rail right-of-way.[52]

In the north, steam **paddlewheelers** continued to operate on the major rivers, opening unroaded areas to visiting hunters and the guide-outfitting operations that served them.[53] In operation on major rivers and lakes across the province since the 1830s, paddlewheelers played an important role in shortening pack train routes and opening new areas to commercial and sport hunting. As guide outfitter and historian Leo Rutledge explains, the packers that met the steamship lines to ferry freight and passengers farther into the Interior formed the origins of the guide-outfitting industry. As oth- er pack trail work tapered off with the extension of rail lines in the 1880s

Steam paddlewheelers like the *Inlander*, which made its last journey down the Skeena River in 1912, preceded the railways in opening access to wildlife refuges in the interior of the province. Royal BC Museum, B-01268.

and 1890s, packers took advantage of new revenue opportunities to employ their backcountry knowledge in guiding and outfitting elite sport hunters from around the world. Beginning in the Kootenays, southern Chilcotin and Mount Robson districts, where paddlewheelers and later rail lines made "game herds . . . readily accessible," guide outfitters and their sport hunter clientele had extended their reach into the Cassiar district near the BC–Yukon border by the end of the nineteenth century.[54]

Across the province, freshwater fish stocks were among the quickest wildlife resources to be depleted. Recognition of the vulnerability of freshwater fish was clear as early as 1859, when Vancouver Island's first Act for the Preservation of Game prohibited the use of nets of any kind to take fish "in any lake, pond, or standing water" in the colony.[55] Fisheries fell under federal jurisdiction after the province joined Confederation in 1871.[56] Federal fisheries wardens, however, were thinly dispersed and often poorly prepared. As a result, federal attempts to restrict overfishing (especially

CPR promotional material for hunting and fishing along the railway line, 1891. Cover image, Canadian Pacific Railway, *Fishing and Shooting on the Canadian Pacific Railway*, 1891. Image courtesy of UBC Rare Books and Special Collections.

among non-Indigenous fishers) were nearly non-existent in this period. The "scramble for protein" in these years led some settlers to dynamite and shoot fish in rivers and lakes, driven in part by a gold rush mentality that saw wildlife left behind not as an investment for the future but as a squandered opportunity that would be taken up by others. Fish stocks in lakes and streams adjacent to growing towns were hit especially hard, buckling under the combined pressure of local food requirements and an export trade to higher-priced urban markets. In other areas, waste disposal from processing plants and sawmills destroyed spawning grounds and depleted fish populations.[57]

At the same time, tourism placed its own demands on wildlife. By the late 1880s, the CPR had found ways to boost flagging passenger revenues by promoting and outfitting southern and eastern travellers for hunting trips to what was billed as the "best big game country in North America, if not in the entire world." Sporting guidebooks promised "deer, bear, mountain sheep, 'panther' (mountain lion), and elk" awaiting "at Hatzic Lake in Mission and near whistle stops at New Westminster, Port Moody, Revelstoke, the Shuswap, and Victoria."[58] And in the early years, at least, the few visiting hunters who travelled to the province were not disappointed. Train passengers and crews shot animals from railcar platforms in the Rockies, and American and British hunters travelling the CPR line and American branch lines in southern BC felt the rush of a bonanza of wildlife for the taking. By the 1890s, however, overhunting along these rail lines led visiting big-game hunters to bypass southeastern BC for the wildlife-rich fields of Alaska or the Cassiar district of northwestern BC, newly accessible by rail and steamship.[59]

SPECIES PROFILE: Brant (*Branta bernicla*)

Once an abundant winter resident along the BC coast, the brant (*Branta bernicla*) declined dramatically as a wintering species over the course of the twentieth century owing to hunting pressure and habitat loss. Market hunter Henry Weaver of Ladner remembered that in his youth in the 1890s, the shores of Mud Bay and Boundary Bay were at times "solid with flocks of Brant." The birds "came in so continuously to decoys," he recalled, that on one occasion he and eight other hunters "took turns shooting from a single blind and picked up 128 birds in the course of a few hours." Business was especially brisk in late December, when market hunters shot large quantities of brant on the east coast of Vancouver Island and on the Fraser River delta to supply Christmas and New Year's Day feasts in Victoria and Vancouver.[60]

By the late 1940s, the wintering population had begun a precipitous decline. A second, separate population of brant continued to visit BC shorelines in spring, stopping to feed on eelgrass (*Zostera marina*) during their annual migration from Mexico to breeding grounds in Alaska. Hunting pressure remained relentless, however, and biologists' warnings of population collapse were ignored by a provincial fish and game agency primarily concerned with enforcing bag limits and retaining public hunting opportunities.[61] Brant hunting was not closed on the BC coast until

Brant near Parksville Bay, Parksville, March 31, 2011. Photo courtesy of Neil K. Dawe.

the late 1970s, when a report by the Fish and Wildlife Branch warned that "if recent trends continue few if any Brant will appear in B.C. prior to the last day of the open [hunting] season." Hunting pressure, the report found, unduly impacted breeding pairs of adults, which arrived from Mexico during the hunting season.[62]

Brant numbers continued to decline in the Strait of Georgia, however, dropping from roughly 25,000 individuals in 1965 to 8,000 by the 1990s. For Canadian Wildlife Service (CWS) habitat manager Neil Dawe—who was stationed at Qualicum Beach, a major stopping point for migrating brant, from 1975 to 2006—the missing piece of the puzzle was habitat: specifically, the threatened and highly productive estuarine and intertidal habitats that were key to the survival of brant and other wintering migratory birds in the province.

For Dawe, the brant provided inspiration for a community celebration of the Parksville-Qualicum Beach area's natural values. The spectacle of this beautiful, "talkative little sea goose" arriving in huge flocks each spring prompted the idea for a wildlife festival along the lines of the annual Waterfowl Festival in Maryland. "I also thought it would be a good tourism draw," Dawe recalled in a 2019 interview; "it was during the shoulder season and . . . there are other wildlife spectacles around the same time: the Pacific herring spawn, for example, which brings in hundreds of thousands of sea ducks and sea lions and seals." Early support from Bashir El-Khalafawi, manager of the Bayside Inn Resort and incoming president of the Parksville Chamber of Commerce, combined with support from the CWS and the BC Ministry of Environment's new Wildlife Watch initiative, led to the launch of the first Brant Festival in Parksville-Qualicum Beach in the spring of 1991.[63]

Under Dawe's initial direction, the Brant Festival succeeded in generating tremendous local and government support for what became a popular annual event, drawing on sponsorship from federal, provincial and municipal governments, environmental organizations such as Ducks Unlimited Canada (DUC) and the Nature Trust of BC, and vital community supports from local businesses, naturalist and fish and game stewardship organizations, and area First Nations. In addition to festival supports, area naturalists contributed thousands of hours of volunteer expertise to assist CWS biologists in monitoring brant populations each spring. Together, the festival and the surveys highlighted the importance of the Parksville-Qualicum Beach area to the brant. In the spring of 1993, provincial Minister of Environment John Cashore and wildlife director Ray Halladay acted on this information by designating the Parksville-Qualicum Beach Wildlife Management Area, protecting over one thousand hectares of estuarine and foreshore habitat. The Brant Festival still attracts tourists to the area each year under the direction of the Nature Trust of BC. As for the brant itself, the numbers of spring migrants through the Strait of Georgia continue to fluctuate, and the little goose remains a species of special concern in the province.[64]

Sport Hunters and Early Fish and Game Protection

Early game protection initiatives took their impetus from a small but influential group of sport hunters whose beliefs about hunting etiquette had shaped the earliest game legislation in the province. As early as 1859, the passage of BC's first game act recognized the importance of hunting as a source of not only food and livelihood but "healthy and manly recreation."[65] This reference, contained in the preamble to the legislation, reflected the views of a small cadre of sport hunters—typically British-born men of means who held property and political influence in the colony. Some of these men and the organizations they later formed played a direct role in advocating for, and often drafting the content of, early game ordinances. Protections were extended to insect-eating birds in 1862, for example, to protect the agricultural interests of southern Vancouver Island's estate owners.[66] The bounty laws of the 1860s further protected these interests by instituting payments for cougars and wolves killed in settled areas.[67]

The influence of the colony's sporting elite is especially apparent in the province's third game ordinance of 1870, which extended protections to non-native species of quail, pheasant and partridge. As native game bird populations plummeted as a result of hunting pressure near populated areas, prominent sport hunters used their wealth and connections to import exotic pheasants and partridges from China and Europe as replacements.[68]

Once the pursuit of a privileged few, interest in the promotion of hunting and fishing as a sport rather than a necessity grew considerably among professional and middle-class British Columbians between 1890 and 1910. Rod and gun clubs and fish and game protection associations proliferated in BC towns and cities after 1890, when an amendment to the Game Protection Act allowed for their incorporation.[69] Building on the work of similar groups in Europe, the United States, and Central and Eastern Canada, these organizations formed in response to what they saw as the wasteful slaughter of wildlife for consumption or commercial use. They promoted instead the development of hunting as a sport, educating their members to shoot discriminately and adopt an etiquette of **"fair chase"** in pursuing their quarry—privileging the patient, skilled shot over more expedient measures such as hunting with dogs or traps.[70]

Leaders of these organizations, often men of considerable wealth and esteem in their communities, used their influence to advocate for game laws and to raise funds to support their enforcement. The creation of the BC Game Protection Association in Victoria in 1895, for example, mobilized a $1 membership fee among its fifty founding members to hire private game wardens for popular hunting areas. By the turn of the century, local fish and game protection associations had formed in Ashcroft, Chilliwack, Fernie, Kamloops, Ladner, Nelson, Vancouver and Victoria.[71] These associations shared a vision of protecting valued wildlife species from the excesses of the market and subsistence hunt to maintain a vigorous sporting culture in the province for local and visiting hunters.

Fish and game associations made some headway in their efforts to rein in unsustainable hunting practices with the passage of new game ordinances in the 1880s and '90s. Ordinances in this period laid out what would become the defining elements of game conservation legislation in BC (and across

North America) for the next half-century: closed seasons and bag limits defined by animal species, age and sex; hunting and fishing licences; predator bounties; and support for the propagation of exotic game species.

One of the principal objectives of the nineteenth-century ordinances was to curb the commercial exploitation of BC game species. With the completion of the CPR and the extension of associated railway lines and roads, new opportunities had arisen for the export of meat, hides and horns. Hide hunting in the southeastern part of the province, for example, led to great declines in mule deer populations. "There was an almost constant stream of wagons passing from the Okanagan Valley across the line into the United States," then hunting guide Bryan Williams recalled, and their "sole freight consist[ed] of mule deer skins."[72] Ice-refrigerated railway cars, meanwhile, allowed visiting hunters to export meat, antlers, and heads of deer, bighorn sheep and grizzly bear on eastbound trains.[73] Indigenous hunters responded to a high demand for wildlife souvenirs among foreign tourists by selling pelts and heads to curio shops, raising the ire of area sport hunters.

In 1890, the province heeded the lobby of fish and game associations by implementing, for the first time, hunting-licence fees and bag limits for non-resident, visiting hunters. In response to the wildlife souvenir market, amendments to the Game Protection Act prohibited the export "in raw state" of animals or portions of animals protected under the law.[74] Commercial freshwater fisheries also came under regulation. By 1898, game legislation took aim at the overexploitation of trout fisheries, prohibiting "any explosive, lime or poison, net, seine, drag net, or other device other than hook and line" in waterways or lakes smaller than 13,000 hectares.[75]

However promising these restrictions may have looked on paper, they were notoriously difficult to enforce. Although private fish and game associations had appointed volunteer and salaried game wardens in more populated parts of the province from the 1890s on, their authority, and their coverage, was extremely thin. Magistrates throughout the province, furthermore, were known to show "excessively leniency" toward those who violated the game laws.[76] A fee paid to informers, introduced in the 1898 Game Protection Act, provided some support to game wardens, but in remote areas of the province especially, hunters, fishers and guides generally turned a blind eye to game regulations.[77]

Exemptions on closed seasons and bag limits for miners, cattle ranchers, Indigenous people and settlers in unorganized districts—provided the

Free miner's certificates, like this one from 1863, granted prospectors unlimited rights to fish and hunt for a small fee. Royal BC Museum, D-09652.

animals killed were for their own immediate use—contributed to a patchwork of applicability and, as Georgiana Ball has noted, considerable abuse. Non-resident hunters, for example, took out **free miner's certificates** to evade the $50 game-licence fee; residents could do the same when they wished to kill game out of season; and Indigenous hunters, who depended on access to fish and game year-round for subsistence and trade, continued to hunt for food and income out of season (in accordance with what would later be recognized as their Aboriginal right).[78] The sale of pelts and heads to tourists and travelling businessmen by Indigenous groups in the Rockies, for example, continued well into the 1920s.[79] By 1900, the cumulative effects of hunting pressure from resident, non-resident and Indigenous hunters raised significant conservation concerns for Rocky Mountain bighorn sheep and other valued game species.

The severity of wildlife depletion in places like the Kootenay and Okanagan districts led local residents and fish and game associations to petition the government repeatedly between 1900 and 1905 for better enforcement of game laws, the initiation of gun licences to fund enforcement and the appointment of a salaried provincial game warden and deputies.[80] Persistent lobbying, coupled with the political influence of fish and game association leadership, finally led the province to consolidate existing game regulations under a newly created Department for the Protection of Game and Forests in 1905. Bryan Williams, an experienced angler and guide from Ireland whose concerns about game protection had earned sport hunters' respect, became the province's first game and forest warden.[81]

Conclusion: Geography Matters

From the end of the HBC monopoly over the wildlife trade in 1858 until the early twentieth century, the dispossession of Indigenous Peoples of their lands and established stewardship regimes had profound consequences for people and wildlife alike. In the Lower Mainland, southeastern Vancouver Island and centres of settlement in the southern Interior, a commons opened wherein valued wildlife species were accessible to all with minimal regulation and enforcement. Dependence on wildlife for food and income in this period generated heavy hunting and fishing pressure and corresponding declines of valued species of freshwater fish, resident and migratory game birds, fur-bearers and ungulates. Much of the coast and the northern and central Interior would be insulated from these developments by their relative isolation and small settler populations. In these parts of the province, the relative persistence of First Nations control over and access to traditional territories (and correspondingly reduced pressure from settler populations) mitigated against an unregulated wildlife commons.

Nineteenth-century responses to the rapid depletion of valued fish and game species were generally ad hoc, locally initiated and sporadically enforced. An important exception lay in the salmon fisheries, where tightening dominion government regulation by the 1890s sought to prioritize access to commercial canneries at the expense of long-established Indigenous fisheries. Elsewhere, early game ordinances were initiated and enforced by local fish and game protection associations seeking, for the most part, to protect local wildlife from the incursions of newcomers and neighbouring townspeople. In the absence of reliable information on animal population numbers, nineteenth-century game regulations aimed mainly to arrest decline rather than promote sustainability. Prominent BC zoologist and conservationist Ian McTaggart Cowan later summed up the general philosophy of protective measures in this period as "one of parcelling out a dwindling supply of wildlife rather than one of maintaining and enhancing a renewable resource."[82] Reliance on private and often unsalaried game wardens, furthermore, resulted in spotty and often unreliable enforcement.

For fish and game protective associations concerned about the viability of local wildlife resources, the ineffectiveness of existing regulations and the known leniency of the courts generated frustration and concern. Beyond the settled regions of the south, nineteenth-century game ordinances drew little attention among Indigenous hunters, settlers and guides in outlying regions. Exemptions for Indigenous Peoples and acknowledgements of the hardships of settlement in unorganized districts of the province, and of the necessity to rely on wildlife for food, meant that game ordinances could generally be ignored. Not until the first decades of the twentieth century, with changes in the revenue and reach of the province's game protection offices, would Indigenous communities and rural settlers in less populated parts of the province begin to feel the burden of increasingly restrictive fish and game regulations.

PART THREE

EARLY WILDLIFE CONSERVATION AND THE RISE OF SCIENTIFIC MANAGEMENT, 1905–1965

4

Conserving Wildlife in the Early Twentieth Century

The period spanning Bryan Williams's two terms as provincial game warden (1905–18) and later provincial game commissioner (1929–34) saw the early expression of principles of conservation or "wise use" of BC wildlife resources. Moving beyond the game protection initiatives of the nineteenth century, which aimed to protect the interests of wealthy sport hunters and avert the collapse of valued game species, the initiatives of the early twentieth century saw the provincial and federal government take an increasingly large role in the development and implementation of fish and game policy and enforcement. New measures, such as licensing requirements for non-resident and later resident hunters and anglers, greatly expanded the revenue and the enforcement capabilities of the provincial Game Department. The experiments and innovations of this period, including the game reserves of the 1910s and '20s, the Migratory Birds Convention Act of 1917 and the trapline registration system of the 1920s, signalled efforts to maintain and enhance wildlife populations to ensure what American conservationist Gifford Pinchot described as "the greatest good to the greatest number of people for the longest time."[1] In the absence of a scientific capacity to systematically and reliably assess game species population numbers, these initiatives showed variable success. Their implementation, combined with growing constraints on commercial and subsistence hunting, would disproportionately affect Indigenous communities and settlers in remote districts.

Provincial Fish and Game Conservation, 1905–1918

While the creation of the province's first game department in 1905 is justifiably recognized as a major turning point in the history of wildlife management in the province, change at the time was slow in coming. Provincial game and forest warden Bryan Williams was doubtless overwhelmed by the scale of the problems he faced and the meagreness of the resources at his disposal. He embarked on the mammoth task of enforcing fish and game protection laws across the province with next to no government support: no operating budget, and just three volunteer deputy wardens to assist him in his work. Income from the $50 game licence purchased by the province's relatively few non-resident hunters counted as his only source of operational revenue.[2] Fish and game associations came to Williams's aid by appointing sixteen deputy wardens to monitor the settled areas of the province (from Vancouver Island to the East Kootenay and as far north as Quesnel). With the exception of two salaried deputy wardens appointed by the Vancouver and Victoria associations, most operated as volunteers. In 1907, Williams appointed three unsalaried deputy wardens for "trouble spots" in Invermere, Fernie and Lillooet. With no remuneration and little guidance, however, these honorary appointments were too often, in Williams's words "worse than useless." As Gerry Lister writes in his history of BC's Conservation Officer Service, "most of these men did not conduct regular patrols and many never apprehended any violators or made any effort to do so."[3] Eighteen salaried fire wardens doubled as game wardens in other areas—cross-appointments that Williams would later describe as an "absolute failure" given the divergent nature of the work and overlaps in the peak periods for fire and game protection.[4]

For Williams and the sport hunters who supported him, the goal was to build a self-sustaining game department underwritten by those who profited from wildlife use. In his first report as provincial game warden, Williams pointed to several successful examples from the United States to argue that wildlife was one of the province's most significant economic assets and that its value should be mobilized to support government conservation and stock improvement programs. Governments could fund conservation initiatives, in other words, by promoting and licensing tourism and sport hunting activities. This was an early expression of what is now a foundational concept of what wildlife management scholars and policymakers have

A hunter with a black-tailed deer (*Odocoileus hemionus columbianus*) on Shawnigan Lake, Vancouver Island, November 1939. Royal BC Museum, F-02490.

labelled the "North American model of wildlife management": the "**public trust doctrine**" wherein wildlife resources are held in trust by the state for the public's "use and enjoyment into perpetuity."[5]

Williams's plan for game protection was twofold: (1) set aside big game for high-paying tourists; and (2) conserve and improve stocks of smaller game near towns for residents. Most resident hunters, he believed, sought small game such as fish, birds and deer taken over "a day or two" of effort; "a very small fraction of the population of this Province has either the time, money, or inclination" to hunt moose, elk, bighorn sheep and grizzly bear. For Williams, these larger animals were better reserved for visiting big-game hunters whose requisite licence fees could support the department's conservation and stock improvement activities.[6] With these objectives, he set about to expand and enforce the province's game laws to rein in what had become chronic wildlife depletion in some parts of the province. His primary targets were day-tripping townspeople who hunted for subsistence and profit, and, outside the towns, primarily Indigenous hunters who sold meat and trophies to wildlife butchers and tourists.

No. 39. A day with rod and gun.

"A Day with Rod and Gun." This photograph, which was produced and sold as a souvenir for tourists, was one of many early twentieth-century photos depicting British Columbia as a "sportsman's paradise." Photo by Gus A. Maves, ca.1920. Royal BC Museum, 198303-041.

The growing problem of urban "pot hunters," as they were known—those taking day trips to hunt animals for food in surrounding streams, forests and marshes—was apparent to Williams from his first year in office, when he estimated a 25 per cent increase in the number of gun-holding residents, especially in the booming coastal cities of Victoria and New Westminster.[7] As populations increased and expanding road networks joined existing rail lines, these numbers continued to grow annually. "Every week," Williams reported in 1911, "scores of hunters [return] by train, car, launches, and every means of conveyance." He estimated that in 1911 alone, 1,000 deer and 1,500 pheasants were hauled back to Vancouver in the first few days of the hunting season. Some of these animals were retained for personal consumption, but many more were sold for profit to restaurants and game butchers.

Pressures from urban hunters led to the formation of new game protection associations in surrounding areas known for their wild fowl, such
as Richmond and Delta.[8] If the sheer number of hunters was one concern,
their lack of experience and knowledge of conservation was another. In 1912,
Williams reported male and female hunters exiting the city in numbers "never seen before" and carrying "every conceivable sort of weapon." With "this
army of hunters scouring the country, many of them not knowing one species of bird from another and shooting at everything they see," he lamented,
"it is really a wonder that there is a head of game left."[9] Williams's emphasis
on lack of skill and knowledge here is significant: unlike experienced sport
hunters who conducted a hunt with judiciousness and restraint, he believed,
day-tripping hunters threatened animal populations with wanton slaughter.

Wildlife depletion was not just an urban issue; it was also felt in the
province's resource hinterlands, particularly in mining towns. Coal-rich
areas such as Nanaimo and Fernie, and the gold rush towns of the Cariboo,
saw settler populations surge in the first decade of the twentieth century. In these places, independent and often poorly resourced miners took
advantage of the province's free mining licence to hunt for food without
restriction. In company-run mines and logging camps, migrant labourers
provisioned their camps by fishing and hunting in surrounding streams
and railway allowances. Explosive population growth, hungry and poorly
paid labourers, game law exemptions in unorganized districts and a general
lack of enforcement led to a rush on wildlife resources. In the Kootenay
district, for example, miners dynamited lakes, speared fish at night, netted bays and creeks, and left the shores of lakes "littered with fine trout."[10]
Alarmed by these abuses, neighbouring communities formed sporting organizations to enforce game regulations and lobby for wildlife protection.
The Coldstream Gun Club in Vernon formed in 1906 likely in response
to the "large appetites of neighbouring mining communities," while the
Grand Forks Sportsmen's Association (1911) responded to the overexploitation of wildlife in the Kettle Valley resulting from rapidly growing copper
mining towns in the neighbouring Boundary region.[11]

A protectionist impulse underlay the formation of these fish and game
associations. As historian George Colpitts has argued, at issue was not only
how wildlife should be obtained—through ethical means or otherwise—
but also *who* should have access to it. Efforts by early sport hunters' organizations to protect fish and game from heedless destruction by newcomers,

in other words, were at the same time efforts to secure access to wildlife for their own use.[12] Newcomers of all countries of origin, Colpitts has shown, hunted and fished more intensively than established settlers with farms. Frustration with mining-licence freedoms, especially, ran high among residents who saw the wealth of the country drained by hungry new arrivals. A desire to protect opportunities for sport hunting and to promote British values of fair chase and sportsmanship became especially acute in response to the influx of non-British settlers and sojourners in resource frontiers. Unlike the coastal cities, which attracted predominantly British-born migrants, coal mining settlements attracted newcomers from a variety of places including the United States, China, Italy and Denmark.[13] Concern about people perceived as "outsiders" robbing the province's forests and streams of game and fish led sport hunters to direct their enforcement activities toward non-British newcomers. Overhunting by newcomers, they feared, would not only deplete the resource for local sportsmen and women but damage their areas' reputations as destinations for wealthy hunters and tourists.

Guide outfitters operating in more remote areas of the province also expressed concern about declining big-game populations in the early twentieth century. Laying blame on the mainly Indigenous suppliers of the "head trade," guide outfitters described the greater time and effort, and corresponding declines in revenue, required to find suitable animals for their clients.[14] While both groups catered to similar demands among non-resident populations for wildlife "trophies," and both had impacts on wildlife abundance, the wealthy hunter clientele of guide outfitters were required to follow provincial bag limits and other regulations related to season and sex in fulfilling their hunts and to pay a licence fee to the province for the pleasure.[15] While some portion of the heads and pelts Indigenous hunters sold were derived from animals hunted for food, market opportunities contributed to unsustainable hunting by both Indigenous and non-Indigenous hunters.[16] The heavy toll on Roosevelt elk on Vancouver Island to supply the market for ornamental elk teeth is one example.[17] For Williams, trade in wildlife trophies was not only illegal; it undermined his goal of supplying wealthy sport hunters with big-game quarry. In 1909, he encouraged railway station agents to inspect permits for each head shipped out of the province (apparently with little success) and ordered taxidermists in Victoria and Vancouver to obtain a licence before exporting trophies.[18]

Funding the Game Department

Williams's strategy of supporting Game Department activities with revenue from wildlife relied heavily on the deep pockets of non-resident sport hunters. To this end, he worked to promote hunting opportunities in the province and to advocate for higher licence fees. With support from rod and gun clubs in different parts of the province, Williams devoted a good portion of his time to the promotion of British Columbia as a "hunter's Eden" abundant with wild game. In his correspondence with foreign sport hunters and European and North American sporting magazines, he positioned BC as a "last refuge" for northern game in the context of wildlife depletion south of the border.[19] Williams seized opportunities large and small in his promotion of hunting tourism in the province—on the one hand, working with rail companies like the CPR to publicize hunting expeditions with trophy specimens of BC wildlife, and on the other, providing detailed personal responses to the inquiries of foreign hunters, advising them on local conditions and connecting them with experienced guides in favoured hunting areas.[20] More income from non-resident hunting licences, he reasoned, would support the salaries of more game wardens, ultimately protecting more game and attracting more sport hunters. This logic saw him advocate successfully for licence fee increases for non-resident hunters: fees doubled to $100 in 1908, and the government approved new non-resident licence fees for spring bear hunts ($25) in 1909 and angling ($5) in 1910. Annual fluctuations, combined with relatively low overall numbers of tourist hunters, however, made this an inconsistent and insufficient source of revenue.[21]

If big-game hunting licences were the most lucrative source of revenue for Game Department activities, a much broader base of potential support lay in the province's large number of resident hunters, trappers and anglers. Fisheries were the first to be licensed, in 1901, when the province passed legislation regulating the licensing and taxing of commercial fisheries and prohibiting unlicensed fishing for all but resident anglers.[22] The new legislation (and its enforcement by provincial police constables) openly contravened federal jurisdiction over fisheries. As historian Georgiana Ball argues, the provincial government's actions reflected long-standing frustration among fish and game protection associations with spotty enforcement by federal fisheries officials, especially in the Interior where market fishing continued to decimate trout populations. When pressure from the federal government forced the repeal of the short-lived provincial fisheries act in 1910, Williams continued to advocate for provincial responsibility over inland sport fisheries. Beginning in 1912, the enforcement of federal fisheries regulations by provincial game wardens extended oversight somewhat. Not until 1937, however, would Williams's call for provincial authority over freshwater fisheries yield an official transfer of authority from the federal government to the Province of British Columbia.[23]

Resident hunters provided another opportunity for revenue generation. From the time of his appointment in 1905, Williams and allied fish and game associations had advocated to expand licensing regulations to incorporate a firearms licence for resident hunters. But licensing generated considerable resistance among legislators concerned about pushback from their constituents. In 1913, ongoing concerns about the depredations of market hunters finally prompted legislators to amend the game act to require all resident hunters to take out a $2.50 annual firearms licence. A rush on licences in the first year caught Game Department staff off guard: initial estimates of 12,000 licences for a provincial population of about 400,000 were far surpassed by the almost 32,000 licences sold. Generating over $99,000 in direct revenue in 1913, the new resident hunter's licence became a major source of funding for Game Department activities.[24] With no limits on the number of licences awarded, however, and no capacity to systematically assess game species population numbers, it contained an inherent bias toward generating revenue at the expense of wildlife.[25] Exemptions for farmers, prospectors and Indigenous residents (who collectively received 7,500 resident licences free of charge in 1913), and for settlers in unorganized districts, only increased hunting pressure.[26] It would become the work of future generations of wildlife managers to try to strike a balance between hunting demand and revenue generation, on the one hand, and sustainable populations of valued game species, on the other.

For trappers and guides in the province, the 1913 licensing requirements generated information in addition to revenue. The newly required $5 annual guiding licence, for example, required that hunting parties employ only licensed guides and that guides attest to the number and sex of each animal species killed. Annual submissions from licensed guides allowed for the beginning of regulatory adjustment in response to animal population impacts. Numbers were certainly skewed by unreported kills, particularly those associated with the ongoing illegal head trade, but the reporting re-quirement was an important first step nonetheless. Efforts to enumerate fur-bearers were less successful. Although $10 annual trapping licences required the submission of an annual return identifying the number and species of pelts taken, exemptions for Indigenous trappers—by far the ma-jority of trappers in the province—meant only about one-tenth of trappers submitted returns. Guiding licences also generated a database of experi-enced guides that Williams could draw on in his role as tourist agent for prospective hunting parties. In his correspondence with guides in the lead up to the 1913 amendments, Williams pointed to the value of the licence in "plac[ing] on record the skill of the guides in obtaining game."[27] The shift to a licensing system for resident hunters, trappers and guides, with its joint inputs of revenue and information, "firmly entrenched game protection as a government responsibility."[28]

The 1913 amendments marked a major turning point in Game Department fortunes. Williams was perhaps too hasty to celebrate the effects of these changes by pointing to "a notable increase of nearly all species of birds and animals" in his 1913 annual report—a claim he would struggle to make in subsequent years. Certainly, a guaranteed annual budget and revenue from licence sales improved the effectiveness of Game Department enforcement activities. By 1914, the department employed thirty-six full-time salaried deputy wardens and recorded 256 convictions for game law violations, up from fifty-four "informations laid" (charges rather than convictions) in 1910.[29] Effects on wildlife populations, however, are more difficult to ascer-tain. Mounting hunting pressure facilitated by rail and increasingly road access, and exacerbated by wartime food shortages, placed a growing toll on wildlife. Although large fires in the 1910s and '20s created new vegeta-tion attractive to moose and other ungulates in the central and southern Interior, the growth of timber and mining operations and pollution from industrial sites reduced viable habitat for other species.[30] Severe winters, dry summer conditions and disease also contributed to fluctuating ungu-late and game bird populations. Williams's annual reports during the 1910s reveal growing anxiety about wildlife scarcity, especially among mule deer, white-tailed deer and grouse and quail populations in the southern Interior and mountain caribou in the Selkirks. Improvements to the capacity of the Game Department in this period, in other words, did not translate into wildlife abundance.

Stocking Desirable Quarry

While enforcement of game laws was the primary role of Williams and his deputy wardens in this period, additional staff and operational funds enabled experimentation with other game conservation initiatives, including species introduction and restocking efforts and the establishment of game reserves. Williams's efforts to support Vancouver Island and Lower Mainland game associations in the introduction and improvement of exotic game bird species, for example, saw government expenditures to acclimatize hatchlings and, by 1918, the establishment of a game bird hatchery on the Saanich Peninsula.[31] In other areas, Williams urged restocking and the filling of presumed-vacant ecosystem niches with indigenous and exotic deer species. In 1911, for instance, government funds supported the transplantation of black-tailed deer from Prince Rupert to Haida Gwaii, a project initiated by game associations as early as 1878 that ultimately led to runaway deer populations on the islands.[32] Less worthy of support, in Williams's view, were efforts by natural history societies in Victoria and Vancouver to import exotic songbirds. Undesirable as game and subject to predation, songbirds like the goldfinches, skylarks and robins imported from New York in 1903 were expensive investments that would fail to take hold, he argued. Political pressure from the influential leaders of the Natural History Society of BC, however, resulted in government support for a second importation of skylarks to the Lower Mainland in 1913.[33]

The notion of valued wildlife species as "crops" to be restocked for harvest was nowhere more apparent than in the freshwater fisheries. Beginning in the late nineteenth century, angling associations sought to improve lakes and rivers through unlimited harvests of so-called "coarse" or "nuisance" fish species such as graylings, suckers and Dolly Varden trout to create more space for desirable sport fishery species including rainbow trout, char and kokanee salmon. Better-quality sport fish, the rationale went, could be achieved by rectifying overcrowded conditions and replacing a diversity of species with a "single crop" of fish best suited to local conditions.[34]

Fish and game clubs began cultivating and releasing desirable fish fry into select lakes and streams in the 1890s. The establishment of trout hatcheries at Cowichan Lake in 1911 and Summerland in 1918 greatly expanded the size of stocking operations. Successes were especially notable in the numerous "fishless" (or at least, trout-free) lakes of the province's dry Interior

STRIPPING SALMON AND COLLECTING OVA, FRASER RIVER HATCHING PENS, B.C.

Men stripping salmon for eggs at a Fraser River hatchery, ca.1890. Bailey Bros. Photo courtesy of Vancouver Public Library, 19960.

plateau—lakes that lacked spawning areas but presented ideal growing conditions for stocked trout. Through these interventions, places like Paul and Pinantan lakes near Kamloops came to attract sport fishers from around the world.[35] The transfer of responsibility for sports fisheries and hatchery operations from the federal government to the province in 1937 led to an expansion of fish culture operations.[36] In the following decades, BC fisheries biologists and angling associations would come to uphold hatchery fry not only as the answer to fishing pressures but also as a more efficient avenue to sport fish abundance. By circumventing the vagaries of nature, such as the loss of eggs or milt in storm events or the loss of small fry to predators, hatcheries could transform streams and lakes into "teeming trout beds."[37]

Enthusiasm for hatcheries also occurred in the coastal salmon fisheries, but with considerably less success. In 1883, declining salmon populations and political pressure from canneries led to the construction of the province's first sockeye salmon hatchery on the Fraser at Bon Accord, across from New Westminster. Other hatcheries followed on the Skeena and Cowichan

Unloading salmon at a cannery on the Fraser River, ca.1900. Canneries employed a diverse workforce, including Chinese, Indigenous and later Japanese men, women and children. Photo by Thompson's Studios. Royal BC Museum, B-04094.

rivers and several locations on the central coast. Designed to replenish, and even enhance, sockeye numbers in the context of the cannery industry's massive commercial catch, and as an alternative to commercial harvest regulations, early salmon hatcheries were large, ambitious operations. In 1910, for example, these hatcheries produced as many as 500 million fish— a quantity that, as former Freshwater Fisheries Society of BC president Donald Peterson has noted, matches "the current [2002] production . . . of all hatcheries, spawning channels, and other [Salmon Enhancement Program] operations combined."[38] Concern about the effectiveness of salmon hatcheries and their potential detriments to native salmon populations, however, ultimately brought about their demise. Scientific studies in the 1920s and '30s revealed no correlation between fish abundance and hatchery production; while hatcheries continued to release large numbers of juvenile fish, the number of adult fish returning to spawn was not increasing. These results, combined with the economic realities of the Depression years, led the federal government to close all sockeye hatcheries in the province in 1936.

Early Conservation Strategies: Game Reserves and Provincial Parks

Another strategy that game associations promoted to restore depleted wild-life populations was the creation of protected areas or "**game reserves**" for animal breeding. This was not a new idea; private game reserves had been financed and guarded by wealthy sport hunters in places like James Island, off the Saanich Peninsula, since the 1890s.[39] In other cases game protection associations sought to introduce or restock diminished game species in existing protected areas, like Stanley Park in Vancouver. Borrowed from the early national parks such as Yellowstone, established in Wyoming in 1872 to protect remnant bison herds, and Banff, established as a reserve for wildlife in 1885, game reserves were understood primarily as "breeding areas" to be protected from both human and animal predation. To this end, game wardens eradicated wolves, coyotes and other predator species in game reserves with the goal of speeding the recovery of depleted game species' populations. Measures like this, however, also reflected widespread societal beliefs in the worthiness of some animals over others. As game and fur-bearer populations increased in protected areas, their numbers would "spill over," promoters argued, to stock adjoining areas for harvest. Provincial game warden Bryan Williams was a strong supporter, as were area residents who saw the reserves as a way of making wildlife both "abundant and fearless."[40] Expanded licensing of mineral and timber extraction activities across the province provided additional impetus for breeding habitat protection.

The implementation of game reserves occurred in the context of a subtle but important shift in game legislation. In 1908, an amendment to the Game Protection Act spelled out for the first time the role of the Game Department as not simply enforcing game regulations but "manag[ing] and supervis[ing] the province's game and those who pursued it."[41] By 1908, Williams had collaborated with local trappers, hunting guides and game protection associations to set aside two game reserves for a period of ten years: the Yalakom Reserve in Lillooet District, established in 1907 to protect California bighorn sheep, and the Elk River Game Reserve in the East Kootenay, established in 1908 to protect mountain goats, Rocky Mountain bighorn sheep, elk and mule deer. Pressure from prominent American big-game hunters and conservationists, such as Theodore Roosevelt and William T. Hornaday, to rein in local and Indigenous "pot hunters" also factored into the creation of these reserves.[42] In the case of the Elk River reserve, one of the underlying objectives was to prevent the Stoney Nakoda First Nation from travelling from their reserve in the Alberta foothills to hunt in the area as they had done historically.[43]

Temporary and limited in their protections—neither designation precluded mineral or timber extraction, for example—the reserves were for Williams the product of compromise. Reflecting growing concern about the effects of logging and mining on wildlife populations, he hoped that these and subsequent reserves would become the foundation for future national parks where "all lands, timber and minerals" could be protected from exploitation. (Williams's wishes would be fulfilled decades later, when some of the early twentieth-century game reserves were incorporated into provincial park designations.)[44] Their success in bolstering ungulate and fur-bearer populations is difficult to gauge. Although Williams made glowing reports of animal increases in and around game reserves in his annual reports through the 1910s and 1920s, the absence of reliable population inventory methods in this period raises doubts about the accuracy of his claims. Yet the knowledge of local game wardens should not be discounted. Deputy game wardens, especially salaried ones, often had a good understanding of the health of local game populations. Deputy J. Russell of Lillooet, for example, submitted in his report for 1907 the number of calves, fawns and lambs born in that season and an assessment of the condition of winter and summer ranges.[45]

Like game reserves, the first provincial parks were created with both wildlife protection and tourism in mind. The establishment in 1911 of Strathcona Provincial Park in the rugged centre of Vancouver Island—the first of thirteen "wilderness parks" that the province created in the 1910s and '20s—went some distance toward meeting Williams's hope for wildlife reserves protected from extractive industries. Tourism, however, was the principal aim. While proponents of game reserves sought to attract wealthy non-resident hunters by seeding adjoining areas with big game, proponents of provincial parks—including hunters, fishers and naturalists but more significantly, railway companies and boards of trade—aimed to attract tourists and future settlers to BC through displays of the province's natural beauty and resource wealth. The challenge of accessing these wilderness parks would ultimately dampen these hopes, however: by the late 1930s, pressure from logging and mining interests led to Park Act amendments permitting resource extraction within most of the province's large wilderness parks.[46] Game reserves and provincial parks were an early expression of what would become a common practice in twentieth-century resource management, that of segregating landscapes for different uses in ways that ignored both the porousness of ecosystem boundaries and the human (Indigenous) history of use and occupation.

The outbreak of war in Europe in 1914 would bring sweeping changes to Williams's fledgling Game Department. By 1916, every unmarried deputy warden and many married ones had enlisted, four had been killed and several wounded. Williams's requests for additional staff went unheeded, and in the fall of 1917 a new-to-power Liberal government proposed to cut costs by turning over the Game Department and its duties to the provincial police. Williams lost his position in the melee. In his place, the government set up an advisory Game Conservation Board and directed the police superintendent to act as provincial game warden, *ex officio*. The Game Department had effectively been gutted and its salaried deputies replaced with overburdened policemen who often lacked the "woods skills," in Williams's words, necessary for the job.[47]

Protecting International Wildlife

Species that crossed provincial and national borders presented special challenges for government monitoring and conservation. The challenges of controlling cross-border hunting pressure generated formal international collaboration for the first time in 1911, when the United States, Great Britain (representing Canada), Japan and Russia signed the North Pacific Fur Seal Convention outlawing open-water seal and sea otter hunting.[48] Alarming declines in migratory bird populations in the same period presented their own challenges, given the wide range of species involved, the continental reach of their annual migrations and the varying hunting regulations and levels of enforcement in the jurisdictions through which they travelled.

For migratory game birds in particular, shooting during the spring mating season and intensive market hunting, especially in the US where populations were larger and transportation networks more developed, had taken a heavy toll. Widespread belief in the superabundance of bird life contributed to the

Hunting waterfowl in the Fraser delta from the vessel *Baby Face*, 1929. Note the birds strung to the ship's rigging. Photo courtesy of Delta Heritage Society and City of Delta Archives, 1983-211.

extinction of once-abundant species like the passenger pigeon in central and eastern North America. By 1900, populations of whooping cranes, curlews, wood ducks and trumpeter swans also approached collapse.

The lucrative millinery industry added to the pressure. Demand for the "colourful plumage of terns, egrets, ibises, bobolinks, rails, and herons to adorn women's hats" led to the annual slaughter of five million birds in the US alone in the 1900s and 1910s.[49] Even songbirds were not immune: economic devastation in the southern US in the years following the Civil War meant many songbirds were hunted for food as well as plumage. Habitat loss also played a role in the depletion of bird life. According to historian Janet Foster, the draining of swamps and sloughs for settlement and agriculture, especially in the US where populations were larger, was "undoubtedly the single largest factor in the decline of North American waterfowl populations," while the clearing of vast areas of forest destroyed song and insectivorous bird habitat.[50]

Concern about the plight of migratory birds developed first in the United States, where birdwatching and field naturalist clubs active since the mid-nineteenth century advocated for an end to the feather trade. Experiments with bird banding in the 1890s provided new information about migratory bird flyways across North America and exposed the consequences of spring shooting: "birds shot on their way north to nesting grounds in the spring resulted in fewer birds returning south in the fall."[51] This knowledge came with the recognition that birds wintering in the southern US and Mexico and travelling the length of the continent to breeding grounds in northern Canada were the property of no single jurisdiction. Their protection would require federal and international intervention.

In 1915, the US government sent a draft treaty to the Canadian government proposing a fifteen-year moratorium on spring shooting.[52] The request was well timed. Questions of national wildlife conservation were already on the national agenda in both countries, with Roosevelt's establishment of the National Conservation Commission in 1908 and Canada's Commission of Conservation, headed by conservationist and former Minister of the Interior Clifford Sifton, established the following year. Both provided valuable forums for dialogue on cross-boundary wildlife concerns and jurisdictional problems. As Neil Forkey has argued, these commissions, combined with advocacy by prominent American conservationists, facilitated an appreciation of national and international wildlife commons in this period. Regulating those commons would ultimately pit local wildlife users against a much wider pool of national and international sport hunting and conservation interests.[53]

By 1916, the Canadian government had secured the support of all provinces with one exception: British Columbia. BC hunters accustomed to spring shooting until March 31 objected to a three-and-a-half-month open season ending February 1; they rejected outright the treaty's proposed moratoriums on hunting rapidly declining populations of wood duck, swans, cranes and curlews. Chief game warden Bryan Williams argued that BC's game regulations provided sufficient protection for these species and voiced the widespread opinion among sport hunters that treaty terms would benefit US hunters to the detriment of those in BC (the closed season coming into effect before geese and other species had migrated to the province).[54] Behind these objections lay a broader unwillingness to surrender control over migratory birds to the federal government.[55] This entrenched opposition from BC hunters and game managers presented one of the most formidable obstacles to finalizing the treaty.

For parks commissioner James Harkin, an early advocate for the treaty, and dominion entomologist Gordon Hewitt, charged with overseeing treaty negotiations, migratory birds provided significant economic benefits to the country: game birds supported tourism and supplied tables, while insectivorous birds aided Canadian agriculture. Eager to finalize the treaty, they convinced their American counterparts to grant sweeping exemptions to secure BC's participation. To satisfy BC's objections to the five-year closed season on critically endangered wood duck, for example, states and provinces were permitted to employ other conservation measures, such as the creation of nest boxes or sanctuaries, in lieu of the moratorium. Objections to spring hunting closures produced similar exemptions: migratory birds "injurious to agriculture" could be killed under permit at any time; and, in a major setback for treaty advocates, the end of the open season was extended from February 1 to March 10.[56]

Signed in August 1916 (by Britain for Canada), the Treaty for International Protection of Migratory Birds was nevertheless a landmark achievement in international collaboration toward wildlife conservation in North America. Significantly, it ended the commercial sale of wild game birds and their eggs, established provisions for the creation of migratory bird sanctuaries (which prohibited shooting but did not protect habitat) and prohibited the destruction of migratory insectivorous birds in Canada and the United States. By transferring control of migratory game, insectivorous and non-game birds to the federal government, it recognized the significance of these birds as the property of a national, and international, commons. Not all migratory birds fell under the treaty's protection, however. The exclusion of migratory hawks, eagles and owls reflected societal perceptions of predatory birds as "vermin" for extermination rather than animals meriting protection.

At a broader level, the treaty served as a catalyst for federal government action on questions of wildlife protection. The need to design and administer policies flowing from Canada's **Migratory Birds Convention Act (MBCA)**, passed in 1917 to ratify the treaty, led to the appointment of a dominion ornithologist under the Parks Branch and the creation of the Advisory Board on Wild Life Protection with a mandate to consider wider wildlife protection needs. Despite its earlier opposition, BC joined most other provinces in amending its provincial game laws to conform to MBCA regulations.[57] Today, North America remains the only continent in the world whose bird populations are protected by an international agreement of this scale.[58]

INITIATIVE PROFILE: The Christmas Bird Count

Initiated by the Audubon Society in 1900, the **Christmas Bird Count** is North America's longest-running citizen science project. Each year, on a single day between December 14 and January 5, volunteer participants from over two thousand localities across the Western Hemisphere count all bird species sighted within a twenty-four-kilometre-diameter circle that stays the same from year to year. Organized locally by birding clubs and naturalist organizations, the counts bring together experienced and novice birders to provide education and greater accuracy in survey results. The resulting information forms one of the world's largest sets of wildlife survey data. Survey results are used by conservation biologists and naturalists to assess the population trends and distribution of bird species.

BC naturalists, hunters and wildlife enthusiasts have participated in the Christmas Bird Count from its inception, with the earliest survey results filed in places like Okanagan Landing, Vernon and Naramata between 1905 and 1908 and at Comox and Courtenay on Vancouver Island beginning in the 1920s. Data from these surveys and the ones that followed, year after year in locations across the province, are freely accessible on the National Audubon Society's website.

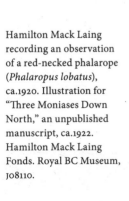

Hamilton Mack Laing recording an observation of a red-necked phalarope (*Phalaropus lobatus*), ca.1920. Illustration for "Three Moniases Down North," an unpublished manuscript, ca.1922. Hamilton Mack Laing Fonds. Royal BC Museum, J08110.

The Christmas Bird Count and its history in the province point to the nascent interest in non-consumptive relationships with wildlife, and the conservation of both game and non-game species, beginning in the early twentieth century. The proliferation of naturalist clubs, natural history museums and wildlife parks across the province in the late nineteenth and early twentieth century, combined with growing concern about declining wildlife populations, generated interest among a growing number of wildlife enthusiasts.[59]

Implications for Indigenous Peoples

The double thrust of early twentieth-century provincial and federal game laws—to prohibit market hunting, on the one hand, and circumscribe the subsistence hunt, on the other—came into direct conflict with established Indigenous economies, which had relied for thousands of years on the consumption and trade of fish and wildlife. These changes came at a time when other conservation measures, like the creation of parks and game reserves, further constrained access to traditional hunting and trapping grounds. Borders also played a role in barring access to traditional territories and exacerbating hunting pressure on BC wildlife populations.

The traditional territory of the Ktunaxa, for example, historically included parts of Alberta, Montana, Washington and Idaho. Following the completion of the Great Northern railway through Montana in 1896 and the associated influx of settlers, Ktunaxa hunters from southeastern BC faced prosecution for hunting in their territories south of the border. The enforcement of game legislation in Montana severed Ktunaxa communities in southeastern BC from their fall hunting grounds, where mule deer and other species were taken in large numbers for winter provisioning, redirecting hunting pressure within a smaller area in the East Kootenay.[60] Changes like this undermined established stewardship strategies such as seasonal rounds, where hunting pressures were distributed throughout the year across large traditional territories.

Regulating Indigenous Hunters

The maintenance of Indigenous subsistence economies in places like the East Kootenay, combined with hunting pressure from settlers and non-resident sport hunters and the natural variability of ungulate populations, heightened concerns about the viability of big-game populations in the early years of the twentieth century. Many conservationists and game officials identified Indigenous hunters and trappers as the most significant threat to wildlife populations in the province. Not only did Indigenous hunters kill wildlife for their own subsistence, critics pointed out, but they also provisioned logging and mining camps with wild meat and sold venison and game birds to game markets and butchers.[61] Complaints tended to coalesce around three kinds of alleged abuses: (1) overexploitation of wildlife; (2) violation of specific game laws, such as hunting out of season or taking female or juvenile members of a species protected by game regulations; and (3) the use of what were considered to be "unsportsmanlike" hunting methods, such as snares and dogs.[62] In discussion of the "Indian problem" at Canada's **Commission of Conservation** conference in 1919, for example, BC representative Dr. Albert R. Baker, chairman of the Game Conservation Board, claimed that Indigenous people on hunting trips in the Atlin and Cassiar area killed a moose "every day for their dogs," while those gathering for potlatches in the Chilcotin country slaughtered California bighorn sheep "just for the love of killing."[63] Other attendees objected to the killing of large numbers of moose and elk out of season when they "are easily lured within range by the use of a call," or expressed outrage at the tendency of Indigenous hunters to slaughter animals and "[take] away the meat for food" while leaving "priceless" heads to rot in the bush.[64] The irony of this was not lost on Indigenous leaders who objected to trophy hunting by outsiders on their traditional territories.[65]

In addition to the racism that fuelled many of these complaints, sport hunters voiced fundamental objections to a system of game legislation that was applicable to some members of the province but not others. Prominent American conservationists like William T. Hornaday added fuel to these debates, pressuring the federal and provincial governments to restrict Indigenous hunting freedoms in areas renowned for big-game hunting, such as the East Kootenay. "With proper protection," the editors of New York's *Forest and Stream* wrote in 1907, "British Columbia should for many years offer the best hunting to be had on this continent."[66] Accounts like these, which cast Indigenous hunters as "unruly and improvident killers of wildlife," were reiterated by sport hunters and game officials for decades.[67] While some of these accounts were unsubstantiated—for example, those that categorically blamed low moose numbers on "Indian depredations"—

the detail in other accounts, and similar observations made by sport hunters and game officials across the province, suggest that some truth lay in claims of large numbers of animals killed by Indigenous hunters for subsistence, trade and sale.

By defining acceptable hunting as a selective sport hunt by non-Indigenous hunters and tourists, conservationists and the game legislation they developed left out an important category of wildlife users with legitimate claims to the resource. Sport hunters' and game officials' complaints demonstrated a failure to understand, or to accept, both the ongoing importance of wildlife as food for Indigenous communities and the long-standing practice of trading or selling game, from the pre-contact trade between Indigenous nations to the provisioning of European fur traders in the eighteenth and nineteenth centuries. As Métis scholar Frank Tough has observed, "the extensive demands generated by a kin-based subsistence economy could not easily be grasped by the sports hunter horrified by 'rotting heads.'"[68]

Adding to the anxiety over Indigenous hunting was the considerable confusion that surrounded government regulation of Indigenous hunting. The colonial history of Indigenous Peoples' nation-to-nation relationships with European powers underlay the assignment of federal responsibility for the regulation of Indigenous affairs. As wards of the federal government, Indigenous hunters, trappers and traders were, in theory at least, subject only to federal laws and, in the few areas of the province covered by treaties, to treaty provisions that granted them rights to hunt and fish on reserve lands and unoccupied Crown lands.[69] Even the federal Fisheries Act (1878) was silent on Indigenous fishers. Instead, fisheries officials followed an informal policy of exempting Indigenous fishers from federal fisheries regulations.[70] The provinces, meanwhile, held authority over provincial lands and wildlife resources according to the terms of the 1867 British North America Act. In the grey area between these jurisdictions lay substantial room for interpretation.

Federal Department of Indian Affairs (DIA) officials themselves presented mixed messages on the applicability of provincial game laws to Indigenous hunters. Rather than upholding provincial game laws' explicit exemption of Indigenous Peoples, they alternated between encouraging adherence to hunting regulations and negotiating exceptions with provincial game officials.[71] Deputy Superintendent of Indian Affairs Duncan Campbell Scott, for example, responded to the vociferous complaints of provincial game wardens at the 1919 Commission of Conservation conference with a promise "to induce the Indians to obey the laws passed by the Provincial authorities for the conservation of wildlife and the preservation of game."[72] As historian Tina Loo argues, Scott and his officials believed that even if Indigenous people did not fall under the jurisdiction of provincial game laws, they should "be made to conform to the spirit of them." For example, Scott urged federal Indian agents to support provincial conservation objectives by refusing to supply ammunition during closed seasons and cautioning against the harvest of fish and birds during the breeding season.[73] The BC Supreme Court upheld exemptions to provincial game laws only on reserve lands; off-reserve, federal justice and Indian Affairs officials permitted game laws to encroach on longer-standing treaty and Aboriginal rights to hunt and fish.[74]

Not all DIA officials shared these views, however. Some Indian agents responded to the hardships they witnessed on reserves by defending Indigenous hunters accused of violating game regulations. In 1921, for example, Indian agent J.F. Smith registered his concern with a lower court's decision to impound a Secwépemc man's gun as part of a sentence for having deer in his possession out of season. "As it is not easy to estimate what an Indian's gun means to him, being practically a part of his being," Smith wrote, "the extreme hardship inflicted in the loss of this main food getter can hardly be exaggerated."[75] Smith's protest reflected broader concerns among DIA officials about the potential effect of hunting restrictions on welfare expenditures. Penalties for violations of the game laws included fines or jail time for those unable to pay—or worse, the confiscation of valuable pelts, traps or firearms that threatened their ability to make a living.[76] If Indigenous people were deprived of the right to hunt, officials believed, the federal government would be legally obligated to provide them with food and clothing.[77]

Restricting Indigenous Fisheries

Similar developments occurred in the salmon fisheries. Since the late 1890s, the owners of coastal canneries and resident anglers had pressured the federal government to reduce competition from Indigenous fishers in the Interior, especially on major salmon rivers such as the Skeena and the Fraser. Ad hoc destruction of traditional fish weirs and traps by settlers

Secwépemc people waiting to meet the game warden coming to remove their fish weirs, 1891. Photo by C.W. Holliday. Photo courtesy of Enderby and District Museum & Archives, edms photo #0281. Reprinted with permission from Splatsín te Secwépemc.

and local game wardens in the 1880s and 1890s became more systematic in the early twentieth century, with federal fisheries officials seizing and destroying the salmon weirs of the Dakelh and other First Nations on the upper Fraser River. For peoples who had long depended on fall salmon harvests as a principal winter food staple, government fisheries policies brought enormous hardship.[78] Ongoing encroachment of commercial and sport fisheries on reserve-based fishing grounds further diminished First Nations' access to ancestral fisheries.

The effects of the combined pressures of industrial development, commercial fishing and federal fisheries policies came into sharp focus on the Fraser River in 1913, when Canadian National (CN) railway construction in the Fraser Canyon triggered a series of landslides that deposited tons of rock into the river at Hell's Gate. The **Hell's Gate slides** narrowed the river channel and increased its flow and turbulence, effectively barring salmon from their upriver spawning grounds. Three decades would pass before the installation of fishways at Hell's Gate allowed passage for spawning fish. In the meantime, the federal Department of Fisheries responded by closing the Indigenous food fishery on the Fraser in 1914. Because sockeye salmon runs peak every four years, the full effect of the slides did not become clear until 1917, when the fish failed to return in expected numbers. Responses by federal officials replicated an established pattern of restricting Indigenous fisheries in order to privilege access to the canneries. While the commercial fishery at the mouth of the Fraser continued unrestricted, upriver food fisheries remained closed until 1922 and heavily restricted thereafter, as new regulations allowed officials to dictate the places, methods and duration of food fishery harvests.[79] As canneries responded to declining runs on the Fraser by shifting their operations to the central and northern coasts, food fisheries restrictions followed in their application to other rivers in the province. In each case, as Cole Harris concludes, Indigenous food fisheries became "the last claim on fish stocks and the first to be questioned if supplies to the canneries diminished."[80]

Declining Access and Management Authority

Indigenous opposition to fisheries regulations joined a tide of discontent regarding the loss of traditional territories and the effects of provincial game regulations in circumscribing sources of sustenance and livelihood. In a 1905 petition in response to the restrictions imposed by the new Game Protection Act, for example, St'at'imc (Lillooet) leaders wrote that "the new game act as a whole is hurting us altogether. . . . Hunting and fishing is our living. It is our daily bread for which we have a right and which no law can take away from us. . . . We have a right to live."[81] Amendments in 1911 prohibiting Indigenous hunters from taking more than three deer per year created further hardship. Although by 1913 game wardens were permitted to issue permits to hunt deer for food, wardens "were often far away . . . or disinclined."[82] Cowichan Chief Joe Eukahalt referenced the suffering that the game laws created in an address to the BC Royal Commission on Indian Affairs in 1914: "white men are making laws that are getting our people in trouble. . . . Our people cannot . . . get their [food] anywhere without being guilty of violating some law." He requested permission to kill "siwash ducks" (white-winged scoters or surf scoters) for food, a species considered undesirable by white hunters.[83]

In the old days, the Pacheenaht people [of southwestern Vancouver Island] depended on their ability as hunters and fishermen to survive. If we didn't catch enough fish and game in the spring and summer, we would not have enough food preserved to last us through the winter.

I was 10 years old when I started to hunt [around 1886]. . . . There were elk, bear, [and] deer . . . all around at that time, and you didn't have to go . . . too far to get any of them— you could get them when they were right down by the river, and then just roll the carcass right into your canoe. . . .

We started hunting with dogs when I was about 15 years old. It was useful to have a dog along with you if you were hunting in the deep bush. . . . If you shot a deer and wounded it, the dog would track the wounded deer and, when the animal died, stand there barking to let you know where it was. . . .

We used to use the skins of the animals we hunted to make things like covers for our beds and rawhide rope, which was made by scraping the hair off and cutting the hide into strips. . . . I can remember seeing my father and grandfather working with the hides.

[In 1905] they passed a law which said that we couldn't catch fish or hunt any kind of animal like elk or deer, except at certain times of year. If we get caught hunting out of season, we get into trouble. After they . . . passed this law, we had to start eating the white man's food, as that was the only way to stay alive. So, to pay for the white man's goods, we had to make money, and the only way we could do that was to work for the white man's companies. . . . In my father's and grandfather's day . . . they had everything they needed right outside their houses. . . . I think that the people were happier in the old days.

—excerpt from Chief Charles Jones with Stephen Bosustow, *Queesto, Pacheenaht Chief by Birthright* (Nanaimo, BC: Theytus Books, 1981), 33–34, 94.

Not only was the right to hunt for food considerably restricted by the game laws of 1905 and after, but the right to participate in the management of wild-life resources was also lost. Nuu-chah-nulth Chief Earl Maquinna George pointedly critiqued these changes in his commentary on the **International Fur Seal Convention** of 1911 that prohibited the hunting of northern fur seals and sea otters, ending a lucrative occupation for the Nuu-chah-nulth and other coastal First Nations. Laws like this, he wrote in 2003, "[gave our people no say] in the disposition of the animals that are part of our world, yet are harvested for commercial gain by other peoples."[84] Others appealed for co-management, or at least shared revenue from the wildlife wealth removed from their lands. The chief and band members of the Spuzzum band in the Fraser Canyon, for example, decried the waste created by white trophy hunters in a 1916 letter to the local Indian agent. They challenged the province's right to wildlife revenue from hunting licences, arguing that the fees should be shared with the Indigenous owners of the territory.[85]

By 1916, the combined effects of land losses and restricted access to fish and wildlife prompted Andrew Paull and Peter Kelly, of the Squamish and Haida nations, respectively, to form the **Allied Tribes of British Columbia (ATBC)**. The organization, which attracted participation from First Nations on the north and south coasts and many in the Interior, became the first to unite BC First Nations in pressing the federal and provincial governments for claims to land and resources.

Conflicting Fur-Bearer Conservation Systems

Nowhere were conflicts over systems of game conservation more pronounced than in the regulation of access to fur-bearers by Indigenous and non-Indigenous trappers. Fur-bearers had historically received less consideration in the province's early game laws than other valued wildlife resources. Unlike angling and big-game hunting, trapping was generally seen as "the vocation of Indians . . . and itinerant prospectors" rather than more politically influential sport hunters.[86] Trappers' quarry, furthermore, was not classified as game by the sport hunters writing the game regulations. The result was a largely unregulated market in fur-bearers that threatened the sustainability of the hunt and the viability of fur-bearer populations. Managed carefully through Indigenous stewardship systems or principles of sustained yield, beaver populations tended to remain relatively stable. As inexperienced settler trappers encroached on Indigenous trapping territories in the 1880s and '90s, however, competition and careless methods (such as the use of poison and the trapping of breeding stock) led to alarming declines in beaver and other fur-bearer populations.[87]

The province was slow to respond. Not until 1896 were amendments made to the Game Protection Act to protect "unprimed [not yet premium] beaver, marten and river otters" in the summer and fall.[88] Ongoing declines led Williams to announce a six-year provincewide closed season on beaver in 1905, a decision that generated stiff opposition from northern Indigenous leaders, Indian agents and the HBC alike. Chiefs in the Cariboo region, for example, argued in a petition to the superintendent of Indian Affairs that such measures disregarded effective and long-practiced stewardship of fur-bearers at the local level: "We have laws of our own which we may call natural by which Beaver is protected. . . . For instance every group of families have a certain special circuit where they do their hunting and they understand that it is their interest to see that the game is not destroyed, to that effect we never hunt [two] years in succession on the same streams."[89]

Petitions by other northern Indigenous groups reiterated the effectiveness of traditional trapping techniques that harvested disparate tracts of territory in rotation, leaving breeding stock in place and allowing areas to regenerate over several years. They also emphasized, as the Cariboo-area chiefs had done, the importance of beaver not only as a source of income but as a vital source of food over the winter months. While big-game populations fluctuated, and the cost of ammunition and weapons was prohibitive, beaver provided a reliable and inexpensively procured source of protein.[90] "Survival," they argued, "was the ultimate conservation motive."[91]

HBC lawyers also weighed in, affirming that family ownership of beaver streams and associated cultural controls on beaver harvests had been "scrupulously observed" from "time immemorial," resulting in "no apparent [diminution] of Beaver" over many years past.[92] A closed season on beaver, HBC and northern Indigenous leaders maintained, inordinately penalized Indigenous trappers who relied on the beaver harvest for their survival, while failing to address the root of the problem: the encroachment of non-Indigenous trappers whose indiscriminate harvesting practices threatened the resource for everyone. Although the HBC and its Indigenous suppliers succeeded in obtaining short-term exemptions from the six-year closed season on beaver, tensions resumed when closures were lifted and competition from white trappers intensified.[93]

Changes in game legislation in the 1910s further exacerbated these tensions. The introduction of licence fees for resident hunters in 1913 enabled anyone who purchased a $10 special firearms licence to claim a trapping territory (with the exception of Indigenous trappers, who were exempt from licensing requirements).[94] Non-Indigenous trappers took advantage of these circumstances to appropriate First Nations' traditional trapping

Setting a lynx snare near Fort Nelson, ca.1913. Royal BC Museum, A-04249. Reprinted with permission from Fort Nelson First Nation.

territories under the protection of provincial law. By the 1920s, the growing popularity of fur among consumers caused fur prices to climb substantially, leading more and more non-Indigenous residents to look to trapping as a source of income.[95] The result, by all accounts, was a "mass displacement" of Indigenous trappers by non-Indigenous trappers and other land uses, such as road and rail development, forestry and mining, and the construction of settlements and townsites.[96] Game Department estimates placed Indigenous trappers at 90 per cent of the total in 1914; by 1936, the ratio had dropped to 40 per cent.[97]

These changes came into focus in places like Prince George, where Constable Thomas Van Dyk reported 600 non-Indigenous trappers operating in the area under 250 trapping licences in 1924. All of the Indigenous trappers in the region, he noted, had lost their territories through non-compliance with game regulations (including failure to report numbers of fur-bearers trapped). The displacement of Indigenous trappers coincided with precipitous declines in fur-bearer populations: Van Dyk reported declines of 90 per cent for otter, fisher and marten since 1911 and 75 per cent for beaver since 1915.[98] The ineffectiveness of closed seasons in addressing conservation concerns, combined with ongoing conflict between

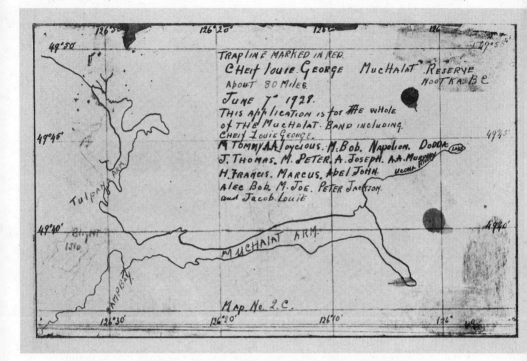

Trapline map accompanying an application for trapline registration, submitted by Chief
Louie George on behalf of members of the Muchalaht band, June 7, 1928. Image source:
Our Wildlife Heritage: 100 Years of Wildlife Management, edited by Allan Murray (Victoria:
Centennial Wildlife Society of British Columbia, 1987). Reprinted with permission from the
Mowachaht/Muchalaht First Nation.

Indigenous and settler trappers, led the provincial government to introduce
new legislation in 1925 requiring the registration of all traplines.

British Columbia's **trapline registration system** was the first of its kind
in North America. Modelled loosely on Indigenous stewardship methods,
the registration system created a geographically bounded territory in which
a resident of the province could claim exclusive trapping rights.[99] More than
a licensing system, trapline registration introduced a new kind of land tenure: registrants received specified rights on defined parcels of land and the
right to designate successors.[100] The idea, historian Brenda Ireland writes,
"was to provide a sense of ownership to a certain area and create an exclusive right to harvest furs in exchange for responsibility for conservation."[101]
Insights into fur-bearer population cycles from Gordon Hewitt's landmark 1921 publication, *The Conservation of Wild Life in Canada*, proved

influential in the establishment of long-term, area-based tenures.[102] While the trapline registration system approximated Indigenous stewardship systems to some extent, it missed important features such as "freedom of access, flexible use, and rotational conservation, which meant that some areas went untrapped for seasons on end."[103] Indigenous stewardship systems, furthermore, applied to all the wildlife in a given area and not just fur-bearers. As Ireland concludes, "restricting hunting activities to a single resource in selected areas while opening hunt[ing] seasons for specific animals in all areas was a foreign and unsustainable management technique for aboriginal people."[104]

Despite its intended aims of mitigating conflict between Indigenous and settler trappers and introducing a conservation management scheme that could be monitored by game wardens, in practice the trapline registration system further marginalized Indigenous trappers. As historian David Vogt has shown, the senior DIA officials in BC who recommended the registration system had the opposite outcome in mind. Following widespread consultations on reserves in 1923, they secured an informal agreement with the Game Conservation Board to give "preferential treatment to Indians" in registering lines, in order to protect the hereditary lines of majority Indigenous trappers from further encroachment.

What they did not anticipate, however, was a boycott of the registration system by many Indigenous leaders (including representatives from the Nisga'a, Tahltan, Kwakwaka'wakw and several Okanagan nations) as an unjustified intrusion into Indigenous trapping and a repudiation of Aboriginal title or, for First Nations in the province's northeast, of treaty rights.[105] Some of the Indian agents charged with compiling and submitting applications also refused to participate, and game wardens reviewing trapline applications varied in their responses. While some followed the Game Board's instructions regarding preferential treatment, "turn[ing] whites away from what they considered to be 'old Indian trapping country,'" others found reasons to reject Indigenous applications based on speculation of fraud or on grounds that settler applications had arrived first.[106] Further losses of Indigenous trapping territories occurred when game wardens rescinded registered traplines for non-compliance. An Indigenous trapper who used the traditional method of rotating trapping territories "risked losing all or part of his line for under-utilization"; others lost lines for failing to commence trapping by the mandated mid-November start of the season.[107]

By the 1930s, the steady erosion of Indigenous trapping rights led to some localized and regional interventions. Joe Colburne, Tahltan hereditary chief at Telegraph Creek, attempted to organize his people to support a Tahltan-run block-ownership system in place of government registration.[108] While Colburne's efforts were largely frustrated by settler registrations that undermined Tahltan control, similar forms of "block" registration were taken up as an informal expedience by game wardens in the Interior, who "regularly approved registrations submitted by Indian 'bands' or house- and family-based 'companies' rather than individuals."[109] Block registrations corresponded more readily with traditional trapping areas, acknowledging the reality that Indigenous trapping rights were allocated within family groups rather than to individuals. Indian agents, too, found it more expedient to register family or group blocks than to map out each individual line. By 1937, "company" or block registrations had been officially incorporated within the trapline registration system.[110] Indigenous trappers developed their own interpretations of trapline registration. As Gitxsan elder Mary Johnson recalls, "my uncle George Williams . . . always understood that he was registering his territory. He never considered that he was only registering a trapline."[111]

Other informal compromises between DIA officials and the provincial Game Department allowed for the limited protection and expansion of Indigenous trapping territories in the 1930s. Northern game officials like Van Dyk, now BC regional supervisor in Prince George, agreed to exempt Indigenous trappers from the requirement to submit an annual renewal and report of furs taken, lowering the number of traplines lost for non-compliance.[112] They also agreed to stop cancelling "Indian lines" without approval from the Indian agent and to notify agents whenever trapline vacancies arose in suitable areas. These provisions enabled DIA officials to purchase numerous lines and return them to Indigenous trappers.

In 1938 DIA purchased thirty-one vacated lines in the Peace River district in areas that had once been Indigenous trapping territories.[113] As Vogt observes, the arrangements arrived at in the 1930s created, at least in practice, two different kinds of traplines: "white" traplines supervised by game wardens for conservation purposes; and "Indian" traplines supervised by Indian agents. For game officials, the compromise (which persisted informally at least into the mid-1960s) constrained their ability to enforce provincial game regulations. Relaxed reporting obligations also meant a loss of Indigenous trapping data to support regional conservation efforts. For the DIA, the arrangement secured an important source of Indigenous economic prosperity. For Indigenous trappers, as Vogt argues, "the arrangement should not be read as an unqualified victory." Far from the Indigenous-run system that Joe Colburne envisioned, "the practical effect was . . . that game wardens outsourced to Indian agents the decision of how best to accommodate Indigenous governance of trapping."[114]

Implications and Opportunities for Rural Settlers

To the extent that they privileged the sport hunt over established subsistence and market hunting practices, provincial game laws also criminalized the activities of rural settlers who depended on local wildlife for food and income. Farmers, for example, often resented game regulations that prohibited the killing of deer and elk—animals that feasted on their fields, orchards and kitchen gardens—except in open season. While game regulations (from 1898 on) allowed a farmer to kill animals out of season if they were "depasturing" their fields, the onus rested on the farmer to prove the necessity of their actions. In an effort to discourage "pot hunting," local game wardens sometimes required farmers to provide an affidavit detailing the circumstances of the shooting and to turn over the deer they had killed "so as not to profit from their actions."[115]

Newly arrived settlers with limited access to cash and livestock were another group who encountered a disproportionate burden in closed seasons and hunting-licence expenses. In a letter to the provincial game warden in response to the game law amendments of 1913, settler Albert J. Wilson spoke for "hundreds of . . . [fellow] pre-emptors" when he noted that "many of us are heavily in debt and half starved having to live for weeks on rabbits and such. . . . If there are laws forbidding us to kill deer for food all I can say is that the men that made them could never have known the hardships we have to suffer when trying to open up this country and live."[116] As historians Tina Loo and George Colpitts have shown, non-white newcomers, including hunters and shopkeepers, were more likely to be prosecuted for Game Act violations than their white counterparts.[117] Some of the practices targeted as unsportsmanlike, like hunting deer with pit lamps at night, had been an expedience for settlers facing the myriad daily tasks of making a living from the land. Logger and author Wallace Baikie recalled of Denman Island that "when the early settlers needed meat for the table they would go out and shoot a deer; however, during the daylight hours, it took time to hunt down a deer, so instead of wasting daylight hours, they would go hunting in the backfield with a pit lamp."[118]

The increasingly rigorous game regulations of the early twentieth century, Loo argues, "[imposed] an urban and bourgeois sensibility about wildlife on rural Canada." Implemented to protect increasingly scarce wildlife populations as common property for all, policies that promoted the non-consumptive use of wildlife served certain interests—those of middle- and upper-class hunters, tourists and naturalists—while marginalizing others. "Members of the rural working class—many of them non-British immigrants—and Aboriginal peoples found themselves prosecuted for doing what they had always done, wresting a subsistence and a living from the woods," Loo explains.[119]

Limited enforcement, especially in remote areas of the province, meant that settlers often succeeded in ignoring game regulations. Others ridiculed or threatened local game wardens when faced with prosecution. Writing about the early years of his work as provincial game warden, for example, Bryan Williams recalled being "frequently subjected to considerable abuse, threats of violence, occasional actual attempts at violence, and sometimes to practical jokes."[120]

Twice in the history of the BC warden service, game wardens were killed by those they charged with violations. Both instances occurred during the Great Depression, when families struggled to provision their tables. The first incident took place in July 1930, when Kootenays game warden Dennis Greenwood was shot and killed in Canal Flats by a man he had charged with poaching deer the previous winter. Two years later, in October 1932, warden Albert Farey was shot twice in the back by a man he had stopped to question about an untagged deer hide in his possession. As in the Greenwood case, Farey had charged and convicted his killer in a separate incident two years previously, apparently seeding resentment. Never popular and sometimes dangerous, the work of local game wardens was, for some, not worth the enmities it generated and the relatively meagre remuneration it offered.[121]

Guiding and Bounty Hunting

As much as game regulations were bitterly resented by some, they also provided new economic opportunities for rural and Indigenous residents. Game regulations requiring non-resident hunters to be accompanied by a licensed guide created opportunities for some residents to market their horsemanship, hunting experience and local knowledge as outfitters and hunting guides. The wildlife wealth of places such as the Bull and Elk River valleys in the East Kootenay supported early outfitters like Charley Stevens, who left a legacy of mountain trail infrastructure in what is now the Top of the World Provincial Park.[122] Exclusionary practices among licensing agents and established guide outfitters often prevented Indigenous hunters from operating as independent operators or head guides, but many took up work as assistant guides, horse wranglers, cooks and store clerks.[123] For Tahltan and Kaska men in the vast Cassiar district of northwestern BC, a growing market in big-game hunting provided an opportunity to supplement their primary incomes as trappers with wages from the fall hunt.[124] (See plate 2.)

Rural residents found other ways to supplement seasonal and often sporadic incomes through government **bounty** payments for predators and other animals classified as undesirable. While bounty payments had existed in settled districts from the colonial period on, primarily for the protection of livestock, Williams succeeded in obtaining a provincewide bounty on wolves in 1907 with the broader goal of protecting wintering moose, elk and caribou populations. For the next six decades, predator control became a standard tool of provincial game protection.[125] Bounty payments fluctuated by species and over time, but they were high enough to constitute a significant expense for government and an important source of revenue for rural residents. Wolf bounties increased from $5 to $10 in 1910, for example, while the bounty for mature cougar peaked at $40 in 1922.[126]

In settled areas like Vancouver Island, bounty hunters like Cecil "Cougar" Smith (1878–1961) earned government income and the respect of local residents for the speed and effectiveness of their work tracking and killing cougars, bears and wolves that encroached on farms or attacked livestock. Cougar populations had expanded considerably on the Island as agricultural settlement, logging and fire brought down old-growth forests and provided forage for growing populations of deer. By the turn of the twentieth century, historian Richard Mackie writes, "every valley or large rural district had its own cougar hunter."[127] Skilful hunters like Smith gained a reputation among visiting hunters and naturalists, allowing them to supplement bounty incomes with guiding fees and sales of pelts and skulls to taxidermists and museum collectors.[128]

Cecil "Cougar" Smith packing the heads and pelts of two juvenile cougars, Comox Valley, ca.1925. Smith shot an estimated 900 to 1,200 cougars in his work as a bounty hunter for the provincial government in the 1920s and 1930s. Photo courtesy of the Courtenay and District Museum and Archives, 977.14.4.

INDIVIDUAL PROFILE:
"Cougar Annie" Rae-Arthur of Hequiat Harbour, Vancouver Island

While the majority of bounty hunters were men, settler women also defended their livestock from predators and collected bounties for the animals they shot. In recent years, "Cougar Annie" Rae-Arthur (1888–1985) has become an emblem of pioneer women's resilience as the inspiration for an ecotourism destination at her former homestead, a 1999 book and a 2017 musical. But her story also points to the role of the bounty in supporting settlers who struggled to make a living on land ill suited to agricultural settlement and the everyday challenges of living in remote areas in proximity to wildlife.

Born in California in 1888 to English military parents, Ada Annie Jordan spent her childhood in South Africa and the Canadian Prairies before moving to Vancouver

"Cougar Annie" Rae-Arthur outside her cabin with her rifle, 1962. Photo by John Manning. Royal BC Museum, C-04904.

with her family at the age of nineteen. The following year, in 1908, she married Willie Rae-Arthur, who was sixteen years her senior. The disgraced son of a Scottish lord, he had been banished to British Columbia with a small monthly stipend to distance himself, and his family's reputation, from his opium addiction. Willie's addiction found new ground in Vancouver, however, and in 1915 he, twenty-six-year-old Annie and their three children left Vancouver to take up a land grant at Boat Basin in re- mote Hesquiat Harbour, fifty-two kilometres northwest of Tofino and accessible only by boat.

The land that greeted them was rugged, rocky and heavily forested. While Willie and their sons took up seasonal work on the telegraph lines on the west coast of Vancouver Island, Annie set to work clearing five acres of land, running a post office and general store on her property and planting the garden that would become the source of her mail-order nursery business. Having learned to shoot at the age of eight, she supplemented her income as a trapper for the Hudson's Bay Company and with bounty payments of $10 to $40 for cougars she tracked and shot or, more unconventionally, as historian Richard Mackie noted, lured to her garden "by tying a goat to a post for use as bait." Her skill as a tracker and markswoman earned her the moniker "Cougar Annie."

Annie and Willie had five more children at Boat Basin before Willie drowned in 1936. After his death, Annie chose to stay on at the remote property with her eight children. As she would do several times in the decades to come, she advertised in farming magazines and newspapers for a new husband to assist her, taking out an ad in the *Western Producer* in 1936: "BC widow with nursery and orchard wishes partner. Widower preferred. Object matrimony." She married three more times between 1936 and 1961, outliving each of her husbands (her second husband died after accidentally shooting himself in the leg while cleaning a gun in 1944; her third died of pneumonia in 1955; the fourth, a violent man who drank and stole from her, she drove off at gunpoint in 1967). Her children fled the endless work and stern discipline of life in Boat Basin as soon as they could.

"Cougar Annie" Rae-Arthur continued to tend her extensive, now renowned garden in Boat Basin into her nineties. In 1955, at the age of sixty-seven, she tallied sixty-two cougars and over eighty bears among her kills. She died in a Port Alberni hospital in 1985 at the age of ninety-seven, having outlived six of her eleven children, survived two cougar attacks and managed a remote homestead, much of the time on her own, for almost seventy years. Her legacy of stern resilience and self-reliance as a woman cutting a living out of BC's rugged west coast points to the exigencies of her time and place. For Rae-Arthur, cougars and bears were not glorious animals to romanticize, or even more neutral co-inhabitants of her wilderness home, as much as they were a threat to her livelihood and a source of necessary income. Her views of and her actions toward predator species were shared by many settlers, especially those living in remote areas of the province in proximity to wildlife.[129]

The persistence of the bounty as a wildlife management tool for almost a century, from its initiation in 1864 to its replacement in the late-1950s with government-run predator control programs of a similar nature, reflected widespread societal beliefs in the moral worthiness of some animals over others. Categorizations of wild animals as "good" or "bad" based on their relative usefulness to humans were entrenched in the wildlife laws of the period, which accounted for animals in only two categories: "game," valuable animals or birds that were hunted; and "vermin," undesirable animals that preyed on game, livestock or "innocent" songbirds, or destroyed crops.[130]

While animals classified as "game" fluctuated over time—bear moved in and out of this category, and small fur-bearers were not extended protection as game species until 1896—those classified as "vermin" remained fairly constant, including large predatory fur-bearers such as wolves, coyotes and cougars, birds of prey, and scavenging or nest-raiding birds such as crows and magpies.

Bounties placed on "vermin" were intended to reduce and even eliminate predatory species, and they enjoyed wide public support.[131] By 1910, game warden Bryan Williams had extended bounties to golden eagles to protect sheep and goat ranges, while a bounty placed on great horned owls was intended to protect grouse populations in the Interior. A firm believer in the effectiveness of the bounty as a tool for game protection, Williams credited the program with "saving the lives of thousands of birds and animals" in his 1911 report.[132] In practice, however, the bounty had a surprisingly limited effect on predator populations. Concerns about wolf predation on deer and elk populations on Vancouver Island's northwest coast, for example, were not abated until the introduction of poison as a method of wolf control in 1914.[133]

INDUSTRY PROFILE: Commercial Whaling in BC

British Columbia's history of wildlife overexploitation did not end with the game laws of the early twentieth century. In its coastal and offshore waters, a competitive industrial hunt for whales decimated baleen and sperm whale populations into the mid-twentieth century. Whaling was not new to the West Coast: the Nuu-chah-nulth and other coastal peoples had hunted small numbers of grey whales and other species for thousands of years. European whalers had targeted grey and North Pacific right whales to render their fat into soap, margarine and lamp oil since the 1860s. By 1900, however, when European whalers had perilously depleted grey and right whale populations, the industrial hunt was only just beginning. Steam-powered ships and explosive harpoons replaced sail power and hand-thrown harpoons, allowing whalers to expand their operations and target faster blue, fin and minke whales.

In 1905, just as Williams was sworn in as the first provincial game warden, the Pacific Whaling Company opened its first whaling station at Sechart in Vancouver Island's Barkley Sound. Stations followed at Kyuquot Sound and Page's Lagoon near Nanaimo, the latter closing after just two years when it decimated the entire

Processing a whale at Rose Harbour Whaling Station, Haida Gwaii, 1918. Royal BC Museum, E-04602.

wintering population of humpback whales in the Strait of Georgia. Two additional whaling stations opened at Rose Harbour and Naden Harbour in Haida Gwaii in the early 1910s, refining the efficiency of the hunt through the use of spotting planes by 1919. Declining whale populations and fluctuating markets, however, made whaling a volatile business. Both the Sechart and Kyuquot stations had closed by 1925; a wartime cessation of whaling forced the closure of the Haida Gwaii stations in the early 1940s.

Commercial whaling operations continued in BC until 1967, when the province's last whaling station at Coal Harbour on northern Vancouver Island closed after two decades of operation. Japanese and Soviet whalers would continue to hunt sperm, sei, fin and North Pacific right whales in BC's offshore waters until 1985, when the International Whaling Commission (IWC) finally enacted a moratorium on commercial whaling for all species.

Since the 1985 moratorium, some whale populations in the North Pacific have slowly recovered. Humpback whales, taken in high numbers off the BC coast until a species-specific moratorium banned their capture in 1966, had recovered from a low of 1,200 to 1,400 individuals to over 18,000 individuals in the North Pacific by

2006. Some grey whale populations have seen similar rates of recovery. Yet other species have not fared as well. Despite legal protections for the North Pacific right whale in 1931, population estimates remained as low as thirty individuals across their range in 2017. Two North Pacific right whales sighted off Haida Gwaii in 2013 were the first to be confirmed in British Columbia since 1951. Blue, fin, sei and North Pacific right whales continue to be listed as endangered in Canada.[134]

Growing Support for Conservation between the Wars

By the end of World War I, local experience with wildlife depletion, combined with the recent and well-known extermination of once numerous species such as the bison and passenger pigeon, saw early beliefs in unending animal abundance give way to a recognition of limits and the need for wildlife protection. "Conservation"—the efficient and wise use of resources to provide, as prominent American forester Gifford Pinchot described, "the greatest good to the greatest number of people for the longest time"—had become the dominant ethos of a new generation of fishery and game managers.

Growing public awareness of conservation principles coupled with the heightened popularity of outdoor pursuits following the war saw significant growth in the membership and incorporation of fish and game associations across the province. The loss of over a million hectares of forest in southeastern BC to the massive fires of 1910 reinforced this sense of limits and created an appetite for fire suppression that would have lasting consequences for land and wildlife management in the province. For their part, Indigenous leaders deputized the newly created Allied Tribes of British Columbia to amplify their demands for land and pursue their rights to control the allocation and stewardship of animals within their traditional territories.

Rising scientific capacity, especially within the federal government, contributed to some important wildlife conservation measures in the interwar years, spurred in part by the success of the Migratory Birds Convention Act (1917) and the federally led Commission of Conservation (1909–21). Rampant overgrazing of range lands in the BC Interior, for example, led to the passage of the provincial Grazing Act in 1919. The act granted the BC Ministry of Lands greater power in regulating range use to prevent overgrazing and soil erosion. Although the act did not mention range-dependent wildlife like elk, the establishment of a federal range

Children learned to hunt as part of growing up in rural British Columbia. Here, a boy
examines a clutch of pheasant, ruffed grouse and mallards near Comox, November 1931.
Photo by Hamilton Mack Laing. Royal BC Museum, I-51805.

research station at Tranquille, near Kamloops, in the mid-1930s supported
further study of range management to keep forage viable for wildlife and
cattle alike.[135] Reinvestment in a wider slate of provincial game conservation
activities had also occurred by the 1930s. In 1928, premier Simon Fraser
Tolmie heeded the growing discontent of police officers responsible
for everything "from licensing vehicles to workmen's compensation to
'counting deer'" by restoring the Game Department and reinstating Bryan
Williams with the new title of provincial game commissioner.[136]

While growing government research capacity produced some benefits
for wildlife conservation, the dominant thrust of this work aimed to identify opportunities for industrialization and development, typically with
detrimental effects on wildlife. Surveying work from the 1890s onward
expanded land classification capabilities in this period, allowing the
Department of Agriculture and other provincial land use offices to better
target resource development on particular tracts of land. The draining of

Sumas Lake in the Fraser Valley in the early 1920s exemplifies these trends. One of several initiatives aimed at expanding agricultural lands for return-ing soldiers, the project removed 30,000 acres of productive wetland and freshwater habitat and forever altered Stó:lō traditional territories.[137]

Among the wider public, interest in and appreciation of conservation principles fuelled the growth of non-consumptive relationships with wildlife in the early twentieth century. Natural history societies in Victoria, Comox-Courtenay, the lower Fraser Valley and the Okanagan Valley attracted men and, increasingly, women to support museum collection and education activities, conduct scientific studies, and promote interest in and knowledge of the natural world.[138] (See plate 3.) The Vancouver Natural History Society, established in 1918, drew on a growing urban membership to protest destructive logging practices and to press for protected areas in the city's surrounding watersheds. In 1922, natural history societies in Vancouver, Victoria and Duncan joined forces to campaign against provincial bounties for predatory mammals and birds of prey—opposition that would gain traction with the support of conservation-minded scientists in the 1940s and 1950s.[139]

Vancouver Natural History Society members at an outing near Caulfield, West Vancouver, ca.1920. Photo by John Davidson. Photo courtesy of City of Vancouver Archives, 660-359.

While most naturalists of the period were also ardent hunters and collectors, some, like writer-adventurer Warburton Pike, had shifted from big-game hunting to wildlife photography in their later years as an alternative form of wildlife appreciation. "Enough blood has been spilt," Pike wrote in *Canada Magazine* in July 1907, "and it is only by laying down the rifle for the camera that one may begin . . . the search for lonely places where wild beasts wander undisturbed."[140] Used to illustrate popular hunting and adventure narratives of the period, wildlife drawing and photography became a way to experience distant landscapes and wild animals in the first decades of the twentieth century. Even Bryan Williams, focused as he was on the economic value of wildlife, recognized its wider significance for all British Columbians: "everybody should realize that wild life [*sic*] is a heritage," he wrote in his 1931 annual report, "not for this generation alone, but for those who come after us, and we have a great responsibility to keep that heritage unimpaired."[141] (See plate 4.)

Despite the growth of field naturalist organizations and other non-consumptive wildlife enthusiasts in this period, the consumptive users—hunters, trappers and fishers—remained the main proponents of conservation or "wise use" of wildlife resources in the early twentieth century.

Conclusion: Subsistence vs. Sport

From the beginning of Williams's term in 1905 to the end of his second term as game commissioner in 1934, a marked shift took place in the nature of game legislation. The role of local fish and game associations as producers and enforcers of game policy gave way to more centralized government game regulation in the early decades of the twentieth century. Nineteenth-century efforts to conserve wildlife as a food resource for all were replaced by increasing emphasis on apportioning game resources to resident and non-resident sport hunters while heavily regulating commercial and subsistence uses. Selling game became illegal in the province by 1920, although limited enforcement permitted some market harvest of game species to continue well beyond World War I. Similar trends emerged in the freshwater fisheries, where regulations against overexploitation and commercial harvest were combined with ambitious restocking programs for desirable game fish species. (A notably different pattern emerged in the coastal fisheries, where commercial uses were privileged over sport and Indigenous fisheries.)

These changes occurred within the context of declining subsistence needs among settler populations, as farms and ranches became more established and beef and other sources of protein became more available and affordable. As Colpitts points out, the persistence of Indigenous subsistence economies widened the gulf between settler and Indigenous communities that had previously depended on each other through the exchange of meat, feathers and furs for other commodities.[142] But many rural non-Indigenous communities, too, continued to rely on wildlife resources for subsistence needs and supplementary income. Rural and especially Indigenous hunters not only became the primary target of enforcement activities in this period but also felt the imposition of game legislation most keenly.

The efforts of Indigenous leaders to protect the interests of their people in this period ultimately resulted in frustration. As the Allied Tribes of British Columbia pressed the provincial and federal governments to respond to their claims to land, water, hunting and fishing rights in the province, Ottawa responded by amending the Indian Act to prohibit all land-claims-related activities. The 1927 amendments prevented First Nations from raising funds or obtaining legal assistance to further their claims. The ATBC dissolved in the aftermath of the new legislation, which would remain in effect until 1951.[143]

Tensions between preserving fish and game to attract tourists and managing a provincial commons of resident users also emerged in this period. Provincial game guardians struggled to support game conservation and enforcement activities by marketing the resource to paying outsiders, on the one hand, and shutting down non-paying outsiders, or "poachers," on the other. The development and expansion of rail, road and trail infrastructure exacerbated these tensions, creating access networks for local and non-resident hunters and facilitating the rapid transportation of game meat and trophies to urban and export markets. While the advent of licensing requirements for residents eased tensions somewhat by bolstering Game Department coffers, the conflicts over wildlife allocations set out in this period between resident and non-resident, Indigenous and sport, and commercial and subsistence users would only intensify in the coming decades as wildlife populations responded to the growth of human settlement and the expansion of extractive natural resource industries in the postwar years.

5

Ian McTaggart Cowan and the Rise of Scientific Wildlife Conservation

This chapter charts the growing role of science in the professionalization and modernization of fish and game management in the years leading up to and following World War II. The systematic collection of British Columbia's vertebrate species in the period between the wars supported scientific research and led to an explosion of knowledge about the province's wildlife. A new generation of university-trained government biologists hired in the years following the war ushered in significant changes in practice and policy. While Game Commission biologists focused primarily on population health and sustainable allocation of popular sporting species, their research and training elicited a growing recognition of habitat as a critical variable in the sustainability of fish and wildlife populations.[1]

More than any other individual in this period, UBC zoologist Ian McTaggart Cowan epitomized this shift from game management to science-based wildlife conservation over the course of his career. From his early experience as a **hunter-naturalist** and field assistant to prominent specimen collectors in the province to his decades of groundbreaking research and collaboration with government game managers at the University of British Columbia, Cowan provided leadership for this transition through the evolution of his own knowledge and experience (see plate 5). Together with UBC colleagues Bert Brink (plant science), Vladimir Krajina (botany) and Tom Northcote and Peter Larkin (fisheries science), he advanced knowledge of BC wildlife characteristics, distribution and habitat needs; trained a new generation of wildlife and fisheries biologists; and played an outsized role in the development of institutions like the Provincial Museum and their reference-species collections.

Revitalizing Wildlife Research and Education
at the Provincial Museum, 1935–1940

Scientific practices came to shape wildlife research and education at least
a decade before they shaped government wildlife management decisions.
The story of the revitalization of the Provincial Museum in the late 1930s,
and Cowan's role in those changes, is emblematic of this shift. Fresh from
the completion of a doctorate in vertebrate zoology under the influential
Berkeley ecologist Joseph Grinnell, Cowan stepped into the role of assistant
curator of the vertebrate collections at the Provincial Museum in 1935.[2] He
brought with him not only the classroom knowledge acquired over three
years at Berkeley but several summers of field experience collecting and
preserving animal specimens as an assistant to the accomplished amateur
scientist-naturalist Kenneth Racey of Vancouver and the naturalist-
collector and writer Hamilton Mack Laing of Comox.[3]

Alan and Kenneth Racey and Ian McTaggart Cowan preparing specimens in the field,
August 1931. Photo courtesy of Special Collections and University Archives, University
of Victoria Libraries.

Provincial Museum collector Charles Guiguet preparing a specimen in Tweedsmuir Provincial Park near Stuie, BC, September 17, 1938. Photo by Hamilton Mack Laing. Royal BC Museum, G-03674.

Languishing since John Fannin's death in 1904 under the lacklustre direction of Francis Kermode, the Provincial Museum was in considerable disarray when Cowan arrived.[4] The wildlife collection so carefully assembled by Fannin was in especially poor condition, with species and location information uncatalogued and specimens deteriorating from lack of care.[5] Cowan set to work cataloguing and conserving the collection and improving the museum's educational outreach through exhibit renewal and a weekly lecture series for local schoolchildren.

Promoted to assistant director of the museum in 1937, Cowan worked to expand the museum's reference collections, conducting summer collection expeditions and drawing on a growing network of naturalist-collectors to produce systematic surveys of bird, mammal, amphibian and reptile specimens from different regions of the province.[6] By the time of his departure in 1940 to take up a position at UBC, he had vastly expanded the museum's collection to over 92,000 specimens (up from roughly 7,000 specimens in 1935), modernized the preservation and cataloguing process, and drawn on his field research to update the museum's handbooks of provincial wildlife species and launch its respected and long-running Occasional Papers series.[7] Cowan's vision for reimagined exhibitions that presented animal specimens within lifelike representations of their natural habitat, rather than in sterile drawers and glass cases, was fulfilled decades later by subsequent curators, many of whom were former students whom he continued to mentor.[8]

Last of the Hunter-Naturalists: Hamilton Mack Laing

At the same time as Cowan was revitalizing the wildlife research and education programs at the Provincial Museum, a schism emerged between an older generation of "hunter" (or "collector") naturalists and a newer generation of what became known as "observer" naturalists—those who eschewed collection in favour of visual observation and, as camera technology improved, photographic capture. Among the former was a mentor of Cowan's, the Comox-based hunter, naturalist and specimen collector Hamilton Mack Laing.

In the words of his biographer Richard Mackie, Laing embodied a philosophy of conservation "that insisted the naturalist be a good man with a gun."[9] Born in Ontario in 1883 and raised on a frontier farm in Manitoba, Laing learned to hunt and trap at an early age, supplying game for the pot and protection for the family's livestock. Like many other Canadians who came of age around the turn of the twentieth century, he immersed himself in the nature writing of Ernest Thompson Seton, Charles G.D. Roberts and their American counterpart John Burroughs, later training in writing and drawing with the goal of following in their footsteps.

By the early 1910s, Laing had turned to nature and travel writing full time. Forging an identity as the "motorcycle naturalist," he embarked on a series of long-distance explorations of the US and Canadian West astride "Barking Betsy," his Harley-Davidson motorcycle. His captivating stories of wildlife and life on the road across the North American West received a wide audience in over seven hundred popular articles for magazines like *Outdoor Life*, *Field and Stream* and *Sunset* over the next two decades. His travels would eventually take him to the wildlife-rich Comox Valley on Vancouver Island, where he settled with his wife, Ethel Hart, in the 1920s.

Hamilton Mack Laing with a great horned owl (*Bubo virginianus*), Juniper Mountain, Ashnola, October 7, 1928. Hamilton Laing Fonds. Royal BC Museum, G-03686.

The "motorcycle naturalist":
Hamilton Mack Laing
hunting cranes at Ebor,
Saskatchewan, 1914. Royal
BC Museum, G-03629.

Laing's skills found another outlet after World War I, when he picked up work as a freelance collector of bird and mammal specimens for museums and private collectors. An intuitive and highly observant naturalist, Laing could devise a trap to attract a rare species of mole just as surely as he could summon a covey of songbirds for collection with the decoy call of a pygmy owl predator. His detailed field notes and precise drawings further recommended him, allowing him to market his expertise to the National Museum of Natural Sciences in Ottawa and the BC Provincial Museum in Victoria. In the years that followed, Laing would develop a reputation as one of the finest freelance collectors in Canada. His work training and mentoring a new generation of biologists, including the influential taxonomists Charles Guiguet and Ian McTaggart Cowan, extended his influence well into the twentieth century.

For Laing and fellow BC collectors, like artist-naturalist Allan Brooks and National Museum ornithologist Percy A. Taverner, the killing and collection of birds and mammals was necessary to produce baseline taxonomies of animal diversity. As Richard Mackie has observed, a pervasive sense of the unknown accompanied the collecting enterprises of the interwar years. Because much of the initial collecting and taxonomic classification had not yet been completed for British Columbia, "taxonomists simply did not know what kind of animals were living out there." Hunter-naturalists like Laing lived by the maxim of "what's shot's history, what's missed mystery." Mackie concludes, "The best hunter made the best collector, and the best scientist was the one with access to the best collection."[10]

Specimens were valued not only as skins for research and education purposes but also for the information their stomach contents provided about their diet, health and habitat needs. Vital as they were to the development of knowledge of the province's wildlife in the 1910s and '20s, specimen collections continue to provide important baselines for biodiversity and human public health (through toxicity and epidemiological studies) in the present. Given the significance of their work, authorized museum collectors like Laing were given the green light from wildlife authorities even for threatened wildlife species. As an exception to the 1917 Migratory Birds Convention Act, for example, museum collectors received near-unlimited provisions (via federal permit) to shoot migratory birds for the purpose of scientific study.

By the 1930s, however, a new generation of university-trained biologists and "observer-naturalists" were expressing growing concern about the overzealous killing of animals by specimen collectors like Laing. Ornithologists such as federal migratory birds officer James A. Munro, nature writer Harry J. Parham of Penticton, and Theed Pearse, Laing's neighbour in Comox, called out collectors for the pressures they placed on already threatened populations (specimen collectors typically took a minimum of twenty individuals of any one species, and double that if the sexes differed in size and appearance).

Another point of contention raised by this more ecologically minded generation of biologists and naturalists was the increasingly outdated attitude toward predators, and especially predatory birds, espoused by the older generation of hunter-naturalists. For Laing, falcons were "destructive little killers" while crows were nest-robbing "pirates" and "vermin." The great horned owl, meanwhile, was a bloodthirsty killer of game birds that every good hunter should seek to rid from the landscape. Laing made a habit of shooting predatory owls, eagles, hawks and crows whenever he had the opportunity, a practice in keeping with a philosophy of "practical conser-

James A. Munro collecting bird specimens at Okanagan Landing, 1928. An early advocate of waterfowl and wetlands protection, Munro oversaw the creation of some of the province's first migratory bird sanctuaries in his role as Canada's chief migratory bird officer for British Columbia. Royal BC Museum, G-03660.

vation" shared by many other hunter-naturalists of his generation. Like his friend and fellow naturalist Allan Brooks, Laing drew on his foundational experiences as a frontier farmer to position humans as natural managers of animal relationships, duty-bound to shoot and trap the "bad" animals in order to preserve the "good" ones.

Debates around these questions produced a lasting schism in the ornithological community between the amateur hunter-naturalists, on the one side, and the "observer-naturalists" and scientifically trained biologists, on the other. The divide between these positions became especially pronounced over the creation of a series of bird sanctuaries in the province in the 1920s and '30s under the leadership of Hoyes Lloyd, superintendent of wildlife protection for the National Parks Branch, and James A. Munro, chief migratory birds officer for the western provinces. For old-school collectors like Laing, these sanctuaries (which prohibited hunting and collecting but contained no provisions for habitat protection) did little more than create "sanctuaries for predatory mammals and birds" while ignoring the effects of industrial pollution and habitat destruction. Human hunting and collecting, in Laing's view, was an insignificant threat to bird and mammal populations compared with "the toll of natural predators" and "the hazards of civilization." The fate of seabirds as a result of oil pollution was especially galling for Laing, an observation that, as Mackie notes, he made some forty years ahead of public consciousness of the issue.[11]

A series of changes evident by the mid-1930s made Laing's form of practical conservation increasingly obsolete. Funding for collection work was dwindling in the face of Depression-era budget shortfalls and the completion of baseline collecting and classification work for many areas of the province. University-trained scientists were beginning to replace the older cohort of talented amateur naturalists in museums, universities and government game departments—a trend that would continue into the 1950s. Perhaps most significantly, the frontier conditions of Laing's youth were rapidly disappearing. A new generation of naturalists, many of whom had grown up in cities and towns rather than remote homesteads, viewed predators less as bloodthirsty competitors than as magnificent wild animals worthy of protection.

Laing retired from both writing and collecting in 1940. His contribution to plant and animal taxonomy in the province lived on, however, laying the foundation for future zoological research. In his eighteen years as a professional collector, Laing contributed more than ten thousand birds, mammals and plants to museums, universities and private collections around the world. In addition to his popular natural history writing, he produced two dozen scientific articles and notes for major ornithological journals. Four species of birds and mammals were named after him, including the coastal subspecies of northern goshawk (*Accipter gentilis laingi*).[12] Laing continued to make daily entries and pen and ink drawings in his "nature diaries" until a few weeks before his death in 1982, noting the weather, the plants in bloom and the animals he encountered. As Briony Penn has noted, he was "one of the last great amateur naturalists-conservationists of the late nineteenth century who were 'captivated by diversity' and poured their energies into documenting and cataloguing it."[13]

Modernizing Game Management

To follow Ian McTaggart Cowan's career in this period is to follow some
of the most significant developments in the knowledge and management
of wildlife populations in the province. In taking up the position of assistant professor of zoology at the University of British Columbia in 1940,
Cowan set out to create the first university program in Canada focused on
the science of wildlife conservation.[14] To do this he drew not only on his
field experience, his training at Berkeley and a growing network of professional contacts but also on his personal specimen collections and those
of his mentor and father-in-law Kenneth Racey: these collections supported decades of teaching and research in vertebrate zoology.[15] Together with
like-minded colleagues, including agronomist Bert Brink and later fisheries biologist Peter Larkin and botanist Vladimir Krajina, Cowan worked
to build a research and teaching program that would educate students in
the taxonomy, diversity and management of wild animals while informing
pressing conservation concerns for the province's wildlife and fisheries.

Cowan's work at UBC and his thinking as a conservationist was partly
informed by his role in a broader North American network of wildlife and
conservation professionals. Beginning with his fieldwork with Racey and
continuing through his years at Berkeley, Cowan had become acquainted
with some of the leading naturalists, scientists and conservation thinkers
in North America. These associations were further solidified by his induc-
tion into a secret society of wildlife professionals, the "Brotherhood of the
Venery," in the mid-1920s.

Formed in 1925 by Hoyes Lloyd, superintendent for wildlife protection
for the National Parks Branch—or the "B," as it was known among its
members—aimed to "advance wildlife knowledge and wildlife protection,
and the spread of the ideals of sportsmanship through friendship, education
and the reviving of the old art of the venery," the latter defined as hunting
for sport.[16] Established at a time when secret societies (typically male and
white) were still popular as forums for open discussion outside of the bounds
of work, family and church, the "B" included among its founding members
prominent American conservationists Aldo Leopold and George Bird
Grinnell. In Canada, Parks Commissioner James Harkin, ornithologist and
author Percy Taverner, federal migratory bird officer James A. Munro and
naturalist-scientists Kenneth Racey and Hamilton Mack Laing, together

with a few women—Munro's wife, Olive (née Bunting), and naturalist Pearl McGahey of Ottawa—held membership alongside Cowan and Lloyd. Cowan would draw support throughout his career from the camaraderie, commitment and professional knowledge of this international group of hunter-conservationists who "worked quietly through networks" to improve public knowledge about wildlife and push for its protection.[17]

Gathering and Applying Wildlife Knowledge

For Cowan, one of the obstacles to effective wildlife conservation in the province was a Game Commission steeped in the tools of an older generation of practical game managers. South of the border, US fish and game managers drew increasingly on insights and approaches from the biological sciences and the new science of ecology to inform decision-making related to wildlife. British Columbia, by comparison, "still behaved like a game-keeper on a Scottish grouse moor. Its fauna consisted of good and bad creatures. A species seen as a sporting target and eatable was 'good'; all those that sometimes killed a 'good' bird or ate its eggs were 'bad'; all else was of little importance." Cowan recalled that "very few" game wardens "had any interest in natural history or in the host of birds and mammals that were not considered game, except those hawks, eagles, owls, crows, magpies, jays, coyotes, wolves and cougars that were marked for destruction as pests."[18]

This exclusive focus on game species, Cowan reasoned, reflected the orientation and authority structure of a department that had since its inception privileged law enforcement over wildlife knowledge.[19] In other words, too much emphasis was placed on policing users and not enough on understanding the animal populations they sought to sustain. The setting of hunting regulations in the 1920s and '30s, for example, had achieved a relatively successful *social* balance by receiving impressions of game species numbers from both area game wardens and fish and game associations (although Indigenous knowledge was generally excluded). From the perspective of biological science, however, its process for determining population numbers and setting harvest rates was "based on guesswork."[20]

World War II marked a turning point for wildlife management in the province, as it did in so many other areas of endeavour. By the end of the war in 1945, wartime scientific innovations were being repurposed for peacetime uses, and publics in Canada and beyond had become sensitized to the role and value of science in improving human societies. The Game Commission was not immune to these changes. As the number of resident and non-resident hunters and anglers grew exponentially in the years after the war, ratcheting up the pressure on wildlife populations, game commissioners Frank R. Butler and James G. Cunningham (who had replaced Bryan Williams in 1934) began to explore opportunities for collaboration and consultation with biologists in the province. Their willingness to connect with scientists drew in part from some successful interactions before the war; in the early 1930s, for example, UBC microbiologist David C.B. Duff assisted the commissioners in addressing problems of disease in provincial trout hatcheries. A series of meetings between the game commissioners and UBC biologists in the months following the war led to the appointment of Cowan and his senior colleague Wilbur A. Clemens, then director of UBC's Pacific Biological Station, as scientific advisers to the Game Commission in 1946.

Together, Butler, Cunningham, Cowan and Clemens ushered in a new period of collaboration between scientists and government game managers. One of the immediate outcomes was a cooperative program for UBC graduate students, wherein students would conduct "research studies of immediate concern to the Game Commissioners" in return for funding for their studies.[21] While the vast majority of these students were men, a few women, including UBC wildlife biologist Iola Musfeldt, made important contributions to knowledge of wildlife health in this period and initiated a decades-long process of reshaping gender expectations surrounding wildlife work.[22] Many UBC graduate students would go on to take up positions with wildlife management agencies in BC and other jurisdictions. Cowan's student James (Jim) Hatter was the first, hired by the BC Game Commission in 1947 as the province's first game biologist. Others soon followed, including fisheries biologist Peter A. Larkin, predatory animal control supervisor W. Winston (Bill) Mair, assistant biologists Donald J. Robinson and Patrick W. Martin, range management biologist Lawson Sugden and regional biologist for the East Kootenay Glen Smith. By 1953, fisheries and wildlife biologists had been appointed in all regions of the province except the far north.

This first generation of government fisheries and wildlife biologists were, as Cowan later recalled, "a pretty select lot." As scientists, they brought new research-based techniques to estimate animal populations and access to research literature and academic networks that allowed them to tap into the accumulated knowledge of other jurisdictions. But they also carried a deep knowledge of the outdoors that earned them the respect of their game warden colleagues (see plate 5). "All of them were hunters, fishermen and naturalists with a lot of outdoor experience," Cowan recalled. "They appreciated the extensive local knowledge and 'woods wisdom' that some of the wardens had, and [they] were eager to learn."[23] The encroachment of biologists into areas formerly controlled by game wardens, such as the setting of hunting and fishing regulations, seasons, and bag limits, produced friction at times.[24] Wartime service, however, created an important source of mutual respect and shared experience between established game wardens—some of whom had served in World War I—and a new generation of university-trained biologists who, in many cases, had gained maturity and life experience through service in World War II. As the late Alan Martin recalled of the generation of his father, biologist Pat Martin, "there was a very strong [bond] between the [game wardens] and the biologists that developed. Once [the wardens] saw the utility of what they were doing, they were fully engaged." These relationships were especially apparent at the Cache Creek game check station, where biologists and wardens worked "shoulder to shoulder" to enforce regulations and collect harvest data from hunters as they travelled out of the Interior to the Lower Mainland.[25]

Provincial game check station at Cache Creek, late 1940s. Source: *Our Wildlife Heritage: 100 Years of Wildlife Management*, edited by Allan Murray (Victoria: Centennial Wildlife Society of British Columbia, 1987). Photo courtesy of Dennis Demarchi.

Cowan and the wildlife biologists he trained also learned on the job
from Indigenous hunters and trappers and local naturalists with deep experience and knowledge of wild animals and their behaviour. During summer field expeditions to Chilcotin (formerly Chezacut) Lake in the early
1930s, Cowan and Kenneth Racey consulted with naturalist Frank Shillaker
and Tsilhqot'in trappers Laciese Cha and Moses Ronsin on the distribution of small mammals and the historical presence of elk in the region.[26]
Jim Hatter, Cowan's student and the Game Commission's first professional
biologist, also consulted with local and Indigenous hunters and guides in
his pioneering research on the movement of moose into the province's central Interior and the ecological factors that shaped their populations.[27] Later
in life, Cowan would take his appreciation of Indigenous knowledge one
step further in recognizing the merits of Indigenous practices of wildlife
conservation. In correspondence with Northwest Territories wildlife biologist and friend Tom Beck in 1994, Cowan acknowledged "that a feeling of
kinship and mutual responsibility between the hunter and his prey [may]
have effects similar to our mathematically based calculations of sustainable
yield."[28] (See plate 6.)

This recognition of the value of local knowledge aided Cowan and
the first generation of provincial wildlife biologists in their relationships
with game wardens and sport hunters. As scientific advisers to the Game
Commission's newly created Scientific Branch in 1949, Cowan and his senior colleague, fisheries biologist Wilbur Clemens, travelled to regional
headquarters to "spread the gospel of science" by advising inspectors and
wardens and giving lectures on wildlife management issues for angling
and sport hunting groups.[29] **Annual game conventions** hosted and funded by the province from 1947 to 1957, when administrative control of the
events passed to the BC Wildlife Federation (BCWF), provided another
venue for knowledge exchange between wildlife biologists and wildlife
users. The annual conventions brought together delegates from fish and
game clubs across the province, Game Commission officials, and representatives from other interest groups, including guiding and trapping
associations, the BC Cattlemen's Association and the BC Federation of
Agriculture, all of whom had interests in the land base that supported
fish and wildlife.[30]

The general absence of representation from BC First Nations at these
events—at least as entities in their own right—was in part a reflection of

decades of marginalization and incapacitation through residential schooling, loss of access to traditional territories and land management practices, and, until 1951, Indian Act prohibitions on organizing or seeking legal counsel to protect their interests. Furthermore, a lack of First Nations representation at fish and game events is not surprising given decades of animosity between Indigenous and sport hunting interests. Indigenous leaders at the time directed their energy to what were for them more pressing concerns. In 1947, for example, the **Native Brotherhood of British Columbia** (which remains one of largest democratic Indigenous organizations in the country) organized a delegation of chiefs from across the province to travel to Victoria to press for extended hunting, fishing and trapping privileges.[31] In most parts of the province, Indigenous hunters required a permit to hunt beyond the small territories of their reserves. Trapping income, furthermore, had fallen precipitously from its wartime peak in 1945. As fur prices fell, expenses rose, and competition from settler trappers pushed some Indigenous trappers out of the industry.[32]

As the face of new science-based approaches in wildlife management, Game Commission biologists sometimes experienced tensions with the commission's long-standing and original advisers, the local rod and gun clubs and game protection associations. Tasked with addressing persistent problems in game management, graduate student researchers and staff biologists produced evidence that sometimes challenged practices that an older generation of hunters and fishers had long revered. For example, research by Cowan's student Ernest W. Taylor in the late 1940s, which reported low survival rates of farm-raised birds, put an end to the accepted practice of raising and releasing pheasants and other exotic game birds to bolster populations in the wild. Methods that had proved successful in the intensively managed British countryside, he found, were not appropriate for conditions in BC.[33] The province acted on his findings by discontinuing the pheasant-rearing program in 1954.

Another Cowan student, Jim Hatter, went up against deeply held sport hunting principles prohibiting the hunting of female animals in his pioneering research on BC moose populations in the late 1940s. Dramatic increases in moose populations in the central and southern regions of the province in the 1920s and early 1930s, Hatter found, were facilitated by the abundance of tender vegetation produced in the wake of fires throughout the region in the preceding decades. Irruptions of moose across the province led to overbrowsing of vegetation on critical winter range habitat, and by 1938, moose numbers had begun to decline. To avert starvation for moose and other species, Hatter recommended reducing moose numbers to meet the carrying capacity of the environment by opening a hunting season not just for bulls but for cow moose as well. Acknowledging the success of such measures in Norway and other northern European countries, game commissioners Frank Butler and Jim Cunningham accepted Hatter's recommendations and instituted an either-sex hunt in the fall of 1952. Either-sex hunting and juvenile hunting have since been used occasionally as a management tool for moose, elk and deer populations.[34]

Challenging the Bounty

No practical management tool was more hotly contested, however, than the bounty on predatory birds and mammals. Extended as a method of game (and not just livestock) protection in the 1910s, bounty payments had resulted in the destruction of a quarter of a million predatory birds and hundreds of thousands of predatory mammals in the province by the early 1940s. In 1922 alone, 17,625 great horned and snowy owls, 7,095 bald and golden eagles and 2,246 magpies were shot for the bounty in British Columbia.[35] Bounties of 10 to 20 cents a bill on ravens and crows encouraged both casual and organized destruction through community "crow shoots" and other competitions. The influence of Jim Munro, chief migratory bird officer for the western provinces, combined with the efforts of naturalists and ornithologists across the province resulted in the gradual elimination of bounties on many predatory birds between 1924 and 1931.[36] Old habits and assumptions die hard, however, and lacking the protection afforded other migratory bird species, hawks, eagles and owls continued to be targeted as pests by farmers, ranchers and sport hunters. Bounties on predatory mammals, meanwhile, continued unabated.

Cowan was among a growing community of conservation-minded biologists and naturalists in Canada and the United States who sought to put an end to what they viewed as the senseless and misdirected destruction of animal life. Beginning in 1942, Cowan and fellow conservationist John R. Dymond, a fisheries biologist at the University of Toronto, embarked on what would become a ten-year campaign of lectures and radio addresses to hundreds of audiences across the country. Drawing initially on data

SERVICE—XIII. MISCELLANEOUS.

No. of Treasury Voucher.............

No. of Cash Book Folio ....

VOTE No... 226.....

No. of Journal Folio.............

GOVERNMENT OF BRITISH COLUMBIA.

A. Bryan Williams

Department of.............

Provincial Game Warden

Post-office address.............Vancouver B.C.

Cr. for the undermentioned, on account of Requisition No.............

Date of Purchase or Service rendered.	Items in Detail.	Rate of each Article.	Amount.	
			$	cts.
1912	— Destruction of Wolves, Panthers, Coyotes etc —			
SEPT.	To Bounty on one Big Horned Owl paid to C.W. Jordan		2	—
	" Do one Do " " J.Snellenberg		2	—
	" Do one Wolf " " D.Pegg		15	—
	" Do one Cougar " " P.Larson		15	—
	Thirty-four dollars...................	TOTAL $	34	—

Provincial Game Warden,
PAID
SEP 30 1912
VANCOUVER, B. C.

Certified correct.

....

Certified correct.

....

Deputy.............

Approved.

....

Minister of the Department.

The provincial game warden's office issued bounty vouchers like this one to rural hunters on receipt of evidence of destroyed coyotes, wolves, cougars and birds of prey such as hawks and owls. BC Game Commission. Royal BC Museum, GR-445-161-1A.

from predation studies in the US, they argued for the vital role of predators in preventing unnaturally high populations of prey species, keeping prey populations healthy by targeting sick and malnourished animals, and reducing rodent populations and the threats they presented to human health and agriculture. In BC, Cowan received support for his efforts from game commissioners Cunningham and Butler. Butler, who had for decades decried the expense and inefficiency of the bounty system, welcomed Cowan's expertise in addressing fish and game associations, ranchers and other stakeholders.

Cowan's research on predator-prey relationships added relevant Canadian findings to the debate. Since the late 1920s, the Rocky Mountain parks had served as lightning rods for the predator debate. While area sport hunters— who viewed the parks as "breeding grounds" for predators—lobbied for aggressive predator reduction programs in the parks to protect surrounding game and livestock, an increasingly ecologically minded parks administration under James Harkin sought further information on the role of predators in park ecosystems. In 1943, Cowan secured federal funding to investigate predator-prey relationships in Banff and Jasper National Parks, a project that would involve two summers of fieldwork and tap the knowledge of area park wardens, trappers and guides, including legendary packer and guide Jimmy Simpson. The result, according to Cowan biographer Briony Penn, was "the most comprehensive inventory of wildlife in Canadian national parks . . . ever undertaken, even to this day."[37]

Published in 1947, Cowan's results skewered assumptions that predators were the principal threat to big-game populations in the parks. Instead, an increase in moose and Rocky Mountain elk moving in from outside the park, combined with grazing pressures from horses, had led to overgrazing and deterioration of critical winter ranges that affected all big game, including Rocky Mountain bighorn sheep, goats, moose, caribou and mule deer. Wolves were present in the park in low numbers, and scat analyses revealed a diet of principally elk, but the influence of their predation was "definitely secondary . . . to the absence of sufficient suitable winter forage." Their impact on other big-game species was, according to Cowan, "inconsequential." In the conditions that Cowan encountered in 1943 and 1944, wild ungulates crowded onto the parks' limited winter ranges were more likely to die of winter starvation or parasites (such as tapeworm and ticks) than they were of wolf predation.[38] Cowan's students would go on to build understanding of predator-prey relationships for other species, including cougar and coyote, in the decades that followed.

For many sport hunters and game wardens, scientific research on predator-prey relationships proved less persuasive than the persistent corruption and waste that plagued the bounty system. Forms of abuse included the substitution of pelts from domestic animals, the submission of "pelts or portions of pelts such as 'ears' cut from the belly of a bobcat," and the repeated submission of the "same threadbare pelts" for bounty claims.[39] Claiming bounties for animals shot in other jurisdictions was another form of abuse. Cowan recalled in a 2002 interview that "the year that the Yukon stopped giving a bounty, there was something like 600 or 700 wolves bountied [across the border] in Telegraph Creek [BC]," an area where previously there had "never been more than . . . a few."[40]

Research in other jurisdictions, furthermore, had exposed bounty programs as not only prohibitively expensive (in 1949, for example, the BC government paid out over $70,000 in bounties) but also surprisingly ineffective. Blanket bounties on predator species failed to encourage hunting of individual "problem" animals, such as those that killed livestock. Bounties offered little precision to game managers seeking to control predators in particular places (like summer game ranges) or times (in cases of disease outbreak, for example). When it came to reducing predator numbers, furthermore, bounties only skimmed the surface, stimulating higher reproduction rates among remaining animals rather than removing entire populations. As Frank Butler noted ruefully in an address to the first annual game convention in 1947, after spending $800,000 over nearly fifty years, "there were just as many predatory animals in British Columbia as when the first bounty payments were made."[41]

In the end, Cowan, Butler and their supporters succeeded in bringing an end to the bounty system in BC. The province removed the bounty for coyotes in 1954, for wolves in 1955 and for cougar in 1957.[42] While opposition to the elimination of the bounty remained, particularly among northern guides and farmers concerned about depredations on wild ungulates and domestic livestock, the broader hunting community took reassurance in the knowledge that an end to the bounty did not mean an end to predator control. Instead, what had been a form of local revenue and responsibility became a provincial government responsibility.

In 1947, seven years before the first bounty closures, the BC Game Commission established the Predator Control Branch to create what

commissioners envisioned as a more efficient, targeted and effective predator control system. Headed by Cowan's former student Bill Mair, the new
program aimed for complete removal of predators in agricultural and built-
up areas and varied levels of control in popular hunting areas, depending
on the status of prey populations and the level of hunting pressure. Remote
wilderness areas, where trappers and guides conducted their own predator
control practices, would receive the least government intervention.[43] The
program's small staff—just five regional predatory animal hunters worked
under Mair in 1947—would be offset by the adoption of technological solutions such as poison (banned in the province between 1905 and 1950) and
aircraft to access rugged terrain.

Throughout the 1950s, the program expanded beyond its initial aims
into a massive control program for coyotes and wolves across the central
and northern reaches of the province. Publicity surrounding the "rabies
crisis" in northern Alberta and British Columbia in the early 1950s, and
concerns that the disease might be "pooling" in wild fur-bearer populations,
contributed to this enthusiasm for extensive predator culls.[44] Baited cyanide
traps ("coyote-getters") and carcasses laced with "Compound 1080"
(sodium fluoroacetate) dropped from aircraft onto ice-covered lakes and
rivers became the principal method of control. Valued for its high toxicity
to canids (a group that includes coyotes and wolves), Compound 1080 was
also water soluble, dissipating relatively quickly in the environment when
poisoned baits fell through the ice in the spring.

For Mair's successor Al West, the enormous success of poisoning campaigns helped to justify the gradual removal of bounties. It was not until
1950, he told an audience of hunters at the 1952 annual game convention,
that "improvement in the predator situation . . . [was] realized" through
"mass destruction . . . by the use of poisons." His choice of words reflected
the societal fascinations of postwar Canada as much as they did the broad
public consensus on the need for predator control. Reports in 1953 of a rabies outbreak among wolves in northern Alberta led to an intensification of
the poisoning campaign in the northeastern part of the province, and by
1958, West could report that "every wild-sheep range in the province" had
been baited with poison to protect the sheep from "outside elements" such
as predators.[45] By the end of the decade, wolf populations on Vancouver
Island, among other areas of BC, had been completely obliterated.

Building a Sport Fishery in BC's Freshwater Lakes

Similar hierarchies of value occurred in the freshwater fisheries. Just as hunters and game managers sought to eradicate "vermin" and "noxious predators," so anglers and fisheries biologists sought to clear inland lakes and streams of "coarse" or undesirable native fish species in order to produce competition-free conditions for game fish species. As with predatory mammal control, these ideas were not new, nor were they limited to British Columbia. Since their establishment in the late nineteenth century, angling clubs had encouraged the eradication of undesirable fish (including white suckers, peamouth chub, carp and northern pikeminnow) through overfishing and other destructive measures. The early 1950s, however, brought new solutions. Experiments with the use of **rotenone**, a plant-derived broad-spectrum poison toxic to insects and fish, enabled what fisheries biologists described as the "rehabilitation" of small inland lakes beginning in 1953.[46]

Just as it did in the case of predator control, language mattered in these initiatives in convincing both the public and the biologists running these programs of the value of their actions. Lakes would be "cleaned" of

Rotenone is still used by provincial fisheries biologists to eradicate invasive fish species in the province's freshwater lakes. Photo courtesy of Steve Maricle, ca.2020.

"infestations" of coarse fish species and restocked with a single game fish species—typically rainbow trout. In the Interior especially, where landlocked lakes often provided the principal fishing opportunities, treated lakes became "the cornerstone . . . of the fishery." As regional fisheries biologist George Stringer recalled of his work in the central Interior in this period, "trout fishing was big business and a monoculture of rainbow trout was a major asset."[47] By 1955, thriving trout populations in treated lakes led the province to liberalize fishing regulations, abolishing closed seasons on all lakes and encouraging previously prohibited activities such as ice fishing.[48]

As the number of anglers continued to climb and demand for tourism destinations increased in the years after World War II, Stringer dedicated himself to the improvement of sport fishing in the region, personally converting fifty multi-species lakes to trout fishing destinations during his tenure in Kelowna between 1954 and 1967. Like the predator control biologists, he was faced with a limited budget and a vast area to cover. Rotenone treatment was a relatively low-cost solution that required minimal effort (several hours spraying chemical solution from a boat) and, unlike previous coarse fish removal efforts, minimal to no assistance from the fish and game clubs. Landlocked interior lakes provided the perfect test environment, obviating the need for barriers to "prevent re-infestation" from connected waterways.

As Stringer turned his attention to larger and deeper lakes in the region, he pioneered the use of toxaphene (the active ingredient in rotenone) as a cheaper and more lethal solution. Like rotenone, toxaphene destroyed all the fish and insect life in the treated lake, including amphipods (shrimp), dragonfly nymphs and midge larvae favoured by trout—species that, Stringer reasoned, could be reintroduced when the lake had "cleared" of toxicity: typically after two to three years. Incidental damage to amphibians and reductions in prey availability for fish-eating birds also diminished as toxicity declined.[49] For Stringer, the benefits of a thriving sport fishery far outweighed the costs: aware "that such chemicals would be banned sometime in the future," he made liberal use of them, going so far as to commission aircraft to "air-bomb" smaller, remote lakes with bags of toxaphene in the late 1950s.[50]

These ideas and methods survived much longer in freshwater fisheries management than they did in game management, where the use of poisons to remove predators and other undesirable species was curbed in the early

1960s and terminated entirely in 1999.[51] Today, fisheries managers continue
to use rotenone periodically to control invasive fish species in BC's freshwater lakes.[52]

Conclusion: Cowan's Legacy

From his work revitalizing the reference collections and education programs
at the Provincial Museum in the late 1930s to his thirty-five years as
professor of zoology at UBC and adviser to the BC Game Commission, Ian
McTaggart Cowan laid the foundation for modern wildlife conservation in
BC. His influence is still felt across these institutions today and in the legacy
of students he trained who took up academic and government wildlife
positions across the province and beyond.[53] From the late 1940s on, a new
generation of wildlife biologists brought scientific training and ecological
perspectives to the study, management and conservation of fish and
wildlife populations in the province. As rates of pollution, land alienation
and resource extraction rose over the same period, their training would
become even more relevant in understanding the overlapping pressures
facing wildlife on a shrinking land base.

6

Land Use Pressures in the Postwar Period

The ascent to power of Premier W.A.C. Bennett's Social Credit government in 1952 ushered in what legal historian Michael Begg describes as a "forceful ethos of economic development" in the decade following the war.[1] While industrial development of the province's forest, mineral, and oil and gas resources had generated greater affluence along the coast, parts of the central and northern Interior were still "in near frontier conditions" by 1950. Many roads in the central Interior were mired in mud for weeks each spring and fall, while electric power and running water were unknown luxuries in many rural parts of the province. Bennett sought to ameliorate these regional disparities by funnelling profits from resource exploitation into infrastructure development in the province's Interior and north.[2] Over the course of his twenty years in power—the longest of any BC premier—Bennett oversaw what historians have described as BC's "Great Leap Forward," rapidly expanding the province's rail and highway systems and nationalizing (or more accurately, "provincializing") transportation and electrical bodies—BC Ferries (1960) and BC Hydro (1963)—to bring electricity and reliable transportation to rural areas. The expansion of highway and rail infrastructure through the 1950s paved the way quite literally for the massive hydroelectric developments of the following decade.

These industrial developments and the economic growth they stimulated were enormously popular with the non-Indigenous settler population.[3] Indigenous residents and a minority population of conservationists and fish and wildlife enthusiasts, however, voiced increasing concern in this period for what they saw as reckless and poorly planned development that would seriously compromise BC's fish and wildlife populations. Especially egregious was the permanent alienation of prime valley-bottom wildlife habitat brought about by the construction of dams on the Columbia and Peace River systems. In response to these developments and the rapid expansion of forestry and mining operations, prominent BC conservationists, including Roderick Haig-Brown, worked to articulate an ethic of **multiple use** that emphasized the maintenance of public access to and enjoyment of Crown lands for a variety of purposes beyond resource extraction.

Forestry, Wildlife and the Ethic of Multiple Use

Looking back near the end of his career as a regional wildlife biologist in the East Kootenay (1954–64) and later chief of wildlife management in Victoria (1963–73), Glen Smith described wildlife management in the province as little more than "a Salvation Army soup kitchen." "Our efforts as wildlife managers," he noted in a 1970 newspaper interview, "have been continually frustrated because we have no say about the land on which the big game species live or die. Our role has been primarily one of doling out a diminishing resource."[4] Smith was referring to the frustrating position the Fish and Wildlife Branch found itself in: charged with managing wildlife, it had no direct say in the management or alienation of Crown lands—the habitat on which wildlife depended. These decisions came under the so-called "dirt ministries": the Departments of Lands and Forests, Agriculture, and Mines. The province's fish and wildlife, Smith and others felt, were too often an afterthought. Where wildlife was considered at all, it was as an "impediment to development" rather than a source of value unto itself.[5]

King Forestry

The notion of fish and wildlife as an impediment to development was especially true in the province's forestry sector. As the dominant industry in the province since 1910, forestry generated prosperity for BC residents and significant revenue for the province.[6] The province's dependence on timber returns made claims for other values on the landscape difficult to sustain. As historian Rick Rajala has written, the provincial government and timber companies were bound together by "a profit-sharing arrangement . . . that left plenty of room for squabbling over the size of the shares but that left them united against any challenge to profitable forest exploitation."[7] The result was near-unregulated conditions for timber extraction in the early decades of the twentieth century. On both private and Crown lands, timber companies had little incentive to pursue anything other than "rapid liquidation of their timber assets."[8] What political scientist Jeremy Wilson has described as the "era of timber liquidation" within coastal forests proceeded until the Great Depression of the early 1930s, when economic conditions prompted a sharp decline in forest exploitation.[9] A three-year pause in production provided opportunity for public reflection. When the industry began to revive its operations in the mid-1930s, it met with a mounting public critique of unregulated timber harvesting.

For fish and game associations, tourism operators and local chambers of commerce on Vancouver Island and the mainland coast, the vast areas of cutover land stood as emblems of rapacious overcutting that left little opportunity for other landscape uses. Despite promises to the contrary, natural reforestation had failed to occur in large portions of the cutover lands.[10] Concern was especially acute among anglers, commercial fishers, and Indigenous fishers, who witnessed the destructive effects of hauling logs along stream beds and the impediments to fish passage created by the enormous piles of slash and debris left behind in streams and rivers. Even more deadly to fish populations, studies would later confirm, was the removal of streamside forest cover. Cutting to the water's edge deprived salmon and other valued fish species of cover, shade and habitat for their insect prey. At a broader landscape level, the creation of vast expanses of deforested land robbed soils of their capacity to hold moisture, exposing streams to damaging fluctuations in flows. "Heavy rains on deforested slopes," Rajala explains, "caused rapid runoff and freshets that scoured spawning beds, killing eggs and fry." In late summer, conversely, "water temperatures rose to dangerous levels" and "stream levels fell dramatically, stranding fish in isolated, shallow pools and dry creek beds."[11]

Public demands to reforest stream banks and regulate forest practices to accommodate fisheries interests gained little traction in the context of a provincial economy "that ranked the returns of timber above those of fish."[12] Fishers and fisheries managers had next to no say in the business of getting the wood out. Jurisdictional divides only complicated the issue. While forests fell largely under provincial control, responsibility for salmon fisheries rested with the dominion.[13] Silence on fisheries habitat protection in the province's 1912 Forest Act and on logging practices in the federal **Fisheries Act** left little legislative backing for federal prosecutions.[14] When Ottawa attempted to address the issue, explicitly prohibiting the deposit of

Log drives like this one on the Bull River in the 1920s unleashed destructive effects on fish and fish habitat until they were phased out in the late 1940s. Royal BC Museum, F-09172.

slash, stumps and other debris in "fish-bearing waters or their sources" in a 1932 amendment to the Fisheries Act, objections by forest industry leaders combined with the challenge of vast enforcement territories meant that the regulations were not well enforced. Debris violations led "to a few prosecutions and small fines in the mid-1930s," but as Rajala concludes, "unfettered forest exploitation" ultimately "meant more to British Columbia than undisturbed streams did to the Dominion."[15]

Complaints by fish and game associations, furthermore, sometimes led to counter-accusations by timber industry representatives. In 1937, for example, an article in the *British Columbia Lumberman* drew on an established trope of public carelessness and endangerment of timber holdings by accusing tourists, anglers and hunters of setting fires and polluting streams, in turn causing "more damage to the haunts of game . . . [and] fishing streams than all the logging operations in the province."[16] Rhetoric like this partly served to counter increasing calls by recreational hunters and anglers for access to Crown lands, a debate that would grow more heated as land uses intensified in the 1950s. While the activities of tourists and outdoor enthusiasts likely caused a small portion of the fires in this period, railway operators and timber and mining companies were more frequently identified as sources of ignition.[17] The massive Bloedel or Comox Valley Fire of 1938, for example, was sparked by a Bloedel, Stewart & Welch timber company locomotive near Campbell River. The fire, still the largest in recorded history on the BC coast, destroyed over 40,000 hectares of cutover land in a 48-by-13-kilometre swath between Campbell River and Courtenay.[18]

The Depression years of the 1930s brought new concerns about wasteful and destructive forestry practices, this time from within the province's Forest Branch. In 1937, the publication of forester Frederick D. Mulholland's multi-year inventory analysis, *The Forest Resources of British Columbia*, supported growing concerns about future timber shortages resulting from the vast scale of forest liquidation and the failure of forests to adequately regenerate. Timber companies, Mulholland argued, were rapidly depleting firstgrowth forest. In the province's accessible coastal forests, where 85 per cent of logging operations occurred, Mulholland estimated overcutting rates of 100 per cent in relation to the forests' sustained annual yield capacity.[19]

Conditions were even worse in the province's private forests, where the absence of government regulation provided incentives to liquidate timber and sell the land rather than retain it as forest. Vancouver Island's 1.9-million-acre **E&N Railway land grant**, for example, had netted enormous wealth for railway and later logging companies when it was parcelled and sold in the 1880s, liquidated of its forest cover, and resold to incoming settlers. (Land grabs like this had prompted the provincial government to prohibit the sale of forest lands and introduce short-term timber licences on Crown holdings in 1888.) Mulholland's 1937 report emphasized the ongoing significance of Crown ownership of forest lands. But ensuring the long-term sustainability of the industry, he argued, would require greater government regulation to prevent waste and to balance the rate of cutting with the rate of replacement. Mulholland's proposed solutions applied a conservation ethic to the timber resource but not to the forest itself and its multiplicity of human and animal users.

E.C. Manning and the Ethic of Multiple Use

Mulholland's report undergirded a growing appetite for forest practice reform within the Forest Service, articulated most notably in the "multiple
use" philosophy of the province's chief forester, Ernest C. Manning. "It is
becoming increasingly clear," Manning wrote in a 1936 opinion piece in the
Victoria Daily Times, "that we must value our forests not only as a source
of our supplies of timber but also for their other uses—as food and shelter
for our game and fur-bearing animals, as regulators of the water flow of
the streams in which we fish, and as attractions for the tourist and other
recreationalists who delight in the great outdoors."[20]

Manning advocated for the authority to regulate forest practices on
Crown and private lands alike, with the goal of putting an end to the industry's tendency to log an area out and leave ghost towns, slash piles and
barren landscapes in its wake. Citing the recommendations of the 1909
Royal Commission on Forest Resources, he argued that government royalties from forestry "be treated as capital rather than revenue" and reinvested
to a much larger extent in "forest protection, research, and enhancement."[21]
Government investment, Manning believed, would not only contribute to
a sustainable forest industry but also allow forests to support a range of
uses. His close relationships with fish and wildlife associations in the East
Kootenay and other parts of the province led to him to describe anglers and
sport hunters as "legitimate forest users" and "sources of revenue capable
of great expansion."[22]

Manning was not alone in these ideas. By the beginning of World War
II, concern about forest industry practices and their effects on fish had led
to petitions and complaints from sport and commercial fishers, tourism
operators and conservationists under the banner of multiple use. In June
1939, for example, the Associated Boards of Trade of Vancouver Island
called on dominion fisheries officials to protect stands of trees along
streams, lakes and roads. Commercial fishermen weighed in with a
more ambitious proposal the same year, when the North Island Trollers
Cooperative Association called on the province to adopt "a comprehensive
conservation policy for the timberlands of the Province which are a part
of the watersheds draining into salmon spawning streams."[23] The trollers'
proposal resulted in an agreement between the federal Department of
Fisheries and the provincial Department of Lands to jointly inspect

instances where logging activities seemed to harm fish runs, but wartime exigencies meant fisheries inspections carried little weight in the years that followed.

At the same time, research on salmon life cycles and habitat needs provided a scientific foundation for multiple-use forest practices. Growing scientific consensus on the "home stream theory," for example, which showed that salmon returned to spawn in the same streams in which they were born, highlighted the need for protection of particular spawning grounds. A loss of faith in salmon hatcheries, closed on the coast by the mid-1930s, further underlined this recognition of the need to protect natural spawning grounds.[24] In the same period, scientific work on the effects of logging on fish-bearing streams bolstered observations that anglers and Indigenous leaders had been making for decades. Complaints of declining runs by the Cowichan Fish and Game Association, for example, led Pacific Biological Station biologist Ferris Neave to begin investigating the effects of logging on the Cowichan River in 1933. His 1941 report highlighted the lethal effects of rapid runoff, siltation and high water temperatures on young fry, changes that reduced the abundance of mature salmon. By the late 1940s, Neave had documented similar deterioration of salmon habitat in streams across Vancouver Island.[25]

INDIVIDUAL PROFILE: Writer and Conservationist Roderick Haig-Brown

Among the most articulate and persuasive advocates for multiple use of BC landscapes was writer and conservationist Roderick Haig-Brown (1908–1976). From the 1940s to the late 1960s, Haig-Brown built a reputation as BC's best-known author through his internationally acclaimed books on fishing and conservation. He used this reputation to promote respect for nature's limits during a time of aggressive industrial development in the province's resource hinterlands.[26]

Born in England in 1908 to an upper-class rural family, Haig-Brown learned to hunt and fish on his mother's family estate after his father died in World War I. He travelled to British Columbia for the first time in the late 1920s, taking up work as a logger and trapper before emigrating permanently to a homestead near Campbell River with his wife, Ann, in 1931. By the 1950s, Haig-Brown had channelled his skill and passion as a fly fisherman into the production of a series of popular fishing and natural history books, including *The Western Angler* (1939), *A River Never Sleeps*

Roderick Haig-Brown fishing in
the Campbell River, ca.1950. Photo
courtesy of Museum at Campbell
River, Van Egan Fonds, image 18056.

(1944) and *Measure of the Year* (1950). His books and magazine articles were
enormously popular in Canada and beyond, leading *Time* magazine to declare him
Canada's "top nature writer and conservationist" in 1952.

But the explosive growth of timber harvesting and commercial fishing during
and after World War II were for Haig-Brown a source of growing concern. The speed
and destructiveness of these activities contradicted what for him was a central
tenet of effective conservation, that of using resources wisely with a sense of responsibility for the future. "Any given generation" of people, he wrote in 1950, "can
have only a lease, not ownership, of the earth; and one essential term of the lease is
that the earth be handed on to the next generation with unimpaired potentialities."
Respecting this arrangement, he argued in his 1961 book, *The Living Land*, meant
"accepting moral and practical restraints that limit immediate self-interest" while
seeking "a measure of wisdom and understanding of natural things."[27]

Especially discouraging for Haig-Brown was the lack of protection for the province's parks. Between 1948 and 1961, the province excised more than 40 per cent
from its park land base, mostly to facilitate resource development. The proposal
in the late 1940s to dam the Campbell River in BC's celebrated Strathcona Park to
generate power for industrial purposes struck especially close to home. The dam

would raise the level of Buttle Lake, destroying fish habitat and flooding valuable Roosevelt elk winter range. Haig-Brown launched a public awareness campaign in the early 1950s in an effort to stop the development, joining forces with tourism interests, fish and game clubs and local naturalists. Their actions were unsuccessful, however, and dam construction went ahead in 1955.

Despite this early defeat, Haig-Brown's influence continued to grow through the 1950s. Through his participation at the BC Natural Resources Conference, an annual meeting of senior government, industry, university and conservation group representatives, and the federal Resources for Tomorrow conference in 1961, he refined his message about wildlife and parks as "recreational resources" worthy of protection.

Vindication came in a second dam battle in the late 1950s. The proposal to dam the Fraser River at Moran Canyon near Lillooet presented different circumstances than a small dam in Vancouver Island's remote interior. The gigantic High Moran Dam, which would have generated more power than almost any dam in North America, would have blocked access to a projected 70 per cent of the Fraser's highly productive salmon and steelhead trout runs. This time, Haig-Brown and sport fishery associations gained a powerful ally in commercial fisheries interests. Determined opposition resulted in the cancellation of the dam in 1972, a notable success for conservationists during the height of North America's dam construction era. BC's Clean Energy Act of 2010 committed the province to a **"two rivers policy"** (referring to the Peace and Columbia) that prohibited future hydroelectric development on the Fraser and all other river systems. Today, the Fraser River continues to support one of the most productive salmon fisheries on the continent.

Haig-Brown's thinking as a conservationist changed over the course of his life. He came to distance himself from the kind of economic evaluation of wildlife's worth that dominated discussion at the BC Natural Resources Conferences and other venues. Instead, like the famous US ecologist Aldo Leopold, he adopted a conservation ethic that, in keeping with Indigenous world views, saw land and wildlife as "a community to which we belong" rather than "a commodity that belongs to us." Instead of taking the role of "independent master and shaper," he wrote in 1961, humans should see themselves as "an integral part of the world environment."[28]

Haig-Brown's influence is still felt in the work of subsequent generations of BC conservationists and environmentalists, many of whom read his books as children. His vision for community awareness and stewardship of local watersheds continues to bear fruit in the work of community groups across the province to restore habitat on salmon-bearing streams.[29]

Changing Priorities after World War II

Canada's participation in World War II generated new urgency for resource extraction at the expense of nascent conservation measures. As Haig-Brown had warned in a 1939 letter to Ernest Manning, war "[brought] to the front the two worst enemies of conservation: profit and expediency."[30] As demand for salmon, timber and other BC resources increased, provincial and federal resource ministries shifted their emphasis from conservation to production. Manning's death in a plane crash in 1941, six years into his career as chief forester, contributed to this bureaucratic reorientation. His successor, Chauncey D. Orchard, sought to create incentives within the forest industry for sustaining the timber resource. Lost in the process was Manning's broader definition of conservation, which aimed to conserve the forest itself for multiple uses, not just timber.

In 1943, a second Royal Commission on Forestry, headed by Chief Justice Gordon Sloan, supported Orchard's vision for a new system of forest tenures based on the principles of **sustained yield**, an approach borrowed from agriculture aimed at balancing the rate of cut with the rate of forest growth. The new forest management licences (precursors to today's tree farm licences) bundled the private land holdings of large logging companies (many of which had bought out smaller operators) with vast areas of adjacent public land, providing these companies with exclusive long-term timber rights on those lands in exchange for the maintenance of local mills and job opportunities. The Forest Act of 1947 enacted these recommendations and set in motion a sustained yield agenda that, for the next three decades, "prioritized maximum timber production to the virtual exclusion of all other considerations."[31]

As Jeremy Wilson has argued, the reassuring notion of "tree farming" associated with sustained yield contributed to public complacency about forest conservation in the years that followed: "sustained yield became a kind of security blanket for British Columbians of the 1950s and 1960s, a seeming guarantee that the province's forests would produce a perpetual even-flow (or perhaps even a perpetually increasing flow) of timber wealth."[32] Little in the period countered these perceptions: rapidly expanding markets and high prices created a steady stream of forestry revenue, while advances in infrastructure and technology opened up previously inaccessible areas to industrial forestry. Inventories, allowable cuts and allocations continued to climb in this context, easing public concern about the sustainability of the timber supply. As forest conservation issues receded from public consciousness in the postwar boom atmosphere of the 1950s, it was possible for governments to neglect ongoing problems such as inadequate reforestation, climbing fire control expenditures and a lack of habitat protection for fish-bearing streams.[33]

For wildlife enthusiasts, concern about forestry practices was less pronounced in the years following the war. Beyond the question of damage to fish-bearing streams, much of the debate among fish and game associations centred around questions of recreational access to Crown lands leased by forestry companies. Much less concern rested with the effects of logging practices on wildlife itself. In fact, the opposite was true: clearcutting seemed to benefit some game species, including deer and grouse—at least in the short term. The growth of new tender vegetation in cutover areas provided important sources of browse for ungulates and game birds, stimulating population growth. As James A. Munro and Ian McTaggart Cowan wrote in their 1947 *Bird Fauna of British Columbia*, "following the removal of the conifer forest . . . perhaps the most spectacular change . . . has been the increase in the blue grouse accompanying this floral revolution. From a primitive population close to nil, this bird now exists in uncountable numbers."[34] By the 1960s, however, it was becoming apparent that clearcut logging offered only temporary benefits to grouse and other game species and that the loss of forested winter habitat was deadly. Cowan's students would later use changes in grouse populations to exemplify the concept of the **"wildlife sink,"** where clearcut logging produces an abundance of habitat for certain species for a short period, followed by sharp population declines when single-aged stands matured and canopies closed.[35]

Despite research findings to the contrary through the 1950s and '60s, early associations of clearcutting with benefits to wildlife were difficult to shake. They were reinforced in policy decisions and government institutional arrangements. When the Fish and Game Branch became part of the newly created Department of Recreation and Conservation in 1957, for example, forestry and wildlife protection became housed in separate and disproportionately resourced ministries. Unlike fisheries management, where federal regulations increasingly required forestry operations to minimize damage to fish habitat, wildlife was, in general, "not seen as a valuable component of forest resources." As forester Bill Bourgeois commented in looking back at this period, "forestry was looked at as an industry; fish and wildlife was looked at as recreation." The lack of habitat provisions in resource ministries reflected a belief shared by many that "wildlife and forestry were fully compatible"—that clearcutting and other forestry practices were, for the most part, good for game species.[36]

Indigenous communities were hit especially hard by the effects of changes caused by logging and other industrial activity on their traditional territories. Chief Queesto (Charles Jones, 1876–1990), hereditary chief of the Pacheenaht people on Vancouver Island's southwest coast, described the effect of accelerated old-growth logging on Pacheenaht territory from the 1940s on and the decline in wildlife abundance as second-growth forests matured:

> In the early days, we used to hunt elk, deer, and bear right here by the San Juan River. They were all so plentiful, you could get anything you wanted. . . . At times, I would go out hunting without taking anything to eat with me, just some bread and salt, because I knew that, with all the game around, I could always depend on being able to catch something for lunch . . . You could just live right off the land. Ever since the logging came, there's been no more deer or wolf or elk or beaver. They've all disappeared. Maybe they've been killed off, or maybe they've just moved on to somewhere else. We don't know where the animals have gone.[37]

For Cowan, Hatter and other wildlife biologists who had deepened their understanding through consultations with Indigenous hunters and trappers, "the economic importance of livelihoods gained from wildlife"— subsistence hunting, trapping and guiding—became "the central (and few) arguments available against destructive, competing uses of the landscape."[38]

Range Land Conflicts

Conflicts over multiple use also affected vulnerable grasslands habitats in the province's southern Interior valleys. Located in low-elevation areas where the rain shadow of major mountain systems to the west and east limits soil moisture and precludes the growth of forests, these grasslands constitute about 1 per cent of the province's land mass. In addition to supporting a wide variety of bird and small mammal species, they

Grasslands locations in British Columbia with areas greater than 500 hectares, 2000

Concentrations of grasslands in the south-central part of the province and in the northeast near Fort St. John form the remnants of larger historical grasslands in these areas. Data source: Herb and Grassland 1:250,000 GeoBase Land Cover, 2000. Map by GeoBC, 2022.

provide important winter range for Rocky Mountain elk, bighorn sheep, mule deer and other wild ungulates. Their additional suitability as range land for cattle and domestic sheep has made them especially vulnerable to overexploitation.

Disputes between ranching and wildlife interests over allocation of forage intensified as the supply of suitable range lands diminished. While about 40 per cent of cattle ranching operations occur on private lands, the majority of summer grazing takes place on provincial Crown lands through the provision of grazing tenures managed by the BC Forest Service. The alienation of public grazing lands for roads and railways, townsites and flooding associated with hydroelectric dams in the postwar years diminished what was already a very limited supply of natural grasslands in the province. Fire suppression also played a role, allowing trees to encroach on grasslands that had once relied on frequent natural and human-set fires for their maintenance. As grazing pressure intensified on remaining lands, ranchers and range managers struggled to mitigate soil erosion, insect outbreaks and invasions of annual cheatgrass (*Bromus tectorum*) and other noxious plants that pushed out native perennial species and increased the risk of fire. In this context of declining forage for wild and domestic animals alike, predators like coyotes and golden eagles were often blamed for the deaths of animals that had succumbed to starvation.[39]

As with other resource conflicts in the province, scientists played an important role in developing and applying knowledge to persistent range management challenges in the years following World War II. UBC professor Vernon Cuthbert (Bert) Brink was a pioneer of early range science, offering the province's first range management course in the early 1940s, the second of its kind in North America.[40] Having completed his master's degree at the BC Range Station near Kamloops in the 1930s, when dry conditions and overgrazing had reduced grasslands to dust in the Cariboo, Thompson and Nicola valleys, Brink was familiar with the effects of overcompetition on a fragile resource. A talented biologist and naturalist, he was also deeply attuned to the multiplicity of species that relied on grassland environments for their survival. Working in collaboration with government agrologists and biologists, he contributed to sweeping changes in range management, such as the implementation of grazing seasons and the regulation of herd sizes, that allowed range lands to recover.

One of the important innovations that Brink and his counterparts at the BC Range Station developed was the addition of timber ranges to the grazing lands complement. Moving cattle into open-canopy timber ranges reduced pressure on low-elevation ranges, Brink recalled in a 2001 interview, helping to restore depleted grass cover. Brink also contributed to broader appreciation of the value of grasslands as vital habitat for birds and other wildlife species. Describing field trips to the Interior that he led for naturalists from the Lower Mainland, he recalled, "I had to point out that the grasslands of BC were . . . valuable for recreation and wildlife. Not only cattle use grasslands."[41]

Vernon Cuthbert (Bert) Brink assessing grassland health at Joe Mountain, Ashnola River watershed, 1964. Photo courtesy of the Nature Trust of British Columbia.

Meanwhile, hunting interests continued to press government range managers to grant greater consideration for wildlife forage needs in their grazing allocations. Especially concerning was the absence of protection of bighorn sheep ranges. Requests by Game Commission biologists to have a larger role in the Forest Service's grazing-licence decisions were rebuffed repeatedly through the 1950s and '60s. An editorial in the April 1956 issue of the *Wildlife Review* lamented a situation wherein "little control can be exercised by the biologists and the availability of range [for wild sheep] rests largely upon the tolerance of the grazier."

Forage allocations remained a regular subject of concern at the BC Wildlife Federation's annual game convention and the annual BC Natural Resources Conference. Hunting advocates argued that grazing legislation was, like forestry legislation, heavily oriented toward single rather than multiple resource use. Multiple use had a double meaning in this context: it applied not only to the rights of hunters to access public grazing lands but also to the rights of multiple species, including wild ungulates, to access grasslands forage.[42] As biologist Don Robinson later reflected, "what the Ministry of Forests does on the forest and rangelands to a substantial degree determines the number and variety of species found over much of British Columbia."[43] Persistent lobbying by hunter-conservationists through the 1950s and 1960s finally resulted in changes to the Range Act in the late 1970s. Their efforts would also prove critical in spearheading broader environmental protections for grasslands in the latter decades of the twentieth century.[44]

SPECIES PROFILE: Chukar Partridge (*Alectoris chukar*)

The introduction of chukar partridges to the Kamloops and southern Okanagan districts in the early 1950s illustrates the effects of range degradation and the ways certain species were able to profit from these conditions. An Old World game bird originally from India, the grouse-sized chukar is readily identified by its striking vertical black bars along its sides and conspicuous black band across its forehead and neck. Valued for their meat, chukars tolerate hot, dry conditions that support few other bird species.

Chukar partridges (*Alectoris chukar*). Drawing by BC writer and wildlife illustrator Frank Beebe, ca.1957. British Columbia Ministry of the Provincial Secretary and Travel Industry, Film and Photographic Branch. Royal BC Museum, 1-29280.

Efforts in the 1890s to introduce the bird to other parts of North America had been largely unsuccessful, with the exception of semi-arid desert regions of the western states. The hot, dry canyon country of the Kamloops and Okanagan districts offered ideal chukar habitat. First released at Harper Ranch east of Kamloops in 1950, the birds thrived and enlarged their range, prompting repeated releases by area game associations. As retired regional wildlife biologist Ralph Ritcey recalled, chukars "did great here because the ranges were all overstocked. They were in very poor shape, and that's just what the chukar needed for its habitat. One of their primary foods is cheatgrass seed, and cheatgrass is a sign of poor range." The chukar's success showed how "[habitat] changes that wipe out some animals are beneficial to others."[45]

In the decades since, chukar partridges have continued to adapt to changing conditions. Better range management has reduced the extent of cheatgrass in the region and, with it, chukar food sources. The reduction of grain freight on rail lines through the region had a similar effect, removing what Ritcey called a winter "food program" for the chukar in sources of spilled grain along the tracks. Although their numbers have decreased, chukars have remained surprisingly resilient. Suburbanization, for example, which has removed critical habitat for pheasants and other bird species, has provided chukars with new sources of food and water: "A lot of people feed them," Ritcey commented, "so they are quite happy for the development." For hunters in the region, the plucky birds are a sign of the resilience of rangeland environments. Recalling his earlier years as a hunter, Ritcey noted that "it was great to be able to go over the foot of the hill and shoot a chukar."[46]

Hydroelectric Development and Habitat Loss

Before the 1960s, most hydroelectric development in the province had been conducted by private mills, smelters and other companies seeking to power their operations. The massive Kenney Dam on the Nechako River in northwestern BC, for example, was completed by the Aluminum Company of Canada (Alcan) in 1954 to provide power and water for its aluminum smelter in Kitimat. The largest hydroelectric project in North America at the time, the resulting Nechako (Ootsa Lake) Reservoir flooded a series of seven lakes and a rich network of rivers and sloughs in the upper Nechako watershed, homeland of the Cheslatta T'En (Cheslatta Carrier Nation). The flooding destroyed habitat for moose and migratory waterfowl, while flow reductions and heightened water temperatures on the Nechako River affected chinook and sockeye salmon runs, valuable Indigenous eulachon fisheries and white sturgeon populations.[47]

Bennett's government brought the public sector into the business of hydroelectric development with the construction of three dams on the Columbia River and a fourth on the Peace River in the 1960s and early 1970s. Bennett's two rivers policy tied the province's economic development to hydroelectric development on two of its major rivers. Damming the Columbia River, which flowed from the southern Rockies through the province's southeast and into the US Pacific Northwest, would provide power to growing industries throughout British Columbia; damming the Peace River, which flowed from the northern Rockies to the province's northeastern border, would fuel northern expansion and development. Transforming these Rocky Mountain river basins into "power trenches," in the words of Minister of Land and Forests Ray Williston, would produce not only electricity but also the ability to regulate flow for flood protection and agricultural purposes.[48]

Publicly owned power generation was the first step in Bennett's policy, allowing the province to seize hydroelectric power opportunities and provide low-cost power to residents and industrial interests.[49] The simultaneous development of the Columbia and the Peace was the second. By creating the possibility for enormous power generation on both rivers, Bennett wagered, British Columbia would gain the economic independence it needed to negotiate favourable terms in an international treaty. The two rivers policy, in other words, would give him the leverage to pressure the federal government to allow BC to sell excess electricity to the Americans. Because power demand in the province was still relatively low, the BC government could use the funds gained by selling its electricity entitlement to the US to offset the costs of dam construction.[50]

Damming the Peace and Columbia

International discussions about flow regulation on the Columbia emerged in the mid-1940s in response to damaging and sometimes deadly seasonal flooding, especially on the US side of the border. Flood protection needs, combined with growing demand for hydroelectric power, led the Canadian and US governments to sign the **Columbia River Treaty** in 1961. The treaty

Columbia River Treaty area, 2022

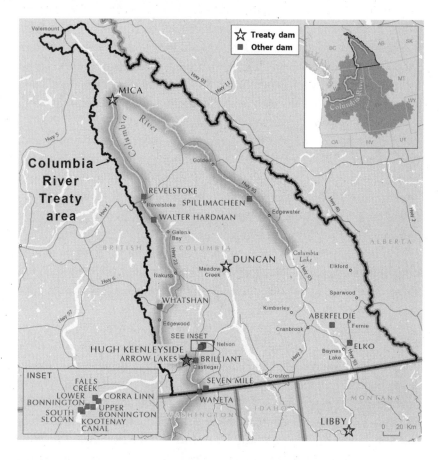

Data sources: BC Dams, 1997, Water Management Branch, Ministry of Forests; and BC Major Watersheds, 2003, GeoBC. Map by GeoBC, 2022.

authorized the development and operation of four dams in the upper Columbia River basin, each of which would flood river valleys within British Columbia: the Duncan Dam at the upper end of Kootenay Lake (completed in 1967); the High Arrow (later renamed the Hugh Keenleyside) Dam at the lower end of the Arrow Lakes (completed in 1968); the Libby Dam in Montana, completed in 1972, which formed the Koocanusa Reservoir extending into BC; and the Mica Dam on the Columbia north of Revelstoke (completed in 1973).

The primary purpose of the three BC dams was water storage and flow regulation for downstream dams in the United States. Of the three dams, only the Mica would be fitted for power generation (the Keenleyside Dam was retrofitted with a hydro generating station thirty-five years later, in 2002). In exchange for providing these benefits, Canada would receive an upfront payment for estimated future flood control benefits in the US and entitlement to half of the estimated electricity generated at downstream hydroelectric generating stations in the United States.[51]

As discussions about the implementation of the treaty continued, Bennett turned his attention to the Peace, initiating construction of the W.A.C. Bennett Dam at "Site A" on the Peace River in 1961. Unlike the dams on the Columbia River, the Bennett Dam was built for the primary objective of power generation. Completed in 1967, it remains one of the largest dams in the world. The corralling of the Finlay, Parsnip and Peace rivers behind the dam produced the province's largest body of fresh water, the 1,650-square-kilometre Williston Reservoir.[52] (In 1980, the completion of the smaller Peace Canyon Dam twenty-three kilometres downstream produced a second reservoir on the Peace at Dinosaur Lake.)

Provincial-federal disagreement over control of Canada's hydroelectric entitlement delayed the ratification of the Columbia River Treaty for three years. When it was finally ratified in 1964, the treaty incorporated a Canada-BC agreement giving BC the right to sell Canada's electricity entitlement to downstream US power authorities.[53] Bennett's gamble appeared to have been successful. Revenue gained through the terms of the treaty would aid in financing dam construction.[54] And a new publicly owned power company, BC Hydro, would manage the construction and annual operation of the dams on the Peace and Columbia, fulfilling Bennett's vision of harnessing the energy of two rivers through the mechanism of publicly owned power.

In the carbon-emissions-conscious calculations of the present, hydroelectric power carries positive associations of "clean power" and renewable energy production. Certainly, the Bennett Dam and the dams on the Columbia have produced a range of benefits for the province, including flood protection, annual revenue from US benefits, employment opportunities in dam construction and operation, the provision of electric power to rural communities and, perhaps most significantly, the prosperity generated by reliably low electricity rates for BC residents and industries.[55] As Bennett biographer David J. Mitchell has argued, the reliable source of

Dam sites on the Peace River by 1980

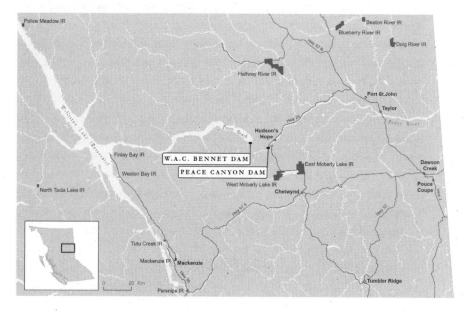

Data source: BC Dams, 1997, Water Management Branch, Ministry of Forests. Map by GeoBC, 2022.

power and revenue that dams on the Peace and Columbia generated helped to even out the boom-and-bust cycles of a provincial economy otherwise dependent on fluctuating global demand for its natural resources.[56]

Consequences of the Dams for People and Wildlife

What Bennett and the Columbia River Treaty signatories failed to account for, however, was the enormous long-term consequences of dam construction and operation for local residents and for fish and wildlife. Both projects proceeded with little to no consultation with area residents. A series of public hearings held throughout the upper Columbia basin in 1961, for example, were limited to water-licence issues and precluded any discussion of the treaty itself.[57] The flooding of roughly 600 square kilometres of fertile valley bottoms in the Kootenays—a region where land use is already constrained by steep mountain ranges—and almost 1,800 square kilometres of forest and mineral-rich land on the Peace affected residents of both regions directly and indirectly. The projects required the relocation of over 1,400 residents in the Columbia basin and roughly 150 in the Peace. While those directly affected received compensation for lands, homes and other inundated assets, such as traplines, many felt the compensation they received was inadequate. Monies received for homes or land could not compensate for the loss of a self-sufficient way of life that some residents experienced on relocation to BC Hydro's newly constructed communities in the Arrow Lakes area.[58]

On the Peace, the failure to clear more than 142,000 hectares of forested land despite promises to the contrary was especially galling for local residents and logging interests. Flooding of Williston Reservoir much sooner than anticipated buried thousands of hectares of forest land in the new lake. Although some of the timber was recovered, as time passed it became impossible to salvage waterlogged trees. Ten years later, the lake remained "barely navigable" because of the danger of submerged trees.[59] Damming also compromised agricultural production. In the Columbia basin, the filling of the Arrow Lakes and Koocanusa reservoirs flooded fertile farm land and dramatically altered high and low water levels—by as much as tens of metres in some areas—resulting in the flooding of arable land in spring and the loss of fertile soil when waters were drawn down for power production in the fall and winter.[60] On the Peace, the enormous expanse of Williston Reservoir produced local climatic changes, causing area grain farmers to complain of increased winds, higher humidity and cooler temperatures.[61]

The loss of livelihoods and homelands was especially pronounced for Indigenous residents of the Columbia and Peace River basins. In the Columbia River basin, the Sinixt (Arrow Lakes band) lost sacred burial grounds when the Arrow Lakes were flooded in the late 1960s.[62] Because no reserve lands were physically affected by the dams in the Columbia basin, the federal Department of Indian Affairs had minimal influence in protecting Indigenous interests. Neither BC Hydro nor Indian Affairs considered in their compensation calculations the economic and spiritual significance of lost hunting, fishing, gathering and sacred grounds throughout the traditional territories of the Okanagan and Ktunaxa nations.[63] On the Peace, the settlements, traplines and traditional territories of the Tsay Keh Dene First Nation, Sekani people then known as the Ingenika, were inundated by the reservoir. Forty to fifty of roughly two hundred Tsay Keh band members were moved several hundred kilometres south to a new reserve near Mackenzie. No one stayed at this new reserve, however. Some joined other families at the Fort Ware reserve at the top of Williston Reservoir; others relocated to urban areas and in some cases ended up destitute.[64] New reserve locations and minimal compensation for property damage did little to address the loss of trails, burial grounds, cultural sites and a way of life deeply dependent on the river and the animal life it supported.

Most devastating for the Tsay Keh Dene and other Indigenous groups of the Peace region were the impacts of the flooding on the once-substantial woodland caribou herd that migrated through the region each spring. The creation of the reservoir blocked the caribou's east–west migration across the Rocky Mountain Trench, drowning many animals and dispersing them into small remnant herds whose numbers continued to decline in subsequent decades. Anthropologist Hugh Brody described the immediate effects of the flooding in his 1981 book about the region, *Maps and Dreams*:

> The water was full of floating trees, debris and turbidity. Whole trees would suddenly shoot up from the bottom. With the migration route cut off, the caribou and moose tried to swim across but they couldn't make it to the bank because the log jams and debris on the shores prevented them. They slipped and drowned because they couldn't get out. The water was full of bloated corpses.[65]

As the reservoir filled, the large number of moose and caribou trapped by the rising waters led the province to declare an open hunting season for two years in order to clear the lake of trapped animals.[66] Fur-bearers such as beaver and muskrat, once an important source of winter income and subsistence for the Tsay Keh and nearby Kadaska First Nations, were also disrupted by the dam. On the Williston Reservoir, winter drawdowns— the release of water to generate electricity and create storage capacity for spring freshets—average about seventeen metres but are sometimes as high as thirty-two metres. Retreating water levels exposed formerly submerged beaver and muskrat lodges to winter elements, greatly increasing mortality rates. Studies of muskrat populations around Williston Reservoir, for example, show a precipitous drop from roughly 250,000 individuals before dam construction to 17,000 after.[67] Rising water levels upstream from the dam also submerged nesting and feeding areas for waterfowl, while downstream reductions in water flow dried out critical wetland habitat at the

Peace-Athabasca Delta in northern Alberta. For area First Nations, a way of life that revolved around the annual migration of caribou and waterfowl and the winter returns of the trapline had been irreparably upended.

On the Columbia, the outcome was equally grim for wildlife. In a region dominated by steep mountain ranges, the flooding of high-value valley habitat within the Rocky Mountain Trench permanently reduced the regional capability to support big-game species such as moose, deer, caribou and elk.[68] In Deer Park on the Lower Arrow Lake, wildlife was dealt two blows: the High Arrow dam flooded habitat, and then BC Hydro relocated displaced residents onto the best remaining white-tailed deer winter range.[69] On the main stem of the Columbia, a study of the effects of the proposed Mica Dam on area wildlife pointed to the steep-walled reservoir and the paucity of nearby alternative habitat as a death sentence for big game, fur-bearers and upland birds such as ruffed and Franklin grouse. In sum, the authors noted, "most of the high-quality wildlife habitat in the valley systems of the reservoir area will be flooded," including productive wetlands, riparian areas and natural meadows impossible to replicate in surrounding areas. The barrier created by the reservoir itself, furthermore, would block the seasonal migration of "most big game species," directly affecting big-game populations occupying tributary valleys "many miles" from the reservoir.[70] Hunters and guides in the region corroborated these predictions in subsequent decades, noting a reduction in the number of ungulates and the incursion of greater travelling costs to access remaining game species.[71]

Even more pronounced than the effects on surrounding wildlife were the effects on fish species within the two river systems. Extreme fluctuations in water and flow levels set in motion a series of changes to plankton, nutrients and sediment loads with effects that reverberated up the food chain. Nutrient-rich sediment, for example, which previously would have flowed downstream to collect in estuaries, became trapped in the reservoirs above the dams, altering river temperatures and clogging spawning grounds.[72] Steep-sided reservoirs, like the Mica Dam's Kinbasket Lake, eroded bank vegetation and eliminated habitat for the bottom-feeding organisms that many fish species relied on.[73] These kinds of changes to river and lake temperatures and substrates made survival increasingly difficult for some fish species. Loss of riparian habitat significantly reduced Artic grayling populations within the Williston Reservoir, while the survival rates of juvenile white sturgeon have declined precipitously in the decades since dams were erected on the Kootenay, Columbia and Nechako rivers.[74]

On the Peace, the failure to remove standing trees prior to flooding the reservoir created not only navigation hazards but also changes to the chemical composition of the lake water. Decomposing trees and vegetation released mercury into the lake's food chain, which concentrated over time in the tissues of predatory fish species. By 1992, mercury levels had become high enough to cause the province to issue a Fish Consumption Advisory for bull trout (*Salvelinus confluentus*) and, later, lake trout (*Salvelinus namaycush*). Mercury levels have since declined. Today, levels are similar to those found in fish in BC's natural lakes and rivers.[75]

Most visible among the effects on fish populations were the barriers the dams created to fish movement and migration. On the US portion of the Columbia, the absence of fish ladders at the Grand Coulee Dam (1942) and, later, the downstream Chief Joseph Dam (1955) blocked the passage of migrating sockeye and chinook salmon into the upper Columbia River, eliminating traditional salmon fisheries for upper Columbia First Nations.[76] Upriver, rainbow trout and other species lost access to spawning grounds on tributary streams owing to flooding or downstream dams. Dam and reservoir construction also affected fish movement downstream. Where river currents had once carried migrating juveniles (fry) to the ocean, reservoirs required fry to exert much greater energy swimming through slack waters. The journey downstream through multiple dam turbines also placed a heavy toll on fry populations.

Kokanee salmon (*Onchorhynchus nerka*), a landlocked variant of sockeye that spend their entire lives in large lakes, fared somewhat better in the new circumstances created by the dams. But while the reservoirs provided suitable habitat for maturing fish, the dams destroyed kilometres of spawning grounds essential to kokanee, bull trout and rainbow trout survival. In the late 1960s, the BC Fish and Wildlife Branch collaborated with BC Hydro and local fish and game associations to construct an alternate spawning channel that replicated kokanee habitat with reasonable success. The three-kilometre Meadow Creek spawning channel, constructed in 1967 at the north end of Kootenay Lake, became the first of three kokanee spawning channels on the lake completed by the 1980s.[77] At least initially, kokanee populations responded well, thriving on the high nutrient levels of the reservoir and attracting large numbers of anglers through the 1970s.

Success would be difficult to sustain, however, as nutrient retention behind the Libby Dam, completed in 1973, combined with growing pressure from anglers caused kokanee populations to crash by 1979. Their maintenance has since required ongoing intervention by fisheries managers.[78]

Conclusion: "Development at All Costs"

As infrastructure and townsite development alienated wildlife habitat in the decades following World War II and resource extraction activities expanded with little consideration for fish and wildlife, conservationists sought new ways to amplify their message, sway decision makers and reach new audiences. The federation of stakeholder groups such as the BC Trappers Association (1945) and the BC Wildlife Federation (1951) reflected a growing need to represent hunting, fishing and trapping interests in infrastructure and resource allocation decisions. New venues for provincewide dialogue around wildlife and resource development concerns, including the BC Natural Resources Conference and the BC Wildlife Federation's annual game convention, provided these organizations with an important platform to shape public policy in the postwar period. While the overwhelming ethos of the two decades following the war was "development at all costs," conservationists of the period used these forums to press for recognition of the vulnerability and value of wildlife populations on the landscape.

7

The Conservation Imperative

The industrial and infrastructure expansion of the postwar period prompted naturalists and hunting, trapping and fishing organizations to articulate with greater urgency a conservation imperative for the province's wildlife. By the mid-1960s, conservationists mobilized arguments for the economic value of wildlife in addition to older arguments for the multiple use of public lands.

At the same time, the growth in numbers of hunters and anglers in British Columbia created its own conservation concerns. Pressures on fish and wildlife populations increased as rising numbers of hunters and anglers capitalized on a booming economy and expanded leisure time. Furthermore, technological and infrastructure developments facilitated access to wildlife. The advent of the bush plane in the 1930s and the completion of the Alaska Highway in 1942, for example, allowed for the growth of the guide-outfitting industry by greatly reducing travel times to prime hunting regions for companies and their foreign clientele. Roads and rail provided similar benefits for the province's resident hunters and anglers. As hunter and angler numbers climbed dramatically in the 1950s and 1960s, stakeholder organizations such as the BC Wildlife Federation and the BC Trappers Association formed to defend hunting, angling and trapping interests against competing Indigenous and commercial claims. Government wildlife managers, meanwhile, struggled to adapt regulations to keep pace with the rapidly changing realities of recreational access and harvesting efficiency.

Educational initiatives also expanded in this period, as conservation officers, biologists and fish and game organizations attempted to square public knowledge of game regulations and hunting and fishing methods with rapidly expanding public interest and participation. The advent of outdoor education classes and Game Commission initiatives like the quarterly

Wildlife Review helped to dispel older ideas about predators and instil a conservation ethic among the province's hunters and anglers. Efforts to educate a broader public about wildlife ecology and conservation took root in the mid-1950s, with the creation of the BC Parks Naturalist Program and Ian McTaggart Cowan's popular *Fur and Feathers* television show. Together with the ongoing research and education work of the Provincial Museum and its affiliated naturalists' organizations, these initiatives shaped public attitudes toward wildlife in the decades following World War II.

A Seat at the Table for Wildlife?

Conflicts over competing land uses in the late 1950s and early 1960s resulted in a series of conferences at the provincial and federal level, including the BC Natural Resources Conference, which met annually between 1948 and 1968, and the federal Resources for Tomorrow conference, which brought together eight hundred university, government and industry representatives from across the country in 1961 (see plate 7). Both conferences emphasized improved planning and use of resources to ensure long-term sustainability, rather than restricting access or "locking up" resources through protective measures.[1] Championed by Prime Minister John Diefenbaker, the 1961 Resources for Tomorrow conference emphasized partnership and information sharing between federal, provincial and territorial officials around parks, wildlife and resource management. One of the major initiatives that emerged at the federal level was the **Canada Land Inventory (CLI)**, launched in 1963 and completed in 1976. The first nationwide inventory of Canada's renewable resources, the CLI assessed the land's capacity to support agriculture, forestry, outdoor recreation and wildlife (sport fish and game) as a basis for land use planning.[2] It would become a critical source of information for government assessment of land use proposals.

At the provincial level, the annual **BC Natural Resources Conference** provided an important forum for communication across resource sectors. Fish and game clubs, naturalists and representatives from commercial fisheries' trade unions expressed concerns about the rapid proliferation of industrial forestry, mining and hydroelectric developments and the threats they posed to fish and game species. This dedicated cross-sector communication resulted in some significant gains for wildlife interests. Improved communication with forestry industry representatives, for example, enabled the BC Wildlife Federation to resolve long-standing demands among its member clubs for public access to logging roads on Crown land. In 1963, Bennett's government passed the Private Roads Access Act, which permitted public access to logging roads and relieved timber-licence holders of the financial responsibility for fires caused by recreational users. By 1970, logging companies had come to accept weekend access to their leased holdings and the Forest Service had begun to expand its picnic and campsite system.[3]

Concerns about water pollution among sport fishing interests also found a larger audience through the BC Natural Resources Conference and the BCWF's annual game convention. In response to anglers' concerns, game wardens began investigating incidents of water pollution in 1952.[4] Research by Peter Larkin, director of the Fisheries Institute at UBC and former chief fisheries biologist for the province, confirmed the detrimental effects of untreated organic wastes and toxic substances on sport fish and their food supply. The Game Commission, however, lacked the legislative authority to prosecute pollution infractions, complicating abatement efforts.[5] Within this context, direct communication and practical solutions yielded some early successes. For example, the destructive effects of cannery wastes on trout-bearing Achelitz Creek, near Chilliwack, led game wardens and biologists to secure an agreement with the cannery wherein solid wastes would be screened out and sold as pig feed and liquid wastes pumped onto a nearby field to use as fertilizer. The successful result produced extra revenue for the cannery and saw the return of cutthroat trout to upstream spawning beds.[6] Persistent lobbying by the BCWF and commercial fishing interests (together with a hotly debated sewage treatment plant proposed for Iona Island on the Fraser River) propelled the passage of the **Pollution Control Act** in 1956 and the province's first concerted efforts to mitigate sources of water pollution.

Identifying an Economic Value for Wildlife

Multiple-use arguments forwarded in the context of resource allocation debates were less effective in responding to the permanent alienation of public lands brought about by hydroelectric development. The singular challenges of dam development, with its associated losses of valley-bottom wildlife habitat and permanent alterations of aquatic systems, saw fish and game associations collaborate with academics to establish an economic value for wildlife itself and the tourism industries it supported.

The effects of large hydroelectric dams on the Columbia, Peace and Nechako rivers, and numerous small hydroelectric and water diversion dams on other river systems, had long raised concerns among BC hunters, trappers, fishers and naturalists.[7] Hydroelectric developments were among the first issues to be tabled at the **BC Wildlife Federation**'s (then known as the BC Fish and Game Council) annual game convention, the first of which was held in 1947.[8]

During the Columbia River Treaty negotiations, BCWF executive director Howard Paish and Kootenay region fish and wildlife biologist Glen Smith visited hydroelectric developments in the US where compensation or amelioration efforts had been implemented to mitigate fish and wildlife losses. Interest in quantifying these losses led to engagement with UBC natural resources economist Peter Pearse, who authored several papers on the value of sport fish and game resources in the 1960s and early 1970s.

Pearse and his wildlife biologist collaborators sought to challenge two prevalent notions that worked against the cause of wildlife conservation in the province: (1) the notion that fish and wildlife held aesthetic, but not economic, value; and (2) the notion that animals could simply relocate to other environments less desirable for human purposes. Wildlife, they argued, and especially waterfowl and big-game animals, depended for their survival on the same highly specific environments (wetlands and valley bottoms) that people found easiest to exploit for agriculture, townsites and hydroelectric development. Furthermore, fish and wildlife supported hunting, angling, guiding and tourism industries that together generated significant annual revenue for the province.[9] Pearse's groundbreaking work, the first to document the economic value of wildlife as a non-marketed resource, estimated that the reservoirs created in fulfilment of the Columbia River Treaty flooded the habitat of 8,000 deer, 600 elk, 1,500 moose, 2,000 black bears and 70,000 ducks and geese.[10] In 1974, the BC Environment and Land Use Committee drew on Pearse's work to estimate a decline of 50 per cent in the value of wildlife resources (excluding waterfowl) in the Mica basin alone— from $10.9 million prior to flooding to $5.6 million after reservoir creation.[11]

Compensation for fish and wildlife losses was slow in coming, but the cost-benefit approach that the BC Wildlife Federation pursued was ultimately successful. Pressure from the BCWF, which often amplified and supported Fish and Game Branch concerns in this period, contributed to BC Hydro's adoption of better practices by the mid-1970s, including the completion of environmental impact studies and public hearings before projects got underway and the granting of water licences on condition that reservoirs be cleared before flooding. In the late 1980s and early 1990s, two decades after the completion of the dams, BC Hydro established fish and wildlife compensation programs to conserve and enhance habitat on affected Columbia and Peace River watersheds.[12] Decades of effort by local residents, tribal councils and regional districts in the Columbia basin finally led to the creation of the Columbia Basin Trust in 1995, which allocated a portion of treaty revenues to the region most affected by the dams and established a regional organization, governed by a board of basin residents, to manage the funds. The Trust continues to support initiatives that enhance social, economic and environmental well-being in the region most affected by the treaty.[13]

Mitigating the Effects of the Dams: The Creston Valley Wildlife Management Area, 1968

With official compensation from BC Hydro still decades away, a collaborative wetland conservation initiative began to take shape in the Creston Valley in the late 1960s. Located on the Kootenay River floodplain south of Kootenay Lake in southeastern British Columbia, the Creston Valley forms part of what was once a seventy-kilometre stretch of wetland habitat along the Kootenay River from Kootenay Lake south into Idaho. Its location on the Pacific Flyway, a major bird migration corridor, and its combination of marshes, lakes, rivers and associated upland habitat make it an important breeding and staging area—a place to rest and "refuel"—for waterfowl and other bird species.

In the late 1940s, farmers of the rich alluvial lands of the Creston Flats extended their reclamation work to the wetlands around Duck Lake, a shallow water body south of Kootenay Lake. The move ignited historic tensions between farmers, wildlife advocates and the Yaqan Nuʔkiy or Lower Kootenay Band, one of the seven bands of the Ktunaxa Nation. Since the 1880s, the Yaqan Nuʔkiy had confronted surveyors and destroyed survey stakes that threatened burial grounds and obstructed their access to the river. Efforts by nineteenth-century settlers to dike and farm the flats

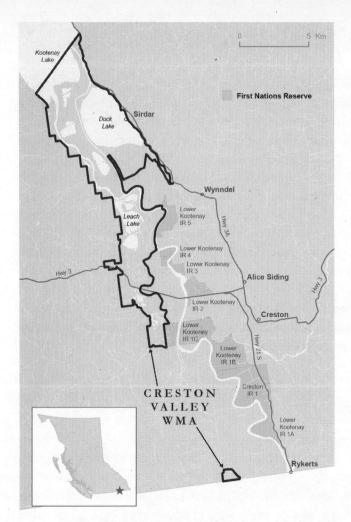

Creston Valley Wildlife Management Area

The Creston Valley Wildlife Management Area lies within the Columbia River basin. Data source: Environment and Climate Change Canada, Canadian Protected and Conserved Areas Database. Map by GeoBC, 2022.

conflicted with seasonal rounds that for millenniums had incorporated floodplain harvests of cattails, dogwood berries and plentiful waterfowl in spring and fall and, later, plots of potatoes and hay on the river flats.

While early reclamation efforts were mostly frustrated by spring floods that washed away crops and destroyed dikes, by the late 1930s outside capital investments enabled farmers to construct a comprehensive system of dikes and drainage ditches and to reclaim large areas of the flats for agriculture. Objections from the Yaqan Nuʔkiy, who faced relocation and limited compensation for reclaimed reserve lands, were joined by protests by local rod and gun clubs arguing the reclamation would endanger local wildfowl populations.[14] By 1947, local clubs could call on a broad base of support from hunter-conservationists across the province and neighbouring states and from game biologists within the provincial and federal government. Research on Creston Valley wildlife populations by dominion wildlife officer James A. Munro, for example, provided evidence that migratory waterfowl populations had dropped to one-quarter of their pre-reclamation numbers. The flats along the Kootenay River, Munro concluded, "constitute the largest and most important resting and feeding ground for waterfowl in the interior of British Columbia." They provided critical habitat not only for local wildlife but for migratory birds protected by international treaty.[15]

Working in collaboration with regional game biologist Glen Smith, the BCWF, **Ducks Unlimited Canada** and a coalition of dedicated West Kootenay rod and gun club members, Munro sketched out a proposal for a wildlife refuge. Conservation, rather than reclamation, they argued, was the best use for the lands surrounding Duck Lake. Their efforts resulted in the passage of the Creston Valley Wildlife Act in 1968, which established the 7,000-hectare Creston Valley Wildlife Management Area (CVWMA) incorporating the lake, surrounding marshes and adjoining mountain slopes. A joint federal-provincial management authority would oversee the restoration and maintenance of the site. Initially excluded from CVWMA negotiations, the Yaqan Nu?kiy worked directly with conservation interests in the following decade.

Intended in part to offset the loss of prime wildlife habitat to the Duncan Dam reservoir farther north, the goal of the CVWMA was to enhance and expand increasingly scarce regional waterfowl habitat.[16] The project represented the provincial government's first attempt at partial voluntary compensation for habitat loss resulting from hydroelectric development; it set an important precedent for mitigating fish and wildlife losses. The story of the CVWMA also points to the inadequacy of habitat protection alone, especially in the context of systemwide changes to water flows caused by hydroelectric development; ongoing management interventions would be required to create and maintain suitable habitat for wildlife. Annual funding contributions from BC Hydro, government grants and wetland restoration expertise from DUC saw the expansion and repurposing of dikes to control seasonal variation in water levels and create much-needed waterfowl nesting habitat. Reconciliation with agricultural interests was part of the strategy: the designers of the wildlife management area built low dikes so that when high water threatens the Creston Flats, the wildlife area floods, protecting adjacent agricultural land.

These efforts to mitigate the effects of hydroelectric development on the Kootenay River and to enhance wildlife habitat have resulted in an increase in the number of species and the size of breeding populations of birds and other wildlife. In 1994, the area was officially declared a Wetland of International Importance (one of over 2,400 sites designated under UNESCO's 1971 Ramsar Convention as wetlands of global significance for waterfowl conservation). Today, the Creston Valley is one of the premier birdwatching destinations in British Columbia.[17]

Accommodation of agricultural and Indigenous interests is ongoing. The Yaqan Nuʔkiy continue to farm some 1,600 hectares of diked flats beside the Kootenay River and are currently working with the BC Wildlife Federation and other partners to restore more than 500 hectares of wetland habitat for waterfowl, moose, elk, grizzly bear, and amphibians.[18] Since the creation of the CVWMA in 1968, the province and conservation partners like Ducks Unlimited Canada have established thirty additional wildlife management areas. The majority are located in the southern half of the province, where development pressures have been most intense.

Rising Recreational Demand

As the province's population grew and resource development expanded in the decades following World War II, many British Columbians enjoyed more wealth, stability and leisure time.[19] Together with the growth of automobile ownership and the Bennett government's investments in roads and infrastructure, these developments produced a heightened demand for recreational facilities and experiences. Fish and game club membership ballooned, as did government licence revenue from a growing number of resident and non-resident hunters and anglers. Parks expansion followed a similar logic of recreational demand. Between 1951 and 1957, the province established over seventy small, easily accessible roadside parks to attract residents and tourists to the province's scenic destinations. In the same period, however, reductions in the area of larger parks, combined with increased industrial activity within their boundaries, prompted a growing coalition of wilderness enthusiasts, including hunter-conservationists like Roderick Haig-Brown, to lobby for the removal of parks from the purview of the Forest Service.[20]

Expanded recreational opportunities for a growing population of hunters, anglers and weekend recreationists not surprisingly placed growing pressure on wildlife populations. Advancements in outboard motor technology and the mass production of aluminum and fibreglass boats and four-wheel-drive jeeps after the war facilitated public access to previously difficult-to-reach hunting and fishing locations. More efficient, affordable and user-friendly rifles and fishing tackle also played a role in increasing the popularity of the sport. Returning World War II veterans repurposed military rifles for sporting use after the war, aided by the emergence of companies like Brownells that supplied affordable tools and components for do-it-yourself gunsmiths. Advances in cartridge technology and, for bow hunters, the advent of aluminum arrow shafts also contributed to the rapid popularization of hunting. Anglers, meanwhile, took advantage of new high-efficiency spinning reels and flexible fibreglass casting and fly rods that quickly made bamboo and steel rods obsolete.[21]

Keeping up with these changes and their effects on targeted fish and wildlife became a perennial challenge for wildlife managers. Earlier adaptations, including the implementation of a tagging system for deer in 1932, became increasingly important as hunting pressure increased. By purchasing a deer tag and cancelling it when a deer (and later moose and elk) was killed, hunters contributed revenue, facilitated enforcement and provided useful baseline data for harvest surveys.[22] Concern over the proliferation of roads and four-wheel-drive vehicles in the late 1940s led managers to secure an amendment to the Game Act in 1950 prohibiting the use of aircraft or (off-road) motor vehicles for the purpose of hunting, trapping or fishing except under prescribed conditions.[23] Ten years later, in response to the growing availability of high-powered pump-action shotguns, a revised Game Act prohibited the use of automatic shotguns of any kind.[24] Game and fishing regulations became more detailed, and more specific, over the same period. Between 1950 and 1961, for example, annual synopses of game regulations evolved from opaque documents that described areas closed to hunting using topographical descriptions to more accessible folded booklets that divided the province into twenty-one "game management areas" (hunting zones) with a map for ease of reference.[25]

In 1957, a new stand-alone Department of Recreation and Conservation took up responsibility for parks and fish and game. The move, which ended over fifty years of oversight by the Ministry of the Attorney General, signalled a transition away from a regulatory and enforcement approach toward a science-based approach to fish and wildlife conservation. With the

Provincial wildlife staff meeting at the Flying U Guest Ranch, 70 Mile House, BC, 1966.
Photo courtesy of Bryan Gates.

retirement in 1962 of Frank Butler, the province's last game commissioner, biologist Jim Hatter became the first in a succession of scientifically trained Fish and Game Branch directors. At the operations level, game wardens were retitled "conservation officers" in 1961 and took on a growing array of enforcement and education responsibilities. By housing the Fish and Game Branch with tourism-related endeavours such as parks, the move also provided an explicit recognition of the value of fish and game to the province's economy. The product of several years of lobbying by the BC Wildlife Federation and representatives at the BC Natural Resources Conference, the move to "Rec and Con" was intended to provide dedicated ministry resources to wildlife conservation. Fundamental ministerial inequities would persist, however, in the absence of specific statutes mandating the consideration of wildlife in the management or alienation of Crown lands.[26]

The prioritization of research within the new department was facilitated by an ongoing close relationship with scientists at UBC. In 1962, the Fish and Game Branch established a research section at the university, a mutually beneficial arrangement wherein the Branch gained access to the university library, research laboratories and graduate student researchers, while the university received financial support and supervision for graduate student research.[27] Ian McTaggart Cowan, now head of UBC's zoology department, continued to support research on fish and game population ecology while expressing rising concern about habitat loss and the effects of DDT and other synthetic insecticides on birds and other wildlife. Research in the late 1940s by Cowan student Arthur Benson had demonstrated the toxicity of pesticides (parathion and DDT) on pheasant populations around orchards.[28] A decade of passionate lobbying by the Canadian Wildlife Service's chief migratory birds officer James Munro, federal entomologist Ronald Buckell, and Okanagan naturalists' and rod and gun clubs had produced no government response by the time of Munro's death in 1958. Cowan would mobilize this research and a growing body of scientific studies from south of the border in his public education work through the 1950s and '60s.

INITIATIVE PROFILE: Territorial Allotments for BC Guide Outfitters

Rising incomes and security after World War II brought new business for the province's guide outfitters. The opening of northeast BC following the Alaska Highway's completion in 1942, coupled with road and infrastructure investments in other parts of the province and the growing availability of float planes and off-road jeeps, made access to guiding areas faster and easier. As costs and time commitments for foreign hunting trips came down, demand for guiding services soared among American and European sport hunters.

BC game wardens responded to this heightened demand by licensing more and more guides. A lack of clear guidelines for awarding guide licences contributed to this situation, in part a reflection of the prewar history of the industry where low numbers of guide outfitters generally kept out of one another's way. With more guides entering the business after 1945, crowding soon became apparent. As Hudson's Hope guide outfitter Leo Rutledge explained in his 2004 memoir, "successful guide outfitting rests upon meticulous planning . . . often two or more years in advance." With an upsurge in business, "too many guides were vying for too little room, and . . . interfering with [one another's] plans."[29]

Changes in the Cariboo region exemplified these trends. Following upgrades to the Cariboo Highway after the war, the region experienced a "tremendous influx

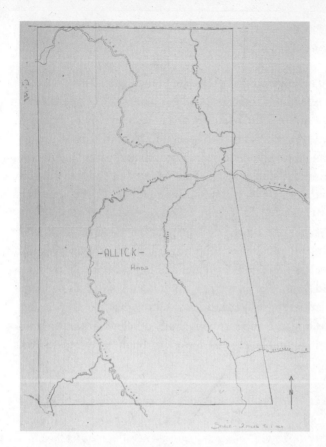

Amos Allick's guiding
territory, Guide's
Files, ca.1966.
Royal BC Museum,
CM/C2054.

of both resident and non-resident hunters" seeking moose and deer. Numbers of
licensed guides increased to the point that "practically every ranch had a guide
or two," generating conflict and exerting undue pressure on game populations.
Recalling similar competition among trappers in the 1920s, BC Trappers Association
president Eric Collier hosted a well-attended meeting for Cariboo region guides,
trappers and BC Game Commission staff. Held in Clinton in the fall of 1948, the
meeting led to the creation of the province's first **guide territories**. By 1950, Cariboo
game warden Leo Jobin had drawn up territories limiting each guide to a radius of
seven miles from the centre of their operation. Problems of overlapping boundaries
led to refinements in the mid-1950s, producing the block-style arrangement that is
still in use across the province today. Under this system each guide was allotted one
block, which generally consisted of "one or two watersheds with the mountain crests
serving as boundaries." Territorial allotments for guide outfitters proved successful
in reducing not only competition among BC-based guides but also encroachment
from non-resident guides. As East Kootenay guide outfitter Dix Anderson recalled,
guide territories "turned out to be the best thing that ever happened" for the guiding

business in the area, as their enforcement meant that Alberta outfitters could "no longer hunt on the west side of the Rockies."[30]

While territorial allotments greatly improved opportunities for planning and game species conservation, guide outfitters still lacked the secure, long-term tenures that their trapper counterparts enjoyed. A guide licence's one-year term and lack of transferability to successors made business investments precarious. In the early 1960s, representatives of the Northern Guides Association spearheaded advocacy for guide tenure security. Efforts to represent guide-outfitter interests in discussions with Fish and Wildlife Branch officials led to the federation of the province's many small guide associations in 1966. That same year, the newly formed Guide Outfitters Association of British Columbia succeeded in securing fifteen-year transferable guide-outfitter tenures. As former Muskwa-Kechika guide outfitter Ross Peck recalls, secure tenures allowed outfitters to invest in improvements to their territories, including trails, cabins, maintenance of associated grazing leases and the use of prescribed burns to improve wildlife habitat. Like the trapline registration system of the 1920s, area allotment produced incentives for guide outfitters to steward the wildlife within their territories. Guide licences became more difficult to obtain and, as a result, "more valuable than ever," placing the industry, and the big-game species on which it depended, on a more sustainable path.[31]

At the federal level, the creation of the **Canadian Wildlife Service** in 1947 led to an expansion of the federal role in wildlife conservation and research through the 1950s and 1960s. A close relationship between the CWS and the National Park Service, for example, saw CWS biologists lead studies of elk and bighorn sheep ecology in Kootenay and Yoho National Parks in the 1950s and '60s. Annual **Federal-Provincial Wildlife Conferences**, initiated by dominion parks commissioner James Harkin and the influential Department of Agriculture entomologist George Hewitt in 1919, continued to shape the agenda for wildlife research and management responses at both the federal and provincial levels.[32]

Migratory birds remained a key area of federal concern, with Jim Munro taking an early lead in this area. In his twenty-nine years as chief federal migratory birds officer, from 1920 until his retirement in 1949, Munro oversaw the selection and creation of five of the province's seven **migratory bird sanctuaries**: Vaseux Lake (1923) in the Okanagan; Victoria Harbour (1923), Esquimalt Lagoon (1931) and Shoal Harbour (1931) on Vancouver

Island; and Nechako River (1944), west of Prince George.[33] Stemming from the terms of the 1917 Migratory Birds Convention Act, migratory bird sanctuaries are limited both in regulatory scope and in geographic area. Essentially, they prohibit shooting in critical estuary habitats but contain no provisions for habitat protection and no restrictions against developments such as marinas. Most of the early sanctuaries, furthermore, including Victoria Harbour and Esquimalt Lagoon, were located within expanding urban areas, in places that had historically been subject to high hunting pressure. As municipal firearms bylaws came to prohibit shooting within city boundaries, these sanctuary designations became increasingly obsolete. The Reifel sanctuary, initiated by the BC Waterfowl Society in 1963 and federally designated in 1967, was the last bird sanctuary in the province established under federal migratory bird legislation.[34]

INITIATIVE PROFILE: California Bighorn Sheep Transplants

British Columbia is home to two subspecies of bighorn sheep: the Rocky Mountain bighorn sheep (*Ovis canadensis canadensis*), occupying the grassy mountain slopes and rugged foothills of the Rocky Mountains from BC's East Kootenay region south to New Mexico; and the California bighorn sheep (*Ovis canadensis californiana*), which historically occupied the dry grasslands and high valleys of BC's southern and central Interior south to California and east to North Dakota.[35]

Slightly smaller and darker than their Rocky Mountain counterparts, and historically less numerous, California bighorns were extirpated from much of their former range in BC and most of the US owing to unregulated hunting, overgrazing and diseases introduced by domestic sheep. By 1950, only about one thousand of the animals remained: a small population in California and ten separate groups at the northern extreme of their range in BC's Chilcotin District.

Beginning in the 1930s, a loose coalition of organizations in the US, including the Boy Scouts and the National Wildlife Federation, set out to restore California bighorns to their former ranges. Meanwhile, in BC, concern was growing about the effects of declining range habitat and disease on the province's isolated and dwindling herds. Collaboration between the BC and Oregon game commissions, with financial support from the US federal government, enabled experimental transplants of sheep to their former ranges in the United States. The goal was to avert the extinction of the subspecies by allowing the sheep to recolonize their former ranges.[36]

California bighorn sheep (*Ovis canadensis*), 2014. Photo courtesy of Jared Hobbs.

In November 1954, BC Game Commission biologist Lawson Sugden and crew used a live trap to capture twenty bighorns at Riske Creek, near Williams Lake, for relocation to the Hart Mountain National Wildlife Refuge (now Antelope Refuge) in southern Oregon. Wild sheep had been trapped in the province before, for shipment to zoos and wildlife parks, but this was the first effort to relocate wild sheep for conservation purposes. The following spring the *Wildlife Review*, published by the BC Game Commission, reported on the success of the initiative: six of eight lambs born that spring had survived; by 1958, the transplanted Oregon population had increased to forty-nine.[37] The success of the 1954 initiative led to subsequent transplants from the Williams Lake area to Montana, North Dakota and other western states. By 1998, California bighorn numbered roughly ten thousand and occupied much of their historic range. This initiative, like the signing of the Migratory Birds Treaty decades before, exemplifies what is possible when wildlife administrations in Canada and the United States work together to conserve species that cross national borders.

The successes of the US transplants also prompted sheep transplants within British Columbia. Originally occupying high grassy slopes throughout the southern and central Interior, California bighorns were extirpated from the Thompson and Nicola watersheds sometime before European settlement. Older residents of Kamloops, for example, had no experience of bighorns in the area when the animals were reintro-duced to the hills above Kamloops Lake in the 1960s. Regional biologist Ralph Ritcey, who monitored the Kamloops transplants in the early years, described the initiative as a success: "as the range improved, they did very well." Bighorns from Riske Creek were also relocated to suitable habitat in the South Okanagan and parts of the Chilcotin.[38] By 1990, the province's California bighorns had more than doubled to 4,650.

In both the United States and British Columbia, however, the initial success of transplant efforts proved difficult to sustain. In BC, California bighorn populations have declined to roughly three thousand since the early 1990s as a result of cycli-cal disease outbreaks, competition for a diminishing supply of winter range habitat and generally poor lamb survival rates.[39] Both of BC's bighorn sheep subspecies have been identified as species of special concern by the province's Conservation Data Centre. Habitat protection and improvement, combined with efforts to reduce disease transmission, have been the driving force of organizations such as the Wild Sheep Society of BC, which has worked in partnership with provincial agencies and land conservancies since 1992 to ensure a future for the province's threatened bighorn sheep populations.

Growing Public Awareness

"Standing room only in Outdoor Classes," reads a column in the April 1958 issue of the *Wildlife Review*. Public interest and participation in hunting, fishing and other forms of outdoor recreation had grown enormously in the decade following the war, facilitated by a growing network of roads and provincial campgrounds. Knowledge of hunting and fishing methods and game regulations, however, had not kept up with demand for these activities.[40] Sensing the need for greater education for hunters and fishers, *Vancouver Sun* outdoors columnist Lee Straight and Vancouver sportsman "Squid" McInnes worked with Vancouver's night school program to develop a permanent course in outdoor education. The course drew on the deep experience of Fish and Game Branch conservation officers and the scientific expertise of chief game biologist Jim Hatter and chief fisheries biologist

R.G. McMynn to offer an education in fish and wildlife management and conservation for Vancouver-area hunters and anglers.[41]

Hatter's and McMynn's participation in the night school course was part of a broader public role for government biologists and conservation officers in this period. Outspoken and articulate advocates for wildlife, government biologists operated as both scientists and public communicators, meeting regularly with regional hunting and fishing organizations and even providing firearms safety training in primary schools. Conservation officers and biologists alike contributed columns to the *Wildlife Review*, the popular and freely distributed public newsletter of the BC Game Commission (which was restructured in 1957 to become the Fish and Game Branch). While the tone and scientific content of their columns varied, they typically spoke with one voice on conservation-related topics. In the September 1955 issue of the newsletter, for example, veteran Fernie game warden Jim Osman drew on a combination of experience and research evidence to argue against the destruction of predatory hawks, the majority of which prey primarily on snakes, grasshoppers and gophers, rather than domestic fowl and game birds. Cougars and coyotes, too, were too often blamed for the deaths of winter-killed deer but deserved recognition for their important role in keeping ungulate populations in check: "I have killed 80 cougars and trailed a good many more and have yet to see any of [the] wanton destruction they are blamed for," Osman observed. "It is with a feeling of genuine remorse that I now look up at a cougar sitting in a tree, big-eyed and bewildered, waiting to be shot like a pig in a pen."[42]

Changing attitudes among government biologists and conservation officers like Osman were the product of research on predator-prey relations by Cowan and US biologists. Government conservation officers and biologists, in turn, helped change public perceptions. In 1957, the province amended game regulations to protect most species of hawks and eagles from hunting and trapping without a permit.[43] A massive control program for wolves continued, however, despite evidence that ballooning moose populations were overbrowsing their range in the Interior. By 1961, recognition that the government control program had become even more costly than the bounty system it had replaced contributed to the cessation of poisoning programs in remote areas. The Predator Control Branch was disbanded two years later. Administration of a more minimal predator control program shifted to the regional offices, where conservation officers responded to direct complaints about problem animals.[44]

INITIATIVE PROFILE: The Wildlife Review

In 1954, the BC Game Commission followed the efforts of state fish and game authorities in the US by publishing its first educational newsletter, the *Wildlife Review*. The
first of its kind in Canada, the quarterly newsletter of Game Commission activities
was compiled and edited by former Kamloops game warden W.T. (Bill) Ward with the
purpose of fostering "understanding and wise use of BC's wildlife resources." Ward,
who had worked as an army reporter during the war, captured the attention of Game
Commission headquarters with his local radio program "Conservation Calling" and
mimeographed periodical, the *Game Patrol*, the forerunner to the *Wildlife Review*.

The newsletter reflected sweeping changes in the work of the Game Commission.
Just five years after the first wildlife biologist was hired in 1949, it had expanded to
incorporate twenty permanent biologists: thirteen in fisheries management, five
in game management and two in predatory animal control. Game wardens and
biologists alike recognized that relationships with the public were critical to their
success, contributing to the need for "an accurate, interesting, and simply written
presentation of our wildlife position and problems."

The BC Game Commission
distributed its quarterly newsletter,
the *Wildlife Review*, to a wide
readership from 1954 to 1985,
providing an important vehicle
for communicating changing
ideas about wildlife management.
Cover of *Wildlife Review* 1, no. 9
(August 1957). Image courtesy
of Dennis Demarchi.

RACCOON

Illustrations like this one aided readers in identifying animal tracks. *Wildlife Review* 1, no. 9 (August 1957). Image courtesy of Dennis Demarchi.

Composed of short essays and original artwork by game wardens and biologists, clippings from wildlife periodicals and state game commission publications from south of the border, poetry and pithy conservation maxims, the *Wildlife Review* provided entertaining and informative reading on topics ranging from firearms safety to hunting and tracking techniques to the positive influence of outdoor activity on the province's youth. Short feature essays by provincial biologists demystified the daily work of game and fisheries biologists and communicated the results of recent research in accessible ways. Complementing the direct outreach work of Game Commission biologists to fish and game clubs, the newsletter provided science education for a broader public, debunking long-held assumptions about the harmfulness of predatory birds to domestic livestock and game birds and building knowledge about wildlife behaviour and habitat requirements. As fisheries biologist Alan Martin recalled of his father Patrick Martin's generation of biologists, "their job was just not biology, [it] was public communications and . . . ensuring that there was public trust in the management of . . . public resources."

The *Wildlife Review* was enormously popular, not only among hunters and anglers but also among schoolteachers and youth groups. By the late 1960s, its circulation had grown to 37,000 readers in seventy countries. Biologist Jenny Feick remembered collecting issues as a high school student in Ontario. Reading it, she recalled, "was one of the things that drew me to move out west."[45]

Publication of the newsletter continued under the new Department of Recreation and Conservation and later the BC Ministry of Environment. In 1983, budget cutbacks to the Fish and Wildlife Branch led to the privatization of publication work. The *Wildlife Review* was discontinued two years later, in 1985.[46]

Cover of *The Mammals of British Columbia*, by Ian McTaggart Cowan and Charles J. Guiguet, Natural History Handbook no. 11 (Victoria: BC Provincial Museum, February 1956). Royal BC Museum.

If Fish and Game Branch staff were one source of wildlife education in the 1950s and 1960s, by far the larger proportion fell to institutions like the BC Provincial Museum, naturalists' organizations and fish and game clubs, magazines such as *Game Trails of BC* (1937–early 1950s) and the *Northwest Sportsman* (1945–77), and prolific outdoors columnists including Lee Straight of the *Vancouver Sun* and Mike Crammond of the *Province*.[47] At the BC Provincial Museum, birds and mammals curator Charles Guiguet contributed to the museum's popular series of natural history handbooks with such titles as *The Crows and Their Allies* and *The Shorebirds* in the Birds of British Columbia series. In 1956, Guiguet co-authored the museum's *Mammals of British Columbia* handbook with Ian McTaggart Cowan. Illustrated by Port Alberni falconer and artist Frank Beebe, the natural history handbooks provided an inexpensive source of wildlife education for amateur naturalists, schoolchildren and wildlife enthusiasts across the province.

The Provincial Museum's long history of mutually supportive associations with the province's naturalists' organizations further bolstered its public education goals. Since 1890, when the Natural History Society of

BC Parks chief ranger Bob Boyd and head of interpretation Yorke Edwards at Manning Park Nature House, ca.1960. Edwards Family photograph. Photo courtesy of Jane Edwards and Anne Wills.

British Columbia was established as an independent auxiliary of the museum, naturalists had served as volunteer docents and instructors of natural history programs for Scouts, Guides and other organizations. Beginning in 1957, museum director Clifford Carl organized a federation of the Victoria, Vancouver and Vernon natural history societies to promote natural history interest and education in other parts of the province. In 1962, the federation became the Council of Naturalists (a forerunner to the Federation of BC Naturalists that formed in 1969) with a joint mission of education and conservation to "know nature and keep it worth knowing."

Another significant development for wildlife education was the launch of **BC Parks Naturalist Program** in 1957. Headed by biologist Yorke Edwards, the program grew from a pilot "nature house" in a makeshift tent at Manning Park to a system of nature houses, trails, interpretive signs and naturalist talks in most parts of the province by the late 1960s. The program not only introduced BC residents and visitors to local natural history but also served as an incubator for new generations of naturalists, biologists and wildlife researchers. Prominent BC ornithologists Wayne Campbell and Richard Cannings, for example, spent many formative summers working as park naturalists in BC parks. As the program developed under Edwards's leadership, it attracted thousands of annual visitors to popular nature houses at Manning Park and Miracle Beach. By the time Edwards stepped down in 1967, the program was widely regarded as a model for park education across the country.[48]

Naturalists' organizations would continue to grow and attract new members from the late 1950s into the 1980s, prompted in part by a steady rise in non-consumptive wildlife activities like birdwatching. As binoculars became more affordable and practical field guides more readily accessible in the 1950s, the Vancouver Natural History Society and other regional naturalists' organizations hosted growing numbers of birders and wildlife enthusiasts in regional field trips and educational lectures.[49] Decades of hands-on work to enhance wildlife habitat complemented educational activities. Here the efforts of naturalists' groups aligned most directly with those of rod and gun clubs, both of which had since the early 1920s planted shrubs for birds, cleared fish-spawning beds, and built and cleared nature trails and wildlife-viewing platforms.[50] Until the late 1960s, when recreational organizations became more explicitly pro-hunting or anti-hunting in their focus, "nature-lovers of all kinds" could be found in both types of organizations.[51]

Not surprisingly, UBC zoologist Ian McTaggart Cowan was as influential in the field of public education as he was in other areas of wildlife management and conservation in this period. Picking up on his public education work in his early years with the Provincial Museum, Cowan was an early adopter of television as a medium to promote wildlife conservation and education in the 1950s and '60s. Even before CBC Television's sixty-year-running *The Nature of Things* debuted in 1960, Cowan's popular *Fur and Feathers* series featured explorations of the province's wildlife across fifty-two live episodes in 1955 and 1956. "The approach," Cowan's students and colleagues recalled, "was to confront a youngster with a natural history object that had never been seen before, and provide facts by responding to the child's questions." Three years later, Cowan collaborated with Guiguet to host the award-winning nature series *Web of Life*, which aired on CBC from 1959 to 1963 before being syndicated for British television audiences.[52]

By stimulating young viewers' interest in the natural world around them, Cowan and his contemporaries created important foundations for the environmental movement of the following decade. Cowan's viewers reached adulthood as pressure from resource development activities continued to intensify. Their heightened concern about the effects of logging, mining and industrial pollution on the province's iconic wildlife species helped to support the growth of land conservancy organizations and government habitat conservation initiatives in the 1970s and '80s.

Conclusion: Early Victories

From the mid-1930s until the mid-1960s, public and professional knowledge of wildlife rose in concert with rising threats to wildlife from resource extraction, hydroelectric development, residential and agricultural development, and industrial pollution. Concerns about habitat loss and degradation and declining recreational access led emerging stakeholder federations to articulate an ethic of multiple use for the province's public lands.

Collaboration between conservation organizations, naturalists' groups and government agencies like the Canadian Wildlife Service and the BC Fish and Wildlife Branch produced some important conservation victories in this period, including migratory bird sanctuaries at Vaseux Lake and the Fraser River delta, the Creston Valley Wildlife Management Area on the Kootenay River floodplain (which today forms the province's largest complex of managed waterfowl habitat), international cooperation in the conservation of California bighorn sheep and advances in range management to accommodate forage for wildlife.

In the years ahead, the rise of anti-hunting sentiment in urban areas, combined with waning numbers of hunters in the province, would lead government agencies to broaden their focus from game species to a much wider definition of wildlife. New interest groups, and new agendas, would shape fish and wildlife management objectives in the province in the 1970s and 1980s.

— PART FOUR —

MAKING SPACE
FOR WILDLIFE,
1966–1991

8

Access and Alienation
Emerging Threats to Wildlife

By the late 1960s, rising development pressure, combined with heightened public consciousness and very limited mechanisms for wildlife habitat protection, had created the conditions for a series of seemingly intractable land use conflicts in the southern half of the province. At the same time, the W.A.C. Bennett government's provincewide investments into rail and highway development spurred the rapid expansion of forestry and mining operations into the BC Interior. The effects of these developments on the province's wildlife coalesced into two central concerns. The first revolved around the question of access to formerly isolated areas. Rail and highway development facilitated access not only to "stranded resources" but also to fish and game species previously protected (from hunters and predators alike) by the challenges of reaching them across difficult, unroaded terrain. Along with the growing availability of off-road vehicles and ever-more-efficient hunting and fishing technologies, access considerations became a perennial challenge for new generations of wildlife managers. The second concern centred on the problem of land alienation: the conversion of wildlife habitat on public lands to private residential, agricultural and commercial holdings. Primarily a southern phenomenon, land alienation concerns mobilized the development of creative solutions to acquire and protect wildlife habitat in the 1970s and 1980s.

This chapter documents a gradual shift within provincial resource agencies from their historical roles as allocators of resources to more active, collaborative managers of conflicting resource uses. For government biologists and fish and wildlife advocates, this shift materialized in a growing emphasis on wildlife habitat in research, policy and enforcement. As habitat loss and degradation threatened animal abundance, fish and wildlife managers responded by expanding regulations to reduce harvest levels and associated recreational opportunities. Some responses, such as adjustments to bag and creel limits and open season durations, followed conservation practices established in the late nineteenth century. Others introduced new approaches, including lottery systems for hunting and angling opportunities. Meanwhile, the growing intensity and complexity of land use conflicts in the southern reaches of the province prompted the first experiments in inter-agency consultation and land use planning, as well as, beyond government, the establishment of the province's first land conservancies.

The "Cascading Effects of Access"

Across the province, the construction of new bridges, highways, rail lines and resource roads facilitated recreational access to previously unroaded areas. In the north, the completion of the Stewart-Cassiar Highway in 1972 linked the province's northwest with the Alaska Highway in the northeast. Together with rail extensions from Prince George to Fort Nelson in the northeast and Fort St. James in the northwest, highway development furthered Premier Bennett's vision of "opening the vast untapped BC north" to agricultural and resource development.[1] Rail and road extensions led to a surge of mineral exploration in the northeast. They also facilitated access for hunters, anglers and recreationalists.

British Columbia's human population more than doubled between 1941 and 1966, from roughly 818,000 to almost 1.9 million.[2] Growing hunting and angling pressure accompanied these changes, facilitated by rising affluence, leisure time and expanding road and camping infrastructure. The number of licensed resident hunters more than doubled between 1947 and 1966, peaking at 7.5 per cent of the total population in 1961. Hunter numbers continued to climb with the province's population until 1981, which marked the beginning of a three-decade decline in hunter numbers and representation in the total population. Resident angler numbers expanded even more rapidly, nearly quadrupling between 1947 and 1966 and continuing to climb before levelling off in the early 1980s.[3]

Technological advancements exacerbated these trends of road proliferation and rising numbers of recreationalists. By the mid-1960s, the growing availability of portable trail bikes, snowmobiles and jet boats expanded

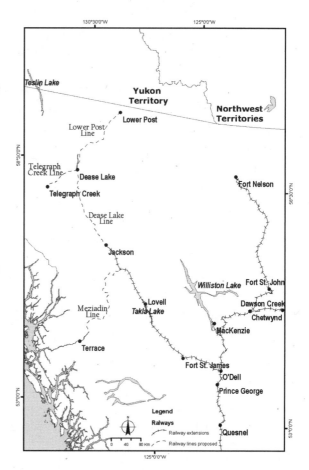

Railway extensions in northern British Columbia completed or proposed in the late 1960s and 1970s

Source: Lawrence D. Taylor, "The Bennett Government's Pacific Northern Railway Project and the Development of British Columbia's 'Hinterland,'" *BC Studies*, no. 175 (Autumn 2012): 52. Map courtesy of Lawrence D. Taylor and *BC Studies*.

existing off-road vehicle options, allowing hunters and anglers to traverse greater distances and more challenging terrain. Advances in hunting and fishing equipment worked alongside vehicle technologies to improve the efficiency and success of the chase. As Bob Hooton has shown for freshwater fisheries in the province, "ever more effective and efficient fishing equipment made each generation of anglers a greater harvesting force than ever before."[4]

These "cascading effects of access" can be seen in the nested consequences of BC Rail's discontinued Dease Lake Extension. Abandoned in 1977 owing to cost overruns and falling mineral prices, BC Rail's partially constructed Dease Lake Extension left over 400 kilometres of abandoned track and roughly 200 kilometres of cleared and graded railbed south of

Dease Lake in the province's northwest. While the trains would turn back at Fort St. James, the abandoned and unmonitored railbed "allowed vehicular access to an area previously only accessible by helicopter or float plane, on foot or on horseback."[5] Fish and Wildlife Branch officials warned in their submission to the 1977 McKenzie Commission that "within a 20 minute walk from the rail grade along the Klappan River, one can be amongst Stone's sheep and mountain goats."[6] The railbed also bordered the new Spatsizi Provincial Park, one of the province's most important remaining habitats for woodland caribou.

As hunting and guiding activity increased along the corridor, recognition of its limited enforcement capacity in the region led the Branch to impose a temporary 200-kilometre no-hunting zone along the length of the Dease Lake Extension. Hunters, however, were not the only threat to wildlife along newly created access corridors. Wolves and other predators also profited from such linear efficiencies, using rail grades and resource roads to access caribou herds previously insulated from predation by deep snow and challenging terrain. Across the province, the proliferation of such corridors of movement—roads, rail and seismic lines—continue to produce "cascading effects of access," providing expanded opportunities for recreationalists, resident hunters, guide outfitters and other tourism operators while at the same time constraining opportunities for refuge for the province's wildlife.

SPECIES PROFILE: Woodland Caribou (*Rangifer tarandus caribou*)

In 1982, Ian McTaggart Cowan singled out woodland caribou as the "most seriously depleted large ungulate in British Columbia." The Dawson's subspecies (*Rangifer tarandus dawsoni*), found only on Graham Island in Haida Gwaii, had succumbed to climate-induced habitat change and hunting pressure and gone extinct as early as the 1920s. By the 1980s, most of the province's fifty-four distinct woodland caribou herds were showing signs of serious decline, and several herds in the Selkirk and Purcell ranges of the province's southeast were unlikely to recover. While early twentieth-century population declines could generally be attributed to a combination of overhunting and predation, declines from mid-century on were increasingly understood as the product of habitat loss and fragmentation, especially in the south.[7]

Woodland caribou herd locations in British Columbia, 2021

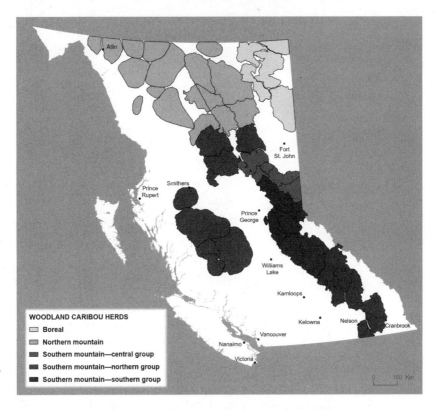

Data source: Provincial Caribou Recovery Program, 2021 herd boundaries. Map by GeoBC, 2022.

All caribou in British Columbia are woodland caribou. Distinguished from other caribou subspecies in Canada by their larger size, relatively short migration distances and dependence on forest or "woodland" habitat, woodland caribou are classified by the province into four major population units: southern mountain, central mountain, northern mountain and boreal. Southern mountain caribou inhabit the deep-snow forests of central BC. Unlike the province's other mountain caribou populations, most of which migrate between low-elevation winter ranges and higher-elevation summer ranges, they occupy high-elevation subalpine forests for much of the winter. Boreal caribou of the province's northeast differ from mountain caribou in that they remain in boreal forests year-round instead of migrating to higher elevations in winter.[8]

If woodland caribou were the most threatened of the province's large mammals, they were also, paradoxically, one of the most understood. Research on the province's most threatened southern populations began in the early 1950s, when wildlife biologists Yorke Edwards and Ralph Ritcey made important breakthroughs in understanding the survival strategies of southern mountain caribou in the wet-belt forests of eastern British Columbia. With assistance from hunting guide Thorbjorn "Ted" Halset and forester Bob Miller, Edwards and Ritcey established the woodland caribou's dependence on mature or old-growth forests through a series of studies in Wells Gray Park.[9] Among the first wildlife studies in the province to employ aerial surveys, their research determined that caribou in the park were high above the treeline in summer and winter, but "in spring and fall the key to survival in times of soft snow seemed to be the old forest deep in the basin about Murtle Lake. There they could move and find food by pawing through the snow or by eating the beard-lichens from old trees." Edwards concluded in a 1981 presentation, "Old forests in the valleys and up the slopes [are] a necessity in these mountains, if there [are] to be caribou."[10]

Biologist Ted Antifeau built on this work in the late 1980s through an intensive study of caribou in the North Thompson River watershed. His research underlined that large, contiguous areas of high-elevation old-growth forests are critically important to caribou survival. In winter, he found, caribou depended "almost entirely" on a single food source: "the lichens which grow on old stands of trees found at high elevations." Each animal required about 4.5 kilograms of lichen a day. Adapted to a landscape of severe climates and slow vegetation growth, caribou also differed from other deer species in grazing lightly, rather than intensively, over large areas. Their movements were both more extensive—over home ranges as large as seven hundred square kilometres—and more complex. At different times of year animals moved not only vertically, from alpine tundra to subalpine forest, but also horizontally, in migrations east and west. Biologists confirmed what Indigenous and non-Indigenous hunters and guide outfitters had long observed: mountain caribou relied on big spaces and a diversity of landscapes, from high-elevation mature forests to lower-elevation movement corridors.[11]

The problem for caribou survival was not overhunting—for many southern mountain herds, hunting had been closed completely since the early 1970s. While illegal kills put pressure on dwindling populations, the main cause of declining caribou numbers was habitat loss resulting from wildfire and human land uses like mining, forestry and ranching. Logging of subalpine forests had accelerated in the late 1970s, rapidly removing winter food sources. In the North Thompson watershed, extensive high-elevation logging meant there were "no large undeveloped drain-ages available to move into as alternatives." As Edwards observed, logging of this kind turned "valley slopes into places fit for fireweed and gophers, but useless to caribou. The forest might return, but probably not the *old* forest."[12]

If present cutting rates continued, Ritcey warned in 1980 in his role as regional wildlife biologist for the Kamloops region, in as little as twenty years "there would be no caribou in south-central BC outside of Wells Gray Park"—and even those within the park would be endangered by crossing park boundaries into areas desig-nated for logging.[13] Since 1965, inventories of southern mountain herds at five-year intervals revealed diminishing populations, with herds declining in steep drops af-ter periods of relative stability. The eventual extirpation of herds from parts of their historical range and the diminishment of others to unsustainable levels reflected ever-mounting fragility for the southern mountain population as a whole. Smaller numbers of animals also reduced a herd's chances of surviving the typical risks in the lives of wild animals: avalanches in winter, predation, injury.[14]

Transportation and energy corridors, as biologists were beginning to under-stand, presented problems of their own. Linear corridors like roads and pipelines—and, in the northeast, seismic lines—interfered with caribou survival strategies. Hunters and recreationalists used resource access roads to penetrate previously inaccessible areas with all-terrain vehicles and snowmobiles. And animal predators found similar efficiencies, travelling linear corridors to access caribou herds once protected by the deep winter snows of unroaded high-elevation and boreal forests. For disturbance-sensitive animals with slow reproduction rates, the cumulative threats and stressors have generally proved too great.

Despite high levels of understanding among scientists and government biol-ogists of the behaviours and habitat requirements of the province's threatened southern mountain caribou herds, little has been achieved toward their protection. Regional negotiations between the Fish and Wildlife Branch and the Forest Service, beginning in 1973, were not successful in maintaining sufficient habitat to support existing caribou populations. A steering committee established in 1978 by the Environment and Land Use Committee failed to reach agreement on tabled options for caribou protection. Proposed selective logging prescriptions in subalpine forests were abandoned as impractical and still overly destructive of forest lichens.[15] As Ritcey observed, "you can [adjust] logging practices to benefit moose or deer, but you can't do that with caribou."[16]

In the north, studies of the relationship between caribou survival and wolf con-trol by biologists Tom Bergerud and John Elliot supported interventions to reduce wolf numbers in the mid-1980s. Elliot and Bergerud were the first managers to link caribou declines with high moose populations that generated correspondingly high numbers of wolves.[17] The links were not as clear in other parts of the province, however, where historical fluctuations in caribou populations occurred seemingly independently of wolf and moose population levels.[18] As scientific data expanded through the 1990s, wildlife biologists like Bruce McLellan came to see that the out-sized role of predation could not easily be dismissed. The loss of old-growth forests to large-scale logging not only removed refuge and important food sources but also recalibrated predator-prey dynamics. Younger forests providing more browse for moose and deer led to higher numbers of wolves and cougars. When a hard winter brought these "alternate prey" numbers down, predators switched to caribou. As McLellan explains, "caribou aren't fast like a deer. They're not strong like a moose. They're just easy to kill once you find them." For an animal whose anti-predator strategy was to live where there is no other prey, the complex effects of large-scale ecosystem change have proved lethal.[19]

Despite localized predator control initiatives and several important protected area designations, almost all of the province's woodland caribou herds had declined significantly by 2000. In 2003, BC's southern mountain and boreal caribou popu-lations were listed as threatened under the federal Species at Risk Act; by 2014, the Committee on the Status of Endangered Wildlife in Canada had designated the southern herds as endangered. Precipitous declines among southern moun-tain caribou herds over the past twenty years, including the extirpation of seven of thirty-one herds, prompted the federal and provincial governments to implement emergency measures, including snowmobile closures in caribou habitats, wolf and cougar control, reductions in alternate prey like moose, penning and protection of pregnant females and translocation of caribou to areas with smaller populations. In 2017, the province announced the multi-year Provincial Caribou Recovery Program with the goal of partnering with First Nations communities in habitat restoration and population recovery.[20]

The elusiveness of caribou recovery in BC to date is matched by experiences elsewhere: woodland caribou have declined across Canada in the same period, and no Canadian jurisdiction has yet implemented a program that has demonstrated sustained success at recovering caribou. For McLellan, rescuing small and isolat-ed caribou populations will require "intensive predator and prey management, for-ever." We have to ask ourselves, he warns, "what are we managing for? Do we want an ecosystem where we've got some caribou and very few moose, deer, wolves, cougars? Or do we want an ecosystem that's got no caribou and all kinds of moose and deer and cougars and wolves?" We cannot have it both ways.[21] For the biologists and First Nations involved in the rescue effort, however, the goal of recovering one of Canada's most iconic species and a mainstay of northern Indigenous cultures for thousands of years is worth the effort.

Responses: Regulating Access to Fish and Wildlife

As valued fish and game populations faced the double threat of habitat loss and heightened hunting and angling pressure, fish and wildlife managers sought to broaden their tool kits beyond bag limits and open season durations. Two regulatory interventions in 1974 aimed to reduce hunting pressure by limiting opportunity and emphasizing the value of the hunting experience over the success of the hunt. The first, for non-resident hunters, saw the replacement of the existing trophy system with a species-licence system. Hunters paid a fee for an opportunity to hunt, regardless of their success, rather than paying a trophy fee. The second, for resident hunters, introduced **limited entry hunting (LEH)**. The LEH system allocated hunting opportunities through a random draw in areas where hunter demand exceeded the availability of a particular species.[22] First introduced for grizzly bears in the Kootenays and southern Interior, the LEH system gave wildlife managers greater control over the number of hunters and the type and sex of species hunted in a particular area.

The success of this trial LEH initiative in reducing pressure on threatened grizzly populations led to the expansion of the system for other species.[23] On Vancouver Island, for example, the implementation of limited entry hunting for Roosevelt elk in 1977 allowed biologists to partially reopen hunting for a species whose declining numbers had required successive closed seasons since the late 1960s. The successful translocation of elk into more suitable habitat on Vancouver Island and the Lower Mainland over the same period also contributed to their recovery. In the decades since, collective management between the Fish and Wildlife Branch and North Island First Nations has seen Roosevelt elk populations rebound to more than seven thousand animals, enough to sustain an annual hunt by tribal members.[24] For the former BC chief of wildlife management, Glen Smith, who had lamented game management practices that doled out a diminishing resource like a "Salvation Army soup kitchen," the LEH system marked

Anglers casting for steelhead (*Oncorhynchus mykiss*) on the Skeena River near Moricetown, 1967. Province of British Columbia, Special Services Branch. Royal BC Museum, I-11693.

an important transition from wildlife allocation to a more robust form of wildlife management, one that considered the limitations of a changing land base, availability of forage and predator-prey relationships in the allocation of hunting privileges.

Fisheries managers also adopted new strategies in this period in an effort to reduce pressure on valued fish populations. At issue was not only the sustainability of the catch but also the quality of the angling experience. Like other popular sport fishing destinations around the world, BC's reputation for world-class stream fishing attracted rising numbers of anglers from within and beyond the province. Crowding on premier streams—for example, the Salmon River on Vancouver Island and the Dean River on the province's central coast—heightened competition among anglers and compromised both the sustainability and quality of the sport. Crowding concerns were especially pronounced on BC's steelhead streams. Between 1966 and 1990, rising demand for limited wild steelhead populations prompted a succession of regulatory responses, each more restrictive than the last.

Annual catch limits dropped from forty steelhead per angler provincewide in 1966 to twenty in 1977 and ten in 1981. By 1976, the precarity of steelhead numbers on five Vancouver Island streams led the province to introduce its first **catch and release (C&R)** regulations for summer anglers. Year-round C&R orders banning bait and prohibiting all but single barbless hooks covered all Vancouver Island steelhead streams by 1980. Similar regulations later blanketed highly productive northern steelhead rivers like the Nass and the Skeena; they extended provincewide by 2007.[25] What was initially viewed as a promising solution for rising demand and limited fish, however, has received criticism in recent years for the physical stress it places on fish that are often caught and released multiple times.

As restrictions on catch limits and methods tightened over the 1970s and 1980s, tensions escalated between resident anglers and a new class of angling guides and their out-of-province clientele. From the introduction of "small game and angling" guide licences in 1966, guide numbers had swelled by 1990 to over three hundred angling guides and almost two hundred assistant guides, the majority operating in the Skeena River watershed.[26] Compared with their hunting guide counterparts, angling guides enjoyed a larger clientele and fewer restrictions to the area of their operations.[27] Early efforts to regulate guiding activity began in 1974, when BC required non-resident anglers to purchase an additional Special Rivers Licence to access thirteen "exceptional quality" steelhead rivers. In 1987, fisheries managers borrowed from hunting policy to create the first limited entry fishery for non-Canadian steelhead anglers on the Upper Dean River.

Licence fees and creel limits proved insufficient, however, in addressing rising pressures on the fish from angler competition, habitat loss and commercial fisheries bycatch. In 1990, the introduction of a more comprehensive **classified waters** system identified forty-two highly productive steelhead and trout streams in wilderness or semi-wilderness settings (mostly in the Skeena region) for special management. The new system, modelled on a similar program in New Brunswick, capped the number of angling guide licences and client days ("rod-days") on each classified stream, giving priority to licensed resident anglers.[28]

In the three decades since its creation, surcharges from the classified waters licence have supported investments in trout research and conservation under the administration of the Habitat Conservation Trust Foundation (HCTF). The River Guardian Program on the Dean River and other classified waters, for example, has produced over thirty years of "catch and effort" data from anglers that have contributed to the maintenance of world-class fishing experiences. The management approach for the Dean River has served as a model for other jurisdictions, especially as angler pressure has increased.[29] By combining classified waters designation with a limited entry fishery for non-guided, non-Canadian anglers, fisheries managers have privileged resident anglers on the Dean while allowing for more informed and responsive management. Perilously low steelhead returns on the Skeena, Thompson and Chilcotin rivers in recent years suggest that similar interventions will be necessary on other steelhead rivers to protect threatened runs from extirpation.[30]

As fish and wildlife managers struggled to manage increasing demand on fluctuating animal populations, competing land use interests in the southern half of the province generated new commitments to planning and coordination within government and the establishment of a new generation of non-governmental land and wildlife protection organizations.

INITIATIVE PROFILE: Wildlife Crossings

The proliferation of roads across BC's landscape brought steady increases in the number of vehicle-wildlife collisions. Usually fatal for wildlife, and sometimes for drivers as well, collisions increased dramatically with new road and highway construction between the 1960s and 1990s. In response to these trends, the province's transportation ministry expanded its system of wildlife warning signs in areas with high wildlife movement. Ongoing threats to drivers and animals led the ministry to consider more effective wildlife exclusion fencing and crossing structures for new highway developments. Following the successful implementation of wildlife overpasses in Europe and the US in the 1960s and 1970s, BC designed and installed Canada's first system of wildlife crossings on the new Coquihalla Highway and on the "Okanagan Connector" between Merritt and Peachland in the late 1980s.[31] Subsequent wildlife exclusion systems on Highway 1 in the Kicking Horse Canyon and on Vancouver Island's Inland Highway have combined roadside fencing, overpasses and underpasses, and one-way gates or "jump-outs" to allow animals trapped on the highway to exit. Together, these systems constitute the largest network of wildlife exclusion works on highways in North America. Placed strategically

A male white-tailed deer (*Odocoileus virginianus*) takes advantage of a wildlife overpass
to cross Highway 97C (the Okanagan Connector) near Peachland, 2019. Built in 1989,
the Trepanier Wildlife Overpass was the first wildlife overpass constructed in Canada.
© Province of British Columbia. All rights reserved. Photo reproduced with permission
from the Province of British Columbia.

along existing wildlife movement corridors, they reduce wildlife collisions by an
estimated 80 to 90 per cent of what they would otherwise be.[32]

Retrofitting existing highways is more costly and challenging. To date, the ministry has avoided large-scale wildlife exclusion work on existing highways. Some
important exceptions exist, such as the collaboration in 1999 between the Ministry
of Transportation, the Insurance Corporation of BC and two area fish and game
associations to construct a wildlife exclusion fence along Highway 97 between
Summerland and Peachland.[33] However, in the Elk Valley in the East Kootenay, one
of the province's most significant wildlife corridors, the CPR line and the adjacent
two-lane Crowsnest Highway (Highway 3) see an average of two hundred collisions
with elk, grizzly bears and other large mammals every year.

In 2010, a team of East Kootenay conservationists and road ecology experts—
including Tony Clevenger, whose research informed the development of Banff
National Park's famed system of wildlife overpasses and underpasses—came together to imagine a solution. Over the next decade, planning and consultation for

the "Reconnecting the Rockies" project drew on the knowledge of area hunters and conservation organizations, the Ktunaxa Nation and professional staff from the province's transportation and natural resources ministries. Information from a companion citizen science initiative, which supplemented government roadkill data with wildlife sightings digitally logged by Elk Valley motorists, helped to identify sections of the road with high wildlife activity.

In 2021, the province broke ground on the first phase of an ambitious wildlife crossing system that will incorporate roadside fencing and nine crossing locations along a thirty-six-kilometre stretch of Highway 3. At the centre of the initiative is a fifty-metre-wide wildlife overpass—the first of its size in the province—that will span the highway and rail line west of the BC-Alberta border. When completed, the project will not only prevent costly collisions for drivers and wildlife but also reconnect critical cross-border wildlife habitat across the Crown of the Continent ecosystem.[34]

"The Squeeze": Land Use Conflicts of the 1960s and 1970s

Wildlife managers and historians have described the period from the mid-1960s to early 1970s as an "era of confrontation" surrounding conflicting land uses in the province. Until the early 1970s, provincial resource ministries took a siloed approach to resource allocation decisions. Existing legislation provided little incentive to assess other values on the landscape: neither the Wildlife Act nor the Forest Act, for example, contained provisions to require consideration of wildlife in resource allocation decisions. Within the regions, few formal mechanisms existed for coordination and consultation among government agencies and between government jurisdictions.

As the province's southern population continued to swell, land alienations—that is, the sale and privatization of Crown land for residential or commercial use—expanded at an alarming rate. Pressures were especially intense within the province's limited and highly valuable low-elevation valleys, riparian corridors and estuaries. Critical to wildlife populations, these environments were also highly sought after for human uses ranging from residential subdivisions, farms and marinas to hydroelectric reservoirs and logging and mining operations. UBC forest ecologist Fred Bunnell described the mounting pressures on high-value wildlife and human habitat in this period as "the squeeze," noting the tendency to "consistently

[take] land or habitat away from wildlife, through our actions big and small."[35] For naturalists and fish and game clubs, the growing frequency and rapidity of land alienations was especially distressing given the absence of any coordinated land use planning.

Places like the Rocky Mountain Trench of the East Kootenay, roughly 202,000 hectares of grassy mountain slopes and forested valley bottoms in the southeast corner of the province, epitomized the effects of "the squeeze." Once richly productive Ktunaxa hunting grounds, the Trench's wildlife-supporting grasslands were threatened by overgrazing of domestic livestock by the 1960s. By 1973, massive losses of productive valley-bottom land to hydroelectric development (the Kinbasket and Koocanusa reservoirs together occupy almost half of the southern portion of the Trench) and ongoing land alienations for residential and commercial purposes dramatically reduced ungulate winter ranges and valuable riparian habitat. On the remaining land base, government aims to "maximize wood fibre, livestock, wildlife and recreation" led to heightened competition for land and resources. These factors, according to former regional wildlife biologist Ray Demarchi, made the East Kootenay "one of the most controversial if not hostile environments in which to practice forestry, operate a cattle ranch or to manage range or wildlife in the province."[36] The absence of a regional land use plan to guide decision-making, combined with the paucity of legislative remedies to protect land from alienation, created an atmosphere of sequential and overlapping battles for wildlife and other resources on a shrinking land base.

Another highly productive ecosystem subjected to the "squeeze" of competing land uses was the province's estuaries. Richly productive coastal areas where fresh water from rivers mixes with salt water from the ocean, estuaries serve as vital nursery and rearing habitat for juvenile fish and important resting and wintering habitat for migratory waterfowl, among other species. As retired Canadian Wildlife Service biologist Neil Dawe explains, "estuaries support a tremendous amount of wildlife. . . . BC has the largest population of wintering [migratory] birds in Canada, and they are dependent on these estuaries. . . . When the inland lakes and marshes and agricultural fields are frozen, [estuaries are] the only place that's open that has a lot of food."[37]

Comprising just over 2 per cent of BC's coastline, estuaries are naturally rare.[38] And yet they also make ideal sites for human developments such as log sorts, pulp mills, shipping terminals and marinas. A case in point is the Lower Mainland's Fraser River estuary, one of the most significant rearing habitats for the province's salmon fishery and supporting habitat for Canada's largest wintering waterfowl population.[39] In the early 1970s, a proposal by the Vancouver Airport Authority to build a new runway in the estuary highlighted the deteriorating condition of the Fraser River wetlands and prompted calls for a moratorium on development until protective measures could be put in place. In both the East Kootenay and the Lower Mainland, as we shall see, acute development pressures in critical fish and wildlife habitats led to some important early steps in habitat protection and land use planning.

These developments occurred against a backdrop of rising public discontent about the effects of urban expansion, infrastructure development and resource extraction on the province's celebrated natural landscapes. Beginning in the late 1960s, a strong anti-development sentiment emerged within the urban areas of the southern coast and pockets of the southern Interior. As W.A.C. Bennett's biographer David Mitchell writes of this period, "before the late 1960s, the word 'environment' had never appeared in the lexicon of B.C. politics. Suddenly, numerous groups were agitating for pollution control and improved conservation of natural resources" with support from the media and opposition parties.[40] A generation of largely urban, middle-class outdoor enthusiasts was prepared to fight for greater protection of natural landscapes within driving range of the province's cities. In 1969, for example, the Run Out Skagit Spoilers (ROSS) Committee organized to oppose Seattle City Light's plans to raise its Ross dam in Washington State and flood the Skagit Valley east of Vancouver. The movement assembled an extraordinarily broad coalition of outdoor recreation and environmental groups, churches, unions and municipal governments to win park protection for the Skagit Valley.[41] Other citizen-led campaigns, like the broad constituency of West Kootenay residents who fought to protect the Purcell Wilderness in the early 1970s, demonstrated the breadth of public concern for environmental protection in different parts of the province.

Environmental and wilderness movements drew on the established work of the two historic constituent groups for wildlife protection: naturalist organizations and fish and game clubs. Both groups had not only grown dramatically in numbers by the early 1970s but also become more organized in support of habitat protection. As UBC zoologist Ian McTaggart Cowan wrote in a *Vancouver Sun* op-ed in 1972, "while our wildlife land has been decreasing in area and in quality, there has been an unprecedented surge of interest in wild species of birds and mammals." Pointing to provincial statistics, Cowan noted a 70 per cent increase in hunters and fishermen since 1945 and estimated at least a fivefold increase in the number of amateur naturalists.

The establishment of the **Federation of BC Naturalists** in 1969 reflected this enormous growth in local club memberships and their desire for co-ordinated advocacy to protect threatened species and habitats. In Cowan's assessment, "the advent of the organized naturalist group" meant that wildlife conservation was "no longer the 'special province' of the hunter."[42] Guide-outfitting organizations also federated in this period: the creation of the **Guide Outfitters Association of British Columbia** in 1966 provided a provincial platform for guide-outfitter interests, including concerns about the impact of wildlife habitat loss and degradation on the industry. At the same time, the well-established BC Wildlife Federation shifted its focus from narrower hunter and fisher advocacy, such as season dates and bag limits, to advocate for broader environmental protections.

Vancouver-based organizations such as the Society Promoting Environmental Conservation (SPEC) and the Sierra Club of British Columbia, both launched in 1969, and Greenpeace, launched in 1971, marked the beginning of a broader environmentalism. These nascent environmental organizations were not simply an outgrowth of earlier movements to protect wildlife. Instead, they captured the energy of a growing constituency of younger British Columbians concerned with the inherent value of "wilderness" and intact ecosystems, for their own sake. They coalesced around a range of environmental threats: clearcut logging, flooding for hydroelectric development, pollution of urban waterways, and others.

Unlike their fish and game and naturalist forebears, these organizations employed much more confrontational tactics to capture public interest and shame offenders. In 1970, for example, SPEC members dressed in seventeenth-century costumes staged a proclamation against forestry company MacMillan Bloedel, depicting the company as the "Tyrannosaurus Rex—King of Polluters" for its discharge of toxic pulp-mill effluents into the province's tidal and freshwater systems. Greenpeace would take provocative, theatrical activism to a new level in its campaigns against nuclear testing, commercial whaling and fur-seal hunting in the years to come. Campaigns like this galvanized public concern for commercial hunting and environmental degradation, but they also seeded divisions between urban environmentalists and typically more rural fish and game advocates, many of whom earned their livelihoods through resource development industries.

Responses: Early Habitat Protection and Land Use Planning Initiatives

Initial government responses to demands for environmental protection were tone-deaf at best. "How can you make an omelette without breaking a few eggs?" Bennett's minister of highways, Phil Gaglardi, famously quipped in response to concerns about the ecological impacts of development.[43] By positioning wilderness and wildlife protection as an impediment to progress, Bennett and his cabinet failed to register what had been a profound shift in public sentiment. The growing role of the media in shaping and amplifying issues of public concern in this period also pressured politicians to act.

Significantly, however, it was the intractable land use conflicts of the period, and not environmental advocacy per se, that led to legislative and policy changes within government. Land use conflicts like those of the East Kootenay Trench pitted historically legitimate resource licensees and government resource agencies against each other, prompting what legal historian Michael Begg describes as a slow transition from a "land allocation" to a "land management" bureaucracy.[44] Beginning in the mid-1960s, two distinct but complementary responses to land use conflicts began to take shape within and beyond government: one approach enabled new forms of protection or acquisition of threatened wildlife habitats; the other aimed to develop land use planning and coordination systems to ensure the best use of resources across BC's public land base.

Protection and Acquisition of Threatened Habitats

Prior to the mid-1960s, few formal mechanisms existed to protect wildlife habitat from development. Provincially designated game reserves, for example, did not preclude logging or mineral extraction, and federally designated migratory bird sanctuaries prohibited shooting but provided no protection for waterfowl habitat. Even parks offered incomplete and insecure protection. Not only had the province excised 40 per cent of its park land base through the 1950s to facilitate resource development, but parks themselves had historically been conceived primarily for their economic value as symbols of the province's resource wealth and attractions for wealthy (and typically non-resident) tourists. This was true for both the large national parks established in the Rockies in the late nineteenth and early twentieth centuries and the early provincial parks of the 1910s and '20s. As historians Michael Begg and Ben Bradley have pointed out, the importance of parks as spaces for public recreation did not become significant until the 1950s, when highway developments made them more accessible to a larger number of people.[45] The small roadside provincial parks created through the 1950s and '60s served tourism and recreation interests first and foremost; there was "almost no thought of preserving land for its inherent value."[46]

The first winds of change came in 1965 with the passing of a new and more protective Park Act. The act realigned Parks Branch objectives by relocating it from the Ministry of Lands and Forests to the more conservation-oriented Department of Recreation and Conservation. Significantly, it allowed for the creation of larger parks with more clearly defined protections from resource exploitation activities. For the first time, the Parks Branch received authority to determine economic activity in parks through a permit system. A clarification of park classifications prohibited resource extraction or disturbance in large Class A and smaller, locally managed Class C parks "unless necessary for the preservation of recreation values." Only Class B parks would continue to permit mining, logging and other forms of development, with the proviso that they not impinge on the recreational values of the park.[47] Furthermore, two new designations—"recreation area" and "nature conservancy area"—allowed for the identification and protection of valued recreation and habitat sites within park boundaries. In Strathcona Provincial Park, for example, where mining exploration and industrial activities continued to mobilize conservationists, conservancy designations came to protect most of the valued recreational areas; mining activities were eventually confined to a small area of the park under Class B designation.[48] Even nature conservancy designations, however, continued to privilege recreational uses over ecological considerations.

In 1968, the Canadian Wildlife Service became the first government agency operating in the province to implement wildlife habitat protection measures. Its **National Wildlife Area** program set out to address the deficiencies of existing migratory bird sanctuary legislation by enabling federal acquisition of wildlife habitat under the 1973 Canada Wildlife Act. By the end of the 1970s, the CWS had designated seven national wildlife areas in British Columbia, including the Alaksen National Wildlife Area in the Fraser River delta and the Vaseux-Bighorn National Wildlife Area in the threatened Okanagan-Similkameen region.[49] Dedicated lobbying by grassroots naturalist and hunting organizations played an important role in the creation of these wildlife areas. In the case of Vaseux-Bighorn, the Okanagan-Similkameen Parks Society—founded in 1966 by South Okanagan naturalists Katy Madsen, Steve Cannings and others—rallied to purchase critical winter range for California bighorn sheep at Vaseux Lake, later selling these lands to CWS. The group went on to secure a number of important victories for threatened grassland and desert habitat in the South Okanagan, including Okanagan Mountain and Cathedral provincial parks.[50]

Pressures within and outside of government led the Bennett administration to follow suit, enacting two pieces of legislation in the early 1970s that provided new mechanisms for habitat protection. The first, the **Ecological Reserve Act** of 1971, allowed for the designation and protection of areas of ecological significance.[51] The second, the **Green Belt Protection Fund Act** of 1972, enabled government to purchase and protect private lands from urban sprawl. Greenbelt reserves, as they came to be known, could be used for agricultural purposes or wildlife habitat acquisitions.[52] Unlike the greenbelt legislation, which was used primarily to acquire land for trails and parks in cities, the Ecological Reserve Act charted a lasting and significant legacy for habitat protection in the province. The first of its kind in Canada, it set the foundation for what would become the world's most comprehensive ecological reserves system.

Vladimir Krajina and the Creation of BC's Ecological Reserves Program

The ecological reserves program was long in the making. In 1965, UBC botanist Vladimir Krajina published what quickly became a highly influential classification system for the province's ecosystems.[53] The result of over forty years of dedicated research, Krajina's system used plant abundance and distribution, climate and soil characteristics to identify eleven distinct biogeoclimatic zones throughout the province.[54]

UBC botanist Vladimir
Krajina recording
observations at a bog
on Haida Gwaii, ca.1971.
Photo courtesy of
Bristol Foster.

Deeply concerned about the pace and destructiveness of logging operations in the 1950s and '60s, Krajina drew on his research to launch what
his students have described as a "one-man crusade" to create an ecological
reserves system as a "genetic bank" of the province's extraordinary
ecological diversity.

In 1969, Krajina and UBC zoologist Ian McTaggart Cowan succeeded
in convincing Minister of Lands and Forests Ray Williston to respond to
an international initiative to create a worldwide system of representative
ecosystems.[55] A series of biologically significant sites identified for this
project became the nucleus of the ecological reserves program. Research
contributions from Provincial Museum biologists Bristol Foster and Charles
Guiguet saw the inclusion of areas of specific scientific interest for birds and
mammals, including critical nesting habitat for the province's seabirds.[56]
In 1971, Williston capitalized on the significance of BC's centennial to
announce the creation of the first twenty-nine sites in what would become
a living museum of the province's natural heritage. By 1975, the province's

Ecological reserves program
coordinator Bristol Foster at
Solander Island Ecological
Reserve, 1976. Photo by R.
Wayne Campbell. Photo
courtesy of the Biodiversity
Centre for Wildlife Studies.

Lands Branch would "set aside one hundred distinctive ecosystems for
present and future scientific study"; the number of sites has since climbed
to a total of 154 reserves across the province (see plate 8).[57]

The ecological reserves program certainly generated excitement from a
scientific standpoint, providing as it did a mechanism to protect, study and
monitor threatened ecosystems and rare or endangered plants and animals
and to educate the public about their significance. In densely populated
areas especially, these included highly threatened lowland ecosystems such
as marshes and bogs, lowland forests, undisturbed grasslands, sand dunes
and tidal flats. When it came to protecting wildlife habitat, however, ecological reserves served more as "nature museums" than viable protection
strategies in and of themselves. With some notable exceptions, such as the
Vladimir J. Krajina Ecological Reserve on Haida Gwaii and the Gladys
Lake reserve in the Stikine, almost all of BC's ecological reserves were less
than one thousand hectares in size, and most were less than two hundred
hectares.[58] As Provincial Museum director Yorke Edwards commented in
a conference presentation in 1982, "most are too small for animals of some

mobility."[59] A lack of funding for enforcement and management of reserves also hindered their success. Bristol Foster, hired in 1974 as the first full-time coordinator of the reserves program, argued in 1980 that there was no use creating ecological reserves "if all we are doing is drawing lines on maps."[60] Later that year, the creation of a volunteer warden program, modelled after a similar program for archaeological sites, provided limited local protection for designated reserves.[61]

Protecting Wildlife Habitat on Private Lands: The Nature Trust of British Columbia

Another centennial initiative, and one that charted a different path for wildlife habitat protection, was the establishment of the National Second Century Fund of British Columbia (now the **Nature Trust of British Columbia [NTBC]**) in 1971. A public foundation, the NTBC aimed to acquire and protect private lands of high wildlife value. Current CEO Jasper Lament explains, "only about 5 per cent of BC is private land, but it is disproportionately important to biodiversity. . . . Landscapes that are attractive to people, such as river valleys and coastal regions, are for the most part the same landscapes that can support high numbers of species."[62] Given the limitations of statutory protections such as parks and ecological reserves, the NTBC provided an important alternative path to acquiring and protecting critical fish and wildlife habitats. In 1971, Ducks Unlimited Canada was the only other non-government conservation organization operating in British Columbia. In this context, the NTBC became the sole organization working outside of wetland landscapes to conserve wildlife habitat. It would grow to become the largest regional **land trust** in Canada.[63]

The NTBC owed its origins to the vision of four Kamloops-area wildlife enthusiasts: Jack Davis, the first minister of the newly formed federal Ministry of Environment, who had grown up on a homestead in the Tranquille Valley outside Kamloops; Len Marchand, member of Parliament for Kamloops, former agronomist and member of the Inkumupulux (Okanagan) First Nation; Dr. Alastair McLean, a federal range scientist based in Kamloops; and Ralph Shaw, a Kamloops school principal and avid outdoorsman. Each had witnessed dramatic changes to the landscapes of the BC Interior and shared a sense of urgency to protect remaining ecologically significant areas for both their value to fish and wildlife and their importance as sites of environmental education. The idea for a land

Nature Trust of British Columbia founders at NTBC's Bull River Conservation Area
in the East Kootenay, n.d. Photo courtesy of the Nature Trust of British Columbia.

trust was not new: models existed in the United States, where local land
trusts had proliferated since 1891, and elsewhere in Canada. The Nature
Conservancy of Canada, for example, had begun acquiring properties in
Ontario in 1962. Davis, Marchand, McLean and Shaw proposed the land
trust idea as a creative use for $4.5 million remaining in federal funds gifted
to the province to commemorate its centennial. This "second century" fund
would form the foundation for the NTBC, with interest and subsequent
donations supporting land purchases.[64]

Forged amid the ascendancy of science in wildlife management, the
NTBC drew on the "the brightest minds in conservation science" to build
the organization and advise on site selection. Chaired for the first twenty
years by retired Major General Bert Hoffmeister, a former forestry executive, conservationist and decorated veteran of World War II, the NTBC's
board assembled the expertise of eight volunteer directors from across
the province. Zoologist Ian McTaggart Cowan, grasslands scientist Bert

Brink, research scientist Alastair McLean, and conservationist and author Roderick Haig-Brown were among those who helped shape the organization's governance structures and land acquisition priorities in its early years. Some, like Cowan, remained a guiding force for the organization for decades. Cowan stepped down from the board in 2002, after thirty-one years of service; he remained a director emeritus until his death in 2010.[65]

More nimble than government agencies, land conservancies like the NTBC avoided both the long process of approvals to secure an area for protection and the subsequent uncertainty caused by changing government policies. Because of the NTBC's status as a private charitable organization, projects manager Pamela Cowtan explained at a 1982 conference on wild lands protection, "a change in government cannot change the fund." Funds to purchase lands, furthermore, could be accessed immediately to purchase properties "as soon as they [came] up for sale, or before," or be banked for future acquisitions.[66] Early NTBC acquisitions included 595 hectares of prime California bighorn sheep habitat at Grand Forks in the Kootenay-Boundary region and portions of the Salmon River estuary near Campbell River on Vancouver Island, vital fish-rearing habitat that also supported a threatened herd of Roosevelt elk.

The NTBC and subsequent BC land conservancy organizations underlined the value of cooperation in conservation initiatives. Here they drew on the long experience of Ducks Unlimited, active for decades in the US and the Canadian Prairies. Ducks Unlimited Canada brought a wealth of experience in wetland restoration and community-based conservation partnerships when it established a BC office in Kamloops in 1968. DUC's successful practice of collaborating with landowners, tenant farmers, and government and non-government agencies to maintain and expand wetland habitat served as a model for land conservancies operating across a wider range of threatened landscapes.

The new ability of the Fish and Wildlife Branch to purchase and administer lands for wildlife, enshrined in the 1966 Wildlife Act, made the provincial government an important partner in early land acquisitions. The NTBC and other conservancy organizations entered into stewardship agreements with both the BC Fish and Wildlife Branch and the Canadian Wildlife Service through the 1970s and '80s. These ninety-nine-year lease agreements saw land conservancies assume the costs of acquiring private lands with high wildlife value, while government agencies took up the work of stewardship and protection. The presence of the **Nature Conservancy of Canada** in the province by the late 1970s initiated new opportunities for co-operation. In the coming decades, conservancies would pool their assets to assemble larger holdings and to purchase properties in increasingly heated urban real estate markets.

INITIATIVE PROFILE: The George C. Reifel Migratory Bird Sanctuary

One of the most significant migratory bird sanctuaries in the province lies just thirty-five kilometres south of Vancouver. Located on Westham Island within the Fraser River delta, the George C. Reifel Migratory Bird Sanctuary provides an important stopover and wintering area for the roughly 1.4 million birds that migrate along the Pacific Flyway from Siberia to South America each year.

The story of the site's creation highlights the interconnected histories of farming, hunting and conservation efforts in the Fraser River delta. When Vancouver businessman and avid sport hunter George C. Reifel purchased the northwest portion of Westham Island in 1927, he took advantage of the natural flood cycles of the Fraser River to create a private hunting retreat, diking the intertidal lands to create about a thousand acres of prime wetland habitat. During World War II, Reifel's son George H. Reifel maintained the hunting tradition on the family's island property while developing a successful sugar beet seed operation on the diked fields. George H. Reifel and his family moved to the farm permanently in 1960, providing his father's grandson and namesake, George C. Reifel, and his siblings with an education in conservation they would carry throughout their lives: "It certainly made us understand that the farm provided an important habitat for migrating waterfowl. We knew when the birds were going to come, where they were going to rest, what they were going to eat, where you could go if you wanted to hunt them." More than that, however, Reifel and his siblings understood how important the place was to the Pacific Flyway. "What happens if these birds didn't have this place to refuel?. . . . We knew that [the snow geese] came from a very long way away and we knew they were hungry and tired when they got here."[67]

In the early 1960s, as industrial development consumed other portions of the valued lands in the Fraser River delta, DUC president Fred Auger asked the Reifel family to consider leasing a portion of their farm to the newly created British Columbia Waterfowl Society to operate as a waterfowl sanctuary. The family agreed to a thirty-year lease, and the Reifel Migratory Bird Sanctuary opened in 1963.

Alaksen National Wildlife Area and Reifel Migratory Bird Sanctuary, 2022

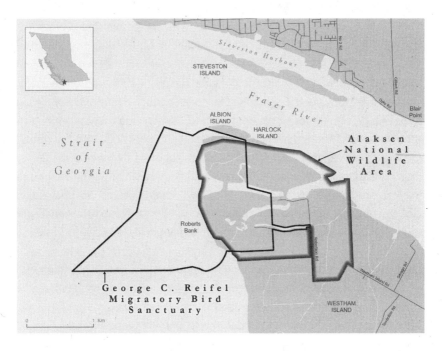

Data source: Environment and Climate Change Canada, Canadian Protected and Conserved Areas Database. Map by GeoBC, 2022.

Ducks Unlimited Canada provided assistance with wetland management and the BC Game Commission stepped in to protect the adjacent intertidal foreshore with a game reserve designation. In 1972, the Reifel family agreed to stave off persistent development interest in the remaining property by transferring the entirety of their holdings, including the sanctuary land, to the federal government through a combination of land sale and donation. Arrangements included a commitment to honour the legacy of George C. Reifel in the sanctuary name in perpetuity and to manage the property primarily for the benefit of waterfowl.

Four years later, in 1976, the federal government designated the Reifel property as the Alaksen National Wildlife Area and bundled the adjacent provincial game reserve and sanctuary lease into the George C. Reifel Migratory Bird Sanctuary. The Reifel family home now serves as the Pacific Region headquarters of the Canadian Wildlife Service—a fitting location for an agency whose biologists had been among the first to emphasize the vital importance of estuaries in the 1950s and 1960s. The

BC Waterfowl Society continues to manage the adjacent sanctuary under a long-term agreement with the CWS.[68]

Farmers remain an important component of the wildlife conservation work at Alaksen. In exchange for farming in a way that benefits waterfowl and other wildlife, the CWS permits local farmers to sell the produce they grow on the Alaksen property. As George C. Reifel, grandson of the original Reifel and former DUC president, explains, "we want grains, vegetables, potatoes, carrots, cabbages," soil-based crops that provide winter forage for waterfowl. "We want to limit the acreage of agriculture that is less waterfowl-friendly, like greenhouses and blueberry crops." The refuge provided for waterfowl at Alaksen also benefits surrounding farmers by luring birds away from their fields. Prohibitions on hunting at the site help to ensure "that the birds are very happy coming here," CWS regional director Blair Hammond explains, "so that they are not flying into jet engines [at the nearby Vancouver International Airport] or hitting [surrounding] farmers' fields too hard."[69]

In 1982, Alaksen became BC's first wetland of international significance to be designated under the Ramsar Convention. Ongoing purchases of adjacent farmland and neighbouring islands under the Pacific Estuary Conservation Program, a private-public partnership formed in 1987 to secure significant coastal estuaries, has furthered the protection of habitat for migratory birds and species at risk on Westham Island and the surrounding Fraser River delta. Despite these developments, the delta remains one of the most threatened and modified estuaries in the province. Ongoing concerns about pollution and land conversion for agricultural and commercial purposes make the Fraser River delta the only Important Bird Area in Canada designated as endangered by BirdLife International.[70]

Westham Island's proximity to Vancouver, furthermore, makes it a popular destination for birders and day trippers. Unlike most national wildlife areas, where conservation objectives prohibit public access, visitors are welcome at the Reifel sanctuary. Visitorship has swelled in recent years: over 100,000 people visited the sanctuary in 2019 to view birds and other wildlife and to participate in the BC Waterfowl Society's popular public education programs. Balancing this growing public interest with the wildlife conservation mandate of the site, and the ongoing wishes of its donors to manage the site principally for waterfowl, remains a central concern for the CWS as it approaches the extension of its tenure agreement with the BC Waterfowl Society in 2025.[71]

Early Land Use Planning

As effective as land conservancies and, to a lesser extent, ecological reserves were at protecting significant wildlife habitats from development,
they protected only a small fraction of the province's land base. By 1982,
ecological reserves occupied roughly 72,000 hectares of the province's
88.7-million-hectare Crown land mass; the holdings of all of the province's
designated wildlife lands, including private lands acquired or leased for
conservation purposes, occupied just 884,000 hectares, or roughly 0.01 per
cent of BC's Crown lands.[72] Across the rest of the land base, agriculture,
residential and commercial development, infrastructure development and
resource extraction activities proceeded with little to no consideration for
the needs of wildlife. For wildlife scientists, subsistence harvesters, sport
hunters and fishers, and those who depended on wildlife for their livelihoods, a scattering of protected areas across the landscape was not enough.
What was needed to address the growing frequency and intensity of land
use conflicts, especially in the province's more densely populated southern
half, was comprehensive land use planning on public lands that accounted
for the needs of wildlife.

Advocacy for a more coordinated approach to resource management
had been building for years. The BC Wildlife Federation and its member
associations were especially persistent on this front, passing numerous
resolutions throughout the 1950s and '60s calling for structural reform to
better manage and coordinate competing land use demands. As early as 1952,
for example, the Vancouver Island Affiliated Fish and Game Association
proposed a "permanent commission of industrial, government, recreational,
and other interests" with the power to "thoroughly investigate any proposed
development of any large area" and to make its recommendations public.
This resolution was adopted by the BCWF in 1961, when it called on the
provincial government to establish a "land use cooperation agency" to
assess and coordinate competing interests."[73]

Experiments in Inter-Agency Consultation

Consultation between resource agencies was not completely absent. Since
the 1950s, the BC Forest Service had accepted input from federal fisheries
officials in its review of timber cutting permit applications. Initially limited

to fish habitat considerations, this "**referral system**" was eventually extended to provincial wildlife officials in 1970.[74] As historian Rick Rajala has shown, however, government and industry foresters resisted any surrender of their land planning authority to fisheries biologists. The absence of any obligation to protect fish and wildlife habitat under the BC Forest Act only reinforced these positions. Government foresters were directed to "[consider] advice but [take] no direction from fisheries officers." As a result, stream protection clauses in timber permit applications were "violated by almost every operation near a stream."[75] Without a legislative framework enabling and requiring multi-stakeholder land use planning, it remained extremely difficult to compel the resource ministries to take fish and wildlife needs into account.

The first shift in this direction came in 1969, when conflict over the alienation of agricultural land in the Vanderhoof area led the Bennett government to establish a Land Use Committee of cabinet. The first of its kind, the committee of resource department ministers set out to improve coordination among resource ministries and establish land use policy guidelines.[76] Their work was supported by BC's participation in the Canada Land Inventory, a national initiative to assess and catalogue land capability for agriculture, forestry, recreation and wildlife (ungulates and waterfowl).[77] With the Vanderhoof area as a test case, the Land Use Committee supported a forward-thinking group of regional managers in Prince George to develop the province's first comprehensive land use planning tool; it would later become known as the **Resource Folio Planning System**. A forerunner to GIS (geographic information system) mapping today, the system drew on CLI data to produce layered, hand-coloured maps of resource capabilities to inform decision-making.[78]

The early success of the Land Use Committee in addressing impasses surrounding land use led the Social Credit government to pass the **Environment and Land Use Act** in 1971. Together with the Ecological Reserve Act of the same year, it constituted the first of the province's environmental laws. The act renamed the Environment and Land Use Committee and charged it with determining "maximum beneficial land use" to "minimize and prevent waste . . . and despoliation of the environment" in resource development decisions.[79] Critically, it permitted cabinet to use its power to override all other legislation and to place a moratorium on land alienations in a specific area to allow consultation and planning to occur. As such, the legislation and the committee it supported carried enormous potential to intervene in land use disputes. The committee became, in mandate at least, the kind of body that the BCWF and other wildlife advocates had been proposing for over a decade. As legal historian Michael Begg has argued, the Environment and Land Use Act marked the beginning of a broader shift in the provincial government's approach to land: from "land allocation" to "land management." Until these changes of the late 1960s and early 1970s, he writes, there were "virtually no policies governing the allocation of land, no guidelines for identifying its most suitable uses, and no rules for resolving conflicts between current and future uses."[80]

Transformative potential, however, did not always translate into transformative practice. Long-established mandates and legislative frameworks of the resource ministries, combined with declining capacity within those agencies with environmental responsibilities, constrained the change-making ability of the Environment and Land Use Committee. The Parks Branch and especially the Fish and Wildlife Branch were seriously under-resourced by the early 1970s. Ian McTaggart Cowan summed up the problem as one of escalating responsibilities and shrinking budgets in a 1972 *Vancouver Sun* article. As the "major source . . . of ecological expertise" within the provincial government, he wrote, the Fish and Wildlife Branch shouldered rapidly expanding responsibilities for inter-agency consultation, a growing population of hunters and anglers and ever-more-frequent public inquiries about environmental protection.[81] Political scientist Jeremy Wilson confirmed these observations, noting that despite its growing management responsibilities, BC's Fish and Wildlife Branch received a significantly lower budget "per capita, per sportsperson, and per square mile" than comparable agencies in other provinces and US states. For BCWF members, especially galling was the fact that the Fish and Wildlife Branch's budget allowances had slipped below the amount it raised through the sale of hunting and fishing licences.[82]

In 1972, the election of the New Democratic Party under premier Dave Barrett not only flushed the depleted coffers of agencies like BC Parks and the Fish and Wildlife Branch but also invested energy and funds into land use planning activities in the province. To support the work of the Environment and Land Use Committee, the new government created regional resource management committees that remained an important mechanism of inter-agency consultation for the next decade. As an alternative to a provincial department of environment, a Secretariat of the Environment and Land Use Committee provided technical support and coordination for a series of multi-agency task forces. One of these task forces, the North West Study, produced what can be considered the province's first land use plan by reconciling timber interests with environmental and recreational concerns in BC's northwest. Another led to the designation of Valhalla Provincial Park northwest of Nelson, celebrated as one of the early successes of BC's environmentalist movement.[83]

Land for Wildlife? The Agricultural Land Commission

One of the most significant developments for habitat protection and land use planning in the province came with the creation of the **Agricultural Land Commission** in 1973. The steady loss of farmland to urban sprawl was a topic of heightened public concern for British Columbians in the lead up to the 1972 election, so much so that each of the four political parties had an agricultural land preservation platform of some kind.[84] By the early 1970s the province was losing some 4,000 to 6,000 hectares of prime agricultural lands annually; the problem was especially acute within the rich agricultural lands of the Fraser Valley in the Lower Mainland. The loss of agricultural lands was a Canada-wide problem, but one that was especially pressing in BC, where only 5 per cent of the land base is considered suitable for agriculture and less than 3 per cent capable of growing a reasonable range of crops.[85]

The establishment of the Agricultural Land Commission in 1973 and the development over the next three years of a system of zoned agricultural land reserves (ALRs) marked a major step forward in the evolution of land use planning in BC and in North America.[86] Previous initiatives, such as the Social Credit government's 1972 Greenbelt Protection Fund, sought to address agricultural land conversions through the acquisition of privately owned farmlands for protection as greenbelt reserves. The incoming NDP government, however, opted for the more comprehensive approach of applying restrictive agricultural land use zoning across the province's twenty-eight regional districts. Agrologist Gary Runka was a driving force in the development of the zoning concept. By 1976, Runka as general manager and chair of the new Agricultural Land Commission had overseen the designation of roughly 4.7 million hectares of agricultural land (5 per cent of the province's land base) concentrated mainly in the southern half of the province.[87] The

Agricultural land reserves in British Columbia, 2008

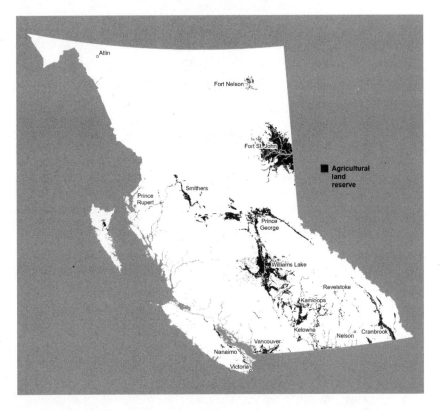

Data sources: Ministry of Forests, Forest Analysis and Inventory Branch, Biogeoclimatic (BEC) Zones, 2014; Ministry of Environment, BC Parks, BC Parks, Ecological Reserves, and Protected Areas, 2008. Map by GeoBC, 2022.

amount of ALR land has remained relatively constant in subsequent decades, although land removed in the south has been replaced with less productive land in the north.[88] The BC Auditor General concluded in 2010 that despite legislative changes and funding challenges, the ALR has been largely success-ful in preserving the province's limited agricultural lands.[89]

An important form of rural land protection, the ALR also mattered for wildlife. Much of British Columbia's prime agricultural lands occupied the same low-elevation valleys that provided critical shelter, breeding grounds and food sources to a wide range of wildlife species. Losing these lands to urban development was also a loss for wildlife. While acquisitions under the Greenbelt Fund had included important wildlife areas, such as the nesting grounds of greater sandhill cranes in the Pitt River Valley, the ALR introduced protections over a broader scale. In the Fraser Valley in particular, the ALR protected large areas of farmland that, over winter, offered flooded or puddled habitat for dabbling ducks and grazing geese.[90] Natural pasture lands provided important habitat for small mammals, raptors and resident and migratory birds, while the hedgerows, woodlands, wetlands and riparian areas interspersed through agricultural landscapes supported a wide range of species.[91] Wildlife species such as bats, birds, raptors and insects offered important benefits for farmers by pollinating crops, controlling insect and rodent pests and breaking down organic matter to provide nutrients for crops.[92]

But wildlife and agriculture, then and now, are not always compatible. Intensive forms of agriculture—such as orchards, vineyards and cropland used for grains, vegetables, sod and berries—leave little viable habitat for wildlife; also, they rely on fertilizers and pesticides that often threaten fish and wildlife health. Fencing used to contain livestock on farms and ranches can block or injure wildlife attempting to pass over or under. For their part, wildlife, and especially waterfowl, can have a devastating effect on farmers' fields, consuming crops, compacting soils and limiting crop choices. Farms in the Fraser River delta, for example, occupy an internationally significant feeding and resting area on the Pacific Flyway that hosts roughly one million migrating and wintering waterfowl and five million shorebirds annually. Agriculture-wildlife conflicts remained high in the Fraser River delta until the early 1990s, when a combination of conservation designations and voluntary stewardship programs created alternative foraging areas for overwintering waterfowl and compensated farmers for their efforts to protect wildlife habitat.[93]

Land Use Planning from the Grassroots: Experiments in the Kootenays

One of the most promising responses to the land use conflicts of the late 1960s and early '70s came from the bottom up, rather than from the top down. Following multiple and frequent land use conflicts in the highly charged Kootenay region, regional range and wildlife managers sought ways to bring land users together to recognize their shared interests and contribute to better decision-making surrounding resource development in the region.

Coordinated Resource Management Planning (CRMP) is a consensus-based planning process that aims to improve land management through collaborative decision-making among landowners, resource permit holders and other stakeholders within a specified watershed or local area. The process originated in eastern Oregon in 1949, as part of efforts to harmonize range improvements across private and public lands. Unlike other early planning processes, which typically took place among government resource managers and industry representatives behind closed doors, CRMP integrates technical expertise with local knowledge and experience. Local resource users are key members of the planning team from beginning to end. As CRMP founder Bill Anderson explains, this depth and consistency of involvement allows participants to "develop a sense of responsibility and confidence in the outcome." Because stakeholders make decisions by consensus instead of voting, "everyone [has] to be able to live with the decision—discussion continues until they can." When CRMP is done well, it results in not only ecological change but social change. By "listening to the viewpoints, experiences and options of others," Anderson writes, participants "increase their awareness of total-resource relationships and interactions. All this helps them amend the viewpoints they had at the beginning, and this is part of the social change that is needed."[94]

For Ray Demarchi, regional wildlife biologist for the Kootenay region, the CRMP process carried a lot of promise for resolving the intractable and increasingly frequent land use disputes over diminishing range lands in the East Kootenay Trench of the Rocky Mountains. When Demarchi arrived in the East Kootenay in 1964, he assessed range conditions in the Trench as occupying one of two extremes: overgrazed or not grazed enough.

Few fences meant that cows, left to their own devices, overgrazed the gentle, low-elevation terrains close to water before snowfall pushed them back to their home ranches in the late fall. The remainder of the range suffered from the opposite problem. Logging and large-scale fires throughout the Trench in the 1920s and 1930s had produced grassland and seral shrublands that supported a wide range of wildlife, including wintering deer, elk and bighorn sheep, abundant sharptailed grouse, and "a proliferation of other birds and small and mid-sized mammals."[95]

Regional wildlife biologist Ray Demarchi explaining the pitfalls of poor land use practices on a joint BC Forest Service and Fish and Wildlife Branch field trip to the Findlay Lower Range, May 19, 1972. *Daily Bulletin* (Kimberley), June 1, 1972. Photo courtesy of the Columbia Basin Institute of Regional History and Kimberley District Heritage Society, item 0158.0018.

In the two decades following World War II, several thousand feral horses had been removed from the Crown lands in the Trench, reducing grazing pressure. By the late 1960s, Demarchi explained, "we could see . . . that forest succession was starting to cut deeply into the forage capital for wildlife." Tree seedlings, historically deterred by Indigenous fire practices and later settler logging, wildfire and livestock grazing, were beginning to take hold on the valued grasslands of the Trench. The solution to the problem—a combination of prescribed burns, thinning and a redistribution of livestock throughout the affected rangelands—would take planning and buy-in from local ranchers, grazing permit holders and government range managers.[96]

With encouragement from CBC resource correspondent Mike Halleran, Demarchi and other Kootenay region resource managers, together with a delegation from the Kootenay Livestock Association, travelled to Oregon in 1974 to meet Bill Anderson and view first-hand the results of CRMP on public rangelands. The trip was a success. The following year, provincial chief of wildlife Glen Smith convinced the BC Forest Service to hire Anderson to implement pilot CRMP task groups in the Kootenay, Okanagan, Thompson-Nicola and Chilcotin-Cariboo regions. Within a few years, eighty-six CRMP processes had been initiated over 570,000 hectares of land in BC's southern Interior.[97] Almost all focused predominantly on conflicts surrounding forage allocations and range conditions for wildlife.[98] Each involved licensed resource users from a defined area, with support and technical expertise from provincial resource planners and managers. Funding from the federal-provincial Agriculture and Rural Development Agreement (ARDA) enabled range improvements, infrastructure and habitat enhancement projects once a CRMP was in place.

Of all the regions, the Kootenay CRMP task group faced what Demarchi described as the most "extreme conditions" within which to test the process: there, competition for a shrinking land base was most intense, and positions among stakeholders most entrenched. As chair of eighteen CRMP processes in the region, Demarchi used the established CRMP structure of reaching agreement on minor issues before tackling the "big ticket" issues, keeping expectations realistic, and focusing on issues where agreement was possible, to build trust among participants and move the planning process ahead. In the end, the Kootenay CRMP task group completed coordinated resource management plans on all but one of the managed range units in the East Kootenay Trench, an area of over 200,000 hectares. Roughly 120 ranchers with public grazing permits actively participated in the planning processes, which aimed to reduce overgrazing by enabling moderate-level livestock use over a larger range area.

With financial support from ARDA, the task group made substantial investments in range improvements, including livestock fences, cattle guards and livestock watering systems. The Fish and Wildlife Branch drew on greenbelt reserve funds to acquire several privately owned ranches in the area, allowing for the redistribution of cattle and the recovery of overgrazed Crown ranges. Other management changes, such as the initiation of burning and thinning programs to restore and protect grasslands from forest succession and the implementation of deferred rotation grazing plans to remove livestock from the ranges earlier in the fall, also contributed to the task group's success. As Demarchi recalls, the ranges "almost immediately showed signs of improvement," with benefits for both cattle and wildlife.

The demise of the CRMP plans in the East Kootenay was in part a result of their success. A series of milder-than-average winters and wet springs in the mid to late 1970s contributed to rapid range improvement, with two immediate results: (1) pressure from ranchers to increase their Crown land grazing allotments (the amount of cattle or sheep they could release to graze in a given area); and (2) an explosion in elk populations within the Trench. Elk populations benefited not only from the milder winters and excellent forage growth but also from an intensive winter feeding program, implemented to avert their starvation when range conditions were poor and carried on through the early CRMP years. By the late 1970s, resident and migratory wintering elk populations had doubled, peaking at roughly 30,000 animals.

Ranchers failed in their bid for increased grazing allotments in part due to growing elk populations that, together with their cattle, placed pressure on the range's ability to support other wildlife species. But ballooning elk populations also affected ranchers in other ways: by eating winter hay stores, trampling and eating cultivated crops and competing with cattle for forage on private range lands. Ranchers' complaints that they unfairly bore the burden of increased elk numbers as an uncompensated expense to their operations led the province to order a reduction of the elk population in the Trench. In 1981, Demarchi oversaw—with considerable misgivings—the first calf elk hunting season in North America. In the years that followed, government support for the pilot CRMP processes withered, and in the absence of ongoing funding and commitment, all but a handful of local CRMP groups disbanded.

Reflecting on the rapid results and ultimate failure of the CRMP process in the East Kootenay, Demarchi concluded that conflicts resulting from range improvements in the Trench were inevitable in the absence of a broader, strategic land use plan for the region. Because CRMPs apply to the operational, or local, level, where management plans are applied, they depend on the direction and backing of agreed-on objectives for the larger region. Had a strategic land use plan been in place to guide the local CRMPs, the value of a large elk population—with its spinoff effects for regional tourism, guiding and hunting revenue—might have been weighed more effectively against the value of beef production in the region. Compensation for ranchers who lost forage to growing elk populations might also have been viewed more favourably within the context of long-term land use planning and the trade-offs it necessitates.

The abandonment of the CRMP process had lasting implications for the quality of range lands in the East Kootenay Trench. Most of the ranches acquired by the province in the 1970s were later sold or leased, and elk-proof fences on private lands replaced more cooperative arrangements between resource users. In the absence of integrated burning, thinning and grazing programs, forest regrowth continued to encroach on grass and shrublands. By the 1990s, a comprehensive study of vegetation and forage use in the Trench found that combined use by cattle and wildlife exceeded the carrying capacity of the grasslands, resulting in ongoing degradation.[99]

The relationships built during the CRMP discussions of the mid-1970s did not completely evaporate, however. For area ranchers, wildlife advocates and resource managers, the persistence of shared concerns surrounding the ongoing alienation of public lands, soil erosion, water quality degradation, unregulated off-road vehicle use and the need for prescribed burns continued to generate support for better land use management. Land use planning processes in the 1990s led to the development of a long-term restoration program for the fire-dependent ecosystems of the Trench. Restoration work, including prescribed burns, thinning and grass seeding, continues as a collaborative effort of government agencies, area First Nations and non-government organizations such as the Rocky Mountain Trench Natural Resources Society. While problems with forage allocation remain—a 2008 Forest Practices Board investigation of grazing management in the East Kootenay concluded that cattle and wildlife continued to exceed grassland carrying capacity—the restoration program has shown promising results in reducing forest encroachment and improving grassland health.[100]

Conclusion: Mounting Pressures in the Postwar Period

Between the mid-1960s and the early 1990s, the intertwined problems of increasing human populations, proliferating access roads and the alienation or degradation of wildlife habitats ratcheted up the pressure on BC wildlife. Fisheries and wildlife managers responded by imposing ever-more-restrictive limits on hunters and anglers and introducing new systems to privilege resident wildlife users and protect threatened animal populations.

Beyond bag limits and seasonal harvest restrictions, increased attention to wildlife habitat also characterized developments in this period. Land use conflicts in areas of high wildlife value, such as the low-elevation valleys of the East Kootenay Trench and the richly productive estuaries of the Lower Fraser River, generated the province's first land conservancies and provided the impetus for its early experiments in land use planning. Don Robinson, director of the Fish and Wildlife Branch in the early 1980s, recognized the relative strengths and weaknesses of these approaches. While land acquisition was "current, clear cut, tangible, simple, and . . . satisfying," he observed at BC's 1982 Land for Wildlife conference, inter-agency resource management planning was "long-term, cooperative, complex, and . . . frustrating."[101] Each of these processes, from the grassroots CRMP process in the province's southern Interior to the more lasting and centralized Agricultural Land Commission, helped to lay the groundwork for the more comprehensive land use planning initiatives of the 1990s.

9

Fisheries, Habitat Protection and Indigenous Rights

I n January 1973, forty Vancouver Island fishers drove a convoy of trucks into Victoria and unloaded piles of slash, debris and dead salmon collected from choked coastal streams onto the lawn of the BC legislature. As representatives of the Save Our Salmon Committee (SOSC), a fisheries advocacy group affiliated with the Pacific Trollers Association, they demanded better logging practices and tougher enforcement of the Fisheries Act. Their protest came just days after the publication of a pointed opinion piece by Roderick Haig-Brown in the *Vancouver Sun* that identified sparse salmon runs on "nearly all coastal streams" as the result of poorly controlled logging.[1]

Haig-Brown's editorial and the SOSC protest highlighted the precarious position of the province's valued trout and salmon populations within a political and economic environment where "forestry was king." Protesters drew on a broad coalition of fisheries workers, environmentalists and Indigenous leaders, deploying strategies that would be taken up on a larger scale in the more famous "War in the Woods" of the 1990s.[2] Their demands for protective forest buffers, or "leave strips," along lakes and waterways appeared to gain some initial purchase with NDP Minister of Forests Bob Williams. However, strong industry objections to any kind of blanket regulations, combined with falling forestry revenues, saw Williams back away from prescriptive stream protection legislation in favour of a promise of "improved planning."[3]

As this chapter shows, efforts to protect freshwater and tidal fish habitat succumbed to the logic of fish production in the decades following World War II. BC's freshwater fish hatchery program grew considerably in this pe-

BC Fish and Game Branch staff stocking live trout in a lake in the Interior of BC, late 1950s.
Photo courtesy of Freshwater Fisheries Society of BC.

riod, with investment in research and the acquisition of new facilities such
as the Kootenay and Fraser Valley trout hatcheries in the mid-1960s.[4] An
expansion of federal salmon hatcheries followed in the late 1970s. Unlike
management of the province's avian and mammalian game species, where
hunting regulation and habitat protection overshadowed and ultimately
replaced game propagation programs, management of salmon and trout
populations placed greater faith in fish production and allocation than in
regulating harvest and protecting habitat.

Conflicts surrounding fisheries allocation were also much more intense,
and much more sustained, than their counterparts in game management.
This was especially true regarding salmon. The value of the salmon resource and the presence of a large and powerful commercial sector created
an atmosphere of historical and ongoing antagonism between commercial,
sport and Indigenous fisheries. More than any other group, Indigenous
communities bore the brunt of fishery conservation measures. Their
efforts to reassert treaty and Aboriginal rights to traditional fisheries laid
the groundwork for a radical shift in Canada's relationship with Indigenous
Peoples in the decades to come.

Fisheries vs. Forestry: The Failure of Multiple Use

In 1965, a heated controversy surrounding the resumption of annual log drives on the Stellako River west of Prince George focused public attention on the tensions between forestry and fishing interests and the failure of multiple-use directives to bring about any meaningful change. A tributary of the Nechako River and ultimately the Fraser, the Stellako was a prime fly-fishing river whose spawning grounds nurtured provincially significant trout and salmon stocks. In 1965, a sawmill company received a federal permit to run logs down the river to its sawmill on Fraser Lake. The log drive that June, the first in seventeen years, produced vocal opposition from area fishing resort owners, rod and gun clubs, commercial fisheries interests and members of the Stellat'en First Nation on Fraser Lake. Each of these groups had depended on the salmon and trout populations that had rebounded after four decades of destructive log driving came to an end in 1948.

In 1966, the federal Department of Fisheries asserted its jurisdiction over fish habitat protection under the Fisheries Act by refusing to reissue a log drive permit. An extensive study of the 1965 drive had concluded that "bark deposits, . . . erosion and scouring of the stream bed" had caused "serious decline in the river's spawning productivity." For BC's minister of lands, forests and water resources, Ray Williston, the controversy presented an opportunity to assert the province's control over the products of its forests and the flows of its rivers. Williston intervened to allow a second log drive in 1966, transforming, as historian Rick Rajala has observed, a local permit dispute into "a constitutional test of strength between Ottawa and Victoria." As it had with the Columbia River Treaty in 1961, the federal government retreated. When log driving finally ceased on the Stellako in 1968, it was due not to government regulation but to a decision by the sawmill company to truck, rather than drive, its logs to mill.[5]

The Stellako River controversy exposed some key tensions that resurfaced in other resource disputes of the period. The first was the hesitancy of the federal government to interfere in provincial resource decisions. Despite express wording in the Fisheries Act that gave the federal minister authority to restrict log drives in the province and to prohibit the deposit of logs in fish-bearing streams, Ottawa proved reluctant to interfere with the province's most lucrative industry. This was especially true in the context of the rapid growth of logging in the BC Interior to supply a growing number of pulp and paper mills.[6] The widening gap in provincial revenues from forestry and fish also contributed to regulatory reluctance at all levels of government: in 1950, forestry-related activities produced close to $400 million in wealth, while commercial fishing produced $63 million; in 1965, the forest industry generated $980 million in revenue, jobs and investment capital for the province, while commercial fisheries generated just $52 million.[7]

Second, Ottawa's retreat from the Stellako controversy also spoke to the uncertainty of its jurisdiction over matters of habitat protection. While the Fisheries Act held potential power in protecting salmon habitat, the courts had not yet tested the extent to which Ottawa could interfere with provincial jurisdiction over forestry and rivers. As Rajala argues, this uncertainty meant that "education and post-logging cleanup" tended to prevail over strict enforcement. Third, the Stellako controversy exposed, as the Columbia River Treaty had just a few years earlier, the tenacity of the provincial government's efforts to claim jurisdiction—and revenue potential—from its natural resources. For provincial Forests Minister Williston, "a few federal fish were well worth sacrificing in the process of asserting BC's control over the flows of rivers."[8]

Finally, Stellako made apparent how disillusioned wildlife advocates were with the language of multiple use. For Howard Paish, the tenacious new executive director of the BCWF, multiple use had in practice meant "trying to accommodate a variety of users after one major unilateral decision has been made." What was needed instead, according to Paish, was a shift toward integrated resource management, a management framework that would reflect a "genuine intention . . . to accommodate a number of resource users on one resource base." None of this was possible, he acknowledged, without a legislative framework that enabled multi-stakeholder land use planning.[9]

Advocacy around fish-forestry concerns was not completely fruitless. Operators began to experiment with the voluntary use of buffer strips along some valuable salmon streams. The tendency of these thin strips of trees to blow over in high winds, however, meant they were not widely adopted in the 1970s. Small advances toward inter-agency cooperation came in the NDP's formal adoption in 1975 of the Resource Folio Planning System tested in the Prince George region in the late 1960s. As Rajala notes, the more flexible, site-specific folio planning appealed much more to industry than efforts to impose what they viewed as rigid habitat protection regulations—a preference that would hold through subsequent government regulatory efforts in the 1990s.[10] Fish and wildlife biologists were not as sanguine. For all its gains in improving the transparency of overlapping resource claims, the folio system and the referrals process it facilitated were often an exercise in frustration. Habitat protection biologist John Dick recalled the process of the mid-1970s:

> We went to all those meetings, we coloured all those maps. . . . but [when] we started asking for reservations of mature timber on Vancouver Island for salmon stream protection and a range of mature forest-dwelling wildlife, the answer was, "you can't do that, you'll affect the AAC [annual allowable cut]." "Oh well," we said, "how about reserving some of this medium-poor site, overmature subalpine for caribou?" And the reply was, " . . . we're having timber supply problems and we're going to need that to sustain the AAC." Suddenly we learned a lesson about participating in planning processes where most of the major decisions had already been made by somebody else at a much higher level.[11]

More substantive change came with legislative reforms in the late 1970s. Amendments to the federal Fisheries Act in 1977 strengthened habitat protection provisions, prohibiting "harmful alteration, disruption or destruction of fish habitat" unless authorized by the federal government. This "**HADD**" provision would become one of Canada's most powerful legal protections for wildlife habitat.[12] Although jurisdictional uncertainty would continue to cloud enforcement efforts in the decades ahead, the evolution of case law in this area would more clearly subject the province's authority over activities on its land base to federal jurisdiction over the conservation and protection of fish.[13] Peter Pearse's emphasis on the value and legitimacy of multiple forest uses in his 1976 Royal Commission on Forest Resources report prompted an overhaul of the BC Forest Act by 1979. The new act required the Ministry of Forests, for the first time, to manage public forest lands for multiple use, including fisheries, wildlife and outdoor recreation.[14] It also mandated public participation in management decisions. In practice, however, the value of timber continued to dominate resource decision-making. This was especially true during the gruelling economic recession of the early 1980s, when forestry standards were again relaxed as part of a policy of revenue generation via "sympathetic administration."[15]

The forest industry, for its part, was not immune to the sea change in public opinion in the late 1960s and early 1970s and the negative publicity its operations attracted. In 1974, MacMillan Bloedel became the first of the BC forestry companies to attempt to accommodate what it referred to as "non-timber resources." The company's three-person land use planning advisory team assembled wildlife, fisheries and forest hydrology and soils expertise to address persistent points of conflict surrounding the protection of fish-bearing streams and deer winter range, as well as concerns surrounding landslides and runoff and their effects on streams. One of the team's lasting contributions was a system for classifying landslides and landslide-prone areas that is still in use today. For forester and team member Bill Bourgeois, the team's success came in part through its productive relationship with the province's Environment and Land Use Committee Secretariat. "Rather than the traditional way, where government said, 'I know the answer and this is the way it will be,'" he recalled, "they were very willing . . . to look at different ways of doing things."[16]

Industry and BC Forest Service demands for "BC-based research" on fish-forestry interactions led to the initiation of the province's first comprehensive baseline study of pre- and post-harvest watershed conditions. Beginning in 1970, a salmon stream on the southwest coast of Vancouver Island became the site of the **Carnation Creek Experimental Watershed study**. Initiated by the federal Department of Fisheries and MacMillan Bloedel, with partnership from the BC Forest Service and the Fish and Wildlife Branch, among other agencies, multidisciplinary research at the site examined the effects of forestry practices on watershed processes and salmon populations. Studies of pre-logging conditions occurred until 1975, followed by logging using a variety of methods designed to permit long-term comparative analysis. The Carnation Creek study was not the first BC-based research on fish-forestry interactions—Ferris Neave and other federal fisheries biologists had investigated the effects of logging on the Cowichan and other Vancouver Island rivers beginning in the 1930s—but its continuous, comparative data collected over multiple years generated scientific insights that would transform forestry regulations in the 1980s and 1990s. Research from the site informed the province's 1988 Coastal Fisheries/Forestry Guidelines and its 1995 Forest Practices Code. Today, the Carnation Creek study constitutes the longest series of continuous data on fish-forestry interactions in the world.[17]

The Carnation Creek Experimental Watershed Study, initiated in 1970, has produced the longest series of continuous data on fish-forestry interactions in the world.

Cover of "Proceedings of the Carnation Creek Workshop, A 10 Year Review, February 24–26, 1982, Malaspina College, Nanaimo, B.C.," edited by G. Hartman (Pacific Forestry Centre, Canadian Forest Service, Natural Resources Canada, 1983). Image reproduced with permission from the Department of Natural Resources Canada, 2022.

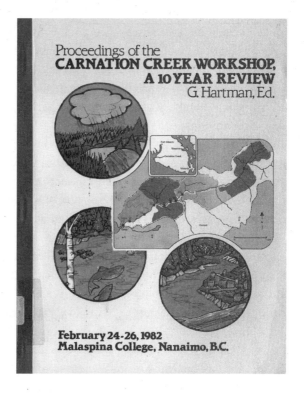

Proceedings of the
**CARNATION CREEK WORKSHOP,
A 10 YEAR REVIEW**
G. Hartman, Ed.

**February 24-26, 1982
Malaspina College, Nanaimo, B.C.**

Carnation Creek laid important groundwork for the future of stream protection in the province, but its results would take time. Until then, frustrated efforts to protect fish habitat led fisheries officials and advocates to consider other methods of bolstering flagging salmon populations. The resulting shift from habitat protection to salmon production would see the revival of two methods popular at the turn of the twentieth century: (1) small-scale, low-tech and relatively low-risk restoration work to improve salmon passage; and (2) large-scale, high-tech and relatively high-risk hatchery production.

This return to older approaches emerged in 1974, when respected UBC fisheries scientist Peter Larkin published an influential essay on salmon enhancement titled "Play It Again, Sam." In it, Larkin called for a return to simple, small-scale efforts to improve salmon habitat. Since World War II, he argued, salmon management had mostly involved regulatory adjustments to control the harvest and failed attempts to protect salmon from the effects of resource extraction. Lost in the process were the efforts of an

earlier generation of fisheries officers and conservationists to increase salmon production through low-tech, site-specific practices, such as the removal of natural and human-made obstructions to salmon migration, the
regulation of stream flow and the construction of artificial spawning channels.

Unlike the hatchery operations of the early twentieth century, which
scientists now suspected had contributed to the spread of fish diseases
and the reduction of genetic resilience among wild salmon, these simple
interventions offered a low-cost and relatively low-risk means of boosting
salmon productivity. Larkin cited the success of the Hell's Gate Fishway,
completed in 1945 to address the effects of a historic landslide that had
blocked fish passage, in restoring pink salmon runs to the upper Fraser. Like
Demarchi in his efforts to restore grassland systems in the East Kootenay,
Larkin recognized that a successful salmon enhancement program would
require "more than anything . . . a commitment to continuity." Participation
and revenue support from resource users, and the engagement of a wider
public as stewards of the resource, would also be critical to program success.
To achieve these ends he called on the provincial government, until then
a "bystander in the salmon business," to become more involved given its
"vital role in maintaining freshwater environments."[18]

Larkin's recommendations contributed to the establishment of the
Canadian **Salmonid Enhancement Program** in 1977, a joint federal-
provincial initiative with the goal of doubling Pacific salmon runs on the BC
coast. Intended in part as an economic development initiative for Indigenous
and coastal communities, the program provided some support for the
habitat rehabilitation and community stewardship methods that Larkin
identified. The bulk of annual funds, however, went to the construction and
maintenance of twenty salmon hatcheries (some new and some constructed
a decade earlier) on the coast and inland rivers. The political and economic
appeal of a program that would address overfishing by manufacturing more
fish proved stronger, evidently, than the history of hatchery failures in the
1930s and the known risks that hatchery-raised fish posed to wild salmon.
Ongoing salmon allocation conflicts between the US and Canada, and
among fisheries sectors in BC, contributed to the push for more fish, as did
the growing technological capacity of the commercial fleet.

Hatchery production did have its successes: it produced large numbers
of fish that supported valuable sport, commercial and Indigenous fisheries
and seeded new recreational fisheries in some areas. By 1992, however, after

fifteen years of enhancement and $500 million in federal government expenditure, the Salmonid Enhancement Program had not yet met its target of doubling salmon catch numbers on the coast. More troubling, the risks of hatchery production had become increasingly clear. Wild coho numbers in the Strait of Georgia had declined by more than 50 per cent since the 1970s—the result, some scientists argued, of competition for food and habitat from the hundreds of thousands of hatchery-raised coho released into the same feeding grounds.[19] Others, including Stó:lō fisheries expert Vince Harper, warned of the dilution of wild gene pools by hatchery fish and the effects of larger, hatchery-fuelled harvests on remnant wild stocks.[20]

UBC fisheries biologist Carl Walters echoed the conclusions of fisheries scientists in the 1920s and '30s in a 1992 interview in the *Globe and Mail*: "Hatcheries don't work. I pray they will all be gone and replaced by small projects, especially those that rehabilitate habitat. That, and better fisheries management." With the collapse of the northern cod stocks on the East Coast occupying the national news, former royal commissioner Peter Pearse made a similar assessment: "The surest, most environmentally friendly and by far the most economical way to rebuild salmon stocks," he commented, "is to let more wild fish reach their spawning grounds. That means catching less. It's as simple as that."[21]

Today, the federal government continues to operate twenty-three salmon hatcheries on the BC coast, despite ongoing concern from scientists and environmentalists. The growth of private salmon aquaculture operations since the 1970s, with their associated risks of disease and parasite transmission, have further depressed wild salmon populations.[22] In 2018, the Committee on the Status of Endangered Wildlife in Canada found that 50 per cent of chinook salmon populations in southern BC were at risk. Salmon returns on the rivers of BC's north and central coasts that year were among the lowest ever recorded, with implications not only for human fisheries but also for the wide range of salmon-dependent animal species, including grizzly bears and dwindling populations of southern resident orcas.[23]

While debates continue to rage about the future of hatchery production in the province, there is little dispute about the advances in knowledge that five decades of consistent federal investment in salmon enhancement enabled. As Larkin advised in 1974, "continuity is key." Research emerging from the Salmonid Enhancement Program has yielded important scientific understanding of salmon biology, migration and genetics. Investing in salmon enhancement, however flawed in implementation, also helped to raise the profile of fish relative to other resource uses. Small-scale initiatives, though less a priority than Larkin might have wished, also benefited from this continuity of support. The program nurtured the development of citizen stream stewardship initiatives still active today and provided the research, funding and political will to protect and restore critical salmon habitat in the lower Fraser Valley and other urban areas.[24]

INITIATIVE PROFILE: Creating a Private Fishery at Pennask Lake

British Columbia, like many other parts of North America, has been celebrated for its relatively democratic access to fish and wildlife. Exclusive game preserves conjure associations with early modern Europe or nineteenth-century South Africa, not twentieth-century British Columbia. Pennask Lake, in the southern Interior, stands as a reminder of a lesser-known history of privatization and exclusion within the province's sport fisheries. Here, the use of private property law to exclude Indigenous fishers in the 1920s has continued to resonate as recreational fishers and hunters have challenged the enclosure and de facto privatization by private landowners of freshwater lakes and the fish populations they support.

Located approximately eighty kilometres south of Kamloops, Pennask Lake is a large, high-elevation lake that today hosts one of the largest remaining runs of wild rainbow trout in the world. Until the late 1920s, its abundant trout populations supported twelve Indigenous communities in the southern Interior, including members of the Nłeʔkepmxc (Lower Nicola), Secwépemc, Lillooet and Syilx First Nations. For generations, these communities had intensively fished the shallows of the lake's inlet and outlet creeks during the spring rainbow trout spawn, drying portions of their catch to last throughout the year and to trade with other groups.[25]

When members of the Upper Nicola Syilx and Lower Nicola Nłeʔkepmxc communities arrived at their ancestral fishing grounds at the lake outlet in the spring of 1929, they were denied access. In the space of the preceding two years, members of the Pennask Lake Fishing and Game Club, an elite group of hunters and fly-fishers founded by Hawaii pineapple magnate James Drummond Dole, had drawn on the support of influential Canadian lawyers and politicians to purchase the entire lakefront and construct a lodge and private access road. As historian J. Michael Thoms has shown, Dole's use of private property to displace what

Access routes to Pennask Lake, ca.1929

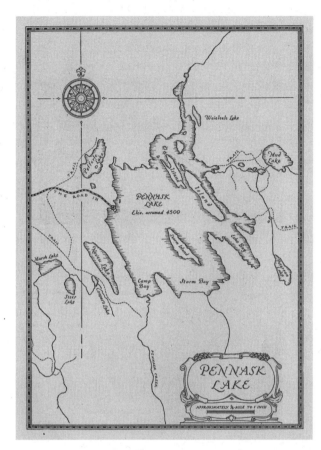

Source: Pennask
Lake Club promo-
tional booklet, 1929.
Image courtesy of
UBC Library
Open Collections.

he viewed as an excessively large Indigenous fishery enclosed and effectively privatized the fishery. While the lake and creekbeds themselves remained in Crown possession, owners of the surrounding lands could point to trespass law to prohibit public access. The provincial superintendent of land's 1930 rejection of renewed Syilx and Nłe?kepmxc requests for two small reserves to protect their ancestral fishing sites ended a collective Indigenous fishery that had supported people in the region for hundreds if not thousands of years.[26]

The Pennask Club's goals to create a "properly protected domain" aligned well with provincial and federal fish and wildlife policy and the interests of its leadership. BC game commissioner Bryan Williams and several UBC professors were among the fifty collective owners of the club and its property. Club efforts to "preserve [the fishery] undiminished" by limiting members' daily catch and permitting "fly-casting only" supported the vision of federal fisheries biologists who saw the lake's "clean, bright, firm, [and] lice-free" rainbows as a source of brood stock for government hatcheries.[27] In 1927, as Dole and the Pennask Club were assembling property holdings around the lake, the dominion government opened its Summerland trout hatchery (purchased by the province in 1937) using eggs from Pennask Lake rainbow trout. Today, the lake's wild rainbow trout continue to support roughly 40 per cent of the hatchery needs across the province. While the creation of Pennask Lake Provincial Park in 1975 provided limited access to the lake for backcountry campers and anglers, the vast majority of the lakefront remains the property of the Pennask Club, which continues to operate a lodge on the site.[28]

As fish and game and outdoor recreation clubs have pressed in recent decades for public access to lakes and waterways enclosed by private lands, the story of Pennask Lake has acquired renewed relevance. The enclosure of an Indigenous and later Crown-owned fishery at Pennask was not anomalous: exclusive fishery leases were granted to other BC fish and game clubs in the late nineteenth and early twentieth centuries, and ranches and other large properties would enclose other publicly owned lakes and river frontages.[29] As the 2021 verdict in *Douglas Lake Cattle Company v. Nicola Valley Fish and Game Club* confirmed, the absence of "freedom to roam" legislation in British Columbia means private landowners have the law behind them when they prohibit access to publicly owned bodies of water on their property.[30]

Fisheries Allocation Conflicts and Indigenous Rights

In British Columbia, the Indigenous rights cases that would come to redefine Canada's relationship with Indigenous Peoples originated in the fisheries. As the province's salmon fisheries moved from a position of relative abundance in the 1950s and 1960s to increasing scarcity from the late 1960s on, conflicts between commercial, sport and Indigenous fisheries became more frequent and more intense. In 1967, federal fisheries officers closed the Indigenous food fishery on the Fraser River from Mission Bridge to Lytton for three weeks in July in order to protect a threatened early sockeye run. Stó:lō and other Fraser River peoples who continued to fish were arrested and had their nets confiscated, but the commercial fishery at the mouth of the Fraser River remained open. When the closure was

Fraser River sockeye returns, 1893–2021

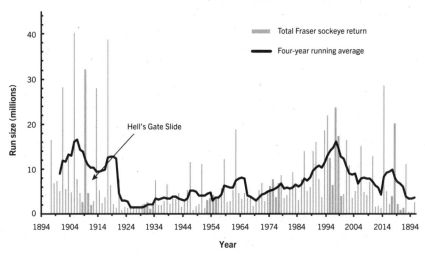

Image courtesy of the Pacific Salmon Commission.

repeated the following year, protests by Indigenous leaders resulted in a single twenty-four-hour opening within the three-week closure. But the crackdowns on the Indigenous food fishery continued. In 1970, Stó:lō and Okanagan communities organized large-scale "fish-ins" in defiance of fisheries closures and what royal commissioner Peter Pearse would later describe as "harassment, intimidation, and unjustified confiscations of fish, cars, and gear" by fisheries officers.[31] For Indigenous communities along the coast and inland rivers, much of the impetus for their groundbreaking court challenges of the next three decades was rooted in what had been a century-long fight for access to traditional salmon fisheries.

Since 1888, when Ottawa introduced the notion of a food fishery by requiring Indigenous fishers to fish only for personal consumption and "not for sale [or] barter," regulation of the food fishery had become increasingly restrictive as competition for salmon stocks intensified. The federal government had consistently denied the existence of an Aboriginal right to fish commercially and interpreted the traditional Indigenous fishery "as a strictly subsistence activity, one to be continued as a privilege, not a right." Any broader Aboriginal or treaty-based right to fish, Ottawa maintained, had been extinguished by successive federal fisheries regulations.[32]

The Fraser River was an especially significant battleground in the fight for Aboriginal fishing rights. Its massive summer and fall salmon runs alone supported over half of the Indigenous food fishery in the province.[33] In 1913, after an extensive rock slide in the Fraser Canyon destroyed upstream salmon runs, Ottawa attempted to eliminate the food fishery altogether by prohibiting Indigenous fishing at customary sites on the Fraser River. These efforts were ultimately abandoned in favour of a more restrictive licensing system. Introduced in 1917, the new system required Indigenous fishers to hold a federal permit to fish for food, subject to the same place, time and equipment restrictions as the commercial fishery. Permits were required even for members of those nations that had signed colonial treaties protecting their fishing and hunting rights. Indian Affairs agents, furthermore, were notoriously subjective in their distribution of food fishery permits, identifying "deserving" recipients and (in keeping with Department of Fisheries policy) denying permits to fishers near urban areas.[34] By the 1960s, as historian Diane Newell argues, fisheries officers treated Indigenous food fishery allocations more as a form of welfare than as an Aboriginal right. Because Indigenous river fishing occurred near the end of the salmon's migrations to their spawning grounds, food fishery allocations were often the first to be reduced or eliminated in the name of conservation.

Indigenous fishers lost considerable ground within the commercial fishery in the same period. In the late nineteenth century, Ottawa's practice of granting the majority of commercial licences to the canneries meant that Indigenous fishers had to work for the canneries in order to sell their fish. In the early years, many coastal peoples took advantage of this source of supplementary income by selling fish to the canneries and working on the canning lines. As immigration increased after 1900, however, non-Indigenous fishers and cannery workers increasingly displaced their Indigenous counterparts, first on the Fraser River and later on the central and north coast. By 1951, only one-third of BC commercial fishers were Indigenous and most commercial licences were held by non-Indigenous fishers. Ottawa's efforts to reduce the number of licensed commercial fishers in the context of conservation concerns in the late 1960s only exacerbated these trends. With the prioritization of larger, full-time operators and the gradual elimination of smaller, less profitable operators through government buy-back programs, many Indigenous fishers lost their boats and their livelihoods.[35]

Conflicts over federal fisheries allocations continued into the late 1980s. Here, a federal fisheries officer inspects a Stó:lō fishing net near Yale in 1988. Photo courtesy of the *Chilliwack Progress* and Chilliwack Museum and Archives, 2019.039.005.

In both the river-based food fishery and the ocean-based commercial fishery, conservation-based arguments had the effect of marginalizing Indigenous fishers while permitting unsustainable commercial catches to continue. This was especially true for the province's most productive salmon fisheries on the Fraser and Skeena rivers. Because inland Indigenous fisheries occurred "at the end of the harvesting chain" for salmon, they became flashpoints in larger conservation battles. For federal fisheries officials and sport fishery advocates, upriver fisheries compromised conservation aims in that they provided "no way to ensure escapement" for returning salmon.[36]

For their part, Indigenous fishers not only sought to uphold an Aboriginal right to fish but rejected the expectation that they would bear the brunt of conservation measures. Ongoing encroachment on reserve-based fishing grounds by non-Indigenous sport and commercial fishers presented another point of contention for Indigenous communities experiencing the steady erosion of access to traditional fisheries (see plate 9). Resource economist

Floyd Joseph's 1985 silkscreen print, *Capilano Fishing Grounds*, commemorates his BC
Supreme Court victory of the same year. Tried five years before the landmark *Sparrow*
decision, *R v. Joseph* held that a Squamish band bylaw permitting band members to fish on
reserve land at any time superseded federal regulations under the Fisheries Act (*R v. Joseph*,
1985 CarswellBC 675). The spring and coho salmon in the print represent "different paths
at different times that native people go through for similar reasons" (Pacific Editions
Artist Statement). Royal BC Museum, Catalogue no. 18204. Reprinted with permission
from Floyd Joseph.

Peter Pearse sided with Indigenous fishers in his 1982 report for the Royal
Commission on Pacific Fisheries Policy. Placing the blame for historically
low salmon returns squarely on overfishing by commercial operators and
an expanding and largely unregulated sport fishery, Pearse recommended
stricter regulation of commercial and sport operators and greater recognition of Indigenous interests.[37]

Fish-ins and localized defiance of fisheries regulations were not
the only ways that Indigenous communities responded to what they
viewed as unfair and unlawful restrictions on their Aboriginal right to
fish. Changes to the Indian Act in 1951 that lifted prohibitions against

seeking legal counsel for land and resource claims, coupled with the extension of the right to vote in federal elections in 1960, had opened new avenues for Indigenous claims—most significantly, the courts. Gains were slow in coming, however, and incremental in their effect. Through the 1960s, plaintiffs claiming an Aboriginal or treaty right to fish were mostly unsuccessful.[38]

The Sparrow *Decision*

Not until the passage of the federal Constitution Act in 1982 did the tides begin to turn for Indigenous plaintiffs. The recognition of "existing aboriginal and treaty rights" in section 35(1) of the act placed new requirements before the courts. ***R v. Sparrow*** was the first case to test the application and significance of section 35. Ronald Sparrow, a prominent elder of the Musqueam First Nation, had been charged in 1984 for fishing with a drift net considerably longer than that permitted by the Musqueam's food fishing licence. Sparrow claimed an Aboriginal right to fish and argued that the net limit regulation violated section 35(1) of the Constitution Act. The Supreme Court of Canada issued its unanimous and groundbreaking decision in 1990: historic government regulations, such as the Fisheries Act and its associated regulations, did not *in themselves* extinguish an Aboriginal right. Instead, the intention of the Crown (i.e., federal and provincial governments) to extinguish an Aboriginal right must "be clear and plain." *Sparrow* established that "existing aboriginal rights" must be interpreted flexibly to acknowledge their evolution over time. It identified the federal government's special trust or "fiduciary" relationship with Indigenous people as the primary consideration in justifying any regulations that interfered with an Aboriginal right. Finally, *Sparrow* confirmed the priority of the Indigenous right to fish for food, social and ceremonial purposes, subject only to valid conservation measures, over the interests of non-Indigenous commercial and sport fishers.[39]

The *Sparrow* decision would have lasting significance for fisheries and wildlife management in British Columbia and across Canada. From 1990 on, provincial wildlife managers would be tasked with attempting to balance constitutionally protected Aboriginal rights with the conservation and allocation rationales undergirding the province's hunting and fishing regulations. Efforts by the federal government to acknowledge its legal obligations resulted in the creation of the Aboriginal Fisheries Strategy (AFS) in 1992, which continues to provide limited commercial harvest rights and fisheries management opportunities for Indigenous communities on the Lower Fraser River and several other major salmon rivers in the province. Pilot initiatives for commercial fish sales by Indigenous people, and the deep resentment those initiatives have engendered among non-Indigenous commercial and sport fishers, mean that the Fraser River salmon fishery remains a flashpoint for concerns over salmon conservation and fisheries allocation and management.[40]

Sparrow's affirmation of the existence of Aboriginal rights and the duty of the Crown to justify any infringement on them, set the stage for a new relationship between Indigenous Peoples and the provincial and federal governments. As Newell has shown, it provided the "crucial underpinnings" for broader claims, both at the negotiating table and in the courts.[41] In 1990, the government of British Columbia finally reversed its long-standing position of refusing to recognize the existence of Aboriginal title and an Aboriginal right to self-government by establishing the BC Claims Task Force. By 1992, the newly formed BC Treaty Commission had set in motion the modern treaty process. Six years later, Canada, British Columbia and the Nisga'a Nation signed the province's first modern land claim.[42]

Conclusion: Production vs. Protection

For commercially harvested salmon and valued sport fish in freshwater lakes and rivers, high demand coupled with the significance of forestry returns in the province led authorities to prioritize hatchery production and allocation over habitat protection and restoration. Significant investments in hatchery production for salmon on the coast and freshwater trout and other species provincewide supported growing commercial and sport fisheries and contributed to BC's reputation as a premium angling destination. However, for salmon especially, the risks that hatchery-released fish pose to remnant wild stocks prompted scientists to revisit the concerns that led to provincewide hatchery closures in the 1930s.

Inequities within the salmon fisheries' allocation process, furthermore, concentrated the burden of conservation measures on inland Indigenous fisheries. A decades-long fight by First Nations in BC for access to and management authority over traditional fisheries laid the foundation for a series of landmark court challenges that would transform the relationship between Indigenous communities and the federal and provincial governments. By mobilizing Aboriginal rights newly entrenched in the 1982 Canadian Charter of Rights and Freedoms, the Musqueam Nation's 1990 *Sparrow* case established the primacy of the Indigenous food fishery and enabled future entitlements to wildlife management authority and decision-making power in the decades to come.

PLATE 1 • Hilda V. Foster's watercolour *The Gathering of the Camas Was a Ceremony* (ca.1965) depicts a group of likely Lekwungen (Songhees and Xwsepsum) women gathering camas near present-day Oak Bay. Victoria's camas meadows were maintained by Indigenous burning practices over thousands of years. Royal BC Museum, PDP-01738.

PLATE 2 • Tahltan and other northern Indigenous hunters took advantage of guiding opportunities beginning in the early twentieth century. Here, renowned Tahltan hunting guide Benny Frank stands with "silver tip" grizzly (*Ursus arctos horribilis*), Telegraph Creek, ca.1920. Royal BC Museum, 01158. Reprinted with permission from the Tahltan Central Government.

PLATE 3 • BC naturalist and mountaineer Phyllis Munday feeding wild birds on the porch of the family cabin on Dam Mountain, North Vancouver, ca.1920. Munday Family Photographs. Royal BC Museum, 1-61717.

PLATE 4 • British Columbians had multiple and varying relationships with wildlife. Here, a boy feeds a deer on the recently constructed road to Hope, ca.1930s. Royal BC Museum, C-08188.

PLATE 5 • Ian McTaggart Cowan packing a black-tailed deer (*Odocoileus hemionus columbianus*), Constitution Hill, Vancouver Island, November 10, 1930. Hamilton Mack Laing Fonds. Royal BC Museum, G-03664.

PLATE 6 • An Indigenous woman fleshing a moosehide, 1942. J.J. Wood Fonds. Royal BC Museum, H-03359.

PLATE 7 • A wildlife-themed stamp commemorating the 1961 federal Resources for Tomorrow conference. Canada Post Corporation. Library and Archives Canada, RG3-1989-565 CPA.

Ecological reserve locations and corresponding biogeoclimatic zones in British Columbia, 2008

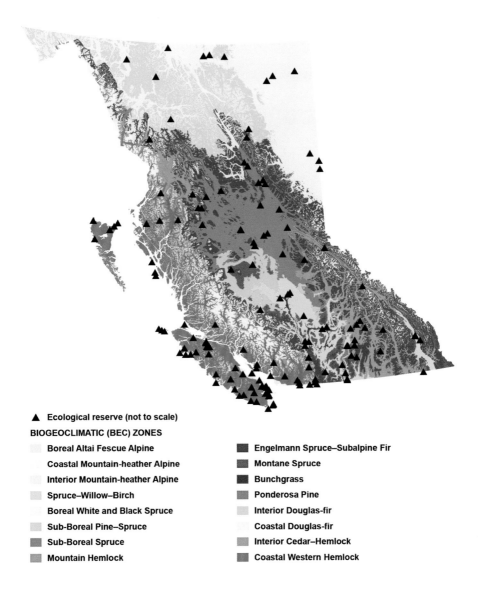

▲ Ecological reserve (not to scale)

BIOGEOCLIMATIC (BEC) ZONES

Boreal Altai Fescue Alpine

Coastal Mountain-heather Alpine

Interior Mountain-heather Alpine

Spruce–Willow–Birch

Boreal White and Black Spruce

Sub-Boreal Pine–Spruce

Sub-Boreal Spruce

Mountain Hemlock

Engelmann Spruce–Subalpine Fir

Montane Spruce

Bunchgrass

Ponderosa Pine

Interior Douglas-fir

Coastal Douglas-fir

Interior Cedar–Hemlock

Coastal Western Hemlock

PLATE 8 • Today, ecologists and soil scientists recognize sixteen distinct biogeoclimatic zones in British Columbia. Data sources: Ministry of Forests, Forest Analysis and Inventory Branch, Biogeoclimatic (BEC) Zones, 2014; Ministry of Environment, BC Parks, BC Parks, Ecological Reserves, and Protected Areas, 2008. Map by GeoBC, 2022.

PLATE 9 • Monique (Basil) McKinnon smoking salmon at her smokehouse on Stuart Lake, Nak'azdli Reserve, 1971. British Columbia, Special Services Branch. Royal BC Museum, I-02890. Reprinted with permission from the Monique (Basil) McKinnon Family and Nak'azd'i Whut'en First Nation.

10

Changing Public Sentiment

For Canadian Wildlife Service biologist Laszlo Retfalvi, the environmental awakening of the 1960s and 1970s "permanently shattered . . . the myth of abundance" that had characterized attitudes toward land and wildlife use for well over a century.[1] An explosion of public interest in British Columbia's wildlife and natural systems stemmed from expansions in postwar wealth and leisure time, as well as a growing urban population seeking recreation and connection with nature. These were countrywide, continentwide shifts in public consciousness. But in BC, heightened public awareness and advocacy for nature were shaped by the province's extraordinary natural heritage and the visibility—to hunters, fishers, naturalists and hikers—of what was being lost. Two decades of rapid industrialization of the province's fisheries, forestry and mineral sectors had not only acquainted British Columbians with problems of pollution, stream degradation and declining salmon runs but also raised public skepticism of the sustainability of these operations.

Television also played an important role in popularizing a more expansive understanding of human relationships with the natural environment. Here again, British Columbians contributed insights shaped by an appreciation of the province's ecological diversity. The launch in 1960 of CBC Television's *The Nature of Things*, hosted by UBC geneticist David Suzuki, exemplified this shift. Like Cowan's groundbreaking wildlife television series of the 1950s and early 1960s, Suzuki brought the findings of biology and environmental science to a wide public audience. His stance was more explicitly environmental, however, emphasizing the reality of ecological limits and the folly of human developments that ignored them. Having recently celebrated its sixtieth season, the series has made an important contribution to the ecological literacy of generations of Canadians. Another British Columbian, television producer Mike Halleran, would later bring a more rural perspective to BC resource management issues in his acclaimed *Westland* series, which aired on the Knowledge Network from 1984 to 2007.

Over the same period, the popular influence of Canadian writers Farley Mowat and Bill Mason contributed to a sea change in public opinion about wildlife. Mowat's 1963 book *Never Cry Wolf* and Mason's 1972 film *Cry of the Wild* fuelled rising public opposition to provincial predator control activities. By the late 1970s, wolves had become emblematic of the polarized positions of the hunting lobby, on the one hand, which generally viewed wolf control as a necessary component of effective wildlife management, and the environmental lobby, on the other, which viewed it as an unnecessary managerial intrusion into a natural system with its own built-in checks and balances.

Writers like Mowat also picked up on a much older desire to understand wild animals as individuals rather than as populations. Drawing on a long tradition of popular works dating back to Ernest Thompson Seton's 1898 *Wild Animals I Have Known*, Mowat generated empathy for a once hated and feared predator by encouraging readers to see wolves as playful, family-oriented animals with legitimate motivations of their own. Instead of wasteful and bloodthirsty killers of livestock and game, wolves in Mowat's telling played a vital ecological role by helping to maintain the health of prey populations. While his methods raised significant doubts among Canadian wildlife scientists, his conclusions roughly aligned with changing scientific thought about the value of wolves and other predators. BC's Predator Control Branch had been disbanded in 1963. By 1979, the Fish and Wildlife Branch had reined in its once liberal use of wolf and coyote poisons to "cases of demonstrated need."[2]

As a new generation of wildlife biologists, many of whom were not active hunters, took up government and university positions, scientific consensus shifted to favour a broader conception of wildlife in research and government policy. The federal government's introduction in 1966 of its groundbreaking National Wildlife Policy and Program, for example, expanded federal responsibilities for migratory birds to include research, education and management roles for all wildlife on federal lands and new management initiatives for species that crossed provincial boundaries, like caribou.[3] Seven years later, the passage of the Canada Wildlife Act enabled the new federal Ministry of Environment to manage or acquire public lands for the purposes of wildlife conservation.

Shifts at the provincial level were more gradual. In 1966, the replacement of the Game Act with the BC Wildlife Act and the removal of the word "game" from the retitled Fish and Wildlife Branch signalled an important shift in the province's approach to wildlife management. In practice, however, not much had changed. Wildlife was still described in the act primarily as game—although the addition to that definition of "and any other species of vertebrates designated as wildlife" opened up possibilities for responsibility to a wider range of species in the years that followed.[4] While the new act gave the Branch statutory authority to purchase or acquire land for the purposes of protecting wildlife, it made no provision to require consideration of wildlife habitat needs in the resource management decisions made by other ministries.

This chapter explores the ways that these changing public attitudes toward wildlife produced schisms between established conservation groups and a new generation of environmental and animal rights organizations that often adopted anti-hunting and anti-trapping positions. By the late 1970s, an oppositional stance had hardened between fish and game organizations and environmental organizations that had once collaborated on habitat protect initiatives. These schisms also appeared within the Fish and Wildlife Branch, as a new cohort of non-game biologists took up positions in regional offices and emphasis shifted to the protection of threatened and endangered non-game species.

INDIVIDUAL PROFILE:
Michael Bigg and the Reimagination of BC's Orcas

Changes in public attitudes toward orcas (*Orcinus orca*), or killer whales, offer a profound illustration of some of the broader shifts taking place in public understanding and concern for wildlife in the province. Before the mid-1960s, orcas were widely understood among settler populations as vicious man-eaters and malevolent predators that threatened local fishing economies. Fishers often shot at surfacing orcas and other marine mammals on sight. Their belief in rising orca numbers led the federal Department of Fisheries to mount a .50 calibre machine gun overlooking Seymour Narrows, northwest of Campbell River, in 1961 for the purpose of shooting

Dr. Michael Bigg analyzing photographs of orca saddle patches
in his office at the Pacific Biological Station in Nanaimo, ca.1985.
Photo courtesy of Michelle Bigg.

orcas. Although the gun was never fired and was removed several months later because of safety concerns, the fact that it was installed at all demonstrates the gulf
in understanding and perception of the province's orcas between then and now.[5]

Ironically, as University of Victoria historian Jason Colby has shown, it was the
capture of orcas for display in aquariums, beginning in the 1960s, that initiated
the transformation of public perceptions. Between 1962 and 1973, forty-five killer
whales were captured off the British Columbia and Washington coasts; at least thirteen others died during capture attempts.[6] Captive whales not only endeared themselves to public audiences with their playfulness and intelligence but also provided
scientists for the first time with live subjects for detailed study. Whale captures for
aquariums—unregulated between 1964 and 1976—also prompted government efforts to determine baseline orca populations.

In 1970, Dr. Michael Bigg, the new head of marine mammal research at the Department of Fisheries Pacific Biological Station in Nanaimo, took up the task of organizing the first-ever population census of orcas on the Pacific Coast. Boaters, lighthouse keepers and fishers participated in the census by recording orca sightings on a single day in late July 1971. The results showed a maximum population of 350 animals in BC waters, far fewer than the thousands anticipated. Surveys in subsequent years corroborated these results, lending support to growing opposition to orca capture among scientists and BC residents.

Bigg's efforts to obtain an accurate count of individuals, rather than an estimate of populations, led to his most significant breakthrough. Following unsuccessful experiments with branding or notching the dorsal fins of captive whales, Bigg and his colleagues discovered that individual animals could be distinguished through close examination of the dorsal fin and "saddle patch" at its base. Photographs taken when a whale surfaced revealed variations such as nicks, tears and pigmentation unique to each individual. By 1975, Bigg and a growing team of researchers and volunteers had assembled a photographic catalogue documenting every individual orca in BC waters (work that continues today under the auspices of the BC Cetacean Sightings Network). The following year, authorities in BC and Washington State halted the capture of orcas for captivity.

Bigg's research—conducted with the assistance of friends and associates after the end of the Department of Fisheries orca study in 1975—revolutionized the study of cetaceans (whales, dolphins and porpoises), enabling long-term studies of individual animals, their migration routes and their social relationships. The ability to discern animals as individuals allowed him to identify four distinct populations of orcas in BC: fish-eating northern residents; fish-eating southern residents; marine-mammal-eating transients; and fish- and shark-eating offshore orcas. His work also demonstrated that orca groups did not orient around adult males, as originally thought, but rather formed matrilineal pods led by mothers and maternal relatives. Over the space of two decades, Bigg and his network of volunteers assembled "one of the most thorough data sets for any wild mammal" and transformed the orca "from one of the least known to among the best understood of all cetaceans."[7] His photo identification methods would later be adapted for use with other wildlife species, including terrestrial mammals such as wolverines and martens.[8]

When Bigg died of leukemia in 1990 at the age of fifty-one, the Robson Bight Ecological Reserve in Johnstone Strait—designated as an orca sanctuary in 1982— was renamed the Robson Bight/Michael Bigg Ecological Reserve in his honour. The reserve protects one of the few documented "rubbing beaches," where northern resident orcas gather to rub against smooth underwater pebbles.

Although shooting and capture for marine parks no longer occur in BC waters, pollution, declining salmon runs and rising maritime traffic continue to threaten the survival of southern resident orcas, whose numbers have fluctuated between seventy and ninety-nine individuals since 1976.[9] In 2001, the Committee on the Status of Endangered Wildlife in Canada formally designated the southern resident population as endangered. Northern residents, transients and offshore orca populations were listed as threatened in the same year.[10]

Setbacks and Shifting Alliances, 1977–1991

The environment of the early 1970s, with its bold experiments in land use planning and generous increases in budget allocations for fish and wildlife work, came to an end with the return to a Social Credit government in 1975 and recession-induced cutbacks within both provincial and federal wildlife programs in the early 1980s. Internal tensions and leadership challenges dogged the Fish and Wildlife Branch through the late 1970s, resulting in significant reforms to its mission and structure.

The problems began in 1975, when the newly formed Sierra Club of British Columbia raised concerns about lax regulation and possible corruption in the issuing of guide licences in the Spatsizi area of northwestern BC, soon to become a provincial park. A public inquiry by Judge J.L. McCarthy revealed serious errors in judgment and Branch-wide failures in administrative oversight. Branch funding was slashed, and director Jim Hatter, who had led the Fish and Wildlife Branch since 1963, lost his job in the process. Though cleared of any personal wrongdoing, Hatter's belief in the values of an older game management ethos was seen as increasingly out of step with changing public attitudes and, by his own admission, with the environmental values of his own staff.[11] Devastating as the inquiry was for the Branch's reputation and budget, it had the benefit of drawing the government's attention to a large and growing wildlife stakeholder group that was not interested in hunting and that wanted wildlife management to reflect concern for ecosystem integrity rather than for only a narrow range of game species.[12]

Tensions within the Fish and Wildlife Branch prompted the Department of Recreation and Conservation to commission a comprehensive review of

Branch operations in 1976. The review invited responses from key wildlife constituencies. The Federation of BC Naturalists and other such organizations took the opportunity to advocate for legal recognition and protection for non-game species, including reptiles, amphibians and small mammals.[13] In his 1977 report, Winston Mair, former chief of the CWS, recommended that the Branch better reflect in practice the nominal shift from "game" to "wildlife" that had occurred eleven years earlier. Inspired leadership and greater support for planning and research would allow the Branch to better fulfil its mandate to maintain and enhance *all* wildlife species in BC and to support their use and enjoyment by consumptive and non-consumptive users alike. Mair stressed the value of ongoing habitat protection work and recommended greater emphasis on wildlife education for the public and the development of avenues for active assistance from and collaboration with Indigenous and non-Indigenous hunters, trappers, anglers and naturalists.

More than any other area of Mair's report, his recommendations for the Conservation Officer Service resulted in lasting changes for wildlife work in the province. As biologists increased in number within the Branch in the 1950s and '60s, they contributed to a fulfilling work environment that rewarded initiative, professional competence and the regard of international peers. Their game warden and, later, conservation officer counterparts, however, experienced deteriorating work conditions over the same period. "The explosive growth of both concern and regulations respecting the environment" meant that conservation officers, or COs, were responsible for enforcing a dizzying array of legislation, from hunting and fishing regulations to pollution and environmental protection measures. In addition, COs in some regions were asked to assist with "game counts, fisheries programs, [and] stream clearing" activities, reducing their time for enforcement activities. As Mair reported, "it became impossible, in short . . . to do a thorough job of anything."[14] The exclusion of senior COs from decision-making in Victoria made these problems difficult to rectify.

In response, Mair recommended a "cautious evolution" toward the separation of management and enforcement work within the Department of Recreation and Conservation. A distinct and reinvigorated enforcement program, Mair proposed, could be achieved with a trained police officer at the helm and a transition to distinctive uniforms with rank insignia. In 1979, the province followed through on these recommendations by appointing Ralph Aldrich, a retired RCMP officer, as the province's chief conservation officer. In the decades that followed, the Conservation Officer Service became increasingly aligned with the culture and structure of policing in the province.[15]

The shift from game management to a broader emphasis on wildlife and environment became more concrete still with the transfer of the Branch to the recently formed Ministry of Environment in 1978.[16] Nominally promising, the new ministry enjoyed little direct control over the land base in practice. With the elevation of the Department of Forests to a stand-alone ministry and the hiving off of both the Parks and Lands branches into a separate ministry, the remnant units within the Ministry of Environment, including the Environment and Land Use (ELU) Secretariat and the Fish and Wildlife Branch, were confined to an advisory role of referral processes and inter-agency studies.

Ian McTaggart Cowan had predicted as much in a 1972 *Vancouver Sun* editorial. Pondering a broader government trend of creating departments of environment, he warned that such a move in British Columbia was likely to be an "empty gesture" with the potential to bury the Fish and Wildlife Branch, "the one group in provincial government . . . uniquely equipped to prevent or respond to wild land environmental problems." Instead, Cowan suggested, "each department [should] be compelled to consider the wild-land values of the land over which it has jurisdiction."[17] The BC Wildlife Federation was more forceful still, describing the 1978 reorganization as "part of a grand design to silence the one government agency anxious to defend the environment against developers and despoilers."[18] In political scientist Jeremy Wilson's assessment, these changes, combined with subsequent dismantling of the ELU Secretariat and its acclaimed regional resource management committees, "effectively derailed" development of a "broader, multi-agency conception of land use planning."[19]

Anti-hunting Sentiment and Environmentalism

The identity crisis within the Fish and Wildlife Branch played out on a broader canvas in the growing polarization between traditional fish and game organizations and a new generation of environmental organizations. Initially aligned in their interests to protect threatened fish and wildlife habitats from development, these organizations began to stake out diverging views, around hunting and trapping in particular, beginning in the late 1970s. From the Sierra Club's exposé of illegal hunting practices by a guide outfitter in Spatsizi Provincial Park in 1975 to the anti-hunting and anti-trapping stance of new media-savvy organizations like Greenpeace, environmental organizations gave voice to a growing distaste for hunting among urban British Columbians.[20] Some viewed hunting, and especially trophy hunting, as wasteful, barbaric and no longer justifiable in the context of abundant sources of domesticated animal protein. Wrapped up in the defence of wild spaces, for many of these organizations, was the right of wild animals to live what Cowan summarized as "a 'natural' life with all its hazards, predators, disease, starvation, winter kill, and competitive expulsion as well as its success—survival."[21]

For the BCWF and its 150 member clubs, which had long been on the forefront of efforts to protect and enhance wildlife habitat, anti-hunting critiques by environmental organizations amounted to, at best, ignorance—and at worst, betrayal. As Canadian historian Jean Manore has observed, "hunters are conservationists not just because they want animals to be available to hunt, but also because they believe that animals should continue to exist as part of the natural order just as much as humans." Hunting itself, she argues, is a way of relating to nature shaped by an ethic of conservation or "wise use."[22] Hunters chafed at what they viewed as judgmental ignorance among an urban majority increasingly disconnected from nature, wildlife and the province's hunting heritage. Their responses were not unfounded. A 1998 Manitoba government survey of urban attitudes toward hunting, for example, found that 80 per cent of respondents associated hunting with poaching and 49 per cent assumed that endangered species were hunted.[23]

Anti-hunting and anti-trapping critiques were especially pointed among the emerging **animal rights movement** in the 1970s. Unlike the animal welfare movement that preceded it, which focused its wildlife-oriented work primarily on the reduction of cruelty in fur-bearer trapping, animal rights activists sought to afford animals the right to their own existence and protection for their basic interests. At the foundation of animal rights arguments was the assertion that animals had the right to be treated as individuals with their own desires and needs, rather than as common property to be disposed of by humans. For hunters, these arguments were incomprehensible. Animal rights activists' use of lurid images and emotional language was especially troubling. It had the effect, hunters argued, of divorcing the perhaps unpleasant reality of the kill from the typically careful and respectful context within which it was conducted, just as surely as packaged supermarket meat placates consumers by removing that reality. While some common ground with environmentalist organizations could still be found in the protection of wilderness areas, and among naturalist organizations who shared a long history of collaboration with fish and game clubs in efforts to protect wildlife habitat, no such bridge existed between animal rights activists and hunting advocates.

In their defence, hunters laid out three central arguments. The first focused on the revenue that hunting generated for the province, and for wildlife conservation specifically. Unlike naturalists, environmentalists and other non-consumptive users of wildlife, resident and non-resident hunters paid licence fees and other taxes that directly supported wildlife conservation and management activities in the province. In addition, their annual hunting trips supported a range of jobs and livelihoods in rural areas.

The second argument centred on the nature of hunting as a biologically sound and sustainable activity. Hunter-conservationists pointed to the fact that with the exception of a few localized examples, there was "no crisis in game populations in British Columbia." As hunter and natural resources journalist Mike Halleran explained, the "properly-regulated presence of the hunter" assists wildlife managers in striking a balance between animal numbers and available habitat. Too many animals in a given area not only threatens the environment on which the animals depend but also produces suffering: "Disease and die-off in wildlife populations are ghastly to behold. The grim prospect of heavy winter kill is equally horrible. When populations get too large, the animals can literally eat themselves out of house and home." Hunting, he argued, "should not occur if it presents a threat to wildlife populations, but, if it does not, there are many sound, biological reasons why it should continue."[24]

The third argument upheld the value of science over sentiment in informing wildlife management decisions. For politically sensitive topics like the annual grizzly bear hunt, decisions should weigh the viability of the hunt for bear populations over objections to the hunt on philosophical grounds.

These three arguments still form the central pillars of hunters' arguments today. Then as now, however, hunters struggled to communicate these messages to a growing urban populace with receding connections not only to hunting traditions but also to nature. A decline in the number

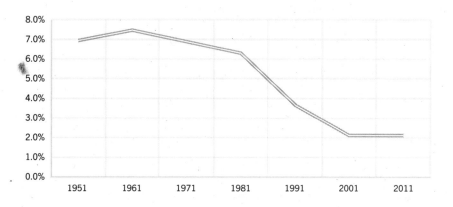

Percentage of BC population that hunts, 1951–2011

Data sources: John Gordon Terpenning, "The B.C. Wildlife Federation and Government: A Comparative Study of Pressure Group and Government Interaction for Two Periods, 1947 to 1957, and 1958 to 1975" (MA thesis, University of Victoria, 1982), 243–44; BC Population Statistics, 1867 to 2018, Statistics Canada, BC Statistics, Ministry of Citizens' Services, 2021; BC Ministry of Forests, Wildlife and Habitat Branch, "Annual Hunting Licence Sales by Type, 1976–77 to 2019–20." Image courtesy of the author.

of hunters in this period only exacerbated the waning influence of hunter-conservationists in the province's wildlife management work. The numbers of licensed resident hunters declined in the mid-1970s for the first time in the history of Fish and Wildlife Branch records. A brief climb in resident hunting licences in the recession period of the early 1980s was followed by a thirty-year decline beginning in 1982.[25] By 1987, BC had fewer hunters per capita than many other Canadian provinces. Halleran commented on these changes in a 1987 article on BC's hunting tradition: "when asked, the lapsed hunters said they quit because of cost, over-regulation, [and] poor hunting," among other reasons. Although Halleran noted that "pressure from anti-hunters did not seem to be a factor," it is difficult to gauge the effects of these broader societal shifts on people's individual choices.[26]

Whatever their cause, the changes had discernible effects on a wildlife management system predicated at least in part on user revenue. Fewer hunters meant less licence revenue, ultimately reducing capacity for research, monitoring and enforcement. Although revenue losses were partially offset by a dramatic jump in the number of resident angling licences over the same period, the closure of the Cache Creek game check station in 1981 came to symbolize the shrinking influence of hunters and the declining effectiveness of the wildlife management agency they had supported for almost a century.

INITIATIVE PROFILE: The Conibear Trap: BC's Contribution to More Humane Trapping Practice

Images of desperate animals caught in leghold traps mobilized a surge in public concern for the welfare of wild fur-bearers in the 1970s and early 1980s. A series of films by the Association for the Protection of Fur-Bearing Animals drew together television personalities and prominent BC scientists, including Ian McTaggart Cowan and David Suzuki, to present anti-cruelty messages that captured significant public attention. Their efforts, however, were just the latest in a decades-long campaign to reduce the suffering of animals killed for their furs. Victoria-based Clara Van Steenwyk, a founding member of the association, had been advocating for a humane alternative to the leghold trap since the 1930s. Her collaboration with northern trapper Frank Conibear and the BC Trappers Association would result in an important made-in-BC contribution to animal welfare.

Conibear, a trapper from the Northwest Territories, had long used the quiet hours walking his trapline to imagine humane alternatives to the leghold trap. In the late 1920s he began experimenting with trap designs. At that point, trappers and inventors in Canada and the United States had presented design ideas and filed patents for decades, with little success. The challenge was to produce a trap that killed an animal swiftly and humanely while meeting the practical needs of the fur industry. The trap needed to be light and strong, easy to carry and inexpensive; it could not endanger the trapper with poisons or explosive attachments.

When she heard of Conibear's experiments, Van Steenwyk offered to back his efforts, providing funds for the construction of prototypes and a patent application. Field tests proved disappointing, however, and Conibear abandoned his experiments. Over a decade later, after a back injury sidelined him from trapping, Conibear moved with his family to Victoria. Renewed acquaintance with Van Steenwyk led him to return to his trap designs, and by the early 1950s he had produced a promising and versatile "body-gripping" design that purportedly killed an animal quickly by snapping over its neck or chest.

Frank R. Conibear fleshing a
beaver pelt, ca.1934. Source:
Frank R. Conibear, *Devil Dog*
(New York: William Sloane, 1954).
Photo courtesy of the author.

In 1953, an unlikely partnership between Van Steenwyk's newly incorporated fur-bearer protection organization, the BC Game Commission, and the BC Trappers Association propelled Conibear's prototype to success. Van Steenwyk's association financed the manufacture of fifty prototype traps, and Chilcotin trapper Eric Collier, president of the trappers' association, worked with Game Commission biologists to field-test and fine-tune the trap's design. By the late 1950s, Conibear had patented his trap in Canada and the US. The higher manufacturing costs of the Conibear trap, however, discouraged widespread adoption by trappers. In BC, however, it was a different story. Collier's advocacy for the trap's effectiveness, combined with a Game Commission program that allowed trappers to exchange their leghold traps for a free Conibear trap, made the province a national leader in the shift from leghold to Conibear traps.

By the early 1970s, Conibear's design was the top-selling "humane" trap in the US and Canada, with over one million traps produced annually. In 1981, seven years before his death, Conibear accepted a prize from the BC government's Humane Trapping Committee for "outstanding creativity in the development of humane animal traps." Ongoing advocacy by the organization Van Steenwyk had helped to found led the province to ban the use of the least humane "toothed" leghold traps in 1982.[27]

A Bright Light in a Time of Austerity: The Habitat Conservation Fund

As an economic recession in the early 1980s introduced a new period of fiscal austerity in both the federal and provincial governments, spending was curtailed on wildlife management and habitat conservation initiatives. Funding cuts to the National Wildlife Area program, for example, meant the federal Ministry of Environment could "barely cover" existing habitat acquisition agreements with the provinces, let alone more recent acquisitions that came to "depend entirely" on the resources of land conservancy organizations like the Nature Trust of BC.[28] Within this context, the creation of BC's Habitat Conservation Fund (now the **Habitat Conservation Trust Foundation**) was a remarkable achievement, and one that would make a significant and lasting contribution to wildlife conservation in the province.

Like the other bold and creative experiments in wildlife management in this period, the idea for the fund emerged from the East Kootenay region, where wildlife advocates were especially vocal in their efforts to protect a shrinking and valuable land base. Carmen Purdy, president of the East Kootenay Wildlife Association and regional director for the BCWF, Ray Demarchi, regional wildlife biologist, and Joe Hall, a Cranbrook-area trapper and hunter, shared frequent conversations about the need for greater investment to enhance fish and wildlife populations and to conserve threatened habitat.

Hall came up with the idea of a tax on resource extraction—perhaps 10 cents a ton on coal, or 10 cents a cubic metre on timber—that could be dedicated exclusively to wildlife conservation initiatives. His idea was loosely based on the US Pittman-Robertson Act of 1937, which allocated an excise tax on firearms and ammunition to state fish and wildlife departments.[29] In March 1979, Purdy took advantage of a planned stopover in Cranbrook by a group of Social Credit cabinet ministers to schedule a meeting between the ministers and a group of local hunters and anglers. Meanwhile, Demarchi learned from a colleague on the Treasury Board that a self-imposed, user-pay tax on hunting and fishing licences was likely to be received more favourably than an extra tax on the resource industries. Purdy's twenty-minute meeting turned into a two-hour discussion. In the end, the parties agreed to a surcharge on hunting, angling, trapping and guide-outfitting licences. Purdy felt confident he could gather support from BCWF members provided that the funds went directly toward habitat acquisition and enhancement.

This was not the first proposal of its kind, and older members of the BCWF had seen similar initiatives run aground in the past. In 1951, the Sportsmen's Council, forerunner to the BCWF, had lobbied successfully for the creation of a game conservation fund drawn from licence revenue surpluses. Little of the money was spent, however, and in 1954 W.A.C. Bennett's government appropriated the fund for general revenues, sparking heated opposition by fish and game organizations. The BCWF's political influence had grown with the size of its membership in the intervening years, however, and with it the confidence that it could hold the government to their promises. Purdy, Hall and Demarchi gathered support among stakeholders while government proponents of the new fund worked behind the scenes to clear a legislative path and bolster its effectiveness.

Inaugurated in 1981, the Habitat Conservation Fund (HCF) relied on an innovative public-private partnership that generated revenue from two sources. An estimated $1.25 million, earmarked for habitat enhancement projects, would come from a new $3 surcharge on all hunting, angling, trapping and guide-outfitting licences; an additional $1.25 million would be drawn from the annual growth of the province's Crown Land Fund to support purchases of ecologically significant private lands. Significantly, in the early years several naturalists' clubs contributed to the HCF by voluntarily donating a $3 annual surcharge for each of their members. Although the HCF allowed for the receipt of donations like this, its position within government likely dampened donor interests.[30]

Problems with government control of the funds, however, began early and shaped the direction of what ultimately became the Habitat Conservation Trust Foundation. In 1983, two years after the HCF was created, widespread government cutbacks led the Bill Bennett government to impede its funds earmarked for habitat enhancement. While the existence of the HCF was never threatened (unlike its 1951 predecessor), its expenditures and staffing allocations could be controlled to balance the books. The public-private partnership that emerged in response to this early crisis created an important model for the future work of the fund. Rod Silver, a government biologist charged with administering the HCF, and Jim Walker, manager of habitat for the Fish and Wildlife Branch, proposed a cooperative venture between the HCF and the **BC Conservation Foundation (BCCF)**, a charitable foundation the BCWF had established in 1969. Formalized in the fall of 1985, the arrangement allowed the HCF to contract the BCCF, and later other not-for-profit organizations, to administer and manage conservation projects with oversight from the Ministry of Environment.

Similar constraints prompted creative solutions in the 1990s. In 1996, government spending restrictions led to the establishment of the fund as a separate trust entity at arm's length from the Ministry of Environment. This transition bolstered the flexibility, fundraising capability and accessibility of the newly titled Habitat Conservation Trust Fund. Where before only government entities could apply to the HCF, after 1996 anyone could apply, including First Nations and conservation and naturalists' organizations with habitat enhancement proposals. By 2001, the fund had directed almost $80 million into conservation education initiatives and vitally important fish and wildlife conservation projects at over one thousand different sites across the province. Former Habitat Conservation Trust Fund manager Rod Silver's knack for leveraging and pooling funds in partnership with land conservancy organizations supported voluntary stewardship arrangements and allowed for significant acquisitions of critical wildlife habitat in an environment of climbing real estate prices. Such funding partnerships became especially valuable after revenue from the Crown Land Account, one of the two pillars of the original fund, dried up in 2002.[31]

Today, the Habitat Conservation Trust Foundation, a stand-alone charitable organization since 2007, owes its remarkable four decades of success in fish and wildlife habitat conservation to the unique circumstances of its evolution. As journalist Ben Parfitt wrote in 2001, the then Habitat Conservation Trust Fund grew to become "one of the most important, reliable and dedicated sources of conservation funding in the history of the province."[32] From the beginning, one of the things that set it apart was the rigour and credibility of its board of directors. Comprising licensees and scientists, and led for the first two decades by the inimitable Ian McTaggart Cowan, the board implemented peer-reviewed, science-based project selection and evaluation protocols. As recently retired HCTF CEO Brian Springinotic explains, "the multi-stage technical review process that we run ... really attracts external investors. . . . [It] gives them confidence . . . that the investments that they're making through us are good value for money, technically sound, and designed to actually make a demonstrable difference for fish and wildlife in the province."[33]

INITIATIVE PROFILE: Is Ogopogo Wildlife?

Not all the creatures that came under the protection of the Wildlife Act were well documented, or even undisputedly real. In September 1989, the *Vancouver Sun* and *Province* newspapers reported that a US news group was planning to visit Okanagan Lake to search for its famed and mythical resident creature, Ogopogo. The team planned to comb the lake with a submersible camera equipped with a harpoon, aiming to film and possibly capture Ogopogo. The story generated both excitement and alarm in BC. Ogopogo was not only a beloved local legend for Okanagan residents and tourists but also an ancient water spirit (known as Nx̌ax̌aitkʷ, N'ha-a-itk or Naitaka) for Secwépemc and Syilx peoples.

Seeking to avert harassment of Okanagan wildlife, real or otherwise, BC Minister of Environment Bruce Strachan and Assistant Deputy Minister for Fish and Wildlife Jim Walker came up with a creative solution: they would include Ogopogo as a protected species in the Wildlife Act. Walker crafted an addition to the act that protected "a vertebrate, over three metres in length, resident in Lake Okanagan, which is not a white sturgeon." Their quick thinking paid off: the US news team called off their hunt, and Ogopogo had new protective status. That status, however, and the creativity and sense of humour that inspired it, was short-lived. Several years later, the protection was removed. However fleeting the protection for Ogopogo, the incident served to raise awareness of Okanagan wildlife and the possibilities of the Wildlife Act as a tool for emergency protections.[34]

The Importance of Wildlife to British Columbians

By the early 1980s, it was clear within government and among the majority of BC residents that the term "wildlife" comprised much more than just "game." A national survey on the importance of wildlife conducted between

Birders scoping a view of a rare spoon-billed sandpiper (*Calidris pygmaea*) at Iona Island at the mouth of the Fraser River, 1978. Brothers Richard and Syd Cannings, both biologists and lifelong naturalists (along with the third Cannings brother, Robert, behind the camera), stand with scopes in the foreground. Photo by Robert A. Cannings. Photo courtesy of the Biodiversity Centre for Wildlife Studies.

1981 and 1991 revealed the prevalence and popularity of non-consumptive wildlife activities, such as wildlife viewing and photography, even among consumptive users. Furthermore, over 80 per cent of Canadians believed in the importance of maintaining abundant wildlife populations and pre- serving endangered species.[35] Many British Columbians, though they inter- acted little with fish or wildlife, took aesthetic or moral gratification in its ongoing existence. A 1977 survey on attitudes to grizzly bears, for example, found that 88 per cent of BC's city dwellers supported bear conservation simply for the pleasure of knowing that the bears "were out there."[36]

The province's revamped Wildlife Act of 1982 reflected these changes in public attitudes, granting greater recognition to non-consumptive inter- ests in wildlife and solidifying the purpose of the legislation to "maintain the diversity and viability of species representative of the major biophysical zones of the province." A new commitment to public involvement was also apparent in the Ministry of Environment's dissemination of a discussion paper soliciting public comment on proposed changes within the act in the year before it was passed.[37]

The inclusion of non-game species in the province's wildlife management objectives also had the effect of weakening cherished economic arguments for wildlife protection, such as Peter Pearse's 1966 study of the economic benefits of big-game hunting in the Kootenays. As US conservationist Aldo Leopold recognized in his famous 1949 essay, "The Land Ethic," "one basic weakness in a conservation system based wholly on economic motives is that most members of the land community have no economic value."[38] Efforts to extend economic arguments to "non-resource" species were never as convincing as the promise of short-term economic gain; these arguments, furthermore, too often strained the credulity of their audiences. Instead, as prominent US biologist David Ehrenfeld argued, rationales for the conservation of non-game species needed to draw on a broader base of values. Wildlife enthusiasts espoused aesthetic and moral values in wishing to conserve the full diversity of wildlife for its own sake and for future human generations. But biological diversity offered a wider range of ecosystem and scientific benefits, too, in promoting ecological resilience, providing a blueprint for environmental restoration efforts and acting as a living laboratory for scientific research and teaching.[39]

Despite the persuasiveness of these alternative viewpoints, economic valuations of wildlife continued to animate policy responses. Growing markets for wildlife viewing, and their spinoff benefits for local tourism economies, were a case in point. In response to expanding public interest in non-consumptive relationships with wildlife and concerns about human-wildlife conflict, the province developed its first **wildlife-viewing program** in 1988. Developed in partnership with the Federation of BC Naturalists and in consultation with regional wildlife biologists, the initiative produced informative brochures identifying wildlife-viewing sites, species and viewing seasons across the province. Corresponding roadside signs bearing binocular icons indicated viewing sites such as Dragon Lake near Quesnel, for migrating sandhill cranes, and Bull River in the East Kootenay, for bighorn sheep. Regional wildlife-viewing brochures not only shared viewing tips ("wear drab clothing" and "approach downwind") but also introduced wildlife enthusiasts to principles of wildlife safety and viewing ethics—the first of their kind in the country.[40]

Stone's sheep (*Ovis dalli stonei*) seeking salt near one of British Columbia's iconic wildlife-viewing signs on the Alaska Highway near Muncho Lake, BC, n.d. (© Province of British Columbia. All rights reserved. Reproduced with permission.)

While the province's 1988 wildlife-viewing program is no longer active, government, private and industry funding continues to support conservation organizations in their public education work. For example, the Somenos Marsh Wildlife Society in Duncan incorporates Hul'q'umi'num language into interpretive signage as part of a collaborative effort with Cowichan Tribes. Photo courtesy of Melissa Collins.

The need to develop viewing guidelines signalled not only a growth in public interest in wildlife (coupled with a growth in leisure time and disposable income to pursue those interests) but also a loss of the kind of knowledge that previous generations of British Columbians had grown up with: what used to be called "woodcraft," or the knowledge of the woods, including the habits and behaviours of wild animals. As the province became more urbanized, residents seeking to admire and learn about its wildlife needed instruction in how to do so safely and successfully.

The growth of the BC Parks Naturalist Program and rising visitorship through the 1960s and 1970s contributed to these goals. The program also trained a growing cadre of educated observers of the province's wildlife, something the editors of the four-volume *Birds of British Columbia* pointed to as accelerating the development of ornithological knowledge between the 1950s and 1980s.[41] As BC ornithologist Richard Cannings recalled of his years as a summer park naturalist in the early 1970s, "under the tutelage of [senior park naturalists] like Michael Shepard and George Sirk, I [became] inculcated with taking more serious bird notes."[42]

The systematic recording of daily observations by park naturalists like Cannings and future Royal BC Museum ornithologist Wayne Campbell came to motivate larger wildlife data projects, including the BC Photo Records File. Initiated by Campbell and naturalist David Stirling in 1970, the project set out to prove that quality photographs could be used to confirm the presence of rare or unusual species in the province, removing the need to shoot and collect specimens of rare birds and other vertebrate species.[43] An early example of citizen science, the Photo Records File took advantage of improvements in the precision and accessibility of photographic equipment to solicit photographs from volunteer, amateur naturalists across the province. By 1987, volunteers had submitted roughly 1,200 prints and slides to the Royal BC Museum for cataloguing. Together, they represented 297 species, 52 of which had never before been recorded in the province.[44]

As an incubator for projects like this, the BC Parks Naturalist Program played a vital role in advancing wildlife research and education in the province. By 1967, the program had expanded to four nature houses across nine provincial parks. It continued to grow, attracting thousands of visitors annually, until budget cuts and the regionalization of BC Parks programs led to the dismantling of the program in the late 1970s and early 1980s.[45]

INITIATIVE PROFILE: BC Nest Record Scheme

The **BC Nest Record Scheme** is the longest-running database of breeding bird nest
records in North America. Initiated in 1955 by Timothy Myres, a graduate student
in zoology at UBC, the program was inspired by a similar initiative launched by the
British Trust for Ornithology in 1939. A series of UBC graduate students kept the
program running through its first decade. Working with naturalists' organizations
and birders across the province, they distributed nest record cards to a growing
number of observers and filed and analyzed incoming records of nest locations,
species, clutch sizes, and hatching and fledging success.

The program received a boost in 1966, when Penticton naturalist Violet Gibbard
took up the role of coordinator. Over the next twenty years, Gibbard oversaw the
expansion of the program into the "largest regional nest card program in North
America." As family friend and ornithologist Richard Cannings recalled, "Violet was
the driving force . . . [in] encouraging people to participate." By the time Gibbard
retired in 1986, annual submissions had grown to about three thousand nest cards
from 120 contributors across the province, with cumulative representation of nearly
three hundred species.

Wayne Campbell, curator of UBC's Cowan Vertebrate Museum from 1969 to
1973, managed the centralized registry of files, which became a highly valued

Volunteers sorting nest record cards at the Royal British Columbia Museum, early 1980s.
From left to right: John Elliot, Lillian Weston, Herbert Van Kampen, Terry Snye, Bernice
Smith, Elizabeth Brooke and Margaret Wainwright. Photo by Grant Hollands. Photo courtesy
of the Biodiversity Centre for Wildlife Studies.

database for researchers. In this pre-computer era, the work of a committed cadre of volunteer naturalists to sort and file the incoming cards was essential to the project's success. When Campbell accepted a position as curator of ornithology at the Royal BC Museum in 1973, he brought the registry of nest records with him. Since 2004, Campbell has housed and administrated the BC Nest Record Scheme through the Biodiversity Centre for Wildlife Studies, a non-government charitable organization. The project continues to process about 28,000 records annually; its roughly one million records constitute the largest nest record database in Canada.[46]

Looking back, Cannings recalled the personal impact of the project: "When I was growing up in the '60s, . . . it was the Nest Record Scheme that really got me interested in biology. [My brothers and I] were out there gathering data on birds' nests and nesting success and how many young fledged and how long the incubation period was for the nestlings." In Cannings's assessment, the BC Nest Record Scheme was "really ahead of its time." Together with the related BC Photo Records File, which documented rare or unusual occurrences of birds in the province, the nest record scheme formed the basis for numerous scientific publications, including the highly regarded four-volume *Birds of British Columbia*. The two initiatives "set the stage," Cannings noted, for broader citizen science efforts such as the global e-Birds program and the Cornell Lab of Ornithology's Nestwatch program, a countrywide nest monitoring program established in 1997.[47]

Like the province's naturalists, wildlife biologists seeking public and political support for habitat protection measures came to understand that "wildlife education" was just as necessary for broader publics as it had been for the earlier, more consumption-oriented readers of the *Wildlife Review*. A crucial component of this education was to apprise public audiences of two facts: first, that wildlife conservation needs land; and second, that "not just any land will do." BC Provincial Museum director Yorke Edwards noted at a 1982 conference the need to fight the common perception that animals just "move elsewhere" when their habitat is destroyed. "It is a great and largely unknown truth," he argued, "that most wild animals lead hard lives on the edge of survival; that they can survive in only certain kinds of places; and that most individuals do not survive long enough to reproduce once." For land to support certain kinds of animals, Edwards elaborated, it must meet their very specific needs:

Bighorn sheep land needs water, grass, and rugged escape terrain like steep slopes and cliffs. . . . The water and grass have to be close enough to the escape terrain for the steep slopes to be really effective retreats from attacks. . . . There must be enough grass in the right places to feed the sheep through the worst storms, with the worst snow and ice conditions in all years. If there is not enough, perhaps a mile down the valley is another area of grass and slopes near water, and perhaps together the two areas can always offer survival to one band of sheep. Each alone would be an eventual death trap. The two together are the lands needed to save the sheep band.[48]

R.H. (Bob) Ahrens of the province's Lands Division made a similar observation about the distance between public perception and reality in the allocation of Crown lands: "despite the illusion of wide open spaces and unlimited resources, the BC land base is finite, heavily committed, and under strong demand." As pressure on the land base increased, biologists began to see that even recreational uses placed pressure on wildlife populations. "Parks are people places," Edwards acknowledged, "and as the people pressure rises . . . [it begins] to push wildlife out of parks, first the most endangered kinds." Not only did wildlife need land, but "some wildlife, to survive, needs land without people."[49]

Within this context of growing scientific understanding of the specific habitat needs of non-game wildlife species, the Wildlife Research Division within the Fish and Wildlife Branch, established in the mid-1960s, directed greater attention to the identification and management of **threatened and endangered species**. This shift in wildlife research and policy reflected the influence of the US government's landmark 1973 Endangered Species Act (ESA), which set out measures to protect and recover species in danger of extinction.[50] The absence of equivalent Canadian legislation led the BC Ministry of Environment to develop a system for designating threatened and endangered species in 1979, the first of its kind in Canada. In 1982, the revised Wildlife Act incorporated the designation system and introduced "critical wildlife areas" as a modest means of protecting small areas of "absolutely essential habitat" (such as dens or nest sites) for designated species. The sea otter, reintroduced to the northwest coast in 1969, joined the Vancouver Island marmot, white pelican and burrowing owl as the first endangered species in the province to receive official designation and support for their recovery. Designations also served an educational function by raising public awareness.[51]

Species dependent on the particular characteristics of **old-growth forests** emerged as a special category of concern in this period. As timber harvests increased throughout the 1980s to peak at almost 90 million cubic metres in 1987, scientists came to recognize the significance of the province's dwindling old-growth forests to particular wildlife species.[52] UBC forest ecologist Fred Bunnell was at the forefront of this research. In his numerous publications and government advisory roles through the 1980s and '90s, Bunnell showed that "the great majority of BC's wildlife—from amphibians through mammals—[were] dependent upon forest cover." Some, including 60 per cent of terrestrial mammals, relied entirely on forest cover; others, including thirty-two species of cavity-nesting birds, required the particular characteristics of mature or old-growth forests.

Bunnell drew out the significance of these findings at a 1982 Land for Wildlife conference. Timber management, he argued, *is* wildlife management: "in B.C. those who manage wildlife most effectively are those who control and give direction to the character of the forest cover; that is, the forester." Any large-scale wildlife goals, Bunnell concluded, must be accomplished through forestry practices. As Fish and Wildlife Branch director Don Robinson recognized in a presentation at the same conference, "what the Ministry of Forests does on the forest and rangelands to a substantial degree, determines the number and variety of species found over much of British Columbia." And if British Columbians wished to protect the extraordinary diversity of its resident and migratory fish and wildlife, forestry practices would need to change dramatically.[53]

Conclusion: Beyond Fish and Game

From the mid-1960s to the early 1990s, changing public attitudes toward wild animals led to a reorientation of provincial and federal wildlife policy to consider the welfare of a much broader range of species. Recognition of the significance of wildlife habitat, and the threats facing it from a growing human population and an economy dependent on natural resource extraction, propelled a series of initiatives within and beyond government to protect and restore critical habitat.

Near the end of the 1980s, the publication of *Our Common Future*, the final report of the World Commission on Environment and Development (known as the Brundtland Commission), stimulated global concerns about environmental sustainability and helped to reinvigorate the citizen activism of the 1970s. The Brundtland report popularized the concept of sustainability, which fuelled discussions in the early 1990s, but it also gave voice to the value of biological diversity—or **biodiversity**, as it came to be known—as an indicator of resilience in natural systems. These concepts would underlie major changes in wildlife and environmental policy in the decade to come. British Columbians' appetite for greater environmental accountability was one of the factors that contributed to the election of Mike Harcourt's NDP government in 1991 and, with it, the promise of more comprehensive, accountable and participatory land use planning processes.

PART FIVE

RISING STAKES, CHANGING ROLES, 1992–2022

11

Forestry and Wildlife

As British Columbia's dominant industry for more than a century, forestry affects more wildlife species in more areas of the province than any other industry. From the removal of critical resting and foraging habitat for ungulates, fur-bearers and cavity-dwelling birds, to the altering of sediments, temperature and debris loads in fish-bearing streams, forestry practices take a toll on wildlife.

For wildlife ecologist Fred Bunnell, prioritizing wildlife and wildlife habitat became a pathway to inform better forestry practices over the course of his forty-two-year career at the University of British Columbia, from 1971 to 2013. By applying decades of research expertise in forestry-wildlife interactions—first in the context of Clayoquot Sound and later in forest industry pilot projects and consultations—Bunnell was at the forefront of efforts to reimagine forestry by prioritizing wildlife and wildlife habitat and the rights of area First Nations. This chapter follows the most influential decades of his career through the 1990s and early 2000s and efforts by the province and forestry companies to reconcile his ideas with economic and political priorities.

Clayoquot Sound: From the War in the Woods to Ecosystem-Based Management

Over the summer of 1993, some 12,000 people from across British Columbia, Canada and beyond gathered to protest clearcut logging in Clayoquot Sound, the largest area of intact old-growth temperate rainforest on Vancouver Island. The protesters who blocked a bridge leading to a logging site in Clayoquot Sound that summer included members of the five First Nations of the Nuu-chah-nulth Tribal Council and a coalition of environmentalists and concerned citizens coordinated by Tofino-based advocacy group Friends of Clayoquot Sound (FOCS). Women played an outsized role from the beginning, from the work of FOCS organizers Valerie Langer and Tzeporah Berman to the participation of the "Raging Grannies," an activist group of older women established in Victoria in the late 1980s. By the end of the summer, over 850 protesters, including youth and elders, had been arrested for defying a BC Supreme Court injunction against the blockade—at the time, the largest act of civil disobedience in Canadian history.

The most high-profile battleground in a larger "War in the Woods" that had escalated through the late 1980s and early 1990s, Clayoquot Sound marked a significant turning point in public awareness and concern about logging practices in British Columbia. Revelations of poor forestry practices in the late 1980s, when annual timber harvests reached an all-time high, coupled with new understanding of the dramatic extent of logging and other industrial development in coastal watersheds, led the province's maturing environmental organizations to shift strategies. Valley-by-valley campaigns—as Langer, the Sierra Club of BC's Vicky Husband and other environmental leaders came to realize—were exhausting and unsustainable. Clayoquot Sound became, in this context, the first in a series of larger regional campaigns for ecological protection epitomized most recently in the fight for the Great Bear Rainforest.[1]

Not only had the scale of the campaign shifted, but the tactics had too. Local actions, like blockades against logging operations, were amplified by sympathetic demonstrations outside Canadian embassies in Europe, Australia, the United States and Japan. An emphasis on consumers also defined the new activism. Greenpeace assisted the FOCS, for example, in launching a sophisticated international campaign targeting forest product markets in the US and Europe. The combined effects of these campaigns—which delivered punitive revenue losses for MacMillan Bloedel, the main timber-licence holder in Clayoquot Sound—succeeded in capturing the attention of industry and government leaders.[2]

The shifting context of Indigenous rights in BC and beyond was another factor that altered the dynamics of forestry debates in the 1990s. For First Nations in the province, the Clayoquot Sound controversy followed decades of frustration and protest against logging activity on their traditional territories. In the mid-1970s, blockades of logging roads by the Nazko and

Lhoosk'uz Dene nations of the upper Fraser set a precedent for Indigenous blockades that would become increasingly frequent in places including South Moresby Island and the Chilcotin Plateau in the 1980s and early 1990s.[3] Nor were the Clayoquot Sound First Nations strangers to protest. The 1993 conflicts could be traced to the early 1980s, when the Tla-o-qui-aht and Ahousaht First Nations, members of the Nuu-chah-nulth Tribal Council, joined forces with the newly formed FOCS to oppose plans to log their ancestral territory of Meares Island. The standoff came to an end in 1985, when the First Nations won a court injunction prohibiting logging on the island until their land claim had been addressed.[4]

The protests that erupted on a much larger scale in the summer of 1993 were initiated in response to the Harcourt government's decision to permit logging in over 60 per cent of Clayoquot Sound's 2,700-square-kilometre expanse. For the five Nuu-chah-nulth nations of Clayoquot Sound, the decision marked another failure to adequately involve them in the management of their traditional territories. Their concerns, bolstered by a warning from the provincial ombudsman, led to the negotiation of an interim measures agreement between the province and Clayoquot Sound First Nations by 1994. The agreement provided the Nuu-chah-nulth nations with a joint management role, subject to cabinet approval, on all resource activities on their traditional territories while treaty negotiations were underway.

At the same time, Harcourt set out to resolve years of conflict in the sound by promising "to make forest practices in Clayoquot not only the best in the province, but the best in the world."[5] In October 1993, he appointed Ahousaht hereditary chief Richard Atleo (Umeek) and UBC forest wildlife ecologist Fred Bunnell to co-chair the seventeen-member **Scientific Panel for Sustainable Forest Practices in Clayoquot Sound**. Composed of Nuu-chah-nulth representatives and a diverse group of specialists in fisheries, biodiversity, ethnobotany, hydrology, engineering and worker safety, the panel was charged with developing a system for sustainable ecosystem management in Clayoquot Sound that represented the "best application of scientific and traditional knowledge and local experience."[6] Drawing on their respective Indigenous and Quaker backgrounds, the panel co-chairs implemented a consensus-seeking approach that guided the panel's deliberations over its two-year existence.

The panel's detailed studies and resulting recommendations consolidated a vision for ecological stewardship and Indigenous co-management that

upended conventional forestry practices in Clayoquot Sound. Its achievements were firsts not only for British Columbia but for the country as a
whole.[7] As an alternative to the conventional clearcut logging that had
decimated old-growth forests across much of Vancouver Island, the panel
proposed smaller openings using "variable retention" practices to protect
important wildlife habitat such as large old-growth trees, snags and downed
wood. Watershed-level or area-based planning, rather than a volume-based,
predetermined annual allowable cut, would be used to determine harvesting levels. In areas with steep slopes or significant wildlife habitat, at least
70 per cent of the forest should remain; in less sensitive areas, the panel
proposed a minimum of 15 per cent forest retention. A proposed network
of reserves throughout the watersheds would bring protected areas across
Clayoquot Sound to a total of 61 per cent.

The result was the province's first detailed articulation of **ecosystem-
based management**. Informed by the Nuu-chah-nulth concept of hishook-
ish-tsawalk (everything is connected), the panel's prescriptions blended
Indigenous and scientific principles to underline the need for a long-term,
multi-generational perspective in decision-making. The sustainability of
the region, panel members concluded, depended on an equal partnership
between area First Nations and the province in the co-management of the
area's forests.[8]

In July 1995, Forests Minister Andrew Petter announced the province's
intention to fully adopt the panel's recommendations. The decision would
reduce timber harvest levels in Clayoquot Sound by more than two-thirds.[9]
Funding from the province's newly minted forest enhancement agency,
Forest Renewal BC, would help companies offset forestry job losses in the
region through silviculture and watershed restoration projects. Moving
forward, new forestry practices were expected to generate more jobs than
conventional practices. In the short term, however, the transition was
rocky. Initial commitments by MacMillan Bloedel to conduct experimental
logging in three locations, with substantial support from Forest Renewal
BC, were soon abandoned. By the end of 1996, the company had suspended
its logging operations in Clayoquot Sound, citing unprofitability.

The future of forestry in Clayoquot Sound, as the scientific panel had
insisted, would lie in co-management. In 1998, MacMillan Bloedel partnered
with the five Clayoquot Sound First Nations in the creation of Iisaak Forest
Resources, a joint venture with majority First Nations ownership that took

its name from the Nuu-chah-nulth word for "respect."[10] The following year, a memorandum of understanding between Iisaak and several environmental organizations in the region effectively ended the War in the Woods: Iisaak executives agreed not to log intact watersheds in exchange for marketing support for the company's sustainably harvested products. In 2000, Iisaak became the first major licence holder in Canada to have its practices certified by the highly regarded Forest Stewardship Council. Entirely Indigenous-owned since 2005, Iisaak is today the only forestry tenure holder in Clayoquot Sound. Its efforts to balance its stewardship commitments with the economic demands of a resource tenure point to the ongoing need for a new kind of "conservation tenure" to ease the pressure to log and pay resource rents to the province.[11]

Provincewide Land Use Planning and Protection Strategies, 1992–2001

Government and industry concessions in the wake of the massive protests in Clayoquot Sound were, from the outset, area-specific. The area's international profile and the threat of renewed protests conditioned the province's July 1995 decision to fully implement the scientific panel's recommendations. The heavy reductions in timber supply and substantive operational changes necessitated by the Clayoquot Sound agreement, however, were considered unworkable for the remainder of BC's forested lands. These lands would instead be subject to a new regional land use planning process and, by 1995, the regulatory rigours of the Forest Practices Code.

Announced in 1992, the province's **Commission on Resources and Environment (CORE)** would oversee the development of a provincial land use strategy and regional planning processes. It focused first on four regions where land use conflicts had become most entrenched: Vancouver Island, the Cariboo-Chilcotin, the East Kootenay and West Kootenay-Boundary. In keeping with demands for greater public participation in planning processes, deliberations at regional tables would rely on a consensus-seeking model of shared decision-making—an approach that had shown some promise in the smaller-scale CRMP processes of the 1970s. Wildlife and ecosystem integrity was just one of a range of interests represented at these planning tables; resource industries and unions, tourism and outdoor recreation, farmers and ranchers, and local governments were among the many sectors vying to have their interests incorporated. Notably absent from most regional tables were First Nations, who noted that in the context of broader claims to Aboriginal rights and title, their stake in the outcome was "qualitatively different than other stakeholders in the process."[12] Their absence, as we shall see, would have lasting repercussions for the overall effectiveness of the planning process.

While fish and wildlife interests competed with other claims at the planning tables, two strategies that informed the planning process took wildlife and ecosystem integrity more fully into account. The first was the **Protected Areas Strategy (PAS)**. Released in mid-1993, the strategy provided a broader provincial context for evaluating regional protected area proposals. It marked a shift from an older approach that emphasized recreational amenity and scenic beauty in designating protected areas to a science-based approach that sought to protect representative examples of BC's diverse ecosystems and cultural heritage. In keeping with the recommendations of the 1987 World Commission on Environment and Development (the Brundtland Commission), it set an overall protected areas target of 12 per cent of the province's Crown land base by the year 2000.[13] This was an ambitious target, doubling the province's existing 6 per cent protected areas.[14]

The second was the development of the province's first **Old Growth Strategy** in 1992. Acknowledging the need to better incorporate wildlife and ecological considerations into forestry planning, the Ministry of Forests assembled a large working group of government and university biologists and foresters and representatives from industry and environmental organizations. Their resulting strategy defined the significance of old growth for the province's biological diversity and set out two methods of protection: the creation of representative old-growth forest reserves and the modification of forestry practices to create or maintain old-growth characteristics in managed forests.

Changing understanding of the land base contributed to these developments. Ministry of Environment biologist Dennis Demarchi's work to develop a system of **ecoregion classification** for the province greatly facilitated understanding of BC's diversity of wildlife habitat by identifying boundaries and relationships between terrestrial and marine ecosystems across five geographic scales. Adopted by the Ministry of Environment in 1985 and periodically revised, the system continues to serve as a foundation for biodiversity protection in the province and research initiatives such as the work conducted to produce the ambitious and highly regarded *Birds of British Columbia*, published in four volumes beginning in 1990.[15] In 1988, collaboration between the two ministries had determined that only 6.7 per cent of remaining old growth on the BC coast fell within protected areas. Forestry consultant Keith Moore's influential inventory of unlogged coastal watersheds (later extended with Ministry of Forests support to cover the entire province) provided further support for an analysis of gaps in the existing system of protected areas.

By the middle of 1995, cabinet had granted approval for each of the CORE regional plans, and roughly one million hectares had been added to the province's protected areas system. A shift to smaller, sub-regional land and resource management planning (LRMP) processes in 1996 produced generally higher participant consensus than within the "mega-regions" tackled by the CORE tables.[16] By 2001, the province succeeded in increasing its protected areas from approximately 6 per cent to 12.5 per cent of the provincial land base, exceeding the 12 per cent target set in 1991.

From a biodiversity standpoint, however, the province's regional land use planning tables were less successful in achieving ecological representativeness in protected area designations. In many cases, pressure from industrial interests led to a greater proportion of "rock and ice" designations. Low-elevation areas critical to wildlife survival, including productive forest, wetland and grassland habitats, remained under-represented. A status report in 1996, for example, concluded that more than a third of the province's terrestrial ecosections had less than 1 per cent protection.[17] Concerns about representation were especially acute within areas of concentrated human settlement, such as the Coastal Douglas-fir biogeoclimatic zone of the southwest coast and the Bunchgrass biogeoclimatic zone of low-elevation valleys in the southern Interior, home to some of the rarest and most endangered species in Canada. For scientists and conservationists assessing these omissions, it was increasingly clear that protected area targets would need to be higher and that conservation measures would need to be applied across the landscape in order to protect BC's most threatened ecosystems.[18]

Perhaps the greatest shortcoming of strategic land use planning exercises in the 1990s, however, was the failure to involve First Nations. Despite government assurances that planning outcomes would not compromise future land claims, most First Nations declined to participate. Their rejection of planning exercises that positioned them alongside other stakeholder groups proved prescient, as a series of court cases over the same decade elaborated on the meaning of constitutionally protected Aboriginal rights and title. As legal scholars Tim Thielmann and Chris Tollefson have argued, the absence of First Nations undermined a key goal of the province's strategic land use planning program: "to enhance investment in Crown land and resources by increasing certainty about future uses of the provincial land base."[19] In 2006, the Province of British Columbia formally recognized these limitations by declaring an end to multi-stakeholder, consensus-seeking strategic land use planning. In keeping with new "duty to consult" obligations that had emerged from a series of recent court decisions, the province changed tack to negotiate directly with First Nations. Several government-to-government strategic land use agreements, whose outcomes supersede existing land use plans, have since been completed.[20]

INITIATIVE PROFILE: Muskwa-Kechika Management Area, 1998

Named for two rivers in the province's northeast, the Muskwa-Kechika comprises over 6.4 million hectares (more than twice the size of Vancouver Island) of northern boreal forest, mountains and plateaus, wide valleys, and lowlands along the northern boundary of the Rocky Mountains. The area is unique in British Columbia for its largely unroaded condition. Unlike neighbouring areas, the very low density of roads and industrial development in the Muskwa-Kechika—in part a product of permafrost and lower oil values than in the Alberta Plateau to the east—has allowed for the persistence of vast areas of intact ecosystems. Its fifty large, adjoining watersheds constitute the largest remaining wilderness area in the province. These conditions—a variety of habitats coupled with low human disturbance—have supported a great diversity and abundance of wildlife species. Large mammals such as black and grizzly bears, moose, elk, mountain goats and Stone's sheep exist here in densities of global significance. The region also supports one of the world's only remaining fully functioning, intact predator-prey systems (for example, between wolves and caribou), earning it a reputation as the "Serengeti of the North."

Humans, too, have lived, worked and profited from the ecological richness of the Muskwa-Kechika for many thousands of years. Nine Indigenous communities within the Kaska Dena, Treaty 8 and Carrier Sekani nations continue to live, hunt

Muskwa-Kechika Management Area, 2021

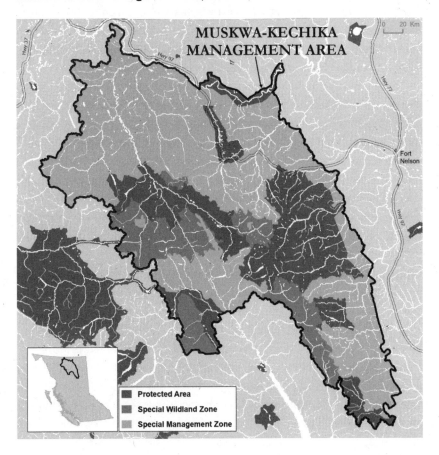

Data sources: Protected Areas: BC Parks, BC Parks, Ecological Reserves, and Protected Areas, 2008; Special Management Zone: BC Lands, TANTALIS—Management Areas (Spatial), 2008; Special Wildland Zone: Environment and Climate Change Canada, Canadian Protected and Conserved Areas Database, 2021. Map by GeoBC, 2022.

and gather foods on traditional territories that fall within and beyond the Muskwa-Kechika. The Cree names for the river systems—Muskwa (bear) and Kechika (Ketchika or Táhdáséh, long inclining river)—are evidence of the long Indigenous presence in the area. Euro-Canadian incursions began in the early 1800s, when North West Company traders established posts in the area.[21] For the next century and a half, however, the northeastern Rocky Mountains remained, in the words of the late guide outfitter and historian Leo Rutledge, a "too distant land." With access restricted to travel by river, on foot or by horseback until the construction of the Alaska Highway in 1942, activities in the area were limited primarily to hunting, trapping and guiding. Even for guide outfitters, who started hunting in the area in the early 1900s, the "two week pack trip, *one way*" to reach the Peace Liard Stone's sheep ranges from Hudson's Hope meant that bookings were few.[22]

The wartime construction of the Alaska Highway through the northeast changed everything. Trophy hunting took off in the region as greater access allowed new and established family guide-outfitting businesses to respond to rising demand from the United States and Europe for wilderness hunting experiences. The area came to support "some of the best guiding-outfitting business in the province." As Rutledge recalled in a 1996 article, the days of the "Great Blue Ram . . . slumbering on his lofty ledge" were over.[23] Oil and gas exploration followed. Beginning in the 1960s, seismic exploration carved ten-metre-wide corridors, or "seismic lines," through forests, tundra, uplands and peatlands. Government financial incentives for mineral exploration in the 1970s led prospectors to scour the area for copper and other minerals, leaving scarred hillsides in their wake. With the exception of a few active mines in the Toad River area, however, exploration in the Muskwa-Kechika yielded little immediate interest, and the area remained largely intact as surrounding areas were fragmented by development.[24]

By the early 1990s, with resource development accelerating across the region, trappers and guide outfitters became increasingly invested in efforts to maintain the wilderness character of the area. As biologist Bill Jex points out, guide-outfitting operations across the north are mostly family-based businesses passed down through generations: "when you are managing your area as an heirloom, as opposed to a business opportunity, . . . the scale of your decisions is much more long term."[25] For Ross Peck, a third-generation guide outfitter who operated in the Tuchodi River drainage of the Muskwa-Kechika Management Area until 2005, the high value that international clients attach to not only the hunt but the hunting experience has for decades supported one of few economic arguments to weigh against competing resource interests. "Gaining an economic value from guide areas," he argues, "is crucial to maintaining wildlife and wilderness."[26]

In 1992, Chetwynd-area wilderness guide Wayne Sawchuk joined forces with George Smith of the Canadian Parks and Wilderness Society to launch the "Northern Rockies: Totally Wild" campaign. At the same time, multi-sectoral land and resource planning processes began in Fort Nelson, Fort St. John and Mackenzie. Together, the Northern Rockies campaign and wildlife interests at the land use planning tables highlighted the unique characteristics of the Muskwa-Kechika. Despite their

often contradictory interests, industry, local government and environmental representatives agreed that the size and character of the region merited treatment as a
special management area.[27]

In 1998, capable shepherding by provincial Ministry of Environment representative Jim Walker saw the Muskwa-Kechika Management Area established
under specific legislation to "maintain in perpetuity the wilderness quality" of the
Muskwa-Kechika and its "diversity and abundance of wildlife." Roughly 25 per cent
of the area would be protected as parks, protected areas and ecological reserves;
resource development would be permitted in the remainder, with 15 per cent zoned
for non-extractive use, such as commercial tourism, and 60 per cent zoned for less
restrictive mining, logging, and oil and gas development. Critically, access within
the management area would be limited to designated routes, and in areas where
development was permitted the long-term objective would be "to return lands to
their natural state" once extraction activities were completed.[28]

In the first decade following the creation of the Muskwa-Kechika Management
Area, the province's $10 million trust fund for the area supported significant plan-
ning and research for wildlife conservation in the area. A multi-year partnership
between the management area's advisory board and the University of Northern
British Columbia (UNBC), for example, produced extensive research on the interactions between oil and gas development and Stone's sheep ranges on the eastern
slopes of the Rockies. Greater understanding of the benefits of prescribed fire in
maintaining habitat for elk and other species also emerged from this research partnership. For Peck, member and later chair of the Muskwa-Kechika Advisory Board
from its inception in 1999 until 2007, these insights support practices that guide
outfitters and Indigenous hunters have employed for decades. This kind of collaborative conservation, however, has seen less emphasis since the restructuring of the
advisory board in 2005. For Peck, the long-term viability of the Muskwa-Kechika
Management Area will depend on a return to active and informed management that
prioritizes wildlife and wildlife habitat.[29]

Shifts within the oil and gas industry over the past twenty years have pulled
development out of the mountains to concentrate on shale gas deposits, relieving
pressure on the wildlife ranges of the eastern slopes. But as some pressures have
eased, others have intensified, including expanded recreational access, accelerating climate change and a heightened frequency and severity of forest fires in the region. A recent study by conservation biologist John Weaver shows that the complex,
diverse terrains of the Muskwa-Kechika Management Area provide adapting wildlife species with a greater range of options for movement in the face of a changing

climate. Protecting a much larger percentage of intact watersheds within the area, he argues, will be essential to the survival of vulnerable species, such as the region's fourteen caribou herds.[30]

Area First Nations have emerged in this context as powerful voices for wildlife conservation and sustainable resource development. Having mostly declined to participate in the multi-sectoral processes of the 1990s that, from their perspective, would have placed them on par with resource stakeholders rather than in a government-to-government relationship with the province, Treaty 8, Kaska Dena and Carrier Sekani nations are taking advantage of a dramatically altered legal climate to claim economic and stewardship opportunities within their traditional territories.

In 2019, the Kaska Dena Council launched Dene K'eh Kusān (Always Will Be There), an Indigenous-led conservation plan to expand protections in the Muskwa-Kechika Management Area while providing greater economic opportunities for Kaska Dena members. At the core of the plan is a new Indigenous Protected and Conserved Area (IPCA) constituting over 4 million hectares of Kaska ancestral territory (an area larger than Vancouver Island). In keeping with the original agreement, the conservancy would honour existing guide and trapping tenures— and by extension, the historical role of these wilderness-based livelihoods in protecting the intact watersheds of the Muskwa-Kechika.[31] The Kaska Dena's timing is fortuitous: federal commitments to protect 30 per cent of Canada's land and oceans by 2030, combined with recent court decisions clarifying provincial obligations to Treaty 8 nations, have laid important groundwork for success.

The Rise and Fall of BC's Forest Practices Code

"Absolutely appalling" was NDP Forests Minister Dan Miller's response to the results of a forestry practices audit in July 1992. Commissioned by the Ministry of Environment, the audit documented excessive damage to fish-bearing streams by logging operations on northern Vancouver Island. Addressing BC's three largest forestry companies, Miller warned, "if you want to continue harvesting timber in the province, obey the rules."[32]

Four years earlier, in 1988, a committee of representatives from the Ministry of Forests, the Ministry of Environment, the federal Department of Fisheries and Oceans (DFO) and coastal logging companies had proudly announced the release of its **Coastal Fisheries/Forestry Guidelines** following fifteen years of study and collaborative policy development. The guidelines identified four classes of fish-bearing waterways, descending in significance from Class 1 to Class 4, and prescribed a corresponding scale of voluntary logging restrictions aimed at protecting fish habitat. Several years after their release, however, problems with forestry practices were still readily apparent. Doubts were especially notable among a new generation of habitat protection biologists who had come to staff regional offices of the Fish and Wildlife Branch beginning in the mid-1980s. In 1991, Doug Morrison, habitat biologist for the Nanaimo office, took the unprecedented step of requesting an audit of forest industry compliance with the new guidelines.[33]

The results of the audit shattered any sense of complacency within government about the effectiveness of the voluntary guidelines. Conducted by biological consultant Derek Tripp, the audit revealed damage caused by non-compliance with fisheries-forestry guidelines in thirty-four of fifty-three streams surveyed on northern Vancouver Island. Of those thirty-four streams, six prime (Class 1 and 2) fish-bearing waterways had suffered "complete habitat loss" as a result of poor logging practices. Streams in these areas, the audit showed, had been logged to their banks; in other areas, inadequate width of "leave strips" had led to streambank erosion, siltation and the sliding of logging debris into stream beds. The guidelines were effective when followed, Tripp concluded, but the level of compliance was "generally poor." For an industry that had repeatedly reassured its critics that the "bad old days" of poor logging practices were behind them, the audit was a public and government relations nightmare.[34]

Miller used the audit to signal a new era of enforcement for forestry practices. He ordered the three large logging companies responsible for the damage—MacMillan Bloedel, Fletcher-Challenge Canada and International Forest Products—to clean it up within ninety days or risk a loss of cutting rights. Directives issued the following month ramped up inspection of logging operations by Ministry of Forests district offices and, for the first time, incorporated adherence to fisheries-forestry guidelines within inspection protocols. The ministry moved to reposition what had been voluntary guidelines into the contractual realm of cutting permits in the same period. For government observers, the response of Miller and his ministry represented a remarkable departure, signalling that the Ministry of Forests (rather than the Ministry of Environment) was prepared to take the offensive in enforcing habitat protection measures.[35]

The Tripp audit marks an important turning point in the development of habitat protections in BC not only for the poor practices it illuminated but also for the extent to which it undermined the Harcourt administration's faith in the effectiveness of a collaborative approach to policy development. The message that Miller sent to industry in the summer of 1992 was that collaboration, in the form of the industry- and government-sanctioned Coastal Fisheries/Forestry Guidelines, had failed. Development of an alternative was already underway, and unlike the existing guidelines, it would be much more prescriptive and enforceable.[36]

In July 1994, two years after the release of the Tripp audit, the BC legislature passed the Forest Practices Code of British Columbia Act. Discussions and consultations surrounding the possibility of a forest practices code had been underway since 1991, when the province's Forest Resources Commission (initiated in 1989) recommended the consolidation of existing legislation, regulations and guidelines into a "single, all-encompassing code of forest practices." One of the drivers of development regarding the **Forest Practices Code** was the recognition that forestry was not covered by existing environmental assessment requirements. The FPC became, in this context, "the environmental assessment of forestry activities."[37] A multi-agency steering committee, including representatives from CORE and the federal DFO, supervised its development. Although forestry companies were consulted at several stages in this process, the decision to exclude them from the steering committee would ultimately undermine the FPC's longevity.

By the summer of 1995, the package of legislation, regulations and guidebooks that formed the Forest Practices Code came into effect.[38] The FPC was the culmination of decades of public concern about the effects of industrial logging on British Columbia's natural environment. It marked a commitment, expressed more forcefully in the work of the Clayoquot Sound Scientific Panel, to improve forest practices for the sustainability of forest ecosystems and forest-dependent communities alike. Incorporating and replacing previously developed fisheries-forestry and biodiversity guidelines, it codified what were once voluntary policies into legally enforceable regulations. Forest companies were obliged to participate in a hierarchy of obligatory planning and public review processes. Operational plans for logging and silviculture, furthermore, had to reflect the objectives of higher-level land use plans.[39] Bolstered government capacity for monitoring and enforcement rounded out this suite of changes, staffing the province's forty-three district forest offices with a new cadre of enforcement officials and forest ecosystem specialists based at the Ministry of Environment. On-the-ground inspections received reinforcement from the Forest Practices Board, an oversight body chaired by respected forestry consultant Keith Moore, which fielded public complaints and conducted independent audits of forest practices.[40]

Pushback from industry was swift, focused primarily on the anticipated 20 to 30 per cent increase in logging costs as a result of FPC requirements. Predictions of associated 10 to 20 per cent reductions in harvest rates would cost jobs and revenue for the province, a 1994 Council of Forest Industries (COFI) report warned.[41] Pressure from companies, the forestry workers' union and the mayors of forest-dependent communities succeeded in convincing Forests Minister Andrew Petter to weaken the FPC's provisions. In 1995, Petter announced that reductions in the annual allowable cut as a result of Forest Practices Code provisions would be capped at 6 per cent (with any further reductions subject to detailed economic analysis).

For the inter-agency working groups developing the FPC's biodiversity, riparian management and wildlife management guidebooks, Petter's 6 per cent cap necessitated what Nancy Wilkin, director of the Habitat Protection Branch for the BC Ministry of Environment, described as a "horrendous mathematical exercise." Biodiversity standards, for example, such as maintaining connectivity, reducing edge habitat and maintaining some old-growth features, could be applied to no more than 10 per cent of the land in a given sub-region.[42] The cap significantly constrained visions of the Forest Practices Code as a mechanism for ecosystem-based management. While stream protection measures and experimental techniques like variable retention would improve outcomes for wildlife in selected sites, limiting the reach of these measures allowed unsustainable harvest levels and associated habitat loss to continue. Forestry on the vast majority of the province's Crown lands, it was clear, would look nothing like the experimental, ecosystem-based and economically challenging forestry in Clayoquot Sound.

Disappointing as these developments were for environmentalists and wildlife advocates, there was still much to celebrate. The confluence of developments within and outside of government in the early to mid-1990s represented significant leaps forward for wildlife habitat protection, planning and research. However watered down it may have been, BC's

Forest Practices Code still provided more comprehensive forest practices legislation, a 1996 Ministry of Forests study confirmed, than that of fourteen comparable international jurisdictions.[43] Regional land use planning tables, meanwhile, established lasting expectations for public involvement in resource management decisions. By 2001, a doubling of protected areas saw the protection of more than 11.9 million hectares of Crown lands, more than in any other Canadian province. Wildlife research within and outside of government also flourished in this period, buoyed by significant injections of funding from Forest Renewal BC.[44] Fisheries Renewal BC, a sister program proposed in the same period by fisheries biologist Alan Martin, made important investments in fish habitat and watershed restoration. Other "made-in-BC" innovations, such as Demarchi's ecoregions classification system, made BC government wildlife work a model for other jurisdictions by the mid-1990s.

Industry Responses: MacMillan Bloedel's "Forest Project," 1998–2003

The forest industry also conducted its own reckoning in response to the conflicts and uncertainty of the early 1990s. This was especially true on the coast, where companies increasingly faced the need to generate public acceptance, or "social licence," in order to continue operations within predominantly old-growth forests. In 1998, MacMillan Bloedel, then the largest forest company operating on the BC coast, made the startling announcement that it would phase out clearcutting over five years across all of its 1.1-million-hectare coastal forest tenures (including both private and public lands). In its place, it would employ a system of stewardship zones and partial cutting or "variable retention" in order to protect components of wildlife habitat within harvested areas. Several other companies followed MacMillan Bloedel's lead, resulting in a significant transformation of forestry practices among coastal operators.[45]

MacMillan Bloedel's new approach arose within the context of novel sources of research funding and an atmosphere of innovation and possibility among university, government and industry-based foresters, biologists and engineers. With financial support from Forest Renewal BC, the company assembled a multidisciplinary team of researchers and practitioners to investigate the economic, social and ecological costs and benefits of adopting new forestry practices. UBC forest ecologist and former Clayoquot Sound

Professor Fred Bunnell at the
University of British Columbia,
ca.2009. Photo courtesy of the
University of British Columbia.

Scientific Panel co-chair Fred Bunnell headed up the biodiversity component of the work. His 1998 study, co-authored with forest habitat ecologist
Laurie Kremsater and forester Mark Boyland, laid out a case for an economically and ecologically viable method of protecting biodiversity across
the forest land base. Prioritizing wildlife and ecosystem integrity, Bunnell
and his co-authors argued, required reimagining forestry practices. Their
study has since been credited as the pivotal publication that changed forest
management in BC and elsewhere in the Pacific Northwest.[46]

Like his previous contributions regarding Clayoquot Sound, Bunnell's
work stands out for its reasoned translation of sometimes opaque scientific
concepts into practical, operational management objectives and practices.
Grappling with the enormity of protecting biodiversity—the full range of
species, known and unknown, within a given area—Bunnell and his co-
authors proposed terrestrial vertebrates as a useful surrogate. Because birds,
mammals, amphibians and reptiles were generally well known, readily
identified and relatively easy to monitor, they formed a practical means
of assessing the presence of a "wide range of other species that cannot be
sampled as readily." Their dependence on specific habitat features, such as
snags and downed wood, and other life forms, such as fungi and plants,
made them useful indicators of broader species diversity.

A cutblock logged with variable retention practices within Western Forest Product's timber licence near Sayward, Vancouver Island, 2019. Photo courtesy of SuavAir and Western Forest Products.

Having established the broad goal of ensuring that "no vertebrate species is lost from MacMillan Bloedel's forest tenure due to forest practices," the scientists proposed a system of three stewardship zones: old-growth management areas, where no harvesting would take place; habitat areas, where harvesting would be reduced; and timber areas, where harvest levels would be highest. To ensure support of a range of vertebrates with different habitat needs, they argued, it was "critical that the same practices not be implemented everywhere." This approach differed from the more standardized measures of BC's Forest Practices Code, where, Bunnell and his co-authors speculated, management zones were unlikely to be "sufficiently disparate" to achieve the desired effect of habitat and species diversity. Instead, they argued, each site required individual, specific assessments of species distribution to determine appropriate responses.[47]

At the core of this system of stewardship zones was the method of **variable retention**. Modelled on experiments with "green tree retention" in the US Pacific Northwest and later adopted by the Clayoquot Sound Scientific Panel, this method involved retaining aspects of the original forest at the time of harvest.[48] Greater habitat diversity and a larger number of organisms could be sustained, proponents argued, by leaving behind patches of high-value habitat features, including "live and dead trees representing multiple canopy layers, undisturbed understory vegetation and coarse woody debris." By maintaining some elements of structural complexity, these methods aimed to "produce future forest stands that more closely resemble conditions that develop after natural disturbances."[49] Success would depend on a complementary system of landscape-level reserves to protect larger areas of undisturbed old-growth and mature forest habitat. Equally critical was a commitment to regular monitoring and "**adaptive management**," a structured process of learning from results on the ground to continually improve management practices.

In 1998, MacMillan Bloedel adopted the recommendations of Bunnell and his co-authors, becoming the first company in the province to attempt variable retention practices on an industrial scale. It established a series of experimental sites on northern Vancouver Island to conduct comparative treatments and was guided by an international panel of scientists to establish an adaptive management program. When Weyerhaeuser acquired MacMillan Bloedel in 1999, it continued the variable retention program, eventually adopting it as part of its long-term Coastal Forest Strategy. Company practices under this strategy, including the creation of old-growth and riparian reserves and the retention of trees and other habitat features, typically exceeded obligatory reserves and retention under the Forest Practices Code. By the end of the phase-in period in 2003, over 90 per cent of harvesting in Weyerhaeuser's coastal operations used variable retention. By 2005, other coastal operators had adopted the method for portions of their holdings, and its promise for diverse forest types had been established through application in the United States, Australia, Argentina and Scandinavia.[50]

One of factors motivating companies was **sustainable forest management certification**. In the years following the 1987 report from the Brundtland Commission and the market-oriented activism wielded by BC environmental organizations, global consumers of pulp, paper and wood products had become increasingly sensitized to the need to purchase forest products from companies that managed forests sustainably. By the mid-1990s, the Europe-based Forest Stewardship Council (FSC) had pioneered the development of a voluntary, third-party assessment system that producers could use to assure buyers of the sustainability of their practices. Specified national or regional standards, however, were slower to develop. In 1995, the Canadian Standards Association (CSA) developed a voluntary, Canada-wide standard. In 1999, MacMillan Bloedel's North Island experimental sites became the first in Canada to achieve sustainable forest management certification by the CSA.[51] The FSC released regional certification standards for British Columbia in 2005. That same year, forestry companies in the United States and Canada collaborated in the development of a third certification body, the Sustainable Forestry Initiative (SFI).

While all three standards included criteria for biodiversity conservation, public involvement and sustainable harvest levels, one clearly set a higher bar than the others. Of the three, the FSC placed the greatest emphasis on biodiversity conservation and primary or original forest protection. As forester Bill Bourgeois recalls, the council's ecological stringency—most notably, its prohibition against converting natural forests to plantations— confined it to a "boutique standard" from the beginning. At the other extreme, the industry-developed SFI standards were widely perceived by environmentalists and sustainable forestry advocates as "greenwashing."[52] CSA and SFI standards aligned roughly with existing standards set by the Forest Practices Code (and later the Forest and Range Practices Act), enabling wide industry participation. Uptake was rapid. By 2010, over 68 per cent of British Columbia's forest land base, or some 54 million hectares, had been certified as sustainably managed—more area than in any other nation in the world (with the exception of Canada as a whole).[53] Significantly, CSA and SFI certified the lion's share of these forestry operations, with FSC accounting for just 2.6 million hectares, or less than 1 per cent.[54]

In the context of relatively lenient certification standards and rising operation costs, MacMillan Bloedel's 1998 goal of eliminating clearcutting in favour of variable retention was never fully achieved. Adaptive management exercises also contributed to this outcome, as damage to retained stands in wind-prone sites prompted coastal operators to revert to a modified form of retention known as "clearcutting with reserves" for a growing percentage of their operations. Between 2006 and 2017, coastal operators applied variable retention practices to just 29 per cent of harvests on public land. Use of the method varied from company to company. Western Forest Products, for example, which acquired Weyerhaeuser's former coastal BC holdings in 2006,

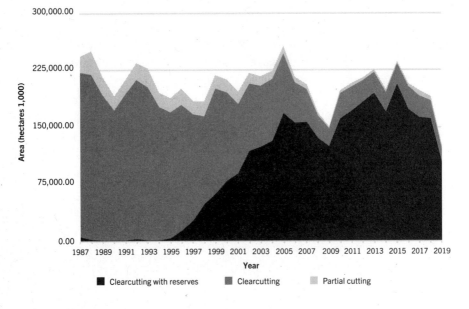

Area harvested by silvicultural method in BC, 1987–2019

Data source: Environmental Reporting BC, Trends in Silviculture in B.C. (1987–2019), Ministry of Forests, Lands, Natural Resource Operations and Rural Development, 2021. Image courtesy of the author.

remains an active proponent of retention forestry, applying the method to approximately 60 per cent of its operations.[55]

These choices are conditioned in part by the nature of the company's forest tenures. Coastal companies credit long-term, area-based tenures (tree farm licences) with providing the ability to plan for the future sustainability of the land base. As one industry forester commented, "when you have an area to manage, you are looking at a land base . . . as forest managers, not forest harvesters. As professionals, you are charged with . . . ensuring that you've met the values that should be met on the land base." While clearcutting has not been eliminated on the coast, the nature of forestry operations represents a dramatic improvement from the routine degradation of streams and forested slopes in the 1980s. Conventional clearcutting (without retention or designation of reserves) dropped from 88 per cent of the harvest on BC public lands in 1998 to 14 per cent in 2017. The average size of clearcuts on the coast has also diminished significantly, from forty-five hectares in 1989 to sixteen hectares in 2017.[56] The industry practice now is to leave more patches of living forest and standing dead trees in each cutblock. Over the past twenty years, one company forester noted, we have left "much more structure in the working forest portion of the land base."[57]

Twenty years of monitoring the effects of variable retention forestry systems within and beyond British Columbia has confirmed significant benefits for species diversity and abundance when compared with conventional clearcutting.[58] Despite these benefits, retention practices have generally been confined to the coast, where area-based tenures predominate. Understanding the ongoing effects of these forestry practices on wildlife populations will require commitments to long-term monitoring—commitments that have waned in the wake of the 2002 elimination of Forest Renewal BC.[59] Sustainable forestry practices also increase the costs of doing business, and many operators are unwilling to sustain those costs without government funding to bridge the gap. The persistence and expansion of variable retention and other practices, and the adaptive management frameworks that supported their ongoing evolution and improvement, will depend on ongoing public pressure to protect forest-dependent fish and wildlife, recreation and other non-timber values across BC's public forests.

SPECIES PROFILE:
Northern Goshawk Laingi Subspecies (*Accipiter gentilis laingi*)

One of the species that became emblematic of the ecological costs of industrial forestry in this period was the northern goshawk (*Accipiter gentilis*). A raven-sized forest hawk known for its deft manoeuvres through forested landscapes in pursuit of prey, goshawks seek out the multi-layered canopies and open understories of mature and old-growth forests for hunting and nesting. Two subspecies exist in British Columbia: the broadly distributed *Accipiter gentilis atricapillus* of the mainland interior and the less numerous, non-migratory *Accipiter gentilis laingi* of the coast. Affected by the accelerating loss of mature coastal forests to commercial logging, the declining population of the laingi subspecies was listed as threatened under the federal Species at Risk Act in 2003.

Until recently, biological distinctions between the two subspecies and the extent of their respective ranges remained uncertain. Research published in 2019, however, revealed a distinct genetic cluster on Haida Gwaii that has been isolated

Northern goshawk laingi subspecies (*Accipiter gentilis laingi*), Bella Coola valley, June 29, 2017. Photo courtesy of Harvey Thommasen.

from mainland populations since at least the last ice age.[60] The conservation implications of these findings are significant. Levels of genetic variation suggest the laingi subspecies may be restricted to Haida Gwaii and not the broader coastal region as biologists initially believed. With as few as fifty individual birds remaining on the archipelago, the findings predict a "high risk of extinction of an ecologically and genetically distinct form of northern goshawk."[61]

The distinctive forest hawks have long held significance for the Haida. Known in the Haida language as stads k'un, or "wings brushing boughs," northern goshawks formed part of the St'aawaas Xaaydagaay (Cumshewa ruling family) culture. In 2017, recognition of this history and the bird's present perilous status led the Haida Nation's House of Assembly to select stads k'un as Haida Gwaii's national bird.[62]

Scientific knowledge and protections for the laingi subspecies have expanded since the mid-1990s, when provincial biologists initiated the first intensive surveys on Vancouver Island and Haida Gwaii. Inventory, monitoring and radio-telemetry work conducted in the 1990s and early 2000s provided for greater understanding of home range sizes, nest occupancy and survival rates. This knowledge has contributed to better habitat protections for the subspecies. Where they are applied, protections for known nest locations within Crown forestry tenures increased from modest 12-hectare "buffer zones" in the 1990s to minimum 176-hectare breeding area reserves by 2015.[63]

Despite these protections, northern goshawks on Haida Gwaii continue to decline, placing the subspecies at high risk of extinction. In addition to the ongoing threat of habitat loss, introduced black-tailed deer (*Odocoileus hemionus columbianus*) have played a role in reducing the abundance of songbird prey by overbrowsing the understory shrubs that many songbird species depend on for nesting and forage. Existing protections are partial and contingent. Breeding area reserves depend on a known nest location; even in places where goshawks have been sighted, the nests of these elusive birds are often exceedingly difficult to find. The birds' much larger foraging habitats, which may range from 7,000 to 11,000 hectares, currently receive no designated protection.[64]

Moving forward, the challenge will lie in securing and managing sufficient habitat over the long term. As the federal recovery strategy noted in 2018, by the time coastal forests reach the structural maturity "suitable for *A. gentilis laingi*," they are also "economically viable for timber harvesting."[65] Coastal forestry companies' adoption of wildlife habitat retention practices may mitigate losses somewhat, but for many observers the success of goshawk recovery efforts will require a more fundamental reimagining of forestry practices.[66] For the Haida, protecting stads k'un is bound up in a larger vision of cultural and territorial sovereignty over their ancestral lands. In 2017, a collaboration between the provincial government and the Council of the Haida Nation produced an islands-based recovery strategy that will combine ongoing nest territory monitoring, inventories of potential habitat, forage habitat protection and restoration, and introduced species reductions.[67] In keeping with Fred Bunnell's findings about the value of terrestrial vertebrates as indicators of forest ecosystem health, the survival of Haida Gwaii's national bird will represent the resilience of the old forests on which it, and the Haida people, depend.

Mountain Pine Beetle Outbreaks, Salvage Operations and Wildlife in the Interior, 1996–2015

If the late 1990s and early 2000s were a time of innovation among logging companies operating on the BC coast, the opposite was generally true in the province's central Interior. Here, forestry practices reverted to large clearcuts and rapid forest liquidation in response to a massive pine beetle infestation that threatened to wipe out BC's commercially valuable lodge-pole pine (*Pinus contorta*). This divergence followed established trends. The disturbance-adapted forests of the BC Interior had typically generated less public and professional concern for large-scale clearcutting and old-growth removal. Since 1995, for example, maximum clearcut sizes had been capped at forty hectares for the south coast and parts of the southern Interior, while clearcuts in the central and northern Interior were permitted to cover as much as sixty hectares.[68] The mountain pine beetle outbreak of the late 1990s prompted a dramatic increase in annual harvest rates in an effort to salvage beetle-killed timber and stop the spread of the insect. The combined impacts of the pine beetle infestations and the subsequent salvage operations continue to affect the region's forests and the people and wildlife that depend on them.

The mountain pine beetle (*Dendroctonus ponderosae*) is a small insect native to North America. Pine beetles attack mature lodgepole and ponder-osa pine (*Pinus ponderosa*) trees by boring through the bark and mining the nutrient-bearing tissue beneath, killing trees within a year of infestation. Periodic outbreaks occur naturally: pine beetle infestations are second only to fire as a cause of major natural disturbance in the Cariboo and Omineca regions of the central Interior.[69] Typically kept in check by the region's cold winters, beetle survival increased over a series of milder winters in the mid-1990s. A history of fire suppression in the region, which allowed for the persistence of an abundant mature pine tree population across the land-scape, helped to set the conditions for the massive pine beetle outbreak that began in the late 1990s.[70] Over the next fifteen years, the outbreak killed 54 per cent of the province's mature lodgepole pine, affecting over 18 million hectares of forest land in the province's central Interior (an area roughly five times the size of Vancouver Island).[71] It remains the largest infestation of forest insects ever reported for Canada.[72]

Little could be done to stop an outbreak of this size and intensity. Modest interventions—the selective removal of infested trees, prescribed fire and insecticide use, for example—were quickly abandoned in favour of "salvage" or clearcut logging operations to recover what remained of the trees' economic value. Such operations, proponents argued, could potentially slow the spread of the beetle to other areas and reduce the fire hazard that large areas of dead pine presented. As one company forester recalled, "the overarching objective was to salvage . . . as much damaged timber as [possible] in the timeframe where it was considered viable."[73] Beginning in 2003, the province expanded timber harvest levels by as much as 18 million cubic metres per year to accommodate salvage operations. In hard-hit forest districts such as Vanderhoof and Quesnel, the annual allowable cut more than doubled, earmarking for immediate harvest trees that had originally been designated for logging decades into the future.[74] Milling capacity expanded in turn, generating volume expectations that would be difficult to sustain once the outbreak had run its course.

Fred Bunnell would play a role here, too, in assessing the likely consequences of these massive disturbances—the outbreak and the salvage operations—for area wildlife. In a 2004 study commissioned by the Canadian Forest Service, Bunnell and two co-authors from UBC's Centre for Applied Conservation Research concluded that the beetle kill itself would likely be beneficial to many terrestrial vertebrates, at least in the short term, given projected increases in important habitat elements such as snags, downed wood, shrubs and other early seral-stage vegetation. Salvage logging, however, with its removal of forest cover, would likely have negative consequences for at least a third of forest-dependent species; mountain caribou, two species of woodpecker and many species of freshwater fish stood to suffer the most. A much broader range of species, including migratory birds, amphibians and small mammals, would be affected by the loss of resting and foraging habitat. To reduce the worst of these effects, Bunnell and his co-authors made two broad recommendations: (1) salvage operations should use selective harvesting, variable retention and riparian buffers to sustain as much forest structure as possible; and (2) road deactivation and other measures should be used to wrap up operations as quickly as possible within salvage areas. Salvage operations, they argued, should be limited to lodgepole pine and avoided entirely in portions of ungulate winter ranges and in areas where pine was not the dominant species.[75]

Bunnell's recommendations to apply the best practices of sustainable forestry to a salvage operation unprecedented in its size and speed seem to have been largely ignored by Interior logging companies and government regulators grappling with the twin problems of beetle spread and fire risk.[76] To incentivize and speed the work, companies received permission to take greenwood and deadwood alike. Even stands containing just 30 per cent pine were logged entirely, stripping the forest cover that provided vital refuge and foraging habitat for wildlife. Widespread use of herbicides to privilege the growth of tree seedlings also ran counter to Bunnell's recommendations of "minimizing vegetation control" to allow for persistent shelter and forage. These practices also affected freshwater fish habitat, increasing sedimentation, altering flow and increasing water temperatures in rivers and streams.[77]

Another departure lay in the extent and nature of road construction through the beetle-damaged areas. Excessive road development for salvage operations had been a concern for wildlife advocates in the central Interior since the early 1980s, but the scale of the outbreak in the 1990s magnified these effects immensely.[78] On volume-based tenures especially, where multiple licensees hold rights to a specific volume of timber within a designated area, rapid access road construction by multiple operators resulted in what one industry commentor described as "a chaos of roads." Early in the salvage regime, he recalled, "roads were being built and then decommissioned." But "because their location was most desirable . . . those same roads were rebuilt again as the pine beetle spread or as salvage opportunities evolved." Eventually, government allowed these roads to be left in a built condition. The result was "a very chaotic, randomized web . . . of road disturbance that occurred over many decades, with no order or particular pattern or design."[79]

For wildlife, the combined effects of extensive forest cover loss and accelerated road development proved devastating. The effects on large, visible and regularly monitored species, such as moose and caribou, were quickly apparent. The Committee on the Status of Endangered Wildlife in Canada reported high levels of habitat loss and associated declines of mountain caribou populations throughout the north-central Interior between 2000 and 2009.[80] Moose populations also declined. As one industry forester observed, the combination of road access and loss of forest cover meant that hunters could "not only . . . see for extended distances [but also] get there in their vehicles. . . . You might have a moose standing in a wetland two kilometres away, and . . . it [didn't] have a chance. . . . There was a high success rate [for hunters] for a number of years."[81] Wolves and other predators made use of the same road networks to access moose and caribou with greater ease. Adjustments to hunting regulations generally could not keep pace with the rate of ecological change in this period. Population surveys conducted in the central Interior between 2011 and 2014 upheld these observations of a significant decline in moose numbers, legitimizing growing concern among wildlife managers, First Nations, hunters and guide outfitters.[82]

Losses were not limited to ungulates. Trappers in the Nazko region southwest of Prince George reported precipitous declines in fisher populations. Their complaints about salvage logging practices that logged streams to their banks and removed healthy fir and spruce—critical denning and resting trees for fishers and other fur-bearers—prompted a Forest Practices Board investigation and ultimately led to the red-listing of the central Interior fisher population by the province's Conservation Data Centre.[83] For Bunnell and other scientists, declines in terrestrial vertebrates like caribou and fishers stood as indicators of much broader, less visible biodiversity losses.

By 2015, the mountain pine beetle infestation had mostly run its course. Reaching its peak in 2004, the infestation declined in step with the shrinking availability of mature host pine trees across the region. Salvage harvesting also declined after 2006, not for lack of beetle-killed trees but rather due to a downturn in lumber markets.[84] Catastrophic wildfires in 2003 and 2004, and again in 2017 and 2018, added to the devastating damage of these decades. The ecological and economic consequences of these forest losses continue to be assessed today. There is good news for some species. Moose populations in salvage-affected areas of the south Chilcotin, for example, have increased in recent years following collaborative efforts by the province and area First Nations to decommission roads and control access.[85]

For some commentators, the events of the late 1990s and the first decades of the 2000s represented a missed opportunity for change. The pine beetle outbreaks occurred at the same time as coastal forestry industry giant MacMillan Bloedel committed to end clearcutting on its tenures by investing, with government support, in variable retention and adaptive management. In the Interior, a few smaller companies, including Lignum Forest Products in the Cariboo region, were using Forest Renewal BC funding to support the application of sophisticated modelling systems to plan for wildlife and other non-timber values within their forest tenures.[86] These pilot initiatives coincided with national and international commitments to maintain the health of forest ecosystems.[87]

The Canada Forest Accord, for example, signed by all Canadian premiers in 1998, presented a call to action to improve understanding of forest ecosystems and promote science-based forest stewardship "for the benefit of all living things."[88] For retired UNBC wildlife biologist Winifred Kessler, "it all just fell apart." From her perspective, concerns about a falling timber supply ultimately overshadowed government commitments to sustainable forestry in BC's Interior. "Wherever you have a massive change" like the pine beetle outbreak of the late 1990s, it presents an "opportunity to adapt, to put . . . experts to use in designing the future forest and integrating wildlife concerns. And that's not what happened." Instead, nascent approaches to sustainable forestry were swept aside in order to "keep the mills afloat at all costs."[89]

The Forest and Range Practices Act, 2003: Regulatory Retraction and Professional Reliance

Despite all the work that went into its complex scaffolding of guidebooks and toothy legal protections, the Forest Practices Code lasted less than a decade. When Premier Gordon Campbell's more business-friendly Liberal government came to power in 2001, it embarked on a major effort to reduce costs and administrative complexity for industry and government alike. In 2003, the **Forest and Range Practices Act (FRPA)** jettisoned many of the prescriptive rules of its predecessor in favour of a results-based system of forest management. By paring back the law's detailed planning and practice requirements, the legislation's emphasis shifted from "how to conduct forest practices" to "what forest practices must deliver."[90] This upending of the regulatory regime for natural resources operations would have significant ramifications not only for the role and size of government but also for efforts to coordinate resource management planning across ministries. The resulting siloed planning within resource industries exacerbated development pressures on the landscape, with consequences for wildlife and the people it supported.

One of the central principles of the new legislation was that of **professional reliance**, which delegated the planning and assessment authority of public officials to credentialed professionals employed by industry (such as foresters, biologists and hydrologists). Professional reliance applies across industrial sectors in BC, but its effects are especially pronounced in the forestry sector, where restrictions on government decision-making went further than in other sectors to reduce government oversight.[91] Through this new regulatory model, government's role in forest management shrank to two central functions: setting the management objectives to be achieved;

and ensuring, through compliance and enforcement programs, that objectives had been met. Opportunities for public input were also curtailed under this model: the FRPA requires tenure holders to make site plans for cutblocks and roads available to the public on request, but they are not required to advertise these plans or to accommodate public input. While much larger-scale forest stewardship plans are publicly available, they are technically complex and often inscrutable to non-professionals. Missing from these documents, for example, are site-specific details such as proposed cutblocks, roads and wildlife habitat protections.[92]

The shift to professional reliance dramatically reduced government research and planning capacity within natural resources agencies. Major staffing reductions occurred in environmental compliance and enforcement across all the resource ministries, significantly diminishing the province's professional and technical workforce. Broader budget cuts in the natural resource ministries further hindered the ability of these agencies to assess industry compliance and ensure appropriate oversight. Highly regarded research programs in the Fish and Wildlife Branch and the BC Forest Service were dismantled, along with long-term wildlife monitoring programs and support for flagship programs like BC's system of ecological reserves. With the 2011 transfer of the Wildlife Branch to the Ministry of Forests, fish and wildlife protection and management was subsumed within a large and predominantly production-oriented ministry.

For wildlife and environmental advocates, deregulation under the FRPA, major cutbacks to government staff and budgets, and reduced opportunity for public feedback significantly weakened public control over forest industry operations on public land.[93] The outsourcing of former core roles— such as the creation of the Freshwater Fisheries Society in 2003 to manage hatchery production and stocking of freshwater "put and take" fisheries— further distanced wildlife work from the core work of government.

From an industry perspective, these were welcome changes, permitting flexibility and innovation in response to changing circumstances on the ground. According to one company forester, a shift to professional reliance meant that those involved "in the decision-making process" were the same people that had their "boots on the ground, doing the work, . . . working with professionals in other disciplines." As such, it was a much more effective model than the government-controlled planning regime that preceded it. Too often, this forester noted, government recommendations were "out of touch," requiring industry staff to "spend a lot of time trying to get [public officials] out to the field to work through these things."[94] Forest Practices Board audits have shown that licensees have generally met forest practices standards in the years following the transition to the FRPA. This is especially true of area-based tenure holders, where licensees often exceed their obligations by carrying out FPC-era riparian, wildlife and hydrological assessments no longer required under the FRPA.[95] Yet even industry representatives acknowledge the need for greater government oversight. "The landlord needs to have authority," a forester operating in the Interior commented. "But at the same time, you need to empower [the] creativity . . . of professionals involved in the management of the resource."[96]

For wildlife managers, the vague nature of forest management objectives under the FRPA and the general inadequacy of government oversight undermined the effectiveness of fish and wildlife protections.[97] The shift to FRPA removed a critical FPC-era test that tied the approval of operational plans to their ability to "adequately manage and conserve" fish and wildlife. As Nancy Wilkin noted, the elimination of this phrase, which "underpinn[ed] the environmental philosophy of the FPC," was a big loss for government fish and wildlife programs.[98]

Like other FRPA regulatory objectives, measures to conserve fish and wildlife habitat and biodiversity were further constrained by the obligation not to "unduly reduce the timber supply." The FRPA also decoupled from the law the detailed guidebooks developed in the FPC era to aid habitat assessment and monitoring. Finally, the new legislation did not require tenure holders to monitor the effectiveness of their wildlife protection strategies, shifting this burden instead to the Ministry of Forests' Forest and Range Evaluation Program. Government-led monitoring and evaluation of outcomes for wildlife, however, did not meet expectations. A 2014 report by the Forest Practices Board expressed strong concern that ten years after the launch of the FRPA, government had not yet made any "appreciable progress" in completing and implementing monitoring protocols for wildlife. In those areas where effectiveness evaluations had been completed, results were not being used to improve forestry practices.[99]

By most accounts, professional reliance is here to stay.[100] Government objectives and oversight mechanisms, however, could be considerably improved. "Where objectives are not clear, or where competing interests and values are in play," the Forest Practices Board concluded, "it is not realistic to expect professionals working for licensees to define the public interest."[101]

Planning Failures: The Cumulative Effects of Resource Extraction

One of the most alarming findings of the Forest Practices Board audit of FRPA forestry regulation was its failure to address the **cumulative effects** of development pressures on the landscape.[102] For the most part, Forest Practices Board chair Mark Haddock concluded, such effects are "unknown and unmanaged." FRPA's outsourcing of government research, planning and oversight functions, coupled with associated staffing reductions, limited the effectiveness of the integrated resource management planning that had gained momentum in the 1990s. Under these conditions, mining or oil and gas operations could negatively affect the activities of a forest tenure holder with little warning or recourse. Even within the forest industry, multiple licensees operating on the same land base often infringed on one another's activities. In a 2018 submission, for example, the Forest Practices Board cited numerous instances wherein one licensee "design[s] access and harvesting to achieve certain results, including retention of wildlife habitat, only to have a subsequent licensee undermine these results by harvesting the retention areas."[103] Efforts to address these problems have been hindered by limitations on the authority of district forest managers that are built into the FRPA legislation.

Significant landscape changes produced by mountain pine beetle infestations, wildfires and industrial development have only compounded the problem of cumulative effects and siloed planning within resource industries. As the Blueberry River First Nation argued successfully before the Supreme Court of British Columbia in 2021, overlapping government permits for oil and gas, forestry, mining, agriculture and hydroelectric projects over many years reduced the health and abundance of wildlife to such an extent as to significantly infringe on their Treaty 8 rights to hunt, trap and fish on their traditional territories.[104] Cumulative effects, the court ruled, constituted an infringement on the Blueberry River First Nation's treaty rights to continue their way of life. The projected effects of climate change on BC's land base further underline the need to adjust the existing regulatory framework to protect Indigenous rights and manage cumulative effects. While professional reliance may be here to stay, it will be exercised increasingly within the context of co-management between provincial and First Nations authorities.

Conclusion: Reimagining Forestry

As Al Gorley and Garry Merkel, authors of a government-commissioned review of BC's old-growth forest management, concluded in 2020, prioritizing ecosystem health and resilience will mean moving from "a timber-based focus with ecological health as a constraint" to "an ecologically-based focus with timber as one of many benefits."[105] Like the province's 1992 Old Growth Strategy, written almost thirty years earlier, the authors communicate an urgent need for a paradigm shift in forest management. *How* we get there, however, has changed considerably. A stark difference between BC's 1992 Old Growth Strategy and Gorley and Merkel's 2020 review is the incorporation of Indigenous perspectives. First Nations declined to participate in the 1992 process to avoid compromising land claims negotiations; the 2020 process, by comparison, was co-chaired by an Indigenous forester (Merkel) and places Indigenous involvement through government-to-government relationships as the top priority in creating conditions for change.

The spring 2022 announcement of a new provincial Ministry of Land, Water and Resource Stewardship that will prioritize shared decision-making with First Nations suggests at the very least a political commitment to the systemwide changes that Gorley and Merkel propose. These developments suggest that there is hope for Fred Bunnell's and Richard Alteo's 1995 vision of a different kind of forestry that supports Indigenous and rural economies and accommodates the needs of wildlife.

12

Changing Faces and Approaches in Wildlife Conservation

This chapter turns from the forestry-dominated debates of the 1990s and early 2000s to focus on the most biologically rich areas of the province: the estuaries, wetlands and low-elevation valleys that provide such productive habitat for humans and wildlife alike. As British Columbia's human population continued to expand, surpassing five million in 2021, pressure on wildlife habitat increased in and around the urban and agricultural landscapes of the southern half of the province. A growing emphasis on non-game species within university and government wildlife programs, meanwhile, contributed to greater clarity on the threats this kind of development poses to resident and migratory wildlife. Maintaining biological diversity, scientists argued, supported the health and resilience of the natural systems on which human societies depend. However, consensus among scientists and conservationists on these questions did not translate into high levels of public awareness. For many urban British Columbians, it was easier to conceive of wildlife habitat loss as a problem of distant resource hinterlands rather than one located in the routine and seemingly benign events of housing, road and infrastructure developments in spaces close to home.

The chapter explores the challenges of assessing and protecting species at risk within the most biologically diverse—and by extension, biologically vulnerable—province in the country. It highlights the tensions between a scientific and conservation community widely acclaimed for its leadership in assessing, ranking and protecting species at risk and a provincial government that lagged behind most others in the scope and power of its endangered species legislation. Responses from conservation organizations contributed to a flowering of partnerships in the 1990s and early 2000s, allowing groups to pool funds and expertise and reduce competition for valuable conservation lands. At the same time, new funding mechanisms and a shift to data-driven approaches enabled organizations to prioritize protection for areas of high biological rarity and richness.

The changing faces of wildlife work in this period also stimulated new approaches. From the 1980s on, rising numbers of women took up positions as biologists, conservation officers, researchers and managers. They asked different questions and pursued different approaches. In university and government settings, women's participation prompted greater consideration of the role of ethics in wildlife research and the social context of wildlife management decisions. Aided by technological advances over the same period, women worked to foster greater appreciation for the significance of wildlife health and pressed for less intrusive forms of wildlife sampling and research.

The movement among First Nations in BC to establish wildlife research, management and conservation programs for their traditional territories brought about their own transformations. Drawing on experience with animals over many generations, Indigenous knowledge keepers and professionals worked independently and in collaboration with government, industry and non-profit organizations to inform wildlife management decisions and conservation efforts. Their growing role as leaders and co-managers of wildlife conservation initiatives are explored further in the final chapter.

From Endangered Species to Endangered Ecosystems

In 1973, the US federal government passed the Endangered Species Act, a watershed piece of legislation that prioritized the welfare of listed animal species above all other interests. The law applies to all land in the country, regardless of jurisdiction, incorporating federal, state, tribal and private landowners. By 2012, the ESA's legally mandated species recovery plans and critical habitat provisions had contributed to the revitalization of 110 critically endangered species, including the black-footed ferret, whooping crane, California condor and short-nosed sturgeon. Nothing of its scope and power exists in Canada, or anywhere else in the world.[1]

Ottawa's response—the enactment, almost thirty years after the passage of the ESA, of the 2002 **Species at Risk Act**—was from the beginning a product of compromise. Designed to meet Canada's commitments under the 1992 United Nations Convention on Biological Diversity, the act was the federal government's fourth attempt at passing endangered species legislation. Nearly ten years of policy and jurisdictional disputes between the federal and provincial governments produced a piece of legislation that, in the end, protected species and habitat within a fairly narrow interpretation of federal jurisdiction.[2] Under SARA, species designated as endangered, threatened or extirpated are automatically protected by two central provisions: the first prohibits the harm, collection or trade in designated species; and the second prohibits the destruction of a species "residence," such as a nest or den. However, these basic prohibitions apply only to aquatic species, migratory birds under the Migratory Birds Convention Act and species found on federal land. Listed species found outside of national parks, national wildlife areas, First Nations reserves, airports and other federal lands—about 1 per cent of the land base in BC— receive no formal protection under SARA. Instead, their protection relies on a patchwork of provincial regulations.

SARA, in other words, left provincial responsibility for wildlife largely intact. While the Province of British Columbia made significant efforts to align its natural resources legislation with the act—incorporating mechanisms for identifying and protecting SARA-listed species into its Forest and Range Practices Act (2004) and Oil and Gas Activities Act (2011)— these efforts were constrained from the outset by assurances that conservation measures would not unduly reduce industrial output. Regulations on timber harvesting, for example, limited the effects of wildlife conservation measures to 1 per cent of the annual range and timber supply. (Amendments proposed in 2004 to align the BC Wildlife Act with SARA were never enacted.)[3] Furthermore, government monitoring of the effectiveness of habitat protection measures has been less than adequate.[4] While a clause in SARA permitted the federal government to "prohibit activities that may adversely affect [a] species and [its] habitat" in cases where provincial protection measures were deemed insufficient, the federal government's reluctance to intervene is consistent with its historical disinclination to employ similar powers under the Fisheries Act.[5]

Home to more species, and more species at risk, than any other province in Canada, BC's shortfalls in legislative protections stood in contrast to the leadership and expertise of its scientific community. University and

Vancouver Island marmot (*Marmota vancouverensis*), 2011. Photo courtesy of Jared Hobbs.

government scientists had convened as early as 1980 to share information about and strategies for protecting threatened species and ecosystems.[6] A decade later, in 1991, advocacy from the Nature Trust of BC and the Nature Conservancy of Canada persuaded the province to establish its celebrated **Conservation Data Centre (CDC)** as a vital clearinghouse for scientific data on BC species and ecosystems. Working with UBC forest ecologist Fred Bunnell and other scientists, the CDC adapted a species ranking system developed by the US-based Nature Conservancy for use within the province. Its resulting conservation status rankings, publicized as the annual blue and red lists for threatened and endangered species, continue to serve as an important springboard to formal designation processes.[7] By the early 2000s, these developments had contributed to BC's position as a national leader in assessing and ranking species at risk.

The success of recovery efforts for the critically endangered Vancouver Island marmot illustrates the conservation community's broader commitment to species at risk in BC. One of the rarest mammals in North America, the Vancouver Island marmot relies on a narrow band of habitat in the subalpine meadows of south-central Vancouver Island. Naturalist groups on the Island first raised the alarm about declining marmot populations in the late 1970s. The causes were complex and interrelated: a rapid expansion of high-elevation logging in the 1970s and 1980s created attractive forage conditions for Columbian black-tailed deer and Roosevelt elk. As deer and elk moved to higher elevations, they drew their predators (cougar, grey wolf and golden eagle) closer to marmot habitat. Like woodland caribou, marmots had based their survival on strategies of avoidance—occupying high-elevation areas where predators were few. Their small population size and low rate of reproduction left them especially vulnerable to rising predation.

By 1997, fewer than one hundred wild marmots remained, scattered across a handful of isolated colonies. The circumstances prompted the province and the non-profit Marmot Recovery Foundation to launch an ambitious captive-breeding program in collaboration with the Calgary and Toronto zoos and several area landowners. In the decades that followed, their collective efforts, combined with the designation of protected areas for marmot habitat, produced one of the most successful species-at-risk recovery programs in Canada. By 2020, marmot populations had expanded to more than two hundred individuals on over twenty mountains. Although populations continue to fluctuate in response to drought and changing climatic conditions, the program has generally succeeded in mitigating the ongoing effects of landscape change and predation.[8]

For some observers, however, the amount of energy and resources directed toward the recovery of a single species like the Vancouver Island marmot was misdirected. UBC zoologist Geoff Scudder was an early proponent of shifting conservation strategies from endangered *species* to endangered *ecosystems*. In a series of papers in the early 2000s, Scudder pointed to two central problems in existing strategies for protecting species at risk: (1) an emphasis on species at risk that ignored biological richness, another vital indicator of biodiversity; and (2) an assumption that protected areas coincided with areas of high biodiversity. By differentiating between areas with high numbers of species at risk—what he called "rarity hotspots"—and areas of high biological diversity, or "richness hotspots," Scudder showed

Conservation priority areas, 2009

Priority levels for
conservation

High

Low

Today, the Nature Trust of BC and other conservation organizations assess a range of data
sources, including ecological communities and species at risk, to prioritize areas of high
conservation concern. This map shows areas of conservation priority based on the number
of species at risk per hectare. Data source: Hectares BC, High Priority Species Count,
December 2009. Map by GeoBC, 2022.

that the two did not always coincide and that neither was well represented
in the province's existing system of protected areas.

Under-representation of lower-elevation and valley-bottom ecosystems
in parks and protected areas, especially in the southern Interior,
contributed to these conclusions. Most of the province's threatened and
endangered species, Scudder showed, occurred in the South Okanagan,
southeast Vancouver Island and the Lower Mainland, areas where urban
and agricultural development had dramatically reduced available habitat
and where most of the remaining biologically rich lands were privately held.
Under these circumstances, he argued, species-at-risk provisions under the

FRPA and other natural resource legislation offered little protection. A 2007 Ministry of Environment report confirmed these findings, pointing to agriculture and urbanization as the most common causes of habitat loss for threatened bird, reptile and terrestrial mammal species.[9] "If there is to be any measure of success" in protecting threatened species, Scudder concluded, the provincial government must "focus on saving species at risk in the context of functioning ecosystems." This could be achieved by prioritizing areas of biological rarity and richness and dispensing with what he viewed as an inadequate target of 12 per cent protected areas. Large-scale, ecosystem-based planning across BC's entire land base would be needed to ensure at least 50 per cent of each ecoregion was managed "for maintenance of . . . ecosystem integrity."[10]

Scudder's work contributed to the development of **Biodiversity BC**, a partnership of government and conservation organizations formed in 2004 to develop a provincial biodiversity conservation strategy.[11] In 2007, following extensive consultation with over one hundred scientists and other experts, Biodiversity BC produced *Taking Nature's Pulse*, a comprehensive report on the status of biodiversity in British Columbia. The report confirmed that for the best-studied vertebrate groups, including threatened birds, mammals and freshwater fish, "more species had experienced a deterioration in conservation status since the 1990s than an improvement." Among these, breeding birds had experienced the largest decline.[12]

The number of species at risk—already larger in BC than in any other province or territory—had continued to increase "as more species [were] assessed and as populations of previously secure species decline[d]." More than one-third of freshwater fish and almost half of the reptile and turtle species in BC, for example, were placed on the provincial red list of species at risk following status assessments in the early 2000s. Habitat loss was by far the greatest threat, affecting over 90 per cent of listed species.[13] With its detailed analysis of cumulative and mounting threats to species and ecosystems at risk, *Taking Nature's Pulse* supported Scudder's 2003 conclusion that the province's conservation strategies were inadequate.[14]

Scientists agree that population recovery for species at risk is generally slow and expensive and that signs of recovery may require several decades to materialize. Species recovery plans, which in BC were completed or underway for most listed wildlife species by 2007, are by nature reactive, "occurring once a species has declined to the point of near endangerment."

Animals that produce only a few young each year require lengthy recovery periods, meaning that changes to forestry and agricultural practices and other habitat protection initiatives will likely require considerable time to bring about improvements in the status of threatened species.[15] The experience of the United States—with its much older endangered species legislation—has borne out, demonstrating that habitat protections applied over several decades can result in significant population recovery.[16]

Species recovery takes time, but experience to date suggests that initial responses must be rapid and monitoring efforts consistent if recovery efforts are to succeed. In this regard there is considerable room for improvement. While charismatic species such as Vancouver Island marmots and resident orcas have generated the public interest, enduring partnerships and cross-sectoral leadership that are vital for recovery efforts, other species have not been as fortunate.[17] For naturalists and conservation biologists—who point to the loss of ecosystem resilience, species interdependencies and vital genetic information with every lost species—adopting a new approach to biodiversity loss is an urgent priority.

In 2011, a provincial task force recommended a shift from a "species by species" approach to an ecosystem approach in terms of recovering threatened and endangered species, echoing Scudder's recommendations from a decade earlier.[18] Canada's participation in a global initiative to identify key biodiversity areas represents an important move in this direction. Building on the national Important Bird Area program initiated in the mid-1990s, the Key Biodiversity Areas (KBA) initiative aims to identify areas of high value for sustaining wildlife and ecological function. Moving away from a historical practice of siting protected areas "with an eye to creating the least possible conflict with resource development or other human interests," the KBA initiative identifies areas of biological richness and rarity as the guiding elements for protected areas design and conservation investment.[19]

Meanwhile, as climate change increases the stakes for many of British Columbia's threatened fish and wildlife species, the call for stand-alone provincial species-at-risk legislation has grown louder. Such legislation, proponents argue, would fill substantive gaps in the existing legislation, allowing for legalized protections of threatened species across the Crown land base. It would also serve to consolidate and strengthen existing legislation, reducing the need for forestry and other resource companies to track wildlife management across several different statutes. The rejection by cabinet of a draft Endangered Species Act in 1992 was followed by several opposition-led bills tabled in the first decade of the 2000s, none of which passed the first reading in the legislature.[20] BC remains one of only four Canadian provinces that lack stand-alone endangered species laws.[21] For conservationists operating in a province with the highest biodiversity and the largest number of species of risk in the country, the absence of legal accountability for protecting and recovering threatened species has been a troubling omission. Furthermore, Scudder's directives remain relevant. With growing recognition of the need for an ecosystem approach to recovering species at risk, the opportunity exists to update and expand twentieth-century endangered species legislation to protect endangered ecological communities.

The Possibilities of Partnership

In the context of limited avenues for legislative protection and steep declines in government capacity, a growing number of not-for-profit organizations have stepped into the breach over the past thirty years to address urgent wildlife conservation priorities. For many wildlife advocates, the reliance on non-governmental organizations to manage a land base that is 94 per cent publicly owned has been less than ideal, producing what former Habitat Conservation Trust Foundation CEO Brian Springinotic described as a "fragmented and uncoordinated approach to managing fish and wildlife."[22] However, working together has helped land trusts, conservation organizations and government wildlife agencies stretch limited conservation dollars. As complexity increased and the costs of land, labour and expertise rose through the 2000s and 2010s, partnerships between various levels of government and sometimes multiple organizations and foundations have provided creative ways of pooling funds and distributing risks.

Pooling Funds and Expertise to Protect Pacific Estuaries

Throughout this period of "War in the Woods" wilderness activism and legislative wrangling to protect species at risk, less adversarial approaches to wildlife conservation and ecosystem stewardship were making quiet gains behind the scenes. As political scientist Jeremy Wilson has pointed out, the environmental movement's near-exclusive focus on forests through the late 1980s and 1990s obscured other serious environmental issues, such as the degradation of wetlands and grasslands.[23] With forestry debates consuming the majority share of public attention, an older generation of naturalist and conservation organizations raised funds and shovels to protect some of the province's most biologically rich ecosystems. From large international partnerships to local, regional and national land conservancy initiatives, conservation organizations worked with governments to secure and improve critical wildlife habitat on private and Crown lands and to educate British Columbians about the actions they could take on their own properties.

Partnership approaches—evident since the 1960s in efforts to protect waterfowl habitat in the Creston Valley and the Fraser River estuary—gathered steam in the late 1980s, when the two dominant land conservancy organizations, the Nature Trust of BC and Ducks Unlimited Canada, found themselves competing for the same parcels of land on the BC coast. Within the context of the urgent need to protect the province's biologically rich coastal estuaries, senior executives from both organizations agreed to work together rather than at cross-purposes. Their agreement ultimately led to the establishment in 1987 of the **Pacific Estuary Conservation Program (PECP)**, which pooled the funds and expertise of federal and provincial government agencies and non-government organizations to jointly identify, acquire and manage coastal estuaries and upland habitat.[24] The program enabled DUC and the NTBC to work with governments to pair small private land acquisitions with larger parcels of adjacent Crown foreshore and then, through lease agreements, designate bundled lands for protection by the province as Wildlife Management Areas (WMAs).

In places like the Fraser River delta, farmers and wildlife alike benefited from these arrangements. Between 1987 and 2019, the global significance of the delta's floodplain and tidal flat habitats stimulated collaboration among governments, farmers and conservation organizations to protect migratory bird habitat. Protected areas increased dramatically in this period, from 1 per cent of the delta in 1987 to 38 per cent by 2019. These legally designated conservation areas benefited farmers by providing alternative foraging sites for overwintering waterfowl. Voluntary wildlife stewardship programs, meanwhile, compensated farmers for farming with wildlife in mind—for example, by planting winter cover crops, protecting native grasslands and planting hedgerows. Seasonal hunting closures, the banning of toxic lead shot on federal properties within the delta and a reduction in the use of several toxic insecticides also improved conditions for migratory birds.

The results have been encouraging: populations of many species of waterfowl, shorebirds and birds of prey have increased; others, such as brant, sandhill crane and greater white-fronted goose, continue to recover.[25] Ongoing threats to delta ecosystems from urban development, conversion to more intensive forms of agriculture, and proposed industrial developments, however, have led to calls for a more effective co-governance structure between the various levels of government and First Nations that oversee the delta and the wildlife it supports.[26]

The PECP's strategy of bundling and designating private and Crown lands remains the dominant model for land conservation in British Columbia. By 1998, the PECP had acquired roughly 1,600 hectares of coastal habitat on private lands and bundled an additional 45,000 hectares of adjacent Crown intertidal areas for protection as provincial Wildlife Management Areas, a 1:28 ratio on investment.[27] Land acquisition partnerships on the coast dovetailed with continental initiatives in 1991, when the PECP became the regional land acquisition and management arm for the broader North American Waterfowl Management Plan (NAWMP), an international agreement between Canada, the United States and Mexico to conserve North American wetlands.[28] Described by DUC as the "largest conservation initiative in history," NAWMP picked up and expanded on a long history of continental work on birds dating back to the 1917 Migratory Birds Convention. At the core of the program, US federal cost-share funding supported habitat acquisition and improvement work across the continent and attracted matching funding from government and non-government sources in Canada, Mexico and the United States. For DUC, these funds provided an important source of annual core funding at a time when contributions from its US-based parent organization were beginning to wane.[29]

Former DUC Western Canada regional director Ian Barnett described the regional and international partnerships generated under NAWMP as a tremendous success. When the program came into effect in 1986, Barnett noted, "waterfowl numbers were the lowest they'd been in thirty or forty years." The program "created this large safety net across the continent for wintering areas, staging areas and breeding areas." Barnett concluded,

Ducks Unlimited Canada's conservation work in the Fraser River estuary has benefited more than just birds. Here, a DUC construction crew works to improve fish passage on Gunn Island, with funding from the federal government's Coastal Restoration Fund. Photo courtesy of Ducks Unlimited Canada, 2022.

"There are many stories that aren't good about wildlife numbers, but waterfowl are . . . a real success story." Part of the success lay in the relative simplicity of wetland conservation work. "We would restore water into some areas that had been drained [decades before]. . . . All of a sudden you're getting bullrush seeds that are germinating twenty, thirty, forty years later. And you're getting birds there. It's really satisfying. We used to joke, 'just add water and stir.' I don't want to be simplistic, but it's a good recipe."[30]

Recognition of the effects of crop harvests and predation on waterfowl led to a greater focus on adjacent upland habitats, including land purchases and incentives for farmers to delay hay cuts to better align with nesting periods. The addition of uplands "enhanced the whole package," according to retired DUC regional director Les Bogdan, providing associated benefits for songbirds and other species.[31] Since its inception more than thirty years ago, NAWMP has expanded to benefit all bird species. "It's [about] more than just ducks," Barnett noted; "it's become a bird plan."

Conservation Innovations on Private Lands

Collaboration and creative problem-solving fuelled conservation successes among a growing number of land trust organizations in the 1990s and early 2000s, funnelling private and corporate donations into the protection of critical wildlife habitat on private land. Pioneers of partnership such as Ron Erickson, NTBC CEO from 1984 to 2001, and DUC regional manager Peter Jones advanced acquisitions of conservation lands in this period and led important innovations in conservation work.

Erickson's emphasis on the need for quality data to establish priorities in land acquisition, for example, transformed the calculus of NTBC conservation priorities. In the threatened desert environments of the South Okanagan, consultations with UBC and Royal BC Museum research biologists allowed the NTBC to map concentrations of rare and endangered species—some of which had never been identified anywhere else in the world. The results informed conservation property purchases in the biodiversity "hot spots" of Vaseux and White lakes and the Okanagan River corridor.[32]

Erickson and the NTBC board used the same information to develop creative partnerships with ranchers in the area. Seeking to avert the sale of ranch lands for more intensive development, NTBC acquired three ranches in these biologically rich areas and worked with ranchers to develop "biodiversity ranches." Management plans developed with support from agronomist Gary Runka allowed ranchers to remain on the land and continue their livelihoods while

Former Nature Trust of BC CEO Ron Erickson and agronomist Gary Runka in the Ashnola River watershed near Keremeos, 2012. Erickson and Runka worked together to develop the "biodiversity ranch" concept to protect threatened Okanagan ecosystems in the 1980s and 1990s. Photo by Rod S. Silver. Photo courtesy of Ron Erickson.

modifying their practices to care for wetlands and wildlife-supporting grass-lands. The success of these data-driven approaches led Erickson to champion the idea of a provincewide conservation data clearing house. BC's respected Conservation Data Centre formed as a result of these efforts in 1991.[33]

However significant they might be for biodiversity protection, land acquisitions constituted a mixed blessing for conservation organizations. When the title transfers for a piece of land acquired through purchase or donation, NTBC CEO Jasper Lament explained, "that piece of property instantly becomes a liability on the Nature Trust budget because now we have to take care of it forever." Nancy Newhouse, BC regional vice-president for the Nature Conservancy of Canada, agreed: "There are tremendous costs to us taking a property. For every project we [take] we raise monies towards a stewardship endowment fund, which helps us provide some of the basic costs of land management moving forward." As a result, large land trusts like the NTBC and the Nature Conservancy of Canada can take on only a small fraction of the lands offered to them. "We have to make sure," Lament explained, that "we select only the very best of what's available to get the most conservation value out of our donors' and partners' conservation dollars."[34]

Within this context, **conservation covenants** emerged as an alternative mechanism to extend already stretched conservation dollars. Advocacy by NTBC and DUC executives produced a significant policy shift in the early 1990s, when the Ministry of Environment created a new legal tool allowing landowners to grant partial interests in land to designated con-servation organizations. Incorporated into the BC Land Title Act in 1994, conservation covenants attached legally binding conservation restrictions to the land title that carried through to subsequent owners. The conser-vation organization, in return, agreed to monitor the property to ensure the intentions of the covenant were maintained. DUC has made especially strategic use of this tool, offering farmers in important habitat areas one-third of the fair market value of their land in exchange for covenants that restrict land uses to waterfowl-compatible crops and practices. For younger farmers seeking access to prohibitively expensive agricultural lands in the Fraser Valley, arrangements like this have provided the means for a down payment. Conservation organizations benefit too, stretching their conser-vation dollars three times as far as traditional (fee simple) land acquisi-tions. Over the past twenty years, however, challenges to the specificity and applicability of restrictive clauses by new property owners have dampened enthusiasm for conservation covenants. Today, conservation organizations are more cautious in their use.[35]

A more flexible donation instrument for conservation organizations has been the use of **creative sentencing** options by federal and provincial courts to allocate damages for environmental, fishery and wildlife offences to habitat rehabilitation projects. BC Crown counsel pioneered these arrangements beginning in the early 1980s, when they persuaded provincial courts to use flexible sentencing provisions within the federal Fisheries Act to direct fines and court-ordered payments to appropriate community-based conservation projects. While fines to individuals or corporations remained the norm in this period, creative sentences issued to logging, oil and rail companies aimed to make environmental prosecutions "more meaningful."[36]

As federal and provincial creative sentencing legislation evolved in the mid-1990s, the province designated two trust funds as direct beneficiaries of court-ordered payments: the Habitat Conservation Trust Foundation, which has received the bulk of the awards, and the Grizzly Bear Trust Fund. Between 1993 and 2009, these organizations invested $1.3 million in court-awarded funds across seventy provincial conservation projects.[37] Funds from creative sentencing for environmental violations continue to expand. As Springinotic explained, "if a person [or corporation] is going to be prosecuted for environmental offences, we've got the optimal mechanism to put those proceeds back on the ground to improve conservation."[38]

INITIATIVE PROFILE: The *Nestucca* Settlement

Settlement funds awarded for international violations also set a precedent for directing proceeds of environmental damage to conservation initiatives on the ground. For example, damages awarded to Canada, British Columbia and the Nuu-chah-nulth Tribal Council following the 1988 *Nestucca* oil spill in Washington State, which had devastating consequences for seabirds and other wildlife off western Vancouver Island and BC's northern mainland coast, funnelled $3.3 million into seabird recovery and monitoring efforts. The bulk of the funds supported a large-scale and highly successful eradication project for introduced rats on Haida Gwaii's Langara Island, allowing for the recovery of what was once the world's largest breeding colony for ancient murrelets (*Synthliboramphus antiquus*).[39] The lasting conservation benefits of the *Nestucca* settlement fund highlight the value of directing damages awarded in environmental lawsuits into funding recovery and research effort for the affected species and ecosystems, rather than into general government revenues.

Despite all the creative funding mechanisms and incentives that land trusts and conservation organizations had at their disposal, their acquisitions, leases and partial interests in land still constituted only a tiny fraction (roughly 0.002 per cent) of the provincial land base and just 0.03 per cent of the province's privately owned lands—what Jeremy Wilson describes as a "small mitigating counterforce" to larger development pressures on the landscape.[40] To address conservation concerns across the large remainder of private lands, government and non-government partners turned to **voluntary private land stewardship programs**—incentives and supports to help landowners maintain and improve wildlife habitat on their properties—beginning in the early 1990s. Wildlife Habitat Canada, a charitable organization perhaps best known for its popular annual "conservation stamp" fundraiser, became an early champion of this approach. Executive director David Neave promoted what the organization described as a "stewardship revolution" in the early 1990s, urging jurisdictions across the country to adopt landowner outreach approaches that had already shown considerable promise in Ontario.[41] "Working with people," Neave argued, could attain some of the same conservation goals as land acquisition without the high costs.

By 1994, the idea had taken hold among conservation advocates in British Columbia, stoked by the well-attended national Stewardship 94 conference held in Vancouver that spring. Later that year, provincial, federal and non-governmental organizations embarked on a collaborative "Stewardship Pledge" to provide tools and training for stewardship practitioners and modest support for on-the-ground pilot projects.[42] By 1995, a partnership with the federal Department of Fisheries and Oceans launched the ambitious Stewardship Series, a peer-reviewed, science-based publication series documenting best practices for private landowners, industry and local governments. Partner efforts coalesced in 2006 in the establishment of the Stewardship Centre for BC, a non-profit organization that continues to support stewardship practice and education in the province.[43]

Federal-provincial collaboration produced the **Environmental Farm Plan (EFP)** program in the same period, which offered farmers and ranchers free and confidential consultations with trained agrologists to reduce the environmental effects of their operations. EFP consultations identify ways to promote biodiversity on farm properties and protect riparian areas from livestock damage. Where the program differs from other voluntary stewardship initiatives is in the funding it provides to help farmers make improvements, such as fencing riparian areas or revitalizing biodiversity-rich wetlands. As BC Cattlemen's Association stewardship coordinator Rick Mumford explained, with as much as 60 per cent of the costs covered by government, "it's too attractive for a rancher to turn down."[44] By 2022, more than 5,700 ranchers and farmers across the province (about 30 per cent of all farms) had completed environmental farm plans for their properties.[45]

INITIATIVE PROFILE: Streamkeepers

Voluntary stewardship initiatives found a ready model of action and engagement in existing community groups dedicated to stream restoration. The Vancouver Salmon and Stream Society, for example, was one of many community groups across BC working to restore the habitat potential of degraded or contaminated local waterways. Beginning in the 1990s, society volunteers secured support from the DFO, the Vancouver Parks Board and the province's Urban Salmon Habitat Program to "daylight," or uncover buried sections of, Spanish Banks Creek on the city's west side. In 2001, years of effort to restore salmon habitat, stabilize creek banks and remove barriers to fish passage were rewarded with the return of spawning coho for the first time in over fifty years.[46]

Local streamkeeper organizations like those at Spanish Banks received a boost in the early 1990s with the development of volunteer training resources and the creation of an umbrella body, the Pacific Streamkeepers Federation, to amplify their concerns and foster cooperation among watershed stakeholders. In 1995, DFO biologist Brian Tutty drew on funds from the Salmonid Enhancement Program to produce the *Streamkeepers Handbook*, a practical guide for restoring and enhancing salmon habitat modelled after stream stewardship programs in the United States. Later incorporated into the Stewardship Centre for BC's respected Stewardship Series, the *Streamkeepers Handbook* remains a valuable training and education resource for citizen conservation initiatives. For groups like the Spanish Banks

West Vancouver Streamkeeper Society volunteers removing silt buildup from a rearing pond for juvenile coho salmon and cutthroat trout on McDonald Creek in Hay Park, West Vancouver, November 26, 2021. Photo courtesy of Joseph McDaniel.

Streamkeepers, an ongoing partnership with the DFO supports stewardship work and the involvement of local schools in rearing chum salmon fry in the classroom for release into the creek. In a city where over thirty historic salmon streams have been lost to urban development, the success of the Spanish Banks project has served as a model of grassroots stewardship.

Maximizing Investment: The Conservation Lands Program

As land trusts continue to struggle with the skyrocketing cost of land in biologically significant areas such as the Lower Mainland, southeastern Vancouver Island and the Okanagan Valley, seed funds from government have become a vital mechanism for stimulating partner investment. The province's 2004 establishment of an $8 million land conservation fund required $3 in matching funds for every dollar granted by government.[47] Three years later, significant reinvestment in private land acquisition by the federal government (after more than twenty years of austerity) allowed organizations like the Nature Conservancy of Canada to attract matching funds from foundations and corporations toward the protection of biologically rich properties.[48]

Together, these investments led to a proliferation of partnership development, stewardship investment and conservation acquisitions among land trusts late in the first decade of the 2000s and early 2010s. One of the results of these developments was a shift away from the traditional model of private land acquisition to place greater emphasis on identifying and designating high-quality habitats on Crown land. As BC expanded its provincial protected area targets in the mid-2000s, land trusts and governments worked to compile bigger acreages with larger proportions of public land. Land trusts also became more innovative in this context, working with private interests on Crown land to buy out timber rights or sub-surface development options.[49] Bundled Crown and private holdings and lease agreements were then transferred to the BC Ministry of Environment for management under its Conservation Lands Program.

Provincial *management* of conservation lands, however, has generally fallen short of expectations. Lands designated as Wildlife Management Areas, for example, are complicated to manage because they do not enjoy the comprehensive protections of more exclusive statutory designations, such as parks or protected areas. Many WMAs permit pre-existing economic uses, like grazing tenures, to continue. The NTBC's Okanagan Falls Biodiversity Ranch, for example, contains Crown grazing licences that existed long before the NTBC acquired the land. In other cases, forestry activities have been permitted in order to protect grassland habitats from forest encroachment. While some of these uses may have been compatible with conservation goals, in 2021 the Office of the Auditor General found

Protected lands in British Columbia, 2021

Black areas indicate "Protected lands" in this map, including all provincial and federal parks, protected areas, conservancies, ecological reserves, wildlife areas and privately and publicly managed conservation lands. Data sources: BC Wildlife and Habitat Branch, Conservation Lands, 2013; Environment and Climate Change Canada, Canadian Protected and Conserved Areas Database, 2021. Map by GeoBC, 2022.

that the Ministry of Environment had failed to manage its Conservation Lands Program effectively. Ministry decisions over the 2010s to issue grazing leases on lands leased to the province by conservation organizations, for example, compromised both wildlife habitat and the trust of long-standing partners like Ducks Unlimited Canada.[50]

As with other aspects of provincial land and wildlife management, the loss of key staff, resources and relationships in the context of deep budget cuts between 2003 and 2012 crippled government capacity. The Ministry of Environment alone lost nearly 30 per cent of its biologist positions between 2002 and 2012.[51] Within this context of declining government capacity

Volunteers from Kootenay-area rod and gun clubs and wilderness societies prepare to install a fence to protect aspen trees from excessive elk browse at the NTBC's Big Ranch conservation property in the Elk Valley, April 2013. Photo courtesy of Rob Neil, former NTBC Kootenay conservation land manager.

and inadequate management, non-government partners have increasingly shouldered more of the management work themselves. The Nature Trust of BC, for example, now employs four full-time conservation land managers who run land management teams across British Columbia.[52] The province's 2021 commitment to reinvest in the Conservation Lands Program suggests a renewed interest in managing for biodiversity on conservation lands within its jurisdiction.[53]

Partnerships with First Nations

The growth of BC First Nations as decision makers, employers and partners in conservation initiatives has also created significant shifts in the land trust sector. Moving "at the speed of trust," conservation organizations, government representatives and local First Nations have identified shared interests in the establishment of new conservation lands. Since the early 2010s, provincial conservation lands have been designated only in consultation with area First Nations.

An example of this is the McTaggart-Cowan/nsək'łniw't Wildlife Management Area, a large, mostly non-roaded area of grassland and rocky outcrop habitat outside of Penticton. Both the NTBC and the SnPink'tn (Penticton Indian Band) sought to protect the California bighorn sheep and numerous other species at risk that depend on threatened South Okanagan grasslands. In 2013, a partnership between the NTBC, the SnPink'tn, and the province established the WMA, adding significant Crown land transfers to a collection of private lands that the NTBC had acquired decades earlier. Named jointly for UBC zoologist and conservationist Ian McTaggart Cowan, who dedicated years of his career to the study of wild sheep, and the Syilx (Okanagan) word "nsək'łniw't," which references an Indigenous trade and medicine-gathering trail in the area, the new WMA demonstrates the possibilities of these new kinds of partnerships.

Other partnerships have involved First Nations in habitat restoration efforts. In 2018, for example, the Nature Conservancy of Canada entered into a joint land purchase and rehabilitation project with the Haida Nation, the first of its kind in Canada, after a creative sentencing procedure released a piece of land damaged by logging practices that violated the Fisheries Act.[54]

Information sharing and capacity development is another feature of collaborations with First Nations. DUC's work over the past twenty years to develop detailed baseline mapping for wetland habitats in boreal zones of northeast BC, for example, has supported northern nations like the Kaska in developing their own comprehensive GIS mapping and land use planning systems. Detailed, current information about ecosystem characteristics on the ground is vital to successful conservation and restoration efforts. As initiatives like these demonstrate, this kind of high-quality, site-specific information is no longer the exclusive purview of governments. Information-sharing has become even more significant in the context of climate change. NTBC partnerships with several coastal First Nations have supported estuary monitoring initiatives, helping both groups to understand how climate change and sea-level rise will affect estuary habitats and associated restoration efforts.[55]

The Future of Conservation Partnerships

Partnerships, in sum, have proved essential in stretching the value of limited conservation dollars. They work best with consistent participation from the provincial government responsible for the land base. As Jasper Lament

explains, "the most effective tool that we have is leverage. Leveraging partner dollars and leveraging donor dollars. In order to effectively leverage
those funds, we need dedicated, reliable sources of provincial and federal
funding for land conservation." The success of other Canadian jurisdictions, including Alberta and Quebec, where robust provincial funding
has allowed conservation organizations to accelerate the pace of land
acquisitions, stands as a reminder of the possibilities. Especially as the
federal government rolled out new funding programs in the 2000s and
2010s, BC organizations found themselves scrambling to find required
sources of matching funds. "Without the province at the table in a meaningful way," one land trust spokesperson commented, "it's very hard for BC
to compete on the Canadian scale. It's a key piece that's missing for us. . . .
Everything we do needs a match." As University of Victoria law professor
Calvin Sandborn argued in 2015, the establishment of a permanent, provincially administered fund for the acquisition of natural lands would allow
resourceful conservation organizations to "dramatically leverage the total
amount of land eventually protected."[56]

Financial contributions are one thing, allowing conservation organizations to take advantage of matching or cost-sharing funds from
other sources. Responsive regulations and statutory protections are
another. But interviewees pointed to institutional memory as the
foundation underpinning this kind of supportive participation. The
partnerships of the 1980s and 1990s relied on senior government staff who
had built relationships with conservation organizations over decades. The
declining number and capacity of staff in these positions over the last two
decades weakened established partnerships. As former DUC executive Les
Bogdan recalled, "[we had] a good relationship . . . with previous people
that retired," but as staff turned over there was a loss of understanding of
"what we [were] trying to do." There was a tendency among incoming staff
to "treat us like [real estate] developers, not as NGOs that [were] going
to benefit agriculture and wildlife." Cultural changes within governments
also contributed to these changes, as directors in the Canadian Wildlife
Service and the provincial wildlife program generally enjoyed less latitude
and decision-making power than their forebears.[57] Yet the longevity of
these partnerships and their common goal of protecting ecosystems and
species at risk carries considerable promise. Like wetlands, they hold great
capacity for renewal.

Changing Faces and Methods of Wildlife Research

For all its noted losses in provincial government funding, staff and political will, the early twenty-first century has also birthed a new kind of
wildlife professional. For wildlife biologists especially, government is no
longer the principal employer; in addition to independent consulting roles,
biologists have taken up positions in industry, First Nations and conservation organizations. The nature of their work has changed dramatically
since Ian McTaggart Cowan and his colleagues ushered in a new era of
scientific wildlife management in the 1940s. From Cowan and his students'
use of telemetry data to model wildlife populations through the 1970s and
'80s, wildlife research has seen significant technological advances. The use
of scat and hair DNA analysis, trail cameras and drones, for example, has
allowed for less intrusive methods of study in animal population and be-
havioural work. Within fisheries science, the growing accessibility of such
tools as environmental DNA detection, which enables scientists to determine species presence by extracting genetic material from water samples,
has the potential to revolutionize fisheries conservation work.[58]

While the copious data generated from these new methods has allowed
biologists to be more exacting in their assessments, older generations of
biologists point to the value of "ground truthing" this kind of information through time in the field. As budgets and staffing for fish and wildlife inventory and research work declined precipitously in the 2000s and
2010s, government biologists in particular found themselves spending most
of their time at their desks. For many observers, the shift has reduced the
ability of biologists to gather insights from extended observation in the
field. As retired wildlife research manager Don Eastman explains, "a lot
of things are happening in the wild that you don't appreciate unless you're
there." Former habitat protection biologist Jenny Feick provides the example of veteran bear biologist Tony Hamilton, who "could tell when he was
in good grizzly bear habitat . . . just by watching band-tailed pigeons. There
was a relationship between the habitat requirements [of the two species]
. . . that is not written in any book." Reduced time in the field not only
removed opportunities for understanding but also hindered the ability to
develop the kind of instincts that first- and second-generation biologists
like Ray Demarchi were famous for. Bear biologist Garth Mowat, for example, points to the field as the place where wildlife managers develop their

Fisheries researchers use acoustic telemetry to track the natural and fishing mortality of wild cutthroat trout (*Oncorhynchus clarkii*) on Cowichan Lake, one of Vancouver Island's most popular freshwater fishing destinations. Photo by Erin Rechisky, 2019. Photo courtesy of the Habitat Conservation Trust Foundation.

judgment: "the better [biologists] are connected to what's going on outside, the better decisions they'll make." Numbers, Feick concludes, "only tell part of the story."[59]

The rising number of women in wildlife research, conservation and management positions has offset these trends in interesting ways. Since the early 1980s, when wildlife biologists like UNBC's Winifred Kessler were among very few women in the field, the number of women has steadily grown. Today, women constitute roughly half of the wildlife management professionals in British Columbia.[60] Their presence has changed not only the culture but also the practice of wildlife management. "We know from the work of Jane Goodall and Dian Fossey," Feick noted, that "women see things differently and interpret wildlife behaviour differently. They're open to different ideas."

Women also make different decisions. For Mowat, the reduction over the past thirty years in hunting allocations for grizzly bears is due in part to the role of female managers. "When it comes to personal judgments, [women] are often more conservative. That, in itself, might slowly reduce the number of animals killed, just because they make slightly more conservative decisions," he explains. "Instead of putting out twelve tags they put out ten." For Kessler, the most profound changes stem from women's relative strengths in communication and collaboration. With their tendency to place greater emphasis on relationships, she explained, women enable more effective collaboration within project teams and committees—"and that's what wildlife and natural resource management is all about. It's solving complex problems collaboratively through team effort [that incorporates] different perspectives and different expertise."[61]

Women's influence has also conditioned a more overt recognition of the human dimensions of wildlife management. Understanding the role of ethics, social and historical inequities, personal experience and geographical positioning in shaping public perceptions about wildlife and wildlife management has become an important component of the wildlife manager's portfolio.[62] Forestry and wildlife management programs at UBC, Simon Fraser University and UNBC contributed to these shifts. As head of UNBC's forestry program in the 1990s, Kessler recognized the need to move beyond siloed training for foresters and wildlife managers in order to model an integrated approach to resource management. "Managing . . . ecosystems is way too complex for any one discipline," she explained. "If you're going to manage by design, you have to build [in] resource objectives upfront." To come up with solutions, "experts [need to] work together as a team. That's the only way it works." She and her colleagues at UNBC constructed a program that placed wildlife, fisheries and forestry majors in teams that, by the end, were tasked with handling "very complex real-world problems." Blending cooperative, interdisciplinary learning with a strong ethics component, Kessler added, equipped students for their future careers by teaching them "to work together in teams to address complex problems that took into account the ecological dimension, the economic dimension, [and] the social dimension" of wildlife management.[63]

Public participation in wildlife management and conservation has also changed. With the shift to professional reliance and the decision to abandon multi-stakeholder land use planning in the early 2000s, opportunities for public involvement in government planning processes have generally diminished. The overturning of consensus-based decisions forged at LRMP tables in some regions has further eroded the willingness of experienced residents, including local hunters and naturalists, to participate in wildlife management forums and other public processes.

The rise of social media over the same period has provided an alternative forum for some. More often a venue to air grievances than to share constructive feedback, social media platforms like Facebook and Twitter have been used by local residents and interest groups to oppose wildlife management decisions made by local or provincial authorities. Conservation officers, who occupy the front lines of wildlife management, have generally felt the pressures of social media more than their biologist colleagues. As senior conservation officer Joe Caravetta explains, officers forced to kill a problem bear that has become habituated to garbage or fruit from neglected fruit trees are too often "raked over the coals on social media." He gave an example from the Kootenay-Boundary region where the decision to shoot a large deer that had become aggressive "went all over social media." The "whole town went after [the CO] and his kids got it at school." COs have always borne the brunt of unpopular wildlife decisions, but social media has amplified the reach and intensity of public opposition.

In its more positive form, social media has amplified the ease and significance of public involvement in wildlife research. The growing popularity of **citizen science** over the last three decades has been fuelled in part by social media channels that have raised awareness and attracted volunteers. Drawing on a century-long history of initiatives like the Christmas Bird Count, organizations like Bird Studies Canada and the BC Wildlife Federation have launched mobile phone applications to facilitate annual counts of a variety of species. The BC Parks Citizen Science Wildlife Monitoring Program is another initiative that relies on trained volunteers to install and monitor trail cameras in Skagit Valley Provincial Park on the US-Canada border. Data gathered from the program, which monitors grizzly bears and other carnivores in the North Cascades recovery zone, supports planning and decision-making by biologists and land managers on both sides of the border.[64]

Citizen science itself is nothing new: volunteer "keymen," as they were called, phoned or wrote in to DUC headquarters with spring and fall water conditions and bird counts beginning in the 1940s, and for at least sixty years hunters have mailed in duck leg bands to an office in Maryland to support North American waterfowl research. New platforms and new technology, however, have sharpened its effectiveness and allowed the data it produces to become "more quickly translated" into research insights and policy responses.[65]

As new generations of wildlife managers tackle the growing complexity of climate change, invasive species and the cumulative effects of resource extraction, finding opportunities to deepen public knowledge of the rising stakes for wildlife survival will be ever more important.

SPECIES PROFILE: Grizzly Bear (*Ursus arctos horribilis*)

British Columbia is home to one of the largest populations of grizzly bears in North America, second only to Alaska. Historically, grizzlies occupied the entire province with the exception of Vancouver Island, Haida Gwaii and other coastal islands. Today, BC's roughly 15,000 grizzly bears occupy about 90 per cent of their historical range. BC's Conservation Data Centre has designated grizzlies as a species of special concern given their slow reproductive rates and sensitivity to human activities. Grizzlies fall into two general population groups, coastal and interior, each with different seasonal movements and food sources. While coastal grizzlies subsist mainly on vegetation, roots and berries in the spring and on live and dead salmon in the fall, interior grizzlies supplement a primarily plant-based diet with winter-weakened and juvenile ungulates, small mammals, fish and insects.

Like other large carnivores, grizzly bears suffered massive population losses over the nineteenth and early twentieth centuries. Euro-Canadian settlers saw them as a serious threat to human life, livestock and property and routinely shot them on sight. Once ranging over most of western North America as far south as central Mexico, by 1920 grizzlies had been extirpated from 98 per cent of their range in Mexico and the United States. Within British Columbia, too, their numbers fell dramatically. By the early 1960s, more than 150 years of aggressive hunting and human settlement had significantly reduced grizzly bear populations and removed them entirely from areas of concentrated urban and agricultural settlement in the Lower Mainland, the Peace River area around Fort St. John and large parts of south-central BC.[66]

The recovery of grizzly bear populations is one of the success stories of human-wildlife relationships in the province. Beginning in the mid-1960s, concern about the vulnerability of grizzly populations in the southern Interior led to the

Female grizzly bear (*Ursus arctos horribilis*) on the Atnarko River near Bella Coola, September 26, 2021. Photo courtesy of Harvey Thommasen.

province's first bear conservation initiatives. Ray Demarchi, who took up the position of wildlife biologist for the Kootenay region in 1964, recognized the effects that decades of commercial hunting, baiting and indiscriminate hunting of females and cubs had had on grizzly populations in the area. Demarchi's advocacy led to a provincial ban on hunting with the use of bait in 1968 and statutory protection of cubs and females with cubs. Restricting grizzly hunting in the southern Interior to a spring season had the effect of further protecting females, in that by spring most were accompanied by cubs, or by a larger male that was more attractive to hunters.

In 1976, the province implemented the first limited entry hunt in the southern Interior, a lottery system that limited the number of available hunting permits. "The bear population started to recover," Demarchi recalled, "and it happened fast." Compulsory inspection—which required non-Indigenous hunters to report all bears killed—followed soon after, allowing wildlife managers to track the harvest. In the space of ten years, grizzlies in the southern half of BC had transitioned from a pest species earmarked for eradication to a valued species meriting conservation concern.[67]

By the late 1970s this shift in perspective toward grizzly bears, first apparent among a new generation of scientifically trained wildlife biologists, had been taken up by proponents of a growing wilderness protection movement. In 1975 the six remaining grizzly populations in the United States were listed as "threatened" under the US Endangered Species Act; while this had no legal effect in Canada, it had a significant social effect in raising public awareness about the status of grizzly bears in BC. Like wolves, grizzly bears had come to symbolize the idea of "undisturbed wilderness" that many British Columbians sought to protect.

The fight to protect the Khutzeymateen Valley, a coastal watershed northeast of Prince Rupert, gave voice to these ideas beginning in the mid-1980s. Home to the largest concentration of grizzly bears on the BC coast, the valley had been proposed for designation as an ecological reserve by UBC plant ecologist Vladimir Krajina and Fish and Wildlife Branch biologist Ken Sumanik as early as 1972. In the early 1980s, a proposal to log the area launched what became a multi-year campaign for its protection. Headed by Friends of Ecological Reserves leaders Vicky Husband and Peter Grant, and bear biologist Wayne McCrory, the campaign stressed the value of protecting an intact coastal grizzly bear and salmon ecosystem.

Grizzlies were, quite literally, the "poster animals" of the campaign: the Western Canada Wilderness Committee's widely circulated poster of a grizzly sow and her cub with the heading "Her Cub Deserves a Future" helped to generate widespread public support—including an endorsement by Prince Philip, Duke of Edinburgh—in the late 1980s. In 1992, following a three-year study, the BC Ministry of Environment announced that the entire 44,000-hectare valley would be protected as Canada's first grizzly bear sanctuary. Today, Khutzeymateen Provincial Park, also known as Khutzeymateen/K'tzim-a-deen Grizzly Bear Sanctuary, is jointly managed by BC Parks, the Coast Tsimshian First Nations and the Gitsi'is Tribe, whose traditional territory encompasses the park.[68]

Grizzlies not only carried wilderness campaigns but also headlined debates about trophy hunting. Beginning in the 1990s, *Vancouver Sun* columnist Nicholas Read published a series of articles about the ethics and sustainability of the grizzly bear hunt, highlighting a lack of certainty in the population estimates of the species that formed the basis for annual hunting allocations. Wilderness and wildlife protection advocates Karen and Ian McAllister mobilized international censure for the hunt from their base on the central coast, in what became known as the Great Bear Rainforest.

Less present in the media coverage were the perspectives of hunters and guide outfitters, whose licence and surcharge fees supported wildlife research and conservation work in the province and who had long relied on government wildlife allocations based on what they described as "science not sentiment." Countering accusations of waste, guide outfitters pointed to provincial meat retrieval laws that ensure "nothing is really wasted." Even historically, when animals were left lying in the bush, the idea of "waste" is misplaced, outfitters argued: "predators and scavengers . . . do pretty well on those sorts of things."[69] Finally, hunters' focus on older male bears served a conservation interest in itself, they argued, by removing a major threat to cubs and young bears. The killing of an average of 250 to 300 bears annually in areas where bear populations were secure, hunters argued, generated important revenue for conservation and wildlife management.

Debates about the sustainability of the hunt rested in large part on the reliability of the province's estimates of specific bear populations. Anecdotal evidence seemed to show that, in most parts of British Columbia, populations were "recovering from a century of overkill." In 1995, the province's Grizzly Bear Conservation Strategy identified nine out of fifty-six grizzly bear subpopulations as threatened— all in the southern part of the province where human populations are highest. Because conservation of these populations was critical in maintaining connectivity with remnant populations south of the border, scientists stressed the importance of geographic specificity in referencing grizzly population health.[70]

Not until the 1990s, however, when population inventories began in the province's southeast, could scientists corroborate their assumptions with actual numbers on the ground. In the mid-1990s, Parks Canada and a team of BC biologists pioneered a method of capturing hair samples and conducting DNA analysis to identify individuals, allowing biologists to estimate population size with high levels of accuracy. (The method is now used worldwide to inventory bears and other carnivores.) Critics of the hunt point out that these sophisticated inventory methods have to date been applied mainly to threatened populations in the southern extremes of the province. This leaves considerable uncertainty elsewhere, where estimates are extrapolated from habitat potential and harvest data. Correlation between the two methods, however, has generally been high. As bear biologist Garth Mowat comments, "we know more about grizzly bears than any other carnivore in the province."[71]

Scientific study of grizzlies has told us a lot more than how many there are. BC Forest Service biologist Bruce McLellan's multi-decade study of grizzlies in the Flathead Valley in southeastern BC, which began in 1978 and continues into the present, yielded numerous insights that have deeply challenged our assumptions about these animals. In contrast to studies in Alaska and Wyoming, which

Conservation status of grizzly bear populations in British Columbia, 2019

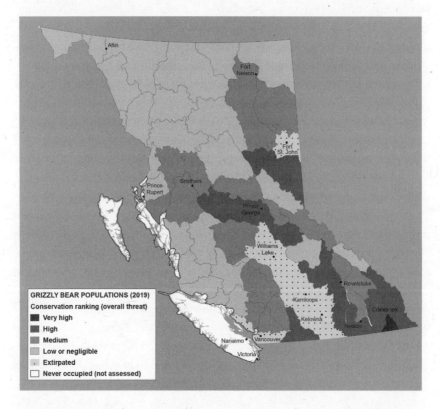

Data sources: DataBC, Grizzly Bear Conservation Rankings, 2019; BC Wildlife and Habitat Branch, Grizzly Bear Population Units, 2012; Tony Hamilton, Garth Mowat, Don Morgan (knowledge experts), Sasha Lees and Rajiv Lalla (GIS analysts), Grizzly Bear Population Units Data Change History 2012 to 2020. Map by GeoBC, 2022.

confirmed hunter suspicions that grizzlies eat large numbers of moose and elk calves, McLellan's dietary analysis of bears in the Flathead showed largely plant-based food sources (over 80 per cent plants and berries and 15 per cent ungulates). Bear population sizes in the Flathead, he found, were tied more to the abundance of huckleberries and other plant sources than to ungulate populations. The difference between the Alaska and Flathead studies, McLellan explains, points to grizzlies' adaptability to different local circumstances. In southern BC, unlike Alaska, ungulate numbers are very low and plant-based food sources are very high: "why . . . risk hunting an elk calf when you can chow down on all these rich herbs?" This dietary flexibility allows bears to subsist in a variety of habitats. It is not so much that habitats modified for agriculture and resource extraction do not support grizzlies, but rather that humans operating in these landscapes do not tolerate bears.[72]

Research has also revealed the significance of roads as sources of human-caused mortality for grizzly bears. Studies have shown that in places with high road density, grizzly bear numbers decline to a third or a quarter of their numbers in similar habitats with low road density. Although roads and rail lines kill a small number of bears in direct collisions, biologists attribute the bulk of population decline to habitat fragmentation and road avoidance behaviours that confine bears to smaller viable spaces. Most significantly, roads facilitate human access into grizzly bear areas. The annual addition of roughly 10,000 kilometres of new resource access roads heightens mortality rates for bears and many other species. As wildlife biologist Grant MacHutchon explains, access roads become recreational corridors for people. And "when people and bears mix, bears get shot."[73] A recent Auditor General's report highlighted that between 2006 and 2015, 389 grizzly bears were killed by conservation officers and armed recreationalists as a result of human conflict with bears. These "non-hunting mortalities" have increased considerably since numbers were first tracked in 1976.[74]

Recognition that most bear problems are people problems is nowhere more apparent than among the province's Conservation Officer Service. After moving or killing 121 grizzly bears and about 400 black bears over a ten-year period, conservation officers in the community of Revelstoke teamed up with wildlife biologists, Parks Canada and the regional district to create the province's first Bear Aware program in 1995. With funding from the Columbia River Basin, they hired a coordinator to educate residents and oversee the removal of fruit trees and other bear attractants from town parks and residential properties. Work with the regional district led to the closure of the town dump to bears by electrifying its perimeter. The project was a success, dramatically reducing the number of bear kills. In 2002, the province developed a Bear Smart Communities program (now WildSafe BC) in partnership with the BC Conservation Foundation and the Union of BC Municipalities. To date, ten communities have received "Bear Smart" designations. Progress has been slow, but participation has grown in recent years among both First Nations and non-Indigenous communities.[75]

Debates over the ethics and sustainability of the grizzly bear hunt have continued to intensify over the past twenty years. Despite the extension of limited entry hunting across the province in 1996 and hunting closures in areas where populations were under threat, the concerns of a growing anti-hunting lobby led the NDP government to impose a provincewide prohibition on grizzly bear hunting in

2001. The political aspect of the debate intensified the following year when Gordon Campbell's Liberals came to power and reinstated the hunt.

In the intervening years, pressures on BC's grizzly populations have also intensified. Declining food sources owing to collapsing salmon runs on the coast and low berry production in the interior have weakened populations in some areas. These factors, combined with advancements in population assessment, led scientists to identify a total of seventeen threatened populations in a recent conservation ranking report.[76] In 2017, NDP premier John Horgan responded to majority sentiment by prohibiting grizzly bear hunting in the province once again. In coordination with recovery efforts in Washington State, the federal government moved the following year to register BC's most vulnerable southern grizzly populations as a species of special concern under the federal Species at Risk Act.

While the question of the hunt seems destined to oscillate with changing political winds, the shift in attitude toward grizzly bears that has contributed to their recovery appears to be here to stay. As MacHutchon observes, in places like the Creston Valley, farmers have become more tolerant of grizzly bears despite occasional losses in their corn fields and chicken coops. Just a few generations ago, bears like this would have been "routinely shot."[77] Five decades of bear research, advocacy and education, however, have contributed to a wider range of outcomes for grizzly bears.

Advancing Understanding of Wildlife Health

As understanding of cumulative effects on wildlife populations has gained ground in recent decades, appreciation for the significance of animal health has grown. While biologists have long been aware of the role of malnutrition and disease in animal mortality, new appreciation of the intersecting effects of disturbance, weather, habitat conditions and disease, in addition to more sophisticated mechanisms for assessing those conditions, has contributed to revolutionary changes in wildlife research.

Bighorn sheep are among the animals most clearly associated with disease risk. As early as the 1850s and 1860s, bighorns died "in huge numbers" after large flocks of domestic sheep were imported to feed miners during the Fraser Canyon and Cariboo gold rushes. As retired provincial wildlife veterinarian Helen Schwantje explains, bighorn sheep evolved to live in small herds, isolated from others except during breeding season. They are not averse, however, to interbreeding with closely related species, such as domestic sheep and goats. Unlike wild sheep, domesticated species are "well adapted to infectious disease. . . . They've been selected for their immunity [and] their ability to live at high densities." When you mix those with a species that evolved in isolation, without exposure or immunity to these diseases, "it's a dangerous combination."[78] Once numerous in North America, wild sheep numbers declined dramatically over the nineteenth and twentieth centuries due to a combination of overhunting, disease exposure and habitat loss. While BC's California and Rocky Mountain bighorns have weathered the storm with greater success than their US counterparts, periodic outbreaks of respiratory and other diseases continue to reduce their numbers.[79]

Schwantje credits one of these outbreaks, in the 1980s, with the origins of her career as a wildlife veterinarian. Contracted to assist regional wildlife biologist Ray Demarchi with pathology work in the aftermath of a bighorn sheep die-off in the East Kootenay region, she went on to report on gaps in the area of wildlife health for the BC Ministry of Environment. Repeated disease outbreaks among wild sheep, combined with safety and security concerns surrounding the use of powerful drugs to immobilize wild animals, eventually led the province to establish a permanent wildlife veterinarian position in 1992. When Schwantje stepped into the role, she became one of the first full-time wildlife veterinarians in Canada, and "certainly the first woman."[80]

Wildlife veterinarians, she explains, "don't necessarily treat animals to make them better." Instead, they seek to understand the factors affecting the health of animal populations. "Looking at wildlife herd health," she explains, "is not that much different from looking at a beef [cattle] or sheep herd and [assessing] their performance. . . . What they are eating? Who is eating them? What is the climate like? What is the snow depth like?" Over the past decade in particular, wildlife professionals have embraced a more holistic definition of health, one that goes beyond diseases and parasites to consider a much more comprehensive suite of effects on a population. Changes in animal handling and research have supported this shift to more comprehensive assessments of wildlife health. Now, researchers and conservation officers handling any wild animal in BC must take a full suite of samples from it, rather than simply "throwing collars on animals and finding out where they go," Schwantje notes. Sophisticated databases and deep-cold freezers allow samples and data to be preserved for present or future research. Such practices have contributed to an information revolution in wildlife research: "we're learning a lot more about the quality of [wildlife] populations: how they are performing; when [an animal] dies; how it dies."

An example of the power of this kind of research emerged with a decline in moose populations in the Omineca and Cariboo regions following a mountain pine beetle outbreak and associated salvage operations in the early 2000s. Samples taken from hundreds of moose collared between 2012 and 2019 complicated the widespread belief that wolf predation was the principal cause of their decline. As the study showed, over half of the cow moose that died over the study period had suffered from malnutrition—in some cases acute. Cow moose fell to predators or hunters, or succumbed to starvation, injury or disease, and their condition often contributed to their vulnerability. As Schwantje explained, "habitat conditions affect [moose] nutrition, trace mineral levels, [and] probably their susceptibility to diseases." Similar sampling techniques are now being applied to assess the range of factors affecting the province's endangered woodland caribou populations. These investments have deepened understanding of the role of landscape change in animal health and vulnerability. Schwantje concludes, "I think we're starting to understand caribou, and moose, far better in this province [by looking at them] in a way that no one else has really [done before]."[81]

As cumulative effects of human development and resource extraction, climate change and introduced species and pathogens have complicated wildlife work in BC, wildlife veterinarians have transitioned from "frill" positions in the early 1990s to essential members of professional wildlife agencies. "With the globalization of travel," Schwantje explains, "we've seen diseases and parasites imported into North America that have become huge [problems] here because wildlife aren't adapted to them." The profession has globalized in step with the problems it tackles. For example, concerns about the spread of white nose syndrome, a fungus that causes mass mortality in bats, have led to collaboration among wildlife veterinarians across North America to better understand the biology of affected bat species "before the impact of the disease occurs."

Sound management decisions, past and present, have contributed to restricting the spread of wildlife diseases in British Columbia. In 1990, for example, when investors eyed game farming as an attractive revenue

Motivated by similar concerns about disease spread and health problems caused by foods that wildlife are not adapted to eat, organizations like the BCSPCA have been working to raise awareness of the hazards of feeding urban wildlife. Photo courtesy of Stuart McFarlane, 2022.

opportunity, members of the hunting and wildlife conservation communities succeeded in passing the BC Game Farm Act. The act allowed farming of fallow deer, bison and reindeer but prohibited farming of native species. Schwantje credits the legislation with reducing the risk of chronic wasting disease among the province's wild deer populations.[82] Foresight and vigilance will remain important mitigating forces as the fatal neurological disease approaches BC's southern border. When evidence of the disease surfaced south of the border in 2019, collaboration with the Ktunaxa Nation and other area hunters enabled rapid surveillance efforts. Mitigating disease risk will also involve reassessing the value of past practices. Supplemental feeding of elk over winter, for example, a practice supported by an earlier generation of hunters and wildlife biologists, has fallen from favour in recent years because of the health risks it presents to congregating animals.[83]

Ongoing health concerns with bighorn sheep, an undercurrent throughout Schwantje's career, have also yielded some rewarding human collaborations. Domestic sheep farmers in particular have stepped up to the plate, Schwantje notes, in efforts to reduce contact between wild and domestic sheep. A recent experimental trial that aimed to clear domestic sheep of dangerous and transmissible pathogens, for example, attracted high participation from producers. The Wild Sheep Society of BC and other conservation organizations have played a large role in these initiatives, raising funds and building awareness. These partnerships will become increasingly valuable as climate change brings new threats to wild sheep, creating favourable conditions for deadly viruses such as bluetongue.[84] Building understanding of the stressors and cumulative effects that weaken animal populations, as well as the conditions that allow them to be resilient, will be critical to their conservation over the long term.

INITIATIVE PROFILE: Get the Lead Out!

Changing sources of environmental pollution affect wildlife health and the complexity of wildlife work in British Columbia. From Ian McTaggart Cowan's early warnings about the effects of orchard insecticides on upland game birds in the 1940s, pollution from urban and agricultural activities and industrial processes like coal mining has proliferated.

One particularly lethal source of pollution has its origins in recreational, rather than industrial, activities. Over the winter of 2020, the death of 182 trumpeter swans at Judson Lake on the BC–Washington State border was a potent reminder of the lasting effects of "legacy lead"—shot fired by hunters decades ago, before the Canadian and US governments banned lead shot for waterfowl hunting in the 1990s. In shallow Judson Lake, birds ingest lead shot by foraging among the roots of aquatic plants. Eagles and other raptors face similar risks when they scavenge the carcasses of animals killed with lead shotgun pellets or fishing tackle.

Consuming even a small amount of lead will slowly poison the birds. While the removal of lead shot from water bodies like Judson Lake is costly and complicated, guarding against new sources of lead toxicity is less so. In 1997, Canada used its jurisdiction over migratory game birds to require waterfowl hunters to use non-toxic shot, such as copper bullets. Lead pellets and bullets are still widely used, however, to hunt large animals and non-migratory game birds such as grouse or pheasant. For the wildlife rehabilitation facilities that treat dozens of lead-poisoned raptors each hunting season, a commitment by hunting organizations and provincial wildlife agencies to phase out lead ammunition would remove a lasting source of toxicity for wildlife.[85]

Conclusion: Expanding Wildlife Knowledge, Expanding Protections

Despite oscillations in government commitment to wildlife conservation in the early twenty-first century, partnerships between conservation organizations, governments, industry and First Nations allowed for considerable gains in the protection of important wildlife habitat. Parks and protected areas in the province have more than doubled in size since the early 1990s, reaching 16.4 per cent of BC's land mass by 2020.[86] Within this larger figure, lands designated for wildlife conservation increased from 884,000 hectares in the early 1980s to almost 2.3 million hectares by 2020, occupying roughly 2.4 per cent of the province's land mass.[87]

Wildlife knowledge expanded considerably in this period, as new technologies and a diversifying profession improved access to information and stimulated new questions and new approaches. The public appetite for wildlife knowledge also continued to grow. A 2012 survey found that nearly one in five British Columbians watched birds, collectively spending over $100 million on birding activities.[88] Similar trends emerged in the growing popularity of whale watching and bear viewing among BC residents and visitors. Many more British Columbians expanded their knowledge through community nature walks, museum exhibitions, television and documentary film, and social media. By the late 1990s, more British Columbians than ever before could recognize a burrowing owl in a publicity poster or comment on the difference between resident and transient orcas. Less apparent, however, was public awareness of the everyday threats to wildlife presented by housing, infrastructure and commercial development. As mentioned in Chapter 10, BC Provincial Museum director Yorke Edwards quipped in 1982, "it is a . . . largely unknown truth" that wild animals need land for their survival, and "not just any land will do."[89] The same could be said in 2022. And yet, the lived reality of climate change has overlaid a new urgency on older arguments about wildlife. Growing environmental literacy around the role of forests, wetlands and grasslands as sinks for climate-warming carbon may further public support for the protection of these spaces.

As First Nations in BC take up a larger role in wildlife research and conservation in the decades to come, possibilities may open to prioritize wildlife protection within and beyond existing protected areas. The final chapter turns to these possibilities and the potential for shared interests in wildlife conservation to form an important pathway to reconciliation between Indigenous and non-Indigenous British Columbians.

13

Indigenous-Led Conservation and Pathways to Reconciliation

As Richard Atleo (Umeek) commented in his 2004 book, *Tsawalk*, the Nuu-chah-nulth and many other northern and remote First Nations in British Columbia experienced their traditional territories as relatively intact into the 1950s.[1] This would change over the 1960s and '70s, when Premier W.A.C. Bennett's "roads to resources" policies opened vast areas of the province to logging, hydroelectric development, mineral extraction and oil and gas development. By the early 2000s, four decades of industrial development in the north had left First Nations communities reeling with the negative aftereffects, and few of the benefits, of natural resource extraction. Responses included a growing number of court challenges and blockades of logging, mining, and oil and gas access roads by First Nations communities. Two examples from the province's north illustrate the varying results of these challenges in the early 2000s. The first, in the province's northwest, saw the Tahltan join allied environmental organizations in protesting a proposed open-pit coal mine and oil and gas development at the headwaters of the salmon-rich Skeena River. The second, in the northeast, saw Treaty 8 First Nations respond to BC Hydro's proposed Site C dam. The third major dam project on the Peace River, Site C threatened to permanently inundate fifty-five square kilometres of irreplaceable river valley habitat and further constrain the hunting, fishing and trapping rights of seven Treaty 8 First Nations.

The outcomes of these developments in the 2010s reflected thirty years of deliberations in Canadian courts on the nature, existence and application of Aboriginal and treaty rights in Canada. Following the recognition of "existing Aboriginal and treaty rights" within the Canadian Constitution in 1982, Indigenous leaders advanced a series of court challenges in the 1980s and early 1990s that delineated Aboriginal rights to fish and wildlife and the extent of permissible infringement by federal and provincial law. A deeper challenge, one that BC First Nations had maintained consistently for well over a century but that had been denied by provincial administrations since the 1870s, was the claim of Aboriginal title, or the right to the land itself. Efforts to establish the existence of Aboriginal title, and to define its scope and implications, would have sweeping ramifications for resource extraction activities and Crown–First Nations relationships around wildlife conservation and management.

The Tahltan's 2012 success in halting mineral and oil and gas development in what became known as the "sacred headwaters" of the Skeena, Nass and Stikine rivers represented for many observers the potential of the federal and provincial governments' newly defined legal and constitutional obligations to reconfigure existing power relationships around resource extraction. The limits of this new order were also apparent, however, in the repeated and ultimately unsuccessful efforts by the West Moberly and Prophet River First Nations to challenge plans for the Site C dam in the courts. As these divergent outcomes demonstrate, First Nations would not enjoy a veto on future developments. By the early 2000s, though, they would for the first time hold the ability to negotiate the terms of proposed developments in ways that reflected their interests and provided compensation for their losses.

This chapter follows the efforts of First Nations in BC to reclaim management authority over fish and wildlife habitat within their traditional territories. It draws on the principles and goals of **reconciliation**, defined by the Truth and Reconciliation Commission of Canada (TRC) as the process of "establishing and maintaining a mutually respectful relationship between Aboriginal and non-Aboriginal peoples in this country."[2] In November 2019, British Columbia became the first jurisdiction in Canada to adopt into law the 2007 United Nations Declaration on the Rights of Indigenous Peoples (UNDRIP) as a framework for reconciliation. Canada followed suit in June 2021. These pieces of legislation represent a commitment to wholesale change in government relationships with Indigenous Peoples. As the Canadian government acknowledges, the legislation demands "nation-to-nation, government-to-government . . . relationships based on recognition of rights, respect, co-operation, and partnership."[3]

The extent to which these changes occur will depend on ongoing public and political will and the ability of First Nations communities to continue to press for change.

The chapter opens by exploring the trail-blazing efforts of BC First Nations to secure rights to land and wildlife use in the courts. A shared interest in wildlife protection emerges as an important counterweight to this narrative, with federal, provincial and Indigenous governments forging alternative pathways to reconciliation through collaborative, government-to-government wildlife conservation agreements. In the second half of the chapter, experiments with Indigenous-led conservation provide an opportunity to examine places of overlap between settler principles of conservation and the Indigenous principles that preceded them and challenge them today. The chapter concludes by highlighting two promising models of Indigenous-led conservation that have taken hold across the province in the first two decades of the twenty-first century.

A Revolution in Indigenous Rights and Title

In October 1984, two years after the entrenchment of Aboriginal and treaty rights within the Canadian Constitution, thirty-five Gitxsan and thirteen Wet'suwet'en hereditary chiefs initiated proceedings against the Province of British Columbia claiming (individually and on behalf of their respective Houses) ownership and jurisdiction over their traditional territories in northwestern BC.[4] For the preceding seven years, Gitxsan leader Neil J. Sterritt and researchers from the Gitxsan-Wet'suwet'en Tribal Council had documented and mapped the territorial knowledge of hereditary chiefs and elders in preparation for the federal comprehensive claims process.

Their frustration with the pace of that process (federal policy limited negotiations to one First Nation at a time) and the lack of political will on the part of the province to negotiate land claims led them to turn to the courts for redress. As Sterritt recalled in 2016, despite years of preparation, "[we realized] we were not going to get to the negotiation table in the foreseeable future and certainly not while many of our elders were still alive." Thirty-four of the forty-eight plaintiffs were in their eighties and nineties and carried vital knowledge of their peoples' lives on their territories before and during colonization.[5] One of the longest trials in the province's history began at the BC Supreme Court in Smithers in May 1987.

The Gitxsan and Wet'suwet'en were not the first to seek court settlement of their land question. Their neighbours to the west, the Nisga'a Nation of the Nass River Valley, had sued the province for recognition of its unceded title to its traditional territories as early as 1967. The *Calder* case, brought by Nisga'a hereditary chief and politician Frank Calder and other Nisga'a elders with representation from lawyer and Indigenous rights advocate Thomas Berger, established the possibility of unextinguished Aboriginal title in Canada. In a landmark 1973 ruling, the Supreme Court of Canada recognized that the Nisga'a held title to their land before British Columbia was established but split evenly on whether colonial and provincial laws had extinguished that title.[6] **Aboriginal title**, the court concluded, was a legal right rooted in Indigenous Peoples' historic "occupation, possession and use" of traditional territories. It "existed at the time of first contact with Europeans, whether or not it was recognized by them."[7]

The case created the foundation for the inclusion of Aboriginal rights in the Constitution and prompted the federal government to launch its comprehensive claims process. Although the Nisga'a Nation was among the first six First Nations in Canada to participate in the process, its land claims were stalled for almost two decades by the province's unwillingness to participate in treaty negotiations or to recognize the ongoing existence of Aboriginal title.

In March 1991, after hearing 387 days of testimony, Chief Justice Alan McEachern dismissed the Gitxsan-Wet'suwet'en case, concluding that Aboriginal title had been extinguished by colonial land legislation before 1871. As Sterritt reported, the hereditary chiefs were incredulous. Not only had their title and rights to the land been extinguished "by a process of which we had no knowledge," but this process had apparently occurred "before any white man had any real knowledge of who we were."[8] The chiefs appealed. In 1997, the Supreme Court of Canada ruled in *Delgamuukw v. British Columbia* that Aboriginal title had never been extinguished in British Columbia and that no province had jurisdiction to do so without an Indigenous nation's consent. The decision clarified the nature of Aboriginal title as more than mere land use and occupation; rather, as a communal and culturally distinct form of ownership, it incorporated jurisdictional authority over *how* the land is used.

Because Aboriginal title continued to exist as a burden on the Crown title, governments were obliged to consult with (and possibly accommodate or compensate) First Nations whose rights would be affected by activities on Crown land. The court laid out a three-part test for determining the ongoing presence of Aboriginal title and noted that a new trial would be necessary to determine if the plaintiffs possessed Aboriginal title to the lands they claimed.[9] The court concluded its comments by urging the parties to use its clarifications to negotiate, rather than litigate, a mutually acceptable land claims agreement.

By the time the *Delgamuukw* case came to a close in 1997, the landscape of Indigenous claims in BC had already shifted considerably. A series of road blockades and other protests by First Nations in response to ongoing logging, mining and oil and gas development within their territories had disrupted resource operations and created uncertainty for investors. In 1990, the Province of British Columbia finally reversed its long-standing position on Aboriginal rights. At long last, it joined in treaty negotiations with the Nisga'a and in 1992, in partnership with Canada and the First Nations Summit, established the BC Treaty Commission to guide a "made-in-BC" treaty negotiations process. Seven years later, in 1998, Canada, British Columbia and the Nisga'a Nation signed the province's first modern land claim.

Roughly 120 of the 198 First Nations in BC submitted statements of intent to negotiate a treaty within the first ten years of the British Columbia treaty process, in turn receiving the right to borrow funds to conduct the detailed research required to enter negotiations. Many of the First Nations, however, rejected a process that involved the surrender of Aboriginal title to large territories in exchange for defined rights and benefits over a much smaller land base. Over the slow and fitful course of treaty negotiation, a number of nations withdrew from the process. By 2012, twenty years after the treaty process began, just three final treaty agreements had been signed.

Meanwhile, through the late 1990s and early 2000s the provincial government continued to issue resource tenures without adequately consulting area First Nations. When the Haida Nation challenged the province's granting of a long-term logging tenure on its territory in the early 2000s, the province argued that "until the Haida people formally prove their claim [to Aboriginal title], they have no legal right to be consulted."[10]

The Supreme Court of Canada rejected the province's position in two 2004 decisions, concluding that the provincial government had a responsibility to consult and possibly accommodate Indigenous interests even where title had not yet been proven through a treaty or court decision. *Haida v. British Columbia* and *Taku River Tlingit First Nation v. British Columbia* established a framework for the **duty to consult**, ruling that First Nations do not have a veto over activities on their territories. Government may make decisions even without consensus, the court ruled, but the consultative process must be fair and honourable.[11] Significantly, Indigenous groups would no longer be required to prove the existence of rights and their infringement; instead, the onus would rest with the Crown to obtain informed consent. The decisions prompted Gordon Campbell's Liberal government to affirm in 2005 that treaty-making would be based on a recognition of Aboriginal rights and title and involve the reconciliation of Aboriginal rights with other rights and interests, rather than the extinguishment of those rights.[12]

In 2014, the Tsilhqot'in Nation, comprising six distinct communities in central BC, became the first Indigenous nation in the province to win a claim of Aboriginal title to a portion of its traditional territory. Having applied the legal test established in *Delgamuukw*—which required regular, sufficient and exclusive use of the claimed area at the time the Crown asserted sovereignty in 1846—the Supreme Court of Canada ruled that the Tsilhqot'in held Aboriginal title to the claimed area, some 1,750 square kilometres of the nation's traditional territory. The unanimous decision marked the first time in Canadian history that a court recognized Aboriginal title to a specific geographical area.[13]

In 2016, the BC government and the Tsilhqot'in Nation signed a five-year framework agreement, the Nenqay Deni Accord (the "People's Accord"), to guide negotiation of a lasting reconciliation between the two parties and to clarify the steps in transitioning the title area to Tsilhqot'in control. The accord outlined provisions for "truly collaborative decision-making" surrounding wildlife, lands and resources over the remainder of Tsilhqot'in territory (an area roughly the same size as the title lands).[14] Treaty settlement lands in BC currently constitute roughly 300,000 hectares, or 0.3 per cent of the provincial land base (see the figure on page 9).[15]

Alternative Pathways to Reconciliation

The years that the Gitxsan, Wet'suwet'en and Tsilhqot'in Nations, and the Nisga'a before them, spent in court to claim Aboriginal title rights had a broader effect. The resulting court decisions established a legal precedent that has aided them and other First Nations in extending their management authority over wildlife and natural resources on their territories and enhancing their economic well-being. By advancing a body of law that defined Aboriginal title and created a legal test for proving it, these decisions blazed a path for litigation by other First Nations in Canada. They also strengthened First Nations' negotiating positions at treaty tables. For the First Nations involved, the court cases demanded years of preparatory research and mapping work. As Neil Sterritt has observed, for the Gitxsan the maps, genealogies and archival material gathered in preparation for their 1984 trial constitute a valuable archive of human experience on their lands, evidence that will continue to serve them in future negotiations and in educating new generations of Gitxsan about their heritage.[16]

Yet Aboriginal title cases are expensive, time-consuming and inherently risky. For many First Nations, the Tsilhqot'in case may prove a difficult path to follow. By confining their claim to a sparsely populated area with little territorial overlap with other First Nations, the Tsilhqot'in enabled a relatively straightforward application of the Aboriginal title test. Furthermore, because they were breaking new legal ground, they qualified for "test case funding" under court order to help cover the more than $30 million cost of litigation. This same source of financial support will not be available to other title claimants.[17]

Faced with the slow, costly and uncertain outcomes of court proceedings, on the one hand, and the lengthy process of treaty negotiations, on the other—negotiations whose land packages have typically comprised about 5 per cent of a nation's traditional territory—a number of First Nations have opted for a different path. For the Tahltan of northwestern BC, for example, the benefits of a collaborative approach to build capacity and decision-making authority have, for now, outweighed the potential longer-term gains of Aboriginal title litigation or treaty agreements.

In 2010, the Tahltan finalized an agreement with the province to establish a government-to-government (G2G) forum, a shared decision-making table that, according to Tahltan Nation Development Corporation CEO

Garry Merkel, "involved us in every aspect of land management and potential development in our territory." The agreement provided the Tahltan
with a share in the provincial taxation revenue from developments on their
territory, set terms for Tahltan partnership in the development of the energy sector in the region and provided supports from a wide range of provincial agencies to assist the Tahltan community in managing the pressures
of that economic transition.[18] The neighbouring Kaska have pursued similar strategies, partnering with Ducks Unlimited Canada to develop highly
site-specific GIS mapping interfaces of scientific and traditional knowledge
to inform decision-making and land use planning on their territories.[19]

For the Tahltan, Kaska and other First Nations that have chosen this
path, building knowledge and skills among their members has been a vital
component of the shift toward a greater decision-making role and a more
"managerial, higher-level role in the economy." Scholarships and placement
opportunities, Merkel explained, form a part of "every agreement that we
negotiate." Tahltan foresters, mining engineers, agrologists and natural resource specialists now guide land use planning and development and "assess every single project that we do." In the end, Merkel reflected, "your
ability to do things is . . . determined much more by your own capacity than
it is by an act of government or a legal decision." He continued, "I mean,
in the end we're all here, right? And we all still have to get along. And once
you've gone to court, often it is hard to rebuild the kind of working relationships that you need to do the things you've got to do. These are complicated problems that require very deep collaboration and cooperation. They
require a will to make it work on all sides."[20] While litigation has a part to
play in any government-to-government relationship, its adversarial nature
makes it a difficult means of achieving reconciliation.

Merkel's optimism and skill in negotiating agreements is evident elsewhere, too, as more First Nations pursue shared decision-making agreements
with the Province of British Columbia. Wildlife allocations and enforcement have been a particular area of strength in this regard. Once known
for its history of enforcement-related conflict with First Nations communities, BC's Conservation Officer Service has emerged over the past two decades as a pioneer of flexible and collaborative approaches to reconciliation.
Acknowledging its limited enforcement capability with respect to Indigenous
hunting and fishing rights, the Conservation Officer Service has shifted its
focus to support Indigenous communities in their own stewardship goals.

Moose conservation is a prominent example. Declining moose populations across the province over the past decade prompted several First Nations in the central Interior to pass community-based laws banning hunting of cow moose by their members. Others have sought assistance in monitoring the activities of non-Indigenous hunters on their territories. **Collaborative enforcement agreements**, which are memorandums of understanding between the Conservation Officer Service and individual band councils, have emerged in this context as a tool to facilitate enforcement partnerships between First Nations authorities and the Conservation Officer Service.[21] The agreements are flexible and First Nations–driven. In responding to offenders, for example, individual First Nations have the choice to turn to the court system or to pursue restorative justice measures within their communities. More in keeping with traditional Indigenous systems of justice, restorative justice allows affected parties to work with offenders to identify and repair the harm they have caused.

Education forms another part of these agreements—on both sides. COs offer training on hunting and fishing regulations to assist First Nations in monitoring activity on their territories. At the same time, they agree to participate in cross-cultural training to better understand the First Nations they are working with. As one Interior First Nations wildlife manager commented, the results for his community have been "very gratifying."[22] First Nations relations CO Andy MacKay agrees. We've "developed a lot of good relationships in the work we're doing. . . . The common goal in it all is protecting the wildlife that's out there."[23]

INITIATIVE PROFILE:
Reducing Moose Mortality from Train Strikes in the Bulkley Valley

The railways that opened the north to resource extraction and fuelled the expansion of guide outfitting in the region still take a toll on wildlife populations. In the Skeena region, moose and other animals are regularly killed in rail strikes along the CN railway. Mortality rates for wildlife are especially high in heavy snow years, when deep snowbanks adjacent to the rail line funnel animals onto the tracks. As former chief forester Jim Snetsinger reported in a 2013 study, an estimated 450 to 500 moose were struck and killed between 2007 and 2012 on a stretch of rail between Endako and Smithers that runs through prime moose habitat. While mortality rates are likely much higher there than on other sections of the line, the numbers give a sense of the potential magnitude of losses of moose and other wildlife along rail lines in other parts of the province. Since 2013, CN investments in wildlife exclusion fencing at three sites in the Bulkley Valley appear to have reduced the number of moose deaths. Railway collisions account for a relatively small percentage of overall moose mortality in the province. For area hunters facing harvest restrictions on declining moose populations, however, the preventable loss of animal life along rail corridors remains a significant source of frustration.[24]

Shared concerns about declining moose populations, it turns out, have inspired broader reconciliation initiatives in the central Interior. For the Tsilhqot'in, the litigation of their twelve-year Aboriginal title case may have been adversarial, but the relationships forged in its aftermath—with government, industry and regional wildlife stakeholders—demonstrate the abilities of all parties to continue to work together. In 2018 the Tsilhqot'in National Government and the Province of British Columbia signed a three-year "Moose Co-management Agreement" to jointly address moose population decline in the region. The agreement involved creation of the Moose Solutions Roundtable, which invited neighbouring First Nations and representatives from a wide range of regional stakeholder groups, including hunters, trappers, guide outfitters, ranchers and forestry companies, to meet to develop solutions for moose recovery.[25] The partners' emphasis on a forward-thinking approach, one that moved beyond "pointing fingers" to work together toward a common goal, is an excellent example of the kind of decentralized and collaborative wildlife management that many wildlife advocates, for all their differences, hope to see more of.

As the Moose Solutions Roundtable demonstrates, for all the promise of collaborative enforcement agreements, collaborative *management* agreements are needed to move toward more meaningful reconciliation. While the Tsilhqot'in hold complete management authority over their title lands, co-management agreements with the province will apply to lands and wildlife over the remainder of their traditional territory. Working together with provincial wildlife authorities will require formalized mechanisms for incorporating local and Indigenous knowledge into management decisions.

The story of moose declines in the Interior illustrates the value of that knowledge: the Tsilhqot'in and many other Interior First Nations, together with non-Indigenous hunters, had registered concern about moose population numbers as early as 2011, before government surveys indicated a problem. As Indigenous governments imposed restrictions on their members to conserve moose populations, they watched with frustration as the province continued to authorize limited entry hunting for moose across their territories. It is a problem felt across the north, as well, where government wildlife population data analysis has often been perceived as being out of step with changing circumstances on the ground.[26] Creating better mechanisms to share information and to generate more rapid management responses, as the roundtable aims to do, will benefit all of those who depend on and care about healthy ungulate populations.[27]

As the province works with First Nations leaders in the coming years to align BC's laws with the standards outlined in the **United Nations Declaration on the Rights of Indigenous Peoples**, these early examples of flexible, collaborative partnerships will provide important models for the kind of shared decision-making in forestry, mining, oil and gas development and environmental assessment that the new legislation will demand.[28] For John Henderson, hereditary chief of the Wei Wai Kum First Nation in Campbell River, building relationships with non-Indigenous guide outfitters and resident hunters on northern Vancouver Island is a working example of "UNDRIP as we see it."

In an effort to move beyond provincial hunting allocation and land use planning processes that tended to separate First Nations from other stakeholders, Henderson and a group of North Island First Nations created the Wildlife Stewardship Council (WSC) in 2011. A non-profit society of First Nations and guide outfitters from across BC, the WSC advocates a "roundtable" approach to ensuring a sustainable wildlife harvest. Henderson's efforts built on a history of local collaboration in support of wildlife population health. Beginning in the late 1990s, he represented Wei Wai Kum chiefs in collaborating with the Nanaimo Fish and Wildlife Branch to bring perilously low Roosevelt elk populations to some 7,000 animals today. Today, North Island First Nations continue to share management authority in monitoring populations and recommending hunting allocations. As Henderson recalls of the process, "it's [one] of the most positive things that has happened in my lifetime. It gives us a voice [in management decisions] and it builds trust."[29]

Indigenous leadership in conservation initiatives like these reflects both the ongoing value of subsistence hunting and fishing to First Nations economies and the responsibility that hereditary leaders assume in stewarding the fish and wildlife of their traditional territories. Henderson confirms that for the Wei Wai Kum and other First Nations, sustenance from the land "is very valuable to us. . . . We've been brought up to survive by the resources of the land." When "we see a place that has historically had wildlife [that has] been decimated by logging, we [have] the responsibility of replenishing the lands by working collectively." The Tsimshian, Gitxsan and Wet'suwet'en First Nations of the Skeena River have exercised similar responsibility, periodically closing or restricting their community fisheries in response to record-low salmon returns over the past two decades.

These decisions to forgo a staple and deeply cultural food source do not come lightly. Gitxsan hereditary chief Bill Blackwater Jr. remembers passing the winter of 2014 without salmon: "whatever little bit of canned salmon people had, they shared with others."[30] Decisions like these—to allow species and systems to recover while at the same time investing in habitat restoration and on-the-land education programs for new generations of First Nations youth—are characteristic of Indigenous stewardship initiatives that are taking hold across the province. As Henderson argues, First Nations wildlife management will "benefit everybody. . . . We want to be a part of the process to ensure that wildlife is there for our children . . . and our children's children, in the future."[31]

Toward Indigenous-Led Conservation

Writing in 1995, wildlife ecologist Valerius Geist speculated that granting Indigenous Peoples greater legal controls over the conservation and management of wildlife "would probably be the best that we could do for wildlife. It might even be a step toward reversing current conditions where wildlife has scant protection from such destroyers as modern agriculture, forestry, and transportation." In jurisdictions like the Northwest Territories, he added, "where native people have de facto control over wildlife, they are exemplary managers."[32]

Today, such endorsements are hardly necessary. Following the court victories of the 1990s and 2000s and the BC government's 2019 passage into law of the **Declaration on the Rights of Indigenous Peoples Act (Declaration Act)**, Indigenous leadership in wildlife conservation is gaining ground across the province. A case in point is the leadership by Saulteau and West Moberly First Nations in the recovery of the Klinse-Za caribou herd in the northern Rockies west of Hudson's Hope. Having endured self-imposed bans on caribou hunting since the 1970s, the two Treaty 8 nations watched with frustration as caribou herds in the region continued to decline. Mining, oil and gas development, and logging made habitats more appealing for moose and elk and introduced roads and industrial corridors that allowed predators to travel faster and farther. Caribou were casualties of these changes: by 2013, the Klinse-Za herd had been reduced to thirty-eight animals and the neighbouring Burnt Pine herd extirpated from the region.

Determined to avert the loss of another herd, the two First Nations collaborated in the launch of an ambitious caribou recovery effort on their homelands. Short-term measures to halt the herd's decline included reducing the number of wolves in caribou habitat and building fenced enclosures to protect pregnant females and their calves. The success of these measures in tripling the herd's population in less than a decade laid the foundation for a landmark partnership agreement with the provincial and federal governments in 2020. The thirty-year agreement not only supports ongoing Indigenous leadership in caribou recovery but also protects 7,900 square kilometres of habitat for the Klinse-Za and five adjacent herds. Habitat restoration work will follow, including the removal of roads and seismic lines that threaten caribou security. For the Saulteau and West Moberly, these short-term successes point the way to a longer-term goal of "rekindl[ing] a culturally meaningful caribou hunt . . . by increasing caribou abundance."[33]

Reconciling the "North American Model" of Wildlife Conservation

As Indigenous stewardship approaches gain momentum, however, they run up against established wildlife laws and policies grounded in a Euro-American world view. The ways that colonial and later provincial wildlife management systems evolved in British Columbia reflect the general principles that Valerius Geist, Shane Mahoney and John Organ described as the "North American Model of Wildlife Conservation" in a 2001 paper. Seeking to differentiate approaches to wildlife conservation in North America from those in other parts of the world, Geist and his co-authors surveyed historical conservation efforts in the United States and Canada and arrived at seven principles that contributed to the success of North American approaches. In general terms, these principles are reflected in BC wildlife legislation and management practice:

- *Wildlife is held in the public trust.* Ownership in fish and wildlife is held by the public through state, provincial and federal governments. Private landowners do not own the wildlife on their lands; instead, wildlife is owned by all citizens.

- *Markets for wildlife are eliminated.* The unregulated killing of wildlife for profit is prohibited.

- *Allocation of wildlife is by law.* The use of wildlife is allocated to the public by law, rather than market principles, landownership or other forms of status.

- *Hunting is democratic.* Every person has an equal opportunity under the law to participate in hunting and other uses of wildlife.

- *Wildlife can be killed only for a legitimate purpose.* Killing wildlife for frivolous reasons is prohibited by law. Wildlife should be killed only for legitimate purposes, such as for food, fur, self-defence or protection of property (including livestock). Use of wildlife by sport hunters is considered legitimate provided that waste is avoided.

- *Wildlife is considered an international resource.* Because many species of wildlife cross political boundaries, state, provincial and national wildlife agencies must coordinate management responses.

- *Science is the proper tool to discharge wildlife policy.* Science, rather than stakeholder interests, forms the basis for informed management and decision-making in wildlife policy.

In the assessment of Geist, Mahoney and Organ, applying these principles in early twentieth-century North America rescued dwindling game species populations from overexploitation, earning recognition as "an exemplary system of 'sustainable development' and one of the great cultural achievements of North America."[34] These claims are legitimate: since the implementation of such principles, "no species has gone extinct because of a regulated hunting season; market hunting pressures have abated, and regulations for both hunting and other environmental activities have created sustainable harvests for most high value game species as well as conservation measures for nongame species."[35] Geist and his co-authors argue that their seven identified principles should not only be celebrated as the basis for historical success but also be used as a framework to guide wildlife conservation approaches into the future. Since Geist, Mahoney and Organ's 2001 publication, the North American model has been upheld and broadly disseminated among hunters' organizations, in wildlife management training programs and within government wildlife policy circles. But it has also garnered some potent criticism.

In the context of ongoing efforts in Canada toward reconciliation between settler and Indigenous societies, Indigenous critiques of the North American model are especially relevant. An important omission from the historical analysis of Geist and his co-authors, Indigenous scholars have argued, is the diversity of Indigenous conservation practices and customary laws regulating wildlife use that existed prior to European settlement and remained in use, especially in places like BC's north, through the twentieth century and into the present.[36]

The incorporation of aspects of Indigenous stewardship systems into celebrated twentieth-century innovations such as BC's registered trapline system go unrecognized in the historical survey that serves as the basis for Geist, Mahoney and Organ's prescriptive model. Furthermore, the North American model's prioritization of sport or recreational hunting fails to capture the historical and ongoing interests of First Nations subsistence hunters. This omission of First Nations perspectives has real consequences in perpetuating conflict over wildlife. In December 2020, for example, a dispute over hunting rights between the BC Conservation Officer Service and the Syilx (Okanagan) people of south-central BC escalated into an armed confrontation.[37] Conflicts such as this perpetuate distrust on both sides and weaken efforts to develop a shared vision for wildlife protection.[38]

In a recent article, "Indigenizing the North American Model," Wyandotte Nation member Mateen Hessami and his co-authors acknowledge significant overlap between the North American model and various models of Indigenous-led conservation across Canada. Both, they argue, share core concerns of "(i) safeguarding wildlife for future generations, (ii) utilizing best available knowledge to solve problems, (iii) prioritizing collaboration between nations, and (iv) democratizing the process of conserving wildlife."[39]

The colonial language and perspectives of some aspects of the North American model, however, continue to serve as barriers to reconciliation. The notion of a public trust in wildlife, for example, makes no allowance for co-management between Indigenous and non-Indigenous governments. The second tenet of eliminating commercial markets in wildlife not only excludes certain species, such as fish and fur-bearers, which continue to be hunted commercially, but also fails to adequately reckon with the ongoing role of trade and reciprocity as a component of Indigenous self-determination. The model's identification of science as the basis for wildlife management neglects the value of Indigenous knowledge systems, the different questions and approaches they bring and the opportunities they present to incorporate detailed local information over long time scales. More generally, its positioning of wildlife as a resource for human allocation "[contradicts] many Indigenous worldviews that instead define wildlife, and people, as an interdependent, connected, and related component of living systems."[40] North American model proponents Shane Mahoney and the late Valerius Geist accepted these critiques, noting the failure to incorporate Indigenous traditions, perspectives and rights as "a historic weakness of the Model and one with enduring implications."[41]

Calls for a more inclusive approach to developing principles to guide wildlife conservation have gathered considerable momentum in recent years. The passage of the BC Declaration Act in 2019 established a provincial framework for reconciliation. The act enables the province to enter into shared decision-making agreements with Indigenous organizations and governments and mandates it to align provincial laws with UNDRIP. The province's Wildlife and Habitat Branch has since made significant moves in this direction through the establishment of five regional collaborative stewardship forums with area First Nations and the creation of a centralized advisory forum to guide amendments to the Wildlife Act and provincial conservation strategies.[42] In keeping with hierarchy of wildlife access established by the Supreme Court of Canada in *R v. Sparrow*, these developments prioritize conservation, followed by Indigenous, commercial and sport hunting and fishing interests, respectively. They reflect the province's responsibility to manage wildlife in the interests of *all* British Columbians, rather than the narrower set of interests reflected in Geist and his co-authors' model. And, significantly, these changes acknowledge the social and ecological context of wildlife management decisions. As critics of the North American model have noted, principles of wildlife conservation for the evolving conditions of the twenty-first century must better assist wildlife managers in weighing questions of social justice and ecosystem health.[43]

Models of Indigenous Stewardship

As First Nations communities work to revive ancestral land stewardship methods and reclaim decision-making authority over their territories, they carry the potential to reimagine existing systems of wildlife conservation and management. For Kaska Dena leader Dave Porter, the problem lies in the "enforcement model" on which wildlife management systems rest: "guys out there with guns making sure people are in compliance." The problem, in his assessment, is not the principle as much as its implementation: "you cannot hire enough bush cops [provincial COs] to have an effective impact." What is needed instead, Porter argues, is a system that places greater emphasis on information and public involvement, one where the "enforcers of good wildlife laws and management practices" are not the "bush cops" but "the resident and visiting public."[44]

By way of example, Porter describes Kaska efforts to disrupt an organized crime ring that had developed in northern BC and the Yukon to rob and illegally sell the eggs and chicks of peregrine falcons. Porter and his Kaska counterparts responded by constructing a series of wildlife-viewing platforms along the Dempster Highway to educate visitors about the birds and allow them to "look across the valley and see the nesting sites." Then, "if they see any [illegal] activity, they are . . . going to want to do their civic duty." Porter explained, "The majority of people care about the environment, care about the wildlife, care about the water. So when you build a management system that incorporates that sense of responsibility, you're going to be . . . a lot more effective."[45]

In BC's north, where Indigenous people constitute 40 to 75 per cent of the population, the "resident public" is often Indigenous.[46] For Porter and other northern Indigenous leaders, empowering First Nations communities to reclaim their historical roles as stewards of land and wildlife in their homelands involves "building a system that incorporates a knowledge base that took thousands of years to accumulate into wildlife [and] environmental management." Over the past decade, Porter's vision to empower local residents in understanding and protecting area wildlife has received expression in a growing number of Indigenous guardians programs across the province.[47]

Indigenous Guardian Programs

The Kaska words "dane nan yé dāh" translate as "person looking after the land." Established in 2014, the Kaska Guardians-Dane nan yé dāh Network aims to revitalize the stewardship responsibilities of the Kaska people for their ancestral lands and waters. Kaska Guardians monitor wildlife health and climate change, manage invasive species, collect harvest data during hunting season and educate community members and the wider public about stewardship goals on Kaska lands. Spearheaded by Porter, the initiative emerged from over ten years of investment in land-based education program for Kaska, Tahltan and Tlingit youth. It fits with Porter's broader objectives of flipping the model of wildlife protection and conservation from top-down to bottom-up.

Across the sparsely populated north especially, Porter argues, the Conservation Officer Service can never be well enough resourced to effectively protect wildlife from overexploitation, illegal trade and other threats. First Nations communities, by contrast, "live out here," he explains, and as a result "we are the most effective managing system." Porter sees Indigenous guardians as "the way of the future for wildlife management in British Columbia." Not only can they take on responsibilities for land, water and wildlife management, but "they are also a critical institution for rebuilding and supporting Indigenous Nations' governance."[48]

The Kaska Guardians drew inspiration from a long history of guardian programs on the north coast. In 1973, well before the creation of the Gwaii Haanas National Park Reserve, a small number of volunteers from the Haida Nation modified traditional watchmen roles by camping at historic

Dane Nan Yě Dāh
Kaska Land Guardian
Kyla Magun collecting
water-quality data near
Good Hope Lake, BC,
2021. Photo courtesy
of Tanya Ball and the
Dena Kayeh Institute.

Haida village sites over the summer months to protect their cultural heritage from a growing number of boaters and tourists. The Skidegate Band
Council formalized the Haida Watchmen program in 1981, and with the
creation of the National Park Reserve in 1988, funding from Parks Canada
supported the Haida Watchmen's dual role of protecting cultural artifacts
and sharing cultural knowledge with visitors. The program expanded to
protect Haida lands and waters according to traditional laws and became
an important source of inspiration for other guardian programs. In 2005,
the Haida joined other stewardship leaders from north and central coast
First Nations in establishing the Coastal Guardian Watchmen Network,
a regional initiative to support member nations in monitoring, stewarding and protecting their respective lands and waters. The program remains
the most established and comprehensive Indigenous guardians initiative
in Canada.[49]

Further afield, the successes of the Innu Nation (1993), Australia (2007) and the Northwest Territories (2008) in implementing Indigenous guardian programs to monitor development activities such as forestry and mining, monitor wildlife populations, restore streams and forests and respond to fire and insect outbreaks have provided a model for similar programs in BC. The federal government's Aboriginal Fishery Guardians Program, established in 1992, was another predecessor that acknowledged the long history of Indigenous stewardship in BC within the confines of a mostly top-down enforcement and monitoring-oriented program. Fisheries guardians worked within their communities to report violations of fisheries and habitat legislation under the Fisheries Act and to monitor the health of fish populations and river systems within their territories. Some First Nations in BC, including the Tahltan and the Ktunaxa, later expanded these roles to full-fledged monitoring and enforcement positions in their communities.

Training and supports for Indigenous stewardship initiatives have grown significantly since the early 2000s. A collaboration between the Coastal Guardian Watchmen and Vancouver Island University produced the Stewardship Technicians Training Program, which provides applied stewardship training for central and north coast First Nations. In 2009, coastal First Nations developed a standardized data collection and monitoring system, enabling guardians to combine traditional knowledge and modern scientific techniques in tracking land use, monitoring wildlife health and water quality, and building relationships with hunters throughout the region.[50] The Kaska have moved in similar ways, combining Western scientific and Indigenous perspectives to identify and protect areas and species of high ecological and cultural value. This **"two-eyed seeing,"** or "walking on two legs," approach is a hallmark of Indigenous guardian programs across Canada and internationally. Originating in the Mi'kmaq language, etuaptmumk, or two-eyed seeing, refers to "learning to see from one eye with the strengths of Indigenous knowledges and ways of knowing, and from the other eye with the strengths of western knowledges and ways of knowing—and learning to use both of these eyes together for the benefit of all."[51]

In the years since the Tsilhqot'in decision in 2014, First Nations in the central and southern Interior have joined their coastal counterparts in establishing guardian programs as a way of reclaiming management and stewardship authority over their territories. The success of guardians as "eyes and ears on the land" has become especially relevant as the country as a whole works to implement the recommendations of the 2015 Truth and Reconciliation Commission. As training grounds for Indigenous youth and supports for broader Indigenous management of traditional territories, guardian programs constitute "reconciliation in action." The favourable reception of these initiatives by British Columbians—a 2020 poll found that almost 70 per cent of respondents supported the expansion of these and other Indigenous stewardship initiatives—suggests that Dave Porter's predictions of a new model of wildlife stewardship are well founded. In 2017, the federal government affirmed the promise of Indigenous-led conservation by dedicating funds toward the development of a National Guardians Program.[52]

INITIATIVE PROFILE: Two-Eyed Seeing in Action: Bears, Salmon and People in Wuikinuxv Territory

At Rivers Inlet on BC's central coast, people and bears have coexisted as consumers of Pacific salmon species for millenniums. Historically, over 3 million sockeye salmon returned to the watershed every year, supporting rich annual harvests by the Wuikinuxv (Owikeno) people and, beginning in the nineteenth century, one of the largest commercial fisheries in British Columbia. This abundance of salmon also supported a large population of grizzly bears. When sockeye runs in the region collapsed in the mid-1990s as a result of overfishing and changing environmental conditions, both people and bears suffered. By 1999, fewer than 10,000 sockeye returned. Rising rates of conflict with hungry bears entering the village of Rivers Inlet led to the destruction of fifteen grizzly bears in that year. While the commercial fishery in the region remains closed, the Wuikinuxv have worked with federal DFO staff to maintain a modest and fluctuating food fishery.

As sockeye populations began to show small signs of recovery in the 2010s, Wuikinuxv leaders sought information about how an increased harvest would affect the fish, the bears and the broader ecosystem.[53] As past research had shown, salmon-fed bears benefit surrounding watersheds by spreading nutrient-rich salmon carcasses that nurture the growth of plants that in turn support songbirds and small mammals. Supplying bears with adequate amounts of salmon also reduces the potential for human conflict with food-seeking bears. A team of scientists and Wuikinuxv wildlife experts took up the challenge of determining how best to manage the food fishery. How much of an Indigenous food harvest, and potentially a future commercial harvest, could fluctuating sockeye salmon populations support, while still providing food and nutrients to other members of the ecosystem?

The Wuikinuxv's concern for the health of the bears was much more than a practical concern for human safety. Bears, for the Wuikinuxv, are family: non-human relatives that warrant respect and consideration. This sense of kinship with bears has deep historical resonance. As researchers have recently shown, the historical territory of the region's three genetically distinct groups of grizzlies overlap in remarkable ways with the region's three distinct Indigenous language families.[54]

For Jenn Walkus, a Wuikinuxv expert on the study, the correlation is not surprising: humans and bears eat the same food. When salmon populations collapsed, grizzlies that had long shown consistent territorial stability began to move to the outer coastal islands in search of food. "If we're not getting enough fish, then they're not getting enough fish," Walkus explained.[55] The Wuikinuxv principle of ńáńakila, meaning to protect or watch over someone, has guided efforts to consider the needs of grizzlies in the future management of the fishery. It aligns with the federal government's Wild Salmon Policy, which since 2005 has acknowledged the need to manage salmon not only for people but also for other, non-human consumers. The two-eyed seeing that has guided Wuikinuxv-led research on salmon and bears is also reflected in Canada's Fisheries Act, which was revised in 2019 to formally incorporate Indigenous knowledge into fisheries management decisions.

For the Wuikinuxv, the combined Indigenous and Western scientific knowledge that informed the salmon harvest study helped them to plan a food fishery that considered the broader needs of the ecosystems that have supported them for thousands of years. The researchers found that by forgoing a modest amount of the harvest, the nation could support a relatively high density of bears. Based on the study's findings, the nation lowered its sockeye harvest a further 10 per cent from the food harvest limit set by DFO to reserve enough food for the bears.[56] Ecosystem-based fisheries management, in this case, considered the needs of bear relatives and the benefits that salmon-fed bears provide to surrounding watersheds.

Shared Authority in Identifying and Managing Protected Areas

Directly connected with the expansion of guardian programs are calls to reimagine the process of identifying and managing protected areas in BC in ways that respect Indigenous rights. These initiatives respond to a history of Indigenous dispossession and exclusion in the creation of parks and protected areas. Rather than conceiving of protected areas as "lands and waters [protected] from human influence," Indigenous leaders promote a perspective where "continued human presence on the land and water is seen as positive and essential."[57]

In British Columbia, several models of collaborative management of protected areas have taken shape in recent decades. An early model of shared governance emerged in the creation of Gwaii Haanas National Park Reserve in the late 1980s. After the Council of the Haida Nation designated the southern portion of the archipelago as a Haida Heritage Site to protect it against logging in 1985, Canada and the council agreed to reserve the area for a national park in 1988. Today, the Haida and Canadian governments cooperatively manage Gwaii Haanas through equal representation on a joint management board.[58] Gwaii Haanas remains British Columbia's longest-standing and most successful example of shared authority in protected areas management.

Negotiations with central coast First Nations over the Great Bear Rainforest Agreement in the early 2000s led to the creation of a new provincial "**conservancy**" designation in 2006—the first designation under the provincial Park Act to explicitly incorporate Indigenous rights. Jointly established and collaboratively managed by Indigenous nations and the Province of British Columbia, conservancies provide a flexible mechanism for government-to-government collaboration in the establishment and management of new protected areas. Like Class A provincial parks, conservancies prohibit commercial logging, mining and large-scale hydroelectric power projects. Where they differ is in their explicit provision for Indigenous cultural uses of land and wildlife in ways that are compatible with the maintenance of biodiversity and recreational opportunities.

The flexibility of these designations has enabled creative problem-solving. In 2022, the Nuxalk and Kitasoo Xai'xais First Nations entered into a pilot project with BC Parks to designate select Indigenous guardians with the same legal authority as BC Parks rangers. Meanwhile, Kaska Dena leaders have pressed for prohibitions against corridor developments, such as roads and rights-of-way, in conservancy designations on their territories. Between 2006 and 2021, the province and area First Nations collaborated in the creation of 158 new conservancies, mostly on the north and central coast. These designations are not insignificant: covering a cumulative area of over 3 million hectares, conservancies constitute the second-largest protected areas designation in number and area, second only to provincial parks.

Indigenous-Led Protected Areas Designations

While the models presented by Gwaii Haanas and provincial conservancies represent promising advances in shared governance, efforts to establish collaboratively managed protected areas have been hindered by insufficient capacity and financial capital. Staff and financial shortages have inhibited planning capacity at BC Parks and limited the options of nations such as Blueberry River, where the creation of protected areas in a territory blanketed with resource tenures will require costly compensation to tenure holders. For some First Nations, the fact that approvals for co-management plans and conservancy designations ultimately rest with the Crown has fuelled the pursuit of Indigenous-led alternatives.[59]

On the BC coast, such alternatives have long been part of Indigenous efforts to protect their traditional territories from clearcut logging, oil and gas, and hydroelectric development. Tla-o-qui-aht hereditary chiefs pioneered the use of Indigenous designations when they declared Meares Island a tribal park in 1984. The court injunction they obtained against logging the island represented the first time in BC's history that the province had been overruled on a land claims issue.[60] The Tla-o-qui-aht have since established three additional tribal parks within their traditional territories in Clayoquot Sound. The Haida Nation's establishment of "Haida Heritage Sites" in 1985 saw similar success in the creation of Gwaii Haanas National Park Reserve and, more recently, eleven new provincially recognized protected areas.[61]

Trail-blazing efforts by the Haida and the Tla-o-qui-aht prompted similar Indigenous-led initiatives in other parts of the province. Following the historic Supreme Court recognition of their Aboriginal title in 2014, the Tsilhqot'in established Dasiqox Tribal Park over 300,000 hectares of forest, meadow and wetland habitat in the south-central Interior. Doig River First Nation, in BC's northeast, used the logic of treaty rights in creating the K'ih Tsaa?dze Tribal Park within its traditional territory in 2011. Pronounced "kih tsad zey," K'ih Tsaa?dze means "old spruce" in the Danezaa language.[62] The 90,000-hectare park straddles the BC-Alberta border, connecting with Chinchaga Wildland Park to protect an important wildlife corridor for the Chinchaga boreal caribou herd.

Surrounded by some 8,500 oil and gas wells and associated road and seismic infrastructure (on the BC side of the border alone), the Doig

A sign on Doig River First Nation traditional territory welcomes visitors to K'ih Tsaaʔdze Tribal Park, established in 2011. Photo courtesy of Rachel Plotkin, 2018. Reprinted with permission from Doig River First Nation.

River First Nation has witnessed the role of habitat loss and disturbance in dwindling caribou and moose populations in the region. In an area of the province with relatively few protected areas, the tribal designation of this highly productive, biologically rich boreal ecosystem provides an opportunity to restore both ecological and cultural integrity. As Doig River community members noted in a vision statement for the tribal park, "K'ih Tsaaʔdze represents a relatively undisturbed part of our land, where we can be ourselves, and pass on our way of life and belief system—our culture— to our youth and future generations." The park's designation "brings the community a sense of relief and confidence in knowing that we have a place to hunt and carry out traditional practices without interference by industrial development."[63]

Like the Tsilhqot'in's Dasiqox Tribal Park, K'ih Tsaaʔdze has yet to be formally recognized by the provincial or federal governments. Still, both industry and Crown governments have refrained from pursuing new industrial developments in the area. As Jack Woodward, an expert in Aboriginal law, commented in a 2016 interview, "declaring a tribal park is a way of putting government and industry on notice that this is the minimum territory required to continue exercising Aboriginal or treaty rights—rights that are ultimately constitutionally protected." For Doig River and other Treaty 8 nations, a treaty right to hunt moose depends on the maintenance of relatively intact moose habitat. In this way, tribal parks are first and foremost about habitat protection. "You declare a tribal park and what you're saying is: 'Cross this line and we're going to get an injunction to stop you from doing the industrial activity.'"[64]

Other nations have rejected the historically loaded terminology of "park" in favour of the more flexible concept of **Indigenous Protected and Conserved Areas** adopted by Parks Canada's Indigenous Council of Experts in 2018 and employed internationally. Defined as "lands and waters where Indigenous governments have the primary role in protecting and conserving ecosystems through Indigenous laws, governance and knowledge systems," IPCAs draw inspiration from the success of Australia's Indigenous Protected Areas system and several pilot initiatives in Canada's Northwest Territories.[65] As opportunities to extend protections over large areas with the leadership and support of First Nations, IPCAs present a promising pathway for meeting Canada's international commitment to protect over 30 per cent of its lands and waters by 2030. The concept holds special promise in British Columbia, where recognition of unextinguished Aboriginal title opens the door to a range of possibilities for collaborative and Indigenous-led land and wildlife protections.

As Indigenous leaders in Australia and New Zealand have found, combining Indigenous protected area designations with the "boots on the ground" model of guardian programs has produced better outcomes for wildlife than state-run wildlife programs. Established in the late 1990s, Australia's Indigenous Protected Areas program was designed to fulfil overlapping government commitments to establish a protected areas system and respond to legal confirmation of Aboriginal title over large portions of the land base. Indigenous governments identify areas for protection within recognized title lands and receive government financial support for their maintenance and management by companion "Indigenous Rangers" programs. Similarly in New Zealand, the Department of Conservation's Nga Whenua Rahui Fund supports Māori landowners in the restoration and conservation of culturally significant ecosystems within their territories. In both places, state recognition and support for the application of Indigenous knowledge in land and wildlife conservation has undergirded program success.[66]

The Kaska Dena, Tahltan, Gitanyow, Ktunaxa and several Vancouver Island First Nations are among a growing number of nations in the province that have identified and formally announced areas for Indigenous-led protection and restoration. Regardless of the designation, these initiatives share the common objective of Indigenous leadership in the long-term protection and conservation of valued ecosystems. Both tribal parks and IPCAs rely on guardian programs as the land-based "eyes and ears" of newly established protected areas. Both seek to revive traditional management practices, like the use of fire to regenerate and expand grassland habitats, as an important component of their conservation and restoration plans. And both espouse sustainable use of lands and wildlife—what some have called a "conservation economy"—within areas designated for protection.

As expressions of Indigenous governance and pathways for wildlife and habitat protection, tribal parks and IPCAs also play a significant cultural role as teaching landscapes. As the Indigenous Council of Experts recognized, "culture and language are the heart and soul of an IPCA."[67] Renewing connections with land, animals and the Indigenous practices that historically supported their health and productivity is in itself a process of cultural resurgence. As Nick Claxton recognized in his work to revive W̱SÁNEĆ reef net fisheries on southern Vancouver Island, connecting Indigenous words with specific animals and practices is a powerful way to teach language and to renew cultural ties to land and wildlife. In this way, restoring Indigenous governance over land and wildlife has the potential to stimulate a much broader process of cultural renewal.[68] To the extent that Indigenous objectives align with those of the Crown, IPCAs have provided an important mechanism for achieving both reconciliation and biodiversity conservation. In BC's north especially, where IPCAs like the Kaska Dena's proposed Dene K'éh Kusān stand to protect large intact landscapes, the carbon-storage capacity of boreal soils and forests will help to mitigate the effects of climate change.

For all the popular support that Indigenous guardian programs and IPCAs have generated among a mostly urban British Columbian public, transitions in the regions where these changes have been felt have not been as smooth. Proposed amendments to residential hunting allocations in the aftermath of the Blueberry River First Nation's 2021 Supreme Court victory in *Yahey v. British Columbia*, for example, have received vigorous critiques from the BC Wildlife Federation and hunters in the province's northeast.

The *Yahey* decision, a landmark victory for Blueberry River, identified the cumulative effects of decades of industrial development as a violation of the nation's Treaty 8 rights. The court prohibited the province from authorizing further activities that would infringe on Blueberry River's rights and required it to overhaul its land use regulations to consider the cumulative effects of development. Significantly, the province elected not to appeal.[69] In the wake of this decision, provincial proposals to halve moose-hunting opportunities and eliminate caribou hunting for resident non-Indigenous hunters in the region have struck a nerve with resident hunters who feel they are being made to "bear [the province's] failures" to address concerns about road density and habitat degradation that they themselves had repeatedly raised. In addition to the maintenance of resident hunter privileges, the BCWF seeks a collaborative process that will involve all wildlife users in protecting and restoring wildlife habitat and establishing sustainable hunting allocations in the region.[70]

It is unlikely to succeed. The implications of three decades of court decisions, combined with Crown commitments to government-to-government relationships with First Nations, mean that the priorities of resident hunters and guide-outfitting operations must fall below the treaty and Indigenous rights of area First Nations. The establishment of regional wildlife forums in other areas, such as the Moose Solutions Roundtable in the central Interior, suggests a way forward. At least in the short term, finding ways to collectively address the legacy of industrial development and prioritize the needs of wildlife in the northeast will likely involve losses of hunting opportunity for everyone.

Conclusion: Reconciliation through Wildlife

In the quarter century since the *Delgamuukw* decision of 1997, First Nations in British Columbia have engineered a transformation of their relationship with the federal and provincial governments. Over a century of petitions, delegations and protests over loss of ownership, management authority and access to land and wildlife had finally borne fruit in recognition of Indigenous and treaty rights in the Canadian Constitution and the elaboration and definition of these rights by the Canadian courts.

This revolution in Indigenous rights has implications for rectifying past injustices. With respect to hydroelectric development alone, BC Hydro and the Province of British Columbia have signed reparations agreements with Peace River valley First Nations for the losses they endured following the construction of the Bennett Dam. Regarding the Nechako River, a 2022 BC Supreme Court ruling recognized the "significant historic and continuing harm to the Nechako River and its fisheries" caused by Alcan's Kenney Dam, stimulating efforts by the regional district and area First Nations to press for new water flow and governance regimes for the river.[71] Recognition of the consequences of cumulative effects in *Yahey v. British Columbia* have placed past practices on trial to powerful effect.

Emerging government-to-government relationships between the Crown and First Nations appear poised to restructure institutions and redistribute authority, following the lead of places like the Northwest Territories and Australia. Concerns around wildlife allocation and management have been paramount in these discussions, as Indigenous communities seek to strengthen their presence on the land and renew their relationships with culturally significant species such as moose, caribou and salmon.

In 2022, the relocation of the province's wildlife programs to a new Ministry of Land, Water and Resource Stewardship loosely mirrored the Department of Recreation and Conservation arrangements of the late 1950s and 1960s. An important difference, however, lies in the new ministry's explicit commitment to work with First Nations on land and wildlife stewardship toward the broader goal of reconciliation. Developments like these have placed wildlife at the centre of reconciliation efforts. While there is no guarantee that collaborative and Indigenous-led initiatives will produce better outcomes for wildlife, the fledgling success of recent initiatives and experience elsewhere suggests that the chances are good.

— CONCLUSION —

In late June 2021, an anomalous "heat dome" scorched the Pacific Northwest and much of southern and central British Columbia. In the southern Interior, temperatures smashed Canadian records, with some areas reaching as high as 49.6 degrees Celsius. More than eight hundred people died across the province, four times as many as the average recorded during the same period over the previous five years.[1] Among BC's wildlife, effects were most visible in the intertidal zones along the coast, where over one billion molluscs and crustaceans baked to death in their shells during low tides.[2] Lightning strikes sparked almost three hundred fires through the southern Interior. On June 30, in the space of a few hours, the town of Lytton was reduced to ashes. The fire also consumed many homes and buildings of the neighbouring Lytton First Nation.

When temperatures finally receded, a global team of scientists began to work around the clock to determine whether the record-breaking, life-threatening heat could be tied to longer-term climate change trends. The conclusions they drew from their detailed modelling exercises left no doubt: heat of this intensity, in this place, would have been "virtually impossible without human-caused climate change." Seeking to dispel denial of the extreme event as merely unusual weather, the scientists worked quickly to drive home the message that severe events such as this would become more frequent with rising global temperatures.[3] Climate change, in other words, was no longer a distant threat.

British Columbians experienced the years of 2020 and 2021 as a time of profound disruption. Catastrophic wildfires, flooding and deadly heat made the realities of climate change increasingly and devastatingly apparent. The global COVID-19 pandemic took the lives of over 3,600 BC residents, seriously challenged the resilience of the healthcare system and suspended or altered social and economic activities. In late May 2021, the discovery of the remains of 215 children buried on the grounds of the former Kamloops Indian Residential School prompted mourning countrywide and renewed calls for meaningful reconciliation between Indigenous and settler societies.

For many, the combined environmental and social effects of events over these two years presented an opportunity to rebuild in ways that prioritize long-term ecosystem health and social reconciliation.

Around the world, scientists, Indigenous leaders and conservationists are reaching similar conclusions. In May 2019, a comprehensive global assessment of biodiversity and ecosystem services warned that biodiversity was declining globally at an unprecedented rate, threatening around one million plant and animal species with extinction—in many cases within decades—and "eroding the very foundations of our economies, livelihoods, food security, health and quality of life worldwide." To avert the worst of these outcomes, the report's 145 expert authors concluded, "transformative change" would be required "at every level from local to global" in order to bring "fundamental, system-wide reorganization . . . [of] paradigms, goals and values." Halting biodiversity loss in places like British Columbia, the report concluded, will require commitments at multiple levels of government to arrest land degradation and wildlife population declines while investing rapidly and substantially in sustainable forest management and land restoration. In addition to reviewing about 15,000 scientific and government sources, the authors drew on Indigenous and local knowledge "for the first time ever at this scale."[4] Both the method and the message of this massive international study resonate with the challenges ahead for British Columbia.

This concluding chapter reflects on the possibilities and limitations of lessons from the past in informing the development of future wildlife policy in the province. A discussion of insights drawn from this analysis of Indigenous (historical and ongoing), colonial and modern relationships with wildlife in British Columbia forms the second part of the chapter. The chapter closes by highlighting the work of three "change makers" whose contributions in different forums and at different scales help to point the way forward.

People and Wildlife in British Columbia over 250 Years

Stewards of Splendour traced a trajectory from Indigenous stewardship of wildlife prior to 1774, through years of oscillating competition and monopoly control over wild animal harvests between European and American trading companies in the eighteenth and nineteenth centuries, to the unregulated market hunting and fishing of the early years of European settlement and the growing emphasis on allocation, regulation and enforcement that followed. With the marginalization of Indigenous access controls in the southern reaches of the province and the withdrawal of the Hudson's Bay Company's trade monopoly in 1858, wildlife became a common property resource, open to everyone. Local fish and game associations and the hunters, anglers and naturalists they represented played an outsized role in pressing colonial and later provincial governments to respond to the resulting decimation of valued game and freshwater fish species. From mule deer and waterfowl to whales and fur seals, prohibitions of commercial hunting succeeded in reining in overexploitation within BC's developing capitalist economy. Permitted exceptions included commercial anadromous and saltwater fisheries and fur-bearer trapping, with the latter generally more sustainably practiced and regulated than the former.

Changes in the land produced by agricultural, townsite and hydroelectric development and the growth of extractive industries such as logging and mining prompted a growing emphasis on wildlife habitat protection by the mid-1960s. Developments in this period illuminated the historical effects of two challenges to wildlife conservation. The first, land alienation, converted valuable wetland, grassland and valley-bottom habitats—places sought after by humans and wildlife alike—to homes and businesses, farms, industrial use and hydroelectric dam reservoirs. The second, proliferating access through the rapid expansion of highways and resource road networks, fragmented habitats, altered stream conditions and removed sources of refuge for wild ungulates and other animals.

Access concerns have been evident since the late nineteenth century when rail lines and steam paddlewheelers opened previously remote regions to prospectors, hunters and anglers; they have intensified greatly over time with growing human populations and improved technology. The creation of linear networks on the land, from seismic line clearing in the northeast to the dramatic expansion of resource roads for salvage logging in the central Interior, facilitated access for hunters, anglers and hikers just as it did for wolves and other predators. Combined with an increasingly affordable selection of all-season off-road vehicles, these developments reduced already precarious chances of survival for threatened woodland caribou populations. Efforts to decommission roads and restore associated habitat will remain pressing needs for moose and caribou conservation into the foreseeable future.

Growing complexity best describes the work of wildlife conservation in the half-century since 1970. While widened definitions of wildlife replaced an exclusive focus on game species beginning in the mid-1960s, these changes became more pronounced as government wildlife programs responded to changing public sentiment surrounding wildlife and expanding scientific knowledge. Beginning in the 1970s, the growth of land trusts and conservation and environmental organizations introduced new tools for identifying and protecting lands of high conservation value and secured legal and financial supports from governments.

Increasing numbers of women entered wildlife work beginning in the 1980s, bringing new perspectives, questions and approaches that changed wildlife research and management. In collaboration and independently, government wildlife programs, university scientists and a growing number of conservation and environmental organizations worked to understand and protect the interests of wildlife on a changing landscape. The expansion of protected areas and the recovery of several endangered animal populations are a tribute to their efforts.

By the turn of the twenty-first century, the cumulative effects of human activities on the land reflected the legal, professional and regulatory complexity of wildlife work. One-time game wardens responsible for enforcing fish and game catch specifications had become conservation officers charged with policing a wide range of environmental violations, from pollution and water diversion to endangered species trafficking. Although this wider range of management activities plays an important role in equitable and effective wildlife management, government funding and capacity has generally not kept pace with the monitoring and enforcement demands of these expanding regulatory regimes.

A revolution in Indigenous rights and title accompanied these changes from the 1990s on. By 2015, gains in the courts over three decades had ushered in a new government-to-government relationship between First Nations and federal and provincial governments. Beginning in the north and extending through the 2000s to other parts of the province, the development of Indigenous-led guardian programs and protected areas strategies revitalized traditional stewardship practices and restored management authority in some regions.

This sea change in land and wildlife governance, with its associated allocation and access restrictions for recreational hunters, has not been well received by everyone. Resident hunters in the northeast, for example, have reacted angrily to provincial plans to eliminate caribou hunting and greatly reduce moose-hunting opportunities for non-Indigenous hunters in response to recent court victories by area First Nations.[5] Periodic closures of recreational fishing opportunities to protect threatened chinook salmon populations on the Fraser and Skeena rivers have resulted in similar censure from resident anglers.[6]

The invitation by some First Nations to open regional roundtables in pursuit of shared goals of wildlife recovery and conservation, backed by the province's 2020 Together for Wildlife strategy, suggests that decentralized responses to shared wildlife concerns may take root in the years ahead. While difficult negotiations remain over resource rights and reparations for the ongoing losses caused by projects like the Site C dam in the Peace River valley, the shift in recent decades toward a renewal of Indigenous land and wildlife stewardship has placed wildlife at the forefront of settler-Indigenous reconciliation initiatives in British Columbia.

Stewards of Splendour?

How effectively have British Columbians shouldered the responsibility of stewarding the great diversity of life in the province? The answer is mixed. Certainly, relationships with wildlife have come a long way from the rapacious market hunting and dynamite-assisted fishing of the late nineteenth century. Yet the acceleration of environmental change after World War II generally reduced wildlife diversity and abundance. Urban and agricultural development removed roughly 50 per cent of the highly biodiverse native grasslands of the southern Interior, for example, and over 75 per cent of wildlife-supporting wetlands in the Okanagan Valley and Fraser River delta.[7] Less than 10 per cent of the province's original low-elevation forest remains. Within freshwater systems, groundwater licensing reduced water flows on many rivers, compromising the survival of fish and aquatic species. The construction of forty hydroelectric dam sites across the province, including massive operations on the Peace and Columbia River systems, permanently inundated valuable valley-bottom and riparian habitat and blocked fish passage to upstream spawning grounds. While regulation and enforcement have curbed the worst abuses, chemical pollution in urban, agricultural and industrial areas continues to threaten water quality and aquatic life. Other threats have worsened, including the proliferation of resource access roads and recreational vehicles and rising numbers of invasive alien fish species in freshwater environments.

Relearning the Same Lessons

Wildlife diversity and abundance has generally suffered in response to these changes. One metric has been the growth in recent decades in species at risk. As of 2022, 245 vertebrate animal species in BC—roughly 25 per cent of all vertebrate species—had received provincial designation as species of conservation concern.[8] As Ian McTaggart Cowan wrote in 1987, "our capacity for damaging habitat and its living creatures has outrun our capacity to respond."[9] While a few especially adaptable species, such as black bear and elk, are likely as abundant or more abundant than they were seventy-five years ago, species that are more sensitive to change have almost certainly declined.

Wildlife conservation as a profession, and a practice, produces lessons that often repeat themselves. What becomes clear in reviewing the recommendations of influential wildlife biologists, such as Cowan and Peter Larkin in the 1960s and 1970s and Fred Bunnell in the 1980s and 1990s, is that we have known for a long time what needs to be done to conserve BC's wildlife. The failure to adequately implement past recommendations to protect and restore fish-bearing streams and riparian habitat, guard against overgrazing and land alienation in grasslands and lowlands, and protect recommended amounts of high-quality old-growth forest across the landscape has brought about the losses in biodiversity and ecosystem resilience that we face today. As foresters Al Gorley and Garry Merkel commented in their recent review of BC's old-growth forest management, had the province's comprehensive, consensus-based 1992 Old Growth Strategy been fully implemented "we would likely not be facing the challenges around old growth to the extent we are today."[10]

We also know *how* to do it. The successful conservation initiatives highlighted in this history, from the reintroduction of sea otters on the West Coast to captive-breeding programs for Vancouver Island marmot and other species, demonstrate the power of collective effort and determination. In each case, scientists, government agencies and conservation organizations worked together to avert the loss of a rare and endemic species or one depleted by commercial hunting. International cooperation has been a significant factor in the maintenance of border-crossing species like California bighorn sheep and the establishment of international agreements prohibiting the destruction or trade of endangered wildlife.

Across this 250-year history, partnerships between and among governments and conservation organizations have been an important mechanism for change, yielding significant and lasting benefits for wildlife. From historic international efforts—for example, the 1916 Migratory Birds Convention Act, which continues to protect migratory birds in Canada and the United States—to local habitat protection and restoration initiatives, working together to pool resources and address cross-boundary threats to species and ecosystems has been a winning strategy for wildlife. Ducks Unlimited, active in Canada since the late 1930s and in British Columbia since 1968, laid important early groundwork for collaborative conservation in its creative work with farmers, governments and other conservation organizations to protect and restore waterfowl habitat. Land trusts have built on this legacy to become masters of partnership approaches over the past fifty years. As this history has shown, however, partnerships are often fragile arrangements, subject to losses of continuity, institutional memory and financial support as government mandates change and key proponents retire. Maintaining and renewing commitments and communicating past successes through periods of transition are the building blocks of successful, long-term conservation partnerships.

While British Columbians have rightly retired many historical wildlife management practices, such as the casual introduction of exotic species or efforts to eradicate predatory birds and mammals, time has shown the value of some older insights about wildlife and ecosystem health. Traditional Indigenous practices, like the use of fire to stimulate early seral vegetation and increase wildlife abundance and diversity, gained recognition beginning in the 1970s. Guide outfitters absorbed these lessons much earlier. For instance, Garry Vince, who held a guiding territory on the Muskwa River in BC's northeast from the late 1950s to the late 1990s, recognized the importance of controlled burns to enhance ungulate habitat and support ecosystem health at a time when fire suppression was unquestioned government policy.[11]

Among land trusts and conservation organizations, insights from an earlier generation continue to guide their activities into the present. Nature

Conservancy of Canada regional vice-president Nancy Newhouse, for example, recalled the origins of her organization's Kootenay Conservation Program in a list of properties that regional biologist Dave Phelps identified in the late 1980s. "What he did on the back of an envelope, essentially, has held up over all the other thinking and planning that has been done over the last thirty years."[12] The same can be said of wildlife research. As much as new research approaches have greatly expanded the accuracy and reduced the intrusive nature of wildlife research and monitoring, insights from an older generation of biologists reinforce the value of ground-truthing knowledge and attending to interconnections that can only be observed in the field.

In other areas, older, more contentious ideas about wildlife management are coming back around. Decisions in the mid-1960s to abandon predator control as a core component of provincial wildlife management have received some reassessment in recent years in the face of declining woodland caribou and moose populations in some areas of British Columbia. The effects of heightened predation facilitated by road access prompted emergency measures, including wolf culls, to improve opportunities for recovery of critically endangered caribou herds. Within this context, hunters, ranchers and some First Nations have advocated for a return to a balanced form of predator control in order to protect livestock and vulnerable ungulates. Considering the extremes of near extirpation of wolf populations from some areas in the 1950s and 1960s, on the one hand, and abandonment of predator control except in emergency circumstances, on the other, many rural residents wish to see management responses that fall somewhere in the middle.[13]

Taking a Long-Term View

Conservation activities stand the best chance of success, this history has shown, under conditions that permit long-term planning and investment. The implementation of a licensing system in the 1910s, for example, allowed BC's first provincial game warden to build a self-sustaining game department underwritten by the economic value of wildlife for tourism and sport hunting. A similar vision guided the development of the international Convention for the Protection of Migratory Birds in 1916.

Since federal and provincial wildlife conservation mandates shifted in the late 1960s to incorporate non-game species, government wildlife agencies have felt the burden of multiple and sometimes conflicting responsibilities.

Retired biologist Rick Marshall recalled of his thirty-five-year career in the Skeena region that the provincial wildlife branch lacked "a long-term vision of where we want to be . . . thirty years from now," and "how we are going to [get] there." Instead, he commented, it has been "a reactive agency" consumed with day-to-day demands.[14] Hunting and angling organizations have characterized a perceived failure of wildlife agencies to set long-term objectives as "managing to zero." Wildlife managers, they argue, have responded to a long-term decline in some animal populations by focusing exclusively on reducing hunting pressure, "continually ratcheting hunting seasons down." This reactionary response fails, in their assessment, to address the range of circumstances contributing to declines in wildlife populations.[15]

Nowhere is this need for a long-term vision more clear than in the decisions surrounding caribou recovery, where dangerous declines in some herds caused by predation and disturbance have led wildlife managers to pursue reductions in predator and "alternate prey" (deer and moose) populations. Former BC Forest Service biologist Bruce McLellan concluded from his research on caribou that a trade-off was necessary between the health of caribou populations and the number of other large wildlife species within an ecosystem.[16] Such a finding makes decision-making extremely challenging for provincial wildlife managers, who must balance their obligations under the federal Species at Risk Act to recover threatened herds of mountain caribou against opposing pressures from hunting groups to maintain large populations of moose and deer on the landscape. While collaboration between the provincial and federal governments and area First Nations has produced some limited signs of recovery in the short term, for scientists like McLellan short-term recovery strategies must be guided by a collective long-term vision that will inevitably involve some difficult choices.

Changing Public Attitudes

Debates like this take place in an atmosphere of changing wildlife constituencies. The number of licensed resident hunters has declined over the past forty years in relation to the total BC population. In 1961, at the peak of hunting popularity, 7.5 per cent of all British Columbians held a basic resident hunting licence. By 1982 this number had fallen to 5.5 per cent, and since the early 2000s it has fluctuated between 2.0 per cent and 2.3 per cent of the population.

Trapper and guide-outfitter numbers have also declined. (The number of licensed resident freshwater anglers, by comparison, continued to climb into the mid-1980s. Following sharp declines in the late 1990s and early 2000s, angler numbers have stabilized at about 5 to 6 per cent of the population.)[17] The province's wildlife branch, accordingly, has shifted from an agency of "hunters managing hunters" to one that aims to reflect broader public views surrounding wildlife. As fewer British Columbians hunt, support for such controversial activities as trophy hunting has dropped to less than 5 per cent of the population—a figure that surely influenced the 2017 decision to prohibit grizzly bear hunting. With fewer hunters and trappers, however, comes the loss not only of direct revenue for government wildlife management and conservation initiatives but also of an important line of defence for wildlife. As an earlier generation of wildlife biologists knew only too well, "the economic importance of livelihoods gained from wildlife" has long been one of "the central (and few) arguments available against destructive, competing uses of the landscape."[18]

For some observers, this decline in practical experience with fish and game species has led to a decline in practical knowledge about wildlife: fewer British Columbians hunt and fish, and as a result, few appreciate the diverse challenges that wild animals face, and few understand their life histories, habitat needs and behaviours. Others rarely think about wildlife at all: at best it offers a pleasing sight, at worst a nuisance or an encumbrance in the pursuit of livelihoods, pleasure and profit. The persistence of tourism slogans like "Super, Natural British Columbia" and the widespread use of orcas and other charismatic wildlife species as mascots for BC's identity only compound the problem by nurturing impressions of uninterrupted abundance in wildlife populations. "Shifting baseline syndrome" contributes to these trends. As each generation of people sees the natural world they grew up in as the "normal state of nature," they fail to recognize longer-term declines in ecosystems or species. Together, these tendencies cloud public perceptions of biodiversity loss and contribute to a sense of complacency with regard to the status of wildlife in the province.

Others find good reasons to be optimistic. Interviewees who remembered the 1940s and 1950s, for example, pointed to the stark contrast between the level of public interest in nature and wildlife conservation in that period and the level of public interest today. The BC Game Commission's *Wildlife*

Review, published quarterly for three decades from 1954 to 1985, introduced scientific perspectives and established a forum for wildlife education for generations of BC hunters and anglers. On a broader scale, public education institutions such as the Royal BC Museum, park naturalist programs, and scientists-cum-television hosts like Ian McTaggart Cowan and David Suzuki played an important role in educating public audiences about wildlife ecology and shaping public attitudes toward wild animals. Collectively, these initiatives served to shift public attitudes toward predatory birds and mammals and generate public and political support for habitat protection measures.[19]

The knowledge traditions of hunters, anglers, naturalists and Indigenous communities have also played a role in cultivating a sense of wonder and appreciation for the natural world. Within each of these communities, knowledge spans generations. Okanagan ornithologist Dick Cannings described his experience growing up within a renowned family of birders and biologists, whose connections to fellow naturalists reached backwards and forwards in time. "Whenever I went out birding with my father as a kid, we'd be walking through the woods and he'd start whistling like a pygmy owl and all the little birds would gather around and mob—so we'd know what kind of chickadees and nuthatches and warblers were around." Cannings's father, Steven, had learned the technique from Summerland neighbour and avid birder Eric Tait, who had in turn learned it from hunter-naturalist Allan Brooks, who had "learned it from his father in India." For Cannings, whistling like a pygmy owl to attract birds represented a kind of "chain of social learning" or intergenerational mentorship.[20]

Since the advent of widespread access to the internet in the 1990s, information (of varying quality) about wildlife has become readily accessible to British Columbians. More so than animal populations, public concern for individual animals—the pair of eagles nesting in the tree at the end of the street, or the survival of the newest calf of a pod of threatened killer whales in the Salish Sea—has been heightened by the proliferation of web cams and social media sites over the past fifteen years. Conservation organizations have picked up on this public fascination with individual creatures. Web and smartphone applications like HappyWhale.com, for example, allow observers to identify named individuals (such as Oscar the humpback whale) and track their movements around the globe. As hunters and anglers, wildlife viewers, or consumers of museum and online programming, British Columbians have access to a range of entry points to wildlife appreciation and education, each of which offers opportunities to recognize the intelligence, beauty and self-determination of other creatures.

Pointing the Way: Change Makers

As this history has shown, individual actors can drive remarkable change. James Munro's efforts in the 1920s as chief migratory bird officer for the western provinces contributed to the elimination of bounties on many predatory birds by the early 1930s. Ian McTaggart Cowan, in his work at the Provincial Museum and later as head of UBC's zoology department, launched the study and practice of scientific wildlife management in the province and contributed to major paradigm shifts in predator control, game management and habitat conservation. Humane trapping advocate Clara Van Steenwyk's collaboration with northern trapper Frank Conibear and the BC Trappers Association led to the gradual adoption of a more humane alternative to the leghold trap beginning in the 1950s. Nisga'a hereditary chief Frank Calder led the fight to have Canadian courts recognize Nisga'a title to their lands in 1973, launching the federal land claims process and the signing of the Nisga'a Treaty—with significant provisions for wildlife allocation and management—almost three decades later.

Change makers operating at different scales, from local to international, continue to build relationships and pioneer approaches that provide the stepping stones for broader systemic change. "You must be the change you wish to see in the natural world," Cowan once held of the role of the individual in conservation work.[21] The following profiles highlight the work of three people whose contributions point the way to a more just and sustainable future that prioritizes wildlife, ecosystem health and reconciliation between Indigenous and non-Indigenous communities. Each was chosen for their passion and commitment to wildlife, their skills in collaboration, and their honesty and humility. Each placed value on the local community as a site of achievable change and demonstrated an ability to move beyond ideological positions. Finally, each stood out for the ability to open hearts and minds to other points of view and let go of their own preferred outcomes to find consensus.

Bill Blackwater Jr. (Mauus): Gitxsan Hereditary Chief, Wildlife
Conservation Advocate and Cross-Cultural Communicator

The late Gitxsan Chief Bill Blackwater Jr. (Mauus) in 2019. Photo courtesy of Laverne Williams.

Gitxsan hereditary chief Bill Blackwater Jr. (Mauus), who passed away in the summer of 2021, was one of those agents of change. A hereditary chief of the Gitxsan Nation since 2001, he worked to build appreciation among his own people and among outsiders of the significance of the ayook, or traditional laws, that govern relationships between the Gitxsan people and the land and wildlife on which they depend. One of the main roles of the hereditary chiefs, he explained, is to make sure that "every beautiful living thing, whether it be wildlife or plants," is available "for the future generations to come. My chief name, Mauus, never goes away. When I pass on, someone else will take that name on. He or she will have the same responsibility." This responsibility, passed down through the generations, to communicate and uphold a shared conservation ethic "is how we survived through the hundreds of years."

Communicating this understanding to non-Indigenous stakeholders and government wildlife managers was part of his legacy. In numerous consultations over the years, he worked to bridge gaps in understanding about the nature of Indigenous knowledge. At a meeting with provincial wildlife managers in Kispiox in 2018, Blackwater's mother commented, "I've lived in Kispiox all my life and this is the first year I've seen a grizzly and her cubs down by the [Kispiox River] bridge." A month after spotting the bears, she was surprised to see a couple of wolves walking up the road outside her kitchen window. When government representatives struggled to grasp the significance of her statement, Bill explained, "what she's telling you is that she's lived here all her life and she's never seen these animals down in the village before. And do you know why they're in the village? Their habitat is wiped out. They have no place to go but to come down to the village." His mother's observations reinforced the knowledge held by many Gitxsan members that "over-logging was decimating . . . wildlife habitat" and removing opportunities to retain former livelihoods, such as trapping. Elders' lived experiences provided important evidence of change.[22]

Chief Mauus's ability to communicate in cross-cultural forums with wisdom, humour and experience made him a valued mentor and leader in collaborative government-to-government wildlife conservation work. As a representative on the First Nations–BC Wildlife and Habitat Conservation Forum from 2018 to 2020, his skilled diplomacy kept discussions "grounded in what matters most." "I think Bill knew that this work [had the potential to] . . . transform how Indigenous governing bodies are seen and understood and how [the province] interacts with them," recalled Hunter Lampreau, a youth member of the Forum and wildlife coordinator for the Qwelminte Secwépemc. "It was more than just . . . putting more wildlife on a landscape and creating better habitat. . . . It was contributing to a culture change and—finally—equity in values." As Forum discussions advanced, Lampreau continued, "we could see that Indigenous values would slowly be understood as the key to how we understand the landscape we occupy." Bill helped the provincial representatives "to understand that [First] Nations want to see not just what's best for our title and rights but also what's best for [all of] our landscapes."[23]

For Lampreau, who would step into a leadership role as co-chair of the Forum, Chief Mauus provided valued mentorship in cross-cultural communication. As "a dedicated practitioner of two-eyed seeing," he understood that "in order to be successful in the modern context of reconciliation, you needed to challenge systems to do better while respecting [both ways of seeing]." He added, "Bill had a very steady, calm presence that ensured that was possible." This kind of principled diplomacy, Lampreau recognized, "is only built from experience. There is no reconciliation handbook." The slow pace of reconciliation has accentuated the value, and the scarcity, of this skill and experience. "As [we lose] Indigenous elders, we are losing [those skills] more rapidly than we can build [them]."[24]

Clearly, however, Lampreau is learning fast. To do this work, he concluded, "we need each other's collective wisdom." He explained, "We get so caught up in the idea of what's next—Is dedicated funding next? Are species objectives next?—[that] we lose sight of what's first. And that's admitting [that Indigenous and non-Indigenous residents of BC] have had an unhealthy [relationship] for a long time." In interactions surrounding wildlife, "we've held a tremendous amount of animosity towards one another." Lampreau concluded, "Coming together for wildlife, for habitat, for the fact that we all give a damn . . . that's got to be [our first priority]. As long as we keep wildlife and habitat first, we can start small. We will build our hope as we go."[25]

Genevieve Singleton: Naturalist and Co-chair, Cowichan Stewardship Roundtable

Genevieve Singleton wears many hats. An active member and leader in several naturalist, nature education and watershed organizations in the Cowichan Valley, she also serves as warden for two area ecological reserves. "I have a knack," she admits, for "bringing together people and making stuff happen."[26] Trained as a naturalist from childhood, Singleton took up her first job as a summer naturalist at Francis Park (now Francis/King Regional Park) at age fourteen, under the mentorship of celebrated Victoria naturalist Freeman "Skipper" King. Once she completed university studies in biology and education, she worked for several summers as a naturalist for BC Parks before moving to the Cowichan Valley with her husband and children in the late 1980s.

Genevieve Singleton holding a western bluebird (*Sialia mexicana*) for banding in May 2018 as part of her work with the Cowichan Bring Back the Bluebirds Project, an initiative to restore extirpated western bluebirds to their former habitat on Vancouver Island. Photo courtesy of Genevieve Singleton.

It wasn't long before Singleton was deeply involved in local conservation and nature education initiatives. A chance meeting with Don Carson, chair of the board of directors for Eves Provincial Park, a small Class C park in the Cowichan Valley, piqued her interest in local park governance. She has chaired or co-chaired the park's board ever since, working with its directors to prioritize park stewardship and nature education. The board's vision and local fundraising success has earned them recognition as a model for other Class C, locally governed parks across the province.

In the early 2000s, several summers of low water flow in the Cowichan River threatened chinook salmon populations and jeopardized the community's water needs. Widespread concern over the health of the Cowichan River watershed led to the establishment of the Cowichan Stewardship Roundtable. As Singleton recalls, it began with "a bunch of people standing around the edge of the river and saying, 'let's get together and see what we can do.'" The roundtable's open membership and ad hoc approach attracted a wide range of partners and participants, including industry, conservation organizations and three levels of government. From the beginning, the involvement of Cowichan Tribes has been integral to its success. As Singleton explains, we "believe strongly in a co-governance approach. . . . We don't move on things until we meet with Cowichan Tribes and hear their perspectives."

An emphasis on problem-solving and mutual aid guides the roundtable's work. Meetings begin with people "just saying what they're doing. Somebody may say, 'I'm working on repairing vegetation, but I need some big woody debris,' and a timber company may say, 'you know, we're just moving some stuff, we can deliver that to you.'" This kind of informal collaboration and mutual concern for the health of the river system has enabled rapid responses to relocate spawning fish in years of low flows, as well as more ambitious initiatives, such as an award-winning restoration project that stabilized an eroding bluff over the river. In 2007, the group completed a twenty-five-year water management plan for the Cowichan basin in collaboration with government, industry and Cowichan Tribes. There have been some bumps along the road in reconciling divergent perspectives around development, but as Singleton notes, "that's what collaborative work looks like." When conflicts arise, she remembers a lesson from a mentor: "be hard on issues, not on people."

For Singleton, working together on watershed issues is part of a long-standing commitment to the practice of reconciliation. "I'm working hard at learning [the Coast Salish language] Hul'q'umi'num," she explained. "I do a lot of interpretive signage in the valley, [and] I use Hul'q'umi'num words for plants and animals whenever I can." In 2018, she led a collaborative initiative with BC Parks, Cowichan Tribes and four other partner organizations (the BCWF, the Cowichan Valley Regional District, the Cowichan Land Trust and the Cowichan Valley Naturalists) to establish a new provincial park in a rare pocket of native grassland south of Duncan. The creation of "Eagle Heights" Provincial Park, which will receive a Hul'qumi'num name, fulfils a decades-long wish of the late Cowichan Valley naturalist Syd Watts to see the area protected. For Singleton, the project's success lay in years of respectful relationship-building; she notes that the "way forward is [to work] with First Nations wherever we are to . . . create scenarios that they are a part of."

Looking forward, Singleton continues to train her focus on the local. "I want to be involved in big issues in my watershed, [and] in educating children." Her faith as a Quaker informs the responsibility she carries for future generations and the consensus-seeking approaches she brings to her work. "I feel if we all worked really hard locally, that's how to make a better world."[27]

Lee Hesketh: Independent Stream and Habitat Restoration Specialist

Lee Hesketh at a river stewardship event in 2014. Photo courtesy of the Stewardship Centre for British Columbia.

Lee Hesketh fixes problems. As a lifelong member of the ranching community in BC's southern Interior, he has spent the past thirty-five years designing and implementing stream restoration projects throughout the Fraser and Skeena river basins. The work requires considerable knowledge of biological systems and stream hydrology. Even more important is the skill it takes in working with people to find common ground in the interests of wildlife and ecosystem health. For Hesketh, there is nothing more rewarding: "My religion is the environment. You can do a lot when you believe."[28]

Hesketh found his way into restoration work in the mid-1980s, when DFO biologist Mel Shang championed an experimental program to support farmers and ranchers in protecting riparian corridors on their properties. Hesketh was hired to work with southern Interior landowners, offering federal funds and an experienced crew to fence off their cattle from sensitive riparian areas, install alternate watering stations and restore damaged sections of creek. He earned a reputation in the process as a skilled and intuitive "bioengineer." Unlike traditional engineering approaches, which employ expensive and intrusive interventions such as berms, dikes and rip-rapping (the use of rocky material along the shoreline to protect stream banks from erosion), bioengineering aims to work *with* the river system to mimic natural features. "The template is there in most creek systems," Hesketh explains, "of what's working and what [the creek] can maintain. You have to replicate that. . . . If I do my job properly, nobody gives you any credit because it looks natural and it functions."[29]

As property owners and operators of often multi-generational family businesses, ranchers gravitate quite readily toward the long-term perspectives that Hesketh espouses. More challenging is the reluctance among older landowners to abandon earlier ways of doing things. Some may insist, for example, that a creek or river be channelled to control seasonal flooding. Hesketh urges the opposite: investment in larger and wider bridges to accommodate flow and protect fish habitat. His familiarity with ranchers' interests and concerns makes these conversations easier. Ultimately, he explains, "I'm there to fix [the rancher's] problem. If they are willing to work with me, I can make things happen." Words matter a great deal, he has found, in the process of reconciling divergent perspectives. "When I take fisheries biologists out to see [a habitat channel I constructed on my property]," they point to the "3.5 kilometres of habitat" it provides. To his rancher friends, however, it is an irrigation ditch. When they ask, "Why does it have all that ugly debris and stuff?" Hesketh replies, "It's for the fish. I can fish and my grandchildren can go fishing." In fact, it's both: "I have all this habitat with all these fish. *And* it's my irrigation system."[30]

Like Singleton, Hesketh has gathered encouragement from collaboration with First Nations over the past two decades. A shared concern for chinook populations in the South Thompson system, for example, led him to work with the Secwépemc Fisheries Commission, the Okanagan Nations Fisheries Commission and several community organizations to lobby for the restoration of fish passage beyond the Wilsey Dam on the Shuswap River. Remediation of the 1928 dam, which obstructs upstream passage for salmon and trout, had been a passion project for Hesketh since the age of twelve. Ten years of technical studies and lobbying paid off in 2018, when BC Hydro agreed to examine methods to repatriate the fish above the dam site.

Decades of work building trust within the ranching community have earned Hesketh the endorsement of the BC Cattlemen's Association; he currently manages its farmland-riparian stewardship program, among other commitments. A strong proponent of local stewardship initiatives that engage community members in contributing to positive change, he sees programs like his as a cost-effective alternative to enforcement. Rewarding conscientious landowners for constructing and maintaining stream protection and habitat enhancement structures requires relatively limited government investment. The dividends from those investments, however, have long-term benefits in improved ecosystem health, landowner awareness and community pride.

British Columbia's extraordinary diversity and historical abundance of wildlife has prompted more than two centuries of passionate involvement by hunters, anglers and trappers, naturalists, scientists, Indigenous leaders and communities, industry representatives, and the non-profit sector. Groups and individuals have overcome divergent political agendas and significant differences in perception and experience to come together to make changes in the interests of wildlife. We can continue to do so.

The considerable momentum achieved on the road to reconciliation between settler and Indigenous residents of British Columbia is likely to continue to transform land and wildlife management and governance into the future, opening economic opportunities for Indigenous communities and setting the terms for government-to-government decision-making. While outcomes to this end may not always benefit wildlife, the ongoing primacy of wild animals in the cultural traditions of many First Nations and the revival of hunting, fishing and associated stewardship practices among many BC groups suggests that wildlife will at the very least receive priority consideration. As regional initiatives such as the Moose Solutions Roundtable, which invited participation from a wide range of concerned parties, suggest, the best way forward is inclusive, locally grounded and informed by a combination of science and local and Indigenous knowledge. Faced with the increasingly apparent ramifications of climate change and global biodiversity loss, revitalizing avenues for local and regional participation has the potential to bring people together to protect and conserve wildlife in ways that honour the ambitious wildlife conservation efforts of the past two centuries.

Appendix | Interviewees

Ackerman, Andy. Retired regional manager, Peace Region, Fish and Wildlife Branch, Ministry of Environment. Former Senior Conservation Officer.

Baccante, Nick. Former regional fisheries biologist, Peace Region, Ministry of Environment.

Barnett, Ian. Chair, Science Advisory Network, BC Regional Board of Directors, Nature Conservancy of Canada. Former director, Regional Operations for Western Canada, Ducks Unlimited Canada. Former vice-president of operations, Nature Conservancy of Canada.

Bergenske, John. Conservation director and founder, Wildsight.

Biffert, Wayne. Representative, Williams Lake Sportsmen's Association.

Blackwater, Bill, Jr. Hereditary Chief, Gitxsan First Nation.

Bogdan, Les. Retired director, Regional Operations, Ducks Unlimited Canada.

Boon, Kevin. General manager, BC Cattlemen's Association.

Bourgeois, Bill. Registered professional forester. President, New Direction Resource Management.

Bunnell, Fred. Professor emeritus, Department of Forest Sciences, University of British Columbia.

Burger, Alan. President, BC Nature (formerly the Federation of BC Naturalists).

Cannings, Richard. Biologist and Member of Parliament for South Okanagan – West Kootenay.

Caravetta, Joe. Retired inspector, Kootenay-Boundary Region, BC Conservation Officer Service, Ministry of Environment.

Conly, Dave. Operations manager, Forest Enhancement Society of British Columbia.

Cooper, John. Ornithologist and consultant, Victoria, BC.

Dawe, Neil. Retired habitat manager and senior wildlife technician, Vancouver Island, Canadian Wildlife Service.

Demarchi, Dennis. Retired habitat assessment specialist, Ministry of Environment.

Demarchi, Ray. Retired BC Chief of Wildlife Conservation. Former wildlife section head, Kootenay Region, Fish and Wildlife Branch, Ministry of Environment.

Eastman, Don. Retired manager, Wildlife Research and Development, Fish and Wildlife Branch, Ministry of Environment.

Feick, Jenny. Retired manager of Habitat Protection, Fish and Wildlife Branch, Ministry of Environment.

Flood, Nancy. Professor, Faculty of Science, Thompson Rivers University.

Fontana, Anna. Retired guide outfitter and wildlife biologist, Elk Valley, Kootenay Region.

Genovali, Chris. Executive director, Raincoast Conservation Foundation.

Hammond, Blair. Regional director, Pacific Region, Canadian Wildlife Service.

Harper, Fred. Retired district agriculturalist, Fort St. John, Ministry of Agriculture. Former regional wildlife biologist, Fort St. John, and regional habitat protection biologist, Okanagan and Thompson-Nicola Regions, Fish and Wildlife Branch, Ministry of Environment.

Hatter, Ian. Retired wildlife manager, Kootenay Region and Provincial Headquarters, Fish and Wildlife Branch, Ministry of Environment.

Henderson, John. Wildlife Stewardship Council, Wei Wai Kum First Nation in Campbell River.

Hesketh, Lee. Coordinator, Farmland-Riparian Interface Stewardship Program, BC Cattlemen's Association.

Hill, Edward. Retired senior environmental coordinator, BC Hydro.

Jamieson, Bob. Biologist and rancher, Ta Ta Creek, Kootenay Region.

Janz, Doug. Retired regional section head for Recreation and Conservation, Vancouver Island Region, Fish and Wildlife Branch, Ministry of Environment.

Jex, Bill. Wildlife biologist, Fish and Wildlife Branch, Skeena Region, Ministry of Forests, Lands and Natural Resource Operations.

Kessler, Wini. Former chair, Habitat Conservation Trust Foundation. Retired professor, Natural Resources, University of Northern British Columbia.

Lament, Jasper. Chief executive officer, Nature Trust of British Columbia.

Lampreau, Hunter. Wildlife strategic coordinator, Qwelminte Secwépemc First Nation.

Lee, Stuart. Fisheries and wildlife manager, Secwépemc – Splatsín First Nation.

Little, Jim. Retired senior land officer, Peace Region, Integrated Land Management Bureau, Ministry of Agriculture and Lands. Former co-chair, Fort St. John Land and Resource Management Plan.

MacHutchon, Grant. Wildlife biologist, A. Grant MacHutchon Consulting.

Marshall, Rick. Retired wildlife section head, Skeena Region, Fish and Wildlife Branch, Ministry of Environment.

Martin, Al. Fisheries biologist and former director, Strategic Initiatives, BC Wildlife Federation. Former director, Kootenay Region, Fish and Wildlife Branch, Ministry of Environment.

McAdam, Steve. Hydroelectric impacts biologist, Ecosystems Branch, Ministry of Environment and Climate Change Strategy.

McBride, Joe. Retired legal counsel, Resource, Environment and Land Law Group, Ministry of Justice and Attorney General.

McKay, Andy. Acting Inspector of the OIC (Officer in Charge) of Restorative Justice of First Nations Relations, Conservation Officer Service, Ministry of Environment.

McLellan, Bruce. Retired wildlife research ecologist, Kootenay Region, Ministry of Forests, Lands and Natural Resource Operations.

Merkel, Garry. Chief executive officer, Tahltan Nation Development Corporation.

Morhart, Tyler. Manager, Agriculture Wildlife Program, Ministry of Agriculture.

Mowat, Garth. Large carnivore specialist and section head, Research Program, Resource Stewardship Division, Kootenay Region, Ministry of Forests, Lands, Natural Resource Operations and Rural Development.

Mumford, Rick. Land stewardship coordinator, BC Cattlemen's Association.

Njenga, Francis. Rangeland stewardship officer, Range Branch, Thompson/Okanagan Region, Ministry of Forests, Lands, Natural Resource Operations and Rural Development.

Notseta, Roslyn. Lands manager, Halfway River First Nation.

Paille, Gerry. Regional president, Peace Region, BC Wildlife Federation.

Peck, Ross. Retired guide outfitter and biologist, Peace Region. Former chair and board member, Habitat Trust Conservation Foundation and Muskwa-Kechika Advisory Board.

Popplestone, Dennis. Regional president, Vancouver Island, BC Wildlife Federation.

Porter, Dave. Kaska Dena leader and chief executive officer, BC First Nations Energy and Mining Council.

Purdy, Carmen. Founder and chair, Kootenay Wildlife Heritage Fund.

Reifel, George C. Founding partner, Reifel Cooke Group. Vice-president, British Columbia Waterfowl Society. Family land donor, George C. Reifel Migratory Bird Sanctuary and Alaksen National Wildlife Area.

Ritcey, Frank. Retired biologist, Northern and Central BC Region, BC Conservation Foundation.

Ritcey, Ralph. Retired regional biologist, Thompson/Okanagan Region, Fish and Wildlife Branch, Ministry of Environment.

Scheck, Joelle. Resource manager, Northeast Caribou Team Lead, Ministry of Forests, Lands, Natural Resource Operations and Rural Development.

Schultze, George. Retired wildlife officer, Skeena Region, Fish and Wildlife Branch, Ministry of Environment.

Schwantje, Helen. Provincial wildlife veterinarian, BC Ministry of Forests, Lands, Natural Resource Operations and Rural Development.

Silver, Rod. Retired biologist and former manager, Habitat Conservation Trust Fund.

Singleton, Genevieve. Co-chair, Cowichan Stewardship Roundtable. Chair, Board of Directors, Eves Provincial Park.

Springinotic, Brian. Chief executive officer, Habitat Trust Conservation Foundation.

Trethewey, Don. Member, Kamloops & District Fish and Game Association.

Vince, Garry and Sandra. Retired guide outfitters, Northeast Region.

Weir, Rich. Carnivore conservation specialist, Ecosystems Branch, Ministry of Environment and Climate Change Strategy.

Wilkin, Nancy. Director, Office of Sustainability, Royal Roads University. Former assistant deputy minister, Environmental Stewardship, Ministry of Environment.

Williams, Mark. Retired senior wildlife biologist, Skeena Region, Fish and Wildlife Branch, Ministry of Environment.

And six interviewees who wished to remain anonymous.

Glossary

Aboriginal title: The Canadian legal system recognizes Aboriginal title as a unique collective right to the use of and jurisdiction over an Indigenous group's ancestral territories. This right is not granted from an external source but a result of Indigenous Peoples' own occupation of and relationship with their home territories as well as their ongoing social structures and political and legal systems.

Act for the Preservation of Game: When the Hudson's Bay Company lost its monopoly rights, wildlife became a common property resource, open to all. Resulting pressures on wildlife in populated areas led to the passage of the province's first game protection laws. The colony of Vancouver Island passed an Act for the Preservation of Game (1859), which prohibited hunting of deer and elk from January to July and outlawed the sale or purchase of a number of waterfowl and upland game birds and their eggs during the breeding season. The colony of British Columbia passed similar legislation in 1865, and a single ordinance for the newly united colonies replaced its predecessors in 1867.

adaptive management: A structured process of learning from results on the ground to continually improve management practices, adaptive management promotes flexible decision-making that can be adjusted as outcomes from actions and events become better understood. Careful monitoring of these outcomes advances scientific understanding and helps in adjusting policies or operations as part of an iterative learning process that recognizes the importance of natural variability in contributing to ecological resilience and productivity.

Agricultural Land Commission: With the steady loss of farmland to urban sprawl, one of the most significant developments for habitat protection and land use planning in BC was the creation of the Agricultural Land Commission. With a mandate to prioritize and protect the land base and its use for agriculture, the 1973 Land Commission Act (the precursor to the Agricultural Land Commission Act) required the province's twenty-eight regional districts to submit an agricultural reserve plan to the commission for consideration.

Allied Tribes of British Columbia (ATBC): The combined effects of land losses and restricted access to fish and wildlife prompted members of the Squamish and Haida nations to form the Allied Tribes of British Columbia in 1916. With the participation of First Nations on the north and south coasts and many in the Interior, the organization was the first in BC to unite First Nations in pressing the federal and provincial governments for claims to land and resources.

anadromous: Fish that are anadromous live in salt water but migrate to fresh water to spawn. In BC, these include salmon and eulachon. These fish hatch in freshwater streams, migrate to the sea to mature, and then return to the same streams where they were hatched to breed and (almost always) die. The spring migration of these anadromous species is critical for Indigenous Peoples and a variety of animals who depend on this protein source.

animal rights movement: The goal of the animal rights movement that emerged in the 1970s was to place animals "beyond use" of human beings, putting an end to exploitative industries and practices. Unlike those in the animal welfare movement that preceded it—with its wildlife-oriented work focused primarily on the reduction of cruelty in fur-bearer trapping—animal rights activists believe animals to be individuals with their own desires and needs, not common property to be disposed of by humans.

annual game conventions: Starting in 1947, annual game conventions provided a venue for knowledge exchange between wildlife biologists and wildlife users, including delegates from fish and game clubs across the province, Game Commission officials, and representatives from guiding and trapping associations, the BC Cattlemen's Association, the BC Federation of Agriculture and other interest groups.

BC Conservation Foundation (BCCF): Founded and incorporated under the Society Act of British Columbia in 1969 by the directors of the BC Wildlife Federation, the BCCF promotes and assists in the conservation of fish and wildlife resources by protecting, acquiring and enhancing fish and wildlife populations and habitat. A federally registered charity dedicated to the conservation and stewardship of BC's ecosystems and species, the BCCF manages projects on behalf of key stakeholders and reinvests funds into programs and initiatives that support these endeavours.

BC Natural Resources Conference: From 1948 to 1968, the annual BC Natural Resources Conference provided an important forum for communication across resource sectors. These conferences attracted fish and game clubs, naturalists and representatives from commercial fisheries' trade unions, who successfully argued their concerns about the rapid proliferation of industrial forestry, mining and hydroelectric developments, and the threats they posed to fish and game species.

BC Nest Record Scheme: Initiated by the UBC Department of Zoology in 1955, the BC Nest Record Scheme is the largest and longest-running database of breeding bird nest records in North America. Its purpose is to collect information on birds' nests discovered by amateur ornithologists and birdwatchers across the province. It files and analyzes incoming records of nest locations, species, clutch sizes, and hatching and fledging success.

BC Parks Naturalist Program: Launched in 1957, the BC Parks Naturalist Program was a significant development in wildlife education. Growing from a pilot "nature house" in a makeshift tent to a system of nature houses, trails, interpretive signs and naturalist talks in most parts of the province by the late 1960s, the program introduced BC residents and visitors to local natural history and served as an incubator for new generations of naturalists, biologists and wildlife researchers. Because of budget cuts and a reorganization of BC Parks programs, the program was dismantled in the early 1980s.

BC Wildlife Federation (BCWF): Incorporated under the BC Societies Act in 1951, the BC Wildlife Federation became a registered charity in 1969 with a mission to conserve and protect British Columbia's wildlife and wild spaces for the benefit of all. Today, the BCWF is the province's leading wildlife conservation organization.

biodiversity: A contraction of "biological diversity" or "biotic diversity," the term "biodiversity" originated in the mid-1980s. Recognized as an indicator of resilience in natural systems, biodiversity refers to the variety and variability of animals, plants, fungi and micro-organisms found in a particular habitat or ecosystem.

Biodiversity BC: Formed in 2004 to develop a provincial biodiversity conservation strategy, Biodiversity BC is a partnership of government and conservation organizations. In 2007, following extensive consultation with over one hundred scientists and other experts, Biodiversity BC produced *Taking Nature's Pulse*, a comprehensive report on the status of biodiversity in British Columbia.

bounty: A bounty is a monetary reward for the removal of animals that are deemed harmful to livestock or game populations and other human interests (such as grain production). Bounties on predatory animals existed as a wildlife management tool for almost a century in BC, representing a significant expense for government and an important source of revenue for rural residents. Although bounties are now regarded as ineffective, inhumane and indiscriminate, they persist as a means of controlling the spread of invasive species.

Canada Land Inventory (CLI): Launched in 1963 and completed in 1976, the Canada Land Inventory was the first nationwide inventory of Canada's renewable resources. The CLI, which assessed the land's capacity to support agriculture, forestry, outdoor recreation and wildlife (sport fish and game) as a basis for land use planning, became a critical source of information for government assessment of land use proposals.

Canadian Wildlife Service (CWS): The Migratory Birds Convention Act of 1917 gave the federal government responsibility for protecting and managing migratory birds in Canada. This task was given to a small unit within the Department of the Interior. In 1947, this unit was expanded to become the Dominion Wildlife Service, which was renamed the Canadian Wildlife Service in 1950. Today, the CWS is responsible for three key areas of focus: migratory birds, species at risk, and habitat monitoring and protection on federal lands.

Carnation Creek Experimental Watershed study: Industry and BC Forest Service demands for "BC-based research" on fish-forestry interactions led to the first comprehensive baseline study of pre- and post-harvest watershed conditions. Beginning in 1970, a salmon stream on Vancouver Island became the site of the Carnation Creek Experimental Watershed, where multidisciplinary research examined the effects of forestry practices on watershed processes and salmon populations.

catch and release (C&R): A recreational fishing system where fish are released live into the water following capture, catch and release is a conservation practice developed to prevent the overharvest of fish stocks in the face of growing human populations and mounting ecological pressure. BC introduced its first C&R regulations for summer anglers in 1976, when steelhead numbers on five Vancouver Island streams became precarious. The practice has received criticism in recent years for the physical stress it places on fish that are often caught and released multiple times.

Christmas Bird Count: Started by the Audubon Society in 1900, the annual Christmas Bird Count is North America's longest-running citizen science project. With counts in more than two thousand localities throughout the Western Hemisphere and sightings logged by thousands of volunteer participants every year, the Christmas Bird Count produces one of the world's largest sets of wildlife survey data, which is used to assess bird population trends and distribution.

citizen science: The practice of public participation and collaboration in scientific research to increase scientific knowledge, citizen science uses the collective power of people to identify research questions, monitor species and habitats, collect and analyze data, make new discoveries, and develop technologies and applications that help scientists and communities to better understand and protect the environment.

classified waters: Introduced in 1990, the classified waters licensing system identified forty-two (later increased to fifty-two) highly productive steelhead and trout streams in wilderness or semi-wilderness settings for special management. The system caps the number of angling guide licences and client days ("rod-days") on each classified stream, giving priority to licensed resident anglers.

Coastal Fisheries/Forestry Guidelines: In 1988, after fifteen years of study and collaborative policy development, a committee of representatives from the provincial Ministries of Forests and Environment, the federal Department of Fisheries and Oceans, and coastal logging companies released the Coastal Fisheries/Forestry Guidelines.

Identifying four classes of fish-bearing waterways, the guidelines prescribed a corresponding scale of voluntary logging restrictions aimed at protecting fish habitat.

collaborative enforcement agreements: Memorandums of understanding between the Conservation Officer Service and individual band councils—known as collaborative enforcement agreements—are a tool to facilitate enforcement partnerships between First Nations authorities and the Conservation Officer Service. The agreements are flexible and First Nations–driven.

Columbia Department: Expanding into the Pacific Northwest when it merged with the North West Company in 1821, the Hudson's Bay Company controlled the fur trade in its immense "Columbia Department"—a 1.8-million-square-kilometre territory that stretched from Russian Alaska to Mexican California and from the Rockies to the Pacific. In 1825, the HBC established Fort Vancouver as the department's regional headquarters.

Columbia River Treaty: In response to flood protection concerns and the growing demand for hydroelectric power, the Canadian and US governments signed the Columbia River Treaty in 1961. The treaty provided Canada with an upfront payment for estimated future flood control benefits in the US and entitlement to half of the estimated electricity generated at the downstream American hydroelectric generating stations.

Commission of Conservation: Established in 1909 to provide Canadian governments with the most up-to-date scientific advice on the conservation of human and natural resources and to help curb the wastefulness of resource exploitation, the Commission of Conservation held a national conference called "Conservation of Game, Fur-Bearing Animals and Other Wild Life" in 1919.

Commission on Resources and Environment (CORE): Established by NDP Premier Mike Harcourt, the Commission on Resources and Environment was tasked with overseeing the development of a provincial land use strategy and consensus-based planning processes for four regions with entrenched land use conflicts: Vancouver Island, the Cariboo-Chilcotin, the East Kootenay, and West Kootenay-Boundary. Between 1992 and 1996, participating stakeholders negotiated agreements regarding regional and local land and resource uses. Although area First Nations generally declined to participate, and levels of agreement varied between regions, the CORE was significant in extending participatory regional planning processes over much of the province in the next two decades. Notable successes included the completion of plans for the central coast (also known as the Great Bear Rainforest) and the vast northern Muskwa-Kechika area. The CORE also initiated BC's Protected Areas Strategy, which doubled the province's protected areas from 6 per cent to 12 per cent of the land base by 2001.

conservancy: Negotiations with central coast First Nations over the Great Bear Rainforest Agreement in the early 2000s led to the creation of a new provincial "conservancy" designation in 2006—the first designation under the provincial Park Act to explicitly incorporate Indigenous rights. Jointly established and collaboratively managed by Indigenous nations and the province, conservancies provide a flexible mechanism for government-to-government collaboration in the establishment and management of new protected areas.

conservation: Originating in the context of unregulated exploitation of natural resources across North America in the late nineteenth century, "conservation" historically described the planned and efficient use of natural resources in order to ensure their permanence. Generally interchangeable with the idea of "wise use," conservation in practice aimed to stamp out wasteful practices and to sustainably allocate wildlife and other natural resources. Today, conservation practice draws on science and changing societal values to respond to the escalating effects of human activities on ecosystems.

conservation covenants: An alternative mechanism to extend conservation dollars, conservation covenants were incorporated into the BC Land Title Act in 1991. Covenants permitted governments and later non-government organizations to hold a partial interest in land. As voluntary, legally binding agreements between a landowner and a conservation organization, covenants attach conservation restrictions to the land title that carry through to subsequent owners. The conservation organization, in return, agrees to monitor the property to ensure the intentions of the covenant are maintained.

Conservation Data Centre (CDC): In 1991, the province established its celebrated Conservation Data Centre, a vital clearinghouse for scientific data on wildlife and ecosystems. Using an adapted species ranking system developed by the US-based Nature Conservancy, the CDC's conservation status rankings—publicized as the annual blue and red lists for threatened and endangered species—continue to serve as an important springboard to formal designation processes.

Coordinated Resource Management Planning (CRMP): Originating in Oregon in 1949, CRMP is a consensus-based planning process that aims to improve land management through collaborative decision-making among landowners, resource permit holders and other stakeholders within a specified watershed or local area. CRMP integrates technical expertise with local knowledge and experience, making local resource users key members of the planning team.

creative sentencing: In the early 1980s, federal and provincial courts provided conservation organizations with a flexible donation instrument through the use of creative sentencing options. These options allow the courts to allocate damages for environmental, fishery and wildlife offences to habitat rehabilitation projects, thus making environmental prosecutions more meaningful.

cumulative effects: Including such impacts as development pressures on a landscape, cumulative effects are changes to environmental values caused by the combined effect of past, present and potential future human activities and natural processes.

Declaration on the Rights of Indigenous Peoples Act: In November 2019, BC became the first Canadian jurisdiction to incorporate the United Nations Declaration on the Rights of Indigenous Peoples (UNDRIP) into law. The Declaration on the Rights of Indigenous Peoples Act establishes UNDRIP as the province's framework for reconciliation, as called for by the Truth and Reconciliation Commission's Calls to Action. The act aims to create a path forward that respects the human rights of Indigenous Peoples while introducing better transparency and predictability. It confirms UNDRIP as an international human rights instrument that can help interpret and apply Canadian law.

Douglas treaties: A series of fourteen land purchases from First Nations on Vancouver Island negotiated by Sir James Douglas between 1850 and 1854, the Douglas treaties constitute the only treaties signed during the colonial era in what would become the province of British Columbia. Disputed as deals made in bad faith—agreements were blank at the time of signing and it is not clear that Indigenous signatories understood what they were signing away—the lands were purchased in exchange for small amounts of cash, clothing and blankets as well as occupation of reserved lands and hunting and fishing rights on unoccupied ceded lands.

Ducks Unlimited Canada (DUC): Active for decades in the US and the Canadian Prairies, Ducks Unlimited established a BC office in Kamloops in 1968 with a mission to conserve, restore and manage wetlands and grasslands to benefit waterfowl, wildlife and people. DUC's successful practice of collaborating with landowners, tenant farmers, and government and non-government agencies to maintain and expand wetland habitat has served as a model for land conservancies operating across a wider range of threatened landscapes.

duty to consult: Integrated into the environmental assessment and regulatory review processes, the duty to consult is a statutory, contractual and common law obligation that the Crown must fulfil prior to taking actions or making decisions that may have consequences for the rights of Indigenous Peoples.

E&N Railway land grant: Vancouver Island's 1.9-million-acre Esquimalt & Nanaimo Railway land grant netted enormous wealth for railway and later logging companies when it was parcelled and sold in the 1880s, liquidated of its forest cover, and resold to incoming settlers. In 1905, the Canadian Pacific Railway paid just over $1 million for the E&N and $1.25 million for the remaining 566,580 hectares of land not yet sold.

Ecological Reserve Act: In 1971, the legislature unanimously approved the Ecological Reserve Act, making British Columbia the first province in Canada to formalize and give permanent protected status to ecological reserves.

ecoregion classification: Facilitating an understanding of the province's diversity of wildlife habitat and small-scale ecosystems, ecoregion classification identified boundaries and relationships between terrestrial and marine ecosystems across five geographic scales. Adopted by the Ministry of Environment in 1985 and periodically revised, the system continues to serve as a foundation for research initiatives and biodiversity protection in BC. (A similar tool, the Biogeoclimatic Ecosystem Classification [BEC] system, was developed by Dr. V.J. Krajina in UBC's botany department. In the 1970s, the Ministry of Forests adopted the BEC system as a method to classify and manage sites on an ecosystem-specific basis.)

ecosystem-based management: Integrating biological, social and economic factors into a comprehensive strategy aimed at protecting and enhancing sustainability, diversity and productivity of natural resources, ecosystem-based management is an adaptive approach to managing human activities that seeks to ensure the coexistence of healthy, fully functioning ecosystems and human communities.

endemic: Species that are endemic are natural to, native to, confined to or widespread within a place or population. Endemic plant and animal species are found only in a limited, restricted and defined area or habitat. Also referred to as indigenous or locally unique, endemic species are isolated in some way (by geography or habitat) and have difficulty spreading to other areas. Often vulnerable, endemic animals and plants are key to their ecosystems and can be a gauge when measuring the state of health of a territory.

Environmental Farm Plan (EFP): Designed to promote biodiversity on farm properties and protect riparian areas from livestock damage, the federal-provincial EFP offers free and confidential consultations with trained agrologists to help farmers and ranchers reduce the environmental effects of their operations. Established in the 1990s and widely embraced by the agricultural community, the program also provides funding for environmental improvements, such as fencing riparian areas or revitalizing biodiversity-rich wetlands.

Environment and Land Use Act: Passed by BC's Social Credit government in 1971, the Environment and Land Use Act (together with the Ecological Reserve Act of the same year) constituted the first of the province's environmental laws. These laws gave cabinet the power to override all other legislation and to place a moratorium on land alienations in a specific area to allow for consultation and planning.

extirpation: Also known as locally extinct, an extirpated species or population no longer exists within a certain geographical location. Unlike extinction—where a species no longer exists anywhere—extirpation means that at least one other population of the species still exists in other areas.

fair chase: The sportsmanlike idea of fair chase—espoused by the rod and gun clubs and fish and game protection associations that proliferated after 1890—was intended to ensure that humans have no unfair advantage over wild game, by balancing the skills and equipment of the hunter with an animal's ability to escape. Historically, sport hunters used this rhetoric to present sport hunting as morally superior to subsistence hunting, where efficiency was considered more important than fairness.

Federal-Provincial Wildlife Conferences: Initiated in the mid-1930s, these annual conferences continue to shape the agenda for wildlife research and management responses at both the federal and provincial levels.

Federation of BC Naturalists: Reflecting an enormous growth in local naturalist club memberships and their desire for coordinated advocacy to protect threatened species and habitats, the Federation of BC Naturalists (now BC Nature) was formally established in 1969. With nine founding clubs, it marked the advent of the organized naturalist group and meant that wildlife conservation was no longer the sole dominion of hunters and anglers.

Fisheries Act: Enacted in 1868, the Fisheries Act is one of Canada's oldest and most important environment laws. It gives the federal government, through the Department of Fisheries and Oceans, the power to conserve and protect fish and fish habitat across the country. Although the Canadian government holds jurisdiction over all marine, coastal and inland fisheries, authority to oversee freshwater recreational fisheries in BC was delegated to the province in 1937. Because the act historically prioritized commercial fishing operations and was often deployed to displace the governance systems, fisheries (particularly salmon) and economies of Indigenous Peoples, the Fisheries Act has had a disproportionately negative effect on First Nations. In 2019, a new and strengthened federal Fisheries Act passed into law. This modernized Act offers more stringent protections for fish and fish habitat and upholds the rights of Indigenous Peoples by requiring consideration of adverse effects of decisions made under the legislation on their collective, constitutional right to fish for food, social and ceremonial purposes.

Forest and Range Practices Act (FRPA): Introduced in 2003, the FRPA scrapped many of the previous prescriptive rules of BC's Forest Practices Code in favour of a results-based system of forest management. The new act required tenure holders to prepare a forest stewardship plan consistent with the government's environmental objectives. However, with few obligations and little to no government supervision, monitoring or evaluation, tenure holders were afforded a high degree of latitude in how they managed their logging operations.

Forest Practices Code: Designed to achieve stewardship of forests based on an ethic of respect for the land, BC's 1994 Forest Practices Code is recognized as the environmental assessment of forestry activities. Acknowledging the requirement for active management and constant evaluation and balancing of values to meet the economic and cultural needs of people and communities, the Forest Practices Code provided the tools, mechanisms and legislated authority to achieve sustainable forest use. It was replaced with the Forest and Range Practices Act (FRPA) in 2003.

Forest Renewal BC (FRBC): From 1994 to 2002 Forest Renewal BC, a Crown corporation, delivered a variety of programs aimed at supporting the forests and forest industry of British Columbia. As a forest enhancement agency, FRBC helped companies offset forestry job losses resulting from reduced timber production through silviculture and watershed restoration projects.

Fraser Canyon War: Triggered by the Fraser River Gold Rush of 1858, the Fraser Canyon War was a military-style conflict waged by encroaching miners in response to scattered Nlaka'pamux defensive attacks. After eight days of fighting and the loss of dozens of Indigenous people's lives, a truce was called when the Nlaka'pamux—under threat of further bloodshed—agreed to grant miners access to their territories and resources.

free miner's certificate: A "free entry" mining system was introduced in 1859 to allow any person sixteen years or older to obtain a free miner's certificate for a nominal fee. The certificate gave the "free miner" the right to freely enter onto and stake a claim on any un-staked area of Crown land—including private property and First Nations territories—and enjoy the exclusive right to conduct exploration and development over their claim. The certificate also granted prospectors unlimited rights to fish and hunt.

game reserves: Game reserves are designated areas intended to replenish game species populations by protecting them from hunting and animal predation. Once used to describe the private hunting estates financed and managed by wealthy sport hunters, game reserves became a category of provincial government protection through an amendment to the Game Protection Act in 1908. Local game protection associations and American big-game hunters played an important role in the establishment of game reserves in the East Kootenay and Lillooet districts, both of which were later incorporated into provincial parks.

Green Belt Protection Fund Act: The Green Belt Protection Fund Act of 1972 enabled the BC government to purchase private lands and protect them from urban sprawl.

Guide Outfitters Association of British Columbia: Established in 1966, this organization gave guide outfitters a provincial platform for their interests, including concerns about the impact of wildlife habitat loss and degradation on the industry.

guide territories: Guiding licences were first issued in 1913, but it was not until the late 1940s that guiding territories were established. These territories initially limited guides to a radius of eleven kilometres from the centre of their operation. This gave way to the block system in the mid-1950s, which still exists today. Now, each guide is allotted one block, which generally includes one or two watersheds with mountain crests serving as boundaries.

Habitat Conservation Trust Foundation (HCTF): A non-profit charitable foundation, the Habitat Conservation Trust Foundation came into existence because its major contributors—hunters, anglers, trappers and guide outfitters—were willing to pay a surcharge on their annual licences to support wildlife conservation work in the province. By funding conservation projects and educating and engaging the public about BC's natural assets, the HCTF helps to improve the conservation outcomes of fish and wildlife and the habitats in which they live.

HADD: Amendments to the federal Fisheries Act in 1977 strengthened habitat protection by prohibiting "harmful alteration, disruption or destruction of fish habitat" unless authorized by the federal government. The HADD provision became one of Canada's most powerful legal protections for wildlife habitat.

Hell's Gate slides: In 1913, CN railway construction in the Fraser River Canyon triggered a series of landslides that deposited tons of rock into the river at Hell's Gate. The slides narrowed the river channel and increased its flow and turbulence, effectively barring salmon from their upriver spawning grounds for three decades.

Hudson's Bay Company (HBC): Chartered on May 2, 1670, the Hudson's Bay Company is the oldest incorporated merchandising company in the English-speaking world. A fur trading business for most of its history, with exclusive trading rights in the territory traversed by rivers flowing in Hudson Bay, the HBC's past is entwined with the colonization of British North America and the development of Canada.

hunter-naturalist: A mutually inclusive idea that developed in the early 1900s was that good hunters—by virtue of their time spent in nature and their necessary study of the natural world—make good naturalists. Because hunting experience fosters a profound and practical understanding and appreciation of nature, the best collectors were understood to be, at the same time, the best natural scientists and conservationists.

Indigenous food fishery: Fisheries regulations introduced in 1888 specifically prohibited Indigenous fishing without leases or licences from the Minister of Marine and Fisheries, despite a centuries-old flourishing salmon economy. Indigenous fishers were permitted to fish with drift nets and spears, but only to provide food for themselves—not for sale, barter or traffic. Restrictions increased in the 1910s, requiring Indigenous fishers to acquire a permit to fish for food. Because Indigenous river fishing occurred near the end of the annual migration of salmon to their spawning grounds, food fishery allocations were often the first to be reduced or eliminated in the name of conservation. Not until the landmark *R v. Sparrow* decision in 1990 would the allocation hierarchy be reversed to privilege the right of Indigenous people to fish for food, social and ceremonial purposes over the interests of commercial and sport fisheries.

Indigenous management: Indigenous management derives its principles, systems and procedures from the natural taxonomies used by Indigenous Peoples to organize their thoughts and actions, construct their realities and design their future, including the economic allocation of natural resources and regulation of human access according to hereditary ownership and authority over a particular territory.

Indigenous Protected and Conserved Areas (IPCAs): Indigenous Protected and Conserved Areas are lands and waters where Indigenous governments have the primary role in protecting and conserving ecosystems through Indigenous laws, governance and knowledge systems. Although they vary in terms of their governance and management objectives, IPCAs share three essential elements: they are Indigenous-led, they represent a long-term commitment to conservation and they elevate Indigenous rights and responsibilities. Indigenous nations determine the lands and waters they want to include in IPCAs, often through extensive community planning.

Indigenous stewardship: Including detailed prescriptions for how the land, waters and wildlife are to be harvested, shared and respected, Indigenous stewardship is an ethical code that embodies the careful and responsible planning and management of resources by Indigenous Peoples and the inherent obligation to answer for their actions to their own people and to the ecological and spiritual authority of the territories they manage.

International Fur Seal Convention: The Convention between the United States and Other Powers Providing for the Preservation and Protection of Fur Seals—known as the Fur Seal Treaty of 1911—was the first international treaty to address the issue of wildlife conservation. Designed to give the resource five years to recover, the convention ended a lucrative and culturally significant occupation for the Nuu-chah-nulth and other coastal First Nations.

land alienation: Land alienation, or the alienation of land, refers to the sale or other disposal of the rights to land. Historically, the colonial government acquired lands from Indigenous Peoples on parts of Vancouver Island, and the Canadian government acquired lands in BC's northeast. The province's decision not to recognize Aboriginal title meant that Indigenous nations across the majority of British Columbia never signed land surrender treaties. Despite these circumstances, the provincial government claimed ownership of these lands and the right to dispose of them for private development. Today, the Crown continues to alienate land through leases and sales to such interests as cattle ranchers; logging, mining and development companies; private individuals; and land trusts.

land trusts are non-governmental organizations that acquire fish and wildlife habitats for the purpose of conservation. As non-profit, registered charities, these organizations raise funds to acquire land or interests in land to protect a property's biological features. The trademark of a land trust is the direct action it takes to protect the land base, which it holds in trust for future generations. Land trusts are supported by the community, through memberships, donations and volunteers, and can be local, regional, provincial, national or even international in scope.

limited entry hunting (LEH): The limited entry hunting system allocates hunting opportunities through a random draw in areas where hunter demand exceeds the availability of a particular species. First introduced for grizzly bears in the Kootenays and southern Interior, the LEH system gives wildlife managers greater control over the number of hunters and the type and sex of species hunted in a particular area during a particular time.

McKenna-McBride Commission: A joint federal-provincial project to adjust the acreage of Indigenous reserves in British Columbia, the 1912 Royal Commission on Indian Affairs in British Columbia, or the McKenna-McBride Commission, recommended cutting 47,000 acres of valuable land from existing reserves and adding 87,000 acres of less valuable land. Indigenous leaders protested, petitioned and boycotted hearings, eventually forming the Allied Tribes of British Columbia in 1916 to represent their case to the public and the government.

Migratory Birds Convention Act (MBCA): The Advisory Board on Wild Life Protection, established in 1909 with a mandate to consider wildlife protection needs, signed the MBCA into law in 1917. In response to concerns on both sides of the Canada-US border regarding the uncontrolled hunting of waterfowl and shorebirds, the act contained regulations to protect migratory birds and their eggs and nests from destruction by wood harvesting, hunting, trafficking and commercialization.

migratory bird sanctuaries: Stemming from the Migratory Birds Convention Act and managed by the Canadian Wildlife Service, migratory bird sanctuaries—which exist only in Canada—help to protect migratory birds by conserving their habitat and making it illegal to hunt or disturb them.

multiple use: Multiple use refers to the use of land for more than one purpose. To be effective, these uses—which can include logging, mining, grazing, farming, gas and oil extraction, recreation, watershed conservation and wildlife habitat—must be managed in a manner that will conserve the basic land resource itself. The theory of multiple use enables sustainable land management that balances a growing list of stakeholders (industry, consumers, local communities, special interest groups and future generations) while at the same time protecting a wide array of natural, cultural and historical resources.

myth of superabundance: The belief that natural wealth is so abundant it cannot possibly be exhausted. This myth holds that the earth has more than sufficient natural resources to satisfy humanity's needs and, no matter how much of these resources are used, the planet will replenish the supply.

National Wildlife Area: In 1968, the Canadian Wildlife Service became the first government agency to implement wildlife habitat protection measures in British Columbia. Its National Wildlife Area program enabled federal acquisition of wildlife habitat under the 1973 Canada Wildlife Act with the purpose of conserving essential habitats for migratory birds and other wildlife species, especially endangered wildlife.

Native Brotherhood of British Columbia (NBBC): A membership organization representing First Nations fishermen, tendermen and shoreworkers, the NBBC was established in 1931 and is recognized as Canada's oldest active First Nations organization.

Natural History Society of British Columbia: In March 1890, BC Provincial Museum curator John Fannin invited forty "gentlemen naturalists" with interests in the study of birds, insects, plants and geological history to form the province's first natural history society. Based in Victoria, the society promoted a systematic approach to the study of BC's natural features and acted as an independent auxiliary to the Provincial Museum. It operated until the early years of World War I.

Nature Conservancy of Canada (NCC): Founded in the 1960s, the Nature Conservancy of Canada is Canada's leading national land conservation organization. A private, non-profit organization, it partners with individuals, corporations, foundations, Indigenous communities and other non-profit organizations and governments at all levels to protect the natural areas that sustain Canada's plants and wildlife by securing properties and managing them for the long term. In 1974, the conservancy began working on the Mud Bay project in Surrey, its first conservation site in British Columbia.

Nature Trust of British Columbia (NTBC): A non-profit land conservation organization, the National Second Century Fund of British Columbia (now the Nature Trust of British Columbia) was established in 1971 to acquire and protect private lands of high wildlife value. Given the limitations of statutory protections such as parks and ecological reserves, the NTBC provided an alternative path that made it possible to build a treasury of wild natural areas to conserve iconic wildlife and species at risk.

old-growth forests: Exhibiting unique ecological features, old-growth forests—also known as primary, virgin, late seral, primeval or first-growth forests—are forests that have attained great age without significant disturbance. As timber harvests increased throughout the 1980s, scientists came to recognize the significance of the province's dwindling old-growth forests to particular wildlife species, making them a special category of concern.

Old Growth Strategy: Acknowledging the need to better accommodate wildlife and ecological considerations into forestry planning, BC developed the first Old Growth Strategy in 1992. Defining the significance of old growth for the province's biological diversity, it set out two methods of protection: the creation of representative old-growth forest reserves and the modification of forestry practices to create or maintain old-growth characteristics in managed forests.

Oregon Treaty: An agreement between Britain and the United States that formalized the border between the US and British North America west of the Rocky Mountains, the Oregon Treaty of June 15, 1846, resolved an important dispute between the two nations. Extending the border along the 49th parallel to the Pacific Ocean and down "the middle" of the channel that separates Vancouver Island from the mainland, it had the effect of reducing competition for furs and pressure on fur-bearer populations.

Pacific Estuary Conservation Program: Pooling the funds and expertise of federal and provincial government agencies and non-government organizations, the Pacific Estuary Conservation Program was established in 1987 to acquire and manage coastal estuaries and upland habitat.

paddlewheeler: Propelled by steam-driven paddlewheels, these passenger boats operated on major rivers and lakes across the province for almost a century, from the 1830s until the 1910s. Preceding the railways, they played an important role in opening unroaded areas in the province's interior to commercial and sport hunters, guide outfitters, settlers and provisioners.

Pollution Control Act: Persistent lobbying by the BC Wildlife Federation and commercial fishing interests—in concert with a hotly debated sewage treatment plant proposed for Iona Island on the Fraser River—led to the Pollution Control Act of 1956, the province's first concerted effort to mitigate sources of water pollution.

preservation: Preservation refers to protecting lands, waters and wildlife from destructive human uses. The term acquired elitist associations beginning in the late nineteenth century, when game preservation societies sought to protect fish and wildlife not for everyone's use but rather for the use of what were considered to be a more disciplined class of sport anglers and hunters. These exclusive connotations of game preservation were carried through in early twentieth-century provincial game legislation, which aimed to protect game species by placing progressive restrictions on local and Indigenous subsistence and commercial hunting while promoting the expansion of sport hunting.

professional reliance: One of the central principles of the 2003 Forest and Range Practices Act, professional reliance reduced government oversight by delegating the planning and assessment authority of public officials to credentialed professionals employed by industry (foresters, biologists and hydrologists).

Protected Areas Strategy (PAS): Released in mid-1993, the Protected Areas Strategy provided a broader provincial context for evaluating regional protected area proposals. It employed a science-based approach that protected representative examples of British Columbia's diverse ecosystems and cultural heritage, committing the province to the goal of doubling the amount of protected areas across its land base from 6 per cent to 12 per cent by 2000.

public trust doctrine: The public trust doctrine is an essential element of North American wildlife law. Considered the foundation of the North American model of wildlife conservation, the doctrine establishes the government's trustee relationship to hold and manage wildlife, fish and waterways for the benefit of the public.

R v. Sparrow: The first court case to test the application and significance of the Constitution Act's section 35, which recognized existing Aboriginal and treaty rights, *R v. Sparrow* landed a groundbreaking decision in 1990 on behalf of Indigenous plaintiff Ronald Sparrow. Finding that historic government regulations, including the Fisheries Act, did not extinguish Aboriginal rights, the decision confirmed the right of Indigenous people to fish for food, social and ceremonial purposes (subject only to valid conservation measures) over the interests of non-Indigenous commercial and sport fishers.

reconciliation: The Truth and Reconciliation Commission of Canada defines reconciliation as an ongoing process of establishing and maintaining respectful relationships. Based on the recognition of rights, respect and partnership, the province is building a renewed relationship with First Nations as the latter work to secure rights to land and reclaim management authority over fish and wildlife habitat within their traditional territories. Using shared concerns around plants, animals and habitat preservation as a springboard for collaboration, federal and provincial wildlife agencies and First Nations governments are forging pathways to reconciliation through the development of government-to-government wildlife conservation and allocation agreements.

referral system: Consultation between resource agencies started in the 1950s with the BC Forest Service accepting input from federal fisheries officials in its review of timber cutting permit applications. Initially limited to fish habitat considerations, this "referral system" was eventually extended to provincial wildlife officials in 1970.

Resource Folio Planning System: The Resource Folio Planning System was the province's first comprehensive land use planning tool and a forerunner to today's GIS (geographic information system) mapping. The system was created by regional wildlife managers in Prince George and supported by BC's Land Use Committee, which was established in 1969 to improve coordination among resource ministries and establish land use policy guidelines. Drawing on data from the Canada Land Inventory, the Resource Folio Planning System produced layered, hand-coloured maps of resource capabilities to inform decision-making.

rotenone: Used as both an effective insecticide and piscicide (fish toxin), rotenone is a naturally occurring compound found in the roots of several plants. Fisheries biologists started using this broad-spectrum poison in 1953 to enhance sport fisheries in small inland lakes by exterminating undesirable fish species and reintroducing desired "sport" fish populations such as rainbow and cutthroat trout.

Salmonid Enhancement Program: This program, established in 1977, was a joint federal-provincial initiative with the goal of doubling Pacific salmon runs on the BC coast. It provided some support for habitat rehabilitation and community stewardship, but most of the funds went to the construction and maintenance of twenty salmon hatcheries on the coast and inland rivers.

Scientific Panel for Sustainable Forest Practices in Clayoquot Sound: Implementing a consensus-seeking approach and comprising Nuu-chah-nulth representatives and a diverse group of specialists in fisheries, biodiversity, ethnobotany, hydrology, engineering and worker safety, the seventeen-member Scientific Panel for Sustainable Forest Practices in Clayoquot Sound (1993–95)—commonly known as the Clayoquot Sound Scientific Panel—was charged with developing a system for sustainable ecosystem management that represented the best application of scientific and traditional knowledge and local experience.

seral stage: The seral stage is a phase in the sequential development of a climax community, the "seres" being the ecological succession of relatively transitory plant communities in an ecosystem. In an unmanaged forest ecosystem, for example, this advancement would begin at bare ground and culminate (climax) in old growth. Although the word "stage" implies a simple linear sequence, succession is actually a cyclical continuum with overlapping seral stages. Natural disturbances such as fire, windthrow, landslides and insect outbreaks create forests containing a full range of seral stages.

shifting baseline: People tend to regard the natural world they grew up in as the "normal state of nature," measuring declining natural abundance or integrity against that baseline. This baseline shifts, as each new generation redefines what is "natural" or normal; thus, longer-term declines in ecosystems or species may go unnoticed.

Species at Risk Act (SARA): Under SARA, federal legislation enacted in 2002, species designated as endangered, threatened or extirpated are protected by two central provisions: the first prohibits the harm, collection or trade in designated species, and the second prohibits the destruction of a species' "residence," such as a nest or den. These basic prohibitions apply only to aquatic species, migratory birds under the Migratory Birds Convention Act and species found on federal land.

stewardship: Stewardship is an ethic and practice to carefully and responsibly manage natural resources and ecosystems for the benefit of current and future generations. It has been used to describe the complex and varied relationships that Indigenous Peoples held, and continue to hold, with the lands and waterways that constitute their traditional territories. Beginning in the 1990s, the term came to describe initiatives by conservation organizations, ranchers and farmers to voluntarily care for their properties with the long-term health of wildlife and ecosystems in mind. Since 2000, it has been associated with efforts by First Nations to reclaim traditional roles of monitoring, protecting and caring for territorial lands and the fish and wildlife that depend on them.

sustainable forest management certification: A best practice in forestry, this certification addresses the ecological, cultural, social and economic aspects of sustainable forest management and provides assurance that timber originates from legal and well-managed sources.

sustained yield: A sustained yield is the extraction level of a resource that does not exceed growth. It also refers to a management system that ensures the replacement of a harvested resource (timber or fish, for example) by regrowth or reproduction before the next harvest.

threatened and endangered species: Endangered species are those that have become so rare they are in danger of becoming extinct. Threatened species are those likely to become endangered within the foreseeable future throughout all or a significant portion of their range.

trapline registration system: In 1925, British Columbia introduced new legislation requiring the registration of all traplines. The first of its kind in North America, the registration system introduced a new kind of land tenure in the province. Registered residents received exclusive rights to trap and harvest fur-bearing mammals on defined parcels of land and, in exchange, assumed de facto responsibility for the conservation of fur-bearers on their territories. Loosely modelled on Indigenous stewardship systems, the system nevertheless imposed a colonial view of land use that many Indigenous leaders rejected.

Treaty 8: Prompted by the Klondike gold rush and the influx of prospectors to the north, Treaty 8 was signed in 1899 by the Crown and First Nations of the Lesser Slave Lake area; at roughly 841,500 square kilometres, it is the largest of Canada's numbered treaties. Written terms provided reserves, annuities and the right to hunt, trap and fish on ceded lands, except those that might be required for settlement, mining, lumbering, trading or other initiatives. Treaty 8 was the last historical treaty signed between the Crown and First Nations in BC until the Nisga'a Final Agreement, the province's first "modern" treaty, was signed in 1998.

two-eyed seeing: Also known as "walking on two legs," the approach of two-eyed seeing is a hallmark of Indigenous guardians and land management programs across Canada and internationally. Originating in the Mi'kmaq language, two-eyed seeing or "etuaptmumk" is a process of learning to see with one eye from the perspective of Indigenous knowledge, and from the other eye from the perspective of Western knowledge, bringing both perspectives together for the benefit of all.

two rivers policy: BC Premier W.A.C. Bennett's two rivers policy in the 1960s tied together the province's economic and hydroelectric development by damming two of British Columbia's major rivers: the Columbia, which would provide power to growing industries throughout the province, and the Peace, which would fuel northern expansion and development.

ungulate: An ungulate is a hoofed mammal. Wild ungulates in British Columbia include woodland caribou, moose, elk, deer, mountain goat, bighorn and thinhorn sheep.

United Nations Declaration on the Rights of Indigenous Peoples (UNDRIP): Establishing a universal framework of minimum standards for the survival, dignity and well-being of the Indigenous Peoples of the world, UNDRIP was adopted by the UN General Assembly on September 13, 2007. The declaration elaborates on existing human rights standards and fundamental freedoms as they apply to the specific situation of Indigenous Peoples and is the most comprehensive international instrument on the rights of those peoples. In Canada, UNDRIP came into force at the federal level on June 21, 2021.

variable retention: A harvesting technique that retains aspects of the original forest at the time of harvest, variable retention allows for greater habitat and wildlife diversity. Leaving behind patches of high-value habitat and maintaining some elements of structural complexity, the method aims to produce future forest stands that more closely resemble conditions that develop after natural disturbances such as wildfire, wind and flood.

voluntary private land stewardship programs: Beginning in the early 1990s, government and non-government partners turned to voluntary private land stewardship programs—incentives and supports to help landowners maintain and improve wildlife habitat on their properties—to address conservation concerns on private lands. By working with landowners, some of the same conservation goals as land acquisition could be achieved without the high cost of habitat purchases.

wildlife commons: The idea of the wildlife commons refers to gifts of nature—air, land, oceans and wildlife—that are accessible to all members of a society. The concept arises from the notion that some sources of wealth, like natural resources, belong to everyone and that these community assets must be actively protected and managed for the good of all.

wildlife management: Wildlife management refers to a prescription to maintain bio-diversity by balancing the needs of wildlife with the needs of people using the best available science. It is a management process that influences interactions among and between wildlife, habitats and humans to achieve predefined objectives.

wildlife sink: Ecologists use the theoretical model of "wildlife sink" to describe how variation in habitat quality may affect the population growth or decline of organisms. For example, clearcut logging produces an abundance of habitat for certain species for a short period, but these species then experience sharp population declines when single-aged stands mature and canopies close.

wildlife-viewing program: In response to expanding public interest in non-consumptive relationships with wildlife and concerns about human-wildlife conflict, the province developed its first wildlife-viewing program in 1988. In partnership with the Federation of BC Naturalists and in consultation with regional wildlife biologists, the initiative produced informative brochures identifying wildlife-viewing sites, species and viewing seasons across the province and introduced wildlife enthusiasts to the principles of wildlife safety and viewing ethics.

Notes

Introduction

1 The coat of arms received royal assent in 1987. Government of British Columbia, "British Columbia's Coat of Arms," accessed June 14, 2022, http://gov.bc.ca.

2 Paul Bramadat and Patricia O'Connell Killen, "Conclusion: Religion at the Edge of a Continent," in *Religion at the Edge: Nature, Spirituality, and Secularity in the Pacific Northwest*, ed. Paul Bramadat, Patricia O'Connell Killen and Sarah Wilkins-Laflamme (Vancouver, UBC Press, 2022), 252.

3 Robert J. Muckle, *The First Nations of British Columbia: An Anthropological Overview*, 3rd ed. (Vancouver: UBC Press, 2014); Canada, Department of Crown-Indigenous Relations and Northern Affairs, "List of First Nations: British Columbia," accessed February 9, 2023, https://services.sac-isc.gc.ca/fnp/; Government of British Columbia, "Writing Guide for Indigenous Content," 2021, accessed February 9, 2023, http://gov.bc.ca.

4 Fred L. Bunnell and R.G. Williams, "Subspecies and Diversity—The Spice of Life or Prophet of Doom," in *Threatened and Endangered Species and Habitats in British Columbia and the Yukon*, ed. Richard Stace-Smith, Lois Johns and Paul Joslin (Victoria: BC Ministry of Environment, 1980), 249. The province's diverse ecosystems are home to 1,138 species of vertebrates including 488 bird species, 142 mammals, 18 reptiles, 22 amphibians and 468 fish. M.A. Austin et al., eds., *Taking Nature's Pulse: The Status of Biodiversity in British Columbia* (Victoria: Biodiversity BC, 2008).

5 The province is home to almost all of the world's mountain caribou and more than half of its mountain goats; it provides breeding habitat for 80 per cent of the world's Cassin's auklets. Austin et al., *Taking Nature's Pulse*.

6 Out of a total of 571 Canadian bird and mammal species, 405 breed in British Columbia. Species diversity is considerably lower in other provinces. Manitoba ranks second to BC, with 341 breeding bird and mammal species, and Ontario third with 340. Bunnell and Williams, "Subspecies and Diversity," 255; BC Ministry of Environment, *Environmental Trends in British Columbia: 2007* (Victoria: BC Ministry of Environment, n.d.), http://gov.bc.ca.

7 Bunnell and Williams, "Subspecies and Diversity," 249.

8 BC Ministry of Environment, *Environmental Trends*. The province's sixteen distinct biogeoclimatic zones include twelve major forest ecosystems, a grassland ecosystem and three kinds of alpine ecosystems. Austin et al., *Taking Nature's Pulse*.

9 Austin et al., *Taking Nature's Pulse*.

10 In 1911, BC and Ontario were the only provinces with more than 50 per cent of their populations living in an urban setting. By 2001, almost 85 per cent of the BC population lived in urban areas (compared with 79.7 per cent for the

country as a whole). In 1971, over 60 per cent of BC's population occupied the southwestern portion of the province; this figure had climbed to over 70 per cent by 2001. Margaret Ormsby, *British Columbia: A History* (Toronto: Macmillan, 1958); Statistics Canada, "Province of British Columbia," *Focus on Geography Series, 2011 Census*, Statistics Canada Catalogue no. 98-310-XWE2011004, last modified March 26, 2019, http://statcan.gc.ca.

11 BC historian Margaret Ormbsy was among the first to recognize these dynamics, in her 1958 book, *British Columbia: A History*. On these dynamics in relation to wildlife management, see Alan Chambers, "Toward a Synthesis of Mountains, People, and Institutions," *Landscape Planning* 6, no. 2 (August 1979): 109–26.

12 Crown land includes "not only upland but also the freshwater, estuarine, and marine foreshore and lands covered by water." R.H. Ahrens, "Crown Land Allocation and Management: The Implications for Wildlife," in *British Columbia Land for Wildlife: Past, Present, Future*, ed. J.C. Day and Richard Stace-Smith (Victoria: BC Ministry of Environment, Fish and Wildlife Branch, 1982), 52.

13 Rock covers almost 10 per cent of the province, the majority occurring in alpine areas. Richard Cannings and Sydney Cannings, *British Columbia: A Natural History*, 3rd ed. (Vancouver: Greystone Books, 2015); M.A. Austin and A. Eriksson, *The Biodiversity Atlas of British Columbia* (Victoria: Biodiversity BC, March 2009), 14.

14 Winifred B. Kessler, "The Canadian Constitution and Wildlife Policy," in *North American Wildlife Policy and Law*, ed. Bruce D. Leopold, Winifred B. Kessler and James L. Cummins (Missoula, MT: Boone and Crockett Club, 2018), 72.

15 The slogan gathered popularity in the late 1970s, when tourism promoters and automobile dealers distributed it on bumper stickers and spare tire covers to market the province's natural attractions. Destination BC, a provincially funded Crown corporation, continues to use the slogan in their logo to support BC's tourism industry. https://hellobc.com/, accessed July 16, 2021; Ben Bradley, personal communication, July 19, 2021.

16 Alan MacEachern, "The Conservation Movement," in *Canada: Confederation to Present*, ed. Chris Hackett and Bob Hesketh (Edmonton: Chinook Multimedia, 2003), n.p.

17 Daniel Pauly, "Anecdotes and the Shifting Baseline Syndrome of Fisheries," *Trends in Ecology & Evolution* 10, no. 10 (1995): 430; J.B. MacKinnon, *The Once and Future World: Nature as It Was, as It Is, as It Could Be* (Boston: Houghton Mifflin Harcourt, 2013), 17–18.

18 See, for example, the Shifting Baselines Ocean Media Project, accessed July 16, 2021, http://shiftingbaselines.org.

19 This definition is drawn from Cathy Beaumont, "Stewardship Works! A Core Funding Model" (Workshop Report, Wosk Centre for Dialogue, Vancouver, May 23, 2007). As Howard Paish points out, historically the term "steward" referred to someone who looked after private property or resources on behalf of a private owner. In its current usage, the term refers to common property resources

that are owned by all and, at least theoretically, managed in everyone's interest. Paish, "An Overview of Fish and Wildlife Stewardship in British Columbia" (unpublished draft report, Stewardship Centre for BC Steering Committee, Vancouver, June 2005).

20 MacEachern, "Conservation Movement."

21 MacEachern, "Conservation Movement."

22 Roderick Haig-Brown, *The Living Land: An Account of the Natural Resources of British Columbia* (Toronto: Macmillan, 1961).

23 C. Meine, M. Soule and R.F. Noss, "'A Mission-Driven Discipline': The Growth of Conservation Biology," *Conservation Biology* 20, no. 3 (2006): 631–51.

24 Aldo Leopold, *Game Management* (New York: Scribner's, 1933; repr. Madison: University of Wisconsin Press, 1987).

25 See, for example, John A. Livingston, *The Fallacy of Wildlife Conservation* (Toronto: McClelland & Stewart, 1981); Farley Mowat, *Never Cry Wolf* (Toronto: McClelland & Stewart, 1963).

Chapter 1 | Wildlife Stewardship among Indigenous Peoples before 1774

1 Wilson Duff, *The Indian History of British Columbia: The Impact of the White Man*, 3rd ed. (Victoria: Royal BC Museum, 1997), 57; Robin Fisher, *Contact and Conflict: Indian-European Relations in British Columbia, 1774–1890*, 2nd ed. (Vancouver: UBC Press, 1992).

2 E. Richard Atleo (Umeek), *Tsawalk: A Nuu-Chah-Nulth Worldview* (Vancouver: UBC Press, 202), 76.

3 On the influence of the commercial fur trade and Christian missionaries in the nineteenth century, the Ridingtons emphasize that neither traders nor priests lived with the people; traders stayed at the posts and priests "came through about once a year to perform baptisms and marriages." Dane-zaa children, furthermore, did not attend school until 1950. Robin Ridington and Jillian Ridington, in collaboration with elders of the Dane-zaa First Nations, *Where Happiness Dwells: A History of the Dane-zaa First Nations* (Vancouver: UBC Press, 2013), 5–6.

4 Neil J. Sterritt, *Mapping My Way Home: A Gitxsan History* (Smithers, BC: Creekstone Press, 2017), 259; Charles R. Menzies, *People of the Saltwater: An Ethnography of Git lax m'oon* (Lincoln: University of Nebraska Press, 2016), 44; Atleo, *Tsawalk*, 76–81.

5 Atleo, *Tsawalk*, 81.

6 Chief Charles Jones with Stephen Bosustow, *Queesto: Pacheenaht Chief by Birthright* (Nanaimo: Theytus Books, 1981); Harry Robinson and Wendy Wickwire, *Write It On Your Heart: The Epic World of an Okanagan Storyteller* (Vancouver: Talonbooks/Theytus, 1989); Chief Earl Maquinna George, *Living on the Edge: Nuu-Chah-Nulth History from an Ahousaht Chief's Perspective* (Winlaw, BC: Sono Nis Press, 2003). See also Margaret B. Blackman, *During*

My Time: Florence Edenshaw Davidson, a Haida Woman (Seattle: University of Washington Press, 1982).

7 Marianne Ignace and Ronald E. Ignace, *Secwépemc People, Land, and Laws: Yerí7 Stsqeys-kucw* (Montreal and Kingston: McGill-Queen's University Press, 2017); Ridington and Ridington, *Where Happiness Dwells*; Richard Daly, *Our Box Was Full: An Ethnography for the* Delgamuukw *Plaintiffs* (Vancouver: UBC Press, 2005).

8 Cecil Paul, as told to Briony Penn, *Stories from the Magic Canoe of Wa'xaid* (Calgary: Rocky Mountain Books, 2019); Nick Claxton, "To Fish as Formerly: A Resurgent Journey Back to the Saanich Reef Net Fishery" (PhD diss., University of Victoria, 2015), 96–97.

9 Muckle, *First Nations of British Columbia*, 56.

10 Duff, *Indian History of British Columbia*, 55–56.

11 Duff, *Indian History of British Columbia*, 15; Muckle, *First Nations of British Columbia*, 55.

12 These categories are adapted from the continental cultural areas defined by anthropologists. Anthropologists divide BC into three cultural areas that correspond with the boundaries I use here: the Northwest Coast, the Interior Plateau and the Subarctic or Sub-boreal. See Muckle, *First Nations of British Columbia*, 54–56.

13 Muckle, *First Nations of British Columbia*, 54.

14 "Eulachon of the Pacific Northwest: A Life History," prepared for the Living Landscapes Program, Royal BC Museum, by Cambria Gordon Consultants, Terrace, BC, January 11, 2006; Government of Canada, "Eulachon (*Thaleichthys pacificus*), Nass/Skeena Rivers Population," Species at Risk Public Registry, November 29, 2011, last modified February 2, 2021, https://species-registry. canada.ca/index-en.html; Mark Hume, "More Than the Loss of a Resource," *Globe and Mail*, June 20, 2007; John Corsiglia, "Traditional Wisdom as Practiced and Transmitted in Northwestern British Columbia, Canada," in *Traditional Ecological Knowledge and Natural Resource Management*, ed. Charles R. Menzies (Lincoln: University of Nebraska Press, 2006), 221–35.

15 Paul and Penn, *Magic Canoe*, 99.

16 BC Conservation Data Centre, "Conservation Status Report: *Thaleichthys pacificus*," BC Ministry of Environment, accessed July 16, 2021, https://a100.gov.bc.ca/ pub/eswp/; Government of Canada, Committee on the Status of Endangered Wildlife in Canada, *COSEWIC Assessment and Status Report on Eulachon (*Thaleichthys pacificus*) in 3 Rivers* (Ottawa, 2011).

17 Rachelle Beveridge et al., "The Nuxalk Sputc (Eulachon) Project: Strengthening Indigenous Management Authority through Community-Driven Research," *Marine Policy* 119 (September 2020), doi:10.1016/j.marpol.2020.103971; Caitlin Thompson, "Bella Coola Sees Biggest Eulachon Run in Almost 20 Years," *Coast Mountain News*, April 17, 2018; Lauren Kaljur, "Sharing Food, Building Resilience," *Hakai Magazine*, August 4, 2020, https://hakaimagazine.com.

18 Muckle, *First Nations of British Columbia*, 55.

19 Muckle, *First Nations of British Columbia*, 55.

20 Nancy J. Turner, "The Importance of Biodiversity for First Peoples of British Columbia," Biodiversity BC Technical Subcommittee for the Report on the Status of Biodiversity in British Columbia (September 2007), 2.

21 Paul Nadasdy, *Hunters and Bureaucrats: Power, Knowledge, and Aboriginal-State Relations in the Southwest Yukon* (Vancouver: UBC Press, 2003), 97–98.

22 Trevor Lantz and Nancy J. Turner, "Traditional Phenological Knowledge of Aboriginal Peoples in British Columbia," *Journal of Ethnobiology* 23, no. 2 (2003): 263–86.

23 Ignace and Ignace, *Secwépemc People*, 180.

24 George, *Living on the Edge*, 87–88.

25 Douglas Deur et al., "Kwakwaka'wakw 'Clam Gardens': Motive and Agency in Traditional Northwest Coast Mariculture," *Human Ecology* 43, no. 2 (April 2015): 201.

26 Nancy J. Turner and Wendy Cocksedge, "Aboriginal Use of Non-Timber Forest Products in Northwestern North America: Applications and Issues," *Journal of Sustainable Forestry* 13, no. 3–4 (2001): 31–58; Muckle, *First Nations of British Columbia*, 62–63.

27 Daly, *Our Box Was Full*, 270.

28 Paul and Penn, *Magic Canoe*, 168–69.

29 Ignace and Ignace, *Secwépemc People*, 176.

30 Douglas Deur, "Salmon, Sedentism, and Cultivation: Toward an Environmental Prehistory of the Northwest Coast," in *Northwest Lands, Northwest Peoples: Readings in Environmental History*, ed. Dale D. Goble and Paul W. Hirt (Seattle: University of Washington Press, 1999), 132.

31 Georgiana Ball, "The Monopoly System of Wildlife Management of the Indians and the Hudson's Bay Company in the Early History of British Columbia," *BC Studies*, no. 66 (Summer 1985): 37.

32 Keith Thor Carlson, "Stó:lō-Xwelítem Relations during the Fur and Salmon Trade Era," in *You Are Asked to Witness: The Stó:lō in Canada's Pacific Coast History*, ed. Carlson (Chilliwack: Stó:lō Heritage Trust, 1997), 44–46. Similar arrangements among the Ktunaxa of southeastern BC allowed sharing of bison hunting and fishing privileges between communities in the upper and lower Kootenay River basin. Harry Holbert Turney-High, *Ethnography of the Kutenai*, Memoir No. 56 (Menasha, WI: American Anthropological Association, 1941), 44, cited in Ball, "Monopoly System," 41–42.

33 Daly, *Our Box Was Full*, 281.

34 Deur, "Salmon, Sedentism," 134–37.

35 Bill Blackwater Jr., interview by the author, Hazelton, BC, July 12, 2019.

36 Deur et al., "Kwakwaka'wakw 'Clam Gardens.'"

37 Deur et al., "Kwakwaka'wakw 'Clam Gardens,'" 208; Douglas Deur and Nancy J. Turner, eds., *Keeping It Living: Traditions of Plant Use and Cultivation on the Northwest Coast of North America* (Seattle: University of Washington Press, 2005).

38 Menzies, *People of the Saltwater*, 149; Deur et al., "Kwakwaka'wakw 'Clam Gardens,'" 208.

39 Laura Cameron, "The Aboriginal Right to Fish," in *You Are Asked to Witness*, ed. Carlson, 141; Emily Walter, R. Michael M'Gonigle and Céleste McKay, "Fishing around the Law: The Pacific Salmon Management System as a 'Structural Infringement' of Aboriginal Rights," *McGill Law Journal* 45, no. 1 (2000): 274. These calculations are based on an average estimated pre-contact catch of 88 million kg/year for British Columbia and an average commercial catch for the province of 70 million kg/year between 1983 and 1997.

40 Michael J. Kew, "Salmon Availability, Technology and Cultural Adaptation in the Fraser River Watershed," in *A Complex Culture of the British Columbia Plateau: Traditional Stl'atl'imx Resource Use*, ed. Brian Hayden (Vancouver: UBC Press, 1992), 178.

41 George, *Living on the Edge*, 74.

42 On the First Salmon Ceremony, see Claxton, "To Fish as Formerly," 96–97; Vince Harper, "Salmon and Aboriginal Fishing on the Lower Fraser River. Present Day Management Issues, Concerns, and Impacts," in *You Are Asked to Witness*, ed. Carlson, 154–55; Kimberly Linkous Brown, "As It Was in the Past: A Return to the Use of Live-Capture Technology in the Aboriginal Riverine Fishery," in *Traditional Ecological Knowledge*, ed. Menzies, 47–63; Daly, *Our Box Was Full*, 276–77.

43 Diane Newell, *Tangled Webs of History: Indians and the Law in Canada's Pacific Coast Fisheries* (Toronto: University of Toronto Press, 1993), 40–41; Walter et al., "Fishing around the Law," 275. Trout fisheries among the Ktunaxa operated on similar principles of hereditary ownership of fisheries technology (such as weirs and traps) at specific sites, with the expectation that harvests would be shared within the community. Turney-High, *Ethnography of the Kutenai*, 44–53, cited in Ball, "Monopoly System," 42.

44 Newell, *Tangled Webs*, 40–41; Walter et al., "Fishing around the Law," 275.

45 Nancy J. Turner and Fikret Berkes, "Coming to Understanding: Developing Conservation through Incremental Learning in the Pacific Northwest," *Human Ecology* 34 (2006): 505.

46 Ignace and Ignace, *Secwépemc People*, 161–62. Interpreter Antoine Gregoire confirmed for the Adams Lake Indian Band in testimony to federal fisheries officers in 1877 that the "chiefs are careful not to destroy, wantonly or wastefully, the mature fish, or to impede their passage to the spawning beds." The weirs are used only temporarily, to "enable the Indians to obtain their necessary winter supply," after which they "are thrown open... to give passage to the ascending fish." Government of Canada, Parliament, *Sessional Papers, 1878*, Appendix no. 1, "Reports of the Fisheries Officers, 1877," cited in Ball, "Monopoly System," 43. Kimberly Linkous Brown notes that "virtually all upriver Aboriginal peoples" in what would become British Columbia employed "live capture" fisheries technologies such as traps, weirs and dip nets. "As It Was in the Past," 52–53.

47 A 2021 study examining chum salmon bones dating from between 400 BCE and 1200 CE from four archaeological sites around Burrard Inlet found that bones from male fish significantly outnumbered those of females at two of the village sites. The archaeological evidence confirmed Tsleil-Waututh conservation practices dating back millienia. Because a single male fish can mate with multiple females, the removal of greater numbers of male fish permits the remaining males to mate with females with "no detriment to the population." "B.C. Study Shows Sustainable Management of Salmon Fishery before Colonization," *Times Colonist* (Victoria), November 10, 2021.

48 Turner and Berkes, "Coming to Understanding," 509.

49 Claxton, "To Fish as Formerly," 96–97.

50 Claxton, "To Fish as Formerly," 112–13.

51 Menzies, *People of the Saltwater*, 148. See also Vince Harper, "Salmon and Aboriginal Fishing on the Lower Fraser River: Present Day Management Issues, Concerns, and Impacts," in *You Are Asked to Witness*, ed. Carlson, 158–60; Brown, "As It Was in the Past," 49.

52 Menzies, *People of the Saltwater*, 138. Menzies concludes that the placement of stone fish traps in relation to local streams meant they were likely used to target pink and dog (chum) salmon, species that travel in dense schools close to shore (unlike sockeye, which run farther off the beach).

53 Steve J. Langdon, "Tidal Pulse Fishing: Selective Traditional Tlingit Salmon Fishing Techniques on the West Coast of the Prince of Wales Archipelago," in *Traditional Ecological Knowledge*, ed. Menzies, 43–45.

54 Menzies, *People of the Saltwater*, 137, 143–44, 148. Drag or beach seines are typically set from a boat and hauled in from sandy beaches, encircling schools of fish swimming in shallow water. Like the stone traps, drag seines allowed for a selective harvest and the live release of non-target species.

55 George, *Living on the Edge*, 74.

56 Walter et al., "Fishing around the Law," 279.

57 Homer G. Barnett, *The Coast Salish of British Columbia* (Eugene: University of Oregon Press, 1955), 68, 88–89, cited in Ball, "Monopoly System," 41.

58 Government of Canada, Reports of the Fisheries Officers, cited in Ball, "Monopoly System," 43.

59 Menzies, *People of the Saltwater*, 133; George, *Living on the Edge*, 73–74; Deur, "Salmon, Sedentism," 139. Secwépemc beliefs and practices also supported the long-term health of the fishery by moving salmon that had spawned back into the river to provide nourishment for their offspring the following season. Ignace and Ignace, *Secwépemc People*, 205.

60 Walter et al., "Fishing around the Law," 274.

61 Ruth Kirk, *Tradition and Change on the Northwest Coast: The Makah, Nuu-Chah-Nulth, Southern Kwakiutl and Nuxalk* (Seattle: University of Washington Press, 1986), 100; Duff, *Indian History of British Columbia*, 15. The Nlaka'pamux (Thompson) people of the lower Fraser Valley adhered to a similar system of

hereditary access to the fences and snares used to trap deer and the mountain passes where they were trapped during their fall migration to lower elevations. Recognized systems of ownership prevented competition and supported discriminate use of the traps. James Teit, *The Thompson Indians of British Columbia*, Memoirs of the American Museum of Natural History, vol. 1, part 4 (New York: G.P. Putnam's Sons, 1900), 293–94, cited in Ball, "Monopoly System," 45.

62 Turner and Berkes, "Coming to Understanding," 498.

63 Risky Creek Productions, *In the Land of Dreamers,* documentary film, CBC Media, 2021, http://gem.cbc.ca; Wayne Sawchuk, *Muskwa-Kechika: The Wild Heart of Canada's Northern Rockies* (Chetwynd, BC: Northern Images, 2004); Gillian Staveley, director of Culture and Land Stewardship, Dena Kayeh Institute, personal communication, March 4, 2022.

64 Daly, *Our Box Was Full*, 272.

65 Henrik Moller et al., "Combining Science and Traditional Ecological Knowledge: Monitoring Populations for Co-management," *Ecology and Society* 9, no. 3 (July 2004): Article 2.

66 Ignace and Ignace, *Secwépemc People*, 282.

67 Joe Stanley Michel, "Testimony during Neskonlith Douglas Reserve Claim, Specific Claims Commission Hearings," file no. 2109-32-01, July 6, 2005, 89, cited in Ignace and Ignace, *Secwépemc People*, 178; Ignace and Ignace, *Secwépemc People*, 193–94.

68 Daly, *Our Box Was Full*, 271–72. Indigenous scholar Mateen Hessami and his collaborators affirm the centrality of an active wildlife harvest within many Indigenous world views. In addition to providing subsistence, they note, "wildlife harvest is associated with keeping traditions alive, intergenerational knowledge transfer, acquiring materials for utility and art, as well as building and maintaining social bonds." Hessami et al., "Indigenizing the North American Model of Wildlife Conservation," *FACETS* 6 (2021): 1293.

69 Shepard Krech, *The Ecological Indian: Myth and History* (New York: W.W. Norton, 1999), 104–5.

70 J.M. Broughton and E.M. Weitzel, "Population Reconstructions for Humans and Megafauna Suggest Mixed Causes for North American Pleistocene Extinctions," *Nature Communications* 9, no. 1 (2018): 5441.

71 Paul S. Martin and Christine R. Szuter, "Megafauna of the Columbia Basin, 1800–1840: Lewis and Clark in a Game Sink," in *Northwest Lands, Northwest Peoples*, ed. Goble and Hirt, 188–204; A.S.R. Laliberte and W.J. Ripple, "Wildlife Encounters by Lewis and Clark: A Spatial Analysis of Interactions between Native Americans and Wildlife," *BioScience* 53 (2003): 994–1003; Domenico Santomauro, Chris J. Johnson and Gail Fondahl, "Historical-Ecological Evaluation of the Long-Term Distribution of Woodland Caribou and Moose in Central British Columbia," *Ecosphere* 3, no. 5 (2012): 1–19; C.E. Kay, "Aboriginal Overkill and the Biogeography of Moose in Western North America," *Alces* 33 (1997): 141–64.

72 Ignace and Ignace, *Secwépemc People*, 168.

73 Arthur Ray, *Indians in the Fur Trade: Their Roles as Trappers, Hunters, and Middlemen in the Lands Southwest of Hudson Bay, 1660–1870* (Toronto: University of Toronto Press, 1974), 95.

74 Sterritt, *Mapping My Way Home*, 71–74. Gitx̱san ant'imahlasxw, narratives used to inform and instruct, often feature a trickster figure named Wiigyet who represents "the essence of human frailty." Wiigyet serves as a warning against selfish or greedy behaviour such as overharvesting. Punished for his actions by fate or natural forces, Wiigyet provides listeners with an opportunity to "reflect on his mistakes and learn from them." John Borrows and Shayla Praud, "Teachings of Sustainability, Stewardship, and Responsibility: Indigenous Perspectives on Obligation, Wealth, Trusts, and Fiduciary Duty" (Discussion Paper, Reconciliation and Responsible Investment Initiative, September 2020), 19–20.

75 Yvette Brend, "Forget Smokey the Bear: How First Nation Fire Wisdom Is Key to Megafire Prevention," *CBC News*, July 17, 2017, http://cbc.ca.

76 Elders remember lighting fires on forested hillsides, in aspen groves and in sage- and grass-covered areas above valley bottoms. Ignace and Ignace, *Secwépemc People*, 192–93.

77 Michael Lewis, Amy Christianson and Marsha Spinks, "Return to Flame: Reasons for Burning in Lytton First Nation, British Columbia," *Journal of Forestry* 116, no. 2 (March 2018): 143–50.

78 Stephen J. Pyne, *Fire: Nature and Culture* (London: Reaktion Books, 2012): 57.

79 Ze'ev Gedalof, "Fire and Biodiversity in British Columbia," in *Biodiversity of British Columbia*, ed. Brian Klinkenberg (Lab for Advanced Spatial Analysis, Department of Geography, University of British Columbia, 2020), http://biodiversity.bc.ca.

80 Sally Thompson, *People before the Park: The Kootenai and Blackfeet before Glacier National Park* (Helena: Montana Historical Society Press, 2015), 5, 80.

81 Stephen J. Pyne, *Awful Splendour: A Fire History of Canada* (Vancouver: UBC Press, 2008), 50–53.

82 Archaeological evidence supports the extensive use of fire to maintain grasslands throughout the Peace River region. Ridington and Ridington, *Where Happiness Dwells*, 70.

83 Alexander Mackenzie and W. Kaye Lamb, eds., *The Journals and Letters of Sir Alexander Mackenzie* (Toronto: MacMillan of Canada, 1970), 265, cited in Ridington and Ridington, *Where Happiness Dwells*, 3, 5.

84 Pyne, *Awful Splendour*, 50–53; H.T. Lewis, "Indian Fires of Spring," *Natural History* 89 (1980): 76–83; H.T. Lewis and T.A. Ferguson, "Yards, Corridors and Mosaics: How to Burn a Boreal Forest," *Human Ecology* 16 (1988): 57–77, cited in "Old Fort Saint John on the Peace River," *Lens of Time Northwest*, n.d., accessed November 12, 2021, http://lensoftimenorthwest.com.

85   Pyne, *Awful Splendour*, 54, 57; Daly, *Our Box Was Full*, 272, 276; Deur and
     Turner, "Introduction," in Deur and Turner, *Keeping It Living*, 19.
86   Deur and Turner, "Introduction," 19; Pyne, *Awful Splendour*, 53; Turner, Nancy
     J., "'Time to Burn': Traditional Use of Fire to Enhance Resource Production by
     Aboriginal Peoples in British Columbia," in *Indians, Fire and the Land in the
     Pacific Northwest*, ed. R. Boyd (Corvallis: Oregon State University Press, 1999),
     195.
87   Ignace and Ignace, *Secwépemc People*, 192.
88   Turner, "Time to Burn," 200–1.
89   Turner, "Importance of Biodiversity," 3. See also Turner and Berkes, "Coming
     to Understanding," 510; Ignace and Ignace, *Secwépemc People*, 206–7: Ridington
     and Ridington, *Where Happiness Dwells*, 45–46.
90   Deur et al., "Kwakwaka'wakw 'Clam Gardens,'" 206.
91   Nadasdy, *Hunters and Bureaucrats*, 83–84.
92   Deur et al., "Kwakwaka'wakw 'Clam Gardens,'" 206.
93   E. Richard Atleo (Umeek), *Principles of Tsawalk: An Indigenous Approach to a
     Global Crisis* (Vancouver: UBC Press, 2012), 36.
94   Paul Nadasdy, "The Gift in the Animal: The Ontology of Hunting and Human–
     Animal Sociality," *American Ethnologist* 34, no. 1 (2007): 31; Turner and Berkes,
     "Coming to Understanding."
95   Nadasdy, *Hunters and Bureaucrats*, 60; Gisday Wa and Delgam Uukw, *The Spirit
     in the Land: The Opening Statement of the Gitksan and Wet'suwet'en Hereditary
     Chiefs in the Supreme Court of British Columbia May 11, 1987* (Gabriola Island, BC:
     Reflections, 1990), 23; Ridington and Ridington, *Where Happiness Dwells*, 45.
96   Ignace and Ignace, *Secwépemc People*, 382.
97   First Nations across the province observed (and in many cases continue to ob-
     serve) a range of cleansing rituals that governed respectful relationships with
     animals. For the Gitxsan, this body of private observances and practices is called
     sestxw, and for the Wet'suwet'en, halh'ala. Cecil Paul describes bathing in water
     infused with devil's club to cleanse before a hunt; Neil J. Sterritt makes the same
     observation about the Gitxsan halayts, or shaman, noting that they "boiled dev-
     il's club and bathed themselves before going hunting." Daly, *Our Box Was Full*,
     273; Paul and Penn, *Magic Canoe*, 59; Sterritt, *Mapping My Way Home*, 71.
98   Ridington and Ridington, *Where Happiness Dwells*, 46.
99   Ignace and Ignace, *Secwépemc People*, 205–7.
100 Gisday Wa and Delgam Uukw, *Spirit in the Land*, 7.
101 Atleo, *Tsawalk*, 63.
102 Paul and Penn, *Magic Canoe*, 188–89; Atleo, *Principles of Tsawalk*, 159, 166.
103 Turner and Berkes, "Coming to Understanding," 501.
104 Claxton, "To Fish as Formerly," 96–97; Turner and Berkes, "Coming to
     Understanding," 509.
105 James A. Teit, "Tahltan Tales," *Journal of American Folklore* 32, no 124 (April–
     June 1919): 230.

106   Nadasdy, *Hunters and Bureaucrats*, 85, 93. Thomas McIlwraith documents sim-
        ilar requirements of respect and reciprocity in relationships with hunted an-
        imals in *"We Are Still Didene": Stories of Hunting and History from Northern
        British Columbia* (Toronto: University of Toronto Press, 2012). See also Sterritt,
        Mapping My Way Home, 71.
107   Krech, *Ecological Indian*.
108   Ignace and Ignace, *Secwépemc People*, 210.
109   Turner and Berkes, "Coming to Understanding," 504.
110   Menzies, *People of the Saltwater*, 149; Daly, *Our Box Was Full*.

Chapter 2 | The Wildlife Trade: Indigenous Hunters and Euro-American Traders, 1774–1858

  1   David R. Hurn, "Wildlife—Our Talent of Silver," in *Our Wildlife Heritage: 100
        Years of Wildlife Management*, ed. Allan Murray (Victoria: Centennial Wildlife
        Society of British Columbia, 1987), 31.
  2   As Gitxaala scholar Charles Menzies reminds his readers, the Gitxaala were
        never "subsistence" harvesters; instead, they were, and remain, "a society that
        values wealth." Our "system of rank and prestige," he explains, is based "in large
        measure on the capacity to harvest surpluses" of fish and marine mammals to
        trade "for economic benefit internally and with nations far removed." Menzies,
        People of the Saltwater, 93.
             Indigenous trade networks extended from the coast into the interior and
        from the Yukon and Northwest Territories south to California. BC historian
        Jean Barman notes that among the Tsimshian peoples of Skeena River alone,
        "over 50 kinds of trade goods and 20 separate trade routes were in use by 1750."
        Barman, *The West beyond the West: A History of British Columbia*, 3rd ed.
        (Toronto: University of Toronto Press, 2007), 17. See also Fisher, *Contact and
        Conflict*, 11; Carlson, "Stó:lō-Xwelítem Relations," 46; Ridington and Ridington,
        Where Happiness Dwells, 69; Daly, *Our Box Was Full*, 217, 222–23.
  3   Barman, *West beyond the West*, 21.
  4   Competition among American and British traders often gave Indigenous bro-
        kers the upper hand in trade interactions. Maritime traders' journals show that
        Indigenous traders not only set the prices but also determined which items were
        marketable. They could choose to hold their furs and wait for the next ship if
        prices were set too high or the goods offered were not in demand. Fisher, *Contact
        and Conflict*, 2–3, 12.
  5   James Hatter, "The Fur Trade: B.C.'s First Industry," in *Our Wildlife Heritage*,
        ed. Murray, 18.
  6   Francisco de Eliza, "Costumbres de los naturales del Puerto de San Lorenzo de
        Nuca," April 1791, cited in Deur, "Salmon, Sedentism," 148n4.
  7   Deur, "Salmon, Sedentism," 148n4.

8   Robin A. Fisher, "Muquinna (d. 1795)," in *Dictionary of Canadian Biography*, vol. 4 (University of Toronto/Université Laval, 2003), accessed June 12, 2020, http://biographi.ca.

9   By the 1820s, American traders reported an annual catch of no more than 600 pelts, down from 15,000 in 1802. Richard Somerset Mackie, *Trading beyond the Mountains: The British Fur Trade on the Pacific, 1793–1843* (Vancouver: UBC Press, 1997), 124, 143.

10 Donald A. Blood, *Sea Otter*, Wildlife at Risk in British Columbia brochure series (Victoria: BC Ministry of Environment, Lands and Parks, October 1993); Linda M. Nichol (marine mammal research biologist, Pacific Biological Station, Fisheries and Oceans Canada), personal communication, May 27, 2022.

11 Iain McKechnie and Rebecca J. Wigen, "Toward a Historical Ecology of Pinniped and Sea Otter Hunting Traditions on the Coast of Southern British Columbia," in *Human Impacts on Seals, Sea Lions, and Sea Otters: Integrating Archaeology and Ecology in the Northeast Pacific*, ed. Todd J. Braje and Torben C. Rick (Berkeley: University of California Press, 2011), 129–66.

12 Linda M. Nichol, "Conservation in Practice," in *Sea Otter Conservation*, ed. Shawn E. Larson, James L. Bodkin and Glenn R. VanBlaricom (New York: Elsevier, 2015), 369–93.

13 A. Doroff, A. Burdin and S. Larson, "Sea Otter (*Enhydra lutris*)," *The IUCN Red List of Threatened Species* (2021): e.T7750A164576728, https://iucnredlist.org/; Linda M. Nichol, personal communication, October 21, 2022.

14 BC Conservation Data Centre, "Conservation Status Report: *Enhydra lutris*," BC Ministry of Environment, accessed July 16, 2021, https://a100.gov.bc.ca/pub/eswp/; Fisheries and Oceans Canada, Pacific Region, "Trends in the Growth of the Sea Otter (*Enhydra lutris*) Population in British Columbia 1977 to 2017," Science Advisory Report 2020/036, Canadian Science Advisory Secretariat, June 2020.

15 Nuu-Chah-Nulth Tribal Council, "Uu-a-thluk: Sea Otter Recovery," n.d., accessed November 22, 2021, uuathluk.ca/sea-otter-recovery/.

16 Ball, "Monopoly System," 49.

17 Daniel Harmon, *A Journal of Voyages and Travels in the Interior of North America* (Andover: Flagg and Gould, 1820), 268, cited in Ball, "Monopoly System," 45.

18 Donald J. Robinson, "Wildlife and the Law," in Murray, *Our Wildlife Heritage*, 44; Fisher, *Contact and Conflict*, 47.

19 Harmon, *Journal of Voyages*, 268, cited in Ball, "Monopoly System," 45.

20 Lorne Hammond, "Marketing Wildlife: The Hudson's Bay Company and the Pacific Northwest, 1821–49," *Forest & Conservation History* 37, no. 1 (1993): 15.

21 Hammond, "Marketing Wildlife," 19.

22 Hammond, "Marketing Wildlife," 17; Ball, "Monopoly System," 51.

23 George Colpitts, *Game in the Garden: A Human History of Wildlife in Western Canada to 1940* (Vancouver: UBC Press, 2002), 16; Hammond, "Marketing Wildlife," 15.

24 Robinson, "Wildlife and the Law," 44.

25 In other parts of the country, HBC conservation measures included strict har-
    vest limits on beaver pelts. These limits—or quotas, as they were called—were
    never applied in the areas west of the Rockies or in the upper Peace River coun-
    try that would later become part of British Columbia, suggesting that beaver
    populations may have been less depleted in BC. Ball, "Monopoly System," 52–53;
    Mackie, *Trading beyond the Mountains*, 246–47. See also Arthur J. Ray, "Some
    Conservation Schemes of the HBC, 1821–50: An Examination of the Problems
    of Resource Management in the Fur Trade," *Journal of Historical Geography* 1
    (January 1975): 49–68.

26 Tina Loo, *States of Nature: Conserving Canada's Wildlife in the Twentieth
    Century* (Vancouver: UBC Press, 2007), 95.

27 Hammond, "Marketing Wildlife," 25, note 46.

28 Ball, "Monopoly System."

29 Mackie, *Trading beyond the Mountains*, 88.

30 Ball, "Monopoly System," 50–51; Loo, *States of Nature*, 97; Hammond, "Marketing
    Wildlife," 17.

31 Colpitts, *Game in the Garden*, 19; Hurn, "Talent of Silver," 36.

32 The murder of five HBC men by the Sekani and Dane-zaa in 1823 hastened the
    closure of the St. John and Dunvegan fur trade posts. Dane-zaa oral histories
    reference the hardships that followed the closure of these posts in the 1820s.
    "With game resources depleted and trade goods difficult to obtain," commu-
    nities experienced hard times until an independent trader restored access to
    trade goods in the 1870s. Ridington and Ridington, *Where Happiness Dwells*,
    122, 128–29.

33 Colpitts, *Game in the Garden*, 20.

34 Ignace and Ignace, *Secwépemc People*, 429.

35 Hurn, "Talent of Silver," 32; Ignace and Ignace, *Secwépemc People*, 431.

36 HBC records show an annual trade of 12,000 to 20,000 fresh and dried salmon at
    Fort Kamloops alone between 1822 and the 1850s. Ignace and Ignace, *Secwépemc
    People*, 429.

37 Carlson, "Stó:lō-Xwelítem Relations," 42, 51; Mackie, *Trading beyond the
    Mountains*, 315.

38 Duff, *Indian History of British Columbia*, 79; Fisher, *Contact and Conflict*, 21.

39 Carlson, "Stó:lō-Xwelítem Relations," 50. See also John Lutz's analysis of the
    coexistence of European capitalist economy with non-capitalist Indigenous
    economies of subsistence, prestige and exchange in *Makúk: A New History of
    Aboriginal-White Relations* (Vancouver: UBC Press, 2008), 23.

40 Mackie, *Trading beyond the Mountains*, 287, 315; Deur, "Salmon, Sedentism," 146.

41 Duff, *Indian History of British Columbia*, 83; Fisher, *Contact and Conflict*, 47:
    Ridington and Ridington, *Where Happiness Dwells*, 77; Ray Izony, Tsay Keh
    Dene Nation elder, personal communication, June 17–24, 2022.

42 Harmon, *Journal of Voyages*, 268, cited in Ball, "Monopoly System," 45.

43 Ball, "Monopoly System," 49.

44 Peace agreements between the Cree and the Dane-zaa followed, once the Dane-zaa had acquired firearms and in the context of smallpox outbreaks among both groups. Ridington and Ridington, *Where Happiness Dwells*, 99.

45 Ridington and Ridington, *Where Happiness Dwells*, 48.

46 Colpitts, *Game in the Garden*, 32–33.

47 Hammond, "Marketing Wildlife," 23.

48 Mackie, *Trading beyond the Mountains*, 245–48.

49 Fisher, *Contact and Conflict*, 98. As Ignace and Ignace report, "gold was initially found by Indigenous miners on Nicomen River near Lytton in 1857 and subsequently at the mouth of the Tranquille River" near Kamloops. *Secwépemc People*, 435.

    Interior peoples like the Secwépemc and Nlaka'pamux actively resisted the initial intrusions of opportunistic miners by expelling them from their territories. As Governor James Douglas reported in an 1857 letter to the Secretary of State for the Colonies, these nations were "determined to resist all attempts at working gold in any of the streams flowing into the Thompson River, both from a desire to monopolize the precious metal for their own benefit and from a well-found impression that shoals of salmon... will be driven off and prevented from making their annual migration to the sea." Douglas to Henry Labouchere, July 15, 1857, A11/76, fol. 655, Hudson's Bay Company Archives, cited in Ignace and Ignace, *Secwépemc People*, 435.

50 Ignace and Ignace, *Secwépemc People*, 98–100.

51 Eric Wright, "Fraser Canyon War," *Canadian Encyclopedia*, article published April 10, 2019, last modified September 10, 2019, http://thecanadian encyclopedia.ca.

52 Fisher, *Contact and Conflict*, 102.

53 Margaret A. Ormsby, "Sir James Douglas," *Canadian Encyclopedia*, article published February 14, 2008, last modified April 29, 2022, https://thecanadian encyclopedia.ca/en/article/sir-james-douglas.

54 Ball, "Monopoly System," 24, 54.

55 An 1859 census of the camps, for example, documented over 2,200 inhabitants, with members of the Haida, Tsimshian and Tlingit Nations among the majority. Greg Lange, "Small Pox Epidemic of 1862 among Northwest Coast and Puget Sound Indians," Essay 5171, HistoryLink.org, April 2, 2003, https://historylink.org/File/5171.

56 Duff, *Indian History of British Columbia*, 59.

Chapter 3 | The Wildlife Commons: Overexploitation in the Early Settlement Period, 1859–1904

1 A large body of scholarly literature exists on common property resources, much of it developed in response to Garrett Hardin's 1968 article "The Tragedy of the Commons." *Science*, 162, no. 3859 (December 13, 1968): 1243–48. Hardin argued that resource depletion was inevitable within common property regimes where resources were "open to all," because individual users would seek to maximize their self-interest. As Nobel-prize-winning economist Elinor Ostrom and others have demonstrated, Hardin failed to account for the locally developed customs and community institutions that regulate access within successful common property systems around the world. In British Columbia, the end of the HBC monopoly and the associated marginalization of customs of Indigenous stewardship created the conditions for an unregulated wildlife commons. On principles of effective commons management, see Elinor Ostrom, *Governing the Commons: The Evolution of Institutions for Collective Action* (Cambridge: Cambridge University Press, 1990).

2 Hurn, "Talent of Silver," 39.

3 George Vancouver, *A Voyage of Discovery to the Pacific Ocean and Round the World, 1790–5*, vol. 1 (London, 1798), 227–29, cited in Turner, "Time to Burn," 195.

4 This patronage policy endured until the 1910s. Barman, *West beyond the West*, 126–27.

5 Of the eighty-seven rail line proposals submitted in the 1890s, only five were actually constructed. But as historian Jean Barman has observed, "even these five grants exceeded six million acres in a province whose potential arable acreage totalled six and one half million and where nearly fourteen million acres had already been alienated in connection with the CPR." *West beyond the West*, 127.

   Grants to railway companies would also play a role in the future of the forest industry in the province, as large swaths of these railway grants were sold to logging companies to be cleared and resold to incoming settlers before provincial policy banned the sale of lands "chiefly valuable for timber" in 1884. On the ramifications of land grants to railway companies in this period, see Robert E. Cail, *Land, Man, and the Law: The Disposal of Crown Lands in British Columbia, 1871–1913* (Vancouver: UBC Press, 1974), 125–52.

6 See the figure on page 9 for land tenure ratios. Similar ratios of Crown to public land appear in Newfoundland (95% Crown land), Quebec (92%) and Ontario (87%). Alberta (60%), Saskatchewan (57%) and Maritime provinces such as Nova Scotia and PEI, where agricultural potential was higher, have much higher levels of private landownership.

7 The first articulation of resource tenures occurred in the province's Land Ordinance, 1865, which granted leases to grazing, timber and mining resources subject to the terms and fees of the Crown. These terms generally favoured settlement (grazing leases, for example, could be withdrawn without compensation

to allow for agricultural development). Not until the 1880s, with the advent of rail and the possibility of large export markets, would the provincial government openly encourage the development of forestry in the province through efforts to retain prime forest land for timber extraction rather than settlement. Michael Begg, "Legislating British Columbia: A History of B.C. Land Law, 1858–1978" (LL.M. thesis, University of British Columbia, 2007), 38–40.

8   Fisher, *Contact and Conflict*, 49.

9   Barman, *West beyond the West*, 166; Joanna Reid, "The Grasslands Debates: Conservationists, Ranchers, First Nations, and the Landscape of the Middle Fraser," *BC Studies*, no. 160 (Winter 2008–9): 93.

10 Turner, "Time to Burn," 203–4.

11 Duff, *Indian History of British Columbia*, 15–16.

12 "Tsilhqot'in Chiefs Hanged in 1864 Exonerated by B.C. Premier Christy Clark," *CBC News*, October 24, 2014, http://cbc.ca.

13 I have used the term "Aboriginal" in association with the legal concepts of "Aboriginal title" and "Aboriginal rights."

14 Duff, *Indian History of British Columbia*, 86.

15 When the Province of British Columbia was created in 1871, it did not recognize Aboriginal title. Instead, provincial policy relegated all issues relating to "Indians" to the federal government. BC First Nations not only saw their appeals for access to traditional territories ignored but were also prohibited from laying pre-emptive claims to land (through occupation and agricultural improvements) in the way that settlers could. Begg, "Legislating British Columbia," 47.

16 Begg, "Legislating British Columbia," 98.

17 Canada, "Treaty No. 8," in *Treaty Texts: Treaty No. 8*, June 21, 1899 (repr., Ottawa: Queen's Printer, 1966).

18 Ridington and Ridington, *Where Happiness Dwells*, 223, 227.

19 Barman, *West beyond the West*, 129–30, 152, 156, 363.

20 Barman, *West beyond the West*, 163; R. Cole Harris, *Making Native Space: Colonialism, Resistance, and Reserves in British Columbia* (Vancouver: UBC Press, 2003), 202, 274.

21 Typically following "a few years behind increased settler interest in a region," reserve allocations began in 1849, with the creation of the colony of Vancouver Island, and continued for seventy-five years until the Dominion and provincial governments agreed on final reserve allotments in 1924. Douglas C. Harris, *Landing Native Fisheries: Indian Reserves and Fishing Rights in British Columbia, 1849–1925* (Vancouver: UBC Press, 2008), 7, 20.

22 Pre-emption involved a claim to land that could be confirmed through purchase or the completion of a survey and "improvements" (such as clearing or the construction of buildings or fences). As Douglas Harris observes, by the late nineteenth century "Native purchase or pre-emption of Crown lands became virtually impossible" beyond the reserves. *Landing Native Fisheries*, 12.

23   R.C. Harris, *Making Native Space*, 273–74; Ignace and Ignace, *Secwépemc People*, 215.

24   Seton Lake hearings, November 5, 1914, RG 10, vol. 11025, file AH7, 18-40 (reel T-3963), Library and Archives Canada (LAC), cited in R.C. Harris, *Making Native Space*, 273.

25   R.C. Harris, *Making Native Space*, 281; Atleo/Umeek, *Tsawalk*, 76; Menzies, *People of the Saltwater*, 44.

26   R.C. Harris, *Making Native Space*, 281–82; Ridington and Ridington, *Where Happiness Dwells*, 5, 229.

27   D.C. Harris, *Landing Native Fisheries*, 26–27.

28   Chiefs of the Shuswap, Couteau and Thompson Tribes et al., "Memorial to the Hon. Frank Oliver, Minister of the Interior," 1911, RB 10, vol. 7780, file 27150-3-1, LAC, cited in Ignace and Ignace, *Secwépemc People*, 475–76.

29   Settler views of Indigenous wildlife use are discussed in greater detail in chapter 4. On early conflicts between wildlife conservation and Indigenous hunting, see Frank Tough, "Conservation and the Indian: Clifford Sifton's Commission of Conservation, 1910–1919," *Native Studies Review* 8, no. 1 (1992): 61–73.

30   Sterritt, *Mapping My Way Home*, 175, 290. In 1887, for example, the Nisga'a and Port Simpson Tsimshian petitioned the BC government "for the return of their lands… and a treaty guaranteeing their rights to those lands forever." British Columbia, Legislative Assembly, *Sessional Papers, 1887*, "Report of Conferences between the Provincial Government and Indian Delegates from Fort Simpson and the Nass River," cited in Hamar Foster, "Honouring the Queen's Flag: A Legal and Historical Perspective on the Nisga'a Treaty," *BC Studies*, no. 120 (Winter 1998–99): 16.

31   Barman, *West beyond the West*, 159. From 1911 until 1951, amendments to the Indian Act enabled the federal government to take reserve land without a band's consent. From 1918 to 1951, the federal government could also lease reserve land to settlers without consent from band leadership.

32   Barman, *West beyond the West*, 156; Fisher, *Contact and Conflict*, 87.

33   See, for example, Ignace and Ignace, *Secwépemc People*, 162.

34   By 1878, eight salmon canneries operated on the Fraser and two on the Skeena. Together they employed nearly 400 boats. When two canneries opened at the mouth of the Nass River in 1881, the Nisga'a petitioned the government to restrict the size of the cannery fleet, noting the reduced availability of salmon upriver. D.C. Harris, *Landing Native Fisheries*, 68, 107.

35   Douglas C. Harris, *Fish, Law, and Colonialism: The Legal Capture of Salmon in British Columbia* (Toronto: University of Toronto Press, 2001), 38–39. Earlier provincial bans on the use of nets in Victoria's inner harbour, for example, were directed at the settler fishery and not the resident Songhees, who relied primarily on reef net fishing beyond the harbour.

36   D.C. Harris, *Landing Native Fisheries*, 109–10, 126–65; Menzies, *People of the Saltwater*, 102–4.

37   D.C. Harris, *Landing Native Fisheries*, 102. Established as a federal service in 1867, the Department of Marine and Fisheries (or Department of Fisheries, as it was known from 1884 to 1892 and 1930 to 1969) became the Department of Fisheries and Oceans in 1979. I have referred to it historically as the "Department of Fisheries" and after 1979 as the "Department of Fisheries and Oceans" or "Fisheries and Oceans Canada."

38   Brown, "As It Was in the Past," 61–62.

39   Deur et al., "Kwakwaka'wakw 'Clam Gardens,'" 209–10.

40   Hurn, "Talent of Silver," 39.

41   Blanche E. Norcross, *The Warm Land: A History of Cowichan* (Duncan, BC: Island Books, 1975), 19, cited in Hurn, "Talent of Silver," 40.

42   Hazel A.E. Hill, *Tales of the Alberni Valley* (Edmonton: Hamly Press, 1952); Winnifred Ariel Weir, ed., *Tales of the Windermere* (self-pub., 1980), both cited in Hurn, "Talent of Silver," 38.

43   A.G. (Adrien Gabriel) Morice, *The History of the Northern Interior of British Columbia (Formerly New Caledonia), 1660 to 1880* (London: Lane, 1906), 3, cited in Hurn, "Talent of Silver," 38.

44   Norcross, *Warm Land*, 24, cited in Hurn, "Talent of Silver," 40.

45   Edgar Fawcett, *Some Reminiscences of Old Victoria* (Toronto: William Briggs, 1912), 284, cited in Hurn, "Talent of Silver," 40.

46   Robinson, "Wildlife and the Law," 44.

47   "A Bill for the Passage of an Act for the Preservation of Game," *Victoria Gazette*, April 23, 1859. By 1883, those killing, selling or buying listed game out of season were subject to a fine of $10 to $25 and imprisonment for up to twenty days.

48   Colpitts, *Game in the Garden*, 77, 85.

49   Colpitts, *Game in the Garden*, 105–6; Ian McTaggart Cowan, "Science and the Conservation of Wildlife," in Murray, *Our Wildlife Heritage*, 87–88; Peter Corley-Smith, *White Bears and Other Curiosities: The First 100 Years of the Royal British Columbia Museum* (Victoria: Royal BC Museum, 1989); Patricia Roy, *The Collectors: A History of the Royal British Columbia Museum and Archives* (Victoria: Royal BC Museum, 2018), 7–9, 214.

50   BC's population nearly doubled in the last decade of the nineteenth century, rising from 98,000 in 1891 to 178,000 in 1901, with much of this gain landing in urban areas in the Lower Mainland and Victoria (Barman, *West beyond the West*).

51   The extension of CN's Yellowhead line to Prince Rupert in 1914 and the Pacific Great Eastern (PGE) line from Squamish to Chasm (north of Clinton) in 1915 continued this pattern of opening new areas to hunting pressure and wildlife exploitation. Leo Rutledge, *That Some May Follow: The History of Guide Outfitting in British Columbia* (Richmond: Guide Outfitters Association of British Columbia, 1989), 7; "A Brief History of the British Columbia Railway and the Pacific Great Eastern Railway," Canadian Toy Train Association, n.d., accessed December 2, 2021, http://canadiantoytrains.org.

52 W.H. Heald's report, 1909, to Williams, BCA, GR 446, box 3, file 2, cited in Colpitts, *Game in the Garden*, 89.

53 Rutledge, *That Some May Follow*, 7.

54 Rutledge, *That Some May Follow*, 9.

55 "An Act for the Preservation of Game," *Public General Statutes of the Colony of Vancouver Island, 1859–63* (Victoria: Queen's Printer, 1866), 199.

56 The federal Fisheries Act protecting fish and fish habitat did not officially apply to the province until 1877.

57 Colpitts, *Game in the Garden*, 82–83, 126.

58 Colpitts, *Game in the Garden*, 73; *Wild Animals I Have Met in the Canadian Rockies*, Soo Line brochure, ca.1910, 3, pamphlet collection, BC Archives; see also Ed W. Sandys, *Fishing and Shooting on the Canadian Pacific Railway*, 3rd ed. (Montreal: Canadian Pacific Railway Company, 1891), Chung Textual Materials, UBC Rare Books and Special Collections, doi.org/10.14288/1.0229063. In 1887, the new CPR rail line to BC was featured in *The Sportsman's Guide to the Hunting and Shooting Grounds of the United States and Canada* (New York: Chas. T. Dilingham, 1888), 190–92.

59 Colpitts, *Game in the Garden*, 115.

60 Barry A. Leach, "The Decline of Geese and Swans on the Lower Fraser River," *BC Studies*, no. 43 (Autumn 1979): 30.

61 BC Conservation Data Centre, "Species Summary: *Branta bernicla*," BC Ministry of Environment, 2010; Canadian Wildlife Service, "Population Status of Migratory Game Birds in Canada," CWS Migratory Birds Regulatory Report No. 45, November 2015; Campbell et al., *Nonpasserines*, 272.

62 W.T. Munro, "Status of Brant," Victoria: Fish and Wildlife Branch, 1977.

63 Neil Dawe, interview by the author, Qualicum Beach, BC, June 24, 2019.

64 Dawe, interview; Brant Wildlife Festival, "Our History," accessed September 8, 2020, http://brantfestival.bc.ca.

65 "A Bill for the Passage of an Act for the Preservation of Game," *Victoria Gazette*, April 23, 1859.

66 By 1892, provincial game legislation guarded landowner investments in imported British songbirds by extending year-round protections to English blackbirds, chaffinches, linnets and skylarks. Georgiana Ball, "A History of Wildlife Management Practices in British Columbia to 1918" (MA thesis, University of Victoria, 1981), 35, 39.

67 Vancouver Island placed a bounty on cougars in 1864. In 1869, bounty payments were extended to cougars and wolves killed in settled areas across the two colonies. Early bounty legislation aimed to protect livestock, rather than other wildlife, from predation. Richard Mackie, "Cougars, Colonists, and the Rural Settlement of Vancouver Island," in *Beyond the City Limits: Rural History in British Columbia*, ed. R.W. Sandwell (Vancouver: UBC Press, 1999), 123; Ball, "History of Wildlife Management," 38.

68 Ball, "History of Wildlife Management," 34–36; G. Clifford Carl and C.J.
    Guiguet, *Alien Animals in British Columbia* (Victoria: Royal BC Museum, 1958).
    California and mountain quail from the US, ring-necked pheasants from China
    and gray partridges from Europe were among the species introduced by land-
    owners on the Saanich Peninsula, the Gulf Islands and the Lower Fraser Valley
    in the 1860s and '70s. While California quail remain common in southeastern
    Vancouver Island and the Okanagan and Kettle Valleys, ring-necked pheas-
    ant and gray partridge populations have declined considerably, and mountain
    quail have been extirpated from the province. P.J.A. Davidson, R.J. Cannings,
    A.R. Couturier, D. Lepage and C.M. Di Corrado, eds., *The Atlas of the Breeding
    Birds of British Columbia, 2008–2012* (Delta, BC: Bird Studies Canada), http://
    birdatlas.bc.ca.
69 Ball, "History of Wildlife Management," 40. Rod and gun clubs were typical-
    ly more social in function; fish and game protective associations tended to be
    more overtly proactive in their efforts to maintain a sporting environment by
    lobbying governments, restocking depleted animal populations and enforcing
    fish and game ordinances.
70 Colpitts, *Game in the Garden*, 126; Jonathan Peyton, "Imbricated Geographies
    of Conservation and Consumption in the Stikine Plateau," *Environment and
    History* 17, no. 4 (2011): 565.
71 Ball, "History of Wildlife Management," 54–55.
72 A. Bryan Williams, *Game Trails in British Columbia: Big Game and Other Sport
    in the Wilds of British Columbia* (New York: Scribner's, 1925), 180, cited in Hurn,
    "Talent of Silver," 40.
73 Colpitts, *Game in the Garden*, 83–84; Ball, "History of Wildlife Management," 41.
74 Game Protection Amendment Act, RSBC 1890, c. 19. In 1898, amendments fur-
    ther restricted wild animal exports by prohibiting fur trade companies from
    handling deerskins and forbidding the wasting of deer flesh.
75 Game Protection Act, RSBC 1898, c. 24.
76 British Columbia, Legislative Assembly, *Sessional Papers, 1906*, "First Report of
    the Provincial Game and Forest Warden of the Province of British Columbia," 5.
77 Rutledge, *That Some May Follow*, 235.
       Informers received half of the penalty obtained for information leading to a
    conviction. Game Protection Act, RSBC 1898, c. 24, s. 22.
78 Ball, "History of Wildlife Management," 43, 61–62.
79 Early twentieth-century reporting and tourism literature lay most of the blame
    for wildlife depletion on Indigenous hunters, ignoring the role of settler and
    non-resident hunters in the reduction of big game. See, for example, "Indian
    Hunters Killing Off Game," *Vancouver Daily Province*, February 24, 1905. The
    Canadian Pacific Railway's 1909 pamphlet *Fishing, Shooting, Canoe Trips, and
    Camping* also references the "heavy toll levied each year by the Stoney Indians"
    on Rocky Mountain wildlife and lists "Indians in the Canadian Rockies" as "the
    Bighorn's most relentless enemy" (10, 19).

80 Ball, "History of Wildlife Management," 54–55.

81 A lack of provincial legislation protecting forests meant that Williams focused almost exclusively on fish and game legislation and its enforcement. Even forest fire protection was primarily a Dominion Forest Branch (federal) responsibility. The four provincial fire wardens appointed in 1905 reported not to Williams but to the Department of Lands and Works. Gerry Lister, "History of the British Columbia Conservation Officer Service," *International Game Warden Magazine*, Summer 2005.

82 Cowan, "Science and the Conservation of Wildlife," 85.

Chapter 4 | Conserving Wildlife in the Early Twentieth Century

1   Gifford Pinchot, *Breaking New Ground* (Seattle: University of Washington Press, 1972), 353.

2   Lister, "History."

3   Lister, "History," n.p.

4   British Columbia, Legislative Assembly, *Sessional Papers, 1908*, "Fourth Report of the Provincial Game and Forest Warden of the Province of British Columbia"; Ball, "History of Wildlife Management," 61; Colpitts, *Game in the Garden*, 89.

5   Bruce D. Leopold, "Wildlife Ownership," in Leopold, Kessler and Cummins, *North American Wildlife Policy and Law*, 27, 29.

6   British Columbia, Legislative Assembly, *Sessional Papers, 1906*, "Second Report of the Provincial Game and Forest Warden of the Province of British Columbia," F10; Colpitts, *Game in the Garden*, 89.

7   British Columbia, Legislative Assembly, *Sessional Papers, 1906*, "Second Report of the Provincial Game and Forest Warden," F10.

8   Colpitts, *Game in the Garden*, 84.

9   British Columbia, Legislative Assembly, *Sessional Papers, 1911*, "Seventh Report of the Chief Game Guardian of the Province of British Columbia," 6, 15.

10 Colpitts, *Game in the Garden*, 140.

11 Colpitts, *Game in the Garden*, 137–38; John Spencer Church, "Mining Companies in the West Kootenay and Boundary Regions of British Columbia, 1890–1900: Capital Formation and Financial Operations" (MA thesis, University of British Columbia, 1961).

12 Colpitts, *Game in the Garden*, 125.

13 Newcomers to the Yale and Cariboo Districts in the first decade of the twentieth century, for example, were over 50 per cent non-British-born. Nanaimo's coal mines had attracted 7,000 "foreigners," mostly Chinese, to join an existing population of 25,000 by 1911. Colpitts, *Game in the Garden*, 137.

14 Colpitts, *Game in the Garden*, 153.

15 Although non-resident hunters were relatively few in number—269 took out licences in 1910, for example—generous bag limits meant their impact on wildlife

populations could be substantial. In 1909, the bag limit for non-resident hunt-ers was two moose, one wapiti (elk), two sheep rams of any one species and no more than three in all, three goats, three caribou, three deer of any one species and no more than than five in all, and 250 ducks. Game Protection Act, 1898, Amendment Act, 1908, RSBC 1908, c. 18, s. 3, cited in Ball, "History of Wildlife Management," 62.

16 Colpitts, *Game in the Garden*, 153.

17 Turney-High, *Ethnography of the Kutenai*, 44. The ivory canine teeth of elk—the evolutionary remnants of the protruding tusks of their ancient ancestors—pro-vided decorative accents on clothing made by Indigenous women. They were also sought after as a sign of membership by Elk Lodge members in the US and for Elks of Canada members after 1912.

18 Colpitts, *Game in the Garden*, 154.

19 Colpitts, *Game in the Garden*, 120.

20 A. Bryan Williams, *Game of British Columbia*, Bureau of Provincial Information, Bulletin 17 (Victoria: King's Printer, 1908), 5, cited in Colpitts, *Game in the Garden*, 117.

21 The 269 non-resident hunters who took out licences in 1910 produced $2,690 in revenue—an insufficient sum to cover Game Department activities. Two years earlier, Williams's requests for government support had finally been heeded with the receipt of a $10,000 operating budget. The removal of forests from his portfolio the following year allowed Williams to focus on wildlife protection as provincial game warden. Gerry Lister notes, "in actuality, any forestry work that had occurred had been under the direction of the Chief Commissioner of Lands… and had not involved any of Williams' staff, with the exception of the cross-appointed fire wardens." "History," n.p.

22 British Columbia Fisheries Act, RSBC 1901, c. 25, cited in Ball, "History of Wildlife Management," 84.

23 The British North America Act placed all fisheries in Canada under federal ju-risdiction. Federal officials' ignorance of local conditions in drafting provincial regulations, and their prioritization of coastal commercial fisheries over inland and sport fisheries, contributed to the frustration by provincial fisheries advo-cates and politicians. In 1910, the province was forced to repeal all fisheries leg-islation with the exception of the $5 non-resident angler's licence. Ball, "History of Wildlife Management," 84–85.

24 Hunters could take out an ordinary licence ($2.50) to hunt birds and deer other than moose, or a general licence ($5) to hunt game birds and animals. Game Protection Amendment Act, RSBC 1913, c. 27, s. 9; Lister, "History"; Colpitts, *Game in the Garden*, 89–90; Ball, "History of Wildlife Management, 64."

25 Ball, "History of Wildlife Management," 113.

26 Unorganized districts were exempt from provincial game laws. In 1906, for ex-ample, only Greenwood, Grand Forks, Similkameen, Kamloops, Okanagan and

Fernie were organized, in addition to cities and municipalities. Ball, "History of Wildlife Management," 61.

27 Williams to Manson, January 18, 1906, Game Warden Correspondence, BC Archives, cited in Ball, "History of Wildlife Management," 63–64.

28 Ball, "History of Wildlife Management," 94.

29 British Columbia, Legislative Assembly, *Sessional Papers, 1915*, "Game Warden Report for 1914," cited in Ball, "History of Wildlife Management," 122, note 120.

30 On the tremendous growth of moose populations in the central Interior in the 1910s and '20s due to the prevalence of fires and resulting habitat improvement, see James Hatter, "The Moose of Central British Columbia" (PhD thesis, State College of Washington, Pullman, 1950), reprinted as *Early Ecology and Management of the Moose in Central British Columbia* (self-pub., 2011), 27–71 (page numbers refer to the 2011 edition). David J. Spalding refutes earlier interpretations that moose were absent in the region before this period; see Spalding, "The Early History of Moose (*Alces alces*): Distribution and Relative Abundance in British Columbia," *Contributions to Natural Science* 11 (March 1990): 1–12.

31 The game bird farm operated until 1933. Ball, "History of Wildlife Management," 76–77.

32 In 1914, Williams oversaw the less successful importation to the islands of exotic red deer from New Zealand. The deer flourished for a few decades before disappearing later in the twentieth century. Ball, "History of Wildlife Management," 78–79.

33 Ball, "History of Wildlife Management," 39, 78.

34 Colpitts, *Game in the Garden*, 146, 157; Jen Corrine Brown, *Trout Culture: How Fly Fishing Forever Changed the Rocky Mountain West* (Seattle: University of Washington Press, 2015), 98.

35 Donald G. Peterson, "A Brief History of Fish Culture in BC and the Current Status of the Current Provincial Hatchery Program," in *Speaking for the Salmon: Hatcheries and the Protection of Wild Salmon*, ed. Craig Orr, Patricia Gallaugher and Jennifer Penikett (Burnaby: Simon Fraser University, June 2002), 9–17.

36 Under the Fisheries Act, the federal government held jurisdiction over all marine, coastal and inland fisheries. In 1937, the federal government delegated authority to BC to oversee freshwater recreational fisheries, including licensing of freshwater fishing and the delivery of hatchery programs to stock lakes and rivers. It retained jurisdiction over freshwater and tidal salmon fisheries and Indigenous, commercial and recreational fisheries in tidal waters.

37 Colpitts, *Game in the Garden*, 159.

38 Peterson, "Brief History of Fish Culture," 9.

39 A syndicate of sportsmen had operated a shooting preserve on James Island for some time before buying the island in 1910. Among them were high-ranking government officials and businessmen, including Lieutenant-Governor T.W. Patterson, Premier Richard McBride, Provincial Secretary and Minister of Education H.E. Young and businessman A.E. Todd of the fish-packing family.

The sportsmen imported exotic game birds and fallow deer for release on the island and hired a private game guardian to protect animals from poaching. Ball, "History of Wildlife Management," 78–79.

40 Colpitts, *Game in the Garden*, 156.

41 Game Protection Act, 1898, Amendment Act, 1908, RSBC 1908, c. 18, s. 4.

42 British Columbia, Legislative Assembly, *Sessional Papers, 1909*, "4th Report of the Provincial Game and Forest Warden, 1908," by Arthur Bryan Williams, 511.

Both reserves prohibited hunting of all game animals and birds for a period of ten years. American hunter and conservationist William T. Hornaday launched an international campaign to protect Rocky Mountain bighorn sheep in the East Kootenay region beginning in 1907. His communications with Bryan Williams supported the Fernie District Game Protective Association's proposal for a game reserve at Elk River. Colpitts, *Game in the Garden*, 134–37.

43 Ball, "History of Wildlife Management," 71–73; Colpitts, *Game in the Garden*, 134–36. The Fernie District Game Protective Association, advocates for the Elk River Reserve, formed in 1906 primarily out of concern about hunting by non-resident First Nations such as the Stoney. Game law amendments made it unlawful for non-resident First Nations to hunt in the province in 1898.

44 Bowron Lakes Game Reserve, established in 1925, provided the foundation for Bowron Lakes Provincial Park in 1961. The White River Game Reserve near Canal Flats, established in the late 1920s, became part of the Height of the Rockies Provincial Park in 1995. The Elk River Game Reserve designation was removed in 1963. Portions of the reserve were absorbed into Elk Lakes Provincial Park (established in 1973) and Height of the Rockies Provincial Park.

45 British Columbia, Legislative Assembly, *Sessional Papers, 1908*, "Game Warden Report," J6, cited in Ball, "History of Wildlife Management," 113, note 12.

46 Only the most wealthy travellers could afford the journey by rail and then horseback into the province's wilderness parks, plus the private lodge or cabin accommodation within them. Failure to meet expectations for provincial tourism revenue, combined with pressure from mining and forestry interests, led to a series of amendments permitting other forms of revenue generation. Mining claims and development were permitted in Strathcona Park by 1918, and amendments to the Provincial Park Act in 1933 permitted modifications to park boundaries. Further amendments in 1939 permitted logging and mining in most of the province's large wilderness parks. Begg, "Legislating British Columbia," 113–18.

47 Precedence for this shift occurred in 1910, when the Game Department was placed under the control of the attorney general, the chief law enforcement officer in the province who also oversaw the operations of the BC Provincial Police. The Game Conservation Board included the provincial museum curator, a chief game inspector (a provincial police officer) and three other appointed members. A few former Game Department deputies received appointments with the provincial police. Lister, "History"; Ball, "History of Wildlife Management," 86–88.

48 The treaty remained in effect until hostilities erupted among signatory countries in World War II. It served as the basis for the subsequent marine mammal protection legislation in the 1960s and '70s.

49 Janet Foster, *Working for Wildlife: The Beginning of Preservation in Canada* (Toronto: University of Toronto Press, 1978), 121–22.

50 Foster, *Working for Wildlife*, 124.

51 Foster, *Working for Wildlife*, 123.

52 This development was preceded by the passage of the US Weeks-Maclean Act in 1913, which placed migratory birds under the care of the US federal government.

53 Neil S. Forkey, *Canadians and the Natural Environment to the Twenty-First Century* (Toronto: University of Toronto Press, 2012), 59–67. See also John Sandlos, "Nature's Nations: The Shared Conservation History of Canada and the USA," *International Journal of Environmental Studies* 70, no. 3 (2013): 358–71.

54 Ball, "History of Wildlife Management," 81.

55 Foster, *Working for Wildlife*, 136.

56 Foster, *Working for Wildlife*, 140–46. The extension of the open season to March 10 occurred largely in response to lobbying from powerful congressmen along the Mississippi Valley flyway.

57 J. Alexander Burnett, *A Passion for Wildlife: The History of the Canadian Wildlife Service* (Vancouver: UBC Press, 2003), 12.

58 Burnett, *Passion for Wildlife*, 148.

59 National Audubon Society, Christmas Bird Count, Historical Results by Count, accessed February 10, 2023, http://christmasbirdcount.org.

60 Charles M. Edwards (Cranbrook, BC) to A. Bryan Williams, May 16, 1907, cited in Jim Cameron, "It's All in the Game: Janus Looks at the History of East Kootenay Hunting," *Cranbrook Daily Townsman*, May 1, 2015.

61 Loo, *States of Nature*, 44.

62 Tough, "Conservation and the Indian," 66.

63 Canada, Commission of Conservation, *National Conference on Conservation of Game, Fur-Bearing Animals and Other Wild Life* (Ottawa: J. De Labroquerie, 1919), 30.

64 Canada, Commission of Conservation, *National Conference*, 21, 30.

65 See, for example, "Petition of Spuzzum band to Indian Agent Graham, Lytton, BC," February 29, 1916, Canada, Department of Indian Affairs, RG 10, vol. 6735, file 420-3A, LAC, cited in Brenda Ireland, "'Working a Great Hardship on Us': First Nations People, The State and Fur Conservation in British Columbia before 1935" (MA thesis, University of British Columbia, 1995), 10, note 18.

66 Colpitts, *Game in the Garden*, 134–37.

67 John Sandlos, *Hunters at the Margin: Native People and Wildlife Conservation in the Northwest Territories* (Vancouver: UBC Press, 2007), 236; Tough, "Conservation and the Indian," 66.

68 Tough, "Conservation and the Indian," 68.

69 Federal laws regulating First Nations' wildlife use included, among others, the Indian Act (1876), the Dominion Forest Reserves and Park Act (1911) and the Migratory Birds Convention Act (1917). Loo, *States of Nature*, 45.

70 J. Michael Thoms, "A Place Called Pennask: Fly Fishing and Colonialism at a British Columbia Lake," *BC Studies*, no. 133 (Spring 2002): 75.

71 The province amended its game laws in 1897 to exempt Indigenous people resident in unorganized districts from fish and game regulations. Further amendments in 1914 and 1924 exempted all Indigenous Peoples in BC from the effects of the legislation. Game Protection Act, RSBC 1897, c. 88, s. 17; Game Act, RSBC 1914, c. 33, s. 6; Game Act, RSBC 1924, c. 98, s. 6.

72 Duncan Campbell Scott, "Relation of Indians to Wild Life [*sic*] Conservation," in Canada, Commission of Conservation, *National Conference,* 21, cited in Tough, "Conservation and the Indian," 66. The federal justice department generally supported this stance by upholding provincial charges against Indigenous hunters. Loo, *States of Nature*, 96.

73 Loo, *States of Nature*, 96.

74 In *R v. Jim* (1915), the BC Supreme Court found that Aboriginal hunting on reserves was subject only to federal laws, and not provincial game laws. As the Supreme Court of Canada would rule later in the twentieth century, in most parts of BC Aboriginal rights (and title) continue to exist, as they were not extinguished by treaty. In general, Aboriginal rights such as hunting and fishing are based "on the continued occupation of lands by Aboriginal peoples since before European settlement." Aboriginal rights, in other words, existed *before* they were officially recognized in the Canadian Constitution Act of 1982; section 35 of the act recognized and affirmed Aboriginal rights, but it did not create them. Erin Hanson, "Constitution Act 1982, Section 35," Indigenous Foundations (UBC First Nations and Indigenous Studies Program), n.d., accessed June 25, 2022, http://indigenousfoundations.arts.ubc.ca; *R v. Jim* (1915) 26 CCC 236.

75 J.F. Smith, Special Report, November 2, 1921, RG 10, vol. 6735, file 420-3A, LAC, cited in Loo, *States of Nature*, 47.

76 Loo, *States of Nature*, 47.

77 The BC Supreme Court came to a similar conclusion six years earlier, when it overturned the conviction of a W̱SÁNEĆ (Saanich) man for possessing venison out of season. *R v. Jim* (1915).

78 Barman, *West beyond the West*, 165.

79 Fishways installed between 1945 and 1966 eventually contributed to the revival of the Fraser River runs. D.C. Harris, *Landing Native Fisheries*, 114; Richard Allan Rajala, "'This Wasteful Use of a River': Log Driving, Conservation, and British Columbia's Stellako River Controversy, 1965–72," *BC Studies*, no. 165 (Spring 2010): 34, 41, 68; Newell, *Tangled Webs*, 117.

80 R.C. Harris, *Making Native Space*, 282.

81 Petition to E. Bell (Agent), Lillooet, September 19, 1905, RG 10, vol. 6735, file 420-3, LAC, cited in Loo, *States of Nature*, 46, note 22.

82 Lutz, *Makúk*, 147.

83 Secretary of the Royal Commission on Indian Affairs for British Columbia to the Attorney General of British Columbia, February 18, 1914, RG 10, vol. 11020, file 516, LAC, cited in Loo, *States of Nature*, 46. The meaning of "siwash duck" is drawn from *The Dictionary of Canadianisms on Historical Principles Online* (DCHP-1 Online), ed. Walter A. Avis et al. (Toronto: Gage Educational Publishing, 1967).

84 George, *Living on the Edge*, 67. The International Fur Seal Convention placed a moratorium on the harvest of northern fur seals (temporary residents in BC waters) and sea otters and placed the management of future harvests under the control of the United States. Exemptions were made for specific Indigenous groups (the Ainu of Japan and the Aleut of Alaska) but only if they employed pre-contact technologies. On the value of the nineteenth-century seal hunt to coastal Indigenous communities, see Lutz, *Makúk*, 201.

85 "Petition of Spuzzum band," cited in Ireland, "Working a Great Hardship," 10, note 18.

86 Ireland, "Working a Great Hardship," 4.

87 Ireland, "Working a Great Hardship," 5. As Georgiana Ball has shown, independent traders "rivalled and often exceeded the HBC" and their Indigenous suppliers in the value of land furs exported annually in the last quarter of the nineteenth century ("History of Wildlife Management," 48).

88 Game Protection Amendment Act, RSBC 1896, c. 22, s. 11, cited in Ball, "History of Wildlife Management," 49.

89 "Petition of the Chiefs of Stuart Lake, Stony Creek, and Fraser Lake tribes to the Superintendent of Indian Affairs," October 30, 1905, RG 10, vol. 6735, file 420-3, LAC, cited in Loo, *States of Nature*, 49.

90 Ireland examines the petitions sent by chiefs from the Fort St. James, Burns Lake, Stuart Lake, Stella and Stoney Creek and Fort George bands in the 1900s and 1910s in "Working a Great Hardship," 9–14.

91 Ireland, "Working a Great Hardship," 12.

92 Drake, Jackson & Helmcken to the Provincial Secretary, February 8, 1905, Game Warden Correspondence for 1905, BC Archives, cited in Ball, "History of Wildlife Management," 66.

93 Acknowledging that beaver population losses were primarily a problem of southern, more populated districts, Williams granted a two-year exemption for northern Indigenous groups and their trading partners from 1905 to 1907. Difficulties in enforcing exemption boundaries, however, led Williams to reinstate a provincewide ban from 1907 to 1911. In 1908, Williams noted the "astounding growth" of beaver populations in southern districts. Extensive trapping in 1911 led to a second provincewide closure, from 1912 to 1913; this second closure

exempted Indigenous trappers and their trading partners in the Stikine, Liard and Peace Districts. Ball, "History of Wildlife Management," 67–68. Further closures followed: in 1914, the Game Department added fox, marten, fisher, mink, muskrat, raccoon and ermine to list of fur-bearers seasonally protected.

94 Prospectors and farmers hunting on their own lands were granted trapping licences free of charge.

95 Barman, *West beyond the West*, 165.

96 David Vogt, "'Indians on White Lines': Bureaucracy, Race, and Power on Northern British Columbian Traplines, 1925–1950," *Journal of the Canadian Historical Association* 26, no. 1 (2015): 164; Ireland, "Working a Great Hardship," 6–7.

97 BC Department of Attorney-General, *Tenth Report of the Provincial Game Warden of the Province of British Columbia* (Victoria: William H. Cullin, 1915), J7; BC Provincial Game Commission, *Report of Provincial Game Commission for the Year 1936* (Victoria: Charles F. Banfield, 1937), Q7, cited in Vogt, "Indians on White Lines," 170. Vogt speculates that Indigenous trappers (and their associated traplines) were likely fewer still by the end of the 1920s, as the estimates for 1936 incorporated new Indigenous traplines registered by DIA officials in the early 1930s.

98 British Columbia Provincial Police, Division "D" District, Fort George, Prince George Detachment, March 21, 1924, GR 1085, box 14, file 1, BC Archives, cited in Ireland, "Working a Great Hardship," 6–7.

99 Glenn Iceton, "'Many Families of Unseen Indians': Trapline Registration and Understandings of Aboriginal Title in the BC-Yukon Borderlands" *BC Studies*, no. 201 (Spring 2019): 67.

100 Vogt, "Indians on White Lines," 165.

101 Ireland, "Working a Great Hardship," 25.

102 C. Gordon Hewitt, *The Conservation of Wild Life in Canada* (New York: C. Scribner's Sons, 1921). Hewitt's work inspired ecology pioneer Charles Elton to begin his studies on population cycling at Oxford in the 1920s and 1930s (George Colpitts, personal communication, October 31, 2022).

103 Hugh Brody, *Maps and Dreams: Indians and the British Columbia Frontier* (Vancouver: Douglas & McIntyre, 1981), 87, cited in Ireland, "Working a Great Hardship," 26.

104 Ireland, "Working a Great Hardship," 26.

105 Vogt, "Indians on White Lines," 168–69; 184, note 28.

106 Vogt, "Indians on White Lines," 169–70.

107 Ireland, "Working a Great Hardship," 30.

108 Peyton, "Imbricated Geographies," 567.

109 Vogt, "Indians on White Lines," 170.

110 Vogt, "Indians on White Lines," 170–71.

111 Sterritt, *Mapping My Way Home*, 302.

112   This waiver of reporting obligations for Indigenous trappers, Vogt observes, continued into the mid-1970s. By way of compromise, Indian agents supplied game officials with updated lists of activity trappers at the beginning of each season ("Indians on White Lines," 186, note 42).

113   Vogt, "Indians on White Lines," 171; Ireland, "Working a Great Hardship," 80. DIA purchased traplines for Indigenous trappers in part because Indigenous trappers were exempted from the $10 trapping licence required to register a trapline. Their efforts succeeded in curbing the losses. By 1949, 56 per cent of the province's registered trappers were status Indians who held 45 per cent of the total traplines—up about 5 per cent from 1936. These numbers were higher in the northern part of the province, where status Indians constituted 71 per cent of registered trappers and held 57 per cent of all traplines. These ratios remain fairly constant today, with "about half" of registered trappers in the province identifying as Indigenous. Vogt, "Indians on White Lines," 166–67.

114   Vogt, "Indians on White Lines," 172.

115   Loo, States of Nature, 42.

116   Albert J. Wilson to Bryan Williams, May 24, 1913, GR 446, box 41, file 5, BC Archives, cited in Loo, States of Nature, 39. "Pre-emptors" were those who claimed or "pre-empted" land before it had been surveyed and released in a Crown land grant. Wilson was likely objecting to the 1913 amendments to the Game Protection Act, which, unlike earlier legislation that had exempted settlers in remote areas from game regulations, required "Indians, resident farmers, and free miners" to obtain a (free) permit to kill deer for their own and their families' immediate use. Such permits gave local game wardens the authority to specify the number of deer that could be killed and the length of time hunters could keep deer meat in their possession. Game Protection Act, RSBC 1911, c. 93; Game Protection Amendment Act, 1913, RSBC 1913, c. 27.

117   Loo, States of Nature, 43; Colpitts, Game in the Garden, 133–39.

118   Wallace Baikie, Rolling with the Times (self-pub., 1985), cited in Hurn, "Talent of Silver," 39. Gerry Lister describes the history of "pitlamping" as a hunting practice first documented in Sooke in 1892, when hunters used miners' head lamps to illuminate the eyes of deer after dark. The bane of game wardens for its lack of sportsmanship and the considerable dangers it caused for other hunters, pitlamping was incorporated as a specific offence in BC game law. In 1918, amendments to the Game Act instituted a mandatory jail sentence for pitlamping, without the option of a fine. Lister, "History."

119   Loo, States of Nature, 40.

120   Williams, Game Trails, 345.

121   William Floyd, Greenwood's killer, was arrested and charged but acquitted by reason of insanity. Both Frank Gott (Farey's killer) and Albert Farey were World War I veterans and experienced outdoorsmen. Gott was shot in the leg after a two-day manhunt by the warden service and area police; he later died of exposure. Lister, "History"; Loo, States of Nature, 53.

122 Bob Jamieson and Pete Lum, "The History of Guide Outfitting in the East Kootenay," 1983, in Rutledge, *That Some May Follow*, 17–19.

123 Peyton, "Imbricated Geographies," 559; Loo, *States of Nature*, 58.

124 As Peyton notes, the $4/day plus board that Tahltan men could earn as assistant guides paled in comparison to the "few hundred to over a thousand dollars" they could earn from a winter's catch of fur. "Imbricated Geographies," 564–65.

125 Ball, "History of Wildlife Management," 69. Williams took over the supervision of bounty payments in 1912.

126 Ball, "History of Wildlife Management," 70. A bounty on coyotes was introduced in 1910. As historian Richard Mackie explains, "the bounty required the hunter to exhibit the [animal], or its hide, to a government official (game warden, justice of the peace, government agent, municipal clerk), who would punch a hole in the left ear and requisition a cheque for the hunter." "Cougars, Colonists," 124.

Bounty payments cost the provincial government an estimated $1 million between 1922 and 1956. D.H. Pimlott, "Wolf Control in Canada," *Canadian Audubon Magazine* 23, no.5 (1961): 146, cited in Loo, *States of Nature*, 156.

127 By 1900, cougars had been eliminated from much of their former range across the continent. Today, Vancouver Island is home to the densest population of cougars in North America. The Vancouver Island cougar (*Felix concolor vancouverensis*) is a slightly larger and darker subspecies of its mainland counterpart, *Felix concolor*. Mackie, "Cougars, Colonists," 121, 124.

128 In 1925, Mackie notes, Smith sold adult cougar skins to taxidermists for $10 and received the same for cougar skulls from museum collectors. He estimated in 1937 that he and his dogs had treed and killed 900 to 1,200 cougars over the course of his career. Mackie describes Smith as a member of Vancouver Island's "bush gentry," part of an "educated rural immigrant group" from the professional and landowning classes of Britain who had rarely farmed before coming to BC. Members of this group often "benefitted from small private incomes in the form of pensions or investments" and, given their education, took up positions in local government offices as game wardens, Indian agents, justices of the peace or magistrates. "Cougars, Colonists," 126, 138.

129 Margaret Horsfield, *Cougar Annie's Garden* (Nanaimo: Salal Books, 1999); Mackie, "Cougars, Colonists," 129.

130 These categorizations were not new: in the 1830s and '40s, the HBC had encouraged the extermination of wolves in the Columbia Department to protect their interests, paying high year-round prices to Indigenous trappers and using strychnine to poison wolves around company farms. Hammond, "Marketing Wildlife," 17.

131 Loo, *States of Nature*, 4, 14. As Ball notes, game legislation in this period treated black and grizzly bears as both a fur-bearer and a trophy animal (and near settlements, a pest). Williams encouraged the hunting of bear for trophies, rather than pelts, given the greater returns from big-game hunters willing to pay $500 to $1,000 for a bear hunt over the $50 a trapper could fetch for the

pelt. Bear species received no protection from game legislation in this period, with the exception of a short closed season introduced in 1911. Ball, "History of Wildlife Management," 69.

132 British Columbia, Legislative Assembly, *Sessional Papers, 1912,* "Game Warden Report," I-10, cited in Ball, "History of Wildlife Management," 70.

133 Ball, "History of Wildlife Management," 69.

134 Linda M. Nichol, E.J. Gregr, R. Flinn, J.K.B. Ford, R. Gurney, L. Michaluk and A. Peacock, "British Columbia Commercial Whaling Catch Data 1908 to 1967: A Detailed Description of the BC Historical Whaling Database" (Canadian Technical Report of Fisheries and Aquatic Sciences 2396, Fisheries and Oceans Canada, Science Branch, Pacific Region, Nanaimo, 2002); Fisheries and Oceans Canada, "Action Plan for Blue, Fin, Sei, and North Pacific Right Whales (*Balaenoptera musculus, B. physalus, B. borealis,* and *Eubalaena japonica*) in Canadian Pacific Waters" (Species at Risk Act Action Plan Series, Fisheries and Oceans Canada, Ottawa, 2017); BC Cetacean Sightings Network, "History of Whaling in British Columbia," n.d., accessed June 15, 2022, http://wildwhales. org; Kate Humble, "BC Whaling—an Uncomfortable History," *Victoria News,* January 7, 2015.

135 Grazing Act, RSBC 1919, c. 30; Reid, "Grasslands Debates," 98.

136 Lynne Stonier-Newman, *Policing a Pioneer Province: The BC Provincial Police, 1858–1950* (Madeira Park, BC: Harbour, 1991), 162, cited in Mica Jorgenson, "'A Business Proposition': Naturalists, Guides, and Sportsmen in the Formation of the Bowron Lakes Game Reserve," *BC Studies,* no. 175 (Autumn 2012): 20, note 56.

137 Begg, "Legislating British Columbia," 83–87. For a history of agricultural improvement projects in this period, see Jamie Murton, *Creating a Modern Countryside: Liberalism and Land Resettlement in British Columbia* (Vancouver: UBC Press, 2007).

138 Vernon C. Brink, "Natural History Societies of B.C.," in *Our Wildlife Heritage,* ed. Murray, 151–52.

139 Susan Fisher and Daphne Solecki, *A Hundred Years of Natural History: The Vancouver Natural History Society, 1918–2018* (Vancouver: Vancouver Natural History Society, 2018), 48–49.

140 Cited in Peyton, "Imbricated Geographies," 575.

141 British Columbia, Department of Attorney-General, *Report of Provincial Game Commissioner, 1931,* by A. Bryan Williams (Victoria, 1932), 6, cited in Jorgenson, "A Business Proposition," 13.

142 Colpitts, *Game in the Garden,* 167.

143 Newell, *Tangled Webs,* 112–13.

Chapter 5 | Ian McTaggart Cowan and the Rise of Scientific
Wildlife Conservation

1   The BC Game Commission was established in 1934 to direct game management
    and enforce game laws in the province. It operated within the Ministry of the
    Attorney General until 1957, when it was replaced by the Fish and Game Branch
    in the Department of Recreation and Conservation. See B.C. Conservation
    Officer Service, "Program Names through the Years," n.d., accessed March 2,
    2023, http://gov.bc.ca.

2   Cowan's doctoral studies at Berkeley were financed by the American sugar heiress
    and pioneering zoologist Annie Alexander, who founded Berkeley's Museum of
    Vertebrate Zoology in 1909, participating in the selection of MVZ director Joseph
    Grinnell and supporting its associated scientific expeditions and students. From
    Grinnell, Cowan learned the importance of statistical analysis of wildlife popu-
    lations and the inseparable connections between a species and its environment.
    He applied this training to his 1935 doctoral thesis on the taxonomy, geograph-
    ic variation and dietary needs of mule and white-tailed deer (genus *Odocoileus*)
    in western North America, likely the first published statistical analysis of a pop-
    ulation of big game animals. Rod S. Silver et al., "A Tribute to Ian McTaggart-
    Cowan, 1910–2010, O.C., O.B.C., PhD, LL.D, F.R.S.C.," *Canadian Field-Naturalist*
    124, no. 4 (2010): 367–83; Briony Penn, *The Real Thing: The Natural History of Ian
    McTaggart Cowan* (Calgary: Rocky Mountain Books, 2015), 51, 115, 132–33.

3   Silver et al., "Tribute," 367–68. Briony Penn provides a fascinating account of
    Cowan's early years as a specimen collector in Part 3 of *The Real Thing*, 91–174.

4   For a detailed discussion of the state of the museum under Kermode in the 1930s,
    see Corley-Smith, *White Bears*, 80–86.

5   Ian McTaggart Cowan, interview by Peter Corley-Smith, 1985, Royal BC Museum
    Collection, cited in Penn, *Real Thing*, 207.
        Wartime budget reallocations also played a role in wildlife work at the mu-
    seum, resulting in the cessation of fieldwork on birds and mammals between
    1916 and 1936. Campbell et al., *Nonpasserines*, 19.

6   Silver et al., "Tribute," 368. For further detail on Cowan's biodiversity surveys for
    the Provincial Museum, see Penn, *Real Thing*, 203–81 (Part 5).

7   The series published twenty-six papers from its inception in 1939 until it was
    discontinued fifty years later in 1989. Silver et al., "Tribute," 368; Penn, *Real
    Thing*, 248.

8   Penn charts Cowan's ongoing involvement as a mentor and supporter to the
    Provincial Museum (later Royal BC Museum) curators and directors who fol-
    lowed him, including director Clifford Carl, curator Charles Guiguet, Guiguet's
    successor Alton Harestad, Carl's successor Bristol Foster, Foster's successor
    Yorke Edwards and Edwards's successor William Barkley (all six of whom were
    former students of Cowan's). Penn, *Real Thing*, 279.

9 Richard Mackie, *Hamilton Mack Laing: Hunter-Naturalist* (Victoria: Sono Nis Press, 1985).

10 Mackie, *Hamilton Mack Laing*, 136.

11 Mackie, *Hamilton Mack Laing*, 149.

12 Mackie, *Hamilton Mack Laing*, 139. The three other species named after Laing, including two subspecies of mice, have since been reclassified as subpopulations.

13 Penn, *Real Thing*, 114.

14 Silver et al., "Tribute," 370.

15 The Cowan Vertebrate Museum, established in 1943, grew to contain over 40,000 specimens representing over 2,500 species, the second-largest scientific collection of birds, mammals, reptiles and amphibians in British Columbia. Today it forms part of UBC's Beaty Biodiversity Museum. "Natural History Collections," Beaty Biodiversity Museum, accessed October 16, 2020, https://beatymuseum.ubc.ca/natural-history-collections/.

16 Cited in Penn, *Real Thing*, 44.

17 See Penn, *Real Thing*, 41–60, for a detailed discussion of the "B" and its influence.

18 Ian McTaggart Cowan, "Moments from the Education of an Ornithologist," *Picoides* 11, no. 2 (November 1998): 21, cited in Penn, *Real Thing*, 100.

19 Originally under the jurisdiction of the Department of Lands and Works, the Game Branch was placed under the Department of the Attorney General in 1910, where it remained until 1957, when it was transferred to the newly created Department of Recreation and Conservation. The law enforcement orientation was especially evident during the "police years" of 1918 to 1929, when the Game Department was disbanded and the role of game law enforcement transferred to the provincial police. Lister, "History."

20 Lister, "History."

21 Cowan, "Science and the Conservation of Wildlife," 95.

22 Musfeldt, who graduated with an MA from UBC in 1947, completed the first study of muskrats and their parasites in British Columbia. "Forging Ahead: Iola Musfeldt Was a Biology Pioneer during World War II," UBC Science, n.d., accessed January 7, 2022, https://science.ubc.ca.

23 Cowan, "Science and the Conservation of Wildlife," 96.

24 University-trained biologists hired by the Game Commission became, like their game warden colleagues, *ex officio* BC Police with all of the legal powers of a police constable. Dennis Demarchi, "Wildlife Biologist and Bird Artist William Glen Smith (1923–1993)," *Wildlife Afield* 12, no. 1 (2015): 75.

25 The Cache Creek Game Checking Station opened in 1946 in response to a dramatic increase in resident and non-resident hunters in the Kamloops, Cariboo and Lillooet districts. A permanent game-check station, constructed in 1955, operated during hunting season at Cache Creek until 1981. The Cache Creek location, which acted as a funnel for almost all southbound traffic moving out

of the Interior, became less strategic as alternate highways were constructed in the 1960s and '70s. Alan D. Martin, interview by the author, April 26, 2019; Lister, "History."

26 Penn, *Real Thing*, 159–61. In the 1950s, the remains of elk antlers found buried near Merritt and Quesnel confirmed the presence of elk across the central Interior in the 1830s. With the exception of the Kootenays and the area north of the Peace River in the province's northeast, where populations remain high, elk were much more numerous in the early nineteenth century than they are today. David J. Spalding, "The History of Elk (*Cervus elaphus*) in British Columbia," *Contributions to Natural Science* 18 (October 1992): 1.

27 Hatter, *Moose in Central British Columbia*; Jenny Feick and Ian Hatter, interview by the author, Victoria, BC, April 25, 2019.

28 Cowan to Tom Beck, September 3, 1994, Cowan personal notes, folio 285, Ian McTaggart Cowan Fonds, Elder Council of BC, University of Victoria Special Collections, cited in Penn, *Real Thing*, 162.

29 Cowan, "Science and the Conservation of Wildlife," 96.

30 The BC Wildlife Federation (BCWF) was informally established in 1947 as the BC Fish and Game Zones Council, a federation of fish and game clubs from Vancouver Island, the Lower Mainland, the Interior and the West Kootenay that formed with assistance from game commissioners Cunningham and Butler (newer clubs in the East Kootenay and northern BC joined the federation in the 1950s and '60s). In 1951, the Council was registered under the Societies Act as the BC Fish and Game Council. By 1965, the newly renamed BC Wildlife Federation was the largest conservation organization in the province, with 175 clubs and 40,000 members (still only a small fraction—roughly 5 per cent—of the province's angling and hunting licence holders) and an annual budget of $1.3 million. While membership fees provided the largest revenue source, the Game Commission and later the Fish and Game Branch contributed grants of $5,000 to $8,000 toward annual operating expenses between 1947 and 1978. John Gordon Terpenning, "The B.C. Wildlife Federation (BCWF) and Government: A Comparative Study of Pressure Group and Government Interaction for Two Periods, 1947 to 1957, and 1958 to 1975" (MA thesis, University of Victoria, 1982), 11, 243; Lee Straight, "Wildlife Societies in B.C.," in *Our Wildlife Heritage*, ed. Murray, 145–46, 150.

31 "Indian Rights," *Native Voice* 1, no. 4 (March 1947): 7. The *Native Voice* newspaper was the official voice of the Native Brotherhood of BC, which formed in 1931 to support Indigenous fishermen and expanded to reflect a range of concerns among coastal First Nations.

32 Lutz, *Makúk*, 202–4. Lutz cites figures that document steep declines in the Indigenous share of BC traplines, from 53 per cent in 1947 to just 10 per cent by 1956. These figures have since been refuted by historian David Vogt, who documented block trapline registrations by the DIA in the 1930s and '40s that corrected earlier losses of Indigenous traplines. By 1949, 56 per cent of the

province's registered trappers were status Indians who held 45 per cent of the total traplines. Vogt, "Indians on White Lines," 166–67.

33 Cowan, "Science and the Conservation of Wildlife," 100; Ernest W. Taylor, "A Study of Factors Affecting Reproduction and Survival of the Ring-Necked Pheasant in the Lower Fraser River Valley of British Columbia" (MA thesis, University of British Columbia, 1950).

34 Cowan, "Science and the Conservation of Wildlife," 99; Hatter, *Moose in Central British Columbia.*

35 Frank R. Butler to Hamilton Mack Laing, February 1924, BC Archives, cited in Mackie, *Hamilton Mack Laing*, 145. The use of poison against problem wildlife was illegal in the province from 1905 until 1950, although some ranchers, guides and farmers made use of strychnine illegally. James Hatter, *Wolves and People: The Management Imperative and Mythology of Animal Rights* (Victoria: Trafford, self-pub, 2005), 7.

36 Cowan, "Science and the Conservation of Wildlife," 100.

37 Penn, *Real Thing*, 310, 315–17.

38 Cowan, "The Timber Wolf in the Rocky Mountain Parks of Canada," *Canadian Journal of Research* 25, no. 5 (1947): 139–74; Penn, *Real Thing*, 344. Cowan's research in the parks also resulted in a number of internal reports, notably "Report on Game Conditions in Banff, Jasper and Kootenay National Parks," CWSC Report no. 313 (Ottawa: Canadian Wildlife Service, 1943). Cowan recommended the culling of elk from the parks, rather than the destruction of wolves, to remove pressure on deteriorating winter ranges. Alan MacEachern, "Ian McTaggart-Cowan in Banff and Jasper: Bringing Wildlife Science to the National Parks," *The Otter*, April 29, 2016, http://niche-canada.org.

39 Penn, *Real Thing*, 302; Lyn Hancock, "The Predator Hunters," in *Our Wildlife Heritage*, ed. Murray, 125, 128; George Stringer, *Before My Memory Fades: My Early Years as a Fish and Wildlife Biologist* (self-pub., 1989), 7.

40 Ian McTaggart Cowan, interview by Valerius Geist, July 9, 2002, for the Wildlife Society's Celebrating Our Wildlife Conservation Heritage project, cited in Penn, *Real Thing*, 302n1122.

41 Hancock, "Predator Hunters," 124.

42 Hancock, "Predator Hunters," 124.
    By 1973, all Canadian jurisdictions except the Northwest Territories had eliminated the bounty system on wildlife. Silver et al., "Tribute."

43 The government Predator Control Branch came into being before the bounties were eliminated; the goal, according to Lyn Hancock, was to "continue [the bounty] until the new policies were found to be working." The eight full-time government hunters hired by Mair in 1949 had already developed strong reputations as predator hunters in their respective regions. Since at least the 1920s, the Game Department had called on hunters such as Adam Monks, Charlie Shuttleworth, Cecil Smith and Jimmy Dewar to assist with predator control. The new positions formalized that role. Full-time government hunters received

support from a Bonus Cougar Hunter System introduced in 1952, which provided registered cougar hunters in "major complaint area[s]" an extra $20 (on top of the regular bounty) for each cougar killed. Hancock, "Predator Hunters," 127–28.

44 George Colpitts, "Howl: The 1952–56 Rabies Crisis and the Creation of the Urban Wild at Banff," in *Animal Metropolis: Histories of Human-Animal Relations in Urban Canada*, ed. Joanna Dean, Darcy Ingram and Christabelle Sethna (Calgary: University of Calgary Press, 2017), 219–53.

45 Hancock, "Predator Hunters," 129–30.

46 Mill Lake, a small lake near Abbotsford, was the first lake in BC to be treated with rotenone. Game Commission fisheries biologist Stuart Smith led the experiment. Despite expectations that the poison would dissipate in the space of a year, it took three years for the lake to clear of poison and be successfully restocked with rainbow trout. As George Stringer explains, monocultures were necessary as rainbow trout "do not successfully co-inhabit waters with 'spiny rays' such as perch, bass, and walleye." *Before My Memory Fades*, 20, 34.

47 Stringer, *Before My Memory Fades*, 16.

48 *Wildlife Review* 1, no. 4 (January 1956): 19.

49 Donald R. Skaar et al., "Effects of Rotenone on Amphibians and Macroinvertebrates in Yellowstone," *Yellowstone Science* 25, no. 1 (July 2017); Roarke Donnelly, "Piscicide Impact Extends beyond Targets and Toxicity," *Restoration Ecology* 26, no. 6 (November 2018): 1075–81; Charles J. Henny and James L. Kaiser, "Rotenone Use and Subsequent Prey Loss Lowers Osprey Fledging Rates via Brood Reduction," *Journal of Raptor Research* 56, no. 1 (2022): 37–54.

50 Stringer, *Before My Memory Fades*, 16–25. Stringer was hired as a fisheries biologist by the Game Commission in 1952. He served as regional biologist for the Okanagan, Thompson and Cariboo regions from 1954 to 1967.

51 The Branch suspended large-scale poisoning in wilderness areas in 1961 but continued to use targeted baiting in areas with livestock and some heavily hunted areas until the use of poisons was officially terminated in 1999. BC Ministry of Forests, "Management Plan for the Grey Wolf (*Canis lupus*) in British Columbia," April 2014, 16.

52 Jessica Greinke, "Invasive Freshwater Fish: What You Need to Know," Freshwater Fisheries Society of BC blog, February 20, 2019, http://www.gofishbc.com/Blog.aspx.

53 The ongoing contributions of Cowan's students are well documented in Ronald D. Jakimchuck, R. Wayne Campbell and Dennis A. Demarchi, *Ian McTaggart Cowan: The Legacy of a Pioneering Biologist, Educator and Conservationist* (Madeira Park, BC: Harbour, 2015).

Chapter 6 | Land Use Pressures in the Postwar Period

1　Begg, "Legislating British Columbia," 96.

2　Barman, *West beyond the West*, 270–71.

3　Ormsby, *British Columbia*, 193.

4　R. Powell, "'Soup Kitchen' Wildlife Management Program: End of the Road unless Crown Land for Game," *Courier* (Cranbrook), 1970, 35, cited in D. Demarchi, "William Glen Smith."

5　D. Demarchi, "William Glen Smith," 77.

6　By 1914, timber "far outranked salmon as a generator of private profit and public revenue." Richard Allan Rajala, "'Streams Being Ruined from a Salmon Producing Standpoint': Clearcutting, Fish Habitat and Forest Regulation in British Columbia, 1900–1945," *BC Studies*, no. 176 (Winter 2012–13): 101.

7　Rajala, "Streams Being Ruined," 95. The relationship between the province and its timber company licensees was set out in the province's revised Forest Act of 1912. The act created a Forest Branch of the Department of Lands and established a system of forest reserves (land reserved exclusively for timber harvesting), providing access to timber through the purchase of short-term licences by timber companies. In return, the province would take the responsibility for "forest protection" (namely, protection of the timber resource from fire) and the perpetuation of the resource through reforestation. Pyne, *Awful Splendour*, 317–18; Byron King Plant, "Forest Tenure and Management in British Columbia," Background Paper 2009-02, Legislative Library of British Columbia, November 2009, 4–5.

8　F.D. Mulholland, *The Forest Resources of British Columbia* (Victoria: King's Printer, 1937), 75–77.

9　Jeremy Wilson, "Forest Conservation in British Columbia, 1935–85: Reflections on a Barren Political Debate," *BC Studies*, no. 76 (Winter 1987): 6; Rajala, "Streams Being Ruined," 109.

10　Mulholland's 1937 report identified inadequate reforestation in coastal forests, where most of the province's logging was concentrated. In the Vancouver Forest District, for example, over 400,000 hectares of cutover land was either devoid of new growth or inadequately reforested. On Vancouver Island's E&N Railway belt, only 25 per cent of the cutover private lands were satisfactorily reforested in 1937. Rajala, "Streams Being Ruined," 124; Wilson, "Forest Conservation," 9–10.

11　Rajala, "Streams Being Ruined," 101, 125.

12　Rajala, "Streams Being Ruined," 95. In 1950, for example, forestry generated $400 million in revenue within the province, almost seven times the $63 million generated by commercial fishing. Rajala, "Wasteful Use," 43.

13　Forested lands were managed by the provincial government, with the exception of the CPR railway belt, a four-million-hectare strip of land along the route of the CPR that the province had ceded to the Dominion as its contribution to the continental railway, along with a block of land in the Peace River region. These lands were managed by the Dominion Forestry Branch. Pyne, *Awful Splendour*, 315.

14 Efforts by the Dominion Department of Marine and Fisheries (DMF) to use the province's 1909 Water Act to prosecute logging companies for stream obstructions were abandoned in the face of legal obstacles mounted by the provincial Water Rights Branch. Rajala, "Streams Being Ruined," 114–15.

15 Rajala, "Streams Being Ruined," 94, 119.

16 "The Tourist Industry and the Lumber Domain," *British Columbia Lumberman* 21 (1937): 14, cited in Rajala, "Streams Being Ruined," 126.

17 Pyne, *Awful Splendour*, 315.

18 Richard Somerset Mackie, *Island Timber: A Social History of the Comox Logging Company of Vancouver Island* (Winlaw, BC: Sono Nis Press, 2000), 272–84; Rajala, "Streams Being Ruined," 126.

19 Mulholland, *Forest Resources*, 45–46, 53; Wilson, "Forest Conservation," 9.

20 E.C. Manning, "Is British Columbia to Be Sea of Barren Hillsides?," *Victoria Daily Times*, November 5, 1936, magazine section, cited in Rajala, "Streams Being Ruined," 124.

21 Wilson, "Forest Conservation," 10. Recommendations from the 1909 Royal Commission on Forest Resources led to the establishment of a Forest Protection Fund emerging from the 1912 Forest Act. Supplied by forestry royalties and separated from general revenues, the fund would support fire control efforts primarily, as well as preventative measures such as the disposal of logging slash. The growing expense of fire protection, coupled with persistent demands for forestry revenue, meant the fund was consistently in arrears. It was abolished by statute in 1956, when the Ministry of Lands and Forests took over direct administration of fire control expenditures. Pyne, *Awful Splendour*, 320–26.

22 This recognition of the value of tourism and the multiple-use potential of forest landscapes is apparent in the Forest Branch's assumption of administrative control over the province's parks in 1939. Rajala, "Streams Being Ruined," 109.

23 J. Robertson to Department of Fisheries, June 20, 1939, GR 435, box 123, BC Archives; "North Island Trollers Report Progress," *Western Fisheries* 18 (1939): 17, both cited in Rajala, "Streams Being Ruined," 128, notes 67 and 68.

24 Rajala, "Streams Being Ruined," 117–18.

25 Ferris Neave, "Cowichan River Investigation," unpublished manuscript, Pacific Biological Station Library, 1941; Ferris Neave and W.P. Wichett, "Factors Affecting the Freshwater Environment of Pacific Salmon in British Columbia," *Proceedings, Seventh Pacific Science Congress* 4 (1949): 555; both cited in Rajala, "Streams Being Ruined," 130.

26 Arn Keeling, "'A Dynamic, Not a Static Conception': The Conservation Thought of Roderick Haig-Brown," *Pacific Historical Review* 71, no. 2 (May 2002): 239–68; Arn Keeling and Robert McDonald, "The Profligate Province: Roderick Haig-Brown and the Modernizing of British Columbia," *Journal of Canadian Studies* 36, no. 3 (Fall 2001): 7.

27 Roderick Haig-Brown, *Measure of the Year: Reflections on Home, Family, and a Life Fully Lived* (1950; repr. Victoria: TouchWood Editions, 2011); Haig-Brown, *Living Land*, 21.

28 Haig-Brown, *Living Land*; Keeling, "Conservation Thought."

29 Mark Hume, "Roderick Haig-Brown," *Globe and Mail*, April 3, 2005.

30 Haig-Brown to E.C. Manning, November 15, 1939, personal collection of Richard Rajala, cited in Rajala, "Streams Being Ruined," 126.

31 Rajala, "Streams Being Ruined," 129. The 1947 Forest Act also created a new Ministry of Lands and Forests, with a separate Lands Service and Forest Service and substantially expanded research capacity. By 1945, each service had its own deputy minister. Begg, "Legislating British Columbia," 105.

32 Wilson, "Forest Conservation," 22.

33 Wilson, "Forest Conservation," 22.

34 James A. Munro and Ian McTaggart Cowan, *A Review of the Bird Fauna of British Columbia* (Victoria: British Columbia Provincial Museum, 1947), 90.

35 Research by James F. Bendell and Fred C. Zwickel in the 1950s and '60s documented the temporary benefits of logging to grouse populations. See, for example, Zwickel and Bendell, "Early Mortality and the Regulation of Numbers in Blue Grouse," *Canadian Journal of Zoology* 45, no. 5 (1967): 817–51. For elaboration on the wildlife sink concept, see Zwickel and Bendell, *Blue Grouse: Their Biology and Natural History* (Ottawa: NRC Research Press, 2003), cited in Penn, *Real Thing*, 25.

36 Bill Bourgeois, telephone interview by the author, August 28, 2019.

37 Jones and Bosustow, *Queesto*, 37–38.

38 Penn, *Real Thing*, 130.

39 Penn, *Real Thing*, 127; Jim Osman, "A Second Look at Predators," *Wildlife Review* 1, no. 3 (September 1955): 4.

40 Niki Paillé, "Profile of a Grassland Afficionado: Dr. Bert Brink," *BC Grasslands: Magazine of the Grasslands Conservation Council of British Columbia*, April 2001.

41 Paillé, "Grassland Afficionado."

42 Terpenning, "BCWF and Government," 9–70, 108. As Terpenning notes, the question of recreational access to public grazing lands—a chronic concern of the BC Wildlife Federation from 1950 on—was never satisfactorily resolved. A provision in the 1966 Wildlife Act permitted hunting on grazing leases, but only if the leased land was not occupied by domestic stock.

43 Donald J. Robinson, "Wildlife Management and Land Use: 'How are we Faring in the Race for Space?" in Day and Stace-Smith, *British Columbia Land for Wildlife*, 76.

44 Reid, "Grasslands Debates," 99.

45 Ralph Ritcey, interview by the author, Kamloops, BC, May 22, 2019.

46 R. Ritcey, interview; "Chukars," *Wildlife Review* 1, no. 3 (September 1955): 3.

47 Penn, *Real Thing*, 224–26; Canada, Royal Commission on Aboriginal Peoples, *Looking Forward, Looking Back*, vol. 1 of *Report of the Royal Commission on*

Aboriginal Peoples (Ottawa: Canada Communication Group, 1996), chap. 11, sec. 3.4 ("The Cheslatta T'En and the Kemano Hydro Project"); Mike Robertson, "The Story of the Surrender of the Cheslatta Reserves on April 21, 1952," Cheslatta Carrier Nation Archives, 1991, accessed March 15, 2022, http://neef.ca; Paul and Penn, *Magic Canoe*.

48 Meg Stanley, *Voices from Two Rivers: Harnessing the Power of the Peace and Columbia* (Vancouver: Douglas & McIntyre, 2010), 7.

49 David Joseph Mitchell, *W.A.C. Bennett and the Rise of British Columbia* (Vancouver: Douglas & McIntyre, 1994), 303.

50 Tina Loo, "People in the Way: Modernity, Environment, and Society on the Arrow Lakes," *BC Studies*, no. 142–43 (Summer–Autumn 2004): 161–96.

51 Province of British Columbia, "Columbia River Treaty: History," accessed February 14, 2023, https://engage.gov.bc.ca/columbiarivertreaty/history/.

52 Stanley, *Voices from Two Rivers*, 3, 17. In 1980, BC Hydro constructed a second hydroelectric facility, the Peace Canyon or "Site B" Dam, twenty-three kilometres downstream. Together, the Bennett and Peace Canyon dams produce about 35 per cent of BC's total electricity.

53 The treaty required the US to pay Canada a one-time cash payment of $69.6 million (CAD) for downstream flood-control benefits. Annual revenue from sales of the Canadian entitlement of downstream power benefits has ranged from $200 million to $300 million in recent decades. Columbia Basin Trust, 2020, "Columbia Basin Trust: A Story of People, Power, and a Region United," Chapter 1: River Power, https://25years.ourtrust.org/.

54 As Meg Stanley notes, the costs of dam construction considerably exceeded the revenue generated from the sale of downstream power and flood-control benefits. In addition to the dam construction, the province had to pay to improve highways and bridges and relocate railways, as well as to compensate people whose properties were expropriated. Dam construction, according to Stanley, drained funds from other government departments, including the Forest Service, highways and water resources. *Voices from Two Rivers*, 49.

55 Water storage provided by dams in the upper Columbia basin also enabled the development of additional hydroelectric generating stations, including the Kootenay Canal Plant (1975), the Revelstoke Dam (1984) and Arrow Lakes Generating Station (2002). Columbia Basin Trust, "A Story."

56 Mitchell, *W.A.C. Bennett*, 256.

57 Columbia Basin Trust, "A Story."

58 James W. Wilson, *People in the Way: The Human Aspects of the Columbia River Project* (Toronto: University of Toronto Press, 1973), 9. See also Joy Parr, *Sensing Changes: Technologies, Environments, and the Everyday, 1953–2003* (Vancouver: UBC Press, 2010), chap. 5.

59 Patricia Marchak, *Green Gold: The Forest Industry in British Columbia* (Vancouver: UBC Press, 1983), 308.

60 Parr, *Sensing Changes*, 104, 132.

61 Tina Loo, "Disturbing the Peace: Environmental Change and the Scales of Justice on a Northern River," *Environmental History* 12, no. 4 (October 2007): 901.

62 Paula Pryce, *Keeping the Lakes' Way: Reburial and the Re-creation of a Moral World among an Invisible People* (Toronto: University of Toronto Press, 1999), 87–98. Population decline and cross-border residency led the Canadian government to mistakenly declare the Sinixt extinct in 1956, a few years before the Columbia River Treaty was finalized and signed in 1961.

63 Stanley, *Voices from Two Rivers*, 234.

64 Several studies have documented the social disintegration experienced by the Tsay Keh Dene community following the construction of the Bennett Dam. Tina Loo notes that the loss of hunting, fishing and trapping territories in the areas surrounding the Bennett Dam led to a 300 per cent increase in social assistance payments to Indigenous residents of the area between 1965 and 1970. Loo, "Disturbing the Peace," 906.

    See also Mary Christina Koyl, "Cultural Chasm: A 1960s Hydro Development and the Tsay Keh Dene Community of Northern British Columbia," (MA thesis, University of Victoria, 1993). In July 2009, the Tsay Keh Dene reached a settlement with the BC government and BC Hydro for damages suffered during the construction and operation of the Bennett Dam and Williston Reservoir. The final agreement provided the First Nation with a one-time payment of $20.9 million and annual payments of approximately $2 million. The previous year, the Fort Ware–based Kwadacha First Nation finalized a similar settlement agreement for damages suffered in the wake of the dam construction. BC Hydro, "Tsay Keh Dene Vote Yes to Williston Settlement Agreement," news release, July 2, 2009, http://bchydro.com; Tim Lai, "First Nation Settles Grievances with BC Hydro, Government," *Vancouver Sun*, October 25, 2008.

65 Brody, *Maps and Dreams*, xi.

66 Marchak, *Green Gold*, 309.

67 Loo, "Disturbing the Peace," 904; Penn, *Real Thing*, 262. Inventory data for muskrat, as a trapped species, was more reliable than for the majority of wildlife species within the reservoir areas.

68 Susan Toller and Peter N. Nemetz, "Assessing the Impact of Hydro Development: A Case Study of the Columbia River Basin in British Columbia," *BC Studies*, no. 114 (Summer 1997): 15. The loss of 42,500 hectares of winter range and other suitable habitat to the Mica Dam's Kinbasket Reservoir, for example, represented approximately one-third of the 137,600 hectares of winter range below 1,000 metres in elevation. BC Environment and Land Use Committee, *Mica Reservoir Region Resource Study: Final Report*, 2 vols. (1974).

69 Rod Silver, personal communication, October 20, 2020; Greg Nesteroff, "Deer Park Lived Up to Its Name," *Nelson Star*, February 16, 2014.

70 G.R. Peterson and I.L. Withler, "Effects on Fish and Game Species of Development of Mica Dam for Hydro-Electric Purposes," Management Publication no. 10, BC Fish and Wildlife Branch, 1965.

The BC Environment and Land Use Committee later estimated that habitat loss to the Mica Dam and Kinbasket Reservoir would reduce populations of moose by 70 per cent, deer by 50 per cent, elk by 40 per cent and caribou by 10 per cent, in addition to displacing "most aquatic animals and waterfowl." BC Environment and Land Use Committee, *Mica Reservoir Region Resource Study*.

71 Toller and Nemetz, "Hydro Development," 15.

72 Stanley, *Voices from Two Rivers*, 192.

73 Peterson and Withler, "Effects on Fish and Game," 17.

74 Ross Peck, interview by the author, Hudson's Hope, BC, July 9, 2019; Steve McAdam, interview by the author, Vancouver, BC, June 3, 2019; Dominic Baccante, interview by the author, Fort St. John, BC, July 9, 2019.

75 Azimuth Consulting Group Partnership, "Williston-Dinosaur Watershed Fish Mercury Investigation: 2016–2018 Final Summary Report," prepared for BC Hydro, Fish and Wildlife Compensation Program, Peace Region, September 2019, accessed 14 February 2023, http://fwcp.ca/mercury.

76 In response to a consultation by US authorities responsible for planning the Grand Coulee Dam in 1934, Canada registered little objection to the projected effects on upper Columbia River salmon populations. They noted the absence of a significant commercial fishery on the upper Columbia, neglecting the significance of salmon for Indigenous groups throughout the upper Columbia basin. Columbia River tribes and First Nations on both sides of the border are currently pursuing efforts to restore fish passage at the Chief Joseph and Grand Coulee dams in the US and at the Keenleyside and upstream dams in Canada, to allow an estimated 16 million salmon to recolonize historical spawning grounds in the upper Columbia basin. Columbia Basin Tribes and First Nations, "Fish Passage and Reintroduction into the U.S. and Canadian Upper Columbia Basin" (Joint Paper, July 2015), 2, http://ucut.org.

77 BC Ministry of Environment, "Spawning Channels," web page archived from August 29, 2011, no longer online. In 2011, the Meadow Creek Spawning Channel supported an average of 250,000 spawning kokanee. It produces an average of 10 to 15 million fry annually with a 45 per cent survival rate from egg to fry. Two additional kokanee spawning channels were constructed on the West Arm of Kootenay Lake in the 1980s with funding from the Habitat Conservation Trust.

78 Toller and Nemetz, "Hydro Development," 14.

Chapter 7 | The Conservation Imperative

1 Public information brochure, Resources for Tomorrow conference, October 1961, Postal History Society of Canada, accessed June 25, 2022, http://postalhistorycorner.blogspot.com.

2 T.W. Pierce and E. Neville Ward, "Canada Land Inventory," *Canadian Encyclopedia*, article published February 6, 2006, last modified December 16, 2013, http://thecanadianencyclopedia.ca.

3 Terpenning, "BCWF and Government," 56; Paish, "Overview of Fish and Wildlife Stewardship." The timber company MacMillan Bloedel set a precedent for access accommodations in the early 1950s, when it provided passes to coastal fish and game clubs with the understanding that individual clubs would monitor access. This arrangement, however, was not provincewide.

4 Lister, "History."

5 The BC Fisheries Act allowed for prosecutions of pollution infractions, but penalties remained too small to constitute a significant deterrent.

6 *Wildlife Review* 1, no. 6 (August 1956): 11; R.G. McMynn, Chief Fisheries Biologist, "Water Pollution and Sport Fish Interests," *Wildlife Review* 1, no. 10 (April 1958): 20.

7 Fisheries biologist Robert Hooton documents the effects of the numerous smaller dams constructed for power and water diversion between 1904 and 1959 on freshwater fish habitats and late summer water flows critical for fish survival. Hooton, *Days of Rivers Past: Reflections on British Columbia's Recreational Steelhead Fishery* (Calgary: Rocky Mountain Books, 2017), 19.

8 In 1948, joint resolutions by the BC Wildlife Federation and the BC Natural Resources Conference led to a 1949 amendment of the Water Act to allow the Ministries of the Attorney General (which housed the Game Commission), Fisheries and Agriculture to file objections to water-licence applications, which, before then, they had typically learned about only after the fact. Terpenning, "BCWF and Government," 107.

9 Government revenue from resident and non-resident angling and hunting licences and tags, for example, increased from $697,000 in 1947–48 to $1,656,000 by 1961. Terpenning, "BCWF and Government," Appendix 13, 243.

10 Peter H. Pearse and Gary Bowden, *Big Game Hunting in the East Kootenay: A Statistical Analysis* (self-published, 1966); see also Pearse, "A New Approach to the Evaluation of Non-Priced Recreational Resources," *Land Economics* 54 (February 1968): 87–99. US economist John V. Krutilla also played an influential role in debates about the economic value of wildlife in the Kootenays. See Krutilla, *The Columbia River Treaty: The Economics of an International River Basin Development* (New York: RFF Press, 1967).

11 BC Environment and Land Use Committee, *Mica Reservoir Region Resource Study.*

12 BC Hydro, Fish and Wildlife Compensation Program, "Our Story," accessed December 2, 2020, http://fwcp.ca. BC Hydro established the Peace-Williston Fish and Wildlife Compensation Program in 1988 and the Columbia Basin Fish and Wildlife Compensation Program in 1993. A coastal restoration fund was added in 1999.

13 Columbia Basin Trust, "Our Story," accessed December 2, 2020, http://ourtrust.org.

14 Anne Dance, "Dikes, Ducks, and Dams: Environmental Change and the Politics of Reclamation at Creston Flats, 1882–2014," *BC Studies*, no. 184 (Winter 2014–15): 11–44.

15 James A. Munro, "The Birds and Mammals of the Creston Region, British Columbia," British Columbia Provincial Museum Occasional Paper no. 8, Victoria, 1950.

16 D. Demarchi, "William Glen Smith."

17 A migration corridor for tundra swans and greater white-fronted geese, the valley attracts the largest population of wintering birds of prey in the province's interior. Biologists recorded 303 species in the area in June 2012, 172 of which breed in the area and one of which—the Forster's tern—breeds nowhere else in BC. The Creston Valley WMA also provides year-round sanctuary to over fifty mammal species, thirty fish, reptile and amphibian species and thousands of invertebrate and plant species. Creston Valley Wildlife Management Area (CVWMA) website, accessed March 15, 2022, http://crestonwildlife.ca.

18 CVWMA website.

19 The editor of the *Wildlife Review*, for example, noted the rising popularity of outdoor recreation in correlation with a declining workweek. By 1957, the average workweek among North Americans had dropped to thirty-nine hours, from a high of almost sixty-six hours in the 1850s. *Wildlife Review* 1, no. 9 (January 1958): 29.

20 In 1957, the Parks Branch was incorporated into the province's new Department of Recreation and Conservation. Eight years later, in 1965, the passage of a revised Park Act provided greater protection against resource extraction within park boundaries and established recreation and conservation as primary considerations for park creation and administration. By 1965, the province's park system had expanded to 239 parks, but the total area of provincial park land had been reduced by almost half of its 1948 area, to 2.6 million hectares. Begg, "Legislating British Columbia," 118–20.

21 Philip Shreirer, "History of the Hunting Rifle in North America," *American Hunter*, 16 May 2018; Hooton, *Days of Rivers Past*, 21.

22 Robinson, "Wildlife and the Law," 49.

23 Game Act Amendment Act, 1950, RSBC 1950, c. 23.

24 Game Act. RS [BC] 1948, c. 135, s. 1.

25 Dan Blower (former provincial ungulate specialist) and Rod Silver, personal communication, May 8, 2021.

26 Paish, "Overview of Fish and Wildlife Stewardship." The move was also a physical one, from Game Commission headquarters in Vancouver to Recreation and Conservation headquarters in Victoria—a move that, for the BC Wildlife Federation and other Vancouver-based stakeholder groups, meant the loss of regular and effective personal contact with Fish and Game Branch staff. Terpenning, "BCWF and Government," 94–95.

27 Cowan, "Science and the Conservation of Wildlife," 97.

28 Cowan, "Science and the Conservation of Wildlife," 98.

29 Rutledge, *That Some May Follow*, 237.

30 Rutledge, *That Some May Follow*, 276.

31 Peck, interview.

32 Foster, *Working for Wildlife*, 199–219. Hewitt's death at the age of thirty-six in 1920, and the dissolution of the Conservation Commission in 1921, destabilized plans for annual federal-provincial meetings on the topic of wildlife. Annual meetings between federal, provincial and territorial wildlife officials resumed in 1922 and continue to be held today.

33 Two additional sanctuaries, Christie Islet in Howe Sound and the George C. Reifel sanctuary in Delta, received federal designation in 1962 and 1967, respectively. Munro was chief migratory bird officer for the western provinces from 1920 to 1933, and for BC only from 1934 to 1949. His title was broadened to dominion wildlife officer for the last two years of his career with CWS, from 1947 to 1949. In addition to establishing sanctuaries and enforcing the Migratory Birds Convention Act in the province, Munro contributed more than 100 published articles on avian life history and ecology. Burnett, *Passion for Wildlife*, 58.

34 Burnett, *Passion for Wildlife*, 90, 96–97; Dawe, interview.

35 Recent genetic analysis has resulted in the absorption of the California bighorn into the Sierra Nevada bighorn subspecies. Today, most scientists recognize two distinct subspecies of bighorn sheep in the province: the Rocky Mountain bighorn sheep (*Ovis canadensis canadensis*) and the Sierra Nevada bighorn sheep (*Ovis canadensis sierrae*). Michael R. Buchalski, Benjamin N. Sacks, Daphne A. Gille and Maria Cecilia T. Penedo, "Phylogeographic and Population Genetic Structure of Bighorn Sheep (*Ovis canadensis*) in North American Deserts," *Journal of Mammalogy* 97, no. 3 (2016): 823–38.

36 R.A. Demarchi, C.L. Hartwig and D.A. Demarchi, "Status of the California Bighorn Sheep in British Columbia" (Wildlife Branch Bulletin B-98, BC Ministry of Environment, 2000); R.A. Demarchi, "Bighorn Sheep (*Ovis canadensis*)," Accounts and Measures for Managing Identified Wildlife, BC Ministry of Environment, 2004.

37 *Wildlife Review* (October 1954, March 1955 and January 1957 issues).

38 Ralph Ritcey and Frank Ritcey, interview by the author, Kamloops, BC, May 22, 2019.

39 Demarchi et al., "Status of the California Bighorn Sheep."

40 Game wardens operating the Cache Creek game checking station, for example, noted an "astonishing lack of knowledge" of game regulations among the hunters and anglers they checked. Lister, "History," n.p.

41 *Wildlife Review* 1, no. 10 (April 1958): 13.

42 Jim Osman, "A Second Look at Predators," *Wildlife Review* 1, no. 3 (September 1955): 4–5.

43 Exceptions included northern goshawks, cooper's hawks and sharp-shinned hawks, which were known to prey on game birds and domestic fowl.

44 J.B. Theberge, "Wolf Management in Canada through a Decade of Change," *Nature Canada* 2, no. 1 (1973): 3–10; Robin Hoffos, "Wolf Management in British Columbia: The Public Controversy," *Wildlife Bulletin*, no. B-52 (BC Ministry of

Environment, May 1987), 3; D.H. Pimlott, "Wolf Control in Canada," *Canadian Audubon* 23, no. 5 (1961): 145–52.

45   Jenny Feick, interview by the author, Victoria, BC, April 25, 2019.

46   Straight, "Wildlife Societies," 139–50.

47   Other popular outdoors columnists of the period included Ernie Fedoruk of the Victoria *Times* and Alec Merriman of the Victoria *Colonist*.

48   Richard Kool and Robert A. Cannings, *The Object's the Thing: The Writings of Yorke Edwards, A Pioneer of Heritage Interpretation in Canada* (Victoria: Royal BC Museum, 2021), 9–10; Richard Cannings, telephone interview by the author, October 29, 2021.

49   Fisher and Solecki, *Hundred Years*, 31.

50   Brink, "Natural History Societies," 151–58; BC Nature: Federation of BC Naturalists, "BC Nature History," accessed December 23, 2020, http://bcnature.org.

51   Straight, "Wildlife Societies in B.C.," 140.

52   Silver et al., "Tribute."

Chapter 8 | Access and Alienation: Emerging Threats to Wildlife

1   Jonathan Peyton, *Unbuilt Environments: Tracing Postwar Development in Northern British Columbia* (Vancouver: UBC Press, 2017), 68–70.

2   K.G. Basavarajappa and Bali Ram, "Population of Canada, by Province, Census Dates, 1851 to 1976," in *Historical Statistics of Canada*, Section A: Population and Migration, Series A1-247, Table A2-14, accessed February 2, 2022, http://statcan.gc.ca.

3   The number of licensed resident hunters in BC climbed from 62,700 in 1947 (6 per cent of the population) to 135,400 in 1966 (7.2 per cent of the population). Hunter numbers reached a high of 177,000 (6.3 per cent of the population) in 1981 before tailing off in subsequent decades. Terpenning provides statistics for resident anglers' and hunters' licences from 1947 to 1981 in "BCWF and Government," 243. Statistics for 1980 to the present are drawn from BC Ministry of Forests, Wildlife and Habitat Branch, "Hunting Licence Sales Statistics, 1976–2021"; BC Data Catalogue, "Angling Licence Sales Statistics, 2010 to Current," published August 3, 2020, last modified July 18, 2022, http://catalogue.data.gov.bc.ca.

4   Hooton, *Days of Rivers Past*, 21.

5   Peyton, *Unbuilt Environments*, 80.

6   BC Ministry of Recreation and Conservation, Fish and Wildlife Branch, "Submission to the Royal Commission on BC Railway," 1977, 17, BC Rail Collection, box 6, file 28, exhibit 181, UBC Archives, cited in Peyton, *Unbuilt Environments*, 189, note 64.

7   Ian McTaggart Cowan, "Faunal Diversity as a Habitat Goal," in *British Columbia Land for Wildlife*, eds. Day and Stace-Smith, 20–30.

8 Environment Canada, *Recovery Strategy for the Woodland Caribou, Southern Mountain population (*Rangifer tarandus caribou*) in Canada*, Species at Risk Act Recovery Strategy Series (Ottawa: Environment Canada, 2014); Bruce McLellan, telephone interview by the author, August 6, 2019.

9 R. Yorke Edwards, "Fire and the Decline of a Mountain Caribou Herd," *Journal of Wildlife Management* 18 (1954): 521–26.

10 R. Yorke Edwards, "Land for What? Are You Kidding?," in *British Columbia Land for Wildlife*, eds. Day and Stace-Smith, 14.

11 T.D. Antifeau, "The Significance of Snow and Arboreal Lichens in the Winter Ecology of Mountain Caribou (*Rangifer tarandus caribou*) in the North Thompson Watershed of British Columbia" (M.Sc. thesis, University of British Columbia, 1987).

12 Edwards, "Land for What?," 14.

13 Ralph W. Ritcey, "Forest Succession and Wildlife in Wells Gray Provincial Park," in *British Columbia Land for Wildlife*, eds. Day and Stace-Smith, 94–98.

14 Environment Canada, *Recovery Strategy for the Woodland Caribou*; McLellan, interview.

15 Geoff B. Swannell, "Caribou in Crisis," in *British Columbia Land for Wildlife*, eds. Day and Stace-Smith, 99–103; Ray Demarchi, interview by the author, Duncan, BC, June 24, 2019.

16 Ralph Ritcey, interview by the author, Kamloops, BC, May 22, 2019.

17 A.T. Bergerud and J. Elliot, "Dynamics of Caribou and Wolves in Northern British Columbia," *Canadian Journal of Zoology* 64 (1986): 1515–28.

18 David J. Spalding, "The Early History of Woodland Caribou (*Rangifer tarandus caribou*) in British Columbia," *Wildlife Bulletin*, no. B-100 (Wildlife Branch, BC Ministry of Environment, Lands and Parks, 2000).

19 McLellan, interview.

20 Environment Canada, *Recovery Strategy for the Woodland Caribou*; Joelle Scheck, telephone interview by the author, April 16, 2019.

21 McLellan, interview.

22 Robinson, "Wildlife and the Law," 54.

23 McLellan, interview.

24 Doug Janz, interview by the author, Nanaimo, BC, June 25, 2019; Jon Henderson, telephone interview by the author, August 13, 2019.

25 Hooton, *Days of Rivers Past*, 237–44.

26 Hooton, *Days of Rivers Past*, 238. Assistant angling guide licenses could obtain licences by 1987.

27 Hooton, *Days of Rivers Past*, 233.

28 The province designated ten additional streams in 2005, bringing the total to fifty-two classified waters located in six regions of the province (the Skeena, Cariboo, Thompson-Nicola, Vancouver Island, Kootenay and Omineca-Peace). There are no classified waters in the Lower Mainland or the Okanagan. R.S. Silver, "Investing in Conservation with Revenue Associated with British Columbia's

Quality Waters, 1997–2012" (Habitat Conservation Trust Foundation, Victoria, November 2015).

29 BC Ministry of Environment, "Lower Dean River Angling Management Plan," May 2, 2005, http://gov.bc.ca.

30 "Interior Fraser Steelhead Face Extinction, Fishery and Conservation Groups Warn," *CBC News*, January 27, 2022, http://cbc.ca; Thom Barker, "BC Closes Skeena Watershed for Steelhead Effective Oct. 12," *Terrace Standard*, October 7, 2021.

31 Richard T.T. Forman, Daniel Sperling and John A. Bissonette, *Road Ecology: Science and Solutions* (Washington, DC: Island Press, 2003).

32 BC Ministry of Transportation and Infrastructure, "Wildlife Management on B.C. Highways," accessed April 28, 2022, http://gov.bc.ca.

33 Since this first retrofit of an existing highway in 1999, the BC Ministry of Transportation has completed at least three additional wildlife exclusion retrofit projects on existing highways. Leonard Sielecki, manager, Wildlife Program, BC Ministry of Transportation and Infrastructure, personal communication, December 7, 2022; BC Ministry of Transportation and Infrastructure, *Wildlife Accident Reporting and Mitigation in British Columbia, 1998–2007: Special Annual Report* (Victoria: BC Ministry of Management Services, 2010), chap. 4.

34 Brian Banks, "Animal Crossing: Reconnecting North America's Most Important Wildlife Corridor," *Canadian Geographic*, November 11, 2021; Wildsight, "Reconnecting the Rockies," accessed April 29, 2022, http://wildsight.ca.

35 F.L. Bunnell, "Wildlife and Land: The Vancouver Island Example," in *British Columbia Land for Wildlife*, eds. Day and Stace-Smith, 117.

36 Raymond A. Demarchi, "The Coordinated Resource Management Planning (CRMP) Process—A Viewpoint," *Rangelands* 10, no. 1 (February 1988): 15–16.

37 Dawe, interview.

38 Samantha Flynn, Carmen Cadrin and Deepa Filatow, *Estuaries in British Columbia*, Ecosystems in British Columbia at Risk brochure series (Victoria: BC Ministry of Environment, March 2006).

39 R. Hunter, "Threatened Coastal Habitats," in *Threatened and Endangered Species*, eds. Stace-Smith, Johns and Joslin, 59.

40 Mitchell, *W.A.C. Bennett*, 407. See also J.I. Little, *At the Wilderness Edge: The Rise of the Antidevelopment Movement on Canada's West Coast* (Montreal: McGill-Queen's University Press, 2019).

41 In 1973, the BC government declared the Skagit Valley a provincial Recreation Area (later Skagit Valley Provincial Park). In 1984, the Canada-US Skagit River Treaty committed BC Hydro to provide lower-priced power to Seattle in return for not raising the water levels in the border-crossing Ross Reservoir for eighty years (until 2065). The treaty also established the Skagit Environmental Endowment Commission (SEEC), the province's first hydroelectric compensation program. Jointly funded by the City of Seattle and the Province of British Columbia, SEEC continues to pursue a mandate to conserve and protect wild-

life habitat and enhance recreational opportunities in the Skagit watershed upstream from the Ross dam. Skagit Environmental Endowment Commission website, accessed February 14, 2023, http://skagiteec.org.

42 Ian McTaggart Cowan, "Land, Wildlife, and People," *Vancouver Sun*, December 26, 1972, 30. In 1946, there were two naturalists' associations in the province, with fewer than 100 members. By 1987, that number had grown to thirty-six naturalists' associations, with a membership of more than 8,000. Campbell et al., *Nonpasserines*, xi.

43 Mitchell, *W.A.C. Bennett*, 407.

44 Begg, "Legislating British Columbia," 164.

45 Begg, "Legislating British Columbia," 201; Ben Bradley, *British Columbia by the Road: Car Culture and the Making of a Modern Landscape* (Vancouver: UBC Press, 2017).

46 Begg, "Legislating British Columbia," 124–25.

47 These changes, still features of the legislation today, were significant: previously, no restrictions had existed on mining and forestry activities in Class B parks; in Class A and C parks, logging had been loosely regulated and mining could be permitted at the discretion of cabinet.

48 Begg, "Legislating British Columbia," 124–28.

49 Declining budgets in the early 1980s led the CWS to surrender management of two of these national wildlife areas to other land conservancies. Currently, there are six national wildlife areas in British Columbia: five established in the 1970s and one, the Scott Islands marine national wildlife area, established in 2018. Canada, "Current National Wildlife Areas," accessed April 10, 2021, http://canada.ca; Laszlo Retfalvi, "Migratory Bird Habitat Preservation in BC and the Yukon Territory," in *British Columbia Land for Wildlife*, eds. Day and Stace-Smith, 67.

50 Richard Cannings, telephone interview by the author, October 29, 2021; Robert A. Cannings, personal communication, June 1, 2022.

51 Quebec passed similar legislation in 1974 and New Brunswick in 1975. Several other provinces have since passed similar acts to designate and protect areas of ecological significance. The system was also studied and adopted in different parts of the world, including Western Australia. BC Parks, "Ecological Reserves," accessed February 23, 2021, http://bcparks.ca; Jenny L. Feick, "Never Underestimate the Power of One: Dr. Vladimir Krajina and B.C.'s Ecological Reserves," *Victoria Naturalist*, May/June 2021, cited in *The Log*, Friends of Ecological Reserves Newsletter, 50th anniversary ed., February 14, 2021, http://ecoreserves.bc.ca.

52 The Greenbelt Act, which remains in force, replaced the Green Belt Protection Fund Act in 1977. It permits the minister responsible to acquire lands from private owners and to reserve Crown land as greenbelt land. Begg, "Legislating British Columbia," 153.

53 V.J. Krajina, "Biogeoclimatic Zones and Classification of British Columbia," in
    Ecology of Western North America, ed. V.J. Krajina (Vancouver: University of
    British Columbia, 1965), 1: 1–17.

54 Krajina's system came to be known as Biogeoclimatic Ecosystem Classification
    (BEC) by the early 1980s. Today, ecologists and soil scientists recognize sixteen
    biogeoclimatic zones in British Columbia, constituting five additional zones
    and some name changes from Krajina's original work. In addition to providing
    a foundation for the ecological reserves program, Krajina's classification sys-
    tem has informed forest and rangeland management in the province since the
    1970s. Mohan K. Wali and Jim Pojar, "The Legacy of Vladimir J. Krajina and
    Contributions to UBC Botany," invited presentation for the centennial of UBC,
    2015, 4.

55 Canada was one of fifty-eight nations to participate in the International
    Biological Program (IBP), a worldwide initiative to describe and conserve rep-
    resentative terrestrial and aquatic ecosystems around the world. BC Parks,
    "Ecological Reserves"; Wali and Pojar, "Legacy of Vladimir J. Krajina," 4; Jeremy
    Wilson, *Talk and Log: Wilderness Politics in British Columbia* (Vancouver: UBC
    Press, 1998), 105.

56 Penn, *Real Thing*, 365, 435. By 1990, most major seabird colonies in BC had been
    protected by ecological reserve or migratory bird sanctuaries. Knowledge of the
    province's breeding seabird populations expanded dramatically in the 1970s
    and 1980s, when the BC Provincial Museum and the Canadian Wildlife Service
    conducted comprehensive surveys that established reliable baseline data for
    coastal seabird colonies. Michael S. Rodway, R. Wayne Campbell, and Moira J.F.
    Lemon, "Seabird Colonies of British Columbia: A Century of Changes," *Wildlife
    Afield* 13, no. 1–2 (2016): 8.

57 Wali and Pojar, "Legacy of Vladimir J. Krajina," 5. Krajina had envisioned a pro-
    gram that would protect 1 per cent of the province's 88.7 million hectare Crown
    land mass. Today, the system's 112,543 hectares constitute 0.001 per cent of the
    province's land mass, or roughly one one-thousandth of Krajina's goal. The sys-
    tem is complemented by other protected areas, which together constitute 14 per
    cent of the province's land mass.

58 Begg, "Legislating British Columbia," 186. The Vladimir J. Krajina Ecological
    Reserve, established in 1973, comprises 9,174 hectares; the Gladys Lake reserve,
    established in 1975, is one of the province's largest ecological reserves at 40,541
    hectares. Today, 14 per cent of the province's 154 ecological reserves are over
    1,000 hectares in size.

59 Edwards, "Land for What?"

60 Bristol Foster, "The Role of Ecological Reserves in Protecting Threatened Species
    and Habitats in British Columbia," in *Threatened and Endangered Species*, eds.
    Stace-Smith, Johns and Joslin, 23–27.

61 Today, volunteer wardens continue to monitor activities and educate area res-
    idents about the significance of local ecological reserves. The warden program

is overseen by BC Parks, which manages and enforces regulations in ecological reserves. Friends of Ecological Reserves, "The Volunteer Warden Program," accessed February 14, 2023, http://ecoreserves.bc.ca.

62 Jasper Lament, telephone interview by the author, May 14, 2019.

63 Lament, interview.

64 Rod Silver, personal communication, March 28, 2022.

65 "Our History," Nature Trust of British Columbia, accessed February 14, 2023, http://naturetrust.bc.ca.

66 Pamela M. Cowtan, "The National Second Century Fund of BC: A Growing Gift," in *British Columbia Land for Wildlife*, eds. Day and Stace-Smith, 84.

67 George C. Reifel, interview by the author, Vancouver, BC, June 4, 2019.

68 George C. Reifel Migratory Bird Sanctuary, "About the Sanctuary," accessed April 5, 2021, http://reifelbirdsanctuary.com; Canada, Ministry of Environment and Climate Change, "Alaksen National Wildlife Area," last modified January 6, 2023, http://canada.ca; Reifel, interview.

69 Blair Hammond, telephone interview by the author, June 19, 2019.

70 Pacific Birds Habitat Joint Venture, "An Updated Ranking of British Columbia's Estuaries," February 4, 2021, http://pacificbirds.org.

71 B. Hammond, interview; Dawe, interview; Reifel, interview.

72 Robinson, "Wildlife Management and Land Use."

73 Terpenning, "BCWF and Government," 72.

74 Wilson, *Talk and Log*, 107.

75 Richard A. Rajala, "Forests and Fish: The 1972 Coast Logging Guidelines and British Columbia's First NDP Government," *BC Studies*, no. 159 (Autumn 2008): 94, 105.

76 Mitchell, *W.A.C. Bennett*, 406–7; Wilson, *Talk and Log*, 107. The Land Use Committee aimed to improve communications among five resource departments: Lands, Forests and Water Resources; Agriculture; Recreation and Conservation; Mines and Petroleum Resources; and Municipal Affairs.

77 The Canada Land Inventory took its impetus from widespread concern about the future of farming and the protection of viable agricultural lands in Canada. Recommendations for a survey of land capabilities at the federal Resources for Tomorrow conference of 1961 laid the groundwork for the national inventory work. The following year, the BC Department of Agriculture established the BC Land Inventory program; inventory work began in 1964. After 1971, the Environment and Land Use Committee ensured the coordination of inventory efforts across departments and the sharing of its results. Begg, "Legislating British Columbia," 166.

78 Wilson, *Talk and Log*, 107; Rajala, "Wasteful Use," 49; Begg, "Legislating British Columbia," 164–66.

79 Environment and Land Use Act, RSBC 1996, c 117.

80 Begg, "Legislating British Columbia," 123, 140. Until the 1960s, government surveys and inventory work focused almost entirely on finding resources for

particular industries to use. Even broader land assessment initiatives, such as the Ministry of Lands' Land Utilization, Research and Survey Division (1946–53), focused on identifying provincial lands suitable for agricultural settlement, with no recognition of other uses.

81   Cowan, "Land, Wildlife, and People."

82   Between 1966 and 1970, budget allocations for the Fish and Wildlife Branch ranged from 73 per cent to 86 per cent of licence revenue. Terpenning, "BCWF and Government," 243; Wilson, *Talk and Log*, 108.

83   Begg, "Legislating British Columbia," 176–78.

84   Barry E. Smith, "A Work in Progress—The British Columbia Farmland Preservation Program" (unpublished paper, Burnaby, BC, 2012).

85   Provincial Agricultural Land Commission, *Ten Years of Agricultural Land Preservation in British Columbia* (Burnaby, BC: PALC, 1983), 4, cited in Smith, "Work in Progress."

86   The 1973 Land Commission Act established a land commission with broader responsibilities for greenbelts and parkland reserves. In 1977, legislation under Bill Bennett's Social Credit government reduced the focus of the agency to agricultural lands under the name of the Agricultural Land Commission.

87   As was the case with the developing resource folio system, the availability of Canada Land Inventory data was a "critical pre-condition" to the designation of ALR lands and to the defence of the program in subsequent decades. The 1971 Environment and Land Use Act also laid important groundwork, enabling cabinet to place a moratorium on the subdivision and development of agricultural lands while the agricultural reserve legislation was put in place. Smith, "Work in Progress."

88   Dubious agricultural land lease programs exacerbated these trends. Beginning in the 1960s and accelerating in the early 1980s, the BC Lands Branch contributed to the growth of marginal agriculture in the Cariboo, Bulkley and Peace regions by permitting applicants to remove the timber on leased lands and convert the cleared lands to agricultural uses that were in many cases unlikely to succeed. The program drew widespread censure from forestry and wildlife interests for effectively removing prime forest lands from the Crown land base. British Columbia, Legislative Assembly, Debates of the Legislative Assembly, *Hansard*, 32nd Parl., 3rd Sess. (June 18, 1981); Rod Silver, personal communication, March 27, 2022.

89   Office of the Auditor General of British Columbia, *Audit of the Agricultural Land Commission*, Report 5, September 2010.

90   Barry Leach, "Waterfowl Habitats of the Lower Fraser Valley Wetlands," in Day and Stace-Smith, *British Columbia Land for Wildlife*, 144.

91   Natural pasture lands are those that have not been cultivated, drained, irrigated or fertilized. In 2011, the composition of agricultural land in British Columbia included 53 per cent natural pasture, 23 per cent cropland and 11 per cent wood-

lands and wetlands. Sarah Jeswiet and Lisa Hermsen, "Agriculture and Wildlife: A Two-Way Relationship," EnviroStats, Statistics Canada, Catalogue no. 16-002-X, March 30, 2015, 1; Elaine Susan Anderson, "Flying on the Wings of Trust: The Story of the Delta Farmland and Wildlife Trust, an Example of Collaborative Community Based Resource Management" (PhD diss., University of British Columbia, 2009), 26.

92 Jeswiet and Hermsen, "Agriculture and Wildlife," 6.

93 Anderson, "Wings of Trust," 27; R.W. Butler, D.W. Bradley and J. Casey, "The Status, Ecology and Conservation of Internationally Important Bird Populations on the Fraser River Delta, British Columbia, Canada," *British Columbia Birds* 32 (2021): 1–52.

94 E. William Anderson, "History of Coordinated Resources Management Planning (CRMP) in Oregon—An Overview," *Rangelands* 21, no. 2 (April 1999): 6–11; Society for Range Management, "Coordinated Resource Management," accessed February 14, 2023, http://rangelands.org.

95 R.A. Demarchi, "CRMP Process," 15–16.

96 R.A. Demarchi, "CRMP Process," 15–16; Demarchi, interview.

97 Robinson, "Wildlife Management and Land Use," 77.

98 Exceptions included two Kootenay-region CRMPs (Lasca Creek and Yahk) that incorporated forestry-wildlife concerns. Dale Anderson, R.O. Planning, Kootenay Lake Forest District, BC Ministry of Forests, "Natural Resource Planning: How to Recognize the Real Thing," PowerPoint presentation, November 9, 2010.

99 D. Gayton and M. Hanson, "Final Report, East Kootenay Trench Agriculture Wildlife Committee" (unpublished report, BC Ministry of Forests, Nelson, BC, 1998), cited in BC Forest Practices Board, "Wildlife and Cattle Grazing in the East Kootenay: Complaint Investigation 060724," FPB/IRC/144, July 2008. A 1988 study on the extent of elk damage to ranching operations led to short-term investments by the BC Ministry of Environment to mitigate the problem. Dan J. Closkey, "A Review of Ranching/Wildlife Conflicts in the East Kootenay Region of British Columbia" (1988), cited in M. Romuld and S.E. Bayley, "Columbia Valley Environmental Resource Database Analysis," report prepared for the Columbia Wetlands Stewardship Partners, Parson, BC, 2017; Rod Silver, personal communication, May 2021.

100 BC Forest Practices Board, "Wildlife and Cattle Grazing"; Gigi Pao, Renata Colwell and Calvin Sandborn, Environmental Law Centre, University of Victoria, letter to Carol Bellringer, Auditor General of British Columbia, "Request for an Audit and Examination of Cattle Grazing Leases on Crown Land, and Related Issues," June 12, 2018.

101 Robinson, "Wildlife Management and Land Use," 73.

Chapter 9 | Fisheries, Habitat Protection and Indigenous Rights

1   Roderick Haig-Brown, "Planning for the Future," *Vancouver Sun*, December 26, 1972, 30.

2   Groups supporting the 1973 SOSC protest included the United Fisheries and Associated Workers Union, the Sierra Club of BC, the Society Promoting Environmental Conservation (SPEC), the Federation of BC Naturalists and the Union of BC Indian Chiefs. Rajala, "Forests and Fish," 108.

3   Rajala, "Forests and Fish," 117.

4   Freshwater Fisheries Society of BC, "A Brief History of Freshwater Fish Stocking and Hatcheries in BC," October 7, 2021, http://www.gofishbc.com.

5   The Nass, Skeena, Wannock and Homathko rivers also suffered from the effects of log driving in this period. Rajala, "Wasteful Use," 34, 68.

6   The province's first pulpwood harvesting agreements, which made smaller Interior timber available to pulp and paper producers, were signed in the early 1960s. Rajala, "Wasteful Use," 37–38.

7   Rajala, "Wasteful Use," 38.

8   Rajala, "Wasteful Use," 73.

9   BC Wildlife Federation, "Submission to the Cabinet," December 12, 1968, 9–10, cited in Wilson, *Talk and Log*, 106.

10 Rajala, "Forests and Fish," 118.

11 John H. Dick, "Strategic Planning for Wildlife in British Columbia," in *British Columbia Land for Wildlife*, eds. Day and Stace-Smith, 41.

12 West Coast Environmental Law, "Fisheries Act," n.d., accessed January 28, 2022, http://wcel.org.

13 *Fowler v. The Queen* ([1980] 2 SCR 213) upheld a provincial court's conviction that regulations under the Fisheries Act interfered with the province's juris-diction over forestry. Shared federal and provincial jurisdiction in non-tidal fisheries management (with provincial authority over activities on its land base subject to federal jurisdiction over the conservation and protection of fish) con-tinues to produce situations that require case-by-case adjudication. Fisheries and Oceans Canada, DFO Legal Services, "Department of Fisheries, Oceans and the Canadian Coast Guard legislative framework," August 19, 2019, http://dfo-mpo.gc.ca.

14 Within the BC government, responsibility for forests has fallen under different departments and ministries over time. From the time the Forest Branch was established in 1912 until 1975, it fell under the Department of Lands (renamed the Department of Lands and Forests in 1945). In 1975, the province created a stand-alone Ministry of Forests. Since 1975, the Ministry of Forests has shifted from an exclusive focus on forestry to a wider responsibility for natural resources, including range lands and mines. I have used "Ministry of Forests" throughout for simplicity.

15 D. Haley, "Forestry Policy," in *Forestry Handbook for British Columbia*, 5th ed., part 1, ed. Susan B. Watts and Lynne Tolland (Vancouver: Forestry Undergraduate Society, UBC Faculty of Forestry, 2005), 6.

16 Bill Bourgeois, telephone interview by the author, August 28, 2019.

17 A similar study was conducted by the US Forest Service in the 1940s. Rajala, "Forests and Fish," 130; Rajala, "Wasteful Use," 70.

18 P.A. Larkin, "Play It Again Sam—An Essay on Salmon Enhancement," *Journal of the Fisheries Board of Canada* 31, no. 8 (1974): 1434–56.

19 Richard Beamish, "Changes in the Dynamics of Coho in the Strait of Georgia in the Last Decade," in Orr, Gallaugher and Penniket, *Speaking for the Salmon*, 56–64.

20 Harper, "Salmon and Aboriginal Fishing," 158.

21 Alex Rose, "High-Tech Hatches a Failure," *Globe and Mail*, August 1, 1992, D8, cited in Newell, *Tangled Webs*, 153.

22 Recent scientific investigations have found that sea lice (*Lepeophtheirus salmonis*) originating in farmed salmon have produced mortality rates as high as 80 per cent in wild salmon populations. See, for example, M. Krkosek, J.S. Ford, A. Morton, S. Lele, R.A. Myers and M.A. Lewis, "Declining Wild Salmon Populations in Relation to Parasites from Farm Salmon," *Science* 318, no. 5857 (December 14, 2007): 1772–75.

23 Pacific Salmon Foundation, "Pacific Salmon Explorer," accessed April 12, 2021, http://salmonexplorer.ca.

24 Al Wood, "The History, Goals and Direction of the Salmonid Enhancement Program (SEP) in British Columbia," in Orr, Gallaugher and Penniket, *Speaking for the Salmon*, 5–8. The British Columbia Salmon Restoration and Innovation Fund, a contribution program funded jointly by the federal and provincial governments, currently supports protection and restoration activities for salmon and other wild fish stocks.

25 Thoms, "Place Called Pennask," 70.

26 Thoms, "Place Called Pennask," 83, 86.

27 *Pennask Lake Club*, promotional booklet, 1929, UBC Library Open Collections, accessed March 9, 2022, http://open.library.ubc.ca.

28 BC Parks, "Pennask Lake Provincial Park," accessed March 9, 2022, http://bcparks.ca.

29 Thoms, "Place Called Pennask," 97.

30 *Douglas Lake Cattle Company v. Nicola Valley Fish and Game Club*, 2021 BCCA 99.

31 Peter H. Pearse, *Turning the Tide: A New Policy for Canada's Pacific Fisheries*, Final Report (Vancouver: Commission on Pacific Fisheries Policy, 1982), 178, cited in Newell, *Tangled Webs*, 172; Laura Cameron, "The Aboriginal Right to Fish," *You Are Asked To Witness*, ed. Carlson, 147.

32 Newell, *Tangled Webs*, 4; D.C. Harris, *Fish, Law, and Colonialism*.

33 Newell, *Tangled Webs*, 146.

34 Newell, *Tangled Webs*, 116–20.

35 Newell, *Tangled Webs*, 84–85, 135.
36 Newell, *Tangled Webs*, 169.
37 Pearse, *Turning the Tide*; Newell, *Tangled Webs*, 154–55, 168.
38 In 1965, the Supreme Court of Canada in *R v. White and Bob* recognized the supremacy of Douglas Treaty rights over provincial hunting regulations. Indigenous claimants were not successful, however, in forwarding treaty rights as a defence against a federal charge (*R v. Cooper*, BCSC 1968). Efforts to claim a more general Aboriginal right to fish, guaranteed by the British Crown in the Royal Proclamation of 1763, foundered in the courts as well. When Westbank First Nation Chief Noll Derriksan was arrested at a massive fish-in on the Fraser River in 1970, the Supreme Court of Canada in *R v. Derriksan* (1976) found his claim to an Aboriginal right to fish was subject to regulations under the federal Fisheries Act.
39 *R v. Sparrow* (1990), 1 SCR 1075; "Aboriginal Fisheries in British Columbia," Indigenous Foundations (UBC First Nations and Indigenous Studies Program), n.d., accessed March 22, 2021, http://indigenousfoundations.arts.ubc.ca; Newell, *Tangled Webs*, 175.
40 Newell, *Tangled Webs*, 179; Peter H. Pearse with Peter A. Larkin, *Managing Salmon in the Fraser*, Report to the Minister of Fisheries and Oceans on the Fraser River Salmon Investigation, Vancouver, November 1992; Canada, Department of Fisheries and Oceans, "Aboriginal Fisheries Strategy," June 1992; Jane Allain and Jean-Denis Fréchette, "The Aboriginal Fisheries and the *Sparrow* Decision" (Report BP-341E, Fisheries and Oceans Canada, October 1993).
41 Newell, *Tangled Webs*, 218.
42 "Aboriginal Fisheries in British Columbia," Indigenous Foundations.

Chapter 10 | Changing Public Sentiment

1 Retfalvi, "Migratory Bird Habitat Preservation."
2 The Branch suspended large-scale poisoning in wilderness areas in 1961 but continued to use targeted baiting in areas with livestock and some heavily hunted areas. The use of targeted baits in response to livestock predation continued until 1999, when the Branch put an end to the use of poisons for predator control. BC Ministry of Forests, Lands and Natural Resource Operations, "Management Plan for the Grey Wolf (*Canis lupus*) in British Columbia," April 2014, 16.
3 Burnett, *Passion for Wildlife*, 131.
4 Wildlife Act, 1966 (BC), s 2.
5 Jason Colby, "Change in Black and White: Killer Whale Bodies and the New Pacific Northwest," in *The Historical Animal*, ed. Susan Nance (Syracuse, NY: Syracuse University Press, 2015), 19–37.
6 Center for Whale Research, "Southern Resident Orca (SRKW) Population," accessed March 11, 2022, http://www.whaleresearch.com.

7   John K.B. Ford and Graeme M. Ellis, "Memories," *Marine Mammal Science* 7, no. 3 (July 1991): 326–28.
8   Alexej P.K. Sirén et al., "Identification and Density Estimation of American Martens (*Martes americana*) Using a Novel Camera-Trap Method," *Diversity* 8, no. 1 (2016): Article 3; Leanne Allison, prod. and dir., *Chasing a Trace: Wolverine Research in the High Alpine of Western Canada*, documentary film, 2018, https://storyhive.com/projects/3976.
9   Center for Whale Research, unpublished research data.
10 BC Conservation Data Centre, BC Species and Ecosystems Explorer, accessed March 12, 2022, http://a100.gov.bc.ca/pub/eswp; Whale Interpretive Centre, Telegraph Cove, BC, August 14, 2019.
11 James Hatter, *Politically Incorrect: The Life and Times of British Columbia's First Game Biologist* (Victoria: O&J Enterprises, self-pub, 1997), 97.
12 Begg, "Legislating British Columbia," 208–9; Wilson, *Talk and Log*, 155–56; Ministry of Environment, "In the Matter of an Examination into the Methods, Procedures and Practices Provided by the Wildlife Act and Regulations for the Granting and Issuing of Guide Outfitters Licences and Guide Outfitters Certificates, Third Interim Report of J.L. McCarthy, inquiry commissioner" (Victoria, 1979).
13 BC Nature, *BC Nature (Federation of British Columbia Naturalists): A Fifty-Year History, 1969–2019*, April 29, 2022, 11.
14 W. Winston Mair, "A Review of the Fish and Wildlife Branch, Ministry of Recreation and Conservation, Province of British Columbia," commissioned by the Ministry of Recreation and Conservation, April 1977, 8, 12.
15 Mair, "Review of the Fish and Wildlife Branch," 26; Lister, "History."
16 Established by order-in-council as the "Department of Environment" in 1975, and renamed the Ministry of Environment in 1976, the ministry has since been renamed several times as the result of government restructuring. It became the Ministry of Environment and Parks in 1986 and the Ministry of Environment, Lands and Parks in 1991. Since 1991, it has retained the same responsibilities under three different names: the Ministry of Water, Land and Air Protection (2001–5); the Ministry of Environment (2005–16); and the Ministry of Environment and Climate Change Strategy (2017–present). For simplicity, I have used the name "Ministry of Environment" throughout.
17 Cowan, "Land, Wildlife, and People."
18 Editorial, *British Columbia Sportsman*, September 1980, 4, cited in Wilson, *Talk and Log*, 156.
19 Wilson, *Talk and Log*, 150, 156. The responsibilities and staff of the ELU Secretariat were distributed to various agencies in 1980; the regional resource management committees were disbanded three years later, in 1983.
20 Rosemary Fox, director of the newly formed Sierra Club of BC, alerted the media to the illegal hunting activities in the park. The guide outfitter was later charged with 116 violations of the Wildlife Act, including the shooting of

non-game species and the taking of undersized animals. The Sierra Club campaign prompted a public inquiry into wildlife management in the province and, ultimately, a significant overhaul of the Wildlife Act in 1982 to reflect non-hunting interests. Amanda Follett Hosgood, "The Life of 'Dynamo' Environmentalist Rosemary Fox," *The Tyee*, June 25, 2021, http://thetyee.ca; BC Spaces for Nature, "The Cassiar Region: Spatsizi Plateau Wilderness Park," accessed January 16, 2022, http://spacesfornature.org.

21 Cowan, "Science and the Conservation of Wildlife," 105.

22 Jean L. Manore, "Conclusion: Learning about Passions, Policies, and Problems," in *The Culture of Hunting in Canada*, ed. Jean L. Manore and Dale G. Miner (Vancouver: UBC Press, 2007), 264.

23 Prairie Research Associates, "Attitudes of Winnipeg Residents to Hunters" (unpublished report, 1998), cited in Tim Sopuck, "The Activists Move West: Recent Experiences in Manitoba," in *Culture of Hunting*, eds. Manore and Miner, 232.

24 Mike Halleran, "The Hunting Tradition," in *Our Wildlife Heritage*, ed. Murray, 81.

25 Terpenning, "BCWF and Government," 243. Migratory waterfowl hunting licences declined by 5 per cent annually in the same period. These changes were echoed at the national level, where participation in hunting declined from close to 10 per cent of the population in 1981 to 7.4 per cent in 1991. Participation in large mammal hunting remained relatively constant at 5 per cent, while participation in waterfowl hunting declined. Paul A. Gray et al., "The Importance of Wildlife to Canadians: Results from Three National Surveys," in *Forests and Wildlife... Towards the 21st Century*, ed. I.D. Thompson (Chalk River, ON: Forestry Canada, Petawawa National Forestry Institute, 1993), 151–57.

26 Halleran, "Hunting Tradition," 77.

27 George Colpitts, personal communication, June 9, 2021; Federal and Provincial Committee for Humane Trapping (FPHT), "Status of Trapping in Canada: Methods Currently in Use," 1981, FPHT Files, 1979–81, RG 1-427, Archives of Ontario; Angie Bevington, "Frank Ralph Conibear (1896–)," *Arctic Profiles* 36, no. 4 (1983): 386; The Fur-Bearers (formerly the Association for the Protection of Fur-Bearing Animals), "History," accessed March 29, 2021, http://thefurbearers. com; "The Search for Humane Traps," *Wildlife Review* 1, no. 8 (May 1957): 99.

28 Retfalvi, "Migratory Bird Habitat Preservation," 67.

29 Informally named for its sponsors, Nevada Senator Key Pittman and Virginia Congressman Absalom W. Robertson, the Federal Aid in Wildlife Restoration Act assisted states in protecting wildlife habitat and enforcing game laws to restore populations of threatened game species.

30 Rod Silver, telephone interview by the author, November 19, 2019.

31 Silver, interview; BC Conservation Foundation, "Forty Years of the BC Conservation Foundation: A Retrospective," 2009, accessed March 31, 2021, http://bccf.com; Terpenning, "BCWF and Government," 96; Straight, "Wildlife Societies in BC," 147.

32 Ben Parfitt, "History of the Habitat Conservation Trust Fund," promotional material for the HCTF's twentieth anniversary (Victoria, 2001), courtesy of Rod Silver.

33 Brian Springinotic, interview by the author, Victoria, BC, April 23, 2019. The HCTF describes donations from individuals and organizations as "investments" in the future of the province's land and wildlife.

34 Lisa Kadane, "Canada's Mysterious Lake Monster," *BBC Travel*, March 10, 2020; "Outside Media Go for Ogopogo," *Vancouver Sun*, September 16, 1989, 29; Bruce R. Strachan, personal communication, June 28, 2017.

35 The surveys were administered by Statistics Canada in 1981, 1987 and 1991 under the sponsorship of the federal and provincial wildlife agencies. See Gray et al., "Importance of Wildlife to Canadians," 152–53.

36 This 1977 study is referenced, without citation, in F.L. Bunnell and R.G. Williams, "Threatened Species and Habitats—Why Bother?" in *Threatened and Endangered Species*, eds. Stace-Smith, Johns and Joslin, 265.

37 Wildlife Act, SBC 1982, c 57; British Columbia, "Discussion Paper on A New Wildlife Act for British Columbia," Ministry of Environment, Victoria, April 1981.

38 Aldo Leopold, *A Sand County Almanac, and Sketches Here and There* (New York: Oxford University Press, 1949).

39 D.W. Ehrenfeld, "The Conservation of Non-Resources," *American Journal of Science* 64 (1976): 648–56, cited in Bunnell and Williams, "Threatened Species and Habitats."

40 Nancy Wilkin, interview by the author, Victoria, BC, April 26, 2019; BC Ministry of Forests, Lands and Natural Resource Operations, "Wildlife Viewing Publications," accessed April 1, 2021, http://gov.bc.ca. A multi-phase study by Gary Runka, Joan Sawicki, Ric Careless and Ken Youds supported the development of wildlife-viewing tourism in BC. See Canada and BC, Economic and Regional Development Agreement, "Wildlife Viewing in British Columbia: The Tourism Potential," prepared by Ethos Consulting, Land Sense Ltd. and Youds Planning Consultants (March 1988).

41 Campbell et al., *Nonpasserines*, xi.

42 Richard Cannings, telephone interview by the author, October 29, 2021.

43 R.W. Campbell and D. Stirling, "A Photoduplicate File for British Columbia Vertebrate Records," *Syesis* 4 (1971): 217–22; Wayne Campbell, personal communication, February 13, 2023).

44 Campbell et al., *Nonpasserines*, 23. The BC Photo Records initiative continues to operate under the administration of the non-profit Biodiversity Centre for Wildlife Studies. Biodiversity Centre for Wildlife Studies, "BC Photo File for Wildlife Records," accessed February 13, 2022, http://wildlifebc.org/bc-photo-file-for-wildlife-records. Campbell and Stirling launched a related initiative, the Sight Records File, in 1971. The project solicited donations of diaries and field notebooks from the families of deceased naturalists, biologists and professors and transferred the data they contained on bird sightings into a central registry. The records served as an important source of historical data for Campbell and co-authors of the four-volume *Birds of British Columbia*. Wayne Campbell, personal communication; Richard Cannings, telephone interview.

45 Kool and Cannings, *Object's the Thing*, 12; Richard Cannings, interview.

46 Wayne Campbell, personal communication.

47 Prior to being digitized in the 2000s, nest records were stored on filing cards in cabinets that once occupied a large section of the Royal BC Museum. Biodiversity Centre for Wildlife Studies, "BC Nest Record Scheme," accessed February 3, 2022, http://wildlifebc.org/bc-nest-record-scheme; Campbell et al., *Nonpasserines*, 21–23; Richard Cannings, interview.

48 Edwards, "Land for What?," 6–19.

49 Ahrens, "Crown Land Allocation," 53.

50 Not until 2002 would the Canadian government pass similar legislation in its Species at Risk Act (SARA); British Columbia is currently developing its own species-at-risk legislation.

51 The Honourable Stephen Rogers, Minister of Environment, "Opening Address," in *Threatened and Endangered Species*, eds. Stace-Smith, Johns and Joslin, iv–v.

52 Environmental Reporting BC, "Trends in Timber Harvest in B.C.," BC Ministry of Forests, last modified May 2018, http://www.env.gov.bc.ca/soe/indicators/land/timber-harvest.html.

53 Bunnell, "Wildlife and Land"; Robinson, "Wildlife Management and Land Use." Bunnell's research on wildlife-forest interactions built on his earlier findings— with students Alton Harestad and Greg Jones and Fish and Wildlife Branch biologists Daryl Hebert and Doug Morrison—on the significance of south-facing forested slopes for ungulate winter range.

Chapter 11 | Forestry and Wildlife

1 Gordon Hamilton, "Clear-Cut Fight: Behind-Scenes Campaign Building for Several Years to Shift Focus North," *Vancouver Sun*, June 4, 1996, C1; Andrew MacLeod, "The Big Dance: Saving the Great Bear Rainforest," *The Tyee*, September 24, 2020, http://thetyee.ca.

2 Keith Moore's 1991 inventory of coastal watersheds provided the first systematic assessment of the impact of logging and other industrial activities on the province's coastal watersheds, which he classified as "pristine," "modified" or "developed." His analysis showed that only one large watershed on Vancouver Island remained entirely undeveloped: the unprotected Megin watershed in Clayoquot Sound. Moore, *Coastal Watersheds: An Inventory of Watersheds in the Coastal Temperate Forests of British Columbia* (Vancouver: Earthlife Canada Foundation and Ecotrust/Conservation International, 1991), cited in Wilson, *Talk and Log*, 247–48. See also David Tindall, "Twenty Years after the Protest, What We Learned from Clayoquot Sound," *Globe and Mail*, August 12, 2013.

3 "Northern Interior Forests Denuded," *Native Voice* 10 (1956): 6; "Skeena Committee under Fire, Some Closure Changes Rumored," *Western Fisheries* 67 (1964): 11; "Trappers Will Seek Damage Compensation," *Prince George Citizen*,

June 14, 1966; "Howard Fights for Trapline Compensation," *Native Voice* 10 (1956): 2, all cited in Rajala, "Wasteful Use," 74, note 80. On the history of blockades in BC by First Nations in the 1980s and '90s, see Nicholas Blomley, "'Shut the Province Down': First Nations Blockades in British Columbia, 1984–1995," *BC Studies*, no. 111 (Autumn 1996): 5–35; John Borrows, "Crown and Aboriginal Occupations of Land: A History and Comparison," submission to the Ipperwash Inquiry, October 15, 2005.

4   Wilson, *Talk and Log*, 194–98.

5   Clayoquot Sound Scientific Panel (CSSP), "Sustainable Ecosystem Management in Clayoquot Sound: Planning and Practices," CSSP, April 1995, 1.

6   CSSP, "Sustainable Ecosystem Management," 153–54.

7   Penn, *Real Thing*, 145.

8   Wilson, *Talk and Log*, 314; Borrows, "Crown and Aboriginal Occupations."

9   Panel recommendations and subsequent adjustments reduced the allowable annual cut (AAC) from 900,000 cubic metres to 290,000 cubic metres. Between 1996 and 2008, annual harvests in Clayoquot Sound averaged roughly 88,000 cubic metres (130 ha/year) under the variable retention guidelines, significantly below the AAC. William J. Beese et al., "Two Decades of Variable Retention in British Columbia: A Review of Its Implementation and Effectiveness for Biodiversity Conservation," *Ecological Processes* 8, no. 1 (2019): 6.

10   American forestry giant Weyerhaeuser took up MacMillan Bloedel's share in Iisaak when it purchased the BC forestry company in 1999.

11   Dionne Bunsha, "What Clayoquot Sound Faces Now," *The Tyee*, August 19, 2013, http://thetyee.ca.

12   Tim Thielmann and Chris Tollefson, "Tears from an Onion: Layering, Exhaustion and Conversion in British Columbia Land Use Planning Policy." *Policy and Society* 28, no. 2 (July 2009): 111–24.

13   Province of BC, "A Protected Areas Strategy for British Columbia: The Protected Areas Component of B.C.'s Land Use Strategy," 1993, 6.

14   Wilson, *Talk and Log*, 256. "Parks and Wilderness for the '90s," an earlier public process jointly managed by the Ministry of Forests and BC Parks, contributed to the Protected Areas Strategy by identifying almost 200 candidate areas for addition to the parks system.

15   At the highest levels, Ecodomains and Ecodivisions place British Columbia globally. The three lowest levels (Ecoprovinces, Ecoregions and Ecosections) are progressively more detailed, relating segments of the province to one another. Within each terrestrial ecoregion, climatic zones support specific soils, plant and animal communities and aquatic systems. Today, these climatic zones are further defined under the province's Biogeoclimatic Ecosystem Classification (BEC) system. Dennis A. Demarchi, "An Introduction to the Ecoregions of British Columbia," 3rd ed. (Victoria: Ecosystem Information Section, Ministry of Environment, 2011), 4; Campbell et al., *Nonpasserines*, xx.

16   Thielmann and Tollefson, "Tears from an Onion"; Wilson, *Talk and Log*, 292.

17   Kaaren Lewis and Susan Westmacott, "Provincial Overview and Status Report," (Victoria: BC Land Use Coordination Office, 1996), cited in Wilson, *Talk and Log*, 300. BC's terrestrial ecosections have since been revised to a total of 116.

18   G.G.E. Scudder, "Species at Risk, Conservation Strategies, and Ecological Integrity," in *Proceedings of a Conference on the Biology and Management of Species and Habitats at Risk*, vol. 1, ed. L.M. Darling (Victoria: BC Ministry of Environment, Lands and Parks; Kamloops: University College of the Cariboo, 2000).

19   Thielmann and Tollefson, "Tears from an Onion."

20   BC Integrated Land Management Bureau, "A New Direction for Strategic Land Use Planning in British Columbia," 2006; Jessica Clogg and Deborah Carlson, *Land Use Planning for Nature, Climate and Communities: Taking Stock and Moving Forward* (Vancouver: West Coast Environmental Law, February 2013).

21   BC Ministry of Environment, "Muskwa-Kechika Wildlife Management Plan. Part A: Strategic Document," October 2009; Muskwa-Kechika Advisory Board, *Muskwa-Kechika Management Area*. 2013–21.

22   Leo Rutledge, "Hunting in a Once Distant Land," *BC Historical News*, Winter 1996–97, 20–24. See also Anthony Kenyon, *The Recorded History of the Liard Basin 1790–1910: Where British Columbia Joins the Yukon and N.W.T.* (Fort Nelson, BC: Fort Nelson News, 2016).

23   Rutledge, "Hunting," 21.

24   Peck, interview; BC Ministry of Environment, "Muskwa-Kechika Wildlife Management Plan."

25   Bill Jex, interview by the author, Smithers, BC, May 6, 2019.

26   Peck, interview.

27   Wayne Sawchuk, "Muskwa-Kechika: Exploring the Wild," accessed February 11, 2023, http://www.muskwakechika.com; *In the Land of Dreamers,* documentary film, Risky Creek Productions, CBC Media, 2021.

28   Silver, interview; Muskwa-Kechika Advisory Board, *Muskwa-Kechika Management Area.*

29   Peck, interview; BC Ministry of Environment, "Muskwa-Kechika Wildlife Management Plan."

30   John L. Weaver, "The Greater Muskwa Kechika: Building a Better Network for Protecting Wildlife and Wildlands," Wildlife Conservation Society Canada Conservation Report no. 13 (Toronto: Wildlife Conservation Society of Canada, July 2019); Yellowstone to Yukon Conservation Initiative, *Muskwa-Kechika Management Area Biodiversity Conservation and Climate Change Assessment: Summary Report*, prepared for the Muskwa-Kechika Management Area Advisory Board (Canmore, AB: Yellowstone to Yukon Conservation Initiative, 2012).

31   Dena Kayeh Institute, *Kaska Dena Conservation Analysis for an Indigenous Protected and Conserved Area in British Columbia*, prepared for the Kaska Dena Council (Lower Post, BC: Dena Kayah Institute, September 2019); Kaska Dena

Council, "Dene K'eh Kusan—Always Will Be There," accessed June 21, 2021, https://kaskadenacouncil.com/dene-k-eh-kusan.

32 Wilkin, interview; Ben Parfitt and Justine Hunter, "Penalties Possible for River Damage," *Vancouver Sun*, July 31, 1992, D8, D18.

33 Wilkin, interview. In the early 1990s, the Ministry of Forests developed guidelines for fish-forestry interactions to support fish and wildlife habitat protection in managed forests in the south and central Interior.

34 Parfitt and Hunter, "Penalties Possible"; Judy Lindsay, "Damage Audit Destroys Industry Claims," *Vancouver Sun*, August 11, 1992, 35; John Massey, "Disturbing Declines of Wild Salmon Runs Are Dire Warnings," *Vancouver Sun*, December 17, 1993, 65.

35 Wilkin, interview; Ben Parfitt, "Logging Rules to Get Contractual Weight," *Vancouver Sun*, August 26, 1992, 43.

36 Wilkin, interview.

37 Wilkin, interview. The province's 1981 Environmental Management Act enabled the Ministry of Environment to require environmental impact assessments for projects likely to have a detrimental environmental impact. A collection of other legislation required environmental review processes for energy and mineral developments. In 1994, the NDP government consolidated this legislation into BC's first Environmental Assessment Act. Mark Haddock, "Environmental Assessment in British Columbia" (Environmental Law Centre, University of Victoria, November 2010).

38 BC Ministry of Forests, Forest Practices Branch, "Evolution of the Forest Practices Code," last modified March 24, 1997, https://www.for.gov.bc.ca/hfp/publications/00222/.

39 Between 1995 and 1997, three regional land use plans (for the Cariboo Chilcotin, Kamloops and Kispiox) were designated as higher-level plans under the Forest Practices Code. After 1997, the definition of "higher-level plan" under the Forest Practices Code was changed to refer to narrower forest and range objectives, rather than entire land use plans. Clogg and Carlson, "Land Use Planning for Nature," 22.

40 A Forest Appeals Commission would hear appeals under the Forest Practices Code.

41 Gordon Hamilton, "Tab for Proposed Forest Practices Code Soars 4-Fold," *Vancouver Sun*, March 3, 1994, cited in Wilson, *Talk and Log*, 309.

42 Wilkin, interview; Wilson, *Talk and Log*, 310–12; Mark Haddock, *Guide to Forest Land Use Planning* (Vancouver: West Coast Environmental Law, 1999, updated 2001).

43 BC Ministry of Forests, "Evolution of the Forest Practices Code."

44 Forest Renewal BC drew on increased stumpage fees and royalty charges from industry to reinvest roughly $400 million annually into forest enhancement and industry transition. By creating a mechanism to reinvest a portion of government forestry revenue back into forest sustainability, FRBC fulfilled a demand that

fish and wildlife advocates and conservationists had been making for decades. Roughly half of the funds would go to support reforestation, silviculture and watershed restoration; the other half would support investments in industry innovation, forest worker training and economic diversification for forest-dependent communities. Forest Renewal BC, *Annual Report, 1994/95* (Victoria, 1995).

45 Fred L. Bunnell and Glen Dunsworth, "Making Adaptive Management for Biodiversity Work: The Example of Weyerhaeuser in Coastal British Columbia," *Forestry Chronicle* 80 (2004): 37–43; Beese et al., "Two Decades of Variable Retention," 33.

46 Fred L. Bunnell, Laurie Kremsater and Mark Boyland, "An Ecological Rationale for Changing Forest Management on MacMillan Bloedel's Forest Tenure" (unpublished paper, Centre for Applied Conservation Biology, University of British Columbia, 1998).

47 Bunnell, Kremsater and Boyland, "Ecological Rationale," 7, 9, 17.

48 See, for example, J.F. Franklin, D.R. Berg, D.A. Thornburgh and J.C. Tappeiner, "Alternative Silvicultural Approaches to Timber Harvesting: Variable Retention Harvest Systems," in *Creating a Forestry for the 21st Century: The Science of Ecosystem Management,* ed. K.A. Kohn and J.F. Franklin (Washington, DC: Island Press, 1997), 111–39. Simon Fraser University forest ecologist Ken Lertzmann, a member of the Clayoquot Sound Scientific Panel, suggested the term "variable retention" to replace "green tree retention," the term used until that point. Beese et al., "Two Decades of Variable Retention," 17.

49 Retention of high-value habitat features in 0.25 to 1 hectare patches, rather than via single dispersed trees, became the most common application of variable retention approaches. Typically incorporating a riparian area, these patches were retained for at least one harvest cycle, though "the intention is that most will never be cut." Beese et al., "Two Decades of Variable Retention," 2, 4–5.

50 Beese et al., "Two Decades of Variable Retention," 3–4.

51 Beese et al., "Two Decades of Variable Retention," 3–4.

52 Bill Bourgeois, telephone interview by the author, August 28, 2019. See also Steve Law, "Pulp Fiction," *Portland Tribune,* August 15, 2013; Council of Forest Industries, "Forest Certification in British Columbia," British Columbia Forest Facts, n.d.

53 BC Ministry of Forests, *The State of British Columbia's Forests,* 3rd ed. (Victoria: Forest Practices and Investment Branch, 2010), 245.

54 BC Ministry of Forests, *State of British Columbia's Forests,* 245–46. The Sustainable Forestry Initiative rose to dominance in the province after 2010. By 2020, Sustainable Forestry Initiative certifications accounted for 44 million hectares, compared with the Canadian Standards Association's 2 million and the Forest Stewardship Council's 1.5 million hectares. Certification Canada, "Forest Management Certification in Canada: 2020 Year-End Status Report, British Columbia" (Forest Products Association of Canada, February 2021).

55 Beese et al., "Two Decades of Variable Retention," 4–5.

56 In 1995, provincial regulations restricted clearcut sizes to a maximum of 40 hectares on the coast and 60 hectares in the Interior. Beese and colleagues note that average cutblock sizes are considerably smaller, averaging 16 hectares on the coast and 23 hectares for the province as a whole. Beese et al., "Two Decades of Variable Retention," 5; BC Ministry of Forests, "Average Cutblock Size on Crown Land from 1988 to 1998, by Region," n.d., accessed May 12, 2021, https://www.for.gov.bc.ca/hfp/publications/00001/1l-harv-cutblock.htm.

57 Anonymous industry forester A, telephone interview by the author, January 9, 2020.

58 K. Fedrowitz et al., "Can Retention Forestry Help Conserve Biodiversity? A Meta-Analysis," *Journal of Applied Ecology* 51 (2014): 1669–79; Beese et al., "Two Decades of Variable Retention."

59 Beese et al., "Two Decades of Variable Retention"; anonymous industry forester A, interview. FRBC was replaced with the Forest Investment Account in 2002, which directed a much smaller proportion of funds to habitat restoration and eliminated FRBC-era land acquisitions for biodiversity protection. In 2016, the province created the Forest Enhancement Society of BC, which funds habitat restoration (among other forest enhancement priorities) in collaboration with the Habitat Conservation Trust Foundation.

60 Armando Geraldes et al., "Population Genomic Analyses Reveal a Highly Differentiated and Endangered Genetic Cluster of Northern Goshawks (*Accipiter gentilis laingi*) in Haida Gwaii," *Evolutionary Applications* 12, no. 4 (April 2019): 757–72.

61 Geraldes et al., "Population Genomic Analyses."

62 Rhonda Lee McIsaac, "Wings Brushing Boughs: Stads K'un Named Haida Gwaii's National Bird," Council of the Haida Nation, November 29, 2017, http://www.haidanation.ca.

63 Erica McLaren et al., "Science-Based Guidelines for Managing Northern Goshawk Breeding Areas in Coastal British Columbia," *Journal of Ecosystems and Management* 15, no. 2 (2015).

64 McIsaac, "Wings Brushing Boughs"; Matt Simmons, "In Search of Haida Gwaii's Forest-Dwelling Hawk, One of the Most Endangered Species on the Planet," *Narwhal*, October 10, 2021, http://thenarwhal.ca.

65 Parks Canada, *Recovery Strategy for the Northern Goshawk* laingi *Subspecies (*Accipiter gentilis laingi*) in Canada*, Species at Risk Act Recovery Strategy Series (Ottawa: Parks Canada, 2018).

66 On Vancouver Island, for example, Western Forest Products has developed northern goshawk management plans for its area-based forestry tenures that exceed provincial requirements. Western Forest Products, "TFL 39—Management Plan #9: Management Plan Overview," August 2016.

67 McIsaac, "Wings Brushing Boughs"; Haida Gwaii Land Use Objectives Order, updated 2017, accessed April 5, 2022, http://haidagwaiimanagementcouncil.ca/land-use-orders/.

68 Beese et al., "Two Decades of Variable Retention," 4; BC Ministry of Forests, "Evaluation of Cutblock Sizes Harvested under the Forest Practices Code in British Columbia, 1996–2002," *FRPA Evaluator*, Extension Note no. 8 (July 2005).

69 Fred L. Bunnell, Kelly A. Squires and Isabelle Houde, "Evaluating Effects of Large-Scale Salvage Logging for Mountain Pine Beetle on Terrestrial and Aquatic Vertebrates" (Mountain Pine Beetle Initiative, Working Paper 2004-2, Natural Resources Canada, Pacific Forestry Centre, Victoria, 2004), 6. Based on dendro-ecological studies, four to five mountain pine beetle outbreaks, with an average duration of ten years, occurred in BC during the twentieth century. Amalesh Dhar, Lael Parrott and Christopher D.B. Hawkins, "Aftermath of Mountain Pine Beetle Outbreak in British Columbia: Stand Dynamics, Management Response and Ecosystem Resilience," *Forests* 7, no. 8 (2016): 171.

70 Dhar, Parrott and Hawkins, "Aftermath," 1.

71 BC Ministry of Forests, "History of the Mountain Pine Beetle Infestation in B.C.," n.d. , accessed May 13, 2021, http://gov.bc.ca.

72 Bunnell et al., "Evaluating Effects," 6.

73 Anonymous industry forester B, telephone interview by the author, January 8, 2020.

74 Dhar, Parrott and Hawkins, "Aftermath," 4; BC Ministry of Forests, *State of British Columbia's Forests*.

75 Bunnell et al., "Evaluating Effects," 7–8, 29–30.

76 A 2009 report by the Forest Practices Board found that the chief forester had provided guidance to licensees intended to conserve more mature forest struc-ture across the landscape. However, no legal objective was established and the desired "conservation uplift" was not achieved. BC Forest Practices Board, "Biodiversity Conservation during Salvage Logging in the Central Interior of BC," Special Report, FPB/SR/35 (November 2009).

77 Dhar, Parrott and Hawkins, "Aftermath," 7.

78 Coordinated Access Management Plans (CAMPs) emerged around 1980, for ex-ample, as an attempt to address concerns about road density, hunting pressure on wildlife and access to outdoor recreation following extensive road develop-ment for pine beetle salvage operations. Haddock, *Guide to Forest Land Use Planning*, 1–18.

79 Anonymous industry forester B, interview. At the time of salvage operations in the 2000s, Crown forest tenures consisted of roughly 80 per cent "volume-based" tenures within timber supply areas and 20 per cent "area-based" tenures, includ-ing tree farm licences, community forest agreements and woodlot licences. Tree farm licences, an older form of tenure, occur mainly on the coast, while timber supply areas constitute much of the forest land base in the province's interi-or. BC Ministry of Forests, "Mid-Term Timber Supply: Conversion of Volume-Based Forest Tenures to Area-Based Forest Tenures," June 11, 2012.

80 Canada, Committee on the Status of Endangered Wildlife in Canada, *COSEWIC Assessment and Status Report on the Caribou* (Rangifer tarandus*)* (Ottawa, 2014), chap. 2.

81 Anonymous industry forester B, interview.

82 Recommendations from BC MLA Mike Morris's 2015 report on the need for improvements to wildlife management following the mountain pine beetle outbreak and associated salvage operations led the Fish and Wildlife Branch to release its "Provincial Framework for Moose Management in British Columbia" in February 2015. The document outlined a strategy for moose population recovery based on regional moose action plans. Morris, "Getting the Balance Right: Improving Wildlife Habitat Management in British Columbia; Strategic Advice to the [BC] Minister of Forests, Lands and Natural Resource Operations," August 2015.

   R.A. (Al) Gorley's 2016 report provided more detailed guidance for moose recovery based on interviews with First Nations and stakeholders. "A Strategy to Help Restore Moose Populations in British Columbia," recommendations prepared for the Ministry of Forests, Lands and Natural Resource Operations, Fish and Wildlife Branch, Victoria, July 8, 2016.

83 Sarah Cox, "British Columbia's Looming Extinction Crisis," *Narwhal*, August 8, 2020, http://thenarwhal.ca; Scott Yaeger and Rich Weir, "Fisher Futures: A Turning Point?" presentation, Smithers, BC, August 14, 2019; BC Conservation Data Centre, "Conservation Status Report: *Pekania pennanti* pop. 5, Fisher—Columbian Population," accessed March 31, 2020, https://a100.gov.bc.ca/pub/eswp/.

84 BC Ministry of Forests, *State of British Columbia's Forests*, 181. Total harvest volume in BC peaked at 92.3 million cubic metres in 2004 and declined 48 per cent to 48 million cubic metres in 2009 as a result of a weak lumber market.

85 Jennifer Psyllakis, director, Wildlife and Habitat Branch, personal communication, August 8, 2021; British Columbia, "Case Study: How Cumulative Effects were Considered in the Context of Cutting Permits," Cariboo Cumulative Effects Assessment, accessed February 26, 2022, http://gov.bc.ca.

86 Bourgeois, interview. Research that contributed to the development of these modelling systems included Jennifer Psyllakis's 2006 dissertation: "A Multi-Scale Analysis of Forest Structure and Vertebrate Diversity" (PhD diss., University of Northern British Columbia, 2006).

87 Beese et al., "Two Decades of Variable Retention," 5. For example, Canada signed the United Nations Convention of Biological Diversity in 1992 and released the Canadian Biodiversity Strategy in 1995.

88 Canada, "Canada Forest Accord" (Canadian Forest Service, Natural Resources Canada, Ottawa, May 1, 1998).

89 Winifred Kessler, telephone interview by the author, June 17, 2019.

90 The FRPA framework consists of three pillars—objectives; plan and practice requirements; and compliance and enforcement—which are supported by two

foundations: professional reliance and effectiveness evaluations. BC Forest Practices Board (BCFPB), "A Decade in Review: Observations on Regulation of Forest and Range Practices in British Columbia," Special Report, FPB/SR/46 (May 2014), 4.

91 Mark Haddock, "Professional Reliance Review: The Final Report of the Review of Professional Reliance in Natural Resource Decision-Making," presented to the BC Ministry of Environment and Climate Change Strategy (May 2018), 102.

92 BCFPB, "Decade in Review," 9–10; Doug Janz, interview by the author, Nanaimo, BC, June 25, 2019.

93 West Coast Environmental Law, "'Timber Rules': Forest Regulations Lower Standards, Tie Government Hands and Reduce Accountability," Deregulation Backgrounder, February 2004; Donald S. Eastman et al., "Trends in Renewable Resource Management in BC," *Journal of Ecosystems and Management* 14, no. 3 (2013).

94 Anonymous industry forester B, interview.

95 BCFPB, "Decade in Review," 15; Haddock, "Professional Reliance Review," 97.

96 Anonymous industry forester B, interview.

97 For example, FRPA eliminated the need for government approval of road and cutblock plans, a role that district forest managers had held since the 1980s (well before the FPC). Instead, government approval was required only for higher-level Forest Stewardship Plans. These plans, which propose results and strategies over large geographic areas, do not provide adequate information to inform government decision makers.

98 Wilkin, interview.

99 BCFPB, "Decade in Review," 23. FRPA identifies eleven forest and environmental values (known as "resource values") that must be maintained: biodiversity, cultural heritage, forage, recreation, resource features, fish/riparian, soils, timber, visual quality, water and wildlife. The Forest and Range Evaluation Program is led by the Ministry of Forests, Lands and Natural Resource Operations in partnership with the Ministry of Environment. The Forest and Range Evaluation Program is a coordinating body that identifies monitoring priorities and protocols and coordinates the monitoring activities of external professionals. Monitoring responsibilities for wildlife pertain mainly to Wildlife Habitat Areas (WHAs) for species at risk and Ungulate Winter Ranges (UWRs).

100 For all his criticisms, Haddock concludes that "relying on professionals outside of government is an inevitable and essential aspect of resource management, and is in the public interest." "Professional Reliance Review," 8.

101 BCFPB, "Decade in Review," 23.

102 See BC Forest Practices Board, "Cumulative Effects: From Assessment towards Management," Special Report, FPB/SR/39 (March 2011); BC Forest Practices Board, *Bulletin 013: The Need to Manage Cumulative Effects*, February 2013.

103 Haddock, "Professional Reliance Review," 106.

104 *Yahey v. British Columbia*, 2021 BCSC 1287.

105 R.A. Gorley and Garry Merkel, "A New Future for Old Forests: A Strategic
     Review of How British Columbia Manages for Old Forests within Its Ancient
     Ecosystems," prepared for the BC Minister of Forests, Lands, Natural Resource
     Operations and Rural Development, Victoria, April 30, 2020, 6, 49.

Chapter 12 | Changing Faces and Approaches in Wildlife Conservation

 1   William Porter, Russ Mason and Kathryn Frens, "Wildlife Protection
     Legislation," in Leopold, Kessler and Cummins, *North American Wildlife Policy
     and Law*, 193–207. While critics of the ESA use species delisting rates to conclude
     that only 1 per cent of listed species have recovered, other analyses have incor-
     porated species' decades-long recovery projections to reach more positive con-
     clusions around the success of ESA listing and recovery plans. See, for example,
     Kieran Suckling, Noah Greenwald and Tierra Curry, "On Time, on Target: How
     the Endangered Species Act Is Saving America's Wildlife," report, US Center for
     Biological Diversity, May 2012.
 2   Species at Risk Act, SC 2002, c 29; Kate Smallwood, *A Guide to Canada's Species
     at Risk Act* (Vancouver: Sierra Legal Defence Fund, May 2003).
 3   An alternate pathway exists to designate species as endangered or threatened
     by order-in-council under the Wildlife Act. To date, four species have received
     legal protection from killing or harassment through this mechanism: the bur-
     rowing owl, the American white pelican, the Vancouver Island marmot and the
     sea otter. Designation and Exemption Regulation (BC Reg. 168/90), Wildlife Act,
     RSBC 1996, c 488, s 108 and Schedules D and E.
 4   Office of the Auditor General of British Columbia (OAGBC), *An Audit of
     Biodiversity in B.C.: Assessing the Effectiveness of Key Tools*, Report 10 (Victoria:
     OAGBC, February 2013), 13, 21.
 5   Species at Risk Act, SC 2002, c 29, s 80.
 6   Stace-Smith, Johns and Joslin, eds., *Threatened and Endangered Species.*
 7   Conservation Data Centres now exist across Canada and North America as part
     of NatureServe's international network of biodiversity data. The CDC's "sub-na-
     tional" rankings (S-ranks) for BC feed into NatureServe's national and global
     ranking system. Andrew P. Harcombe, "The Conservation Data Centre: For the
     Greatest about the Least," in *Proceedings of a Conference*, ed. Darling, 13–18.
 8   Canada, Committee on the Status of Endangered Wildlife in Canada, *COSEWIC
     Assessment and Status Report on the Vancouver Island Marmot (*Marmota van-
     couverensis*)* (Ottawa, 2019); Marmot Recovery Foundation, "Current Status,"
     accessed April 20, 2022, http://marmots.org.
 9   BC Ministry of Environment, *Environmental Trends*; Scudder, "Species at Risk."
10   Scudder, "Species at Risk"; Scudder, "Biodiversity Conservation and Protected
     Areas in British Columbia" (2003), commissioned by the Sierra Legal Defence
     Fund.

11 Biodiversity BC began as an independent committee of the BC Conservation Lands Forum, a partnership of conservation organizations and provincial, federal and municipal governments mandated to improve the acquisition and management of public and private lands for biodiversity conservation. Funding for the initiative stemmed from the BC Trust for Public Lands, a one-time funding commitment from the provincial government initiated in 2004. Austin et al., *Taking Nature's Pulse*, xxvii.

12 Austin et al., *Taking Nature's Pulse*, 60; BC Ministry of Environment, *Environmental Trends*, 292. For the few listed species that showed improvement, the majority comprised peripheral bird species expanding their range into the province and marine mammals whose populations had recovered owing to conservation measures.

13 Austin et al., *Taking Nature's Pulse*, 218; BC Ministry of Environment, *Environmental Trends*, 301, 314.

14 Biodiversity BC's ambitious initiative *Taking Nature's Pulse* resulted in little immediate change. Its five-year Biodiversity Action Plan, scheduled for completion at the end of 2008, was never produced. OAGBC, *Audit of Biodiversity in B.C.*, 25.

15 BC Ministry of Environment, *Environmental Trends*, 298, 320.

16 Suckling, Greenwald and Curry, "On Time, On Target."

17 A.R. Westwood et al., "Protecting Biodiversity in British Columbia: Recommendations for an Endangered Species Law in B.C. from a Species at Risk Expert Panel," report prepared for the BC Ministry of Environment and Climate Change Strategy, 2018.

18 British Columbia, "Report of the British Columbia Task Force on Species at Risk," January 31, 2011.

19 Key Biodiversity Area Canada website, accessed May 6, 2022, http://kbacanada.org.

20 These included the Wildlife Protection Act, 2008, by Shane Simpson of the New Democratic Party (NDP); the Species at Risk Protection Act, 2010 and 2011, by Rob Fleming (NDP); the Endangered Species Act, 2017, by Andrew Weaver (Green Party); and the Species at Risk Protection Act, 2017, by George Heyman (NDP). Wilson, *Talk and Log*, 306; Westwood et al., "Protecting Biodiversity."

21 Nova Scotia, New Brunswick, Quebec, Ontario, Manitoba and Newfoundland and Labrador have specific endangered species laws, while British Columbia, Alberta, Saskatchewan and Prince Edward Island do not.

22 Springinotic, interview.

23 Wilson, *Talk and Log*, 49.

24 PECP partners included the provincial Ministry of Environment, the Habitat Conservation Trust Foundation, Wildlife Habitat Canada (an Ottawa-based non-governmental organization), the Canadian Wildlife Service and the Department of Fisheries and Oceans.

25 Butler, Bradley and Casey, "Status, Ecology, and Conservation"; Jeswiet and Hermsen, "Agriculture and Wildilfe."

26 Laura J. Kehoe et al., "Conservation in Heavily Urbanized Biodiverse Regions Requires Urgent Management Action and Attention to Governance," *Conservation Science and Practice* 3 (2021): e310.

27 Pacific Estuary Conservation Program, archived backgrounder, 1998. Private properties acquired by DUC or NTBC were typically leased to the provincial Ministry of Environment, Fish and Wildlife Branch, which took on the responsibility for managing the lands as part of larger Wildlife Management Areas. These agreements took the form of a $1 lease over a ninety-nine-year term.

28 British Columbia hosts three of the NAWMP's twenty-two bird habitat joint ventures: the Pacific Coast Joint Venture, the Canadian Intermountain Joint Venture in the south and central Interior and the Prairie Habitat Joint Venture in the Peace and boreal forest regions of the province's northeast. Of these, only the Pacific Coast Joint Venture is international in scope, encompassing the area from northern California to southern Alaska and Hawaii. Pacific Birds Habitat Joint Venture website, accessed June 7, 2021, http://pacificbirds.org.

29 Each year, bird habitat joint ventures under the NAWMP provide roughly US$25 million to Canada for wetland conservation. BC receives roughly 10 per cent of the Canadian allocation, which supports the construction and maintenance of water control structures, land purchases and long-term interests in land. Ian Barnett, interview by the author, Kamloops, BC, May 22, 2019; Canadian Wildlife Service, "North American Wetlands Conservation Council (Canada), http://nawcc.wetlandnetwork.ca/nawca.html, archived from June 9, 2013.

30 Barnett, interview.

31 Barnett, interview; Les Bogdan, interview by the author, Duncan, BC, June 25, 2019.

32 These conservation priorities formed the basis for the South Okanagan Similkameen Conservation Program (http://soscp.org), a partnership program established in 2000. NTBC, "Conversations on Conservation with Ron Erickson," April 7, 2021, http://naturetrust.bc.ca.

33 The BC Conservation Data Centre was officially created on December 31, 1990, by an agreement among the Province of BC (Ministry of Environment), the Nature Conservancy (US), the Nature Trust of British Columbia and the Nature Conservancy of Canada. Under the leadership of its first coordinator, BC Wildlife Branch biologist Andrew Harcombe, the CDC set out to produce a centralized inventory of rare and endangered species and ecosystems in order to inform conservation priorities. It joined the NatureServe network of over sixty similar organizations in Canada, the US and Latin America. Andrew Harcombe, Sharon Hartwell, Syd Cannings, Carmen Cadrin, George Douglas and Leah Ramsay, "The British Columbia Conservation Data Centre: Progress from 1991 to 1993," Conservation Data Centre, Wildlife Branch, BC Ministry of Environment, November 1993.

34 Lament, interview; Nancy Newhouse, telephone interview by the author, May 13, 2019.

35 Land Title Act, RSBC 1996, c 250, s 219(3); Springinotic, interview; Judy Atkins, Ann Hillyer and Arlene Kwasniak, "Conservation Easements, Covenants, and Servitudes in Canada: A Legal Review," Report no. 04-1, North American Wetlands Conservation Council (Canada) and the Canadian Wildlife Service, Environment Canada, 2004; William J. Andrews and David Loukidelis, *Leaving a Living Legacy: Using Conservation Covenants in BC* (Vancouver: West Coast Environmental Law Research Foundation, January 1996).

36 Subsection 41(2) of the Fisheries Act (later replaced by section 79.2) gave a court discretion "to make an order to refrain or take action in addition to *any other penalty imposed by it.*" John D. Cliffe, "Creative Sentencing in Environmental Prosecutions, the Canadian Experience: An Overview" (paper prepared for the Canadian Institute of Resources Law Symposium on Environmental Education for Judges and Court Practitioners, Dalhousie University, Halifax, February 21–22, 2014), 4; R.S. Silver, "Investing in Conservation with Revenue from Creative Sentencing: The Characteristics of the Court Award Portfolio Managed by the BC Habitat Conservation Trust Foundation, 1993–2009," Habitat Conservation Trust Foundation, Victoria, March 2011, 8, courtesy of R.S. Silver.

37 In 1995, the federal government took the lead in formalizing creative sentencing provisions by establishing the Environmental Damages Fund. Creative sentencing provisions incorporated into seven distinct statutes—including the Fisheries Act, the Migratory Birds Convention Act and the 1999 Canadian Environmental Protection Act—enabled judges to direct payments to the fund. A competitive application process then distributed funding to conservation organizations in affected regions. In 1996, BC followed suit, enacting creative sentencing provisions across five environmental statutes, including the Wildlife Act, Water Act and Waste Management Act.

38 Springinotic, interview.

39 British Columbia, "The Canada-British Columbia Nestucca Agreement," Order of the Lieutenant Governor in Council, Order in Council No. 955/1992; Douglas F. Bertram, "Oil Spill Settlement Funds Directed to Seabird Conservation," *Marine Policy* 108 (2019): 1–5.

40 Jeremy Wilson, "For the Birds? Neoliberalism and the Protection of Biodiversity in British Columbia," *BC Studies*, no. 142–43 (Summer–Autumn 2004): 264. In 2015, non-government-owned conservation lands constituted 159,424 hectares (excluding overlaps with federal and provincial conservation lands) out of a total provincial land base (including fresh water) of 94,646,000 hectares and a total privately owned land base of 4,608,000 hectares. BC NGO Conservation Areas Database Technical Working Group, "Annual British Columbia Conservation Areas Summary Report 2015," August 16, 2016; Brad Smith, Kelly Vijandre, Jim Johnston, and Nathan Hagan-Braun, *Crown Land: Indicators and Statistics Report, 2010* (Victoria, BC Ministry of Forests, Lands and Natural Resource Operations, 2011).

41 University of Guelph social scientist and land resources planner Stewart Hilts piloted some of these approaches in his extension work with farmers and other landowners in southern Ontario. Stewart Hilts faculty web page, Ontario Agricultural College, University of Guelph, accessed June 11, 2021, http://uoguelph.ca/oac; Rod Silver, telephone interview by the author, November 19, 2019.

42 The Stewardship Pledge was a three-year cooperative venture between the BC Ministry of Environment, Wildlife Habitat Canada, the Canadian Wildlife Service and the Habitat Conservation Trust Foundation. In 1995, Fisheries and Oceans Canada and the Ministry of Municipal Affairs joined Pledge partners to form a Stewardship Committee. T. Duynstee and R.S. Silver, "The *Stewardship Pledge Program* (1994–1997): Draft Final Report" (Victoria, BC: Habitat Conservation Trust Fund, 1997).

43 Publications within the Stewardship Series are still accessible through the Stewardship Centre for British Columbia. "BC Stewardship Series," accessed January 24, 2023, http://stewardshipcentrebc.ca.

    They also serve as resource materials for the Habitat Conservation Trust Foundation's WildBC Education program. HCTF, "Community Education," accessed June 14, 2021, http://hctfeducation.ca.

44 Rick Mumford, interview by the author, Williams Lake, BC, July 23, 2019.

45 Kelsi Stiles, Investment Agriculture Foundation of BC, personal communication, April 28, 2022.

46 Spanish Banks Creek, accessed March 22, 2022, http://urbanstreams.org.

47 The BC Trust for Public Lands operated from 2004 to 2009 with a one-time contribution from the provincial government. Robust attempts to renew this funding failed. Rod Silver, personal communication, June 4, 2022.

48 Barnett, interview. Between 1984 and 2002, Environment Canada did not allocate any funds for acquisition of conservation lands such as Migratory Bird Sanctuaries and National Wildlife Areas. Inadequate management and enforcement, meanwhile, threatened the ecological integrity of existing sites. Canadian Nature Federation, *Conserving Wildlife on a Shoestring Budget* (Ottawa: Canadian Nature Federation, 2002). In 2007, the federal government's Natural Areas Conservation Program awarded $225 million for acquisition of private conservation lands across Canada. The Nature Conservancy of Canada received the majority of these funds, followed by Ducks Unlimited Canada and other land trusts. The program's 1:1 matching funds requirement saw considerable investment in BC conservation lands purchases. Program funding was renewed in the federal government's 2013 budget.

49 Newhouse, interview.

50 The Office of the Auditor General of British Columbia concluded in 2021 that the BC Ministry of Environment had failed to "effectively manage the Conservation Lands Program." Management plans for the majority of WMAs had not been updated for decades and as many as 70 per cent had never been approved. Furthermore, regional offices writing the plans had not ensured that activities

very   g..

..

within wildlife areas, such as livestock grazing, were compatible with conservation goals. Office of the Auditor General of British Columbia, *Management of the Conservation Lands Program* (Victoria: OAGBC, May 2021).

51 Eastman et al., "Trends in Renewable Resource Management," 9.

52 Bogdan, interview; Lament, interview.

53 BC Ministry of Forests, *Together for Wildlife: Improving Wildlife Stewardship and Habitat Conservation in British Columbia*, Action 11 (Victoria: Ministry of Forests, Lands, Natural Resource Operations and Rural Development, August 2020).

54 Newhouse, interview; Lament, interview; Council of the Haida Nation and the Nature Conservancy of Canada, "Press Release: Healing a Hurt Land," March 5, 2018, http://haidanation.ca.

55 Bogdan, interview; Lament, interview.

56 Calvin Sandborn, Megan Presnail, Erin Gray and Matt Hulse, "Finding the Money to Buy and Protect Natural Lands," prepared for the Ancient Forest Alliance (Environmental Law Centre, University of Victoria, December 2015), 5.

57 Bogdan, interview.

58 S.M. Baillie, C. McGowan, S. May-McNally, R. Leggatt, B.J.G. Sutherland and S. Robinson, "Environmental DNA and Its Applications to Fisheries and Oceans Canada: National Needs and Priorities," *Canadian Technical Report of Fisheries and Aquatic Sciences* 3329 (2019).

59 Donald S. Eastman, interview by the author, Victoria, BC, April 25, 2019; Jenny Feick, interview by the author, Victoria, BC, April 25, 2019; Garth Mowat, telephone interview by the author, May 1, 2019.

60 Mowat, interview.

61 Kessler, interview; Feick, interview; Mowat, interview.

62 University of Calgary wildlife ecology professor Valerius Geist was an early proponent of educating students in the social, historical and ethical dimensions of wildlife management. Too often, he pointed out in 1995, technically capable graduates proved "remarkably ill-informed about conservation policy," its history and the "all-too-human factors" that influence its implementation. Appreciation for the limitations of science as the primary foundation for wildlife management programs began in the United States in the 1970s. By the early 1990s, wildlife management programs at UNBC and elsewhere were incorporating courses in ethics and communication into their curriculum. Geist's call for a broader *humanities* education for wildlife managers—one that incorporates history and literature—has yet to be realized within Canadian programs. Geist, "An Introduction," in *Wildlife Conservation Policy: A Reader*, ed. Valerius Geist and Ian McTaggart Cowan (Calgary: Detselig Enterprises, 1995), 12.

63 Kessler, interview.

64 Office of the Auditor General of BC, *Conservation of Ecological Integrity in BC Parks and Protected Areas*, Report 3 (Victoria: OAGBC, August 2010), 10–11; Rob Wilson, "Citizen Science Wildlife Monitoring in the Skagit Valley," BC Parks

Blog, July 17, 2019; Crystal Mason, "BC Parks Made Me a Citizen Scientist!," BC Parks Blog, February 19, 2020, https://engage.gov.bc.ca/bcparksblog.

65 Barnett, interview.

66 Les Gyug, Tony Hamilton and Matt Austin, "Grizzly Bear, *Ursus arctos*," Accounts and Measures for Managing Identified Wildlife, Accounts V, BC Ministry of Environment, 2004; D. Morgan, M. Proctor, G. Mowat, B. McLellan, T. Hamilton and L. Turney, "Conservation Ranking of Grizzly Bear Population Units—2019" (Ministry of Environment and Climate Change Strategy, August 26, 2019); Mowat, interview.

67 Demarchi, interview; Gyug, Hamilton and Austin, "Grizzly Bear."

68 Wilson, *Talk and Log*, 54, 223–25.

69 Peck, interview; McLellan, interview.

70 James Peek, John Beecham, David Garshelis, Francois Messier, Sterling Miller and Dale Strickland, "Management of Grizzly Bears in British Columbia: A Review by an Independent Scientific Panel," submitted to the BC Ministry of Water, Land and Air Protection, March 6, 2003.

71 Mowat, interview; Demarchi, interview.

72 McLellan, interview.

73 Grant MacHutchon, telephone interview by the author, April 16, 2019; G. Mowat, C.T. Lamb, L. Smit and A. Reid, "The Relationships among Road Density, Habitat Quality, and Grizzly Bear Population Density in the Kettle-Granby Area of British Columbia," Extension Note no. 120, BC Ministry of Forests, Lands and Natural Resources Operations (July 2017).

74 Office of the Auditor General of British Columbia, *An Independent Audit of Grizzly Bear Management* (Victoria: OAGBC, October 2017).

75 McLellan, interview; OAGBC, *Independent Audit*.

76 Morgan et al., "Conservation Ranking"; Environmental Reporting BC, "Grizzly Bear Population Ranking in B.C.," State of Environment Reporting, Ministry of Environment, 2020.

77 MacHutchon, interview.

78 Helen Schwantje, telephone interview by the author, September 12, 2019.

79 Schwantje, interview.

80 Schwantje, interview. The Canadian Wildlife Service and the Wildlife Branch in the Northwest Territories each employed a wildlife veterinarian in the early 1990s. Veterinary colleges in Saskatoon, Guelph and Quebec also employed veterinarians with wildlife specializations. South of the border, veterinarians held positions in wildlife agencies in California, Idaho, Colorado and Wyoming. Most US wildlife agencies now employ veterinarians and support significant wildlife health programs.

81 Schwantje, interview; G. Kuzyk, C. Procter, S. Marshall, H. Schindler, H. Schwantje, M. Scheideman and D. Hodder, "Factors Affecting Moose Population Declines in British Columbia, 2019 Progress Report: February 2012–May 2019"

(Wildlife Working Report no. WR-127, Ministry of Forests, Lands, Natural Resource Operations and Rural Development, Victoria, December 2019).

82   Schwantje, interview; Game Farm Act, SBC 1990, c 48.

83   Hunter and wildlife advocate Carmen Purdy and regional wildlife biologist Ray Demarchi initiated a supplemental feeding program for elk in the East Kootenay in 1971. By 1985, the program had significantly increased elk numbers in the region. Carmen Purdy, interview by the author, Cranbrook, BC, June 28, 2019; Demarchi, interview; Schwantje, interview.

84   Changing winds and environmental conditions carried Culicoides biting flies across the border to the Grand Forks area in the summer of 2021. Vectors of the deadly bluetongue virus, the flies rapidly infected and killed dozens of California bighorn sheep in the region. "Disease Wipes Out at least 20 Wild Bighorn Sheep in Quick Succession in B.C.'s Interior," *CBC News*, August 28, 2021, http://cbc.ca.

85   Simon Little and Julia Foy, "BC Man Calls for Lead Shot Ban after Hundreds of Swans Die on Cross-Border Lake," *Global News*, June 20, 2021, http://global news.ca; Brenna Owen, "Switch Ammo to Stop Lead Poisoning in Birds, BC Wildlife Experts Tell Hunters," *CBC News*, November 15, 2019, http://cbc.ca.

86   This figure includes national, provincial, regional and municipal parks and protected areas and private conservation lands. BC NGO Conservation Areas Database Technical Working Group, "Annual British Columbia Conservation Areas Summary Report 2020," July 14, 2021.

87   This figure includes National Wildlife Areas and Migratory Bird Sanctuaries (1.16 million ha), provincially administered conservation lands (276,600 ha), temporarily designated conservation lands under the Lands Act (640,000 ha) and non-governmental organization conservation areas (208,485 ha). BC NGO Conservation Areas Database Technical Working Group, "Summary Report 2020." The 1982 figure is from Robinson, "Wildlife Management and Land Use."

88   Federal, Provincial and Territorial Governments of Canada, *2012 Canadian Nature Survey: Awareness, Participation, and Expenditures in Nature-Based Recreation, Conservation, and Subsistence Activities* (Ottawa: Canadian Councils of Resource Ministers, 2014).

89   Edwards, "Land for What?"

Chapter 13 | Indigenous-Led Conservation and Pathways to Reconciliation

1   Atleo, *Tsawalk*, 76.

2   Truth and Reconciliation Commission of Canada, *Honouring the Truth, Reconciling for the Future: Summary of the Final Report of the Truth and Reconciliation Commission of Canada* (Ottawa: TRC, 2015), 6.

3   The BC government passed the Declaration on the Rights of Indigenous Peoples Act (Declaration Act) into law in November 2019. In June 2021, the federal United Nations Declaration on the Rights of Indigenous Peoples Act came into force.

4   Mary C. Hurley, "Aboriginal Title: The Supreme Court of Canada Decision in *Delgamuukw v. British Columbia*," Report BP-459E, Parliamentary Research Branch, January 1998, rev. February 2000.

5   Sterritt, *Mapping My Way Home*, 302–8.

6   *Calder et al. v. Attorney-General of British Columbia*, [1973] SCR 313.

7   Hurley, "Aboriginal Title."

8   Sterritt, *Mapping My Way Home*, 316.

9   Sterritt, *Mapping My Way Home*, 318; Hurley, "Aboriginal Title"; Erin Hanson, "Aboriginal Title," Indigenous Foundations (UBC First Nations and Indigenous Studies Program), n.d., accessed May 21, 2021, http://indigenousfoundations. arts.ubc.ca.

10 *Haida Nation v. British Columbia (Ministry of Forests)*, 2004 SCC 73 at para. 8.

11 *Taku River Tlingit First Nation v. British Columbia (Project Assessment Director)*, 2004 SCC 74.

12 BC Treaty Commission, *Changing Point: Annual Report 2005*, n.d., 5, http:// bctreaty.ca.

13 *Tsilhqot'in Nation v. British Columbia*, 2014 SCC 44; Sterritt, *Mapping My Way Home*, 319.

14 British Columbia and Tsilhqot'in Nation, "Nenqay Deni Accord," February 11, 2016; Laura Cundari, "The Tsilhqot'in Decision: What Has Changed and What Is Next," *BarTalk* (Canadian Bar Association, BC Branch), April 2016, https:// cbabc.org/BarTalk.

15 British Columbia, Data Catalogue, First Nations Treaty Lands dataset (Implementation and Land Services, 2016).

16 Sterritt, *Mapping My Way Home*, 320.

17 Bradford W. Morse, "Tsilhqot'in Nation v. British Columbia: Is It a Game Changer in Canadian Aboriginal Title Law and Crown-Indigenous Relations?," *Lakehead Law Journal* 2, no. 2 (2017): 64–88; BC Treaty Commission, *Annual Report 2014*, n.d., 25, http://bctreaty.ca.

18 Garry Merkel, telephone interview by the author, July 16, 2019.

19 Bogdan, interview.

20 Merkel, interview.

21 In the north, the Conservation Officer Service's Aboriginal Liaison Program funds First Nations representatives to act as liaisons between their communities and provincial natural resource ministries. Liaison staff accompany COs and other enforcement staff on inspections and monitoring activities and then report back to their communities with first-hand knowledge of key points of concern, such as the number of moose shot by licensed non-Indigenous hunters on their territories. Andy MacKay, telephone interview by the author, July 16, 2019.

22 Anonymous First Nations wildlife manager, interview by the author, May 23, 2019.

23 MacKay, interview.

24 Jim Snetsinger, "Strategic Review of Wildlife Mortality on the CN Rail Line in North Central British Columbia," prepared for Kevin Kriese, Assistant Deputy Minister, Northern Operations, Ministry of Forests, March 2013; Wendy Stueck, "BC Residents Demand Action to Reduce Moose Deaths along CN Railway Tracks," *Globe and Mail*, April 11, 2016.

25 Tsilhqot'in National Government and BC Ministry of Forests, "Meeting Summary: Moose Solutions Roundtable," Williams Lake, BC, April 1–2, 2019.

26 Several regional wildlife managers expressed frustration with centralized habitat capability mapping, which might suggest that a given area could support more moose, or fewer grizzly bears, than local managers and hunters knew to be present. Andy Ackerman, interview by the author, Fort St. John, BC, July 9, 2019.

27 Al Gorley's 2016 report on enhancing moose populations in BC reinforces this need to combine local and Indigenous knowledge with scientific methods for population assessments and monitoring. See Gorley, "Strategy to Help Restore Moose."

28 Both the federal and provincial governments have committed to fully implementing the United Nations Declaration on the Rights of Indigenous Peoples (UNDRIP). Under UNDRIP, Indigenous Peoples have the right to determine how their territories and resources are used to "enable them to maintain and strengthen their institutions, cultures and traditions, and to promote their development in accordance with their aspirations and needs." United Nations Declaration on the Rights of Indigenous People, A/RES/61/295 (September 13, 2007).

29 John Henderson, telephone interview by the author, August 13, 2019; Wildlife Stewardship Council, "About Us," accessed June 30, 2021, http://wildlife stewardshipcouncil.com.

30 Bill Blackwater Jr., interview by the author, Hazelton, BC, July 12, 2019.

31 Henderson, interview; Matt Simmons, "Skeena Sockeye Returns Jump 50 Per Cent in Three Years Thanks to Indigenous Leadership," *Narwhal*, October 15, 2020, http://thenarwhal.ca.

32 Valerius Geist, "Introduction," 18.

33 Clayton Lamb, "Indigenous-Led Conservation Aims to Rekindle Caribou Abundance and Traditions," *The Conversation*, May 23, 2022, http://theconversation.com; Hessami et al., "Indigenizing the North American Model," 1295; British Columbia, "Overview of the Draft Partnership Agreement between British Columbia, Canada, West Moberly First Nations and Salteau First Nations to Recover the Central Group of Southern Mountain Caribou: A Primer to Support a Conversation with British Columbians" (February 2021).

34 Geist, "Introduction," 8. On the seven "pillars" of North American wildlife conservation, see Valerius Geist, Shane P. Mahoney and John F. Organ, "Why Hunting Has Defined the North American Model of Wildlife Conservation," *Transactions of the North American Wildlife and Natural Resources Conference*

66 (2001): 175–85; Mahoney and Geist, eds., *The North American Model of Wildlife Conservation* (Baltimore: Johns Hopkins University Press, 2019).

35 Hessami et al., "Indigenizing the North American Model," 1286; Mahoney and Geist, *North American Model.*

36 Lauren Eichler and David Baumeister, "Hunting for Justice: An Indigenous Critique of the North American Model of Wildlife Conservation," *Environment and Society* 9, no. 1 (2018): 75–90; Hessami et al., "Indigenizing the North American Model."

37 Kelsie Kilawna, "'They Are Jeopardizing Our Lives': Okanagan Chief Calls for Change after Clashes with B.C. Conservation Officers," *APTN National News*, December 30, 2020, http://aptnnews.ca.

38 Hessami et al., "Indigenizing the North American Model," 1290.

39 Hessami et al., "Indigenizing the North American Model," 1291.

40 Hessami et al., "Indigenizing the North American Model," 1291.

41 Shane P. Mahoney, "The Model in Transition: From Proactive Leadership to Reactive Conservation," in *North American Model of Wildlife Conservation*, eds. Mahoney and Geist, 132.

42 BC Ministry of Forests, "Together for Wildlife." The advisory forum, formed in December 2018, captured the perspectives of First Nations forum participants in its July 2021 report, *Cultivating Abundance: First Nations Perspectives from the BC-First Nations Wildlife and Habitat Conservation Forum.*

43 Michael P. Nelson, John A. Vucetich, Paul C. Paquet and Joseph K. Bump, "An Inadequate Construct? North American Model: What's Flawed, What's Missing, What's Needed," *Wildlife Professional* 5 (2011): 58–60; Thomas L. Serfass, Robert P. Brooks and Jeremy T. Bruskotter, "North American Model of Wildlife Conservation: Empowerment and Exclusivity Hinder Advances in Wildlife Conservation," *Canadian Wildlife Biology & Management* 7, no. 2 (2018): 101–18.

44 Dave Porter, telephone interview by the author, August 27, 2019.

45 Porter, interview.

46 Statistics Canada, "Percentage of Aboriginal Population by Census Division, 2001," *Atlas of Canada*, 6th ed. (2010).

47 Porter, interview.

48 Porter, interview; Dena Kayeh Institute, Dane Nan Yé Dāh Network Strategic Plan 2018–2022.

49 Indigenous Leadership Initiative, "Indigenous Guardians," accessed May 20, 2022, https://ilinationhood.ca/guardians; Fisheries and Oceans Canada, "Aboriginal Fisheries Guardian Program," September 6, 2019.

50 Coastal First Nations, "Tracing the Roots of the Coastal Guardian Watchmen," November 27, 2020, http://coastalfirstnations.ca.

51 Mi'kmaq Nation elder Albert Marshall, cited in Parks Canada, Indigenous Council of Experts, *We Rise Together: Achieving Pathway to Canada Target 1 through the Creation of Indigenous Protected and Conserved Areas in the Spirit*

and Practice of Reconciliation, The Indigenous Circle of Experts' Report and Recommendations (Gatineau, QC: Parks Canada, 2018), 57; Hunter Lampreau, virtual interview by the author, November 16, 2021.

52   Indigenous Leadership Initiative, "BC Poll Report on Indigenous-Led Conservation," December 22, 2020, and "Indigenous-Led Conservation: IPCAs and Guardians," October 8, 2021, both at https://ilinationhood.ca/publications.

53   Megan S. Adams et al., "Local Values and Data Empower Culturally Guided Ecosystem-Based Fisheries Management of the Wuikinuxv Bear–Salmon–Human System," *Marine and Coastal Fisheries* 13, no. 4 (2021): 362–78.

54   Lauren Henson et al., "Convergent Geographic Patterns between Grizzly Bear Population Genetic Structure and Indigenous Language Groups in Coastal British Columbia," *Ecology and Society* 26, no. 3 (2021): Article 7.

55   Interview with Walkus from Chris Morgan and Matt Martin, "'Two-Eyed Seeing' as a Way to Decolonize Western Science," June 7, 2022, in *The Wild with Chris Morgan*, podcast, http://kuow.org.

56   Adams et al., "Local Values and Data."

57   Parks Canada, *We Rise Together*, 43.

58   Parks Canada, *We Rise Together*, 77.

59   David Suzuki Foundation, "'Let Us Teach You': Exploring Empowerment for Indigenous Protected and Conserved Areas in B.C.," Report of the September 27, 2018, IPCA Workshop (Vancouver: David Suzuki Foundation, 2018), 15, 23–25; Parks Canada, *We Rise Together*, 86–87; BC Parks, "Summary of the Parks and Protected Areas System," December 15, 2021, last modified June 3, 2022, http://bcparks.ca.

60   Barry Gough, *Possessing Meares Island: A Historian's Journey into the Past of Clayoquot Sound* (Madeira Park, BC: Harbour, 2021), 192. The court injunction against commercial logging on Meares Island remains unchallenged. Neither the provincial nor the federal government has formally recognized Meares Island's status as a tribal park.

61   Parks Canada, *We Rise Together*, 85.

62   Emma Gilchrist, "'It's the Last Place We Have for Our People': Doig River's Last Stand amidst Fracking Boom," *Narwhal*, April 14, 2016, http://thenarwhal.ca.

63   "Ki'h Tsaaʔdze Tribal Park," Doig River First Nation website, accessed June 6, 2022, http://doigriverfn.com.

64   Jack Woodward, cited in Gilchrist, "'It's the Last Place.'"

65   Parks Canada, *We Rise Together*, 5.

66   Parks Canada, *We Rise Together*, 89; E. Ens et al., "Putting Indigenous Conservation Policy into Practice Delivers Biodiversity and Cultural Benefits," *Biodiversity and Conservation*, 25 (2016): 2889–906; Richard Schuster et al., "Vertebrate Biodiversity on Indigenous-Managed Lands in Australia, Brazil, and Canada Equals That in Protected Areas," *Environmental Science & Policy* 101 (2019): 1–6.

67   Parks Canada, *We Rise Together*, 35.

68 Claxton, "To Fish as Formerly."

69 *Yahey v. British Columbia*, 2021 BCSC 1287; BC Attorney General, "Attorney General's Statement on Yahey v. British Columbia," news release, July 28, 2021; Justine Hunter, "How a Tiny First Nation Forced an Overhaul of Land Use," *Globe and Mail*, March 8, 2022.

70 Jesse Zeman and Chuck Zuckerman, BC Wildlife Federation, to Katrine Conroy, Minister of Forests, March 24, 2022.

71 David Carrigg, "Supreme Court of BC Rules Nechako Dam a 'Nuisance' to Indigenous Fishing Rights," *Vancouver Sun*, January 9, 2022.

Conclusion

1   Andrew Weichel, "Number of Deaths Recorded during B.C.'s Heat Wave up to 808, Coroners Say," *CTV News*, July 16, 2021, http://bc.ctvnews.ca.

2   UBC marine biologist Chris Harley estimated that more than one billion animals, including mussels, clams, sea stars and snails, perished along the Salish Sea coastline. Alex Migdal, "More than a Billion Seashore Animals May Have Cooked to Death in B.C. Heat Wave, Says UBC Researcher," *CBC News*, July 5, 2021, http://cbc.ca.

3   World Weather Attribution, "Western North American Extreme Heat Virtually Impossible without Human-Caused Climate Change," July 7, 2021, http://worldweatherattribution.org.

4   Intergovernmental Science-Policy Platform on Biodiversity and Ecosystem Services (IPBES), *Global Assessment Report on Biodiversity and Ecosystem Services of the Intergovernmental Science-Policy Platform on Biodiversity and Ecosystem Services* (Bonn, Germany: IPBES Secretariat, 2019). On biodiversity specifically, see "Life on Land," goal 15 of UN Sustainable Development Goals (2015); United Nations, "UN Report: Nature's Dangerous Decline 'Unprecedented'; Species Extinction Rates 'Accelerating,'" news release, May 6, 2019.

5   Zeman and Zuckerman to Conroy, March 24, 2022.

6   "Recreational Anglers Rally against Chinook Fishery Closures," *CBC News*, July 6, 2020.

7   Austin et al., *Taking Nature's Pulse*, 38, 160; Kristi Iverson, *Grasslands of the Southern Interior*, Ecosystems at Risk in British Columbia brochure series (Victoria: BC Ministry of Sustainable Resource Management, 2004).

8   BC Conservation Data Centre, BC Species and Ecosystems Explorer.

9   Cowan, "Science and the Conservation of Wildlife," 103.

10 Gorley and Merkel, "New Future for Old Forests," 6, 49.

11 Garry and Sandra Vince, interview by the author, Creston, BC, June 27, 2019.

12 Newhouse, interview with the author.

13 Heffelfinger, Geist and Wishart, "The Role of Hunting in North American Wildlife Conservation," *International Journal of Environmental Studies* 70, no. 3 (June 2013): 399–413.

14 Rick Marshall, interview by the author, Smithers, BC, July 21, 2019.

15 Mark L.R. Hall, "Are We 'Managing Wildlife to Zero' in British Columbia?," Hunting BC Forum, January 4, 2018, http://huntingbc.ca/forum.

16 McLellan, interview.

17 Terpenning, "BCWF and Government," 243; Michael Stone, "British Columbia Freshwater Results of the 1985 National Survey of Sport Fishing," Fisheries Technical Circular no. 79 (Victoria: BC Ministry of Environment and Parks, 1988); Freshwater Fisheries Society of BC, *Annual Report, 2019/20* (2020).

18 Penn, *Real Thing*, 130.

19 See, for example, Mark V. Barrow, "Science, Sentiment, and the Specter of Extinction: Reconsidering Birds of Prey during America's Interwar Years," *Environmental History* 7, no. 1 (2002): 69–98, doi.org/10.2307/3985453.

20 Richard Cannings, telephone interview by the author, October 29, 2021; Mackie, *Hamilton Mack Laing*, 137.

21 R. Wayne Campbell, Ronald D. Jakimchuk and Dennis A. Demarchi, "In Memoriam: Ian McTaggart Cowan, 1910–2010," *The Auk* 130, no. 4 (2013): 807–9.

22 Blackwater Jr., interview by the author.

23 Lampreau, interview.

24 Lampreau, interview.

25 Lampreau, interview.

26 Genevieve Singleton, interview by the author, Duncan, BC, April 24, 2019.

27 Singleton, interview.

28 Lee Hesketh, interview by the author, Enderby, BC, May 24, 2019.

29 Hesketh, interview.

30 Hesketh, interview.

Bibliography

Case Law

Calder et al. v. Attorney-General of British Columbia, [1973] SCR 313.
Delgamuukw v. British Columbia, [1997] 3 SCR 1010.
Fowler v. The Queen, [1980] 2 SCR 213.
Haida Nation v. British Columbia (Ministry of Forests) 2004 3 SCR 511, 2t para. 8.
R v. Cooper, I DLR (3d) 113 (BCSC 1968).
R v. Derriksan (1976) CanLII 1270 (SCC).
R v. Jim (1915), 26 CCC 236.
R v. Sparrow (1990), 1 SCR 1075.
R v. White and Bob [1965] CanLII 643 (SCC).
Taku River Tlingit First Nation v. British Columbia (Project Assessment Director), 2004 SCC 74 (CanLII), [2004] 3 SCR 550.
Tsilhqot'in Nation v. British Columbia, 2014 SCC 44 (CanLII), [2014] 2 SCR 257.
Yahey v. British Columbia, 2021 BCSC 1287 (CanLII).

Government Documents

British Columbia
BC Conservation Data Centre. Conservation Status Reports.
—. Species Summaries.
BC Forest Practices Board. Complaint Investigations.
—. Special Reports.
BC Hydro. Fish and Wildlife Compensation Program Reports.
BC Treaty Commission. Annual Reports.
Department of the Attorney General. Provincial Game Warden Reports.
—. BC Game Commission Reports.
Department of Recreation and Conservation. Fish and Wildlife Branch. Annual Reports.
Environment and Land Use Committee. Reports.
Environmental Reporting BC. State of Environment Reports.
Forest Renewal BC. Annual Reports.
Ministry of Environment.
—. Accounts and Measures for Managing Identified Wildlife Series.
—. Angling Management Plans.
—. Conservation Ranking Reports.
—. Ecosystems in British Columbia At Risk Series.
—. Environmental Trends Reports.
—. Wildlife Branch Bulletin Series.

—. Wildlife Management Plans.
Ministry of Forests.
—. Extension Notes.
—. Silvicultural Trends Reports.
—. State of BC Forests Reports.
—. Wildlife and Habitat Branch. Management Plans.
—. —. Discussion Papers.
—. —. Wildlife Viewing Publications.
—. —. Wildlife Working Reports.
Ministry of Transportation and Infrastructure. Wildlife Management Reports.
Office of the Auditor General of British Columbia. Audit Reports.
Sessional Papers.
Statutes of British Columbia.

Canada

Committee on the Status of Endangered Wildlife in Canada (COSEWIC).
    Assessment and status reports.
Crown-Indigenous Relations and Northern Affairs Canada. Treaty Texts.
Environment Canada.
—. Species at Risk Act Recovery Strategy Series.
—. Canadian Wildlife Service. Migratory Birds Regulatory Reports.
—. —. Technical Report Series.
Fisheries and Oceans Canada.
—. Aboriginal Fisheries Strategy.
—. Canadian Science Advisory Secretariat. Science Advisory Reports.
—. Canadian Technical Report of Fisheries and Aquatic Sciences Series.
—. National Indigenous Fisheries Institute Reports.
—. Species at Risk Act Action Plan Series.
Parks Canada. Species at Risk Act Recovery Strategy Series.
—. Indigenous Circle of Experts. Report and Recommendations.
Statistics Canada.
—. Atlas of Canada.
—. Catalogue Reports.
—. Census Documents.
—. Envirostats Reports.
Statutes of Canada.

Magazines and Newspapers

American Hunter
APTN National News

BC Grasslands
BC Historical News
British Columbia Sportsman
Canadian Encyclopedia
Canadian Geographic
CBC News
Coast Mountain News
Conversation
Courier (Cranbrook)
CTV News
Cranbrook Daily Townsman
Dictionary of Canadian Biography
Fort Nelson News
Global News
Globe and Mail
International Game Warden Magazine
Narwhal
Native Voice
Nature Canada
Nelson Star
Prince George Citizen
Terrace Standard
Tyee
Vancouver Daily Province
Vancouver Sun
Victoria Naturalist
Victoria News
Victoria Times Colonist
Western Fisheries
Wild with Chris Morgan
Wildlife Review

Theses and Dissertations

Anderson, Elaine Susan. "Flying on the Wings of Trust: The Story of the Delta Farmland and Wildlife Trust, an Example of Collaborative Community Based Resource Management." PhD diss., University of British Columbia, 2009. doi.org/10.14288/1.0069381.

Antifeau, T.D. "The Significance of Snow and Arboreal Lichens in the Winter Ecology of Mountain Caribou (*Rangifer tarandus caribou*) in the North Thompson Watershed of British Columbia." M.Sc. thesis, University of British Columbia, 1987.

Ball, Georgiana. "A History of Wildlife Management Practices in British Columbia
    to 1918." MA thesis, University of Victoria, 1981.
Begg, Michael. "Legislating British Columbia: A History of B.C. Land Law, 1858–1978."
    LL.M. thesis, University of British Columbia, 2007.
Church, John Spencer. "Mining Companies in the West Kootenay and Boundary
    Regions of British Columbia, 1890–1900: Capital Formation and Financial
    Operations." MA thesis, University of British Columbia, 1961.
Claxton, Nick. "To Fish as Formerly: A Resurgent Journey Back to the Saanich Reef
    Net Fishery." PhD diss., University of Victoria, 2015. https://dspace.library.uvic.ca/
    handle/1828/6614.
Hatter, James. "The Moose of Central British Columbia." PhD thesis, State College of
    Washington, Pullman, 1950. Reprinted as *Early Ecology and Management of the
    Moose in Central British Columbia*. Self-published, 2011.
Ireland, Brenda. "'Working a Great Hardship on Us': First Nations People, the State
    and Fur Conservation in British Columbia before 1935." MA thesis, University of
    British Columbia, 1995.
Taylor, Ernest W. "A Study of Factors Affecting Reproduction and Survival of the
    Ring-Necked Pheasant in the Lower Fraser River Valley of British Columbia."
    MA thesis, University of British Columbia, 1950.
Terpenning, John Gordon. "The B.C. Wildlife Federation and Government: A
    Comparative Study of Pressure Group and Government Interaction for Two
    Periods, 1947 to 1957, and 1958 to 1975." MA thesis, University of Victoria, 1982.

Unpublished Papers and Reports

Beaumont, Cathy. "Stewardship Works! A Core Funding Model." Workshop Report,
    Wosk Centre for Dialogue, Vancouver, May 23, 2007.
Borrows, John. "Crown and Aboriginal Occupations of Land: A History and
    Comparison." Submission to the Ipperwash Inquiry, 15 October 2005.
Borrows, John and Shayla Praud. "Teachings of Sustainability, Stewardship, and
    Responsibility: Indigenous Perspectives on Obligation, Wealth, Trusts, and
    Fiduciary Duty." Discussion Paper, Reconciliation and Responsible Investment
    Initiative, September 2020.
Bunnell, Fred L., Laurie Kremsater and Mark Boyland. "An Ecological Rationale
    for Changing Forest Management on MacMillan Bloedel's Forest Tenure."
    Unpublished paper. Centre for Applied Conservation Biology, University of
    British Columbia, 1998.
Bunnell, Fred L., Kelly A. Squires and Isabelle Houde. "Evaluating Effects of
    Large-Scale Salvage Logging for Mountain Pine Beetle on Terrestrial and Aquatic
    Vertebrates." Mountain Pine Beetle Initiative, Working Paper 2004-2. Natural
    Resources Canada, Pacific Forestry Centre, Victoria, 2004.

Cambria Gordon Consultants. "Eulachon of the Pacific Northwest: A Life History." Prepared for the Living Landscapes Program, Royal BC Museum, Terrace, BC, January 11, 2006.

Clayoquot Sound Scientific Panel. "Sustainable Ecosystem Management in Clayoquot Sound: Planning and Practices." Clayoquot Sound Scientific Panel, April 1995.

Cliffe, John D. "Creative Sentencing in Environmental Prosecutions, the Canadian Experience: An Overview." Paper prepared for the Canadian Institute of Resources Law Symposium on Environmental Education for Judges and Court Practitioners, Dalhousie University, Halifax, February 21–22, 2014.

Clogg, Jessica and Deborah Carlson. "Land Use Planning for Nature, Climate and Communities: Taking Stock and Moving Forward." Vancouver: West Coast Environmental Law, February 2013.

Day, J.C., and Richard Stace-Smith, eds. *British Columbia Land for Wildlife: Past, Present, Future.* Proceedings of the Symposium held at Simon Fraser University, Burnaby, BC, October 23–24, 1981. Victoria: BC Ministry of Environment, Fish and Wildlife Branch, 1982.

Demarchi, Dennis A. "An Introduction to the Ecoregions of British Columbia," 3rd ed. Victoria: Ecosystem Information Section, Ministry of Environment, 2011.

Federal, Provincial and Territorial Governments of Canada. "2012 Canadian Nature Survey: Awareness, Participation, and Expenditures in Nature-Based Recreation, Conservation, and Subsistence Activities." Ottawa: Canadian Councils of Resource Ministers, 2014.

Fisher, Susan, and Daphne Solecki. *A Hundred Years of Natural History: The Vancouver Natural History Society, 1918–2018.* Vancouver: Vancouver Natural History Society, 2018.

Gedalof, Ze'ev. "Fire and Biodiversity in British Columbia." In Biodiversity of British Columbia, ed. Brian Klinkenberg. Lab for Advanced Spatial Analysis, Department of Geography, University of British Columbia, 2020. http://biodiversity.bc.ca

Gorley, R.A. "A Strategy to Help Restore Moose Populations in British Columbia." Recommendations prepared for the Ministry of Forests, Lands and Natural Resource Operations, Fish and Wildlife Branch, Victoria, July 8, 2016.

Gorley, R.A., and Garry Merkel. "A New Future for Old Forests: A Strategic Review of How British Columbia Manages for Old Forests within Its Ancient Ecosystems." Prepared for the BC Minister of Forests, Lands, Natural Resource Operations and Rural Development, Victoria, April 30, 2020.

Government of Canada. Commission of Conservation. *National Conference on Conservation of Game, Fur-bearing Animals and Other Wild Life.* Ottawa: J. De Labroquerie, 1919.

Government of Canada. Royal Commission on Aboriginal Peoples. *Looking Forward, Looking Back.* Vol. 1 of *Report of the Royal Commission on Aboriginal Peoples.* Ottawa: Canada Communication Group, 1996.

Gray, P.A., P.C. Boxall, R. Reid, F.L. Filion, E. DuWors, A. Jacquemot, P. Bouchard and A. Bath. "The Importance of Wildlife to Canadians: Results from Three

National Surveys." In *Forests and Wildlife: Towards the 21st Century*, Proceedings of the International Union of Game Biologists XXI Congress, August 15–20, 1993, Halifax, Nova Scotia, edited by I.D. Thompson, 151–57. Chalk River, ON: Forestry Canada, Petawawa National Forestry Institute, 1993.

Haley, D. "Forestry Policy." In *Forestry Handbook for British Columbia*, 5th ed., part 1, ed. Susan B. Watts and Lynne Tolland. Vancouver: Forestry Undergraduate Society, UBC Faculty of Forestry, 2005.

Harcombe, Andrew P. "The Conservation Data Centre: For the Greatest about the Least." In *Proceedings of a Conference on the Biology and Management of Species and Habitats at Risk, Kamloops, BC, February 15–19, 1999*, Vol. 1, edited by L.M. Darling, 13–18. Victoria: BC Ministry of Environment, Lands and Parks; Kamloops: University College of the Cariboo, 2000.

Hatter, James. *Politically Incorrect: The Life and Times of British Columbia's First Game Biologist*. Victoria: O&J Enterprises, 1997.

—. *Wolves and People: The Management Imperative and Mythology of Animal Rights*. Victoria: Trafford, 2005.

Moore, Keith. "Coastal Watersheds: An Inventory of Watersheds in the Coastal Temperate Forests of British Columbia." Vancouver: Earthlife Canada Foundation and Ecotrust/Conservation International, 1991.

Morris, Mike. "Getting the Balance Right: Improving Wildlife Habitat Management in British Columbia; Strategic Advice to the [BC] Minister of Forests, Lands and Natural Resource Operations." August 2015.

Munro, James A. "The Birds and Mammals of the Creston Region, British Columbia." British Columbia Provincial Museum Occasional Paper no. 8, Victoria, 1950.

Orr, Craig, Patricia Gallaugher and Jennifer Penniket, eds. *Speaking for the Salmon: Hatcheries and the Protection of Wild Salmon*. Conference proceedings. Burnaby: Simon Fraser University, June 2002.

Paish, Howard. "An Overview of Fish and Wildlife Stewardship in British Columbia." Unpublished draft report. Stewardship Centre for British Columbia Steering Committee, Vancouver, June 2005. Courtesy of the Stewardship Centre for British Columbia.

Pearse, Peter H. "Turning the Tide: A New Policy for Canada's Pacific Fisheries." Final Report. Vancouver: Commission on Pacific Fisheries Policy, 1982.

Pearse, Peter H. and Gary Bowden. "Big Game Hunting in the East Kootenay: A Statistical Analysis." Self-published, 1966.

Romuld, M. and S.E. Bayley. "Columbia Valley Environmental Resource Database Analysis." Report prepared for the Columbia Wetlands Stewardship Partners, Parson, BC, 2017.

Rutledge, Leo. *That Some May Follow: The History of Guide Outfitting in British Columbia*. Richmond: Guide Outfitters Association of British Columbia, 1989.

Scudder, G.G.E. "Biodiversity Conservation and Protected Areas in British Columbia." Unpublished paper. Commissioned by the Sierra Legal Defence Fund. March 2003.

—. "Species at Risk, Conservation Strategies, and Ecological Integrity." In *Proceedings of a Conference on the Biology and Management of Species and Habitats at Risk*, Kamloops, BC, February 15–19, 1999, Vol. 1, edited by L.M. Darling, 1–12. Victoria: BC Ministry of Environment, Lands and Parks; Kamloops: University College of the Cariboo, 2000.

Silver, R.S. "Investing in Conservation with Revenue Associated with British Columbia's Quality Waters, 1997–2012." Habitat Conservation Trust Foundation, Victoria, November 2015.

—. "Investing in Conservation with Revenue from Creative Sentencing: The Characteristics of the Court Award Portfolio Managed by the BC Habitat Conservation Trust Foundation, 1993–2009." Habitat Conservation Trust Foundation, Victoria, March 2011.

Smith, Barry E. "A Work in Progress—The British Columbia Farmland Preservation Program." Unpublished paper, Burnaby, BC, 2012.

Stace-Smith, Richard, Lois Johns and Paul Joslin, eds. *Threatened and Endangered Species and Habitats in British Columbia and the Yukon*. Proceedings of the Symposium held in Richmond, BC, March 8–9, 1980. Victoria: BC Ministry of Environment, 1980.

Stringer, George. *Before My Memory Fades: My Early Years as a Fish and Wildlife Biologist*. Self-published, 1989.

Suckling, Kieran, Noah Greenwald and Tierra Curry. "On Time, on Target: How the Endangered Species Act Is Saving America's Wildlife." Report, US Center for Biological Diversity, May 2012.

Turner, Nancy J. "The Importance of Biodiversity for First Peoples of British Columbia." Biodiversity BC Technical Subcommittee for the Report on the Status of Biodiversity in British Columbia, September 2007.

Wali, Mohan K., and Jim Pojar. "The Legacy of Vladimir J. Krajina and Contributions to UBC Botany." Invited presentation for the centennial of the University of British Columbia, 2015.

Books and Articles

Adams, Megan S., Brendan Connors, Taal Levi, Danielle Shaw, Jennifer Walkus, Scott Rogers and Chris Darimont. "Local Values and Data Empower Culturally Guided Ecosystem-Based Fisheries Management of the Wuikinuxv Bear–Salmon–Human System." *Marine and Coastal Fisheries* 13, no. 4 (2021): 362–78. doi.org/10.1002/mcf2.10171.

Ahrens, R.H. "Crown Land Allocation and Management: The Implications for Wildlife." In Day and Stace-Smith, *British Columbia Land for Wildlife*, 52–58.

Anderson, E. William. "History of Coordinated Resources Management Planning (CRMP) in Oregon—An Overview." *Rangelands* 21, no. 2 (April 1999): 6–11.

Atleo, E. Richard (Umeek). *Principles of Tsawalk: An Indigenous Approach to a Global Crisis.* Vancouver: UBC Press, 2012
—. *Tsawalk: A Nuu-Chah-Nulth Worldview.* Vancouver: UBC Press, 2004.
Austin, M.A., D.A. Buffett, D.J. Nicolson, G.G.E. Scudder and V. Stevens, eds. *Taking Nature's Pulse: The Status of Biodiversity in British Columbia.* Victoria: Biodiversity BC, 2008.
Austin, M.A., and A. Eriksson. *The Biodiversity Atlas of British Columbia.* Victoria: Biodiversity BC, March 2009.
Ball, Georgiana. "The Monopoly System of Wildlife Management of the Indians and the Hudson's Bay Company in the Early History of British Columbia." *BC Studies,* no. 66 (Summer 1985): 37–58.
Barman, Jean. *The West beyond the West: A History of British Columbia.* 3rd ed. Toronto: University of Toronto Press, 2007.
Beese, William J., John Deal, B. Glen Dunsworth, Stephen J. Mitchell and Timothy J. Philpott. "Two Decades of Variable Retention in British Columbia: A Review of Its Implementation and Effectiveness for Biodiversity Conservation." *Ecological Processes* 8, no. 1 (2019): Article 33. doi.org/10.1186/s13717-019-0181-9.
Bergerud, A.T., and J. Elliot. "Dynamics of Caribou and Wolves in Northern British Columbia." *Canadian Journal of Zoology* 64, no. 7 (1986): 1515–28.
Bertram, Douglas F. "Oil Spill Settlement Funds Directed to Seabird Conservation." *Marine Policy* 108 (2019): 1–5. doi.org/10.1016/j.marpol.2019.103622.
Beveridge, Rachelle, Megan Moody, Grant Murray, Chris Darimont and Bernie Pauly. "The Nuxalk *Sputc (Eulachon) Project*: Strengthening Indigenous Management Authority through Community-Driven Research." *Marine Policy* 119 (September 2020): Article 103971. doi.org/10.1016/j.marpol.2020.103971.
Bevington, Angie. "Frank Ralph Conibear (1896–)," *Arctic Profiles* 36, no. 4 (1983): 386–87.
Blomley, Nicholas. "'Shut the Province Down': First Nations Blockades in British Columbia, 1984–1995," *BC Studies,* no. 111 (Autumn 1996): 5–35.
Bramadat, Paul., and Patricia O'Connell Killen. "Conclusion: Religion at the Edge of a Continent." In *Religion at the Edge: Nature, Spirituality, and Secularity in the Pacific Northwest,* edited by Paul Bramadat, Patricia O'Connell Killen and Sarah Wilkins-Laflamme, 241–53. Vancouver: UBC Press, 2022.
Brink, Vernon C. "Natural History Societies of B.C." In Murray, *Our Wildlife Heritage,* 151–57.
Brody, Hugh. *Maps and Dreams: Indians and the British Columbia Frontier.* 2nd ed. Vancouver: Douglas & McIntyre, 1992.
Broughton, J.M., and E.M. Weitzel. "Population Reconstructions for Humans and Megafauna Suggest Mixed Causes for North American Pleistocene Extinctions." *Nature Communications* 9, no. 1 (2018): Article 5441. doi.org/10.1038/s41467-018-07897-1.
Brown, Jen Corrine. *Trout Culture: How Fly Fishing Forever Changed the Rocky Mountain West.* Seattle: University of Washington Press, 2015.

Buchalski, Michael R., Benjamin N. Sacks, Daphne A. Gille and Maria Cecilia T. Penedo. "Phylogeographic and Population Genetic Structure of Bighorn Sheep (Ovis canadensis) in North American Deserts." *Journal of Mammalogy* 97, no. 3 (2016): 823–38.

Bunnell, Fred L., and Glen Dunsworth. "Making Adaptive Management for Biodiversity Work: The Example of Weyerhaeuser in Coastal British Columbia." *Forestry Chronicle* 80 (2004): 37–43. doi.org/10.5558/tfc80037-1.

Burnett, J. Alexander. *A Passion for Wildlife: The History of the Canadian Wildlife Service*. Vancouver: UBC Press, 2003.

Butler, R.W., D.W. Bradley and J. Casey. "The Status, Ecology and Conservation of Internationally Important Bird Populations on the Fraser River Delta, British Columbia, Canada." *British Columbia Birds* 32 (2021): 1–52.

Cail, Robert E. *Land, Man, and the Law: The Disposal of Crown Lands in British Columbia, 1871–1913*. Vancouver: UBC Press, 1974.

Campbell, R. Wayne, Neil Dawe, Ian McTaggart Cowan, John M. Cooper, Gary W. Kaiser and Michael C.E. McNall. *Nonpasserines: Introduction and Loons through Waterfowl*. Vol. 1 of *The Birds of British Columbia*. Vancouver: UBC Press, in cooperation with Canadian Wildlife Service, Environment Canada, 1990.

Campbell, R. Wayne, Ronald D. Jakimchuk and Dennis A. Demarchi. "In Memoriam: Ian McTaggart Cowan, 1910–2010." *The Auk* 130, no. 4 (2013): 807–9. doi. org/10.1525/auk.2013.130.4.807.

Cannings, Richard, and Sydney Cannings. *British Columbia: A Natural History*. 3rd ed. Vancouver: Greystone Books, 2015.

Carl, G. Clifford, and C.J. Guiguet. *Alien Animals in British Columbia*. Victoria: Royal BC Museum, 1958.

Carlson, Keith Thor, ed. *You Are Asked to Witness: The Stó:lō in Canada's Pacific Coast History*. Chilliwack: Stó:lō Heritage Trust, 1997.

Chambers, Alan. "Toward a Synthesis of Mountains, People, and Institutions." *Landscape Planning* 6, no. 2 (August 1979): 109–26.

Colby, Jason. "Change in Black and White: Killer Whale Bodies and the New Pacific Northwest." In *The Historical Animal*, ed. Susan Nance, 19–37. Syracuse, NY: Syracuse University Press, 2015.

Colpitts, George. "Howl: The 1952–56 Rabies Crisis and the Creation of the Urban Wild at Banff." In *Animal Metropolis: Histories of Human-Animal Relations in Urban Canada*, ed. Joanna Dean, Darcy Ingram and Christabelle Sethna. Calgary: University of Calgary Press, 2017, 219–53.

—. *Game in the Garden: A Human History of Wildlife in Western Canada to 1940*. Vancouver: UBC Press, 2002.

Corley-Smith, Peter. *White Bears and Other Curiosities: The First 100 Years of the Royal British Columbia Museum*. Victoria: Royal BC Museum, 1989.

Cowan, Ian McTaggart. "The Timber Wolf in the Rocky Mountain Parks of Canada." *Canadian Journal of Research* 25, no. 5 (1947): 139–74.

Daly, Richard. *Our Box Was Full: An Ethnography for the* Delgamuukw *Plaintiffs.*
Vancouver: UBC Press, 2005.

Dance, Anne. "Dikes, Ducks, and Dams: Environmental Change and the Politics of
Reclamation at Creston Flats, 1882–2014." *BC Studies,* no. 184 (Winter 2014–15):
11–44.

Demarchi, Dennis. "Wildlife Biologist and Bird Artist William Glen Smith (1923–
1993)." *Wildlife Afield* 12, no. 1 (2015): 71–101.

Demarchi, Raymond A. "The Coordinated Resource Management Planning (CRMP)
Process—A Viewpoint." *Rangelands* 10, no. 1 (February 1988): 15–16.

Deur, Douglas, Adam Dick, Kim Recalma-Clutesi and Nancy J. Turner.
"Kwakwaka'wakw 'Clam Gardens': Motive and Agency in Traditional Northwest
Coast Mariculture." *Human Ecology* 43, no. 2 (April 2015): 201–12. doi.org/10.1007/
s10745-015-9743-3.

Deur, Douglas, and Nancy J. Turner, eds. *Keeping It Living: Traditions of Plant Use
and Cultivation on the Northwest Coast of North America.* Seattle: University of
Washington Press, 2005.

Dhar, Amalesh, Lael Parrott and Christopher D.B. Hawkins. "Aftermath of Mountain
Pine Beetle Outbreak in British Columbia: Stand Dynamics, Management
Response and Ecosystem Resilience." *Forests* 7, no. 8 (2016): 171. doi.org/10.3390/
f7080171.

Donnelly, Roarke. "Piscicide Impact Extends beyond Targets and Toxicity."
Restoration Ecology 26, no. 6 (November 2018): 1075–81.

Duff, Wilson. *The Indian History of British Columbia: The Impact of the White Man.*
3rd ed. Victoria: Royal BC Museum, 1997.

Eastman, Donald S., Ralph Archibald, Rick Ellis and Brian Nyberg. "Trends in
Renewable Resource Management in BC." *Journal of Ecosystems and Management*
14, no. 3 (2013). doi.org/10.22230/jem.2013v14n3a556.

Edwards, R. Yorke. "Fire and the Decline of a Mountain Caribou Herd." *Journal of
Wildlife Management* 18 (1954): 521–26.

Eichler, Lauren, and David Baumeister. "Hunting for Justice: An Indigenous Critique
of the North American Model of Wildlife Conservation." *Environment and Society*
9, no.1 (2018): 75–90.

Ens, E., M.L. Scott, Y.M Rangers, C. Moritz and R. Pirzl. "Putting Indigenous
Conservation Policy into Practice Delivers Biodiversity and Cultural Benefits."
Biodiversity and Conservation, 25 (2016): 2889–906. doi.org/10.1007/s10531-016-
1207-6.

Fedrowitz, K., J. Koricheva, S.C. Baker, D.B. Lindenmayer, B. Palik, R. Rosenvald,
W. Beese, J.F. Franklin, J. Kouki, E. Macdonald, C. Messier, A. Sverdrup-
Thygeson, L. Gustafsson and C. Baraloto. "Can Retention Forestry Help Conserve
Biodiversity? A Meta-Analysis." *Journal of Applied Ecology* 51 (2014): 1669–79. doi.
org/10.1111/1365-2664.12289.

Fisher, Robin. *Contact and Conflict: Indian-European Relations in British Columbia,
1774–1890.* 2nd ed. Vancouver: UBC Press, 1992.

Ford, John K.B., and Graeme M. Ellis. "Memories." *Marine Mammal Science* 7, no. 3 (July 1991): 326–28. doi.org/10.1111/j.1748-7692.1991.tb00110.x.

Forkey, Neil S. *Canadians and the Natural Environment to the Twenty-First Century.* Toronto: University of Toronto Press, 2012.

Forman, Richard T.T., Daniel Sperling and John A. Bissonette. *Road Ecology: Science and Solutions.* Washington, DC: Island Press, 2003.

Foster, Hamar. "Honouring the Queen's Flag: A Legal and Historical Perspective on the Nisga'a Treaty," *BC Studies*, no. 120 (Winter 1998–99): 11–36. doi.org/10.14288/bcs.voi120.1475.

Foster, Janet. *Working for Wildlife: The Beginning of Preservation in Canada.* Toronto: University of Toronto Press, 1978.

Geist, Valerius. "An Introduction." In *Wildlife Conservation Policy: A Reader*, edited by Valerius Geist and Ian McTaggart Cowan. Calgary: Detselig Enterprises, 1995.

Geist, Valerius, Shane P. Mahoney and John F. Organ. "Why Hunting Has Defined the North American Model of Wildlife Conservation." *Transactions of the North American Wildlife and Natural Resources Conference* 66 (2001): 175–85.

George, Chief Earl Maquinna. *Living on the Edge: Nuu-Chah-Nulth History from an Ahousaht Chief's Perspective.* Winlaw, BC: Sono Nis Press, 2003.

Geraldes, Armando, Kenneth K. Askelson, Ellen Nikelski, Frank I. Doyle, William L. Harrower, Kevin Winkler and Darren E. Irwin. "Population Genomic Analyses Reveal a Highly Differentiated and Endangered Genetic Cluster of Northern Goshawks (*Accipiter gentilis laingi*) in Haida Gwaii." *Evolutionary Applications* 12, no. 4 (April 2019): 757–72. https://onlinelibrary.wiley.com/doi/full/10.1111/eva.12754.

Gisday Wa and Delgam Uukw. The Spirit in the Land: The Opening Statement of the Gitksan and Wet'suwet'en Hereditary Chiefs in the Supreme Court of British Columbia May 11, 1987. Gabriola Island, BC: Reflections, 1990.

Goble, Dale D., and Paul W. Hirt, eds. *Northwest Lands, Northwest Peoples: Readings in Environmental History.* Seattle: University of Washington Press, 1999.

Gough, Barry. *Possessing Meares Island: A Historian's Journey into the Past of Clayoquot Sound.* Madeira Park, BC: Harbour, 2021.

Haig-Brown, Roderick. *The Living Land: An Account of the Natural Resources of British Columbia.* Toronto: Macmillan, 1961.

—. *Measure of the Year: Reflections on Home, Family, and a Life Fully Lived.* 1950. Reprint, Victoria: TouchWood Editions, 2011.

Hammond, Lorne. "Marketing Wildlife: The Hudson's Bay Company and the Pacific Northwest, 1821–49." *Forest & Conservation History* 37, no. 1 (1993): 14–25. doi.org/10.2307/3983815.

Hardin, Garrett. "The Tragedy of the Commons." *Science* 162, no. 3859 (December 13, 1968): 1243–48.

Harris, Douglas C. *Landing Native Fisheries: Indian Reserves and Fishing Rights in British Columbia, 1849–1925.* Vancouver: UBC Press, 2008.

—. *Fish, Law, and Colonialism: The Legal Capture of Salmon in British Columbia.* Toronto: University of Toronto Press, 2001.

Harris, R. Cole. *Making Native Space: Colonialism, Resistance, and Reserves in British Columbia.* Vancouver: UBC Press, 2003.

Heffelfinger, Jim, Valerius Geist and William Wishart. "The Role of Hunting in North American Wildlife Conservation." *International Journal of Environmental Studies* 70, no. 3 (June 2013): 399–413. DOI:10.1080/00207233.2013.800383.

Henny, Charles J. and James L. Kaiser. "Rotenone Use and Subsequent Prey Loss Lowers Osprey Fledging Rates via Brood Reduction." *Journal of Raptor Research* 56, no. 1 (2022): 37–54.

Henson, Lauren, N. Balkenhol, R. Gustas, Megan S. Adams, Jennifer Walkus, W. Housty, A. Stronen, D. Reece, B. vonHolt, B. Koop and Chris T. Darimont. "Convergent Geographic Patterns between Grizzly Bear Population Genetic Structure and Indigenous Language Groups in Coastal British Columbia." *Ecology and Society* 26, no. 3 (2021): Article 7.

Hessami, Mateen A., Ella Bowles, Jesse N. Popp and Adam T. Ford. "Indigenizing the North American Model of Wildlife Conservation." *FACETS* 6 (2021): 1285–306. doi:10.1139/facets-2020-0088.

Hewitt, C. Gordon. *The Conservation of Wild Life in Canada.* New York: C. Scribner's Sons, 1921.

Hooton, Robert S. *Days of Rivers Past: Reflections on British Columbia's Recreational Steelhead Fishery.* Calgary: Rocky Mountain Books, 2017.

Horsfield, Margaret. *Cougar Annie's Garden.* Nanaimo: Salal Books, 1999.

Iceton, Glenn. "'Many Families of Unseen Indians': Trapline Registration and Understandings of Aboriginal Title in the BC-Yukon Borderlands." *BC Studies,* no. 201 (Spring 2019): 67–91.

Ignace, Marianne, and Ronald E. Ignace. *Secwépemc People, Land, and Laws: Yerí7 Stsqeys-kucw.* Montreal and Kingston: McGill-Queen's University Press, 2017.

Jakimchuck, Ronald D., R. Wayne Campbell and Dennis A. Demarchi. *Ian McTaggart Cowan: The Legacy of a Pioneering Biologist, Educator and Conservationist.* Madeira Park, BC: Harbour, 2015.

Jones, Chief Charles, with Stephen Bosustow. *Queesto: Pacheenaht Chief by Birthright.* Nanaimo: Theytus Books, 1981.

Jorgenson, Mica. "'A Business Proposition': Naturalists, Guides, and Sportsmen in the Formation of the Bowron Lakes Game Reserve." *BC Studies,* no. 175 (Autumn 2012): 9–34.

Kay, C.E. "Aboriginal Overkill and the Biogeography of Moose in Western North America." *Alces* 33 (1997): 141–64.

Keeling, Arn. "'A Dynamic, Not a Static Conception': The Conservation Thought of Roderick Haig-Brown." *Pacific Historical Review* 71, no. 2 (May 2002): 239–68.

Keeling, Arn, and Robert McDonald. "The Profligate Province: Roderick Haig-Brown and the Modernizing of British Columbia." *Journal of Canadian Studies* 36, no. 3 (Fall 2001): 7–23.

Kehoe, Laura J., Jessie Lund, Lia Chalifour, Yeganeh Asadian, Eric Balke, Sean Boyd, Deborah Carlson, et al. "Conservation in Heavily Urbanized Biodiverse Regions Requires Urgent Management Action and Attention to Governance." *Conservation Science and Practice* 3 (2021): e310. doi.org/10.1111/csp2.310.

Kew, Michael J. "Salmon Availability, Technology and Cultural Adaptation in the Fraser River Watershed." In *A Complex Culture of the British Columbia Plateau: Traditional Stl'atl'imx Resource Use*, edited by Brian Hayden, 177–220. Vancouver: UBC Press, 1992.

Kirk, Ruth. *Tradition and Change on the Northwest Coast: The Makah, Nuu-Chah-Nulth, Southern Kwakiutl and Nuxalk*. Seattle: University of Washington Press, 1986.

Kool, Richard, and Robert A. Cannings. *The Object's the Thing: The Writings of Yorke Edwards, A Pioneer of Heritage Interpretation in Canada*. Victoria: Royal BC Museum, 2021.

Krajina, V.J. "Biogeoclimatic Zones and Classification of British Columbia." In *Ecology of Western North America*, vol. 1, edited by V.J. Krajina, 1–17. Vancouver: University of British Columbia, 1965.

Krech, Shepard. *The Ecological Indian: Myth and History*. New York: W.W. Norton, 1999.

Laliberte, A.S.R., and W. J. Ripple. "Wildlife Encounters by Lewis and Clark: A Spatial Analysis of Interactions between Native Americans and Wildlife." *BioScience* 53 (2003): 994–1003.

Lantz, Trevor, and Nancy J. Turner. "Traditional Phenological Knowledge of Aboriginal Peoples in British Columbia." *Journal of Ethnobiology* 23, no. 2 (2003): 263–86.

Larkin, P.A. "Play It Again Sam—An Essay on Salmon Enhancement." *Journal of the Fisheries Board of Canada* 31, no. 8 (1974): 1434–56. doi.org/10.1139/f74-174.

Leach, Barry A. "The Decline of Geese and Swans on the Lower Fraser River." *BC Studies*, no. 43 (Autumn 1979): 29–44.

Leopold, Aldo. *Game Management*. New York: Scribner's, 1933. Reprint, Madison: University of Wisconsin Press, 1987.

—. *A Sand County Almanac, and Sketches Here and There*. New York: Oxford University Press, 1949.

Leopold, Bruce D., Winifred B. Kessler and James L. Cummins, eds. *North American Wildlife Policy and Law*. Missoula, MT: Boone and Crockett Club, 2018.

Lewis, Michael, Amy Christianson and Marsha Spinks. "Return to Flame: Reasons for Burning in Lytton First Nation, British Columbia." *Journal of Forestry* 116, no. 2 (March 2018): 143–50. DOI:10.1093/jofore/fvx007.

Lewis, H.T. "Indian Fires of Spring." *Natural History* 89 (1980): 76–83.

Loo, Tina. "Disturbing the Peace: Environmental Change and the Scales of Justice on a Northern River," *Environmental History* 12, no. 4 (October 2007): 895–919.

—. "People in the Way: Modernity, Environment, and Society on the Arrow Lakes." *BC Studies*, no. 142–43 (Summer–Autumn 2004): 161–96.

—. *States of Nature: Conserving Canada's Wildlife in the Twentieth Century.*
    Vancouver: UBC Press, 2007.

Lutz, John. *Makúk: A New History of Aboriginal-White Relations.* Vancouver:
    UBC Press, 2008.

MacEachern, Alan. "The Conservation Movement." In *Canada: Confederation
    to Present*, edited by Chris Hackett and Bob Hesketh. Edmonton: Chinook
    Multimedia, 2003. CD-ROM.

Mackie, Richard Somerset. "Cougars, Colonists, and the Rural Settlement of
    Vancouver Island." In *Beyond the City Limits: Rural History in British Columbia*,
    edited by R.W. Sandwell, 120–41. Vancouver: UBC Press, 1999.

—. *Hamilton Mack Laing: Hunter-Naturalist.* Victoria: Sono Nis Press, 1985.

—. *Island Timber: A Social History of the Comox Logging Company of Vancouver
    Island.* Winlaw, BC: Sono Nis Press, 2000.

—. *Trading beyond the Mountains: The British Fur Trade on the Pacific, 1793–1843.*
    Vancouver: UBC Press, 1997.

MacKinnon, J.B. *The Once and Future World: Nature as It Was, as It Is, as It Could Be.*
    Boston: Houghton Mifflin Harcourt, 2013.

Mahoney, Shane P., and Valerius Geist, eds., *The North American Model of Wildlife
    Conservation.* Baltimore: Johns Hopkins University Press, 2019.

Manore, Jean L., and Dale G. Miner, eds. *The Culture of Hunting in Canada.*
    Vancouver: UBC Press, 2007.

Marchak, Patricia. *Green Gold: The Forest Industry in British Columbia.* Vancouver:
    UBC Press, 1983.

McIlwraith, Thomas. *"We Are Still Didene": Stories of Hunting and History from
    Northern British Columbia.* Toronto: University of Toronto Press, 2012.

McKechnie, Iain, and Rebecca J. Wigen. "Toward a Historical Ecology of Pinniped
    and Sea Otter Hunting Traditions on the Coast of Southern British Columbia."
    In *Human Impacts on Seals, Sea Lions, and Sea Otters: Integrating Archaeology
    and Ecology in the Northeast Pacific*, edited by Todd J. Braje and Torben C.
    Rick, 129–66. Berkeley: University of California Press, 2011. doi.org/10.1525/
    california/9780520267268.003.0007.

McLaren, Erica, Todd Mahon, Frank I. Doyle and William L. Harrower. "Science-
    Based Guidelines for Managing Northern Goshawk Breeding Areas in Coastal
    British Columbia." *Journal of Ecosystems and Management* 15, no. 2 (2015). doi.
    org/10.22230/jem.2015v15n2a576.

Meine, C., M. Soule and R.F. Noss. "'A Mission-Driven Discipline': The Growth of
    Conservation Biology." *Conservation Biology* 20, no. 3 (2006): 631–51.

Menzies, Charles R. *People of the Saltwater: An Ethnography of Git lax m'oon.* Lincoln:
    University of Nebraska Press, 2016.

—, ed. *Traditional Ecological Knowledge and Natural Resource Management.* Lincoln:
    University of Nebraska Press, 2006.

Mitchell, David Joseph. *W.A.C. Bennett and the Rise of British Columbia.* Vancouver:
    Douglas & McIntyre, 1994.

Moller, Henrik, Fikret Berkes, Philip O'Brian Lyver and Mina Kislalioglu. "Combining Science and Traditional Ecological Knowledge: Monitoring Populations for Co-management." *Ecology and Society* 9, no. 3 (July 2004): Article 2. doi.org/10.5751/ES-00675-090302.

Morse, Bradford W. "Tsilhqot'in Nation v. British Columbia: Is It a Game Changer in Canadian Aboriginal Title Law and Crown-Indigenous Relations?" *Lakehead Law Journal* 2, no. 2 (2017): 64–88.

Muckle, Robert J. *The First Nations of British Columbia: An Anthropological Overview.* 3rd ed. Vancouver: UBC Press, 2014.

Mulholland, F.D. *The Forest Resources of British Columbia.* Victoria: King's Printer, 1937.

Munro, James A., and Ian McTaggart Cowan. *A Review of the Bird Fauna of British Columbia.* Victoria: British Columbia Provincial Museum, 1947.

Murray, Allan, ed. *Our Wildlife Heritage: 100 Years of Wildlife Management.* Victoria: Centennial Wildlife Society of British Columbia, 1987.

Nadasdy, Paul. "The Gift in the Animal: The Ontology of Hunting and Human–Animal Sociality." *American Ethnologist* 34, no. 1 (2007): 25–43. doi.org/10.1525/ae.2007.34.1.25.

—. *Hunters and Bureaucrats: Power, Knowledge, and Aboriginal-State Relations in the Southwest Yukon.* Vancouver: UBC Press, 2003.

Nelson, Michael P., John A. Vucetich, Paul C. Paquet and Joseph K. Bump. "An Inadequate Construct? North American Model: What's Flawed, What's Missing, What's Needed." *Wildlife Professional* 5 (2011): 58–60.

Newell, Diane. *Tangled Webs of History: Indians and the Law in Canada's Pacific Coast Fisheries.* Toronto: University of Toronto Press, 1993.

Nichol, Linda M. "Conservation in Practice." In *Sea Otter Conservation*, edited by Shawn E. Larson, James L. Bodkin and Glenn R. VanBlaricom, 369–93. New York: Elsevier, 2015. doi.org/10.1016/B978-0-12-801402-8.00013-5.

Ormsby, Margaret. *British Columbia: A History.* Toronto: Macmillan, 1958.

Ostrom, Elinor. *Governing the Commons: The Evolution of Institutions for Collective Action.* Cambridge: Cambridge University Press, 1990.

Parr, Joy. *Sensing Changes: Technologies, Environments, and the Everyday, 1953–2003.* Vancouver: UBC Press, 2010.

Paul, Cecil, as told to Briony Penn. *Stories from the Magic Canoe of Wa'xaid.* Calgary: Rocky Mountain Books, 2019.

Pauly, Daniel. "Anecdotes and the Shifting Baseline Syndrome of Fisheries." *Trends in Ecology & Evolution* 10, no. 10 (1995): 430.

Pearse, Peter H. "A New Approach to the Evaluation of Non-Priced Recreational Resources." *Land Economics* 54 (February 1968): 87–99.

Penn, Briony. *The Real Thing: The Natural History of Ian McTaggart Cowan.* Calgary: Rocky Mountain Books, 2015.

Peyton, Jonathan. "Imbricated Geographies of Conservation and Consumption in the Stikine Plateau." *Environment and History* 17, no. 4 (2011): 555–81.

—. *Unbuilt Environments: Tracing Postwar Development in Northwest British Columbia*. Vancouver: UBC Press, 2017.

Pryce, Paula. *Keeping the Lakes' Way: Reburial and the Re-creation of a Moral World among an Invisible People*. Toronto: University of Toronto Press, 1999.

Pyne, Stephen J. *Awful Splendour: A Fire History of Canada*. Vancouver: UBC Press, 2008.

—. *Fire: Nature and Culture*. London: Reaktion Books, 2012.

Rajala, Richard A. "Forests and Fish: The 1972 Coast Logging Guidelines and British Columbia's First NDP Government," *BC Studies*, no. 159 (Autumn 2008): 81–120.

—. "'Streams Being Ruined from a Salmon Producing Standpoint': Clearcutting, Fish Habitat and Forest Regulation in British Columbia, 1900–1945." *BC Studies*, no. 176 (Winter 2012–13): 93–132. doi.org/10.14288/bcs.voi176.182928.

—. "'This Wasteful Use of a River': Log Driving, Conservation, and British Columbia's Stellako River Controversy, 1965–72," *BC Studies*, no. 165 (Spring 2010): 31–74.

Ray, Arthur. *Indians in the Fur Trade: Their Roles as Trappers, Hunters, and Middlemen in the Lands Southwest of Hudson Bay, 1660–1870*. Toronto: University of Toronto Press, 1974.

Reid, Joanna. "The Grasslands Debates: Conservationists, Ranchers, First Nations, and the Landscape of the Middle Fraser." *BC Studies*, no. 160 (Winter 2008–9): 93–118.

Ridington, Robin, and Jillian Ridington, in collaboration with elders of the Dane-zaa First Nations. *Where Happiness Dwells: A History of the Dane-zaa First Nations*. Vancouver: UBC Press, 2013.

Robinson, Harry and Wendy Wickwire. *Write It on Your Heart: The Epic World of an Okanagan Storyteller*. Vancouver: Talonbooks/Theytus, 1989.

Rodway, Michael S., R. Wayne Campbell and Moira J.F. Lemon. "Seabird Colonies of British Columbia: A Century of Changes." *Wildlife Afield* 13, no. 1–2 (2016).

Roy, Patricia. *The Collectors: A History of the Royal British Columbia Museum and Archives*. Victoria: Royal BC Museum, 2018.

Sandlos, John. *Hunters at the Margin: Native People and Wildlife Conservation in the Northwest Territories*. Vancouver: UBC Press, 2007.

Santomauro, Domenico, Chris J. Johnson and Gail Fondahl. "Historical-Ecological Evaluation of the Long-Term Distribution of Woodland Caribou and Moose in Central British Columbia." *Ecosphere* 3, no. 5 (2012): 1–19. doi.org/10.1890/ES11-00371.1.

Sawchuk, Wayne. *Muskwa-Kechika: The Wild Heart of Canada's Northern Rockies*. Chetwynd, BC: Northern Images, 2004.

Schuster, Richard, Ryan R. Germain, Joseph R. Bennett, Nicholas J. Reo and Peter Arcese. "Vertebrate Biodiversity on Indigenous-Managed Lands in Australia, Brazil, and Canada Equals That in Protected Areas." *Environmental Science & Policy* 101 (2019): 1–6.

Serfass, Thomas L., Robert P. Brooks and Jeremy T. Bruskotter. "North American Model of Wildlife Conservation: Empowerment and Exclusivity Hinder Advances in Wildlife Conservation." *Canadian Wildlife Biology & Management* 7, no. 2 (2018): 101–18.

Silver, Rod S., Neil K. Dawe, Brian M. Starzomski, Katherine L. Parker and David W. Nagorsen, "A Tribute to Ian McTaggart-Cowan, 1910–2010, O.C., O.B.C., PhD, LL.D, F.R.S.C." *Canadian Field-Naturalist* 124, no. 4 (2010): 367–83.

Sirén, Alexej P.K., Peter J. Pekins, Peter L. Abdu and Mark J. Ducey. "Identification and Density Estimation of American Martens (*Martes americana*) Using a Novel Camera-Trap Method." *Diversity* 8, no. 1 (January 2016): Article 3. doi.org/10.3390/d8010003.

Skaar, Donald R., Jeffrey L. Arnold, Todd M. Koel, Michael E. Ruhl, Joseph A. Skorupski and Hilary B. Treanor. "Effects of Rotenone on Amphibians and Macroinvertebrates in Yellowstone." *Yellowstone Science* 25, no. 1 (July 2017).

Spalding, David J. "The Early History of Moose (*Alces alces*): Distribution and Relative Abundance in British Columbia." *Contributions to Natural Science* 11 (March 1990): 1–12.

—. "The History of Elk (*Cervus elaphus)* in British Columbia." *Contributions to Natural Science* 18 (October 1992): 1–24.

Stanley, Meg. *Voices from Two Rivers: Harnessing the Power of the Peace and Columbia.* Vancouver: Douglas & McIntyre, 2010.

Sterritt, Neil J. *Mapping My Way Home: A Gitxsan History.* Smithers, BC: Creekstone Press, 2017.

Teit, James A. "Tahltan Tales." *Journal of American Folklore* 32, no. 124 (April–June 1919): 230.

Thielmann, Tim, and Chris Tollefson. "Tears from an Onion: Layering, Exhaustion and Conversion in British Columbia Land Use Planning Policy." *Policy and Society* 28, no. 2 (July 2009): 111–24. doi.org/10.1016/j.polsoc.2009.05.006.

Thompson, Sally. *People before the Park: The Kootenai and Blackfeet before Glacier National Park.* Helena: Montana Historical Society Press, 2015.

Thoms, J. Michael. "A Place Called Pennask: Fly Fishing and Colonialism at a British Columbia Lake." *BC Studies*, no. 133 (Spring 2002): 69–98.

Toller, Susan, and Peter N. Nemetz. "Assessing the Impact of Hydro Development: A Case Study of the Columbia River Basin in British Columbia." *BC Studies*, no. 114 (Summer 1997): 5–30.

Tough, Frank. "Conservation and the Indian: Clifford Sifton's Commission of Conservation, 1910–1919." *Native Studies Review* 8, no. 1 (1992): 61–73.

Turner, Nancy J. "'Time to Burn': Traditional Use of Fire to Enhance Resource Production by Aboriginal Peoples in British Columbia." In *Indians, Fire and the Land in the Pacific Northwest*, edited by R. Boyd, 185–218. Corvallis: Oregon State University Press, 1999.

Turner, Nancy J., and Fikret Berkes. "Coming to Understanding: Developing Conservation through Incremental Learning in the Pacific Northwest." *Human Ecology* 34 (2006): 495–513.

Turner, Nancy J., and Wendy Cocksedge. "Aboriginal Use of Non-Timber Forest Products in Northwestern North America: Applications and Issues." *Journal of Sustainable Forestry* 13, no. 3–4 (2001): 31–58.

Thompson, Sally. *People before the Park: The Kootenai and Blackfeet before Glacier National Park*. Helena: Montana Historical Society Press, 2015.

Vogt, David. "'Indians on White Lines': Bureaucracy, Race, and Power on Northern British Columbian Traplines, 1925–1950." *Journal of the Canadian Historical Association* 26, no. 1 (2015): 163–90. doi.org/10.7202/1037201ar.

Walter, Emily, R. Michael M'Gonigle and Céleste McKay. "Fishing around the Law: The Pacific Salmon Management System as a 'Structural Infringement' of Aboriginal Rights." *McGill Law Journal* 45, no. 1 (2000): 263–314.

Westwood, Alana R., Sarah P. Otto, Arne Mooers, Chris Darimont, Karen E. Hodges, Chris Johnson, Brian M. Starzomski, et al. "Protecting Biodiversity in British Columbia: Recommendations for Developing Species at Risk Legislation." *FACETS* 4, no. 1 (June 2019): 136–60. doi.org/10.1139/facets-2018-0042.

Williams, A. Bryan. *Game Trails in British Columbia: Big Game and Other Sport in the Wilds of British Columbia*. New York: Scribner's, 1925.

Wilson, James W. *People in the Way: The Human Aspects of the Columbia River Project*. Toronto: University of Toronto Press, 1973.

Wilson, Jeremy. "Forest Conservation in British Columbia, 1935–85: Reflections on a Barren Political Debate." *BC Studies*, no. 76 (Winter 1987): 3–32. doi.org/10.14288/bcs.voi76.1275.

—. "For the Birds? Neoliberalism and the Protection of Biodiversity in British Columbia." *BC Studies*, no. 142–43 (Summer–Autumn 2004): 241–77.

—. *Talk and Log: Wilderness Politics in British Columbia*. Vancouver: UBC Press, 1998.

Zwickel, Fred C., and James F. Bendell. "Early Mortality and the Regulation of Numbers in Blue Grouse." *Canadian Journal of Zoology* 45, no. 5 (1967): 817–51.

Index

Figures, illustrations, and tables indicated by page numbers in bold

Fraser River: canneries, 77, **108**, 121; closures of recreational chinook fishery, 415; delta (estuary), 234, 238, 246, 252, 350–51, **352**; estuary land use, **plate 7**; eulachon and, 29; gold rush, 65–67, **66**, 374, 468n49; hatchery, **107**; Hell's Gate slides, 120–21, 445; Indigenous fisheries, 119–21, 270–71, 272, 276; Moran Canyon dam proposal, 175; salmon (sockeye) returns, **271**, 480n79

Fraser Valley, 74, 139, 250, 252, 268, 354

free miner's certificates, 92, **92**, 444

Freshwater Fisheries Society, 336

Friends of Clayoquot Sound (FOCS), 308, 309

Friends of Ecological Reserves, 370

Fur and Feathers (TV show), 194, 214–15, 279

fur trade. *See* wildlife trade

G

Gaglardi, Phil, 236

Game Act (BC), 89, 104, 121, 129, 201, 281, 483n118

Game Commission (BC): about, 486n1; BC Wildlife Federation and, 488n30; Conibear's trap and, 291; Predator Control Branch, 161–62, 209, 280, 489n43; Reifel bird sanctuary and, 245; water pollution and, 195; wildlife biologists and shift to scientific management approach, 143, 153–56, 157–58, 165, 487n24; *Wildlife Review*, 181, 193–94, 207, 208, 209, 210–11, **210–11**, 301, 420–21, 498n19. *See also* Fish and Wildlife Branch; Game Department

Game Conservation Board, 111, 127, 478n47

game conventions, annual, 156–57, 161, 162, 181, 192, 195, 196, 436

Game Department (BC): about, 97; enforcement capabilities, 98, 105; establishment, disbandment, and restoration, 98, 111, 138, 478n47, 487n19; game reserves and, 109; Indigenous trapping and, 125, 128, 481n93; predator

control and, 489n43; public trust doctrine and, 98–99; revenue from licence fees, 97, 98, 103, 104–5, 141, 418, 476n21. *See also* Game Commission

Game Farm Act (BC, 1990), 377

game farming, 376–77

game legislation, early: about, 16; enforcement challenges, 91–93; exemptions, 82, 476n26; fines and imprisonment, 472n47; impetus and scope, 81–82, 89–91, 93–94; rural settlers and, 129–30, 483n116; songbirds and, 473n66. *See also* Game Protection Act; licences

Game Patrol (periodical), 210

Game Protection Act (BC): on fish and game associations and rod and gun clubs, 90; on fur-bearing animals, 123; on Game Department, 109; on hunting permits, 483n116; Indigenous Peoples on, 121; on informers, 91, 474n77; on wild animal exports, 91, 474n74

game protection associations. *See* fish and game protection associations

game reserves, 16, 97, 109–10, 111, 236, 444, 478nn42–44

Game Trails of BC (magazine), 212

game wardens, 98, 105, 121, 130, 153, 155, 202

Garry oak savannahs, 44, 70

geese, 34, 58, 80, 113, 196, 252; greater white-fronted, 351, 498n17; snow, 244

Geist, Valerius, 392, 393–95, 396, 397, 528n62

George, Earl Maquinna, 24, 35–36, 38, 122–23

George, Louie, **126**

George C. Reifel bird sanctuary, 206, 244–46, **245**, 499n33

Gibbard, Violet, 300

Gisday Wa, 46

Gitanyow First Nation, 407

Gitsi'is Tribe, 370

Gitxaala Nation, 465n2

Gitxsan Nation: about, 27; colonization and, 24; hereditary chiefs, 33, 36;